JOB #:

Author Name:

Title of Book:

ISBN: 1438429401

Publisher:

Trim Size: 6 x 9

Bulk in mm: 28

Process Approaches to Consciousness in Psychology, Neuroscience, and Philosophy of Mind

SUNY series in Philosophy

George R. Lucas Jr., editor

Process Approaches to Consciousness in Psychology, Neuroscience, and Philosophy of Mind

Edited by

Michel Weber
and
Anderson Weekes

Production by Cathleen Collins
Marketing by Anne M. Valentine

Library of Congress Cataloging-in-Publication Data

Process approaches to consciousness in psychology, neuroscience, and philosophy of
  mind / edited by Michel Weber and Anderson Weekes.
      p. cm. — (SUNY series in philosophy)
  Includes bibliographical references and index.
  ISBN 978-1-4384-2941-0 (hardcover : alk. paper)
  ISBN 978-1-4384-2940-3 (paperback : alk. paper)
  1. Consciousness.   2. Process philosophy.   3. Psychology.   4. Neurosciences.
5. Philosophy of mind.   I. Weber, Michel.   II. Weekes, Anderson, 1960–

  B808.9.P77 2010
  126—dc22   2009010131

10 9 8 7 6 5 4 3 2 1

In memoria ingentis ingenii,

dedicamus librum hunc ad

Alecem

MDCDLXXVI – MMVII

For much of the twentieth century, all sciences, including biology, were obsessed with reductionism: viewing the world at all levels, from the smallest to the largest, as merely a machine made of parts. Take the machine apart, examine the individual pieces, and we would understand how the world works. Reductionism has had many triumphs in understanding the nature of the parts and how some parts fit together. It enabled us to build computers and devise powerful medicines for example. But some scientists admit that reductionism falls short of its ultimate goal: understanding how the world works. It falls short because it fails to recognize the connectedness, the unity, that is the deep essence of nature in all realms. Not in the sense of physicists seeking the ultimate fundamental particle or the theory of everything. There is a oneness in nature in the sense of interdependence.

—Irene Pepperberg, *Alex and Me*

Contents

Figures and Tables

Key to Abbreviations
of Whitehead's Works

AI *Adventures of Ideas*, 1933/1967 (New York: The Free Press)

CN *The Concept of Nature*, 1920/1964 (Cambridge: Cambridge University Press)

ESP *Essays in Science and Philosophy*, 1947 (New York: The Philosophical Library)

FR *The Function of Reason*, 1929/1958 (Boston: Beacon Press)

MT *Modes of Thought*, 1938/1968 (New York: The Free Press)

PM *Principia Mathematica*, 1910–13/1925–1927 (Cambridge: Cambridge University Press)

PNK *Principles of Natural Knowledge*, 1919/1982 (New York: Dover)

PR *Process and Reality*, 1929/1978 (Corrected edition, New York: The Free Press)

PRel *The Principle of Relativity*, 1922 (Cambridge: The University Press)

S *Symbolism, Its Meaning and Effect*, 1927/1985 (New York: Fordham University Press)

SMW *Science and the Modern World*, 1925/1967 (New York: The Free Press)

UA *A Treatise on Universal Algebra*, 1898/1960 (Cambridge: Cambridge University Press)

Introduction

Michel Weber and Anderson Weekes

We introduce this volume with a brief preview of its overall concerns (Section I), followed by a précis of the individual contributions (Section II) and an overview of the most important literature with a similar or related focus (Section III). The preview will show that this is not a collection of specialty scholarship, but a volume rightly intended for the broadest possible learned readership. The uniqueness of its approach is tempered by the generality of its concerns. The précis then situate each contribution in the larger context of the book's philosophical and interdisciplinary ambitions, while the last section situates the book in the broader context of today's intellectual landscape, where a growing body of literature reinforces its cause without anticipating its results.

In this Introduction, we adopt the following conventions in referring to the chapters that follow. (1) Chapters are identified by authorship. Contributors' proper names, including those of the editors, refer to their respective contributions to Parts II–V. Proper names do not reference the contributions to Part I, which resulted from collaboration (chapters 1 and 2) or consensus (chapters 3 and 4) between the editors. These chapters in Part I we refer to simply as the contributions of "the editors." "Contribution(s) of the editors" does not refer their individual contributions in Parts IV and V. (2) Source and locus will not be given for quotations if they are taken from the chapters that follow. Unless otherwise indicated, all quotations in this Introduction are from the named author's contribution to the present volume.

Main Themes of the Book

Alfred North Whitehead's philosophy was a protest against the compartmentalization of knowledge. A specialized subfield of philosophy focused on Whitehead interpretation is therefore something of a paradox. Given the daunting complexity of Whitehead's writing, literal exegesis and historical scholarship aiming at an "immanent" interpretation of his thought have a continuing and obviously important role to play, but Whitehead himself would scarcely recognize such activities as his rightful legacy. A failure of Whiteheadians to be sufficiently Whiteheadian in this regard may well be the reason Whitehead's ideas have seemed at times to be threatened with extinction and mostly available in fossil form. If this is changing, it is at least partly because outsiders are storming the museum. Straightaway this has opened vast avenues of new dialogue with unsuspected partners, to which this book bears witness.

This volume brings multiple disciplinary perspectives to bear on Whitehead's psychology (which, in a way, is his whole philosophy—a metaphysics of experience) in order to analyze it in terms of relevance to contemporary consciousness studies. Accordingly, we have gathered contribution from scholars whose areas of research are diverse and often do not include Whiteheadian process philosophy as a subfield of expertise, but whose own intellectual paths have led them to recognize an important kinship with Whitehead.

The area of consciousness studies proves to be a busy intersection: a place where one can't help but meet everything from metaphysics to psychotherapy. This is not happenstance. It reflects the nature of the beast we are tracking, and we have not shied from it. This accounts for both the broad scope of the volume and the diversity of its contributions.

In important respects, this book complements David Griffin's *Unsnarling the World-Knot: Consciousness, Freedom, and the Mind-Body Problem* (1998), which grew out of an interdisciplinary conference sponsored by the Center for Process Studies at the Claremont Colleges in 1994, "Consciousness in Humans, Animals and Computers. A Scientific-Philosophical Conference." Bringing a Whiteheadian perspective to contemporary consciousness studies, Griffin effects a broad synthesis of the issues currently under debate and at the same time provides an excellent introduction to Whitehead's psychology. We reverse directions. Bringing different contemporary perspectives (including Griffin's) to bear on Whitehead's psychology, we replace synthesis with analysis and highlight the richness and polyvalence of Whitehead's ideas. Of particular concern to this volume is the role that Whitehead's process philosophy can play in providing an interpretive framework for neuropsychology, and, conversely, the role that neuropsychology can play in providing an empirical model for Whitehead's concept of process and an empirical confirmation of his theory of consciousness. According to Whitehead, consciousness is a process—a very specific kind of process that, despite its uniqueness, holds the key to understanding process as such. Consequently, a number of important findings of neuropsychology, some of them familiar, but some of them quite new and even startling, will figure decisively in these pages.

The contributions to this volume can be grouped according to a number of shared themes. Several contributors (David Griffin, Katzko, Shields, Pachalska, and MacQueen, and the editors in Part I) show that some recognizably Whiteheadian issues are at stake in the current debates about consciousness and that Whiteheadian ideas can be exploited—sometimes in ways that Whitehead could not have anticipated—to advance the debate beyond some well-known sticking points. Two of the contributors (Rosenberg and Weekes) explore the curious connection Whitehead alleges between consciousness and causation. One author proceeds by a conceptual analysis of the structure of explanatory theories, the other proceeds phenomenologically, but they both lend support to Whitehead's signature idea, refereed in chapter 4, that scientists and philosophers find consciousness very difficult to explain for the same reason that they have a problem understanding the nature of causation and the basis for induction: due to inherent constraints, the theoretical activity known as explanation tends to suppress the specifically processual aspect of becoming, which Rosenberg calls the receptive face of causation and Whitehead calls concrescence. The argument in brief: By suppressing the dynamic aspect of becoming, explanatory theories render essentially processual phenomena inscrutable. The paradigm of an "essentially processual phenomenon" would be, according to Whitehead, *experience*, of which *consciousness* is only the most sophisticated (and deceiving) sort. Others (Verley, Weekes, and the editors in chapters 3 and 4) expand systematically on Whitehead's scholarly critique of modern philosophy, which Whitehead casts almost entirely as a critique of its favorite concept, consciousness. But there are really three main themes that connect the contributions to this volume.

First, running through all the contributions to this volume is the critical insight that consciousness is *not* the *sui generis* phenomenon it is usually taken to be—in philosophical and scientific discussion as much as in the everyday understanding informed by lay sensibilities. Closely related to this principal theme is a secondary theme that connects more than half of the contributions to the volume (David Griffin, Donald Redfield Griffin, Shields, Velmans, Rosenberg, Weekes, and the editors in chapter 4). It is the question of the distribution of consciousness in the natural universe. Approaching the question from very different angles, each of the contributors just named argues that consciousness (or something much more primitive, but in the same category) is more widely distributed than customarily supposed. At the opposite extreme from the assumed exclusiveness of human consciousness is the position usually referred to as "panpsychism." In the contributions by David Griffin, Weekes, and the editors in chapter 4, Whiteheadian arguments for the universal distribution of some kind of extremely rudimentary (pre- or proto-conscious) experience are explored. In the contributions by Shields, Velmans, and Rosenberg, the possibility of such a distribution is supported with robust and original arguments that will give many readers pause.

The principal theme first: in different ways, each contribution to this volume seeks to relativize the concept of consciousness that is normally taken for granted. The reflective and attentionally focused consciousness that tends to be identified with consciousness absolutely belongs to a wide and multidimensional spectrum of conscious states—or, if someone insists on reserving the word *consciousness* for the particular apex of human experience that is reflective and attentionally focused (as, indeed, Whitehead allows), then we must say that consciousness belongs to a wide and multidimensional spectrum of experience, most of which is "unconscious" or only partially or obliquely conscious. (To know whether the word consciousness is being used in its broader or narrower sense, the reader of this volume will have to be attentive to contexts: we have not thought it appropriate to legislate uniformity in this matter on our contributors.) The point is that "paradigmatic" consciousness is only one of many kinds of consciousness/experience. Its isolation as a paradigm is the result of a variety of organic, psychological, social, and historical processes of development, refinement, and selection (some necessitated by survival and social existence, others contingent, but ossified as dogma). Its view of the world is therefore not absolute or final, but conditioned by these processes.

Weber argues that everyday consciousness of the natural attitude is not an absolute *given*, but an artifact of socialized ontogeny. It results from the constraints of utilitarian and social rationalization that operate on the individual in mostly unconscious ways. Verley, Weekes, and the editors in chapters 3 and 4 expose important ways that the preferred concept of consciousness is an artifact of biases peculiar to the modern philosophical tradition. Pachalska and MacQueen and Schweiger et al. discuss varieties of consciousness revealed by brain pathology in humans. These varieties of consciousness differ markedly from the usual paradigm of reflective and attentionally focused awareness of objects *qua objects*. The authors argue, moreover, that these varieties of consciousness are not abnormal. On the contrary, they are the normal subphases in the moment-to-moment microgenesis of consciousness, with the qualification that they are abnormally exposed because pathology has arrested the microgenetic process at a preterminal phase of realization. Velmans also stresses ways that human consciousness results from and is conditioned by processes of refinement or selection operating on a spectrum of broader and more basic kinds of consciousness/experience. He goes so far as to suggest that what we normally think of as consciousness in humans may be the sophisticated result of a highly selective release from inhibition of what is in reality a pervasive and primitive kind of awareness intrinsic to all organic matter or even to all matter, *period*. In fact, the startling generality of this conclusion is something to which Rosenberg's analysis of causality led him for reasons wholly unrelated to Velmans' argument: there is, Rosenberg concludes, a primitive experiential aspect in every causal nexus, and that means in every event, *period*. Velmans wonders if the purpose of centralization in complex nervous systems isn't to prevent overload by inhibiting this primitive consciousness throughout most of the system, allowing for a selective focus on information of critical relevance. The late Donald Redfield Griffin's examination of consciousness in animals relativizes human consciousness in a more straightforward, if no less controversial way. Although he is mainly concerned with documenting ways that animals can be seen to have consciousness similar to ours, its wider distribution in the animal kingdom means that consciousness is a genus of which human consciousness is only a specific kind. Reflective human consciousness may indeed possess an epistemological privilege, but this is no longer something it can take for granted on the grounds that it defines and exhausts what consciousness is. Nor can we assume any longer that the minimum identity conditions of consciousness/experience are in any way obvious—and least of all obvious from self-conscious reflection or introspection in human beings.

The secondary theme: Since the distribution of consciousness/experience in the universe bears in an obvious way on the relative or absolute status of "paradigmatic" human consciousness, the distribution question becomes another connecting theme in this volume. The distribution of consciousness/experience cannot be divorced from the question of the minimal conditions for the existence of consciousness/experience. The more complex the conditions, the less distributed it will be. Conversely, the more distributed it is, the more the complexity of human consciousness must appear as the result of specialized constraints that exclude other, more basic kinds of consciousness/experience (or at least their foregrounded manifestation). The distribution of consciousness, alluded to by Weekes and the editors in chapter 4), is a thematic focus of contributions by David Griffin, Donald Redfield Griffin, Velmans, Shields, and Rosenberg, and it naturally leads to the hot-button issue of panpsychism, notoriously associated with Whitehead's metaphysics. This special case of the distribution question brings us to the third unifying theme of our volume.

The signature thesis of Whitehead's metaphysics is that the core of actuality is always some kind of experience. Avoiding the misnomer "panpsychism," David Griffin has aptly dubbed this thesis *panexperientialism*.[1] It has long been common to dismiss Whitehead's panexperientialism hastily on the grounds that it is patently absurd to suggest that things like rocks and toasters have experience or that subatomic particles are conscious. But this conflates panexperientialism with panpsychism. As Griffin shows in his contribution, these objections are misdirected. First, panexperientialism distinguishes between conscious and nonconscious experience (in the same way that Velmans, for example, distinguishes between very high-grade and very low-grade "consciousness"). While all entities that are genuine individuals (including subatomic events) are postulated to have some kind of experience, only the most complexly organized of compound individuals have conscious experience. The simplest individuals, presumably Planck-scale units of nature, have an extremely rudimentary kind of "experience" that would consist in little more than a sensitivity or responsiveness to their environment that was not 100% predictable. Second, drawing on an important clarification made by Charles Hartshorne, panexperientialism distinguishes between compound individuals, such as organisms, which are genuine integral individuals and thus have a coherently unified experience, and merely cohesive aggregates (like rocks and toasters), which have individuals as their micro-constituents, but are not themselves integral individuals and as such have *no* experience.[2]

It is also important to keep in mind that, according to panexperientialism, individuals *per se* are momentary events and do not endure for more than the briefest possible duration. Enduring entities, such as electrons or psyches, are made up of many such durational individuals forming a temporal series that is cumulative and characterized by overwhelming similarity between any two consecutive members. Consequently, panexperientialism does not attribute a mind or soul to anything but enduring compound individuals.[3] It is only the small differential of a momentary experience that panexperientialism attributes to every individual regardless of status—compound or simple, bound within a cumulative series or not.

A number of contributors to this volume explore arguments, both logical and empirical, for taking panexperientialism seriously. Logical arguments of various types (metaphysical, transcendental, conceptual) are advanced by David Griffin, Shields, Rosenberg, and the editors in chapter 4. Empirical arguments must appeal to scientific evidence about the distribution of consciousness/ experience. Given the roughly inverse relationship between complexity and distribution of consciousness/experience, a number of contributors take up the critical question that unavoidably arises in this context and that any serious assessment of Whitehead must address: how far downscale in complexity of organization can types of individuals be found that still appear to have some kind of experience? As Thomas Nagel has put it, "if one travels too far down the phylogenetic tree, people gradually shed their faith that there is experience there at all" (Nagel 1979, 168). David Griffin alludes in summary form to the growing range of evidence available on this important topic. Three of our contributors, Donald Redfield Griffin, Velmans, and Shields, observing a division of labor naturally suggested by their respective areas of expertise (biology/animal ethology; psychology/neuropsychology; philosophy/physics), examine empirical evidence that is in many cases startling.

Of course, as an empirical question, how far downscale in organizational complexity experience goes is something that could be answered only indirectly, by inference from decisive clues. As Donald Redfield Griffin notes, prejudices on this question are likely to disguise themselves as disagreements about the criteria for validly inferring the existence of consciousness/experience in other life forms. Donald Redfield Griffin and Velmans both dispatch a number of specious objections to less-than-human consciousness simply by insisting that the same standards of interpretation we apply to other human beings be applied to other organisms: similar behavior and similar brain anatomy and physiology cannot be relevant in the one case and not in the other.

Regarding how far down the scale of complexity experience goes, David Griffin notes that Descartes set the cutoff point right below human beings, but that natural science has been pushing it down ever since—animal ethologists pushing it as far down the phylogenetic tree as bees, biologists as far down as single cell organisms or even as far as bacteria or DNA, and some physicists right down to the Planck-scale units of nature. In this light, panexperientialism looks like a position toward which empirical science is tending all by itself under the weight of the evidence. But it is also a position increasingly under reassessment for strictly philosophical reasons. Part of the reason for this volume is the fact that this slighted position is beginning to garner mainstream consideration. As the deadlock between dualism and materialism in consciousness studies becomes more tiresome, appreciation for the important differences between the less plausible panpsychism and the more plausible panexperientialism grows. To many, panexperientialism is looking more and more like a viable *via tertia* (or "third way").

And we note last that an answer to an important objection to panexperientialism also emerges from this volume. The demand is rightly made: what other meaning can "experience" possibly have than the experience human users of language are readily familiar with in themselves? Consequently, if the concept of experience is attenuated and generalized so that it no longer designates what human speakers normally mean in one language or another, how can it mean anything at all? If the experience of a bacterium or an electron is totally unlike ours, what point is there in calling it experience at all? It seems that we are either saying something obviously wrong or not really saying anything at all.

A great deal of empirical research into the distribution of experience in the universe is addressed in this volume, and it suggests a much wider distribution than is traditionally conceded. But our contributors also show that within its own compass human experience is rich and multiform enough to supply the semantic Rosetta Stone needed to talk meaningfully about these nonhuman manifestations of experience. By noticing that even human experience encompasses kinds of awareness that fall far short of the lucid, objectifying consciousness of the well-socialized adult, we can free ourselves from the conceit that consciousness as such must be narrowly construed as something uniquely human (Weber, Weekes, and the editors in Part I). If there is, even within human consciousness as we experience it now, the vestiges of qualitatively distinct kinds of consciousness corresponding to each evolutionary stratum of our brain (Pachalska and MacQueen and the work of Jason Brown they draw on), then there is no reason to think that we do not share these more basic forms of consciousness with those species that have only the more primitive brain formations. If human consciousness passed through more primitive stages in its own evolution, if it passes through cumulative phases in the recovery from unconsciousness, if it passes through distinct phases in the early motor development of the individual and its subsequent socialization, if it passes through a nested hierarchy of phases as it emerges moment by moment from the neural activity of the brain (Schweiger et al., Weber, and the literature they reference), then it makes no sense to deny that we have any criteria for generalizing an attenuated concept of consciousness beyond human experience. The important question that remains open is not whether, but how far the concept of experience can be meaningfully generalized.

In order to set the individual contributions to this book in the context of its overarching themes, the editors supply the following précis. As for the arrangement of the contributions, the editors hoped to order them in a way that would allow each to benefit the most from being read in the sequence settled on, but to some extent the order is unavoidably arbitrary, and each contribution does, in fact, stand on its own.

Précis of the Contributions

David Griffin not only provides a lucid, jargon-free overview of Whitehead's theory of consciousness, but he also manages to bring it directly into the arena of current debate. The fact that there are conceptual common denominators allowing for a meaningful, if virtual debate between Whitehead and contemporary theorists may surprise many who have, perhaps understandably, stumbled at the outset over Whitehead's dense and idiosyncratic language.[4]

Griffin enlarges on an idea very important to Whitehead: that the philosopher may not deny in theory what she presupposes in practice. Griffin notes that this fallacy involves what Apel and Habermas call a performative contradiction: asserting something that violates the conditions of possibility of making the assertion in question.[5] Accordingly, Griffin elaborates four criteria having to do with the conditions of the possibility of theorizing. These performatively undeniable facts Griffin calls ideas of "hard-core common sense," and any adequate theory of consciousness must account for them: the idea "that conscious experience exists, that it exerts influence upon the body, that it has a degree of self-determining freedom, and that it can act in accord with various norms."

It's obvious how a statement such as "Consciousness does not exist" involves a performative contradiction,[6] but a statement such as "Consciousness is merely an epiphenomenon" runs afoul of performative consistency, too. If the uttered statement means what the speaker intended, then it must be conceded that her mind has had an effect on her body. If the statement was affirmed because the speaker thought it was true, then she must have had the freedom to let herself be motivated by an ideal such as truth.[7]

Griffin takes a broad survey of the important players in current debates and finds that the discussion remains boxed in by the traditionally dominant paradigms of reductionist materialism and Cartesian dualism. Assessed against his four performative criteria, neither of these positions is acceptable. Materialism runs afoul of all four, and dualism runs afoul of all but the first. The contemporary debate is therefore framed by what amounts to a false dilemma. The overlooked third option or *tertium quid* would be a naturalism that was not reductionistic or, by the same token, an interactionism that was not dualistic. According to Griffin, Whitehead's position meets this requirement: "With dualists, Whitehead agrees that consciousness belongs to an entity—a mind or psyche—that is distinct from the brain, and that genuine freedom can, partly for this reason, be attributed to conscious experience. With materialists, Whitehead shares a naturalistic sensibility, thereby eschewing any even implicitly supernaturalistic solution to philosophical problems, and, partly for this reason, rejects any dualism between two kinds of actualities. Like materialists, in other words, he affirms a pluralistic monism. He thereby regards consciousness as a function of something more fundamental. And yet he, like dualists, rejects the reductionism involved in functionalism as understood by materialists."

What makes this *tertium* possible is Whitehead's theory of experience as the core of actuality. In other words, panexperientialism is uniquely qualified to avoid the pitfalls of the materialism-dualism dichotomy. This yields an essentially transcendental argument for panexperientialism: an argument based on performative consistency as a condition of the possibility of conscious activity. Griffin alludes to two subsidiary arguments, as well. For one, he notes the trend in empirical science to cast the net of experience more and more widely. In the absence of a sufficient reason to draw a hard line at a particular point (as Velmans discusses in his contribution, as well) a *prima facie* presumption of validity should be granted to the logical extrapolation of this trend. For another, Griffin (like Velmans) notes the difficulties that arise once we draw such a hard line. It creates a discontinuity and a dualism difficult to square with the theory of evolution. Griffin even makes the case that panexperientialism alone can explain how consciousness could arise in the course of evolution. This is no bluff since he charts the intervening phases that would lead to the gradual or staggered evolution of consciousness from the unconscious or merely incipient intentionality of experience in its most rudimentary shape. But Griffin stresses that his most important argument is the transcendental one: that *only* panexperientialism can satisfy the four performative criteria he sets out.

Michael Katzko offers us a complementary survey of current debates on consciousness, looking especially at three influential philosophers who strongly disagree with one another: David Chalmers, Daniel Dennett, and John Searle. On the surface it would seem that the positions of these three philosophers have relatively little in common, but Katzko argues that they share fundamental presuppositions. This becomes evident when we examine how each philosopher construes the problem he thinks a theory of consciousness is obligated to solve. In each case the problem defining his objective is essentially the same: the difficulty of understanding how the physical could possibly give rise to the mental. (Notice that the question is essentially about causation.) The answers they and many others in the literature give to this question are to be sure quite different. Some answer that it's *not* possible: either because there's really no such thing as the mental or because the mental isn't caused or created by the physical at all, even if it always somehow corresponds to it. Others answer that it's possible, but as yet incomprehensible, or that it's possible, but inherently incomprehensible, and so on. But all these solutions start from the same conception of the problem. Katzko sees them as so many attempts to make a virtue of necessity—having uncritically embraced false dilemmas bequeathed to them by the seventeenth century, contemporary philosophers have no choice but to countenance one side or another. As a whole, the contemporary discussion takes it for granted that what we need to do is rethink our understanding of the mental in order to render its relation to the physical unproblematic. The homogeneity and one-sidedness of the contemporary discussion becomes evident when we compare Whitehead's philosophical conviction that what we need is a new concept of the physical. Why after all should our concept of the mental do *all* the accommodating, especially when the concept of the physical to which accommodation is demanded was discredited by physics a century ago? (In this connection Shields rightly speaks in his contribution of a "cultural lag.")

Looking at the contemporary debate with the eyes of a clinician, Katzko sees a disordered discourse, hamstrung by arbitrary and unacknowledged limitations. Using Whitehead's framework of concepts to make this diagnosis, he shows how the operative concepts of the current debate (mind, the physical, intentionality, qualia) illustrate many of the fallacies described by Whitehead (misplaced concreteness, simple location, vacuous actuality).

The common denominator of these fallacies is the methodological mistake of commencing investigation with abstractions to which one subsequently attempts to reattach what was left out by appealing to other abstractions. The alternative is to begin inquiry with the complete context of the concrete experience in which theoretical investigation operates (including such things as what the investigation presupposes "in practice"), seeking from the outset a generalization that is inclusive rather than exclusive. Whitehead agrees with thinkers such as Bergson, James, and Bradley that prereflective experience is characterized by an unbroken wholeness to which reflection must always do justice. Whenever analytic abstractions precind[8] from this wholeness and treat the world as a set of typological isolates that can be recombined to "explain" concrete phenomena—which the reader will recognize as the resolutive-compositive method that inaugurates modern thought—it will subsequently be difficult, not to say impossible, to understand how things are nevertheless interconnected in nontrivial ways. Katzko shows how well the now popular concept of intentionality illustrates this problem. It reflects an attempt to reattach the contextuality and relatedness that was left out of "mind" when it was conceived as a kind of substance to begin with. And whenever it is supposed, for example, that the "content" of experience does not entail the existence of the "external" world, the mind (or consciousness) is being treated, at least implicitly, as an autonomous entity—that is, as a substance.

Whitehead does not deny the great practical and technological triumphs of the resolutive-compositive method, but he thinks it contributes little to philosophical understanding. It is not possible to explain concreteness—what Aristotle called *tode ti*—as a collocation of abstractions. The task of philosophy is therefore not to explain the concrete by means of the abstract, but to explain how abstractions arise from the analytic partitioning of concrete experience. Katzo shows how the partitioning of experience preferred by the current debate, lacking a self-conscious methodological grounding in the holism of prereflective experience, is often an arbitrary throw-back to platitudes of the seventeenth century.

The late Donald Redfield Griffin's contribution goes a long way toward assuaging the uneasiness noted by philosopher Thomas Nagel that "if one travels too far down the phylogenetic tree, people gradually shed their faith that there is experience there at all" (Nagel 1979, 168). Griffin does not make the specifically Whiteheadian distinction between conscious and unconscious experience, although he does not rule it out either.[9] Defining consciousness as "subjectively experiencing feelings or thoughts," he shows that accumulating evidence strongly suggests that many species of animals have consciousness. His discussion touches on apes, parrots, dolphins, and bees.

Griffin suggests that evidence of animal consciousness is routinely ignored because of an overriding philosophical prejudice "that there is no conceivable way in which valid, objective evidence about conscious experiences of other species can ever be obtained." With regard to species very unlike our own, the prejudice takes the stronger form that conscious thinking simply could not be possible. The result is a double standard, where something naturally accepted as evidence of conscious thinking in the case of humans is dismissed in the case of animals. Griffin reviews evidence from neuropsychology, fieldwork in animal ethology, and experimental work where animals have been trained to communicate.

The evidence from neuropsychology is arresting. Human consciousness does not appear to be associated with any neural structure or function unique to the human brain, but rather with widely distributed, but coordinated activity engaging large areas of the brain. There is no obvious reason why activity of this sort must be limited to brains of the highest complexity. In any case, the close similarity between animal and human nervous systems "means that there is no inherent reason why animal brains cannot produce conscious experiences."

But there is also positive neuroscientific evidence of animal consciousness, at least in monkeys. Just as the phenomenon of blindsight in humans has been used to clarify the important difference between registering and responding to information from the environment, on the one hand, and being conscious of it, on the other, so, too, the evidence of blindsight in monkeys warrants a similar interpretation. Furthermore, the discovery of "mirror neurons" in monkeys suggests that they sometimes entertain possibilities, thinking about behaviors they could or would like to perform. If this interpretation is correct, it has important consequences. It is very hard (maybe impossible) to understand counterfactual ideation as information processing or as stimulus-response conditioning, and Griffin draws very near to Whitehead's technical understanding of consciousness when he suggests that mirror neurons, in providing evidence that monkeys sometimes think about what is *not* the case, but possible, provide evidence of consciousness. There is, moreover, direct evidence that monkeys are conscious when attentionally focused on what *is* the case. It is commonly claimed that monkeys, while they may "know" many facts that are important in their lives, do not *know* that they know them. Reflexivity is thus taken to be a necessary condition of consciousness that monkeys supposedly lack. However, an ingeniously designed experiment demonstrates that monkeys are able to know whether they have remembered a particular piece of useful information and to optimize their strategies for getting food in light of this higher-order knowledge.

It cannot be stressed enough how close Griffin's discussion of consciousness in monkeys comes to Whitehead's very abstract analysis of consciousness. For Whitehead, experience is conscious in one of two basic cases: (1) when we "feel" the absence of a difference between a thing and the description it satisfies or (2) when we "feel" the difference between a thing and a description it doesn't satisfy. To take an arbitrary example (the old cat and the mat), the verbal transcription in the former case would be *the cat is on the mat*; in the latter case, *the cat is not on the mat*. But *the cat is on the mat* is actually abbreviated. Something logically irrelevant, but psychologically crucial has been left out. The verbal analogue of the *consciousness* that the cat is on the mat would have to reflect the actual state of affairs as the absence of a (potential) difference between the thing indicated and its description: the cat is *not* not on the mat. In other words, ideation cannot be conscious unless it involves a counterfactual element. The counterfactual element is denied, but the unrealized possibility of its truth is what makes consciousness of facts possible. To be conscious of a fact is to "experience" that the possibility of its falsehood exists, but is not realized (note that what is experienced is therefore a proposition). Such an experience is possible, according to Whitehead, because there is, in addition to the physical element that supplies the basis of experience, a purely mental element that supplies the necessary modal and logical functions.[10]

In the case of Griffin's monkeys, they apparently understand that their recollection *could be wrong* (possibility), but are confident in specific cases that it is *not wrong* (unrealized possibility), and in other cases they understand that they no longer recall or that the recollection is no longer reliable. In the former case, where error is the unrealized possibility, they are conscious of knowing. In the latter case, where knowledge is the unrealized possibility, they are conscious of not knowing.[11]

Griffin makes his strongest case on the basis of animal communication. He asks only that we accept as evidence of consciousness in animals what we take as evidence of consciousness in humans. Even conceding a single standard, however, many will deny that animal communication has the requisite parity: it is not symbolic, lacks semantic content, and lacks displacement. ("Displacement" means "convey[ing] information about something displaced in space or time from the situation where the communication takes place.") Let the reader note that we are here talking about the "decisive clues" alluded to earlier that would warrant an inference from patent behavior (in this case: communication) to the existence of consciousness, which is necessarily something latent. The decisive features communication must have to warrant such an inference appear to be (1) a symbolic character, (2) semantic content, and (3) displacement. For it is precisely the prominence of these three features in human communication that compels us to view it as expressing subjective experiences, and these three features, so it is alleged, are conspicuously absent from animal communication. But, in fact, these features *are* attested. The alarm calls of vervet monkeys convey specific semantic information about the types of predators, not just emotional arousal, and the famous "waggle dance" of honeybees displays all three critical features. The waggle dance is an elaborate symbolic code, specific enough to convey precise semantic content that is displaced, flexible enough to serve multiple purposes (e.g., finding the best nectar or finding the best location for a new hive), and it involves an extensive exchange of information among dancers leading through reciprocal adjustments to a final group decision.

Griffin concedes that most examples of animal communication, such as the alarm calls of the vervet monkeys, are indeed examples of direct reactions to the current situation in which the animal finds itself, whereas humans "often think and communicate about past occurrences or what may happen in the future." Consciousness is strongly associated with displacement for the same reason it is strongly associated with counterfactual ideation. It is hard to see how sensitivity and responsiveness to what is *not* present could be a matter of unconscious information processing or stimulus-response conditioning. Finding displacement in the communication of social insects therefore poses significant challenges to conventional assumptions about consciousness.

George W. Shields makes skillful use of the methods and resources of Analytic philosophy to argue for panexperientialism, thereby disarming some of its most self-confident critics—Anglo-American philosophers who think panexperientialism violates basic sureties of logically rigorous and scientifically informed analysis. Sophistication in formal logic and command of hard science often make Analytic criticism formidable. Shields meets this criticism on its own terms, presenting formally rigorous arguments and hard empirical evidence in favor of panexperientialism.

The first part of his paper focuses on logical and philosophical arguments for panexperientialism. Shields examines what panexperientialism means and proposes the following as minimal criteria: that every genuine individual has a physical presence in space-time and is related internally to its environment.[12] Whitehead's analytic unit of experience—the prehension—is therefore an internal relation. Following Hartshorne, Shields argues that internal relations translate logically into strict implications. From this analysis he infers what the denial of panexperientialism amounts to: an ontology of exclusively external relations and a logic of entirely open possibilities. There would be no restrictions on the conjunction or separation of individuals in this world (this is what is meant by "open possibilities" in this context). The only necessity would be the completely symmetrical logical necessities of identity and noncontradiction.

Shields is happy to continue the strain or argument begun by David Griffin when he analyzed the idea of performative consistency in terms of "hard-core common sense." Shields calls "assumptions which we presume in our practice universally or nearly universally" "deep protocols of common sense" and under this rubric extends Griffin's list to include four more items:

"that (1) our experience as temporally conceptualized into 'past,' 'present,' and 'future' is coherent; (2) the act of remembering is in principle not the same as the act of imagining; (3) causal influence is objectively real; and (4) a 'skeptical solipsism of the present' is false." Shields presents what he calls a "reduction to pragmatic absurdity" by showing that the external relations ontology violates these four common sense commitments. Since the relation between any two events is wholly external and contingent it becomes impossible to understand how the present could have anything to do with the past. A present event, such as the act of remembering the past, would necessarily be independent of anything that actually happened in the past, undercutting the concepts of "past," "memory," and "causal influence" at one stroke and sealing present consciousness hermetically in the present moment. Panexperientialism, by accepting internal relations, avoids these difficulties. Shields notes that panexperientialism also avoids the cardinal problems typically afflicting materialism and dualism, namely, the emergence of qualia out of matter and the possibility of the mind acting causally on matter.

Shields considers and rebuts in some detail six objections raised against panexperientialism: (1) that it implies that things like rocks have thoughts (only it doesn't), (2) that it implies that the behavior of the elementary constituents of matter would not be predictable through their physical properties alone (only they aren't), (3) that elementary particles are completely identical whatever their past histories and thus could not have any interior states (only they aren't and so could), (4) that attributing any kind of feeling, however qualified or attenuated, to micro-constituents of matter violates the linguistic protocols for meaningful use of terms such as feeling (but not just the concept of feeling is generalized—the criteria for its attribution are generalized as well, yielding predicates such as "openness to the environment" or "internal relatedness," which are still "psychological" predicates without being strained usage), (5) that any adequate physicalism must be tantamount to epiphenomenalism (but epiphenomenalism cuts *against* physical science because it is anti-evolutionary, implying that "animals and humans evolved with persistent natural selection of entirely superfluous mental entities"); and (6) that the existence of unproblematic forms of emergence, such a liquidity from molecules, shows that proto-experiential "elements" are not needed to explain the emergence of the experience we are familiar with (but experience is unlike liquidity in the relevant respect because the latter is a kind of emergence that can be understood and predicted from its antecedent elements, while experience notoriously cannot).

The second part of Shields' paper looks at arresting empirical data in support of panexperientialism. In pushing down the lower threshold of "conscious" experience, Donald Griffin got us to social insects. Velmans, arguing that even single cell organisms might have some kind of phenomenal awareness, got us to the very bottom of the phylogenetic tree. Shields, drawing on startling but well-confirmed empirical findings, provides the final turn of the screw that anchors experience in the Planck-scale units of nature. He cites first the phenomenon of neuroplasticity. Although it had long been dogma that the brain is hardwired once and for all in early childhood, recent research has documented ongoing alterations in the adult brain, including the growth of new neurons, as a result of sensory and cognitional input. Important to Shields' argument is the remarkable discovery that the brain's plasticity is susceptible to clinical manipulation. Attentional therapies, involving such exercises as "observing" undesirable thoughts and emotions in an impartial manner and then refocusing attention repeatedly on alternative thoughts, have not only been shown to work, but PET scans have now revealed altera- tions of the brain's neural system corresponding to the behavioral changes. Shields argues that this is just a special case of the weird but documented quantum phenomenon known as the "Quantum Zeno Effect," where obser- vation increases the probability that a given quantum state will *not* change: "the more frequently and rapidly you observe a physical system in a certain selected way, the more you 'lock in' a certain physical state of the system." The power of attentional therapies to decrease the probability of unwanted thoughts and emotions would thus result from "locking in" the alternatives by repeated ideational exercises. Shields' appeal to quantum mechanics is not entirely speculative since, as he points out, the release of neurotransmitters is regulated by processes so microscopic that quantum mechanical principles do indeed apply. The provocative conclusion is that attention to one's own thinking, like the observation of experimental setups, has the power to alter the probability that one rather than another superimposed wave function will be actualized. This kind of "top-down" causal influence is precisely what Whitehead's panexperientialism is designed to explain. Shields doubts that classical materialism can make any sense of these phenomena at all.[13]

Max Velmans also takes up the critical question of how far downscale in complexity types of individuals can be found that still have some kind of experience. Velmans approaches the question in the context of a larger ques- tion about the evolution of consciousness. Which sorts of entities are thought to have consciousness determines to a large extent when consciousness must have evolved and what biological refinements to the evolving organism are specifically responsible for it. Velmans notes that theories about the distribu- tion of consciousness range from the ultraconservative (only humans have it) to the extravagantly libertarian (everything has it—panpsychism). While ultraconservative theories traditionally drew their support from theology, more contemporary versions "are based on the supposition that higher mental processes of the kinds unique to humans are necessary for consciousness of any kind." Velmans is skeptical not only of these ultraconservative views, but ultimately of any degree of conservatism on this point. He examines a variety of rationales for the claim that consciousness depends on brain complexity or higher order cognitive processes and argues that "[s]uch views confuse the necessary conditions for the *existence* of consciousness with the added conditions required to support its many *forms*."

While Velmans ultimately endorses the "extravagantly libertarian" view, it must be noted that his vocabulary does not strictly conform to the usage of Whitehead or contemporary Whiteheadians. Although he does distinguish between conscious and unconscious information processing (and elsewhere [2000] between conscious and unconscious *mind*), he does not make the terminological distinction between conscious and nonconscious experience or between panpsychism and panexperientialism. Nevertheless, he makes nearly equivalent distinctions by stressing the widely differing degrees of complexity manifested by the forms that consciousness takes: from mere feeling to conceptually articulated consciousness of self and world. At the lowest extreme, consciousness in Velmans' acceptation is tantamount to Whitehead's nonconscious experience. Accordingly, the form of panpsychism he advocates is very close to panexperientialism. This becomes evident when we revisit his distinction between conscious and unconscious information processing in light of his final reflections on the nature of focal-attentive consciousness. As we discuss below, Velmans marshals an arresting reason why unconscious information processing may simply be information processing in which a diffuse, primitive consciousness has been suppressed. So in the end, feeling may well be a naturally occurring feature of all biological processes, which regulate themselves through information extracted from their internal and external environments.

Velmans advances two principle arguments against conservative distribution theories. First, following a tradition that includes Thomas Huxley and Charles Sherrington, he points out that conservative distribution implies a discontinuity theory of evolution. At some point consciousness must "appear [...] (out of nothing) through some random mutation in complex life forms that happen[s] to confer a reproductive advantage." Typically, it is thought that consciousness is linked to the evolution of the neocortex. However, there is nothing unique to cortical cells that might be responsible for consciousness. Indeed, as Sherrington observes, cells in the frog embryo destined to be brain can often be replaced with others, such as skin cells from the back, and still develop into brain. This leaves us with the assumption that consciousness must have something to do with neural *organization*. But the strong evidence for the gradual evolution of the human brain makes it unlikely that consciousness sprang fully formed at any point in the brain's slow accretion of structural/functional complexity.

Velmans' second argument against conservative distribution theories is, by contrast, so untraditional that it upends conventional objections to panexperientialism. Velmans brings neurophysiology and phenomenology together in a startling way. He reminds us that a great number of the synapses in the brain must be inhibitory. Otherwise the nervous system would be in a constant state of universal excitement after the first signal. At the same time we know that consciousness would be impossible if the vast amount of simultaneous information streaming in to the mind/brain were not limited and filtered down to something that it could manageably attend to.[14] From this Velmans infers the possibility that consciousness may be a naturally occurring feature of all neural representations. However, the more complex the nervous system, the more necessary it would be to *inhibit* consciousness of all but the most important information to prevent overload and confusion. In this case, rather than adding something to unconscious representations to make them conscious, attention[15] would correspond to a highly selective release of consciousness from inhibition.

The implications of this argument are dramatic. As Velmans notes, cognitive psychology has demonstrated that most human information processing takes place unconsciously. Naturally, this leads cognitive psychology to seek the specific conditions that distinguish conscious from unconscious processing. It asks, in other words: why does consciousness emerge at some particular threshold in the mind/brain's cognitive functioning? This question is perhaps no less vexed than the question of the threshold at which consciousness emerges in the course of evolution. Both questions presuppose a discontinuity: on the one hand, a discontinuity in the evolution of consciousness (a diachronic discontinuity), on the other, a discontinuity in the distribution of consciousness (a synchronic discontinuity). The synchronic discontinuity takes two forms. There is the discontinuity between organisms that do and those that do not have consciousness, and, within the nervous system of organisms that do have consciousness, there is the discontinuity between conscious and unconscious processes. These two kinds of synchronic discontinuity are closely related. Without having to make any particular assumptions about the relation between organic processes *available* to consciousness and organic processes that *result* in consciousness, we can nonetheless say it is only because consciousness does not extend (in either sense) to the vast majority of organic processes in our own brains and bodies that we resist the idea that very similar processes in other life forms might be conscious (in either sense).

But if what human beings normally experience as consciousness is only the selective release of an aboriginally pervasive consciousness from its systemic inhibition in complex nervous systems, then unconscious information processing would not be different in kind from—that is, discontinuous with—conscious processing. Unless specifically inhibited, a kind of rudimentary "consciousness" would attach to all organic information processing. Neither at some point in evolutionary history nor at some level of neural activity would consciousness come into being *de novo*.

Of course this rudimentary consciousness would not involve attention or any kind of reflective, objectifying, or thematically motivated awareness. It would be a diffuse, nonconceptual, nonobjectifying, and nonreflective feeling of qualia—just the sort of experience Whitehead calls "unconscious" and generalizes to all events in nature. On this telling, discontinuity—the abrupt emergence of consciousness from something unconscious—would be an illusion arising from attentional consciousness, the necessary flip side of which is the suppression or exclusion of diffuse consciousness. The highly restricted access of our own consciousness to what it's like to be a living organism then leaves us in a poor position to appreciate what we have in common with less complex forms of life.

We see how this argument leads to a new opening in the vexed problem of the evolutionary value of consciousness. It would not be consciousness, but complexity of information processing that confers a reproductive advantage on certain organisms in certain environments. Such complexity would go hand in hand with increasing complexity of the attendant consciousness. But increasing complexity in the nervous system would actually become counterproductive for the organism unless the attendant consciousness of all but a narrow selection of the increasingly diffuse aggregate experience embraced in this complexity was suppressed, thus yielding our familiar attentionally focused consciousness as well as the illusion that it is the addition of something altogether new on top of an otherwise unconscious cognitive processing.

For Velmans, an evolutionary account of human consciousness is therefore possible, but only by upending the way the question is usually posed. It would not be consciousness so much as its suppression that under certain circumstances confers a selective advantage. Attentional consciousness evolves when diffuse consciousness begins to pose a selective *disadvantage*. We should note in passing how close this comes to Whitehead's thesis that complexity of experience, which he calls width and depth through harmony and intensity, requires a great deal of the data actually given to an entity to enter into its experience only negatively, that is, as something excluded, suppressed, diminished, or transmuted.

This unanticipated turn of the argument stands Thomas Nagel's reservations on their head. What needs to be explained is not how there possibly could be simple phenomenal consciousness at the low end of the phylogenetic tree, but why it is lacking throughout most of the nervous system of organisms at the high end. "[P]henomenal consciousness (of any kind) might only require representation. If so, even simple invertebrates might have some rudimentary awareness, in so far as they are able to represent and, indeed, respond to certain features of the world." Empirically, it is as yet impossible to rule out even more remote seeming possibilities: "If the ability to represent and respond to the world, or the ability to modify behavior consequent on interactions with the world are the criteria for consciousness then it may be that consciousness extends not just to simple invertebrates (such as Planaria) but also to unicellular organisms, fungi and plants." The upshot of the continuity theory of the evolution of consciousness is essentially panexperientialist: "In the cosmic explosion that gave birth to the universe, consciousness co-emerged with matter and co-evolves with it. [...] On this view, evolution accounts for the different *forms* that consciousness takes. But, consciousness, in some primal form, did not emerge at any particular stage of evolution. Rather, it was there from the beginning. Its emergence, with the birth of the universe, is neither more nor less mysterious than the emergence of matter, energy, space and time."

Gregg Rosenberg also focuses on the case for panexperientialism, but he takes a very different approach from our other contributors. In a precisely executed analysis of the semantic structure of explanatory theories and of causality in particular, Rosenberg surprises us with an altogether original argument for panexperientialism. Rosenberg observes that Whitehead's panexperientialism is "a reaction to the void created by his rejection of Vacuous Actuality," which he explains with admirable lucidity: "A Vacuous Actuality would be a fundamental reality that is purely structural and quantifiable, with no intrinsic nature of its own that escapes the formal description of a pattern. The rejection of Vacuous Actuality amounts to the assertion that the entities of fundamental physics, for instance, are more than mere dynamic quantities, mere information structures in the vacuum. It is the rejection of the now popular information-theoretic 'It from bit' view for understanding the essential nature of the physical world."

Rosenberg notes that the rejection of Vacuous Actuality and the endorsement of panexperientialism by process philosophy look on the surface "like positions of insight, or even faith, not sufficiently motivated by argumentation." The purpose of his paper "is to put more argumentation in place to support the rejection of Vacuous Actuality and the panexperientialist reaction to that rejection."

Rosenberg begins with a logical analysis of different kinds of relations. He is especially interested in the kind of relationships that define the explanatory structure of scientific theories. He illustrates how they are typically conceptual relations in which the relata mutually presuppose one another. For example, in economics, goods and services are things that consumers and producers barter. But consumers and producers are, in turn, simply people occupying distinct positions in the system of bartering goods and services. In biology, a heritable characteristic (gene) is one that parents pass from their generation to the next, but a parent is an organism that passes along its genes. Rosenberg argues that such circularity is logically harmless and metaphysically possible only because the relationships are in these cases carried by items individuated by properties external to the circular relation. The roles of the two players in a game of checkers, for example, are defined in a circular way because they presuppose one another, but their distinction is possible only because they are carried by a difference that is not circular, namely the difference between the colors of the pieces. This leads Rosenberg to identify one kind of circularity as merely contrastive, like "on" and "off"—just as the players in a game of checkers are sufficiently defined simply by stipulating that they are different from one another. Here each term is defined by nothing more than the negation of the other. Another kind of circularity he calls compositional because the items presuppose one another in a positive way as components of each other's natures. He proposes that causality exhibits this kind of circularity, involving a nexus between effective properties, which can determine an event to happen, and receptive properties, which allow such determination to happen. To prevent them from being logical *impossibilia*, both kinds of relations, contrastive and compositional, need carrier properties external to the circles they define.

It may be that these external properties are internal to some other, more fundamental circularity, but ultimately there must be carriers external to any circularity. Rosenberg thus throws light on the hierarchical order of the sciences familiar since Comte, which corresponds to twentieth-century expectations of reduction. Rosenberg mentions the following sequence: economics, sociology, psychology, ecology, and biology, chemistry, physics. The circularity of the higher science is carried by properties external to the circularity of that science, but internal to the circularity of the more fundamental science. This leads Rosenberg to the critical question what the ultimate carriers are. We needn't agree with the reducibility thesis of the unified science program to agree that physics will be the lowest order science in this scheme of grounding. Physical reality in space and time is what finally individuates the operative terms of the higher sciences. So Rosenberg poses the pointed question: what carries the circular relations that define physics? These carriers must have several interesting properties. "What the world needs from a carrier of physics are properties whose being would be extrinsic within *every* such system and yet which still have the requisite internal relations to one another. For physics, we need *ultimate carriers*. The properties best answering to this description are best thought of as properties that are intrinsic *tout court*. A property whose categorical nature is extrinsic within every *system* of properties is simply one whose being is intrinsic at least partly to *itself*, rather than to its contextual relationships. That is, it is a property that we cannot understand in purely systematic terms without leaving something out." At the same time, in order to be "carriers of the effective properties described by physics, these intrinsic properties must have internal contrasts with one another that mirror the features and relations of physical properties: patterns of distinctness, variations in magnitude, and relations of compatibility, incompatibility, and requirement." Rosenberg suggests that the most plausible candidates for the role of such ultimate individuals are the much talked about qualia. On the one hand, they have identities that are noncontextual (the subjective feel of lavender is knowable only through itself and is not implied by any facts of physics). On the other hand, they have definite logical and quantitative relations with one another (such as mutual incompatibility or intensity differences). This leads Rosenberg to his provocative thesis about the identity of the "ultimate carriers" of causation: "Things in the world are natural individuals if, and only if, they are experiencing phenomenal individuals."

If, as seems plausible, the only thing that could be external to every context was something that was at least partly "internal to itself," then we have a strong reason to believe that "self" is a meaningful and indispensable predicate of the ultimate bearers of relations in the world. Rosenberg does not pursue his line of thought in this way, but his logical analysis of a property which is "external *tout court*" in terms of "internal to itself" seems already to lend credence to Whitehead's concept of the ultimate constituents of the world as "actual occasions" understood as possessing an incipient reflexivity or selfhood. There is something self-referential about them by dint of an experience, however attenuated, of self-enjoyment, which implies a modicum of being-for-self happening privately in an interior world. If this argument holds, then we could say that just as Shields gave the panexperientialist argument a last turn of the screw, Rosenberg gives the response to the classic objection to panexperientialism a last turn of the screw. For we have specified the criteria that will allow us to generalize the concept of experience not only to other forms of life without losing the semantic justification for calling it experience, but also, beyond what are normally considered to be organisms, to inorganic nature: experience is the entry of something at least partly internal to itself into an internal relation with something other than itself. We have, furthermore, identified compelling logical and metaphysical reasons for making such a generalization.

Maria Pachalska and Bruce Duncan MacQueen point out that the science most qualified to elucidate the mind-body problem and consciousness in particular is *neuropsychology*, but that the requisite interdisciplinary collaboration between neurology and psychology has largely stymied because the dominant view of brain function in the neurosciences makes a theory of consciousness impossible: "A modular mind/brain made up of discrete processors shuttling bits of data back and forth does not need to be conscious in order to do its job. If computers were to become conscious they would by the same token cease to be useful as computers, and if we conceive of our brains as organic computers, as is fashionable nowadays, then the same applies to them."

Proposing microgenesis as a more promising paradigm in neuropsychology, they provide a straightforward and largely nontechnical overview of the microgenetic theory of consciousness developed by Jason Brown (New York University Medical Center). Brown draws equally on Whiteheadian process thinking and acute clinical observations of brain pathology. According to microgenetic theory, mind-brain states such as consciousness arise as a rapid volley of overlapping waves of activity that can be measured in milliseconds. Drawing *inter alia* on Paul MacLean's theory of the "triune brain" (MacLean 1967 and 1991), microgenetic theory proposes that each wave originates from a core in the anatomically deepest and phylogenetically oldest parts of the brain, the brainstem formations we share with reptiles, and radiates outward through the limbic system (paleomammalian brain) to the cortex (neomammalian brain), and finally to the neocortex of the specifically human brain. Because neurologists tend to think of consciousness as a phenomenon of the cortex, it becomes difficult to understand how consciously initiated activity, supposedly originating in the neocortex, can be integrated with activity originating in the "reptilian" brain stem, where the stimulus-response arc is closed with extreme rapidity. Although the authors don't quite say so explicitly, this integration problem is none other than the "mind-body problem."

It is crucial to understand that on Brown's model nothing is initiated in the cortex—what arises there is always a modification of activity already begun. Corresponding to each of the three evolutionary levels reflected in brain anatomy is a wholly functional brain: the outer/later functions are parasitic on the inner/older ones they enclose, but not *vice versa*. Thus, all processing of stimuli or other response activity originates in the brain stem. The limbic system and the cortex, each in turn, have only the power to sculpt what has already commenced. Depending on the functional/anatomical level at which the cycle of activity is closed, it manifests as reflex (brainstem), emotion (limbic system), or discriminating and objectifying consciousness (cortex, neocortex). But since the cycles are slower the farther out they are from the core, the higher brain functions require the interruption of the faster inner cycles in order to allow the activity initiated in the reptilian brain to be prolonged and shaped by the emotional loading of the limbic system, or for the limbic brain response to be further prolonged and channeled through the more refined constraints of the neocortex. One is reminded of Bergson's thesis that perception is a kind of interruption of action or the prolongation of its incipience, making its enhancement by memory possible. For Brown, each higher function is an enhancement made possible by the disruption or retardation of the more primitive function.

A number of thorny problems in cognitive psychology, such as the binding problem or the murky relationship between cognition and emotion, can be elegantly solved by this analysis, which is supported by extensive pathological data. But it must be stressed that Brown's fascinating analysis implies a concept of consciousness very different from the acceptation common in the current literature: "Consciousness is not purely a cortical phenomenon [...] but emerges precisely from the process of evolution, passing from an undifferentiated core, through an animist dream world, to a world of self and objects. It is the whole process, not its just endpoint, that constitutes and creates consciousness."

Avraham Schweiger, Michael Frost, and Ofer Keren also advance Brown's idea that consciousness is the moment-to-moment product of nested phases of realization, corresponding roughly to the nested evolutionary strata of the brain just described. But they adopt a broader perspective to argue for the process view of consciousness. The authors focus on comparing the development of consciousness at different time scales: phylogeny, ontogeny, and microgeny (the process that sustains consciousness from moment to moment). They note that regardless of scale the same pattern characterizes the process through which consciousness develops. In each case the process unfolds from the global unity of a diffuse whole to the differential individuation of an objectified diversity. Schweiger et al. then show how pathological data on the stages of recovery from coma are consistent with Brown's theory of microgenesis and reflect the same pattern of development on a time scale slow enough to be easily detected. Furthermore, their analysis supports Whitehead's idea that consciousness as we usually think of it is a late-phase development preceded by phases of more primitive experience, which we could, using language not found in their paper, call pre-, proto-, or perhaps demi-conscious, depending on the level of development. Their analysis also supports the Whiteheadian idea that consciousness is a refined, high-level manifestation of a very basic and pervasive type of process that structures nature at all levels, forming nested hierarchies in which higher levels of process incorporate and recapitulate the lower ones. They note that the process view of consciousness is opposed to "the current zeitgeist in cognitive science, according to which phenomenological appearances of objects/events represent properties of 'reality.'" If consciousness unfolds through developmental stages, at each stage "reality" will have a different cast to it, none of which have the right to displace the others and lay claim to exclusive reality.

Michel Weber undertakes a process-oriented phenomenology in order to analyze the normal, everyday consciousness of the "natural attitude." Weber's approach to consciousness is mainly influenced by James and Whitehead. James insisted that the focal consciousness of everyday existence is not the only kind of consciousness. For one thing, it is always enveloped by a fringe of unthematic awareness whose own irremediable vagueness is essential to the clarity and effectiveness of focal consciousness. For another, it is only one of a number of alternate possible states, each with its own cognitive value. Weber brings one of Whitehead's deepest intuitions to bear on these insights of James'. According to Whitehead, permanence and flux (including both arising *and perishing*) are the two most important features of the world that metaphysics must account for, and, accordingly, worldviews can be classified in terms of the distribution and relative importance they accord to each. We can imagine a sort of spectrum, with Parmenides (Everything is permanent) at one end and Heraclitus (Everything flows) at the other. Substantialism is the view that accords metaphysical primacy to permanence. Weber suggests that substantialism is defined by a rigid metaphysical reading—inspired by everyday consciousness—of the principles of Aristotelian logic (Law of Identity, Law of Non-Contradiction, Law of Excluded Middle). Accordingly, substantialism manifests itself in psychology as the assumption that consciousness is also a thing defined by these three laws. Weber argues that this has the unfortunate effect of absolutizing consciousness in its normal and everyday manifestation to the exclusion of the fringe and alternative modalities that exercised James. For it forces us to assume, first, that consciousness is a thing with a fixed identity—an identity that is, moreover, clear and distinct. Second, it forces us to assume that consciousness must—on pain of contradiction—be this thing and nothing else (here we may glimpse part of the rationale for the modern prejudice that consciousness must be all and wholly conscious, through and through). Third, it forces us to assume that there is nothing remaindered or intermediate between consciousness, so understood, and what is unconscious in the sense of dead or inanimate. The implication of this is that normal consciousness is the only kind of consciousness there is. In the context of Weber's Whiteheadian reflections on permanence and flux, clinical evidence from psychotherapy and hypnosis (to say nothing of religious experience or "mind-altering" drugs) that normal consciousness does not exhaust what consciousness is militates against substantialism in psychology and points the way toward process paradigms that allow consciousness to enjoy a more fluid reality.

Weber is mainly engaged by the third assumption (that something is either normal consciousness or simply unconscious). He argues that what normally counts as empirically or phenomenologically "given" consciousness is an artifact of instrumental, linguistic, and social rationality. An alternative—more provocative—title for his paper might have been "The Social Construction of Consciousness." He seeks to relativize the normally absolutized concept of everyday consciousness by exposing the machinery that leads to its construction as a stable thematic nucleus within a rich and ever-flowing multidimensional experience. Through an iterated process of abstraction in which the more thematic features of consciousness are peeled away to reveal the less thematic, but more fundamental ones, Weber arrives at a kind of map of the tacit dimensions. His analysis is organized by the hypothesis that the two faces of consciousness, public and private, are isomorphic in structure so that each element in the cartography of the one corresponds like a mirror image to a similarly embedded element in the cartography of the other. But he also argues that the corresponding elements are interdependent. Consequently, what stabilizes privately as "consciousness" (but is really just *normal* consciousness) cannot be independent of what is established socially as sane or rational consciousness. Once normal consciousness is exposed in its relativity it is possible to appreciate its important contributions to our cognitive life without building a metaphysics around it.

Xavier Verley examines the concept of consciousness native to early modern philosophy and the dialectical consequences it brings on itself as a result of its logico-metaphysical prejudices. He supports Whitehead's view that a peculiar emphasis on consciousness led modern philosophy into the quagmire of solipsism and that an appropriate valorization of memory is the only solution. According to Whitehead the characteristic problems of modern philosophy result from a set of false assumptions and persistent fallacies ultimately running deeper than its fascination with consciousness. While a cause of the problem of solipsism, the modern concept of consciousness is also a symptom of more fundamental errors. Verley referees the deep fallacies of modern thought that Whitehead saw as the most damaging: the logical primacy ascribed to the subject-predicate form of the proposition, the metaphysical primacy ascribed to the universal-particular and substance-quality dyads, and the Aristotelian principle that a primary substance is always a subject, never a predicate. Whitehead opposes to these characteristic assumptions of modern thought a novel set of principles intended on the one hand to avoid the pitfalls of the philosophy of consciousness and on the other to ground a new philosophy of organism. Verley's contribution provides a concise overview of Whitehead's critique of Descartes, Locke, Hume, and Kant, and along the way he names and elucidates the numerous fallacies and counter-principles Whitehead invokes in this critique, showing how consciousness gains its prominence from these fallacies and loses its prominence by their correction.

Verley answers the question: how is it that consciousness emerges as the substance or form of the subject in modern philosophy? He notes that Descartes' peculiar meditation on himself has the effect of substituting for the "me" (that inhabits the world through its body and inhabits time by inheriting the past reality of things) the "I" (that is the subject of doubt and the agent of mental acts). Thinking becomes the fundamental type of mental act, and a judgment, executed by the will in the present moment, becomes the way the subject is supposed to (re)establish a relation to its body, its habits (including its personality and character), the world, and the past. The self is thus defined by a relation to itself, rather than by a specific kind of relation to the world. Once the self is reduced to the consciousness it has of itself in the instant, consciousness itself is confined within this solipsism. What is gained is modest: the self's certainty of being itself in the instant of reflection. What is lost is nothing less than sanity and common sense. Descartes' seeming return to good sense at the end of his meditations to the contrary, all that has been lost cannot be recovered. If time is not physical inheritance, then the "me" will have no ontological inertia. The "I" must remain locked in the solipsism of the present moment and—just as Descartes in fact teaches—only God will have the power to weld together the successive instants of time. The self will remain dispossessed of good sense because it will never be anything more than the "I" grasping after its unobtainable "me." The integrity of the "I" and the "me" is only possible through memory, where perception of the past is understood not as presentation of the past, but as a prolongation of it. In this case, perception is a physical inheritance that is felt (from the past), not "represented" (in the present). This establishes a real continuity of the "I" with the evolving world and the "me" it includes. One important consequence of this valorization of physical inheritance is that consciousness and the "I" it likes to foreground become inessential aspects of experience. Thus, just as starting with the "I" led to the idea of consciousness as the form or essence of the subject, starting with the "me" leads to consciousness being denied such a privileged status.

Anderson Weekes takes advantage of a provocative discussion occurring in the *Journal of Consciousness Studies* to bring an ancient philosophical problem into contemporary focus and to show how Whitehead thought he solved it. The skeptical critique of causality advanced at one point or another in every major philosophical tradition received strong endorsement and indirect empirical support in a paper by Eleanor Rosch on the psychology of explanation. M.C. Price subsequently applied her results to the specific problem of explaining consciousness. Price argues that the prospects for solving the mind-body problem cannot be any greater than the prospects for solving the old riddle of causation. After all, what we are looking for is the mechanism by which the body gives rise to, causes, the mind or consciousness. We are, in effect, looking for the necessary connection Hume claimed could never be found between any two distinct things. If the idea of necessary connection between distinct things is unintelligible, as Rosch and the skeptics contend, then the mind-body problem must be unsolvable.

Weekes contends that Whitehead's thinking, from *Process and Reality* to *Modes of Thought*, is immersed in this problem and that Whitehead offers a breathtakingly original solution that may not deserve our allegiance, but deserves closer scrutiny than it has received. After refereeing the arguments of Rosch and Price and placing them in a large historical context, he examines Whitehead's doctrine of "perception in the mode of causal efficacy" and its own historical pedigree. Whitehead wants to claim that the experience of causation is so fundamental as to be pervasive and undeniable. Supposing this is true, the question becomes aggravated: if causation is pervasive and undeniable, how can it be so elusive that its reality has escaped those observers who were most avid about finding it? According to Whitehead, the answer has to do with the nature of consciousness.

On the one hand, consciousness—if not by nature, then at least when it is seeking knowledge—is objectifying; on the other hand, consciousness always involves a performative dimension that cannot be objectified as such, but is nevertheless always experienced. The two most important aspects of this performative dimension are time and the animal body, and what they reveal, according to Whitehead, is the causal emergence of "immediacy of self-enjoyment" (i.e., "mind") out of what is past and already "second hand" (i.e., "body"). However, when anything tacitly lived or performed (performed "in the first person") is *objectified*, an unwitting substitution occurs. Because we assume parity between objectifying an object and objectifying the self, we think we have captured the intended actuality in the focus of our objectification, just as we would a live specimen, which doesn't cease to live simply because it is subject to observation. But in the case of objectifying one's own performance, what is found at the focus of objectification is never the intended actuality, but a representation that is precisely lacking the character of performance. Thus, since objectification renders the *actuality* of causation (as opposed to the "representation" of it), like anything else performed or tacitly lived, *invisible*, objectifying consciousness obscures the process of its own emergence and cannot help but wonder where in the world it came from. Far from being that thing whose true nature is fully revealed in self-objectifying reflection, objectifying consciousness is always a stranger to itself. By the same token, objectifying consciousness deprives itself of the only possible means to understand causal connection. Valorizing the performative dimension of consciousness thus allows Whitehead to offer an original solution to the mind-body problem as well as to the causation problem in its most general form: the question, namely, "How are synthetic judgments *a priori* possible?"

Weekes stresses that Whitehead's account of causation and of consciousness in its bearing on the issue of causation is essentially phenomenological. In light of this it is remarkable that there has not been more intercourse between process philosophy and Phenomenology. Having at least some goals in common, they could benefit from mutual adjustment and critique. Weekes has set this process going by tightening up Whitehead's loosely conceived analyses with sharply defined concepts borrowed from the Phenomenological tradition (performance, objectification) and by using Whitehead's decisive critique of modern philosophy as a template to isolate the critical failure in Husserl's Phenomenology that led him absurdly to a form of absolute idealism.

Related Literature

This volume fills a noticeable gap in the literature. Given the importance accorded to the concept of consciousness in modern (and contemporary) philosophy and the originality of Whitehead's critique of consciousness-centered philosophy, it is surprising that there is so little literature devoted to the exposition and development of Whitehead's theory of consciousness. A brief overview of the most closely related literature will highlight the unique ambitions of the present book.

Craig Eisendrath's *The Unifying Moment* (1971, reissued 1999) is a comparative exposition of the psychologies of William James and Whitehead. Besides being a James-Whitehead comparison, Eisendrath's book is quite different from ours in that it aims to be a faithful and clarifying exposition. Ours is partly an exposition, but more importantly a development and application of Whitehead's ideas that dovetails with contemporary research and discussions, taking advantage of work that has appeared only in the last ten to twenty years. Furthermore, Eisendrath's book looks synoptically at Whitehead's psychology and devotes only a few pages to the specific topic of his theory of consciousness.

We have already mentioned David Griffin's *Unsnarling the World-Knot* (1998), a broadly conceived exposition of Whitehead's psychology that directly engages the contemporary literature in consciousness studies. Griffin offers a Whiteheadian critique of current leading theories, arguing specifically that they fail to solve the mind-body problem. Griffin's book is not, however, focused *specifically* on Whitehead's theory of consciousness, and while his treatment of Whitehead is not limited to exposition, it is largely a defense rather than a development of Whitehead's ideas. Griffin's contribution to the present volume picks up here his own book left off. He recapitulates the main arguments of his *Unsnarling the World-Knot* and brings them to bear specifically on Whitehead's theory of consciousness.

Jason Brown's *Mind and Nature* (2000) is a work in metapsychology that applies Whitehead's process philosophy to neuropsychology. The result is a Whiteheadian process theory of consciousness that is empirically supported by extensive clinical data. Brown's erudition can be daunting. Drawing on an extensive philosophical literature, he valorizes the phenomenological insights of British Idealism and Buddhist psychology to delineate the distinctive challenges that a theory of consciousness must meet, and in proffering process philosophy as the foundation of a theory adequate to the challenges, he draws on a lifetime of experience in neurology. We are very pleased to be able to feature in our collection the contribution by Pachalska and MacQueen, which presents an overview of Brown's ideas that presupposes no specialized knowledge of medicine or neglected areas of intellectual history and will be readily accessible to scholars in process philosophy and consciousness studies.

Ralph Pred's *Onflow* (2005) is an ambitious book. He argues, first, that certain ideas of William James, John Searle, and Whitehead can be exploited to generate a phenomenology of consciousness that is unprecedented in its nuance and accuracy. Second, he argues that Whitehead's metaphysical categories provide an adequate theoretical model of consciousness and, conversely, that consciousness adequately described illustrates a concrete application of Whitehead's metaphysical categories. Finally, he argues that Gerald Edelman's neurobiological theory of consciousness can be read consistently as a physical interpretation of this model and hence as a physical explanation of the phenomenology.

There are a number of themes common to our book and Pred's (the phenomenology of consciousness, causation, and the neurobiological realization of a Whiteheadian process theory of consciousness), but the treatment in each case is different. Pred exploits Edelman's neurobiological theory of consciousness to show that a neurobiological interpretation of his Whiteheadian theory of consciousness is *possible*. Our book looks to the neurobiological theory of Jason Brown, rather than Edelman, to show that a Whiteheadian interpretation of neurobiology is possible and why it is philosophically promising. Pred looks at the phenomenology of the stream of consciousness, in particular at its actional context. Phenomenologically, our book looks at the performative presuppositions of conscious experience, especially in relation to the nature of time and temporal experience. Pred looks at what the stream of consciousness tells us about causation. Ours looks at what the structure of explanatory theory tells us about causation. These differences in treatment lead directly to the topics featured in our volume that fall outside the purview of Pred's work: panpsychism, nonhuman consciousness, consciousness as organized on a continuum of complexity, causation *per se* as a form of experience.

This brings us to two last books deserving mention, dealing not with consciousness but the single issue of panpsychism: D.S. Clarke's *Panpsychism and the Religious Attitude* (2003) and David Skrbina's *Panpsychism in the West* (2005). The appearance of these two monographs could not be more timely for our own project. Both books complement ours insofar as they help bring the topic of panpsychism into the mainstream. Each has sections discussing

Whiteheadian and process philosophy panpsychism, situating it in a wide historical or critical context.

Clarke's monograph is a sophisticated and hard-hitting defense of panpsychism. Clarke has a strong command of the Anglo-American tradition of analytic philosophy and builds his case entirely with the methods and insights of this tradition, which prides itself on its rigor and no-nonsense sobriety. The fact that panpsychism can be cogently argued with the tools of the tradition most inclined to scoff at it guarantees it a seat at the discussion table.

Skrbina's book is a survey of panpsychism from the pre-Socratic philosophers up to the present day. His thesis is that panpsychism has, until the twentieth century, always been one among well-respected mainstream philosophical positions. Its frequent present day characterization as the fringe position of an idiosyncratic few he shows to be false. The most compelling part of Skrbina's exposition is his treatment of the nineteenth and twentieth centuries, where he documents panpsychist thinking, especially among respected natural scientists, with a degree of prevalence so widespread that even its present supporters will be taken by surprise. The cumulative weight of his documentations makes it difficult to deny the seriousness of panpsychism as a philosophical position. In a final chapter, Skrbina attempts a comprehensive catalog of arguments for and against panpsychism, which takes full cognizance of the arguments of process philosophers. Notably, however, our book contains at least one argument for panpsychism (arguably more) that is entirely new and therefore absent from Skrbina's survey.

Notes

1. Griffin suggested this terminology as early as 1977. See Griffin's "Whitehead's Philosophy and Some General Notions of Physics and Biology," in Cobb and Griffin 1977, 122–134.

2. See Hartshorne's "The Compound Individual," in Northrop et al. 1936, 193–220.

3. The concept of an "enduring compound individual" is of course found in Whitehead, but his terminology is more cumbersome than Hartshorne's. Whitehead speaks of a "socially ordered nexus" with a single "regnant" occasion, and to indicate the perdurance of its order over time he speaks of a "personally" ordered social nexus.

4. The list of the first-rate philosophers who have been put off by the immersion in abstract categoreal thinking required by *Process and Reality* would be quite long, the best-documented case being perhaps Hans Jonas (1986).

5. This fallacy, identified already by Socrates, has been beautifully highlighted by Arendt in her *Life of the Mind*.

6. Let us remember that the point of James's famous 1904 paper "Does Consciousness Exist?" was not to deny the existence of consciousness, but to insist that it was a function rather than some special kind of thing (James 1912, 1–38).

7. As Whitehead remarks, "Scientists animated by the purpose of proving that they are purposeless constitute an interesting subject for study" (FR 16).

8. In Scholasticism "precision" (*praecisio*) designates abstraction that excludes whatever it does not expressly include. "To precind" is always to form an abstraction by exclusion.

9. In his book *Animal Minds* (1992) he does makes a similar distinction between purely "perceptual consciousness" and the "reflective consciousness" of human beings (7–8).

10. As summarized here, Whitehead's theory of consciousness may seem to have the peculiar implication that one cannot be conscious of necessary truths. Whether this is implied is a moot point since Whitehead does not believe there are any strictly necessary propositions (MT 90–95).

11. Since this appears to be a case where Whitehead's abstruse speculations have a clear relevance to experimental science, we should perhaps draw this out as explicitly as possible. Let us, for the sake of didactic simplicity, define belief minimally, as behaviorism would, as a disposition to behave in a certain way and say that a belief is true when the behavior does or would lead to satisfaction of the relevant desires. Then we can say that the monkeys' beliefs appear to be conscious because their behavior appears to be influenced by the following: the possibility that their belief may be wrong; the confidence in some cases that it nevertheless is not wrong; the lack of confidence in some cases that it is not wrong. But there is nothing in sense experience corresponding to such things as possibility, negation, or contingency. Unless we can succeed at the unlikely prospect of describing the monkeys' behavior as the result of operant conditioning alone, it seems that we must admit that in addition to having conditioned dispositions to behave in certain ways ("beliefs" as here defined), they also have consciousness of these dispositions. Otherwise we leave unaccounted for how they go on to develop more sophisticated dispositions to behave that seem to result at least in part from the modalities of counterfactual ideation and logical negation.

12. If we concede that the *reductio* arguments advanced by Shields (and Weekes) prove that experience must be internally related to its environment, we still have an interesting question to settle: whether this is a sufficient or only a necessary condition of experience. Certainly not sufficient, since not every strict implication is a case of experience. By adding the condition of having physical space-time presence, has Shields produced sufficient criteria for experience? This seems *prima facie* implausible. However, a case can be made that the only way something with physical space-time presence can be internally related to its environment is by experience. Weekes in his contribution attributes this very position to Whitehead, pointing out that for Whitehead when experience/concresence is terminated; what is left are items that are only externally related. Only as long as something is still in the act of experiencing an object can the former be internally related to the latter. On the other hand, if Shields' two criteria are found to be too lax to constitute a *sufficient* condition of experience, then Rosenberg's contribution can be seen to take the next

step, isolating a very plausible candidate for the missing constraint: that which experiences must have a nature that is at least partly "internal to itself" (see pp. 20–22 above). It is very possible, however, that Whitehead would have regarded Shields' and Rosenberg's respective formulations as logically equivalent on the grounds that nothing with space-time presence could be partly internal to itself without being internally related to its environment and *vice versa*.

13. The editors note that Stuart Hameroff's concurrence on this point can be found in the first volume of the WPN Studies, *Searching for New Contrasts* (Riffert and Weber 2003, 61–86).

14. Peirce, Bergson, and James seem to have expressed this idea first. It also plays an important role in Whitehead.

15. James' understanding of the role of attention in shaping consciousness has obvious relevance here.

References

Arendt, Hannah. 1978/1971. *The Life of the Mind.* 1-vol. ed. San Diego: Harcourt Brace Jovanovich.

Brown, Jason W. 2000. *Mind and Nature: Essays on Time and Subjectivity.* London and Philadelphia: Whurr Publishers.

Clarke, D.S. 2003. *Panpsychism and the Religious Attitude.* Albany: State University of New York Press.

Cobb Jr., John B., and David Ray Griffin, eds. 1977. *Mind in Nature: Essays on the Interface of Science and Philosophy.* Washington, DC: University Press of America.

Eisendrath, Craig R. 1971. *The Unifying Moment: The Psychological Philosophy of William James and Alfred North Whitehead.* Cambridge, MA: Harvard University Press.

Griffin, David Ray. 1977. "Whitehead's Philosophy and Some General Notions of Physics and Biology." In Cobb and Griffin 1977, 122–134.

Griffin, David Ray. 1998. *Unsnarling the World-knot: Consciousness, Freedom, and the Mind-body Problem.* Berkeley: University of California Press. Reissued 2008 by Wipf and Stock Publishers, Eugene, Oregon.

Griffin, Donald Redfield. 1992. *Animal Minds. Beyond Consciousness to Cognition.* Chicago and London: University of Chicago Press.

Hanlon, Robert E., ed. 1991. *Cognitive Microgenesis: A Neuropsychological Perspective.* Springer Series in Neuropsychology. New York: Springer-Verlag.

Hartshorne, Charles. "The Compound Individual." In Northrop 1936, 193–220.

James, William. 1912. *Essays in Radical Empiricism.* New York: Longmans, Green, and Co.

Jonas, Hans. 1987. "Wissenschaft als personliches Erlebnis." Conference given on the 15th of October 1986 in Heidelberg. Göttingen: Vandenhoeck and Ruprecht.

MacLean, Paul D. 1967. "The Brain in Relation to Empathy and Medical Education." *Journal of Nervous and Mental Disease* 144:374–382.

MacLean, Paul D. 1991. "Neofrontocerebellar Evolution in Regard to Computation and Prediction: Some Fractal Aspects of Microgenesis." In Hanlon 1991, 3–31.

Nagel, Thomas. 1979. *Mortal Questions.* Cambridge: Cambridge University Press.

Northrop, F.S.C. et al. 1936. *Philosophical Essays for Alfred North Whitehead.* February fifteenth, nineteen hundred and thirty-six. London: Longmans, Green, and Co.

Pred, Ralph. 2005. *Onflow: Dynamics of Consciousness and Experience.* Cambridge, MA: MIT Press.

Riffert, Franz G., and Michel Weber, eds. 2003. *Searching for New Contrasts. Whiteheadian Contributions to Contemporary Challenges in Neurophysiology, Psychology, Psychotherapy and the Philosophy of Mind.* Frankfurt am Main: Peter Lang.

Skrbina, David. 2005. *Panpsychism in the West.* Cambridge, MA: MIT Press.

Velmans, Max. 2000. *Understanding Consciousness.* London/Philadelphia: Routledge.

Part I

Setting the Stage

Part I consists of four chapters. In the first chapter, we introduce the Whitehead Psychology Nexus (WPN) and its scholarly mission. We briefly illuminate the background, motivation, and orientation of the present volume of the WPN Studies before addressing ourselves to some fundamental questions of terminology and method that bear on the heuristic approach to be found in these pages. Consciousness, we claim, is a phenomenon that resists anything but an interdisciplinary approach, while Whitehead-inspired process thinking offers an integrative heuristic that can bring coherence to multidisciplinary studies. We situate our approach in relation to some recognizable coordinates: empiricism, radical empiricism (in James' sense), Phenomenology (in Husserl's sense), empirical science (with special reference to neuropathology and abnormal psychology), and critical doxography (which remains relevant to the extent that early modern European philosophy defined the phenomenon that we still refer to as *consciousness*). These preliminary remarks we follow with three introductory chapters dealing with the background and context of Whitehead's philosophizing. These chapters form a whole, but can also be read and appreciated separately. In turn, these examine (a) Whitehead's place in twentieth-century philosophy, (b) the origin of our Western *concept* of consciousness and the history of "consciousness" as a topic of European philosophical reflection, and (c) Whitehead's renegade approach to this venerable topic.

1

Process Thought as a Heuristic for Investigating Consciousness

Michel Weber and Anderson Weekes

Background, Motivation, and Orientation of the Present Volume of WPN Studies

The Whitehead Psychology Nexus (WPN) is an international scholarly society that takes its immediate mandate from issues important to contemporary philosophy and psychology, but seeks creative (possibly daring) solutions, drawing its inspiration from the process-oriented thinking that emerged in the late nineteenth and early twentieth century, which includes the thought of Henri Bergson, Charles Sanders Peirce, and William James, but is most closely associated with the organic philosophy of Alfred North Whitehead (1861–1947).[1] WPN promotes dialogue and is not shy of controversy. The present volume of the WPN Studies places consciousness at the focus of disciplinary cross-elucidation. It taps leading researchers and theorists in the study of consciousness and Whitehead scholars to explore an interface between process thinking and the burgeoning field of consciousness studies. The rationale for such a project has at least two facets worth mentioning by way of introduction. They have to do with the state of an educated debate that seems, first, unproductive and peculiarly burdened by its deep modernist origins and, second, marked more by disciplinary rivalry than interdisciplinary synthesis.

A good part of what fuels the current boom in consciousness studies is the robust progress of cognitive psychology and neuroscience toward reaching consensus explanations of just about anything *except* consciousness. Psychology, neuroscience, and artificial intelligence have produced many astonishing results and upset many old beliefs. Nevertheless, it remains controversial what implications these discoveries have for a general theory of consciousness. Despite hopes that empirical research and computational modeling would constrain theory, consciousness (to judge from a literature in which the most cited figure continues to be Descartes!) is a topic that still lies wide open to speculation. Indeed, the literature is fond of noticing that the contemporary discussion is defined by the same set of theoretical options that became established in early modern philosophy, ranging from materialism to epiphenomenalism to various forms of attribute or substance dualism. Even idealism remains on the table if we include the extreme forms of social and linguistic constructionism, where the world-creating subject of traditional modern philosophy is replaced by the world-creating language or social praxis. In short, it seems that scholarly debate has not so much reached an impasse as remained at one reached in the seventeenth century. Given the massive effort currently invested in research and debate, the lack of progress toward a general (and generally accepted) theory of consciousness begins to make consciousness look like a kind of twenty-first-century Philosopher's Stone, whose hidden nature seems to hold the key to the greatest mysteries, but continues to elude us.

This situation explains one part of the rationale for the present volume. A philosophical intervention in the consciousness debate that does not take for granted the same assumptions that define and limit traditional approaches should not be unwelcome, especially if the goal is a more positive accommodation with empirical research than is achieved by many current models of consciousness. For example, an objection to functionalist models that will emerge from discussions in this volume is that they imply that *consciousness* per se *has no evolutionary or even any cognitive value.* If this assessment is correct, it is easy to see why empirical research in biology or psychology has had relatively little impact on the construction of theoretical models of consciousness and why the philosophical debate continues to be exercised by ideas that predate the very existence of psychology and biology as sciences. Because it provides ways to understand how consciousness has cognitive and evolutionary value, process thought has attracted the attention of a number of researchers whose work is featured or discussed in this volume.

Due to its continuing dominance within the discipline of cognitive psychology, functionalism looms largest over those who seek to reject it. In fairness, then, we should, here at the outset, give the reader some idea of the sorts of arguments and provocative suggestions she can expect from the later chapters of this book. How do our authors propose to deal with the vexed problem of the evolutionary value of consciousness, and why do we claim that this topic poses an insuperable problem for functionalism?

Consciousness could confer a selective advantage only if it enhanced an organism's ability to survive, allowing it to adapt better or more flexibly to its environment. But the computational paradigms of cognitive science have led us to the following impasse: any function, even biological ones, can in principle be executed mechanically; consequently, consciousness cannot be necessary to the performance of any function. In fact, any function consciousness appears to perform (unless perhaps it can do something "supernatural") is superfluous since the underlying neural architecture is *ipso facto* already sufficient to enable this operation, leaving consciousness with no possible role to play. This conclusion follows directly from the computational understanding of a "function." It is therefore *impossible* for conscious as such to have any function. What this finally means is that consciousness is not the sort of thing that could be selected for in the course of evolution: an evolutionary account of consciousness is impossible.

At the point where cognitive scientists arrive at the insight (as David Chalmers does; see 1996) that consciousness, whatever it is, cannot have any function or survival value—at this point we might want to step back and ask if we haven't taken a wrong turn. Since the conclusion follows inexorably from the computational paradigm according to which any function is by definition Turing machine computable, other ways of understanding neurocognitive function may prove to be well worth looking in to.

Neuropathology makes it clear that consciousness depends on the functional architecture of the brain, as damage to specific areas of the brain correlates with specific impairments of consciousness. But some of the phenomena of neuroplasticity adduced by Shields in his contribution (specifically, those that appear to result over time from the deliberate control of one's attention) suggest that the functional architecture of the brain is also, in part, dependent on consciousness! It is easy to see that neuroplasticity is something that could confer an evolutionary advantage, as it would allow for more adaptive behavior. But if, at least in some cases, neuroplasticity depends in part on consciousness, then these are cases where consciousness itself confers a selective advantage. It is certainly possible that the intervention of consciousness in the evolution of an individual brain's plastic infrastructure could turn out to be illusory—just a case of the brain affecting itself according to a predetermined neurofunctional program in which consciousness plays no causal role. But this is hardly a foregone conclusion.

Although it is often asserted as fact, it is by no means clear—and certainly not clear *a priori*—that any function the brain performs could indeed be achieved computationally (Putnam 1992). And even if a given function *could* be achieved computationally, it is not necessarily the case that it *is* achieved computationally. The role of quantum indeterminacy in synaptic activity (also discussed by Shields) and the peculiar causal role the "observer" plays in the collapse of the probability wave function (and hence in the calculation of further probabilities of synaptic activity) suggest a functional role for consciousness that does not fit neatly into the framework of computationalism, and this suggests one way that consciousness might confer a selective advantage.

Drawing on ideas of Karl Popper, David Griffin's contribution will suggest another way that consciousness might confer an evolutionary advantage: consciousness allows an organism to conduct thought experiments, that is, to try out possible strategies for survival without exposing itself to real risks, by imagining what their differential outcomes might be. The critical element here is counterfactual ideation. In effect, the organism poses the question: if I were to do such and such, then what? Behaviorism almost certainly cannot explain counterfactual ideation (it needs rather to deny its existence). What about cognitive science, behaviorism's heir to the mechanistic agenda in psychology? It seems unlikely that strictly computational functionalism, which is only interested in a program that generates real outputs from real inputs through real operations, could provide what Hilary Putnam (1992) calls a "perspicuous representation" of this peculiar process—the cognitive process of counterfactual ideation—and if it cannot, then we would have another good candidate for a neurocognitive function that confers an evolutionary advantage, but is not (and possibly *cannot* be) a computational function.

Now the question may be raised: what does that have to do with consciousness? Is there any reason why such a neurocognitive process must be conscious, seeing that most neurocognitive processes are not? Regardless of the conclusion one ultimately draws, here is a point where Whitehead's ideas could stimulate productive debate in contemporary cognitive science, for Whitehead claims—to a rough approximation—that counterfactual ideation is precisely what consciousness *is*. There is no need to add something to such a process to make it conscious, and nothing could be removed that would render it unconscious. If Whitehead is right about this, then Donald Redfield Griffin is entirely justified in his contribution to see evidence of counterfactual ideation in monkeys as evidence of consciousness.

For their part, Pachalska and MacQueen offer a comprehensive theory of brain function that is noncomputational. Consequently, in their account of consciousness as an activity or function of the brain, no conflict with evolutionary biology need arise. In fact, their account is altogether evolutionary. According to the model developed by Jason Brown, brain function in humans organizes progressively over three levels, corresponding to the evolutionary strata of the brain (brain stem, limbic system, and cortex, which correspond to the reptilian, paleomammalian, and neomammalian brains). Activity occurs in a dense volley of overlapping waves that radiate from the phylogenetically oldest and anatomically deepest part of the brain, the brain stem, toward the youngest and outermost part, the neocortex. Consciousness is not so much the property of a system in a steady state, as something the brain brings about, moment by moment, through a microgenetic process (measured in milliseconds) that must unfold over all three levels. Continuity of phenomenal consciousness results from the overlapping waves of microgenesis.

Because this theory of brain activity is holistic, not modular, consciousness cannot occur at higher levels of activity without being implicated in some way at lower levels. Consciousness is only refined at higher levels; it does not arise *de novo*. This puts the question of the evolutionary value of consciousness in an entirely different light. Consciousness is not something purely cortical that attends to or even commandeers functions that are already executable unconsciously. Consciousness is integral to function because it is the overall unity of function that can be realized at one of three levels: wakefulness (facilitating globalized, essentially reflexive responses), emotion (facilitating more differentiated and purposeful responses), and articulated perception (facilitating separation of self from a world of enduring, independent objects).

A distinct kind of consciousness thus correlates with each level of activity, and its evolutionary value lies in the discriminating response to the organism's environment that it facilitates, with a higher, more adaptive degree of discrimination arising in the outer, more evolved strata. Most important, the higher functions do not supplant the lower ones: we do not cease to be awake because we feel emotion, or cease to feel emotion because we enjoy articulated perception. Rather, the higher functions build on the lower ones, incorporating them as more basic phases in their own genesis. Since microgeny recapitulates phylogeny, the value of consciousness is nothing less than the cumulative value of the organism's adaptive evolution.

As with the radical theory of consciousness advanced by Velmans in his contribution to this volume, so too with microgenetic theory: what needs explaining is not so much how or why consciousness arises at the highest levels of brain function, as why it appears largely absent from lower levels of functioning. According to Brown's model, primitive functions appear unconscious because they no longer occupy the terminal point in the moment-to-moment microgenesis of consciousness. They have been reduced (through a kind of neoteny of microgenesis) to early and incomplete phases in the genesis of a more complex and differentiated consciousness. They recede from foreground to background, becoming the global backdrop presupposed by the more sophisticated function. It follows that they remain present in higher consciousness vestigially, even if this is not obvious from the phenomenology of normal consciousness.

The crucial contribution of primitive brain functions to higher consciousness is precisely what breaks to the surface in the neuropathological symptom. Depending roughly on the depth of the brain lesion along the radius from brainstem to any point on the cortical surface, the genesis of normal conscious behavior is interrupted at a more or less primitive phase.

Deeper lesions cause more global pathologies; more superficial lesions, closer to the brain's outer shell of gray matter, cause more specific and localized pathologies. What appears to be a deficit, however, is really the abnormally exposed competence of a more primitive level of information processing. Disturbed behavior does not replace normal behavior. Rather, the normal process through which conscious behavior comes about is derailed before completion, exposing a less differentiated competence than expected, but a competence nonetheless—one that informs normal consciousness and without which normal consciousness would be impossible.

For example, the patient sees the word *cat*, but reads it as *dog*. It is not by accident that the categorization is correct (four-legged domestic animal). The disrupted ability to fully differentiate meaning exposes the ability to categorize as a more primitive and independently functioning competence. What neuropathology shows, then, is that the importance of a competence's contribution to consciousness is inversely related to how noticeable it is. The more fundamental the competence, the more removed it is from the foregrounded differentiation of conscious attention. It is not categorically unconscious, but its presence in normal consciousness is so global and diffuse that its noticeability is pathological.

Reminiscent in some respects of Kurt Goldstein's (1995) application of the categories of Gestalt psychology to biology, this model leaves no berth for functionalist theories that would deprive consciousness *per se* of cognitive function or survival value. It has the advantage of being an empirical theory, based not on an *a priori* conception of what a physically instantiated function "must be," but on neuroanatomy, evolutionary biology, and neuropathology. Even if further research should leads us back to a more modular understanding of brain function, Velmans in his contribution offers a coherent account of how consciousness could evolve—and how, in particular, diffuse consciousness could evolve into attentional consciousness—without having to be directly subject to natural selection.

In sum, while computational paradigms are hard pressed to assign any evolutionary value to consciousness, the present volume offers no less than four arresting possibilities. If nothing else, this fecundity demonstrates that models based on a Whiteheadian process approach can be a valuable heuristic in developing an evolutionary account not just of the brain, but even of consciousness.

Another reason for approaching the study of consciousness from a Whiteheadian organic or process thought perspective has to do with the unique complexity of consciousness as an object of study. For a single object of study, consciousness lies at the intersection of an unusual number of disciplines—many of them are represented by contributions to this volume, which draws on philosophy, psychology, psychiatry, psychotherapy, zoology, neurobiology, neuropathology, and even physics. This disciplinary polyvalence tells us something about the complexity of consciousness. Any attempt to approach consciousness from one discipline alone is bound to result in a reduction both obvious and unacceptable to the other disciplines. Indeed, for this reason many of the individual contributions to this volume are themselves interdisciplinary in perspective. But once we acknowledge the disciplinary polyvalence of our topic, we face an important philosophical question, one that was uppermost in Whitehead's mind in defining a continuing role for philosophy in the age of empirical science and its multiple specializations. If consciousness can be understood only through the convergence of many different kinds of knowing, then the old problem of the one and the many comes back as a methodological challenge: How are the different approaches to be coordinated? How do we ensure that the convergence of so many perspectives results in a coherent model? How do we resolve conflicts between their different presuppositions—and in a nonreductive way? Whitehead's process philosophy was animated by this problem.

The contributors to this volume are not all "process philosophers" or even Whitehead specialists, and by no means do they share a single point of view. However, they do share the conviction that dominant, mainstream approaches to the study of consciousness, whether philosophical or empirical, have failed to integrate the relevant perspectives in a way that does justice to important evidence—indeed, that these approaches lack an appropriate framework that would allow them to do this. Lacking such a framework, each of these dominant approaches may come up short in different ways, but their shortcomings reflect a common failure to integrate diverse perspectives. This was Whitehead's diagnosis of the intellectual scene of his own day, and the situation does not seem to have changed. Our contributors' sympathies with Whitehead come from the shared sense that his philosophical theories, right or wrong, were a painstaking and often insightful response to the same limitations that still hamper contemporary philosophy and psychology.

The disciplinary rivalry alluded to above illustrates this point. In its *most* acute form this rivalry takes shape as a conflict between scientific and humanistic outlooks, each contesting the primacy of the other. In this case, the failure to integrate relevant perspectives seems obvious. There can be no denying that here we still see the disconnection between different disciplinary approaches that Whitehead deplored. It results from a long-standing stalemate, the origins of which can be traced to the seventeenth century (Descartes' substance dualism, Spinoza's attribute dualism, Leibniz's preestablished harmony, or the contrasting roles played by *perception* and *reflection* in the British empiricists) and to Kant, who cast the problem in the form it has since retained. Kant tried to resolve the tensions between the two domains *by separating them from one another* (Weekes 2003, 347–366). As though they were squabbling children who resented sharing, Kant established rigid boundaries, giving each of them nonoverlapping domains of safe space, forbidding them, in effect, to talk to one another. As any parent knows, this solution is only temporary: ultimately the world is something we all must learn to share. The insularity of different domains of discourse that nevertheless bear on the same topic is a problem more than ever now that the children are grown up.

Whitehead is famous for having constructed a solution to the philo-sophical problems he diagnosed that seems highly artificial. How much of this intricate construction is useful is a matter for debate. However, all of our contributors agree that Whitehead's motives are sound and that his critique of modernity is especially relevant to the issues currently under debate in the consciousness literature. But they also agree that at least some of Whitehead's constructive proposals can and should be rehabilitated and brought to bear on this topic. This may turn out to be the needed expedient to enable theories of consciousness to profit from a positive accommodation with the historical and phenomenological evidence valued by humanists and the empirical research valued by scientists, *both* of which must be integrated if we are to move beyond speculations of the seventeenth century that still control so much of the discussion.

In short, although our contributors do not agree on how much of Whitehead's approach can be endorsed without significant reconstruction, to a greater or lesser extent they all exploit aspects of Whitehead's "categoreal scheme" because they share the conviction that the conceptual and analytic framework of Whitehead's process philosophy offers the outlines of something that mainstream approaches often lack: a promising schematic for assessing and integrating the *full* range of evidence relevant to the nature of consciousness. As noted, the diversity of evidence includes not just the results of empirical research. To be exact, it includes two other important sources: the uncon-trolled, but ubiquitous evidence of everyday experience and the evidence to be found in the history of philosophical opinions about consciousness. Of course, philosophical opinions cannot be taken at face value any more than the conceits of everyday experience, but in both cases an adequate theory of consciousness must be able to make sense of prevailing opinions and reconcile them with an accurate phenomenology. The hermeneutic principle here is the Aristotelian one that includes "opinion" among the phenomena that an adequate explanation must "save": if things are not as they seem, to philosophers or ordinary folks, there nevertheless must be a good explanation why things seem to them other than they are. In sum, the contributions to this volume use a broadly conceived process framework to draw on three sources of evidence about consciousness, often confronting one with another: empirical research, phenomenology, and philosophical doxography.

Methods and Definitions

Since we have yet to define our terms or set specific methodological con-straints, we should say a few words in advance about how we understand phenomenology, how empirical research and doxography will bear on our investigation, and above all what we mean by consciousness.

By "phenomenology" we mean a methodologically self-conscious proce-dure of description, which takes as its object not the way things are thought to be "in themselves" or independent of any particular manner of access, but the way they appear in experiential real time in some actual mode of given-ness: for example, how something is given (appears) to vision, or hearing, or memory, or the imagination. It is a difficult phenomenological question how some things we *obviously experience* are *actually given*—the animal body, for example, or mathematical certainty. It is a very difficult phenomenological question whether some things are given at all—for example, the reality of the past or the external world. And, it is a matter for phenomenological description if some things are habitually imbued with phenomenological misinterpretation—a possibility Whitehead was not alone in seeing. We also use "phenomenology" to designate the object of phenomenological description—the same way "psychology" can mean not only the clinical science of the way people think but also the typical or characteristic way a particular person or group of people thinks. Thus, for example, we refer below to the "phenomenology of certainty," meaning: *how certainty appears* to the consciousness experiencing it (second meaning of phenomenology). Describing this appearance yields (at least some of) the specific experiential conditions under which something can be given as certain (first meaning of phenomenology).

It will become clear as we proceed, but let us note at once that our understanding of phenomenology differs from that of its best-known prac-titioner, Edmund Husserl. Nothing in the preceding description presupposes the specifically Husserlian method of the *epoché*. Unlike Husserl, we are not convinced *a priori* that the transcendent reality of the empirical world is not something that could appear to us as a primitive phenomenological datum, that it must be something consciousness "constitutes." Consequently, we do not see the *epoché* as a precondition of successful phenomenological description. We must look to how things are actually given, yes; but we need not assume in advance that their existence depends on their givenness. To avoid confusion, therefore, we will always capitalize "phenomenology" and its cognates when we have in mind the more specific interpretation of phenomenology made famous by Husserl and lease as lowercase our own more general use of the term, which seeks not to prejudice the answer to this important philosophical question.[2]

One of the most important targets of phenomenological description is the everyday world of ordinary experience and social existence—what Husserl calls the life-world. Because it is pragmatically and performatively presupposed by everything we say and do, it constitutes in some sense a transcendental condition. The significance of this kind of pragmatic presupposition is of course far from obvious (not to say controversial) and requires elucidation. Description of how the life-world is given and how its givenness is habitually understood (i.e., how it seems to be given in discursive reflection if this is different from how it is *actually* given in immediate experience) must form one part of such an elucidation. An idea that Whitehead shares with Husserl is the implicit or nonthematic way in which the life-world is actually given, as well as the elusiveness of this fact. This has important methodological implications that might be brought out best if we briefly compare Husserl and Whitehead, for both philosophers came to this discovery unwillingly.

Husserl originally thought of Phenomenology as a way to transform philosophy into an exact science: "reduced" to pure phenomena, the world of experience could be handled in a precise and rigorous way on the model of the mathematical theory of manifolds. Husserl eventually abandoned the idea of philosophy as rigorous science, saying famously that the "dream was dreamed out" (Husserl 1969, 508). He did not abandon the idea of a foundational stratum of experience that Phenomenology could access and assess, but only the idea that it could be fixed like a specimen in formaldehyde, delineated with morphological exactitude, and rendered conceptually without ambiguity. It is clear from Husserl's fantastic comments on Manifold Theory in the "Prolegomena" to his *Logical Investigations* (1900) that this had been his ideal of scientific rigor, and the fact that just a few years later he describes the methodology of his new science, "Transcendental Phenomenology," in similar terms lets one know that Manifold Theory was his original paradigm for Phenomenology.

Similarly, Whitehead was intoxicated at first with the idea that a mathematically formal analysis of the world, what he later calls "morphology," could be the epistemologically recovered foundation of our knowledge and experience of the world.[3] But in the years following the publication of his three great works on the philosophy of natural science (PNK, CN, PRel) he comes instead to the opposite conclusion—that the decisive and indispensable foundation of experience is everything that morphology leaves out! Like Husserl, he became convinced that what is fundamental always has the character of background, horizon, or tacit presupposition: "The necessities are invariable, and for that reason remain in the background of thought, dimly and vaguely" (MT vii). But this means that what is "foundational" in experience is incapable of focal objectification and must be accessed indirectly. This same realization led Husserl to his method of indirection or "questioning back from the pre-givenness of the life-world" (Husserl 1969, Part III A, 105–193). Whitehead advocated a similar kind of questioning back to find fundamentals. His philosophy looks to the "presuppositions of language rather than its express statements" (MT vii) and to the "generalities which are inherent in literature, in social organization, in the effort towards understanding physical occurrences" (MT 1). Philosophy's "ultimate appeal," he says, "is to the general consciousness of what in practice we experience. Whatever thread of presupposition characterizes social expression throughout the various epochs of rational society must find its place in philosophic theory" (PR 17). This explains the stress Whitehead lays on the fundamental importance of "unscientific" sources of information such as poetry, religion, or collective anthropological experience. The evidence they provide is indirect, but indispensable. Because this indirection is the manner in which the life-world is actually given, we do not hesitate to call its description *phenomenological*.

What do we mean by consciousness? Because some of the proposals that follow, both in these introductory chapters contributed by the editors and throughout the book, are highly unorthodox, it bears stressing at the outset that the consciousness we—the editors and the contributors—seek to circumscribe, understand, or explain is the same one that is at stake in the current debates in philosophy and psychology. We share in the large consensus of opinion that sees consciousness as the qualitative feel of an experience impressed with such hallmarks as unity, intentionality, reflexivity, perspectivity, and personality. But we seek more vigorously than some of our colleagues to find explanations of consciousness that preserve the phenomenology of these features of our experience. Also like other parties to the consciousness debates, we understand the phenomenon targeted in this standard description to be the consciousness experienced (post-infancy) by any "normal" human being.

However, "abnormal" consciousness is by no means irrelevant to our inquiry. On the contrary, a great deal can be learned about normal consciousness from the altered or diminished consciousness consequent to trauma or impairments (e.g., neuropathology, psychopathology, coma, catatonia, anesthesia, intoxication), to say nothing of states of consciousness that are clinically normal yet marginalized in the usual understanding of normal consciousness (e.g., sleep, fatigue and duress, yogic meditation, religious and aesthetic experience, consciousness at its lowest thresholds, implicit or nonobjectifying consciousness, animal consciousness). This explains the prominence given in this volume to findings of empirical research, on the one hand, and to phenomenology, on the other. Empirical research teaches us about states of consciousness that fall outside the compass of clinically normal consciousness (or outside the compass of *human* consciousness in the case of animal studies), while phenomenology teaches us about modalities of normal consciousness that are often omitted (suppressed or overlooked) in the lay, scientific, or philosophical descriptions.

Among the contributors addressing the former topic, Schweiger et al. focus explicitly on what can be learned about normal consciousness from the stages through which consciousness passes during recovery from coma; Weber looks at clinical experience with mental illness, Pachalska and MacQueen at brain pathology, Shields at meditation and attentional therapy, Donald Griffin at experiments assessing consciousness in animals, Velmans at the assumed biological and evolutionary thresholds of consciousness, and so on. Addressing the latter topic, several of our contributors draw attention to implicit or performative aspects of ordinary consciousness that are easy to ignore or even to deny precisely because they are normally operative without being thematic. David Griffin, Shields, and Katzko look at the implicit performative presuppositions of objectifying, theoretical consciousness; Verley, Shields, and Weekes examine the implicit performative conditions of time consciousness and memory; Weber looks as the implicit social aspects of rational consciousness.

In this circumspection we are radicalizing a fundamental precept of Whitehead's; it is well known but worth quoting again:

> In order to discover some of the major categories under which we can classify the infinitely various components of experience, we must appeal to evidence relating to every variety of occasion. Nothing can be omitted, experience drunk and experience sober, experience sleeping and experience waking, experience drowsy and experience wide-awake, experience self-conscious and experience self-forgetful, experience intellectual and experience physical, experience religious and experience sceptical, experience anxious and experience care-free, experience anticipatory and experience retrospective, experience happy and experience grieving, experience dominated by emotion and experience under self-restraint, experience in the light and experience in the dark, experience normal and experience abnormal. (AI 226)

The motive for this broad approach has its roots in an insight of William James:

> Some years ago I myself made some observations on this aspect of nitrous oxide intoxication, and reported them in print. One conclusion was forced upon my mind at that time, and my impression of its truth has ever since remained unshaken. It is that our

normal waking consciousness, rational consciousness as we call it, is but one special type of consciousness, whilst all about it, parted from it by the filmiest of screens, there lie potential forms of consciousness entirely different. We may go through life without suspecting their existence; but apply the requisite stimulus, and at a touch they are there in all their completeness, definite types of mentality which probably somewhere have their field of application and adaptation. No account of the universe in its totality can be final which leaves these other forms of consciousness quite disregarded. How to regard them is the question—for they are so discontinuous with ordinary consciousness. Yet they may determine attitudes though they cannot furnish formulas, and open a region though they fail to give a map. (James 1902, 387–388)

The lesson Whitehead took from James was perhaps more sober, but daring nonetheless. It becomes possible to dismiss a vast amount of evidence about ourselves and the world as "unscientific" or "not really empirical" simply by restricting what counts as cognitively relevant consciousness to states that are in fact exceedingly rare:

We [. . .] objectify the occasions of our own past with peculiar completeness in our immediate present. We find in those occasions, as known from our present standpoint, a surprising variation in the range and intensity of our realized knowledge. We sleep; we are half-awake; we are aware of our perceptions, but are devoid of generalities in thought; we are vividly absorbed within a small region of abstract thought while oblivious to the world around; we are attending to our emotions—some torrent of passion—to them and to nothing else; we are morbidly discursive in the width of our attention; and finally we sink back into temporary obliviousness, sleeping or stunned. Also we can remember factors experienced in our immediate past, which at the time we failed to notice. When we survey the chequered history of our own capacity for knowledge, does common sense allow us to believe that the operations of judgment, operations which require definition in terms of conscious apprehension, are those operations which are foundational in existence either as an essential attribute for an actual entity, or as the final culmination whereby unity of experience is attained? (PR 161)

The present volume carries forward Whitehead's program of developing a more adequate understanding of normal consciousness by attending to occurrent states that are excluded by normal consciousness or marginalized by our usual *understanding* of normal consciousness. To the extent that it only radicalizes the bias inherent in normal consciousness, philosophical and psychological reflection attempts to "epiphenomenalize" these normally excluded or marginalized states. This is closely related to the modern tendency, noted by (among others) Dewey and Heidegger, to think of consciousness as a spectator. Probably because it is reinforced by the phenomenology of (epistemic) certainty, this tendency is still palpable in much of the literature on consciousness. Certainty about the characterization of an object attaches to consciousness at the moment of optimal focus and peak acuity. Consciousness at this moment is indeed very much like a dispassionate spectator. Its attitude is fact-oriented, which means that it is objectifying and theoretical, possessed of acute self-consciousness and analytic attention. The question is whether this particular delineation of consciousness—which consciousness arrives at because it is indeed in this state when it goes looking for itself and what it is—captures its base form, its "essence" so to speak, representing a sort of "pure consciousness" presupposed by its other forms.[4] If so, then all other forms would constitute so many *modifications* of this fundamental sort of consciousness: attenuations, perturbations, accretions, distortions, etc. This has been the implicit (or even explicit) position of the mainline tradition of modern philosophy. It should perhaps not surprise us that consciousness, seeking certainty about what consciousness is, ends up by identifying itself with the limited certainty it can have.

Like Bergson, Whitehead thinks that consciousness as it has come to be known and come to understand itself in the sharp delineation that it owes to modern European thought yields a filtered, straitened, and truncated experience. In its notion of scientific objectivity, European philosophy unwittingly canonized as normative and definitive an extreme idealization of that way of experiencing the world that allows us to maximize our power over nature: above all, to exercise power with algorithmic certainty. As a result, information from other modalities of experience (which certainly occupies a great part of our consciousness, even if it cannot or normally does not take pride of place at the objectified focus of attention) was—and still is—devalued. It is customarily assumed that the information provided by marginal and alternative modalities of consciousness, to the extent that it differs from what normal consciousness does or would disclose directly in otherwise similar circumstances, is simply normal content degraded by "subjectivity" (inattention, suboptimal function, dysfunction, emotions, prejudice, etc.). Such modalities are seen as offering nothing of objective value that could not become the focus of deliberate and thematizing attention, resulting, moreover, in an experience of greater cognitive value. In other words, the nonpreferred modalities of consciousness are treated as "deficient modes" of an assumed normative state, which, uncorrupted, possesses (would possess) the world as a crystalline cognitum.

We are tempted to say this modernist prejudice is refuted by Impressionist and post-Impressionist painting, to say nothing of the magical phenomenology of writers such as Proust or Virginia Woolf, which discovers in every banality a suppressed ontological nimbus, an unsuspected abundance of detail overflowing the thing of "normal" consciousness and indispensably qualifying how the thing exists. What these works of art do is make directly available to normal consciousness the information that would otherwise remain unthematic, marginal, and fleeting. The fact that they reveal so much important information that conditions normal consciousness without being directly available to it is the reason they astonish us. If they exposed nothing more than a degraded form of something perfectly accessible to normal consciousness, they would not, as they so often do, seem like revelations. It goes without saying that when marginal information is revealed in this artificially direct way to objectifying consciousness, it is no longer performing its proper function, which explains why it is art rather than life. But it also explains how an artwork can be more or less "true" even though it is entirely fictional. As a mapping of the marginal onto the focal, it can be more or less faithful, even if such a focal objectification of the marginal is impossible in the real performance of an activity and its execution necessarily an exercise in make-belief. In short, marginal information possesses a preeminence that is unique to its marginal status, and far from being the degraded content of (a possible) direct normal consciousness, it is only through the degradation of its preeminent function that it can ever be turned into the content of direct normal consciousness. Degradation of precisely this kind is characteristic of artistic representation, and we might go so far as to say that here lies the cognitive value of art. (A question that does not belong to the compass of this investigation, but certainly to its horizon, is whether religion does not perform a function similar to art. It makes directly available to normal consciousness something that is otherwise necessarily marginal in one of two ways: it can be directly available to consciousness, but only in extreme and exceptional states of consciousness; or available to normal consciousness, but only indirectly, remaining fugitive and implicit, despite being somehow fundamental.[5])

Whitehead rejects these modernist prejudices. To name one of his reasons: a significant consequence of these assumptions is none other than the famous mind-body problem. As we will detail in the last chapter of Part I, the world as disclosed to "normal" consciousness is a medium in which consciousness of any sort could not arise and cannot exist. How then consciousness is related to this medium that excludes it becomes the greatest of philosophical puzzles.

Needless to say, no philosophical discussion can avoid presupposing normal consciousness. The question is whether we shall do this uncritically, accepting the narrow interpretation of normal consciousness bequeathed to us by modern philosophers along with their assumption that it is uniquely cognitive. One very Whiteheadian aim of this volume is to find out and critically assess just what we are thereby presupposing. We need to know, above all, what such a presupposition excludes. The fact that we must begin with normal consciousness does not mean we have to remain there. Whitehead thinks that marginal experience offers an opportunity to circumscribe a very different concept of subjectivity than the one we are accustomed to—a *weak* subjectivity, which is only faintly like the strong subjectivity of consciousness. If he is right, it may turn out after all that consciousness is the Philosopher's Stone. For if we can find within consciousness (or at its fringes), in its liminal, implicit, or fugitive states, or in states deviant, weakened, or disturbed on normal accounting, the vestige of a world differently disclosed and no longer incompatible with the existence of consciousness, then we can use consciousness against itself to transmute the false show of objectivity into something possibly less transparent, but probably more real. If what we lose is the transparency of the world dear to normal consciousness, what we gain is the meaningfulness of that world. Whitehead thinks this process of transmutation, which after all is just a biological critique of normal consciousness, is indeed possible and that it reveals to us a world urged on from countless centers of weak subjectivity, whose evolving interactions are the course of nature alive with possibilities. This is a nature in and from which the coming-to-be of the strong subjectivity of consciousness is no longer impossible. If the epiphany of such a world flickers in the meditations of philosophers or in the margins of everyday experience, it might be better described not as a transmutation, but as a reversal—however brief, partial, or unstable—of the transmutation already wrought upon the world by normal consciousness.[6] The dramatic implication for psychology, however, is that clear and distinct consciousness requires elucidation from more primitive (and usually marginal or transmarginal) forms of awareness, not the other way around.

With these comments we hope to have clarified not only what we mean by consciousness, but also the role played in our investigations by the various sources of evidence on the nature of consciousness. Because contemporary *theories of consciousness*, like the contemporary *self-understanding of ordinary consciousness*, owes so much—so much that Whitehead rejects—to the intellectual accomplishments of modern European philosophy, it is necessary for us to take account of this influence doxographically and critically. Verley's and Weekes' contributions, which look at early modern figures and Whitehead's critique of them, fall in this category, while David Griffin, Katzko, and Shields bring this doxography up-to-date with the current literature.

To some extent the critique of modern philosophy and its contemporary legacy can be an immanent one, assessing their success in terms of their own goals by their own criteria. But ultimately we must question the validity of the phenomenology they presupposes. To do this, we must have recourse to a description of conscious experience that is not hamstrung by modern ideology. The Phenomenology of Husserl fails on this account, while the radical empiricism of William James presents a promising alternative. Several of our contributions make use of a description of everyday experience in tune with Jamesian radical empiricism. The result is the critique of modern and contemporary accounts of consciousness implicit in David Griffin's appeal to "hard-core common sense notions," in Shields' "deep protocols of common sense," and in the descriptive account of memory deployed by Shields, Verley, and Weekes. The agreement between Shields and Weekes on this point is noteworthy given the wide differences in their backgrounds and in the figures they examine. Shields approaches Whitehead from a generally Analytic perspective and focuses his critique on Russell and current Anglo-American literature; Weekes approaches Whitehead from a generally continental perspective, focusing his critique on early modern philosophy and Phenomenology.

If phenomenology brings us to the margins of consciousness, empirical research on abnormal consciousness brings us to what is normally beyond the margins, but nevertheless always there, shaping the contours and coloring the content of normal consciousness. In their contributions, Schweiger et al. and Pachalska and MacQueen argue that these normally transmarginal modes of experience are not so much an alternative to normal consciousness as its concealed foundation. They are simply the lower tiers in the substructure of normal consciousness, which have become directly exposed because the genesis of normal consciousness finds itself arrested at a preterminal phase. In other words, the clinical presentation of abnormal consciousness gives descriptive phenomenology unique access to the genetic process by which normal consciousness comes to be.

Notes

1. For an overview of process philosophy, see Rescher 1996 and 2000, Weber 2004 and Weber and Desmond 2008. The term "process philosophy" appears to have been coined by Bernard Loomer (1949).

2. What Husserl calls phenomenology is more specific than our definition because Husserl has already taken a decisive position on the question of the givenness of transcendent things. As transcendent, Husserl believes, they *are not* given—he seems to regard this not as a phenomenological finding, but as a sort of analytic truth: if

transcendent, not given, if given, not transcendent. In Husserlese: *Erlebnisse* (lived experiences) are *ipso facto* immanent, and the act of meaning, which interprets (apperceives) some of them as the appearances of transcendent things, is equally immanent, *ergo etc.* Husserl thinks it is a *non sequitur* to suppose that one of the things capable of being given to a description that makes no *assumptions* about the independent being of objects might be . . . the independent being of objects! It follows from this initial commitment that any description that does not, for the sake of methodological purity, *deny* the independent existence of objects is *ipso facto* unphenomenological. (For reasons that cannot be addressed here, Anglophone readers of Husserl are unlikely to recognize in this précis the philosopher they think they know.) There is, however, no need to exclude *a priori* the possibility of transcendence being given, and it will be licit to admit transcendence as long as we can describe its particular manner of givenness. Perhaps it is not given; perhaps its givenness is phenomenologically impossible, but this is surely not a logical impossibility. The important upshot of these differences between Husserl and us is that properly phenomenological statements for Husserl will always be "transcendental" statements—statements about the unworldly Absolute Consciousness—while properly phenomenological statements for us could very well turn out to be ordinary empirical statements—statements about things given to consciousness, but not dependent on consciousness, or about consciousness itself insofar as it is given to itself, but not dependent on its own self-givenness. It is only so as not to prejudice these questions in advance that we must reach for the word "phenomenology" at all. Otherwise, "precise empirical description" would do just fine. This and other differences between a Whiteheadian and a Husserlian phenomenology are broached in chapters 4 and 15. It should be noted that Husserl has no monopoly on phenomenology. It was practiced by Brentano, Stumpf, Hodgson, Bergson, Bradley, James, Mach, and many others. Perhaps none of these figures qualify as Phenomenologists, but all of them are phenomenologists.

3. This parallelism is not coincidental. Both Whitehead and Husserl had been stimulated by the seminal paper of Riemann's, "*Über die Hypothesen, welche der Geometrie zu Grunde liegen*," which first introduces into mathematics the abstractly defined multidimensional manifold, to develop the idea of a deductively generated formal ontology/meta-theory of theoretical models. See Husserl's *Formal and Transcendental Logic*, § 30 (1981, 81–82) and Whitehead's early *Treatise on Universal Algebra* (UA 13).

4. For example, Hans Thomae: "That this 'actual individual totality' [of consciousness] indicates an actual reality [*Wirklichkeit*] can only be demonstrated by pointing to the particular experience of self-observation [*Selbstbeobachtung*]. Thus, we can only *point* to self-observation and the inner reality it grasps if we want to make the factual existence [*Tatbestand*] of this totality in someone else's thinking the logical subject of judgments regarding its characteristics. But precisely in this way this concept reveals itself as the description of a thoroughly concrete reality [*Tatbestand*] to which all other 'modes,' 'forms,' or varieties of consciousness are to be reduced" (1940, 540).

5. This is a recurring theme in William James' *Varieties of Religious Experiences*: "Rationalism insists that all our beliefs ought ultimately to find for themselves articulate grounds. Such grounds, for rationalism, must consist of four things: (1)

definitely statable abstract principles; (2) definite facts of sensation; (3) definite hypotheses based on such facts; and (4) definite inferences logically drawn. Vague impressions of something indefinable have no place in the rationalistic system, which on its positive side is surely a splendid intellectual tendency, for not only are all our philosophies fruits of it, but physical science (amongst other good things) is its result. [. . .] If you have intuitions at all, they come from a deeper level of your nature than the loquacious level which rationalism inhabits. Your whole subconscious life, your impulses, your faiths, your needs, your divinations, have prepared the premises, of which your consciousness now feels the weight of the result; and something in you absolutely *knows* that that result must be truer than any logic-chopping rationalistic talk, however clever, that may contradict it. This inferiority of the rationalistic level in founding belief is just as manifest when rationalism argues for religion as when it argues against it" (James 1902, 73).

6. Note that besides being the fabled process sought by alchemists, transmutation is also a category in Whitehead's metaphysical scheme of basic concepts having to do with the emergence of aggregate effects—such as the qualitative continuity of passively displayed appearances—from the activities of a manifold of discrete micro-constituents.

References

Brown, Delwin, Ralph E. James Jr., and Gene Reeves. 1971. *Process Philosophy and Christian Thought.* Indianapolis: Bobbs-Merrill.

Chalmers, David. 1996. *The Conscious Mind.* New York: Oxford University Press.

Goldstein, Kurt. 1995/1934. *The Organism.* New York: Zone Books.

Griffin, David Ray. 1998. *Unsnarling the World-Knot: Consciousness, Freedom, and the Mind-Body Problem.* Berkeley: University of California Press. Reissued 2008 by Wipf and Stock Publishers, Eugene, Oregon.

Husserl, Edmund. 1969. *Die Krisis der europäischen Wissenschaften und die Transzendentale Phänomenologie. Eine Einleitung in die phänomenologische Philosophie.* 2. Auflage. Haag: Martinus Nijhoff.

Husserl, Edmund. 1981/1929. *Formale und transzendtale Logik. Versuch einer Kritik der logischen Vernunft.* 2. Auflage. Tübingen: Max Niemeyer Verlag.

James, William. 1902. *The Varieties of Religious Experience: A Study in Human Nature. Being the Gifford Lectures on Natural Religion Delivered at Edinburgh in 1901-1902.* New York: Longman, Green, and Co.

Loomer, Bernard MacDougall. 1949. "Christian Faith and Process Philosophy." *The Journal of Religion* 29:181–203. Reprinted in Delwin et al. 1971, 70–98.

Putnam, Hilary. 1992. *Renewing Philosophy.* Cambridge, MA/London: Harvard University Press.

Rescher, Nicholas. 1996. *Process Metaphysics: An Introduction to Process Philosophy.* Albany: State University of New York Press.

Rescher, Nicholas. 2000. *Process Philosophy: A Survey of Basic Issue.* Pittsburgh: University of Pittsburgh Press.

Thomae, Hans. 1940. "Bewusstsein und Leben: Versuch einer Systematisierung des Bewusstseinsproblems." *Archiv für die gesamte Psychologie* 105:532–636.

Weber, Michel, ed. 2004. *After Whitehead: Rescher on Process Metaphysics.* Frankfurt/ Lancaster: Ontos Verlag.

Weber, Michel, and Will Desmond, eds. 2008. *Handbook of Whiteheadian Process Thought.* Frankfurt/Lancaster: Ontos Verlag.

Weekes, Anderson. 2003. "Psychology and Physics Reconciled: Whitehead's Vision of Metaphysics." In *Searching for New Contrasts: Whiteheadian Contributions to Contemporary Challenges in Neurophysiology, Psychology, Psychotherapy and the Philosophy of Mind*, Franz G. Riffert and Michel Weber, eds., 347–374. Frankfurt am Main: Peter Lang.

2

Whitehead as a Neglected Figure of Twentieth-Century Philosophy

Michel Weber and Anderson Weekes

The world of academic philosophy knows Whitehead as a brilliant but eccentric figure, outside the intellectual mainstream, whose ideas are not often taken seriously. Any worthwhile assessment of Whitehead's intellectual contributions must have something to say about this state of affairs. But first we should note that the characterization is not altogether true anymore.

The unexpected developments in physical theory that launched the twentieth century, because they challenged so much of our "default" metaphysics, invited philosophical exploration from the start, even if the results were often greeted with skepticism. Like the philosophical ideas of de Broglie, Bohr, or Heisenberg (and like the more daring ideas of Pauli and Wigner), Whitehead's ideas emerged in this early period of skeptically received speculative ferment. Unlike most of his contemporaries, however, what Whitehead championed was a full reconciliation of physics with common sense (Weekes 2003, 347–365).[1] Despite his profound knowledge of mathematical physics, this deference to naïveté cast him at once as an outsider in an intellectual world defined by the preeminence of modern physics. But the scene has changed. Prominent figures in the hard sciences are now actively promoting the rapprochement with humanistic outlooks that an earlier generation mocked as unscientific.[2] This is due in part to a growing sense of urgency, but in part as well to growing confidence that theoretical models in physics are close to the level of sophistication required to breach the fortress of the mind and reconcile with naive common sense (Weekes 2003, 366–370). Attempts to harvest the remarkable developments of twentieth-century physics for insight into traditional philosophical problems such as free will or the mind-body problem remain highly controversial, but have clearly taken a quantum leap in respectability since the early 1980s.[3] By the same token, intellectual curiosity about the scientific details of Whitehead's own attempt at such a rapprochement is growing into a recognized area of worthwhile scholarship.[4] Indeed, compared to Whitehead scholarship of just twenty years ago, the present volume and the WPN series to which it belongs are in a more fortunate position. It is not necessary to work toward creating an audience with interests broader than specialized Whitehead exegesis. Such an audience already exists and continues to grow.[5]

Nevertheless, the historical reasons for Whitehead's marginalization are important because they quickly lead us to his most distinctive ideas. The perception of Whitehead as an anomaly in the twentieth century rests mainly on his attitude toward metaphysics, but also—because differing attitudes toward metaphysics reflect and are reflected in differing attitudes toward the history of philosophy—on his attitude toward the history of philosophy. Early in the twentieth century the vanguard in both continental and Anglo-American philosophy had proclaimed metaphysics to be bankrupt. Much of the animus against metaphysics came from the sense that it was an unchecked form of speculation that could not in principle be subjected to any rigorous constraints or empirical control. It was claimed that the history of philosophy demonstrated the sterility of metaphysical speculation, and Whitehead began work on constructing a grand metaphysical system at a time when it seemed to many that metaphysics had been discredited for good. Recognition of the bankruptcy of metaphysics was often looked upon as the chief mark of the twentieth-century philosopher's intellectual superiority to a tradition in thrall to *a priori* speculation and other kinds of "armchair" system building.

There can be no question that Whitehead thought of metaphysics as a legitimate discipline productive of important knowledge, and while it draws in part on evidence that can never be "clear and distinct," it nevertheless is able to meet well-defined standards of cogency and methodological control. Thus, while he adopted a highly critical position toward the philosophical tradition, he did not think its metaphysical claims were meaningless, as Positivism claimed, but *false* and therefore capable of correction. This explains why he eschewed wholesale dismissal and sought always to learn from the tradition by way of close, systematic interpretation. In particular, White-head acknowledged the validity of the problems traditionally at the focus of philosophy—such as the mind-body problem, free will and determinism, the reality of the "external world," the objectivity of knowledge claims, the source of values, the justification for induction—and he presented his own organic philosophy as the outgrowth of a long tradition of engagement with these perennial issues.

The tendency to see philosophy—and especially metaphysics—in a large-scale historical context is characteristic of Whitehead's thought and tells us something about his view of philosophy. Besides the more rigorous constraints on philosophical theory to be discussed below, Whitehead thought of the history of philosophy as a kind of experiment in speculative thought subject to the unique control of collective anthropological experience—the experience of societies, civilizations, and cultural traditions. His book *Adventures of Ideas* argues that the jostle of these different forces over the course of time, which empowers some ideas at the expense of others, has definite apophantic value. (Whitehead was an optimist.) This expansive view of verification allowed Whitehead to think of metaphysics as empirical in a way that may not be entirely strange to historians—especially if they harbor Hegelian or even Jungian sympathies—but was impossible to reconcile with the positivism current in Whitehead's time.

However, Whitehead also thought there were other, more rigorous constraints on philosophical theory and a *raison d'être* for metaphysics more compelling than anthropology. We can make sense of this if we look at the idea of disciplinary polyvalence introduced above (chapter 1) in connection with consciousness as an object of study. The problem of interdisciplinary coordination is not unique to the investigation of consciousness and under specialized constraints gives rise to a second-order discipline charged with the very task Whitehead assigns to metaphysics.

All knowledge begins with an approach to experience that involves abstraction, simplification, and elimination of context or detail. As the subsequent refinement and specialization of knowledge progresses, different sciences recover complexity and nuance, but in ways that tend more and more to diverge. As a result, the diversity and aggregate complexity of the world may be understood, but its coherence is not. At best, its unity is viewed from the perspectives of diverse single sciences—a multiplicity of reductions rather than a reduction of multiplicity. Furthermore, questions arise about the relationship between scientific models of the world and prescientific experience, which has multiple dimensions of its own—historical, social, religious, ethical, aesthetic. Science presupposes this everyday, prereflective experience in an obvious way, but the philosophical significance of this fact is far from obvious.

According to Whitehead, bringing the different areas of empirical knowledge back into convergence, both with one another and with the prescientific experience they start from and seek to illuminate, is a task of vital importance to any civilization, failing which it risks a kind of cultural schizophrenia (Weekes 2003, 361–363). Nowhere is such schizophrenia more evident than in the modern (and postmodern) understanding of consciousness and the human individual, where one and the same instance of behavior comes under a multitude of conflicting interpretations, from being an expression of freedom or conscience to being determined in one of many ways that are themselves not always mutually compatible. To name a few of the latter, the same action will, depending on the context of our own interests, be described as issuing from character, or from habit, or from an uncontrollable emotion, or from the controlled, but unconscious sublimation of that emotion, or from instinct, or chemistry (balance of hormones or neurotransmitters perhaps), or from beliefs (that may or may not be true), or from a commanding religious experience, or from a "simple" law of physics, such as entropy, constraining what happens in the brain. Some of these explanations are mutually consistent; some are not. It is difficult or impossible to reconcile any of them with classical notions of freedom, responsibility, or conscience. And if anyone thinks the old problem of "free will vs. determinism" is dead or irrelevant, she needs to consider the ongoing debates in psychiatry between those who endorse biological models of mental illness and those who endorse psychodynamic models.[6]

Whitehead advanced the unsurprising and obviously dated (but not obsolete) view that the task of coordinating and reconciling different kinds of experience falls to philosophy, and his own philosophy was animated by this task. Its principle objective was the elaboration of what he called a "speculative scheme" of concepts that allowed the evidence from divergent perspectives to be integrated into a coherent picture of the world. One familiar view of philosophy holds that it deals with a different subject matter from the empirical sciences. Another holds that it deals with questions empirical science is not yet able to answer. According to Whitehead, philosophy does not distinguish itself from empirical science by having a special (pre-empirical or possibly nonempirical) subject matter, but only by virtue of its greater inclusiveness and interdisciplinary approach. Indeed, by embracing an empiricism more radical than the narrowly focused empiricism of specialized natural sciences, Whitehead's approach cannot avoid being interdisciplinary, and this distinguishes it from the sciences it seeks to coordinate.

This is not really a view that should provoke hostility from advocates of scientific empiricism. In outline, it's the same view of philosophy that was advanced by the apostle of Positivism, Auguste Comte (1798–1857): philosophy is simply the final stage in the widening of scientific perspective. And this, in fact, is just how Whitehead came to philosophy in the course of his long career—through a progressive widening of perspective that evolved through stages not unlike those of Comte's developmental hierarchy of the sciences (i.e., mathematics, physics, chemistry, biology, physiology, philosophy). Trained in pure mathematics and teaching applied mathematics, Whitehead was first focused on logic and projective geometry. Then he became interested in physics and sought systematic ways to apply formal systems to the physical world. He subsequently expanded this program into a philosophy of nature and finally into a metaphysical cosmology with a theological coda. The move from pure mathematics to physical theory—however formal—meant accommodating empirical constraints. The move to a philosophy of nature meant accommodating the initially neglected nonformal aspects of the physical world. The move to metaphysics meant accommodating what his philosophy of nature had explicitly excluded, "the how [...] and [...] the why of thought and sense awareness." Instead of a "philosophy of the thing perceived," the "metaphysics of reality [...] embraces both perceiver and perceived" (CN 28). (We note in passing that this pattern of development reflects Whitehead's distaste for intellectual parochialism. Piqued no doubt by an inner drive toward generalization, Whitehead's ever-expanding speculation was facilitated by the wide range of extracurricular readings and interests he kept alive throughout his life—from his student days to the end of his professional career (see, e.g., Lubenow 2001). Whitehead was always mindful of what had still been left out of his expanding professional focus.

For Comte, of course, philosophy as the highest stage of knowledge was really nothing more than a generalization and comparative taxonomy of scientific concepts. By the same token, Comte's philosophy could hardly be expected to issue in a challenge to scientific orthodoxy, whereas Whitehead's ultimately does. The reasons for this important difference have to do with the formal constraints Whitehead imposes on philosophy. Whitehead identifies four (PR 3–4). Two are "rational" (consistency and coherence), and two are "empirical" (applicability and adequacy). Coherence and adequacy both have special meanings for Whitehead that play the decisive role in legitimizing what he calls metaphysics. Adequacy means universal applicability; that is, all-inclusiveness of application, and coherence means that all parts of the theory must be biconditional. In the case of consciousness, to take the relevant example, the investigation must draw on *all* perspectives as sources of evidence, both scientific and "prescientific"; it must seek a theory that is not only consistent internally, but also consistent with the evidence proffered by each possible empirical perspective. Furthermore, the resulting "unified" theory must render the differing perspectives conceptually interdependent.[7]

It must be stressed that when Whitehead speaks of a theory's applicability and adequacy to experience, he has in mind not just the vaguely defined experience of civilizations, but also the well-defined experience of special sciences. A critical element in the empirical controls on metaphysics is thus the ever-growing body of knowledge resulting from empirical research. Philosophical theory must (minimally) be consistent with scientific knowledge and ideally should incorporate it into a "coherent" view of the whole world. This explains the strong strain of "scientism" in Whitehead that makes humanistically minded thinkers wary of him.

However, another critical element in the empirical constraints is the ubiquitous background experience that science presupposes as its context

and starting point in everyday life. This explains the strong phenomenological strain in Whitehead—an approximation to existentialist concerns that
makes scientific empiricists wary of him. Whether directly or not, this side
of Whitehead's thinking is deeply influenced by Bergson's psychology—his
theory of intuition and his phenomenological description of immediate
experience—and James' philosophy of radical empiricism.[8] Modern science
is empirical because it looks to the data of sense-perception to control and
corroborate its theorizing. But it limits itself to the content of sensory exteroception, objectified at the focus of attentional consciousness, thus neglecting
a variety of information sources that are no less "empirical." These include
interoception, proprioception, and emotional affect; the manifold forms of
tacit knowledge or ineffable pragmatic know-how encoded in social, linguistic,
and motor competence; and all the fugitive or vague experiences occupying
the fringes of consciousness or crossing the threshold of consciousness only in
retrospective analysis. It is absolutely wrong to think that these experiences,
because they are "marginal," do not make an indispensable contribution to
experience and can be ignored by philosophy.

Honoring (i.e., acknowledging the simultaneous validity of) both of
these very different strains of evidence, scientific and phenomenological, is
the main thrust of Whitehead's *adequacy* requirement. Since the untutored
phenomenology of prescientific experience has its disciplinary counterpart in
the humanities and in the human and social sciences, adequacy can be defined
in terms of a cross-disciplinary requirement, encompassing both natural and
human(istic) disciplines. Integrating both of these strains of evidence into
a single, rather than a dualistic worldview (i.e., construing their joint validity as mutual interdependence) is the main thrust of Whitehead's *coherence*
requirement. Such an integration poses a vexing challenge all too familiar
to the history of philosophy and not inappropriately called "metaphysical."
For Whitehead, therefore, it is the combination of adequacy as a uniquely
understood empirical constraint and coherence as a uniquely understood
rational constraint that legitimizes metaphysics as a discipline focused on
a well-defined problematic and subject to well-defined controls (Weekes
2003). Its task is the construction of a model of the world consistent with
the specialized knowledge of different disciplines, yet general enough to
encompass them all and complex enough to bring them together in a way
that is coherent and mutually compatible. Whitehead was not afraid to
call this project metaphysics because it aims to understand the nature of
things—their complexity and coherence—both individually and as an ordered
totality. Whitehead was well aware that this was not a goal that could be
definitively satisfied. His constraints are normative criteria for evaluating
candidate theories as better or worse and for guiding hypothesis formation.
Metaphysics, like science, will never be perfect, but it will always be capable

of improvement. The most strident objection to Whitehead's metaphysics has always been that it is metaphysics, but his was emphatically not a metaphysics set up to challenge empirical sciences. What makes Whitehead's metaphysics a challenge to scientific orthodoxy is not a disdain for empiricism, but his insistence that the empirical evidence be accommodated in a way that satisfies the specialized constraints of adequacy and coherence.

With these two requirements we have pinpointed the commitments most responsible for Whitehead's strong deviations from mainstream thinking in the twentieth century and most likely to set the present volume apart from much of the recent literature on consciousness. There is nothing unusual about requiring consistency, but requiring it across all disciplinary borders, which is what Whitehead means by adequacy, and requiring what he means by coherence lead to a characteristically Whiteheadian kind of philosophical theory. This is evident if we consider the following question: Will all theories of consciousness generated from different disciplinary standpoints, assuming each of them is consistent with the evidence from its own perspective, automatically be mutually consistent? If so, there would be, logically speaking, an effortless way to meet the goal of *consistency*. We could offer as a general theory of consciousness the *set* of theories formed by simply conjoining them all. But this would fail Whitehead's coherence test. It is not enough for the unified theory to consist of several independent theories that are simultaneously true. They must presuppose one another biconditionally as interdependent aspects of a single theory. Clearly, Whitehead's coherence requirement creates a mandate for the sort of higher-order synthesis that only philosophy could provide and goes a long way toward explaining what he means by metaphysics. But even apart from the coherence requirement, we have an interesting problem if mutual consistency of the first-order perspectives is lacking at the outset. Conceptual refinement and reconciliation then become necessary, and Whitehead's concept of philosophy as a cross-disciplinary hermeneutic can be justified even without recourse to his coherence requirement.

Of course, we can easily guarantee the consistency of the whole set simply by disqualifying troublesome perspectives. For example, we could disqualify the deliverances of ordinary consciousness and its explication by the human and social sciences as "folk psychology" that mistakenly takes at face value various subjective illusions (autonomy, free will, etc.), or we could disqualify the findings of objectifying science as "historical constructs" constrained by ideology and social praxis rather than interest-neutral facts. This kind of disqualification was the strategy of the original project of "unified science," which was to be a unification of the sciences under the aegis if classical physics, disregarding data from social sciences and the humanities as epiphenomena. Needless to say, those advocating the disqualified perspectives always return the favor, thus creating a dispute impossible to adjudicate. We see a standoff of this sort in the early twentieth century between the program of unified science and its various nemeses (Philosophy of Life, Phenomenology, Existentialism). This may explain why debates about consciousness, despite extraordinary advances in empirical research, have yet to advance beyond the philosophical alternatives established in the seventeenth century or the stalemate between them. The early modern doctrine of materialism finds its twentieth-century heir in the philosophical orientation sometimes referred to as *scientism*, which looks to natural science or at least to methods modeled on natural science to generate the only possible knowledge of things, including mind or consciousness. Behaviorism and Cognitive Science are the paradigm examples of this approach to consciousness.

The early modern doctrine of idealism finds its twentieth-century heir in social or linguistic constructionism, where the world-creating subject of traditional modern philosophy is replaced by the world-creating language or social praxis. This approach, implicit in Phenomenology, becomes explicit and even polemical in post-Structuralism or its American counterpart, the "strong program" in the sociology of knowledge. But it is also the upshot of Wittgenstein's argument against the possibility of a private language.[9] We should not forget that the autonomy of language as a social phenomenon, coupled with the dependency of knowledge on language, was the fundamental insight that inspired Anglo-American philosophers of an entire generation to adopt linguistic analysis as the only way to obtain philosophically fundamental knowledge about the world. The difference between idealism and materialism or between their twentieth-century successors is that each disqualifies the evidence the other prizes (Weekes 2003, 358–361).

What Whitehead means by metaphysics is a unified science that encompasses rather than takes sides in this old controversy. This is the reason his empirically committed philosophy grapples with a problem unimaginable to Positivism and ultimately issues in metaphysical proposals challenging to scientific orthodoxy. The divisive question is: Are everyday consciousness, practical reason, and "folk psychology" to be included among perspectives relevant to an "adequate" theory of consciousness? Whitehead's answer to this question—shared in one way or another by all our contributors—is emphatically *yes*. But unlike other voices in the twentieth century who answer this question affirmatively, Whitehead does not include these perspectives by unilaterally excluding the perspective of natural science. This dual commitment creates the principle conflict motivating Whitehead's concept of philosophy as a project of interdisciplinary reconciliation.[10] If this is what makes his voice so distinctive in the twentieth century, it is also the reason he is taken as an inspiration by our contributors. They are equally unwilling to reject empirical science as a way to preserve humanistic attitudes—or vice versa.

While this double commitment may pit Whitehead against the scientific establishment of his time, it places him squarely in the philosophical tradition. In this respect, Whitehead is very much a traditionalist. His voice was distinctive because he honored tradition at a time when the convention was to denounce it. Philosophers since Parmenides have recognized experience as the locus of a fundamental contradiction from which philosophy draws its mandate. Originally it took the form of a contradiction between opinion and truth or seeming and being. As it took on modern shape it became the tension between descriptions of the world undertaken in the first person and those proffered in the third person. Since consciousness itself appears to be one of the things in the world, we quickly discover that consciousness *explained* as an object of cognition and consciousness *understood* as a subject of experience and action are perspectives hard to reconcile. We know this problem under many names: Kant's antinomy of freedom and causation, free will and determinism, Schopenhauer's world-knot, the mind-body problem, Chalmer's "hard problem," the tension between final and efficient explanation in Leibniz or Aristotle, etc. Metaphysics is simply the name Whitehead gives to the responsibility we still have to take this problem seriously.

Notes

1. Kant is an obvious comparison to make here. Like Kant, Whitehead wants to make room for (most of) the different ways human beings relate to the world: it's not a matter of one field swallowing the others. But, unlike Kant, Whitehead does not see a solution in sharply differentiating disciplines so as to resolve their conflicts once and for all by establishing mutually exclusive territories of jurisdiction.

2. Davies and Gribbin 1992, Pribam 1996, Prigogine 1997, Prigogine and Stengers 1984.

3. Atmanspacher 1992, Atmanspacher and Fach 2005, Atmanspacher and Dalenoort 1994, Bohm and Nichol 2004, Bohm and Peat 1989, Finkelstein 1996, Lockwood 1989, Malin 2001, Penrose 1994, Penrose and Isham 1986, Polkinghorne 1984 and 1988, Russell et al. 1994, Satinover 2001, Sheldrake 1991, Shimony 1993, Smolin and Kaufman 1997, Stapp 1993, 1999, 2007, Trundle 1994, as well as contributions by Amoroso and Martin, Frohlich and Hyland, Gould, Hiley, Stapp, and Vitiello in (King and Pribam 1995), by Conrad, Hameroff and Penrose, Jibu et al., Nunn et al., Tollaksen, Wolf, and Zohar in (Hameroff, Kasniak, and Scott 1996), by Clarke, Hameroff and Penrose, and Stapp in (Shear 1997), by Beck, Hameroff and Scott, Squires, and Stapp in (Hameroff, Kasniak, and Scott 1998), by Hameroff in (Taddei-Feretti and Musio 1999), by Beck, Bierman, Globus, Hameroff, Marcer and Mitchell, McGinn, Pitkanen, Pribram, Prigogine, Van Loocke, and Walker in (Van Loocke 2001), by Pribram, Vitiello, Werbos in (Yasue, Jibu and Senta 2001), and by Beck and Eccles, Hameroff and Woolf, and Scott in (Osaka 2003).

4. Atmanspacher 1997, Atmanspacher 1995, Atmanspacher 1996, Brown 2005, Busch 1993, Clarke 1993, Code 1985, Eastman 1997and 1998, Eastman and Keeton 2003 and 2004, Epperson 2004, Hampe 1990, Kather 1992, Kirk 1993, Kortright 1994, Löbl 1996, Malin 1988, Rust 1987, Saint-Sernin 2000, Stapp 1999, and Stolz 1995.

5. Indeed, it is growing worldwide. Xie and Derfer 2005 testifies to the efflorescence of Whitehead scholarship in China, and the nascent centers in Romania, Bulgaria, Hungary, and Poland testify to the spread of interest in process philosophy to Eastern Europe.

6. For a recent assessment of the controversy that places the clinical issues in their larger philosophical context, see Schechtman 1996.

7. We omit *necessity*, which is not so much a fifth criterion as a way of clarifying the meaning of the other four. Whitehead's reasoning (PR 3–4) appears to be the following: *Adequate* means applicable not just to known facts, but to all possible facts; in other words, adequacy is *a priori* applicability. How can anything be applicable *a priori*? One solution would be the Kantian one. But Whitehead's commitment to empiricism prevents him from taking *a priori* in the Kantian sense of *transcendental* (a condition of possible experience built in to the faculty of experience). An alternative possibility that Whitehead is also *not* interested in would be the case where all still unknown facts were simply logical consequences of the facts already disclosed. Weirdly, this construal of *a priori* would simply eliminate the need for any further experience: whatever had not yet been experienced could, without experience, simply be deduced (a strange possibility that Husserl seems to toy with in his discussion of Manifold Theory in the *Logical Investigations*). Whitehead sees a third alternative: A theory could be applicable *a priori* if it were known to be empirically applicable to *some* facts and all facts were mutually coherent in the *narrow* sense Whitehead defines. A semantic analysis of any one stated fact would then lead, at least in principle, to the universal structure embracing all facts. In other words, if the universe is coherent in Whitehead's sense, then no analysis of *any* fact could be adequate unless it were (already) applicable to *all* facts. Insofar as it applies to still undiscovered facts, this knowledge would be necessary because it would be *a priori* in the traditional Scholastic-Aristotelian sense of knowledge derived from what is prior by nature (the essence or formal cause of the facts), albeit posterior in the order of investigation or inquiry. That there is such an essence to the universe is the postulate of speculative philosophy. *Necessary* describes the applicability of what is prior by nature to what is posterior by nature. Whatever the ultimate status of knowledge of essences may be in Aristotle, for Whitehead it is always hypothetical and a regulative ideal of inquiry. What Whitehead does share with Aristotle is the idea that finding such an essence is a goal and always comes last in the order of inquiry.

8. The publication in 1884 of an article by James entitled "On some Omissions of Introspective Psychology" (incorporated in 1890 into his *Principles of Psychology* as the chapter on "The Stream of Thought") and in 1889 of Bergson's doctoral dissertation, *An Essay on the Immediate Data of Consciousness*, convulsed the world of psychology, which had evolved a formidable science based on the study of discrete mental contents (ideas, representations, *Vorstellungen*) and the laws governing their interconnection. What James and Bergson brought to the world's attention was star-

tling, yet obvious once exhibited: there were no such discrete contents in the mind, except as artifacts of abstraction. What is concrete is the whole of experience in its richly textured unfolding, which James called *the stream of consciousness* and Bergson *duration*. (Husserl's Phenomenology, as originally conceived, was an attempt to deal with this unsettling realization in a scientifically rigorous way—to keep it contained.) We concede that an eminent Whitehead scholar has denied that Bergson or James exercised a significant influence on Whitehead (Lowe 1949), but find this implausible. Whitehead's indebtedness to their discovery can scarcely be denied. It may *to some extent* not be direct, but it is nevertheless very evident in the way he operates with the concepts of *concretion* and *abstraction* and especially *organism*. Whitehead's concept of organism is not that of contemporary biology, but that of Kant's third Critique, familiar to him indirectly from the Romantic tradition he cherished: a system in which all the parts mutually presuppose one another. In such a system, only the whole is concrete. Bergson's insight can be summed up as: *experience* has a unity that is organic in this sense. James' crucial insight can be expressed methodologically: what is *radically empirical* (and therefore methodologically primary) cannot possibly be discrete data; it can only be the whole of experience in which the various parts are not yet abstracted from their mutual relations. By granting this phenomenological application of the Romantic concept of organism to experience and its methodological primacy for philosophy, Whitehead, like Bradley (and possibly to some extent *via* Bradley), is clearly under the influence by Bergson and/or James. We note that Whitehead at one point explicitly acknowledges Bergson's influence in "introduc[ing] into philosophy [. . .] organic conceptions" (SMW 148). By "philosophy" Whitehead obviously intends to include his own, making this statement a direct acknowledgement of his indebtedness to Bergson in this regard. Whitehead's acknowledgments of James are more plentiful and have been collated by Weber (2002 and 2003). On the relation of Bergson, James, and Whitehead, see Auxier 1999, Brougham 1995, Capek 1953, 1964, 1950, Devaux 1961, Hurley 1976, Levi 1964, Stahl 1955.

9. See Bernard Williams' article, "Wittgenstein's Idealism" (1974). Objections to Williams' interpretation of Wittgenstein by Analytic philosophers (e.g., Malcom 1982 and Bolton 1982) misfire to the extent that the critical method defining the later phase of Analytic philosophy—the linguistic analysis of ordinary usage—presupposes the very sort of "idealism" Williams is talking about. For suggestions that language (or the "grammar" of its correct usage) is in some sense "transcendentally ideal" and that linguistic analysis can be a means to synthetic *a priori* knowledge with transcendental purchase, see Vendler (1967, 1–33) and Cavell (1976, 1–72). We are tempted to say the distinction between the later Wittgenstein and "idealism" that Williams' critics are insisting on is *verbal*, but they would score an entirely valid point simply by agreeing.

10. Whitehead's development clearly reflects the dual commitment of his outlook because he grapples with the issues first in staggered phases. He understood his first inquiries as a formal ontology (not a formal logic), which provided a methodical foundation for natural science. When he turned to metaphysics, the concerns of his earlier approach are not obliterated, but absorbed into a wider systematic context that now includes an existential ontology. The epistemological foundation of natural science (establishing in particular the objectivity of physical measurement) remains

intact and appears in PR as the "theory of extension." It differs from Whitehead's earlier formal ontology because it is now supplemented by and systematically correlated with the "theory of prehensions," which provides the foundation and context for the dynamics of subjectivity. The challenge is to make the theory of extension and the theory of prehensions cohere in such a way that they constitute one theory with two mutually interdependent parts.

References

Atmanspacher, Harald, and Eva Ruhnau, eds. 1997. *Time, Temporality, Now: Experiencing Time and Concepts of Time in an Interdisciplinary Perspective*. Berlin: Springer-Verlag.

Atmanspacher, Harald, and G.J. Dalenoort, eds. 1994. *Inside Versus Outside*. Berlin: Springer-Verlag.

Atmanspacher, Harald, and Wolfgang Fach. 2005. "Akategorialität als mentale Instabilität." In Belschner 2005, 74–115. Reprinted in Gebser 2005, 1–36.

Atmanspacher, Harald, G. Wiedenmann, and A. Amann. 1995. "Descartes Revisited—The Endo/Exo Distinction and its Relevance for the Study of Complex Systems." *Complexity* 1 (3): 15–21.

Atmanspacher, Harald. 1992. "Categoreal and Acategoreal Representation of Knowledge." *Cognitive Systems* 3 (3): 259–288.

Atmanspacher, Harald. 1996. "Exophysics, Endophysics, and Beyond." *Revue de la pensée d'aujourd'hui* [Japan] 24 (11): 347–354. Reprinted in *International Journal Computing Anticipatory Systems*, 1998 (2:105–114).

Auxier, Randall E. 1999. "Influence as Confluence: Bergson and Whitehead. *Process Studies* 28:301–338.

Belschner, W., ed. 2005. *Psychologie des Bewußtseins* Band 1. Münster: LIT-Verlag.

Bergson, Henri. 2001/1889. *Time and Free Will: An Essay on the Immediate Data of Consciousness*. Authorized Translation by F.L. Pogson, M.A. Mineola: Dover Publications.

Bohm, David, and Francis David Peat. 1989/1987. *Science, Order, and Creativity*. New York: Bantam Press.

Bohm, David, and Lee Nichol. 2004/1996. *On Creativity*. With a new preface by Leroy Little Bear. University of Lethbridge. Ed. by Lee Nichol. London and New York: Routledge.

Bolton, Derek. 1996. "Life-form and Idealism." In Vesey 1996, 269–284.

Brougham, Richard L. 1995. "Reality and Appearance in Bergson and Whitehead." *Process Studies* 24:39–43.

Brown, Jason W. 2005. *Process and the Authentic Life: Toward a Psychology of Value*. Process Thought 2. Frankfurt: Ontos Verlag.

Busch, Elmar. 1993. *Viele Subjekte, eine Person: das Gehirn im Blickwinkel der Ereignisphilosophie A. N. Whiteheads*. Würzburg: Königshausen and Neumann.

Capek, Milic. 1950. "Stream of Consciousness and 'Duree Reele.'" *Philosophy and Phenomenological Research* 10 (3): 331–353.

Capek, Milic. 1953. "The Reappearance of the Self in the Last Philosophy of William James." *The Philosophical Review* 62:526–544, reprinted in Capek 1991.

Capek, Milic. 1964. "Simple Location and Fragmentation of Reality." In Reese and Freeman 1964, 79–100.

Capek, Milic. 1991. *New Aspects of Time: Its Continuity and Novelties. Selected Papers in the Philosophy of Science.* Boston Studies in the Philosophy of Science, vol. 125. Dordrecht: Kluwer.

Cavell, Stanley. 1976. *Must We Mean What We Say? A Book of Essays.* Cambridge: Cambridge University Press.

Clarke, C.J.S. 1993. "Process as a Primitive Physical Category." In Fraser and Rowell 1993, 53–69.

Code, Murray. 1985. *Order and Organism: Steps to a Whiteheadian Philosophy of Mathematics and the Natural Sciences.* Albany: State University of New York Press.

Davies, Paul, and John Gribbin. 1992. *The Matter Myth: Dramatic Discoveries that Challenge Our Understanding of Physical Reality.* New York: Simon and Schuster/Touchstone.

Devaux, Philippe. 1961. "Le bergsonisme de Whitehead." *Revue Internationale de Philosophie* 15 (nos. 56–57, fasc. 3–4): 217–236.

Eastman, Timothy, and Hank Keeton, eds. 2003. *Resource Guide for Physics and Whitehead* (*Process Studies Supplement*).

Eastman, Timothy E., and Hank Keeton, eds. 2004. *Physics and Whitehead: Quantum, Process, and Experience.* Albany: State University of New York Press.

Eastman, Timothy, ed. 1997 and 1998. *Process Thought and Natural Science.* Special Focus Issues. *Process Studies* 26 (3–4) and 27 (3–4).

Epperson, Michael. 2004. *Quantum Mechanics and the Philosophy of Alfred North Whitehead.* New York: Fordham University Press.

Finkelstein, David Ritz. 1996. *Quantum Relativity: A Synthesis of the Ideas of Einstein and Heisenberg.* Berlin: Springer-Verlag.

Gebser, Jean, ed. 2005. *Beiträge zur Integralen Weltsicht* 29. Schaffhausen: Novalis Verlag.

Hameroff, Stuart R., Alfred W. Kaszniak, and Alwyn C. Scott, eds. 1996. *Toward a Science of Consciousness I: The First Tucson Discussions and Debates.* Cambridge, MA: MIT Press

Hameroff, Stuart R., Alfred W. Kaszniak, and Alwyn C. Scott, eds. 1998. *Toward a Science of Consciousness II: The Second Tucson Discussions and Debates.* Cambridge, MA: MIT Press.

Hampe, Michael. 1990. *Die Wahrnehmungen der Organismen: über die Voraussetzungen einer naturalistischen Theorie der Erfahrung in der Metaphysik Whiteheads.* Göttingen: Vandenhoeck and Ruprecht.

Hurley, Patrick J. 1976. "Bergson and Whitehead on Freedom." *Proceedings of the American Catholic Philosophical Association* 50:107–117.

James, William. 1950/1890. *The Principles of Psychology.* Authorized ed., in 2 vols. New York: Dover Publications.

Kather, Regine. 1992. "Selbsterschaffung und die Irreversibilität der Zeit bei A.N. Whitehead." *Philosophia Naturalis* 29 (1): 135–159.

King, Joseph, and Karl H. Pribram, eds. 1995. *Scale in Conscious Experience: Is the Brain Too Important To Be Left to Specialists to Study?* Mahwah: Lawrence Erlbaum.

Kirk, James. 1993. *Organicism as Reenchantment. Whitehead, Prigogine, and Barth.* New York: Peter Lang.

Kortright, Enrique V. 1994. "Philosophy, Mathematics, Science and Computation." *Topoi* 13 (1): 51–60.

Levi, Albert William. 1964. "Bergson or Whitehead?" In Reese and Freeman 1964:139–159.

Löbl, Michael. 1996. *Wissenschaftliche Naturerkenntnis und Ontologie der Welterfahrung. Zu A. N. Whiteheads Kosmologiemodell im Horizont von Relativitätstheorie und Quantentheorie.* Frankfurt am Main: Peter Lang.

Lockwood, Michael. 1989. *Mind, Brain, and Quanta.* Cambridge: Basil Blackwell.

Lowe, Victor Augustus. 1949. "The Influence of Bergson, James and Alexander on Whitehead." *Journal of the History of Ideas* 10 (2): 267–296.

Lubenow, W.C. 2001. *The Cambridge Apostles, 1820–1914. Liberalism, Imagination, and Friendship in British Intellectual and Professional Life.* Cambridge: Cambridge University Press.

Malcolm, Norman. 1996. "Wittgenstein and Idealism." In Vesey 1996, 249–269.

Malin, Shimon. 1988 "A Whiteheadian Approach to Bell's Correlations." *Foundations of Physics* 18 (Oct.): 1035–1044.

Malin, Shimon. 2001. *Nature Loves to Hide. Quantum Physics and Reality, a Western Perspective.* New York: Oxford University Press

Osaka, Naoyuki, ed. 2003. *Neural Basis of Consciousness.* Amsterdam/Philadelphia: John Benjamins.

Penrose, Roger, and Chris J. Isham, eds. 1986. *Quantum Concepts in Space and Time.* Oxford: Oxford University Press.

Penrose, Roger. 1994. *Shadows of the Mind: A Search for the Missing Science of Consciousness.* New York/Oxford: Oxford University Press.

Polkinghorne, John C. 1984. *The Quantum World.* London: Longman Group.

Polkinghorne, John C. 1988. *Science and Creation: The Search for Understanding.* London: SPCK.

Pribam, Karl H. 1996. "Quantum Information Processing in Brain Systems and the Spiritual Nature of Mankind." *Frontier Perspectives* (Fall/Winter): 7–16.

Prigogine, Ilya, and Isabelle Stengers. 1984. *Order out of Chaos: Man's New Dialogue with Nature.* Foreword by Alvin Toffler. New York: Bantam Books.

Prigogine, Ilya. 1997/1996. *The End of Certainty: Time, Chaos, and the New Laws of Nature.* In collaboration with Isabelle Stengers. New York: The Free Press.

Reese, William L., and Eugene Freeman, eds. 1964. *Process and Divinity: Philosophical Essays Presented to Charles Hartshorne.* La Salle: Open Court.

Russell, Robert John, Nancey Murphy, and Chris J. Isham, eds. 1994. *Quantum Cosmology and the Laws of Nature: Scientific Perspectives on Divine Action.* Indiana: University of Notre Dame Press, Vatican Observatory Foundation.

Rust, Alois. 1987. *Die Organismische Kosmologie von Alfred N. Whitehead.* Frankfurt am Main: Athenäum Verlag.

Saint-Sernin, Bertrand. 2000. *Whitehead: un univers en essai.* Paris: Vrin.

Satinover, Jeffrey. 2001. *The Quantum Brain: The Search for Freedom and the Next Generation of Man.* New York: John Wiley & Sons.

Schechtman, Marya. 1996. "The Story of the Mind: Psychological and Biological Explanations of Human Behavior." *Zygon. Journal of Religion and Science* 31 (4): 597–614.

Shear, Jonathan, ed. 1997. *Explaining Consciousness—The Hard Problem.* Cambridge, MA/London: MIT Press.

Sheldrake, Rupert. 1991. *The Rebirth of Nature: The Greening of Science and God.* New York: Bantam Books.

Shimony, Abner. 1993. *Search for a Naturalistic World View.* Vol. I, *Scientific Method and Epistemology*; vol. II, *Natural Science and Metaphysic.* Cambridge: Cambridge University Press.

Smolin, Lee, and Stuart A. Kauffman. 1997. "A Possible Solution to the Problem of Time in Quantum Cosmology." www.edge.org.

Stahl, Roland Jr. 1955. "Bergson's Influence on Whitehead." *Personalist* 36:250–257.

Stapp, Henry P. 1993. *Mind, Matter, and Quantum Mechanics.* Berlin: Springer-Verlag.

Stapp, Henry Pierce. 1998. "Whiteheadian Process and Quantum Theory." Paper read at *Process Thought and the Common Good*, The Silver Anniversary International Whitehead Conference, Claremont, August 4–9.

Stapp, Henry Pierce. 1999. *Quantum Ontology and Mind-Matter Synthesis: Quantum Mechanics and the Participating Observer.* Berlin: Springer-Verlag.

Stapp, Henry Pierce. 2007. *Mindful Universe.* In *Proceedings of the 10th Max Born Symposium*, Blanchard and Jadczyk, eds. Berlin: Springer-Verlag.

Stolz, Joachim, 1995. *Whitehead und Einstein: Wissenschaftsgeschichtliche Studien in Naturphilosophischer Absicht.* Frankfurt am Main: Peter Lang.

Taddei-Feretti, C., and C. Musio, eds. 1999. *Neuronal Bases and Psychological Aspects of Consciousness.* Singapore: World Scientific.

Trundle, Robert C. 1994. "Quantum Fluctuation, Self-Organizing Biological Systems, and Human Freedom." *Idealistic Studies* 24 (3): 269–281.

Van Loocke, Philip, ed. 2001. *The Physical Nature of Consciousness.* Amsterdam/Philadelphia: John Benjamins.

Vendler, Zeno. 1967. *Linguistic in Philosophy.* Ithaca: Cornell University Press.

Vesey, Godfrey, ed. 1996. *Idealism Past and Present.* Royal Institute of Philosophy Lecture Series 13. Supplement to *Philosophy 1982.* Cambridge: Cambridge University Press.

Weber, Michel. 2002. "Whitehead's Reading of James and Its Context." Part I. *Streams of William James* 4 (1): 18–22.

Weber, Michel. 2003. "Whitehead's Reading of James and Its Context" Part II. *Streams of William James* 5 (3): 26–31

Weekes, Anderson. 2003. "Psychology and Physics Reconciled: Whitehead's Vision of Metaphysics." In *Searching for New Contrasts: Whiteheadian Contributions to Contemporary Challenges in Neurophysiology, Psychology, Psychotherapy and the Philosophy of Mind*, Franz G. Riffert and Michel Weber, eds., 347–374. Frankfurt am Main: Peter Lang.

Williams, Bernard. 1981. "Wittgenstein and Idealism." In *Moral Luck: Philosophical Papers 1973-1980*, 144–163. Cambridge: Cambridge University Press.

Xie, Wenyu, Zhihe Wang, and George Derfer, eds. 2005. *Whitehead and China: Relevance and Relationships*. Process Thought 4. Frankfurt: Ontos Verlag.

Yasue, Kunio, Mari Jibu, and Tarcisio Della Senta, eds. 2001. *No Matter, Never Mind. Proceedings of Toward a Science of Consciousness: Fundamental Approaches* (Tokyo '99). Amsterdam/Philadelphia: John Benjamins.

3

Consciousness as a Topic of Investigation in Western Thought

Anderson Weekes

It is a very curious and noteworthy fact that before the modern period what we now refer to as consciousness was not recognized in Western thinking as a unified topic of investigation (Hamanaka 1997). To be sure, many specific types of consciousness were named and in limited contexts received philosophical attention. Aristotle, for example, had drawn attention to important types of consciousness when he distinguished the awareness that one is seeing from awareness of the color seen, or when he pointed to the experiential togetherness (*sensus communis*) implied by the ability to distinguish from one another (to contrast) qualities from different sense modalities (*De Anima* 3.2). Beginning in the Hellenistic period, philosophy became more introspective, resulting in a more nuanced understanding of psychological phenomena. Both the Stoics and Plotinus were interested in aspects of reflexivity and identified various ways (feeling, perceiving, thinking) that the soul can be conscious of itself.[1] And from the time of Cicero, with whom Latin philosophy began, through the Reformation, pagan and then Christian authors devoted extraordinary attention to the meaning and manifestations of ethical consciousness (in our sense of *conscience*).[2] Nevertheless, a concept of consciousness encompassing and consolidating all these types is not attested. Consciousness does not appear to have been recognized in Western thought as a univocal and unitary phenomenon before the seventeenth century, when it abruptly became the all-absorbing topic of philosophy. Its status as the primary object of study virtually defined the discipline of philosophy, and a topic was "philosophical" to the extent that it needed to be approached as a problem of and for consciousness. If the concept of consciousness is uniquely implicated in modern philosophical thought, it is not implausible to suggest that it is colored by a history that should not go unquestioned. In the present chapter we examine certain aspects of that history relevant to Whitehead.

Consciousness: Some Words and the Concept

The place to begin is with language, with a history of words that seem most likely to have designated consciousness, or at least a prehistory of words that eventually did come to designate consciousness. Looking at Greek, Latin, English, German, and French, what we will find is that before the seventeenth century there was no word whose meaning corresponds to our concept of consciousness. In ancient Greek a single, embracing name for conscious phenomena is lacking altogether (Siebeck 1882, Jung 1933). It is also lacking in Medieval Latin and, more surprisingly perhaps, even the Latin of the early modern period (Jung 1933, Hamanaka 1997). One could argue that it is marginally recognized in classical Latin since *conscientia* comes closest to having the necessary scope, but it is never thematized as such: words from the *conscientia* group have a wide variety of uses, but the (possible) overall solidarity of these uses is not something connoted by any of them. Around the turn of the millennia (ca. 50 BCE–100 CE) the solidarity of *some* of these uses is of course recognized and corresponds to our concept of *conscience*. The fact that we distinguish clearly between consciousness and conscience, even if the latter falls within the compass of the former, imputes a telling ambiguity to classical Latin, which did not make this distinction. If consciousness was not distinguished from conscience, it is because the possibility of a solidarity of conscious phenomena more encompassing than conscience was not envisioned. In Medieval Latin the situation is more aggravated. For the most part, it knows *conscientia only* in its meaning as conscience (Jung 1933, Hennig 2006), leaving us to wonder what became of consciousness. Finally, European languages all developed words that corresponded to *conscientia*, and their usage is revealing: premodern usage tends to repeat the same semantic and syntactical patterns we find in Greek and Latin and offers nothing that could correspond to the modern concept of consciousness.

How these linguistic findings support the stronger contention that the concept itself was lacking is something that will emerge from the details of our analysis. Other recent analyses have drawn somewhat similar conclusions (Hamanaka 1997, Wilkes 1988), but their arguments have been based on semantic considerations alone. Semantic considerations leave much room for interpretative disagreement (e.g., Zeman 2002, 32–34) and in any case are only as reliable as they are exhaustive in tracking individual uses of the relevant terms. We will begin our inquiry with semantic considerations, but we will quickly discover that the modern concept of consciousness is really the concept of something preeminently nameable and, specifically, that it requires a name with distinctive grammatical properties. If available language was unable to fulfill the requisite grammatical functions before philosophers of the seventeenth century forced the issue, then we have reason to suspect the concept itself was not yet possible. It is not simply the case that there was no *name* for consciousness. There was no *place* for it—no way for a potential name to take up residence in the expressive medium of language.

In the ancient world, it is not until the Hellenistic period that the interior, reflective dimension of human experience takes on sufficient importance—primarily in Stoicism—to require a dedicated vocabulary. This vocabulary, telling in its variety, is evident in the later, Roman works of Stoicism that are still written in Greek: the reflections of Epictetus (ca. 55–ca. 135) and Marcus Aurelius (121–180). As we know, the discourses of Epictetus were recorded by Arrian, but those of Marcus Aurelius were supposedly recorded by the Emperor himself, captioned with the simple, but unprecedented title *EIS HEAUTON*: to himself. Here, if nowhere else, we should expect to find consciousness circumscribed by reflection as an autonomous and interior domain. But what we find in Epictetus and Marcus Aurelius both are words that suggest supervenient awareness as a feature bound and particular to the awareness upon which it supervenes, as diverse and disjoint as the host modalities happen to be: *synaisthēsis/synaisthanesthai* (con-perception, i.e., something that is supervenient upon and concurrent with perception),[3] *syneidēsis/syneidenai* (con-science, i.e., something supervenient upon and concurrent with knowledge),[4] or verbs and participles formed from *parakolouthein* (to follow along side of something—evidently, to follow along side of something perceived or thought about with the mind).[5] Mention must also be made of the odd Stoic term *summnemoneusis* (con-recollection), attested, but not well explained, by Sextus Empiricus (fl. ca. 200).[6] The diversity of these terms, none of which encompasses the meaning of the others, suggests that—despite the inward turn of Hellenistic thought—consciousness as a focal, homogenous phenomenon was not in the offing.[7] In particular, there is no hint that consciousness might be a subject in the Aristotelian sense—something self-supporting, autonomous, or substance-like, and quite different from all other things in the world. A similar conclusion can be drawn from the writings of Galen (ca. 130–ca. 200), who practiced in Rome and was physician to the Emperor Marcus Aurelius. By acknowledging that sensory or psychological events can remain unconscious if not engaged by appropriate activities of the soul, Galen clearly recognizes consciousness as a distinct phenomenon. But he does not recognize it as a

unitary phenomenon, as he assigns one kind of consciousness (*diagnōsis*) to
the organic event of sensation and another (*parakolouthein*) to strictly mental
events (Kühn 2001, 4:444, 5:644).

The fact that Latin could reasonably render all of the Greek terms
mentioned with *conscientia* raises the question that will concern us most:
whether *conscientia* (or comparable words in other languages) might not
adequately capture our concept of consciousness. The importance of *conscientia* directs our attention to the obviously corresponding words in European
languages (*conscience* in English and French, *Gewissen* in German), and it
also redirects our attention to the corresponding Greek word *syneidēsis*, whose
diminished importance in Stoicism is no measure of its overall importance
Greek literature. By taking some care to see why *syneidēsis* and *conscientia*,
as well as their premodern European successors, *conscience* and *Gewissen*, do
not mean consciousness in our sense, we will also get clearer about what
"our sense" of consciousness is.

The Latin word group *conscire* (v.),[8] *conscius* (adj.), *conscientia* (n.). is not
cognate with the Greek word group *syneidenai* (v.), *syneidēsis* (n.), *to syneidos*
(substantival participle), but it is semantically related by etymological parity.
In fact, words similar to one another in meaning and having this distinctive construction—a prefix meaning *along with* plus a verb of knowing—are,
without necessarily being cognate, common in many Indo-European languages
(Zeman 2002, 32–34). *Gewissen* is one example of this.[9] The question then
is if and when such Indo-European word groups designate something like
our concept of consciousness.

From our perspective the most striking thing about *syneidēsis* and
conscientia is the ambiguity already alluded to. Where Latin and Greek (or
modern French, for that matter) have one word, modern English has two, with
clearly distinguishable meanings: *conscience* and *consciousness*. While *conscience*
is limited in its contemporary connotations to the ethical sphere and has to
do with a feeling of or inner knowledge of guilt or innocence, *consciousness*
carries a more general and neutral cognitive connotation. Conscience denotes
the activity or the ever-vigilant readiness of a faculty of internal moral feeling
or judgment; consciousness denotes the content as well as the activity of an
ongoing and at bottom involuntary psychological reflection encompassing all
of our actual experience.

It is of no small significance, however, that this discrimination was
not made terminologically until the late seventeenth century, occurring
first in English and soon thereafter mimicked in German (*Gewissen* vs.
Bewusstsein). In each case the disambiguation was the deliberate work of
philosophers. They isolated the concept of consciousness, separating it from
conscience, and crafted a new word to identify it. This pattern is evident in
the way the concept of consciousness makes its linguistic debut in French

as well—also in the late seventeenth to early eighteenth centuries—even if French vernacular was never willing to absorb the philosophers' neologisms. This raises the obvious question: Why did consciousness have to wait until the seventeenth century to receive a proper baptism? What does it mean that European languages, before the seventeenth century, did not find the resources to resolve the ambiguity already strikingly evident to *us* in *syneidēsis* and *conscientia*? Before trying to answer these questions, we should document the facts they presuppose.

Before Ralph Cudworth's *True Intellectual System of the Universe* (1678), "consciousness" appears to be attested in English only once.[10] Before Christian Wolff's *Vernünftige Gedancken von Gott, der Welt und der Seele des Menschen, auch allen Dingen überhaupt* (1720), "Bewusstsein" is not attested in German at all.[11] The appearance of the neologisms is not without effect on the meaning of the older vocabulary. Both writers continue to use the older terms, conscience and *Gewissen*, in a sense that is clearly limited to conscience in the modern sense, thus creating, at least implicitly, the now classic contrast between conscience and consciousness.[12] At some point in the prior history of both languages we find the older terms associated with both ethical and cognitive meanings. Retaining the older terms for the ethical meaning allows the neologisms to perform a differential function, taking control of and consolidating any nonethical (purely cognitive or psychological) meanings that had been associated with the older terms. We will see that in English this meant reassigning to consciousness some senses that were still current in the usage of conscience, whereas for German it meant recovering and assigning to *Bewusstsein* senses of *Gewissen* that had long been lost to current usage.

Although Cudworth was one of the Cambridge Platonists, his arguments make it clear that his concept of consciousness is heavily indebted to Descartes. Ostensibly, Cudworth proposed "consciousness" as a way to render the Stoic/Neo-Platonic term *synaisthēsis* in English, but *synaisthēsis* is given a distinctly Cartesian interpretation. There is an emphasis on unmediated self-consciousness that is traceable only to Descartes' idea that there is nothing in the mind of which we are not immediately conscious. Cudworth may sound vaguely Hellenistic when he speaks of "[. . .] that *Duplication*, that is included in the Nature of συναίσθησις, *Con-sense* and *Consciousness*, which makes a Being to be Present with it self, Attentive to its own Actions, or Animadversive of them, to perceive it self to Do or Suffer, and to have a *Fruition* or *Enjoyment* of it self" (Cudworth 1678, 159) but he sounds distinctly modern when he speaks of "*Redoubled Consciousness* or *Self-perception*" (173) and describes its plenary self-possession: "the Souls being All *Conscious* of It Self, and *Reflexive* upon its *whole Self* [. . .]" (774). An essentially Cartesian definition of consciousness can be inferred from the following equation: "the *Phancy*, *Apparition*, or *Seeming* of *Cogitation* [. . .] is The *Consciousness* of it [. . .]" (846). He often seeks to clarify the new word by pairing it in explanatory apposition with "con-sense" or "self-perception" (159–162, 173, 190, 198). But consciousness is the term he prefers and standardizes with its remarkably frequent use throughout his long work.[13]

Cudworth's concept of consciousness turns out to be a concession to Descartes made necessary by his project of a modern rehabilitation of neo-Platonism. This becomes evident in the way the concept of consciousness functions in a two-way contrast: on the one hand, Descartes was right that "local motion" cannot explain consciousness (36); but, on the other, Descartes was wrong to deny "any *Action* distinct from *Local Motion* besides *Expressly Conscious Cogitation*" (159). According to Cudworth, the organic activities of "plastic nature" also cannot be explained mechanically, but nor are they consciously executed. Cudworth's book is an apology for theism and a Neo-Platonic concept of nature based on acceptance of the Cartesian definitions of mind and matter and the principle that nothing comes from nothing (31–33): mind and matter, so understood, are insufficient to explain the plasticity of nature with its multiform and highly organized vitality, which must therefore come from "something" other than conscious mind and inert matter (Q.E.D.) (159–162, 830–832). From this précis we see that the concept of consciousness functions primarily as a negative (or "failed") *explanans* for Cudworth: it is relevant as something that needs to be ruled out of natural philosophy because it is specifically *not* able to explain nature.

One very important thing we need to keep in mind is that Cudworth does not in fact introduce consciousness as an English rendering of the Latin *conscientia*. Furthermore, however much his conception of consciousness may be influenced by Cartesian ideas, he does not introduce consciousness as the express translation of any Cartesian term. He offers consciousness as the translation of *synaisthēsis*, albeit under a Cartesian interpretation. It is not self-evident that this corresponds to a featured concept in Descartes' own philosophical vocabulary. We should not, therefore, rush to conclusions about the contemporaneous meaning of the Latin word *conscientia*. We shall come back to the meaning of *conscientia* in Descartes at the end of this section.

The new word "consciousness" gained the widest possible currency through its use in Locke's much-read *Essay Concerning Human Understanding* (1690). Like Cudworth, Locke uses the term *consciousness* in a sense implicitly discriminated from *conscience*, for, like Cudworth, he retains conscience in a sense clearly limited to ethical significance (Locke 1959, 1:71 and 464) while introducing the neologism to designate something like self-perception: "Consciousness is the perception of what passes in a man's own mind" (1:138). But in Locke's *Essay*, consciousness has made the remarkable stride from being evaluated in the role of a potential *explanans* to being a singularly important philosophical *explanandum*. We see this happen in the famous chapter, added in the second edition (1694), on the idea of personal identity (ch. 27).

Circumstances were similar in German literature, where the word *Bewusstsein* was completely unprecedented when introduced by Wolff in 1720. Wolff employs the word in its fully developed modern sense: consciousness is the totality of an individual's self-disclosed awareness. Wolff draws obviously on Descartes in stressing the self-certainty of consciousness (Wolff 1983b/1720, §§ 1–9), but more so on Leibniz in taking pains to prove the identity of consciousness with clarity and distinctness of representation: we are unconscious of things affecting us to the extent that we do not (or are unable to) represent them clearly and distinctly (§§ 727–733). However, Wolff goes beyond Leibniz in emphasizing clarity and distinctness as a function of discrimination (§§ 734–737). This explicitly introduces discriminating reflection as an essential mediating element of consciousness, which is noteworthy because it is inconsistent with the Cartesian idea of immediate, automatic, and plenary self-possession. It leads instead in the direction of the Kantian concept of consciousness as a synthetic activity. One striking consequence of this difference is that Descartes' consciousness is the coincidence of thought with itself in the moment, while Wolff's consciousness is impossible without the synthetic identity of consciousness with itself over time (§§ 734–737).

It may seem obvious to a contemporary reader that Wolff, with his neologism *Bewusstsein*, thought he was translating *conscientia* and hence that the meaning of *conscientia* in contemporary Latin was also consciousness as we understand it (consciousness in its fully developed modern sense), but the situation is not so simple. Several things militate against a straightforward equation of *Bewusstsein* and *conscientia*. In the first place, Wolff, aware that he was writing metaphysics in a language in which philosophy had no precedent, helpfully provided the reader with a German-Latin glossary, where one would naturally expect to find his most peculiar German coinage assigned to its proper Latin forebear. And yet, remarkably, *Bewusstsein*, although it is important enough to find its way into the author's index, is absent from his glossary! In fact, no German word is given as the equivalent of *conscientia* at all because *conscientia*, too, is conspicuously absent! *Conscientia* can be found only in the glossary to his German language work on ethics (Wolff 1976/1720), where it appears as the Latin equivalent of *Gewissen*. This should make us wonder if Wolff's model for *Bewusstsein* was any Latin noun at all. If we turn to Wolff's Latin language works (which appeared from 1728 until his death in 1754) to find out how he did denominate consciousness, we make an interesting discovery. For Wolff makes frequent use of *conscius* as a reflexive predicative adjective,[14] but for nouns he avails himself of language that he acknowledges has been recently invented or at least partly redefined by stipulation: the role of *Bewusstsein* is taken over by Leibniz's *apperceptio* (discussed below) or by *cogitatio* in the special sense stipulated by Descartes (also discussed below).[15] Moreover, it turns out that the relationship between *conscientia* and Wolff's own terminology is something Wolff himself explicitly addresses. Having quoted Descartes definition of *cogitatio* as "everything in us of which we are conscious insofar as we have consciousness (*conscientia*) of it," he asserts that Leibniz's *apperceptio* coincides with the meaning of *conscientia* introduced by Descartes *in this context*: "Apperceptionis nomine utitur Leibnitius: coincidit autem cum conscientia, quem terminum in praesenti negotio Cartesius adhibet" (Wolff 1968/1732, § 25). From this statement and the fact that Wolff elects not to use *conscientia* in this sense at all it would appear that *apperceptio* does not coincide with the meaning of *conscientia* in any context *other* than the Cartesian definition of *cogitatio*. *Conscientia* in this sense is therefore a no less peculiar usage than *Bewusstsein* and consequently useless, if not misleading, as a clarification of it.[16] Moreover, we will argue below that it is only in the context of a *post*-Cartesian assessment of Descartes' definition of thought that *conscientia* can mean consciousness. For whatever Descartes' definition of *cogitatio* may *imply* about consciousness, consciousness is not a thematic term in Descartes' writing.

A second thing that militates against *Bewusstsein* as a direct translation of *conscientia* is Wolff's sometimes curious orthography.[17] Among variant spellings found in the first edition, we find one that is especially striking. The spelling *das bewusst Sein* (in §§ 733 and 736) suggests that Wolff was not thinking of *conscientia*, whatever it may have meant in Descartes (or to readers of Descartes) or in contemporary usage, but rather that he intended to make a substantive out of the Latin *conscius esse*, that is, to make an entity out of being conscious. As we will argue below, this is just what Locke's peculiar use of consciousness had done. At the same time, this would explain why *Bewusstsein* is missing from Wolff's glossary. While in German, as in Greek, it is easy to make a noun out of an infinitive simply by prefixing an article, the grammatical impossibility of doing this in Latin means that an equivalent for *das bewusst Sein* could not be given.

The situation is somewhat different in French. First, vernacular French never made the terminological distinction between conscience and consciousness. Second, although conscience and consciousness were not explicitly discriminated in German and English until philosophers forced the issue, usage tending toward both meanings (that is, both cognitive and ethical meanings) is attested at some point in the prior history of those languages. In French, however, a cognitive meaning is not attested before the seventeenth century and betrays the influence of Cartesian philosophy (Rey 1992, entry for "*Conscience*"). Attempts in French to give *conscience* a cognitive meaning therefore parallel the roughly contemporaneous introduction of neologisms in English and German and are equally deliberate. We see this in Malebranche, who spoke of "*sentiment intérieur ou conscience*,"[18] using *conscience* in a restrictive pairing much the way Cudworth had recourse to the pairing "con-sense and consciousness" to create a newly focused meaning.[19] When so paired, Malebranche's *conscience* evidently means consciousness in a sense very close to the one Locke will carve out: the self-perceived domain contained by inner sense. The extent to which Malebranche is struggling against existing usage is evident. For when Malebranche wants *conscience* to have this novel meaning, he almost always feels obliged to pair it in this way, making "*sentiment intérieur ou conscience*" a fixed and recurring set phrase throughout his writings. When not so paired, Malebranche's *conscience* can also still mean moral conscience, plain and simple (Malebranche 1997, 326, 328, 637; 1979, 1:470, 472, 940).

The attempt in French to give *conscience* a cognitive meaning in addition to its ethical meaning was obviously successful since the result was to create an ambiguity that infiltrated the vernacular and, unlike English and German, has never been resolved at the level of common usage, although the need for disambiguation was certainly felt. But once again, it was philosophers who felt this need and attempted to give consciousness its own proper designation. In his translation (1700) of Locke's *Essay*, Pierre Coste renders consciousness either as "*con-science*," always hyphenated and italicized to distinguish it from *conscience* (Fr.) being used as a rendering of conscience (Eng.), which Locke also employs (Locke 1959, 1:71 and 464), or, influenced no doubt by Malebranche, as *sentiment* or *sentiment intérieur* (apart from a few deviations such as *connoissance* or *conviction*).[20] In his *Nouveaux Essais*, a critical commentary on Locke's *Essay* written in 1703–1705, but published posthumously in 1765, Leibniz invents both *consciosité* and *apperception* to denominate consciousness,[21] the latter term gaining currency in philosophical usage only because it appeared in published writings such as the *Monadology*[22] (1714) or the *Principles of Nature and Grace* (1714), which defines consciousness very clearly as the reflexive knowledge of one's interior state: "[I]l est bon de faire distinction entre la *Perception* qui est l'état interieur de la Monade representant les choses externes, et l'*Apperception* qui est la *Conscience*, ou la connoissance reflexive de cet état interieur."[23] In all these cases it is clear that philosophers of the late seventeenth and early eighteenth centuries found the available words to be inadequate for their purposes. Existing words needed to be paired up in an explanatory apposition, or italicized and hyphenated, or, ideally, replaced by a neologism if the phenomenon of consciousness was to be rightly designated.

What was the semantic composition of the relevant word groups before the explicit terminological discrimination between the concepts of conscience and consciousness? What exactly did the words *Gewissen, conscience,* (Fr.), and conscience (Eng.) mean in premodern usage? Just what did the words *syneidēsis* and *conscientia* mean in antiquity? A detailed lexical history must be reserved for a different place, but some striking patterns need mention. What we will find is that the original meaning of the word groups was neither consciousness nor conscience *in our sense*. But it will be best to arrive at this conclusion by exclusion of the more obvious alternatives: if the concept of consciousness, as we know it, dates from the seventeenth century, then perhaps the older and original meaning of the words was conscience, in the sense familiar to us. Upon examination we find that this is not the case. Alternatively, if conscience is not the original meaning, then perhaps we are wrong to date the concept of consciousness from the seventeenth century. Perhaps consciousness as we know it is after all the original meaning. This, too, will prove obviously false, forcing us to look for a third alternative. Our point of departure will be the earliest documented uses of the word groups in question.

The original meaning of the word groups in Greek and Latin,[24] in German,[25] and (with an important qualification) in English,[26] was not conscience in the ethical sense, but *firsthand knowledge shared with another*: one is conscious *with* another of something. A moral connotation was not absent, however, since the knowledge in question was very often the knowledge a witness has of a criminal act, from which the sense of *complicity* or the *confidence* of a *shared secrete* develops. Connected with this meaning or perhaps following upon it is a crucial extension of meaning: because one is always aware of (witness to) one's own acts, our word groups come to designate the knowledge each person has of her own actions—the knowledge a person as agent shares with herself as knower. The idea that one cannot help but "share" such knowledge with oneself appears to form the vernacular point of departure in Greek and Latin for the earliest concepts of conscience as a kind of inescapable inner judge of one's actions.[27] We see this concept taking definite shape in the first century before and after the start of the current era, when both *conscientia* and *syneidēsis* begin to have this meaning. *Conscientia* plays an important role in the writings of Cicero and Seneca. *Syneidēsis*, if not more frequent, is arguably more important still in Philo and St. Paul. It is important to keep in mind, however, that the shared knowledge denoted by *syneidēsis* and *conscientia* did not *have* to be ethical in its connotations; it could be cognitive in an ethically neutral sense. Such uses are well attested. The situation is different, however, from the early Middle Ages on, when Latin became the language of Christianity.

Conscientia became the Vulgate translation of St. Paul's *syneidēsis*. Accordingly, any neutral or purely psychological sense of consciousness that *conscientia* may have enjoyed along side of its ethical meaning was largely displaced in Medieval Latin usage by the dominance of the concept of *conscience* so important to the New Testament and its theological exegesis

(Jung 1933 and Hennig 2006). A similar phenomenon occurs in German. The oldest meaning of *Gewissen* in Old High German[28] (*gewizzani*) is not religious or moral, but cognitive, although as with *syneidēsis* and *conscientia* the context is often legal or moral (and possibly but not necessarily intersubjective). However, *Gewissen* acquires the possibility of a collateral meaning as conscience when it becomes Notker's (950–1022) translation of *conscientia* in his German rendering of the Vulgate Psalms. This appears to be the oldest documented use of *Gewissen* in the sense of conscience that is peculiar to Christian exegesis of the Bible. Nevertheless, alongside this ethical-religious meaning, *Gewissen* retains the possibility of a cognitive meaning until Luther's (1483–1546) powerful influence stabilizes *Gewissen* as the equivalent of St. Paul's *syneidēsis*, at which point the cognitive meaning becomes obsolete. We thus find in each case—Greek, Latin, and German—that *conscientia* evolves from something originally intersubjective and ambivalent vis-à-vis distinctions between ethical and cognitive contexts into conscience as we know it—an individual's faculty of involuntary self-assessment in the moral or religious sphere. In French the situation is different, and in English more complex.

In French the oldest documented uses of "*conscience*," dating from the twelfth century, signify the individual moral conscience (Huguet 1977, entry for "*Conscience*"). From the start, it is already something private and exclusively moral. Neither a cognitive nor an intersubjective meaning appears to be attested in Medieval French. The word continues to have this limited meaning until philosophers deliberately attach *consciousness* as a second meaning, which abrogates the limitation of "*conscience*" to ethical relevance, but not its privacy. In English we find two patterns: one similar to French and one to German and the classical languages. *Firsthand knowledge shared with another* is indeed the oldest meaning attested (early seventeenth century) in connection with "conscious," but not in connection with "conscience," the oldest occurrences of which (thirteenth century) already attest to a sense of *private* knowledge or inner awareness, often but not always involving moral judgment or feeling (OED 1989, entries for "Conscious" and "Conscience"). Thus, English does in a way recapitulate the semantic evolution we found in German, Latin, and Greek. Albeit over a much shorter span (only one century), the use of *conscious* evolves like the use of *Gewissen*, *syneidēsis* and *conscientia*. It evolves from an original intersubjective meaning of *privity* or the *shared knowledge of a witness* into the meaning we find attested in Cudworth and Locke: it describes something individual and private. Conscience, on the other hand, enters the vernacular of both French and English around the thirteenth century with the approximate meaning that the Latin *conscientia* had by then arrived at, for in both languages conscience denotes something essentially private. In fact, in thirteenth-century French *conscience* has exactly the same meaning *conscientia* has in thirteenth-century Latin, denoting something private, exclusively moral, and individually countable. However, we will see below that in a critical respect even the English conscience follows the pattern evident in German, Latin, and Greek rather than, like French, engaging an already developed meaning of the corresponding Latin term. For, while it begins its career already denoting something private, it is neither exclusively moral nor countable. The decisive importance of this last qualification will become clear as we proceed.

As documented in the Oxford English Dictionary, usage of conscience in Middle and early English (medieval and Renaissance English, respectively) have a noteworthy peculiarity. *Conscientia* and *Gewissen* both suffer from a narrowing of usage that eventually excludes any purely cognitive meaning, and *conscience* in French excludes it from the start. This might make us think that the need for a new word to designate something cognitive resulted from a narrowing of usage that left a familiar phenomenon without a name. But English, the language in which consciousness first got its name, belies this suspicion. Conscience does not evince this narrowing of usage, but into the seventeenth century suggests a scope and flexibility comparable to *conscientia* in classical Latin (inasmuch as moral and cognitive meanings are both attested, even if, unlike classical Latin, the sense in both cases is limited to something private). Nevertheless, English philosophers in the seventeenth century felt the need to coin a new word to designate consciousness in clear contradistinction to conscience. The decisive question is whether the need for the new word was felt because the old word had indeed lost some of the original suppleness of its meaning and was no longer adequate, or because a new concept was abroad demanding a new name—in short, whether the phenomenon of consciousness (as we know it) was recognized in the centuries before it was denominated "consciousness." Since English does not seem to have suffered any semantic loss, aren't we entitled to surmise that a new denotatum—something never before named—had obtruded itself? What could the new denotatum be? We already have what we need to answer this question. The clues are to be found in the early history of our word groups. We will discover the same patterns of early usage in both English and German that we find in Latin and Greek, and we will see how these patterns repeat themselves in different registers of meaning, resulting first in the concept of conscience now familiar to us, and much later in the concept of consciousness that we are now investigating.

There can be no doubt that the earliest uses of our word groups were very often ethical in their implications. This is the case in English and German as much as in Greek and Latin. Nevertheless, their original meaning was not conscience in our sense, but consciousness, with, however, the important qualification that the object and context of such consciousness was usually moral, ethical, religious, or legal. This may seem a distinction without difference. What distinguishes "conscience" from "moral consciousness"? In fact, there are clear differences, and bringing them out will also lead us to the crucial difference between the consciousness in question and *our* concept of consciousness. For one thing, conscience takes on the qualities of its content, but consciousness does not. Where "*conscientia* of guilt" is treated by an author as equivalent to a "guilty *conscientia*," then we are dealing with conscience; otherwise, we are dealing with consciousness. Consciousness is removed from its object by the intentional relation implicit in the objective genitive: always innocent; a witness, but not involved. Conscience, by contrast, is involved and implicated. It is always complicit, either as an accomplice to the commission of impropriety or as a concerned authority culpably omitting to prevent the commission of the act. Unlike consciousness, conscience either *is and should not have been* or *should have been but is not*—an agent. Precisely because an agent is subject to the moral qualities for which he is responsible, his "consciousness of guilt" (or of innocence) becomes a subjective rather than an objective genitive.

Because the crucial semantic distinction between ethical consciousness and conscience can be specified grammatically, we can document with some certainty the semantic evolution of the word groups. Conscience is a faculty possessed in the telling distribution of one and only one per person. It is an enduring, individuated phenomenon associated with each person. It is, therefore, something designated by a noun and specifically by a count noun. It can be qualified by an adjective but also function absolutely, as well as function as the subject of active verbs. The ethical consciousness denoted by the earlier usage is by contrast episodic, individuated as an event; or it is not individuated at all, being rather a quality or state which one can possess more or less of, but cannot count (except as episodes of possession). In the former case, when consciousness is episodic, it is indicated by verbal constructions; in the latter, where it is a quality, it appears in the guise of an adjective (e.g., *conscius*) qualifying a noun rather than as a noun being qualified, or as a mass noun rather than a count noun. The history of our word groups is indeed marked by these grammatical differences. Until the first century BCE Greek employs, almost exclusively, verbal constructions denoting an event. When the verbal noun (*syneidēsis*) and the substantival participle (*to syneidos*) make their appearance, they tend at first to have their natural verbal meanings, designating the *occurrence* of some ethically relevant cognizance. In Latin the adjective is extremely common, and the prominence of the noun is mitigated by the fact that, true to its formation as an abstract noun derived from an adjective, it tends at first to function as a mass noun, designating a quality rather than an individual. The "entified" concept of conscience that we now take for granted emerged only gradually in the first centuries of the Christian era, as New Testament scholars such as Eckstein (1983) and Bosman (2003) have carefully documented. Decisive for our interpretation is the fact that Middle English usage of *conscience* reflects the same pattern of development from mass noun to count noun: "The word [conscience] is etymologically, as its form shows, a noun of condition or function [...] and as such originally had no plural: a man or a people had *more* or *less* conscience. But [...] it came gradually to be thought of as an individual entity, a member or organ of the mental system, of which each man possessed *one*, and thus it took *a* and *pl.*" (OED 1989, "Conscience"). The transition of *Gewissen* in German from a possibly intersubjective state to an instance of a privately possessed faculty testifies to the same development.

This analysis yields several results important for understanding the history of the concept of consciousness. The general conclusion is that we must examine more than one variable in looking at the evolution of the meaning of the word groups in question. Besides the cognitive/ethical contrast we have noted a contrast between intersubjective and private, but above all between states (named by mass nouns) and individuated entities (named by count nouns). In Greek, Latin, English, and German, the oldest meanings are *stative*. In each case we saw that it could be moral or cognitive, and usually either public or private. Only later do the terms *syneidēsis*, *conscientia*, conscience, or *Gewissen* become count nouns that designate a personally individuated phenomenon. But we saw that when they first make this transition, the designated phenomenon is what we know as conscience and is something limited to ethical significance. Before they came to mean conscience (and to some extent continuing afterwards in a parallel usage that remained true to the older meaning) the word groups in question were used with a cognitive meaning. Often the context or content of the cognitive state in question was ethical, but not always. It is certainly the case that the context and content of such cognitive uses were sometimes completely nonethical. The unavoidable conclusion is that in such cases our word groups do indeed designate consciousness as a purely cognitive phenomenon. What is critically important, however, is that there is no evidence the consciousness designated in such nonethical contexts was ever thought of as a countable entity. It was always stative. Furthermore, when the entification of consciousness first occurs, it is always ethical consciousness that is entified, resulting in the concept of conscience. Cognitive consciousness is initially unaffected and continues to be denoted as a state and, with one exception, eventually ceases to be denoted at all. We saw that, except in English, the emergence of the entified ethical meaning sooner or later displaces the possibility of a concurrent stative-cognitive meaning, and that this happens long before neologisms for consciousness make their appearance.

The outstanding question then is: When does an entified concept of cognitive consciousness (consciousness proper as opposed to conscience) make its first appearance? When does the purely cognitive sense attested in the early usage of our word groups make the transition, already documented for their ethical sense, from state to entity? When do we first encounter consciousness as an individuated psychological reality, as the subject and/or totality of the individual's cognizance? The linguistic evidence suggests that this did not happen until the seventeenth century, when consciousness was finally named by a count noun. Obviously this could not happen before consciousness had been given a proper name at all, a name that distinguished it from the thing named by conscience (or, what is the same thing, before conscience was factored out of consciousness as but one of its special cases—as moral cognition achieved through internal affect—giving consciousness wider scope but also a new specificity as something essentially cognitive, not involving morality or affect *per se*, but necessarily presupposed by the moral affectivity of conscience). But nor could it happen if using such a name grammatically as a count noun made no sense. It may not have been possible (may not have made sense to exploit a purely grammatical possibility in this way) to name consciousness with a count noun before consciousness experienced *itself* as a countable thing. Our thesis, then, is the following: it was *cognizance as a countable entity* that was unprecedented and obtruded itself upon the seventeenth century, requiring the creation of not only a new name, but also a new philosophy. We will examine this transformation as a historical event in the following sections. For now we can gloss "cognizance as a countable entity" in more familiar terms: knowledge was now essentially understood as the property of an individual, as one of its "accidents," and therefore contingent on its being, subject to the same limitations and corruptions as the substance of which it was being predicated. The newly discovered entity in the early modern period was just this: an individuated and hence corruptible subject of knowledge.

If the imperative to give consciousness a proper name came—at least linguistically—from its being construed as a countable thing, then we come at last to the pivotal role of Descartes in this development, for Descartes was the first philosopher to construe consciousness as the essential and defining attribute of a *thing*. Descartes' role, however, is easily exaggerated. First, it is not so much a question of how consciousness was interpreted as how it experienced itself, and this will certainly have depended on more than a philosophical definition. As we will see in subsequent sections, Descartes' definition of the mind as a thing only codifies in concepts historical changes already long underway. But second, and more pertinent to our present purpose, is the question of the correct terminus *a quo* for the naming of consciousness by a count noun and the conceptually explicit reification this implies. Descartes, in fact, did not say that consciousness was a thing, but that the mind was a thing defined by consciousness. It is highly debatable whether the transformation of consciousness into a thing has really taken place in Descartes.[29] In light of the common tendency to associate Descartes with a philosophy of consciousness it is worthwhile looking at how consciousness actually functions in his philosophy.

The fact is that Descartes rarely uses the word *conscientia*. Perhaps its rarity is balanced by the importance it bears as a result of Descartes' thesis *that there is nothing in the mind of which we are not conscious* (Descartes 1964–1976, 7:107; Descartes 1984, 2:77). Since this is an essential feature of what it is to be "in the mind," *conscientia* and *conscius esse* figure prominently in Descartes' definition of thought, which is the name he gives to everything that is properly speaking "in the mind." From the "Arguments [. . .] arranged in geometrical fashion" appended to the Second Set of Objections and Replies (1641): "The word *thought* includes everything that is in us in such a way that we are immediately conscious of it" (1964–1976, 7:160; 1984, 2:113). From the *Principles* (1644): "By the word *thought* I understand everything that is in us when we are conscious insofar as we have consciousness of it" (1964–1976, 8A:7; 1984, 1:195). From the reply to Hobbes' second objection (Third Set of Objections and Replies [1641]): "There are other acts, which we call *thoughts*, such as to understand, will, imagine, sense, etc., which are all comprehended under the common notion of thought, or perception, or consciousness, and we say that the substance in which they inhere is a *thinking thing*, or *mind* [. . .]" (1964–1976, 7:176; 1984, 2:124). For Descartes it appears that consciousness may be an act or a state that *defines* a certain kind of entity, but it does not seem to *be* an entity (or to *name* an entity). Also, as with Cudworth, the concept of consciousness belongs in general to the theoretical category of *explanantia* rather than *explananda*.

What is historically noteworthy about Descartes' use of *conscientia* is not that it designates consciousness as an entity (because it doesn't), but the fact that it means *consciousness* at all. Once *conscientia* became a count noun designating *conscience* as an enduring moral faculty within the individual, any concurrent use of *conscientia* as a mass noun to mean *consciousness* or as a count noun to name discrete episodes of cognizance virtually disappears from Medieval Latin, although Hennig has found some interesting exceptions (Hennig 2006). How unusual was Descartes' usage? Because *conscience* in French conformed closely to the contemporaneous meaning and usage of *conscientia* in Latin, we can gauge to some extent the strangeness of Descartes' use of *conscientia* by looking at the difficulties it created for his French translators. Translations of both the *Meditations* (with the *Objections and Replies*) and the *Principles* appeared in 1647. Clerselier renders the definition of thought appended to the Second Set of Responses without recourse to *conscience* or its cognates at all: "Par le nom de *pensée*, ie comprens tout ce qui est tellement en nous, que nous en sommes immediatement connoissans [=immediate conscii simus]."[30] Similarly, Picot does not seem to think *conscience* is an appropriate candidate for rendering what Descartes has in mind with *conscientia*. In the definition of thought in the *Principles*, Picot replaces the noun *conscientia* with a verbal periphrasis: "Par le mot de penser, j'entends tout ce qui se fait en nous de telle sorte que nous l'apperceuons immediatement par nous-mesme [= quatenus eorum in nobis conscientia est]."[31] In fact, *conscience* appears in these translations only once. In rendering Descartes' response to Hobbes's second objection, Clerselier does use *conscience* for *conscientia*—but only in a restrictive pairing with *connoissance*![32] What these renderings show is that recovering a cognitive or psychological concept of consciousness in the mid-seventeenth century posed difficulties for both French and Latin. Most important, we see from *connoisans* as a predicate adjective and *se appercevoir* as a verbal periphrasis for *conscientia* that we are unquestionably dealing with states and episodes, not with entities.

Nevertheless, even if Descartes has not entified consciousness, with hindsight we see the inevitability of such a development prefigured in his insistence that thought is inherently conscious at the same time that it *defines* a unique kind of substance.[33] Descartes, in effect, has already determined the fate of a concept that will gain ascendancy and demand a name. We still cannot say that the transition has been fully realized in Cudworth. To be sure, Cudworth has (like Descartes) isolated the neutral cognitive meaning of *conscientia* threatened by Pauline conscience and (unlike Descartes) assigned it its own name, thus allowing for an easy verbal discrimination between conscience and consciousness. But, significantly, Cudworth tends to use consciousness as a mass noun. Something *has* consciousness (not *a* consciousness) or is done *with* consciousness.[34] In contrast to this, Locke and, shortly thereafter, Samuel Clarke use consciousness as an obvious count noun to designate something that endures within each person; it is something numerically individuated and distributed one (and only one) per person. Each one of us has "a consciousness."

Locke's famous discussion of personal identity documents the semantic transformation of consciousness into an entity. We encounter, for example, the otherwise unintelligible formation of the plural, *consciousnesses*, referred to, moreover, as *agents*: "Could we suppose two distinct incommunicable consciousnesses *acting the same body* [*sic*], the one constantly by day, the other by night [. . .]?" (Locke 1959, 1:464, emphasis added). Also remarkable is the ease with which Locke passes from the term *consciousness* to another neologism, *self-consciousness*, and from there to a reified concept of the self: "I being as much concerned, and as justly accountable for any action that was done a thousand years since, appropriated to me now by this self-consciousness, as I am for what I did the last moment. *Self* is that conscious thinking thing [. . .] which is sensible or conscious of pleasure and pain, capable of happiness or misery, and so is concerned for itself, as far as that consciousness extends" (1:458–459).[35] Samuel Clarke, in the *Letter to Mr. Dodwell* (1706) and its *Defenses* (1706–1708), makes the crux of his argument the insistence that consciousness is an "individual power," that is, a countable thing (Clarke 1706, 33–35 and 1707, 4–5, 25–28, 31–32, 51–53).

The philosophical lesson from this word history is clear. If the many problems—metaphysical, psychological, epistemological, ethical, religious—that we have since the seventeenth century associated with consciousness were not previously seen as forming a naturally cohesive class centered on one fundamental problem, at least part of the reason is that consciousness itself was not recognized as a unitary and encompassing phenomenon: because it was not individuated, consciousness could not totalize the individual's experience. This state of affairs naturally gives rise to the question why consciousness almost suddenly emerged to absorb the complexity of human life into the simplicity of an all-embracing problem. The extent to which this had actually taken place is reflected in the epic form taken on by the modern search for knowledge and certainty, which distinguishes itself in this respect from the otherwise similar preoccupations of Hellenistic philosophy. Almost a hero to modern philosophy, consciousness (with or without "consciousness" as its proper name) was the featured protagonist of more than one intellectual odyssey in which the terrible perils posed by the uncertainty of subjectivity were braved and overcome, bringing reality, like an exotic foreign land, under the dominion of consciousness and rendering the rightfulness of that dominion beyond dispute. Think of Descartes' *Meditations*, Hegel's *Phenomenology of Spirit*, or—with certain modulations—the brooding internalized quests of Romantic poetry.[36]

Subjectivity: Old and New

If by subjectivity we mean the uncertainty that results from the distortion or possible distortion in the manifestation of the world to the knower, then the "problem of subjectivity" is coextensive with the old "problem of appearance," and we cannot say that the problem of subjectivity is uniquely modern. What is understood as the problem of subjectivity, however, is usually more narrowly construed to mean cognitive uncertainty due specifically to the inadequacies of the subject (the experient subject of knowledge, that is). The problem of subjectivity is therefore the problem of appearance insofar as it has this specific etiology. In this case, appearance is understood as a kind of refraction of the world by the imperfect medium of subjectivity.

This restriction allows us to draw a very straightforward contrast between certain ancient and modern attitudes. According to a view widely documented in the philosophy of Greece prior to the Hellenistic period, the problem posed for science is not the subjectivity of consciousness, but the shabbiness of the things that offer themselves to cognition: How could anyone know something that won't stop changing? The difference between the Ancients of Classical antiquity and the Moderns on this point is whether the shabbiness of the object or the shabbiness of the subject is what jeopardizes knowledge and thus whether the remedy is to seek out more reliable objects or more reliable access to objects (Weekes 2007, 57–80). Shabby objects constitute a class of things about which one could only have opinions, never knowledge, and there is no remedy for this except to avoid them. A shabby subject, on the other hand, is one that musters only opinions about things that can actually be known—a condition for which there should be a cure.

But even if we restrict what we mean by the problem of subjectivity in this way, we still cannot say that it is uniquely modern. It is customary to date the beginning of modern philosophy from Descartes' so-called "discovery of subjectivity." But this discovery was in part the rediscovery of ancient ideas and in part the surfacing of a long, tortuous, and often submerged tradition stretching back to similar ideas in Greek antiquity. These were ideas intimated in part by the Sophists, the historical Socrates and the schools of his companions (the so-called Lesser Socratics), vehemently opposed by the Eleatics, Plato, and Aristotle, and developed, sometimes flamboyantly, but often with penetrating insight by the great Hellenistic and early Roman schools of thought, Stoicism, Epicureanism, and above all Pyrrhonism and Skepticism. As Plato had realized early on, these were dangerous ideas. They clustered around the problem of finding an objective standard for knowledge or facing up to the relativity and subjectivity of beliefs in the absence of such a standard.[37]

So the radical departure from tradition taken by seventeenth-century thought cannot be due to an alleged "discovery of subjectivity." In this respect it was a Hellenistic atavism. The recent recovery in Europe of ancient learning was not a recovery of Aristotle, whose works had already enjoyed canonical status since the sixth century in logic and the thirteenth century in metaphysics and natural philosophy. Rather, it was the fragmentary recovery of everything *not* Aristotelian. It thus brought, as a counterthrust to Scholasticism (with its roots in the attitudes of the philosophy of Classical Greece), the concerns of Hellenistic philosophy to the fore. The recovery of Hellenistic Skepticism in particular formed the last phase in the revival of classical learning we call the Renaissance.

The rediscovery of these ideas was occasioned largely by the recovery and publications of the writings of the Hellenistic skeptic, Sextus Empiricus (Schmitt 1983). The decisive events were the Latin translation of his *Outlines of Pyrrhonism*, which appeared in 1562, and the subsequent promulgation of the skeptical arguments contained in this book by Montaigne in his *Apology for Raymond Sebond*. Written in vernacular French and appearing in 1580, Montaigne's *Apology* anticipates the issues that will dominate modern philosophy to such an extent that it seems to set its whole agenda and deserves to be considered the inaugural text of modern philosophy. The fact that it contains almost nothing new gives us something to think about.

But we have also alluded to a *submerged tradition*. Indeed, such a tradition can be traced through the influence of Hellenistic skepticism on the Empiric school of medicine in the early Roman period. The transmission of Greek medical knowledge from Rome to Islam carried, like a Trojan Horse, the skeptic critique of causality, which was subsequently elaborated in the service of a theology of divine omnipotence, first in the Islamic theology of al-Ash'arī (d. 935) and al-Ghazālī (1058–1111) and then, after the European reception of their ideas, in the fourteenth-century Nominalism of the Latin West (Sorabji 1983, 297–306; Groarke 1990, 125–131). How these ideas traveled from the fourteenth to the seventeenth centuries remains unclear, but however indirect, the influences of fourteenth-century Nominalism on Hume or, more startlingly, al-Ghazālī on Descartes,[38] cannot be dismissed.[39]

If so many of the ideas we associate with the problem of subjectivity are not really modern, what makes the modern treatment of this topic so radically new? What makes it so much more than a rediscovery of a Hellenistic sensibility? Our first clue is the strange epic pretensions of modern philosophy. The idea that consciousness must undergo great intellectual labors and rise to an act of near-heroism to transcend itself and become one with its object—slaying subjectivity in the process—is a modern conceit. If we want to understand what suddenly makes consciousness a universal experience and a focal thematic in the modern world, then we should try to understand the reasons for its epic role in modern philosophy. To do this we must examine the sort of threat that was thought to be posed to the subject by its subjectivity. We will argue that consciousness is an extreme form of subjectivity generated in part by an unprecedented threat to the security of the individual and in part by an extreme response to that threat.

The subjectivity in need of remedy is variously circumscribed by Renaissance and early modern thinkers. We see it from two perspectives—from the outside looking in and from the inside looking out. It is circumscribed from the outside in the often cynical observations on human psychology in Machiavelli, Shakespeare, or La Rochefoucauld. Reflection on the "true" motives of the social animal's behavior in society discovers duplicity as its innermost possibility. The true being of the human being is therefore something that lurks behind the public appearances, which can just as easily conceal as reveal it. But being publicly hidden is what it means for something to be private. In the eighteenth century Rousseau will give the consummate expression to this new sense of human subjectivity when he suggests that being in society is precisely what turns the being of the individual into something private. The assumption is that appearances are opaque so that being for another (i.e., appearing) already implies a furtive being that is in truth only for itself (being, but not appearing).[40]

But the opacity of appearances also circumscribes subjectivity from the inside. Instead of being the true self that others cannot reach, it is the uncertainty that the individual cannot get beyond. What the individual has in truth is only itself and its own uncertainty about everything else. Subjectivity is the being to which the individual is consigned if the truth of every appearance (and hence the cognitive possession of anything not self) is doubtful. This sense of subjectivity is implicit in most of the major figures of the early modern era—wherever the appearing of the world to the individual is suspected of concealing rather than revealing the world as it is "in itself." This suspicion figures prominently in the thought of Montaigne, Bacon, Galileo, Descartes, and Locke, even if the language of subjectivity does not. We will look more closely at these figures, beginning, however, not with the earliest figure, but with the one whose historical situation is most familiar and captures the problem of subjectivity in a way that is obvious and compelling: Galileo (1564–1642), for whom subjectivity is concentrated in perception.

In Galileo's case the problem of subjectivity had unhappy consequences that are well known. Nowhere is the nondiaphanous character of appearance more evidently problematic than in Galileo's repeated failures to persuade the learned world of his discoveries and the resulting vacillations in his appraisal of experience as a source of knowledge (Blumenberg 1965 and 1981, 452–502). In his epistemology, Galileo draws on and develops some of the same ideas of pre-Socratic philosophy (in this case, ideas of Democritus and Zeno of Elea) that made Plato and Aristotle go on the offensive to save the objectivity of experience. For Galileo, subjectivity consists in perceptual relativity—the relativity of perceived motion to a reference frame, which was noted by Zeno, and the relativity of secondary qualities to the percipient organism, noted by Democritus.[41] What this means for the mature Galileo is that the truth about things is not something that can be perceived by the senses (Tamny 1980). Renaissance Aristotelians had rebuffed the Copernican hypothesis on the grounds that it contradicted "manifest experience." Thus, in Galileo's *Dialogues Concerning the Two Chief World Systems* (1632), the Peripatetic Simplicio is represented as stubbornly resting his case on appeals to the supposedly unambiguous deliverances of perception: "sensible experience," "manifest experience," "experience," and "manifest sense."[42] But far from repudiating this doctrine of *esperienze manifeste*, Galileo originally endorsed it![43] We know from his correspondence with Kepler that Galileo had been convinced of the Copernican hypothesis long before he broke his silence on matters of astronomy. He had even written out his arguments, but refused—despite Kepler's insistence—to publish or even discuss them publicly (Blumenberg 1965). Not until 1610, when Galileo was 46 years old, did he publish his first book on astronomy, *Siderius Nuncius, The Starry Messenger*. Why had Galileo—so skittish about defending Copernicus—broken his silence? Because the Starry Messenger had brought the truth to light, made it "manifest to the very senses," "revealed it to our senses," "plainly to the eye" (Galilei 1957, 27–28). The Starry Messenger was the telescope, and the message it brought was that Aristotelian cosmology was wrong. Only the deliverances of the telescope emboldened the timorous Galileo to make a public move against the Peripatetics because he was suddenly able to take his stand on their own ground. In 1610 Galileo apparently believed without reservation that the telescope threw the whole weight of manifest experience on his side. He had no doubt that those who placed their trust in manifest experience would draw the appropriate conclusions. In this optimism he proved to be sorely mistaken. The bitter lesson from this failure of truth to be visible and compelling is reflected in the *Dialogues* of 1632, where the idea of manifest experience is repudiated altogether. Salviati shows that experience does not manifestly support Aristotle any more than it manifestly controverts Aristotle (Tamny 1980). Truth is simply not manifest to the senses (even when technologically improved).[44]

In place of manifest experience, we have the subjectivity of secondary qualities and the relativity of primary ones. This means that the world as we are directly conscious of it is entirely suspect, an appearance in the pejorative sense: a show whose ambiguity conceals, rather than reveals what it is the appearance of. Ordinary consciousness is no better off than old Don Quixote, unable to discern illusion from reality, inhabiting a world of his own imagining. This is, moreover, the lesson Husserl presses us to learn from Galileo's innovations in the *Krisis*: his postulate that qualities are "really" quantitative relations in disguise—what Husserl calls the "mathematization of the plena"—estranges appearance from reality, making the life-world something counterfeit and immediate consciousness an obstacle rather than a means to cognition (Husserl 1969, Part Two [18–104]). If this analysis is correct, we can say that consciousness comes to the fore in the history of philosophy precisely when it comes between us and the real world as something opaque and subjective, something not justified by its immediate object and possibly feigning it.

Turning to Montaigne (1533–1592), we cannot miss the new topic of self. Montaigne's "essays of himself" are significant for their questioning turned inward, their need to find truth through critical self-assessment. Teachings consecrated by institutional authority fail to quell private doubts, isolating Montaigne as a being "subject" to uncertainty vis-à-vis all that was traditionally known. Montaigne's subjectivity thus appears as a failure not just of perception, but also of learning and tradition. Instead of institutional authority, integral tradition, and public disputation—things that characterized the Medieval university—science is a private trial motivated by personal crisis.

With Francis Bacon (1561–1626), the second man in history to write "essays," science-as-trial is developed into a putatively rigorous methodology intended to overcome the obstacles to knowledge posed by ordinary consciousness, which Bacon generously catalogs as so many idols, modalities of appearance that conceal, rather than reveal the real. What these appearances conceal according to Bacon are the "true divisions of nature" (Bacon 1960, 56), which only the experimental method is able to reveal because it forces separation upon items that, despite being distinct, seemed otherwise inseparable. Bacon thus demonstrates his familiarity with the Scholastic doctrine of the *distinctio realis*, and makes clear in several passages that his method is intended to ferret out the latent "real distinctions" in things (Bacon 1960, 20, 128–129, 151–152, 185).

Bacon disavows total skepticism, especially in regard to the senses, which, despite their defects, he regards as our only source of knowledge (Bacon 1973, 126–127). He also disavows the lonely path that Descartes will share with his earlier compatriot, Montaigne (Bacon 1960, 23–24). Instead, the advancement of science is to be a widely concerted public work, devoted entirely to the slow accumulation of data from experimentally controlled induction. But like Montaigne, Bacon recognizes the severe limitations of the human being's ability to know. There are the spontaneous distortions due to the inherent nature of sense and intellect, as well as the arbitrary distortions due to the vagaries of the individual and the authority of a corrupt tradition. Nevertheless, all this for Bacon simply exacerbates the underlying problem: only by subjecting nature to what Aristotle would have called violence (and what Bacon himself often describes in terms suggesting torture) can we discover the true divisions of nature and, by the same token, the *truly* unbreakable connections between distinguishable things.[45] Subjectivity for Bacon thus appears particularly as a failure of naive phenomenology—the kind upon which Aristotle based all physical and biological science—to yield knowledge, resulting in the need for a strenuous artificial method.

Like Bacon, Descartes (1596–1650) also proposes an artificial method to remedy the problem of subjectivity. He shares with Bacon and with Montaigne the subjectivity precipitated by the failure of learning and tradition. Hence, suspending of the validity of the teachings of tradition constitutes the precondition of his Method.[46] He shares with Galileo as well as with Bacon and Montaigne the subjectivity precipitated by the failure of perception.

Hence, the first step of the Method, which Descartes depicts autobiographi-
cally as a long-sought and momentous breakthrough, involves suspending the
validity of the teachings of nature (sense perception and anything dependent
on it).[47] But Descartes' subjectivity is also manifest in the alienated residue
of these suspensions, in the fact that finding truth means first losing the
whole world.

Last in our list is Locke (1632–1704), for whom subjectivity manifests
itself in the habitual abuse of words arising from their *natural* imperfections—the referential slippage (and ultimately the referential confabulation)
that occurs because words name ideas that are not all equally clear, distinct,
real, adequate, and true.[48] Within the leeway for abuse created by the various natural shortcomings of ideas arises a manifestation of subjectivity so
pernicious that Locke deems it a form of "madness" that affects *all* men—the
association of ideas by custom or chance rather than by natural affinity
(Locke 1959, 1:528–529).

Consciousness and the Problem of Justification

As the examples in the previous section illustrate, modern philosophy is
distinguished by the extreme predicament it seeks to address, which we
could call the radical subjectification of human existence in consciousness.
Subjectivity is what results from the failure of perception, tradition, intellect,
phenomenology, and language—a condition so severe and yet so unavoidable that it constitutes a kind of universal madness. If subjectivity *is* failed
cognition, consciousness is also awareness of this failure. Consciousness seems
to be the name for an experience of self and world defined by these many
failures of immediacy and the urgent need to overcome them.

Whitehead reveals shrewd insight when he points out that the all-
embracing problem of modernity is justification and that justification becomes
a problem precisely when the individual is forced to fend for itself—socially,
cognitively, spiritually:

> Modern philosophy is tinged with subjectivism, as against the
> objective attitude of the ancients. The same change is to be seen
> in religion. [. . .] At the Reformation, the Church was torn asun-
> der by dissension as to the individual experiences of believers in
> respect to justification. The individual subject of experience had
> been substituted for the total drama of all reality. Luther asked,
> "How am I justified?"; modern philosophers have asked, "How
> do I have knowledge?" The emphasis lies upon the subject of
> experience. (SMW 140)[49]

From the Reformation (1517) to the French Revolution (1784), it was a crisis of justification and the individual's anxiety in the face of this crisis that fomented historic changes: the manner of man's justification before God, the possibility of justifying God's ways to man, the possibility of science (that is, of justifying our claims to knowledge), the justification of faith (which the justification of knowledge seemed to threaten), the justification of our particular faith (jeopardized by the multiplicity of faiths), the justification of property, slavery, monarchy, the social contract, the Church, the State. Many of the reasons for the modern crisis of justification are not hard to find. The breakdown of the structured medieval society and the loss of the security offered by feudalism, along with the emergence of large, socially unstructured urban centers with a mercantile bourgeoisie, engendered the first modern individuals:

> The collapse of the Middle Ages was [. . .] a revolt against coordination. The new keynote is expressed in the word "competition" [. . .]. Private life now dominated the social life of Europe in all its special forms—The Right of Private Judgment, Private Property, The Competition of Private Traders, Private Amusement. (AI 31)

Whether the Reformation and the political chaos of the catastrophic religious wars in France, Germany, and England are to be seen as collateral causes in the emergence of the individual, or as proximate effects of this emergence suddenly catalyzing the whole process, it is clear that the authority of Church and State was no longer beyond doubt. From now on the propriety of such authority had to be established, not taken for granted. This is the arena in which consciousness emerges as a thematic phenomenon in western thought. Consciousness is that which needs, but finds itself naturally lacking, justification.

What this development meant for philosophy in particular is well known: *knowledge* becomes the only certain authority, while lack of authoritative knowledge appears to be the default condition of human existence. Thus, despite its many important and often underestimated continuities with medieval thought, modern philosophy is distinguished by a sudden overriding concern with epistemology. How knowledge is to be justified—and not least the knowledge *about knowledge* in which philosophy itself consists—assumes an urgent priority, so that epistemology displaces metaphysics as "first philosophy." The question *How is it possible to know?* replaces *What is it "to be"?*

Let us now return to the question that led us to this digression about the modern experience of subjectivity: What makes it modern? As we noted above, even if we restrict what we mean by subjectivity to cognitive uncertainty due to the constitution of that *to* which things appear rather than to the constitution of the things that do the appearing, subjectivity was not a new discovery. The language of subjectivity wasn't available, but the dative of manifestation was named in one way or another, and its shabbiness was a theme developed already by the Hellenistic philosophers. The contrast of two concepts is relevant here: *doxa* and *phantasia*. When, in the Classical period of Greek philosophy (by which we mean philosophical activity from Parmenides to Aristotle), the object was faulted for our cognitive uncertainty, that uncertainty was called *doxa*. But when the Hellenistic and early Roman philosophers faulted that *to* which things appear, they called it *phantasia*, which they understood so broadly that it is tantamount to our concept of representation (Weekes 2007, 57–64). The urgency with which the Hellenistic philosophers sought the criterion of truth reflected their understanding of *phantasia* as something subjective and the acquisition of truth as something inherently artificial—not a question of accommodating the right kind of objects, but of applying the right method and criterion to the intrinsically dubious material of *phantasia*. So if the shabbiness of the subject was already a thematic problem in Hellenistic thought, what makes the shabbiness of the modern subject so unique? Alternatively, why was consciousness and its justification not an embracing and overriding concern already in Hellenistic antiquity? Why was this potentiation, so evident in the modern figures we have just discussed, reserved for the modern era?

We can take our cue from Kant on this question. Emblematic of the modern concern with justification is the transcendental motto of the *Critique of Pure Reason*: "the conditions of possibility . . ." Kant's transcendental deductions appear to be modeled on early modern jurisprudence in that they seek to establish a subject's right to something (Henrich 1989). Just as a jurist would argue from the relevant *quid juris* and *quid facti* to the deductive conclusion that a person before the court has the right to possess, say, a certain estate as his legal property, so Kant argues for the subject's right to possess (lay claim to) certain kinds of experience as its validated objective knowledge. But in this respect, Kant's critical philosophy is remarkably similar to the declared intentions of Hume's "science of man," Locke's "survey of the understanding," Descartes' "rules for the direction of the mind," and his later "method for rightly conducting reason and seeking truth in the sciences." They all seek a way to adjudicate conflicting truth-claims.[50] They all seek within the private experience of the individual mind a self-legitimating authority able settle disputes about "the truth" in the same way a natural-law jurist would settle a contest of right. Natural light replaces natural law, and the demonstration of being right replaces the demonstration of having a right.

Since finding itself on trial in this extreme way is what seems to define the subject as modern, another way of posing our present question is to ask what this tribunal is before which the subject now finds itself. We suggest that it is an all-consuming and socially stranded form of *conscience*.[51] If this is correct, then consciousness arises not so much by differentiating itself from its close cognate, conscience, as, first, by expanding the purview of conscience so as to embrace things hitherto considered "purely theoretical" (hence "all-consuming"), and, then, by reducing everything practical to a theoretical problem (hence "socially-stranded").

Let us remember that Aristotle had distinguished the theoretical, in contrast to the practical, as that about which one could not "deliberate." The theoretical is, at least for Aristotle, existentially neutral and can incite neither apprehension nor remorse. If we recall that the primary example of theoretical knowledge for Aristotle was the existence and nature of God, we can appreciate how different our experience of "human nature" is from Aristotle's. Unaware of the possibility of extreme and dramatic divergences between intelligent views about "how things really are" (the subject-matter of theoretical knowledge), Aristotle was particularly insensitive to the way theoretical commitments have practical relevance. For the same reason, "subjectivity" for Aristotle is entirely a practical matter. The "I" in "I know the Pythagorean theorem" is something impersonal, indifferent, and irrelevant to praxis. Unlike the "I" of "I want . . ." or "I do . . ." or "I make . . ." the "I" of "I know . . ." denotes nothing in or particular to the individual. If by consciousness we mean, among other things, the "subjective locus" of knowing, we see why there is no such thing as consciousness in Aristotle: there is no subjective locus of knowing. The theoretically knowing soul is simply not located "in itself"—it is actually *in the world* because it "*is* its objects [. . . and] in a way all existing things" (*De Anima* 431b17, 431b21).

We conclude that there was no such thing as "theoretical subjectivity" for Aristotle. What we mean nowadays by "subjectivity" is precisely the destruction of the impassive and impersonal knower envisioned by Aristotle and the essential dependence of all cognition on the personal, contingent, individual "I" of praxis.

Bringing theoretical knowledge claims irretrievably within the purview of conscience (or what Aristotle called deliberation) was an accomplishment of Hellenistic philosophy that the moderns felt compelled to rehabilitate. Perhaps the most striking example of this Hellenistic influence on the formation of modern sensibility is Descartes' unreconstructed appropriation of important elements of Stoic psychology. According to the Stoics the will must intervene for cognition to take place. Cognition (*katalēpsis*) is the affirmation (*synkatathesis*) of a uniquely clear and distinct (*tranē* and *ektypon*) impression (*phantasia*), which they called a cognitive (*katalēptic*) impression.[52] The crucial moment here is that affirmation is construed as an act of volition, not of knowledge.[53] The benefit of this, for the Stoics as well as for Descartes, is straightforward: it explains how error is possible *without incriminating the faculty of understanding itself.* This, of course, is the goal. If, as the Skeptics claim, we make mistakes because the understanding is incorrigibly defective, then knowledge is a lost cause. The only path to salvation then lies in willing to renounce knowing altogether. But if we make mistakes only because the will disregards the (limits of the) evidence provided by the understanding, then knowledge remains possible. In this case it is necessary only to discipline the will so as to conform our *"synkatatheseis"* to *"kataleptic"* impressions—or, in Descartes' language, to conform our judgments to ideas that are materially true. The possibility of knowledge is thus preserved, but only by subordinating understanding to the will, which means subordinating everything theoretical to practical subjectivity.[54] *If affirmation is an act of volition, then knowledge is something ethical.* This subordination of *theoria* to *praxis* was not unique to Stoicism. It was a point of agreement among all the schools of Hellenistic philosophy that error resides chiefly in the will, namely, the will to know (and act as if known) things that cannot be known—which may or may not be everything.

This insinuation of the ethical into speculative cognition gives rise to theoretical subjectivity: a domain in which every judgment is an action initiated by an act of will, and the truth is a personal issue—a question, in fact, of justification. Wherever justification is lacking, it has to be achieved by a deliberate and hence quasi-practical effort, which therefore requires the practical guidance of a "criterion" (Hellenistic) or a "method" (modern). The modern potentiation of theoretical subjectivity into consciousness seems to involve a process complementary to the first that ends up by leaving nothing beyond the need for such justification. Hellenistic philosophers experienced their theoretical commitments as practically relevant and subject to the deliberations of conscience. In this way we can speak of a subjection of theory to practice, subsequent to which it becomes possible to "deliberate" about such things as whether to believe in God or the afterlife (a possibility to which Epicurus appears to have been the first to bear especially poignant testimony). But even if every judgment was now a kind of covert action, not every action was necessarily a disguised theoretical judgment. By the same token, the subject was not necessarily alienated from the norms and performative presuppositions of the wider community to which it belonged. This is evident in the Stoic doctrine of *synētheia*, which can be rendered as "shared ethos" or "customary experience" or "the common sense of the community."[55] The fact that (at least some of) the Stoics postulated *synētheia* as one of their valid criteria of truth means that the individual was not completely isolated by needed and wanting justification—there were important things it did not have to justify through its private intellectual resources, things whose cogency could be accepted at face value without a crisis of conscience.

If our hypothesis is correct, and consciousness is the complete inter-penetration of the two realms (theory and practice), then, in addition to the subordination of theory to practice, consciousness presupposes the destruction of *synētheia* through a complementary subjection of practice to theory. And, to be sure, modern philosophers experienced their practical commitments as essentially theoretical propositions lacking intrinsic validation and requiring "demonstration" or "deduction." Herbert of Cherbury's *De Veritate* (1624) offers an arresting example of this: he seeks to justify ethical and religious beliefs by deducing them from universal first principles inherent in reason and thus available to the private reflection of the individual. Cherbury's demonstration of a natural religion and a natural-law type ethics serves to justify individual conscience in a world of wildly divergent claims of con-science. Cherbury's theoretical justification of *practical* knowledge was soon followed by Descartes' similarly conceived theoretical justification of *theoretical* knowledge—a similarity noted already by Cassirer (Cassirer 1969, 62–63). In both cases we have the characteristically modern project of *theoretical justification*: because, on the one hand, all judgment is conceived as a kind of latent action with ethical consequences for the individual, justification is necessary; because, on the other hand, all action is conceived as a kind of disguised proposition about what is right or good, its justification needs to be theoretical, that is, a discursive exercise in pure reason.[56]

What seems to make all the difference between modern and Hellenistic outlooks is, therefore, a very different distribution of theory and practice. Indeed, to judge from the extant literature, the epistemological crisis at the focus of Hellenistic philosophy was almost entirely theoretical, while the remedy sought was essentially practical—cultivating equanimity and peace of mind in the face of unanswered questions. The modern crisis, however, was overwhelmingly practical and the remedy theoretical. The individual found itself buffeted by a world in which the Skeptic precept *One side is not more right than another* was acted out in violence on a scale so massive that no tradition, no authority, no social institution remained unscathed. If the modern predicament was unique, so was the response. Modern philoso-phy sought a remedy to practical problems that was derived entirely from theoretical reflection.

We are postulating a connection between the all-inclusiveness of the practical need and the theoretical purity of the response. Because the unsatisfied practical need for justification was impossibly urgent and all encompassing, the alienation of the individual from its world was also complete. If subjectivity got its foothold on cognition because the Hellenistic philosophers, over the protest of Aristotle, followed certain pre-Socratics in construing the mind as something corporeal (see below), this Hellenistic subjectivity, which consisted in the corporeality of the mind (however fleet or subtle a body it may be), preserved a certain continuity of the mind with the world. What we have tried to highlight in our review of the seventeenth century is how the last vestiges of this continuity disappear, and subjectivity becomes weirdly transformed at the start of the modern era. It vanishes from among the contents of the physical universe and becomes something categorically incapable of outward (i.e., worldly) manifestation. With the possibility of justified thought, action, and faith suspended and the very being of the apparent world held in a kind of metaphysical abeyance, what was left was something estranged and displaced from the world. The great crises of modernity accomplished something Hellenistic philosophy had not: the precipitation of consciousness as a new kind of extramundane being. What makes the modern manifestation of the problem of subjectivity specifically modern is the way subjectivity becomes identified with consciousness as a unique sort of entity, one that is by nature dispossessed of the world. The epic of modern philosophy is the quest, at once both practical and theoretical, to recover the world.

The hypothesis proposed here is bold. In the following section we first document the reification of the subject in early modern philosophy and then suggest a rationale to explain why an exaggerated need for justification should result in that reification and then in an equally exaggerated effort to provide justification by purely theoretical means.

Consciousness: An Agent of Cognition Renouncing its Agency

We argued above that the first philosopher to use the word *consciousness* as an obvious count noun was John Locke in his *Essay Concerning Human Understanding* (1690).[57] As a mass noun, *consciousness* names the state (quality, condition, attribute) of *being conscious*. It can designate the state of being conscious absolutely, as in modern English when we speak of consciousness as something one can lose or regain ("he only partially regained consciousness"),[58] or it can designate it under the limitation of an objective genitive, as when we speak of consciousness as a state of specific cognizance that we may lack ("consciousness of wrongdoing"). In the latter example, consciousness is no more countable than its possible contraries: ignorance or innocence. In the former example we recognize one of the hallmarks of the mass noun: continuous rather than discrete quantification (i.e., more *vs.* less rather than many *vs.* few). While the nominalization of conscious into conscious*ness* is attested before Locke (in Massinger and Cudworth), it is clear that in these earlier uses consciousness normally functions as some kind of mass noun. To take the earliest attested use of consciousness in English as an example, Massinger writes in 1632 "the consciousness of mine own wants."[59] While this seventeenth century naming of consciousness is peculiar insofar as it is historically unprecedented, it is a grammatical possibility whose realization, while consistent with and even suggestive of a metaphysical innovation, does not directly imply one. But Locke's use of consciousness as a *count noun* is different. It makes the nominalization of *conscious* into consciousness extremely odd, for now it no longer names a quality, but rather something so qualified. This could be a thing or an event. The usage would still not be so odd if what it designated was an event (a cognitive episode) qualified by consciousness, as in, for example, "he came to *a* consciousness of his sin" or "He never again came to *a* consciousness of his identity." Conceivably, this could have been what Massinger had in mind in "Maid of Honour:" *an* event (or *a* moment) in which "the consciousness of mine own wants" is realized. But Locke evidently does not use consciousness in this way either. Rather, in Locke's usage, consciousness clearly designates a thing that finds itself in the state of being conscious. Many things could be said to be in such a state without arousing controversy—a human being, a divine being, a living being, a person, the person's soul, and so on. Such attributions are extremely frequent in Cudworth's *True Intellectual System*. But if consciousness itself names a thing, not just a thing's attribute, then it is a unique sort of thing, quite unlike all the others that one could possibly talk about. This is not too hard to demonstrate. Consciousness would have to name the very thing that is *by definition* conscious. But then consciousness would seem to be the only thing that is strictly and properly speaking conscious, and the relationship between consciousness and all the things one was accustomed to calling conscious—persons, souls, human beings—becomes an unprecedented problem. Naming consciousness as a thing destines these other things to take their place sooner or later as objects of consciousness, as consciousness itself looms up as the only proper subject of consciousness, and the problem of idealism is born. But if consciousness (the thing) is the only true subject of consciousness (the state), then it is a truly singular phenomenon: the only thing that is, in effect, subject to itself. This would appear to be the conceptual genesis of the modern idea of "self."[60]

That such a strange thing had never been named or even noticed before in the history of Western thought was alleged by the anonymous author of the 1735 treatise, *An Essay on Consciousness*: "*Consciousness* denominates *Self* [...] concerning *Self* [...] there is something extraordinary in the Notion of it, as not being reducible to any kind of Being or Existence yet taken Notice of" (Psuedo-Mayne 1983, 12 and 20). Actually, we must allow that Descartes, without calling it consciousness or self, had taken notice of it. His *res cogitans* is *by definition* conscious, and it is emphatically a *thing* (*res*), subject to its own consciousness (and nothing else). Descartes also recognized the singularity of such a thing. Noticing that it had gone unnoticed, he created a new ontological niche for it: a thing the thinghood of which is essentially and exclusively thinking. A precedent for the idea of a *"thing* that thinks" can be found in materialist theories of the mind such as the Stoics and Epicureans proposed, but in their case the thing that was supposed to think and in which thought or consciousness inheres was the *body*. Bodies were the only *things* in their ontology. The idea that thinking should be its own subject of inherence, in short, that it should be a thing, was truly unprecedented. In fact, Scholastic psychology was founded on a metaphysical principle handed down from Aristotle: that *to which* things appear (the mind) is itself necessarily not a thing (Weekes 2004, 259–262). Aristotle had wanted to correct what he saw as the mistakes of his predecessors that led to the unappealing conclusions that *the mind is nothing more than the organically embodied soul* and hence that *truth is nothing more than whatever appears to sense-perception to be the case.*[61] In order to touch the being of objects, to receive it unadulterated into itself, the mind must become one with them. But the mind, he declared, in order to be capable of becoming one with its object, cannot be anything *in itself* (*De Anima* 429a18). It must be "nothing before it thinks (*all' entelecheiai ouden, prin an noēi*)" (429b30). The mind, in short, is *not a thing* (429a23: "not one of the beings"—*outhen tōn ontōn*). It is hard to believe that Descartes was not deliberately contradicting this principle with his declaration that the mind was a kind of thing (Weekes 2004, 259–262) and that the mind *must* be a kind of thing because "that which thinks is not nothing" (1964–1976, 7:175; 1984, 2:123). Critics of the new way of ideas certainly made this connection right away and responded by reiterating the Scholastic-Aristotelian notion that thought is not really anything "in itself"—certainly not the *mode* of a *special kind of thing* (a thing that thinks).[62] Rather, it is an "extrinsic denomination" of an ordinary worldly thing—its happening to be thought about.[63] "Thought" simply means that *something-or-other is being thought (about)*, and this "being thought" is not a real predicate of the something-or-other or of anything else in the world—certainly not of the mind. For these traditionalists, the dative of manifestation is itself a declension of the thing manifesting itself. It is not a subject of experience, indeed, not a subject at all. It should not surprise us, then, that before Descartes the phenomenon of consciousness was typically not designated by a noun functioning absolutely in the nominative case, but that after Descartes the need for a word that could play this grammatical role was felt acutely. Before consciousness was a thing, it didn't need a proper name.

Whitehead seems to have put his finger on this very issue in *Adventures of Ideas* when he surprisingly exploits the characterization of the Receptacle in Plato's *Timaeus* epistemologically (AI 187–188, see also 134–135). For this, in fact, is just what Aristotle had done! Aristotle's characterization of passive mind (*De Anima* 3.4) is taken almost verbatim from Plato's characterization of the Receptacle (*Timaeus* 48e2–51b6), which cannot, says Plato, have any nature of its own or it would not be fully receptive to the nature it is meant to receive. The rejection of the epistemology modeled on this doctrine is as central to the formation of modern sensibility as its rehabilitation is to Whitehead's breakaway from the modern tradition. Montaigne's *Apology for Raymond Sebond* (1580), for example, is a sustained polemic against the Scholastic-Aristotelian concept of "passive mind,"[64] of which Bacon's catalogue of Idols in his *Novum Organum* (1620) is a judicious compendium (Bacon 1960, 47–66). Bacon attributes the urgent need for a new, *remedial* organon of knowledge to the very fact that the mind is *not* a kind of Platonic Receptacle, but something with a positive nature of its own, always somewhat refractory to whatever it might receive: "And the human understanding is like a false mirror, which, receiving rays irregularly, distorts and discolors the nature of things by mingling its own nature with it."[65]

Whitehead is surely right to describe this fateful innovation of modern philosophy as the transfer of the Aristotelian concept of subject (*hypokeimenon*) to that which experiences, bestowing upon the mind a substantial nature of its own (PR 157–160; also 30, 50, 137–138). This transference appears already underway in Montaigne and Bacon, and it becomes explicit in Hobbes' surprising use of the world "subject" to designate the mind.[66] Just as no one called the mind a "thing" before Descartes, it appears that no one called the experient a "subject" prior to Hobbes. For Hobbes, the experient is quite evidently a quasi-Aristotelian substance, a subject in which experience inheres as an accident. This is, of course, the very analysis that Descartes gives, albeit without ever using the term subject in this novel way.[67] For the early modern philosophers, subjectivity is simply the thinghood of the mind—and the practical-theoretical problem it creates.

Since its unworldly thinghood seals and cements the separation of the mind from the world and alienates the individual from both community and truth, we should not be too surprised to find that the remedy is equally extreme. Bacon's eloquence leads him to describe his method in terms that suggest the administration of violent purgatives,[68] religious purification and spiritual rebirth,[69] and, not least, the heroism of self-sacrifice with intimations of religious ecstasy: his method is the "true and legitimate humiliation of the human spirit" (Bacon 1960, 13). An old doctrine of mystical theology gets an epistemological interpretation: transcendence (*excessus mentis*) is possible only through self-denial. In this case, the transcendent beyond is simply that which is actually true and *a posteriori*. The theme of ascetic self-discipline as the only possible remedy for the otherwise refractory thingliness of the mind reaches an extreme in Descartes. Just like Bacon's experimental method, Descartes' method of radical doubt is also a purgative intended to expel all the impurities from the mind—to annihilate its thinghood, as it were—and reconstitute it as something functionally equivalent to Aristotle's passive mind. Also like Bacon's method, Descartes' achieves its goal by forcibly actualizing the latent real distinctions in things (see below). What distinguishes Descartes' method from Bacon's is its transposed application from the world into the subject: Descartes experiments on the mind, not on nature. If we may borrow Bacon's language, it is *ideas* that are to be "constrained and vexed, forced out of their natural state, squeezed and molded" (Bacon 1960, 25). A crucial element in this process, which the secondary literature tends to ignore despite the enormous stress that Descartes himself lays upon it,[70] is the utter quietism he imposes upon himself. Here Descartes has clearly learned from Montaigne, who saw in radical skepticism and its issue in resigned quietism the only way to "humiliate" the human spirit.[71] But Montaigne's goal is the (suspiciously Protestant-sounding) acquiescence of the individual to the will of God, while Descartes' is the acquisition of truth. Descartes' journey therefore has a different goal, but the means of conveyance is similar. We see this in a remarkably telling aside where we learn what consciousness purified of subjectivity becomes: "I did nothing but roam about in the world, trying to be a spectator rather than an actor in all the comedies that are played out there" (Descartes 1964–1976, 6:28; 1984, 1:125). It seems that the closest a *thing* can get to being *tabula rasa*—an Aristotelian passive mind—is to resign its agency in the world altogether. Aristotle's passive mind becomes the world, and it can become the world because it is not a thing (and so *a fortiori* not an agent); Descartes' consciousness, being a thing, cannot become the world, but it can become passive by renouncing its agency. It thus becomes a pure spectator whose relation to the world is something theoretical.

Whitehead does not entirely disagree with the modern position. He accepts with enthusiasm what he calls the "subjectivist bias" of modern philosophy, according to which the point of departure for philosophy can never be—as it was for Classical Greek[72] and Scholastic philosophy alike—impersonal facts about the world or nature or the individual beings they disclose (PR 166–167). That is to say, philosophy cannot justify itself if it begins with facts having the form *S is P*. Like the early modern philosophers, Whitehead accepts experiential subjectivity as a phenomenological fact and an epistemological problem. Philosophy must therefore begin with facts of the form *my experience of S being P* (PR 157–159). Whitehead calls this the Subjectivist Principle,[73] the discovery of which by Descartes he considers the most important advance in philosophy since the time of Plato and Aristotle.[74] But Whitehead thinks the discovery was no sooner made than obscured by a perverse interpretation: "like Columbus, who never visited America, Descartes missed the full sweep of his own discovery, and he and his successors, Locke and Hume, continued to construe the functionings of the subjective enjoyment of experience according to the substance-quality categories" (PR 159).[75] In a sequence of subtle and acute critical analyses, Whitehead shows how the distinctive character of modern philosophy results, like a system of repercussions from as single blow, from the misguided attempt to construe *my experience of S being P* as a fact having the form *S is P* (PR 157–160). This leads to the idea that the mind is a substance, and experience an accident qualifying that substance (PR 48–50 and 137–139).

This is the point at which Whitehead objects to the modern interpretation of experience as subjectivity. He objects to the explicit or implicit use of the Aristotelian concept of subject (*hypokeimenon*) to define this subjectivity. Inevitably, the Aristotelian concept of subject implies the substantiality, independence, and self-sufficiency of the subject of experience and hence a monadic construal of experience based on the logic of quality inherence rather than a polyadic construal based on the logic of relations (both internal and external). Whitehead's attitude toward modern philosophy is therefore ambivalent. We could say, in short, that Whitehead accepts subjectivity but squarely rejects its thinghood.[76]

Aristotle himself had insisted that in perception the perceiving mind and the thing perceived share a common actuality.[77] But this community of the mind with the world presupposes his doctrine of passive (purely potential) mind. Such community vanishes as soon as the Aristotelian concept of subject is applied where Aristotle himself insisted it should not be applied: to the mind. The rupture of this community is formalized in early modern philosophy with its unique employment of the Scholastic *distinctio realis*. An invigorated real distinction is used to cut the world up in phenomenologically untenable ways. Descartes argues that the mind depends on neither the body nor the world in which it finds itself nor even its own past history and that through a process of methodical doubt he can prove the "reality" of these distinctions. He thus finds that he is metaphysically separate from and independent of everything from which he can distinguish himself. Remarkably, Hobbes, the avowed materialist, proceeds in a very similar way. He begins his *Human Nature* of 1640 with an equivalent separation of the objects of experience from the subject experiencing them: the subjective representation of the world (which he refers to as "imagination," obviously rendering the Stoic *phantasia*), would remain *unchanged in content* even if the world itself were suddenly annihilated.[78] Neither making nor being able to make a distinction in kind between sense and imagination, Hobbes' annihilation of the world—a likely inspiration for Husserl's use of the same language to explain his phenomenological reduction almost three centuries later—isolates the subject of experience in very much the same way Descartes does in his *Meditations* published a year later.[79] This isolated subject of experience, which is an entirely unworldly thing, is what modern philosophy knows as consciousness.

The reification of consciousness as a being characterized by the loss of something it never had (certainty) has a flip side. Because subjectivity now takes all the blame for error and uncertainty, the object emerges as faultless and perfectly knowable. The ancient idea that some things are intrinsically less knowable than others—things that change, for example, or otherwise inhabit time—began its erosion with the Hellenization of Judeo-Christian theology by Philo and Augustine.[80] God knows the whole world, and God's knowledge is perfect, so everything must be perfectly knowable. The idea that no knowledge—including human knowledge when it is attainable—is qualitatively different from this sort of divine knowledge is fundamental to the modern outlook (Weekes 2007, 64–80). It was expressly argued by Galileo in his Dialogues and played a decisive role in his condemnation.[81]

There is an interesting biographical parallel between Galileo and Descartes that comes to light here. We know that Descartes had completed his book on cosmology, *The World*, by 1633, but hearing of the condemnation of Galileo, refused to let it be published. In this book Descartes was careful to hedge his new physics as being the physics not of our world, but of an entirely imaginary one he was making up as he went along. His strongest claims on behalf of this mechanistic universe were that it could be clearly imagined by anyone, that it was possible for God to create such a world because He can create anything we can clearly imagine, and that it would in no way differ in appearance from the world we know. In other words, it fully satisfied the requirement of saving the appearances without recourse to "occult" qualities. Despite having qualified his cosmology as a sort of fantasy with interesting modal and phenomenological properties, Descartes was nonetheless wary of publication and not until 1637, at the age of 41, did he finally publish his first book, the *Discourse* and *Essays*. What had changed in the intervening four years?

Like Galileo, Descartes was unwilling to take his stand until he could do it on the very ground of his adversaries. He waited till, like Galileo, he was sure he had an unanswerable argument. Galileo's views were condemned on the august theological grounds that his claims to scientific certainty implied that God was not omnipotent, that, given the appearances and the dictates of human reason, He could have created the world *only* in the way Galileo claims to have explained it (Cassirer 1969, 119–120). Descartes' ingenuity consists in having found an argument that makes the cognitive certainty of the new science of the seventeenth century a consequence rather than an implied limitation of the omnipotence of God. For if God is not a deceiver (because that would imply some degree of impotence), then clarity and distinctness become hallmarks of knowledge and knowability the hallmark of everything God has created. This was the triumph of a new ontology in which there were no intrinsically shabby objects. There was only one shabby thing, and that was the subject trying to know. Shabbiness was a symptom of deficient knowing, not of deficient being (Weekes 2007, 64–80).

The careful reader may have noticed that we culled from our reading of Whitehead not one, but two explanations for the appearance of consciousness as a focal thematic in the seventeenth century, one having to do with the individual's newly acquired need for justification and the other with a continued preoccupation with predicative logic and acceptance of the substance-quality metaphysics it implies. Whitehead himself does not elaborate on the relation between the two etiologies of modern thinking that he advances. We have tried to tie them together. We now summarize our results.

What was true and right in the Middle Ages possessed a public reality that—at least when compared with the turmoil of early modern Europe— seems monolithic in solidity, stature, and coherence. The lack of emphasis on the individual in the Middle Ages is closely related to this phenomenon. The individual was able to absorb in good conscience the publicly available standards of conduct and belief, effacing to some extent its individuality and individual responsibility. We could say, in effect, that the human being of the Middle Ages enjoyed the possession of something like Aristotelian passive mind, with its capacity for unresisting assimilation to external standards.

The social, religious, and political upheavals of the sixteenth and seventeenth century both expressed and exacerbated a crisis of justification, denying individuals the luxury of reliance on external authority in a situation where all rights were contested and even theoretical commitments had practical consequences (as the case of Giordano Bruno shows paradigmatically). The impossibility of distinguishing commitment from risk created an acute and almost total need for justification. This historical disruption of passive mind created a hospitable environment for the appropriation and development of the Hellenistic psychology recovered in the sixteenth century, which recognized the insinuation of practical agency into speculative cognition. In one sense this development was not unwelcome. It takes the burden and blame for falsehood and uncertainty off of the world as an object of potential knowledge and puts it entirely on the subject seeking knowledge. This is a recognizably Augustinian theme, and we see here part of the reason for the kinship felt by many Reformers with Augustine. But if this development solves some problems, it creates others. It solves an obvious theological problem (imperfection exists only as a consequence of human will), and also an epistemological one (it guarantees, the skeptics notwithstanding, that knowledge is not, as they claimed, impossible on purely theoretical grounds). But if it guarantees that everything is in principle fully knowable, it does so by creating a theoretical subjectivity in which it has both concentrated and amplified the problem of justification. Whatever it is that executes judgment and decides action and belief is now isolated as a cognitive agent *with no worldly collateral*. We noted in our discussion of the origin of conscience as an individual faculty how agency (or the implicit agency of complicity) turns ethical consciousness into a countable entity that assumes (or becomes subject to) the qualities that previously characterized its object (consciousness of guilt or innocence becomes a guilty/innocent conscience). Similarly, we now suggest that agency in the theoretical domain turns speculative consciousness into an entity that takes on (becomes subject to) the essential qualities characterizing its object, which are certainty and uncertainty (primarily the latter, of course). Being without worldly collateral means that this agent must execute its judgments unsecured by any external guarantees and that it is, moreover, a thing defined by this predicament.

While this development reflects a recurrence of Hellenistic attitudes, the extreme to which it tended reflects the severity of the crises defining the sixteenth and seventeenth centuries. But it is especially in the remedy sought that we see the critical differences between the Hellenistic and modern sensibility. Having conceded that dire practical risks attach to theoretical commitment, they both stress the bright side—that the insinuation of the will into cognition empowers the subject (at least in principle) to avoid defective cognition. But from here out the Hellenistic and early modern philosophers take very different paths. This becomes clear if we compare the skepticism of the ancients with the skepticism of Montaigne, which seems at first indistinguishable from the former, borrowed as it is almost entirely from the ancient sources. But in Montaigne's rehabilitation of skepticism there is a strange new twist. For Montaigne the fatal problem with knowledge is not so much that it cannot be *theoretically* justified as that it cannot be *practically* justified. Here is where Montaigne's modernity appears, and it appears as an unacknowledged debt to modernity's first great firebrand, Martin Luther. Luther claimed that man is justified only by faith, not by works. Montaigne's (supposedly counter-reformatory) insight is that the attempt to know, indeed, any judgment at all, is really just a *covert work*. Just like action, theoretical judgment is an effort of the individual towards self-responsible accomplishment. It presumes the possibility of the individual accomplishing something apart from God. For Montaigne, therefore, humanly attained knowledge is just another gesture of individual pride, and for *this* reason unjustifiable. In effect, Montaigne agrees that it is works that cannot be justified. If knowledge that is not a work could be found, it would be justifiable, and this is the very definition of faith: knowledge that is not an achievement of the human subject. Thus, while ancient skepticism is designed to lead to the renunciation of all *knowledge*, leaving a purified agency, Montaigne's skepticism is designed to lead to the renunciation of all *agency*, leaving a purified knowledge, in other words, faith. Descartes' theoretical attitude has in common with Montaigne's faith the desire to neutralize the subject's individuality through the disciplined renunciation of all agency, thus undoing its separation from Truth.

Practical agency, insinuated into the execution of all cognition, has the desirable consequence that it exonerates God and the knowable universe from any imperfection, but by the same token it has the undesirable consequence of alienating consciousness from God or the world it sought to know. In this context it is possible to understand why the systematic *renunciation of agency* and the cultivation of an objectifying neutrality should appear to be a mechanism of reconciliation with a world now assumed to be completely and perfectly knowable—and so, too, why even practical matters should now be approached as abstract theoretical problems. A practical solution to practical problems would require agency to come first, before or without theoretical (i.e., nonagentive) justification. But that would be presumption. Agency unjustified by theory implies subjectivity, fallibility, uncertainty, and error. This would explain why the project of foundationalism emerged in the peculiar form characteristic of modern philosophy. Descartes and his posterity took the *personal fact* of *my experience of S being P*, which the subject can know about only by participating in it, and tried to turn it into an impersonal fact (of the form *S is P*) that can (and, to be justified, *must*) be recovered and objectified by myself as a purely theoretical spectator. By the end of the seventeenth century the proper name of this spectator was *consciousness*.

Consciousness: Beyond the Seventeenth Century?

After its dramatic role in modern philosophy, consciousness fell on hard times in the early to mid-twentieth century, only to enjoy a renaissance as the century came to its close. The reasons for its changing fortunes are telling. Modern philosophy for the most part took it for granted that theories of consciousness could not be experimentally verified, and this was rarely seen as a disadvantage. A more powerful method seemed available, called *reflection* or—if something more empirical sounding was wanted, as happened especially in the nineteenth century—*introspection*. Kant's Transcendental Analysis and Husserl's Phenomenology were sophisticated refinements of this approach, with their roots in the concept of reflection shared by empiricists and rationalists in the seventeenth century. Since consciousness had originally been defined (or at least circumscribed) by the operation of reflection (Cudworth's "duplication," Locke's "self-consciousness," Hartley's "reflex act," etc.), it is not surprising that philosophers assumed that its true nature should be fully available to reflection.

The decline of "consciousness philosophy" had much to do with the ascendancy of a new consensus about the nature of knowledge. It was a consensus of trained experts sharing a common asset, touted as *the* scientific method—the hypothetico-deductive method of verifying theory by controlled and repeatable experimentation. While modern science has its origin in the seventeenth century, the isolation of a heuristic methodology that could be exported from the area of its first success (mechanics) and applied in any domain where knowledge was sought was the pride of the nineteenth century, when the scientist—a term coined by Whewell in 1840—was finally set apart from the philosopher by his adherence to the patently successful "scientific method." What was not clear was if or how the scientific method could be applied to consciousness. The fledgling attempts of nineteenth-century psychology to subject the data of introspection to experimental constraints achieved no wide consensus or lasting recognition.

It cannot be stressed enough that consciousness became scientifically taboo in the early twentieth century not because the concept of consciousness had changed, but because the concept of knowledge had changed. Focus shifted from consciousness to language and behavior because these were accessible to an objective methodology and could be treated in ways that counted as scientific under the new consensus. But a tacit assumption seems to have given this shift in focus a metaphysical twist: that what really exists in the world are the things science studies (or at least *can* study), which exist in just the way that science finds them to exist. Thus, if consciousness is not something science can study, it doesn't exist. This implied that the concept of consciousness, like the concepts of sunrise or sunset, did not really denote anything matching the usual descriptions. This traditional concept of consciousness had to be turned over to folk wisdom—whence it presumably came—as a prescientific notion of everyday life.[82]

The taboo against consciousness lifted in the latter half of the twentieth century. The sterility of Behaviorism became increasingly apparent, while at the same time advances in computer science and computer technology were abundant. Excitement surrounded the development of computers with ever-greater processing power and computer languages with ever-greater suppleness. The apparent success early in the second half of the century at modeling languages computationally (Noam Chomsky's work at MIT)—because it suggested that natural language all along was a computer language—sealed the alliance between mind and computer. The thesis, first proposed by Hilary Putnam (1960), that the mind is the brain's software was called functionalism. It seemed to provide a framework for integrating the results of empirical research on brain function and overt behavior (which includes verbal reports about internal states) and, most important, for extracting from that research information about consciousness. The functionalist hypothesis did for cognitive psychology what Weber's Law did for nineteenth-century psychophysics: it made something not directly accessible to an objective method of investigation seem indirectly accessible. Confidence that computational models would bring consciousness under the control of experimental research made it once again respectable to talk about.

It is very curious, however, that what we find ourselves talking about are the same spectrum of possibilities and problems that defined the philosophical discourse of the seventeenth and eighteenth centuries—reductionism, epiphenomenalism, mental causation, free will, determinism, monism, dualism, parallelism, interactionism, and so on. One likely reason for this is not hard to find. There appears to be a growing consensus that consciousness is precisely what functionalism cannot explain. There is no necessary reason for any computationally executable program of information processing to be conscious. This suggests that the hardware-software metaphor is not suited to the intended purpose. We seek a model that is sensitive to empirical data. Differential results should differently constrain the model. The functionalist paradigm, however, appears to insulate consciousness from empirical research and to take its place among competing but unfalsifiable theories of consciousness.

Another reason for this apparent stagnation is perhaps that our concept of consciousness has not changed significantly since the seventeenth century. Whitehead is among those who find the origin of many contemporary problems in the way questions were posed in the seventeenth century—and the fact that we continue to pose them in the same way. What Whitehead challenges is, first, the idea of the subject as a thing rather than a process, secondly, that it is something "really separate" (i.e., separated by a *distinctio realis*) from the world it experiences and seeks to understand and, thirdly, the idea of a purely objective world beyond appearance that could be described in an entirely extensional language. These three cardinal ideas of modernity are more intimately related than may seem at first glance. If consciousness is a special sort of "subjective" being—that is, a unique kind of "thing"—then it differs from the things it experiences as a thing differs from another thing. This is, of course, the classic definition of a *real distinction* as the difference that separates a thing from another thing. Any relation between them is therefore of necessity external.[83] Rejecting the first idea is therefore what allows Whitehead to reject the second one as well. The role of the third idea deserves special consideration.

Whitehead's recovery of a quasi-Aristotelian concept of passive mind and the possibility of the mind's being internally related to the world it experiences might seem to lead straight to the modern ideal of unadulterated cognitive possession of an absolute objectivity. But notice that appearance in modern thought is blamed (so to speak) on the defect of subjects who cannot incorporate the "real thing." The thinghood of the dative of manifestation and its real distinction from the thing experienced guarantee that things always remain separate and fundamentally aloof from their own appearing to other things. The appearance is therefore a property of the subject experiencing, externally related to the appearing thing. According to Whitehead's relational ontology, however, appearing is what it means to be a real thing.[84] Appearing to others is a fundamental part of what it means to be. Hence, appearance cannot be separated by a real distinction from what it is the appearance of, and it is absurd to think that science can or should factor appearance out of its experience of the world.

Whitehead does justice to the modern meaning of subjectivity and even signs on to the modern philosophical quest when he says, "Philosophy is the self-correction by consciousness of its own initial excess of subjectivity" (PR 15). But for Whitehead this does not mean eliminating appearance or somehow achieving an entirely third-person description of the world. What characterizes the modern project is the idea that metaphysical coherence is to be found by transcending or somehow factoring out appearance and perspective. Consequently, the only path to objective knowledge was the heroic one of self-denial. Consciousness had to transcend its own perspective, overcome itself, destroy its subjectivity, and finally coincide with its other, the object. But Whitehead understands the coherence of the world as the interlocking of perspectives. His model for ontology is not mathematics, but intersubjectivity.[85] One of the fundamental properties of subjectivity for Whitehead is its internal relatedness to a world whose essence involves appearing. Consciousness, as we will learn in the following chapter, is something that distorts and largely conceals this state of affairs. In some ways Whitehead's project is the very opposite of the modern project. He does not want consciousness to transcend its subjectivity: rather than seek a consciousness no longer tainted by subjectivity, he wants to recover (in some fashion *for* consciousness) subjectivity as it was before being tainted by consciousness.

If the key to Whitehead's rejection of modern epistemology is the modified rehabilitation of the Aristotelian passive mind (*nous pathetikos*), then needless to say he has an obligation to give this elusive notion an interpretation that an educated modern need not balk at. The most difficult question for Aristotle's psychology—just as for Plato's cosmology—is how there can be something that is "nothing" in itself—a faculty with no intrinsic being. It is one thing to say the possibility of *x* resides in the actual features of *y* (the actual stone is potentially a sculpture); it is quite another to say that there is (or "must be") such a thing as a transcendental possibility *tout court*, with no intrinsic actual being of its own at all. Its nature is simply to be the possibility of everything actual: in the case of Plato's Receptacle and Aristotle's prime matter, it is the possibility of all physical things coming to be; in the case of Aristotle's passive mind, it is the possibility of all forms becoming actual in separation from matter. In both cases the first principle is something "purely" potential—"pure" here meaning uncompromised by any vestige of actual being. Actually, it *is* only what it becomes. Since its whole being is to be potential, it is "nothing" in itself. (For this reason passive mind is also known as the "potential intellect.")

In a characteristically brilliant conceptual synthesis, Whitehead suggests how to make sense of such a notion in the context of a naturalistic worldview by standing an argument of Lucretius' on its head: "The creativity of the world is the throbbing emotion of the past hurling itself into a new transcendent fact. It is the flying dart, of which Lucretius speaks, hurled beyond the bounds of the world" (AI 177). Whitehead is referring to Luctretius' argument for the infinity of space: "The universe must be infinite [. . .]. [I]f we grant the universe to be finite, what would happen if someone went to the very edge, the outermost limit, and threw from there a flying spear?"[86] Lucretius assumes that every boundary is, at least in principle, transgressible. After all, it would not be a boundary if it did not proscribe access to something. From this he infers that nothing cannot be a boundary. And thus, since there will always be "something" beyond every boundary, the world must be infinite in extent.

Lucretius to the contrary, Whitehead invites us to think that the world *is* finite in a very important sense. In our cosmic epoch, for example, the four-dimensional space-time manifold is limited at least in its forward extension on the axis of time. Beyond this limit there is indeed nothing. Paradoxically, this limit is very real, and yet it doesn't proscribe access to anything. It is a boundary *sui generis*: a boundary between being and nonbeing. For Lucretius, the conceivability of the flying dart transgressing every boundary proves the infinity of the world, for where access to something real is not proscribed, transgression is not possible. Nevertheless, at every moment the universe performs this inconceivable feat, breaching a limit bounded by nothing. This, for Whitehead, is the meaning of time. The modal dynamic of time, in which something possible becomes actual, provides the means to naturalize the Platonic-Aristotelian concept of pure potentiality.

At present, the future is "nothing in itself," and yet in its imminence it is the medium out of which something new becomes present when the boundary of being is breached. To Whitehead's way of thinking, the fact that the immediate future is imminent, that is, the fact that it is always becoming present, means that something is always overtaking it, encroaching on it. Something is transgressing the limits of the present by invading what does not (yet) exist. This transgressive power is creativity. Time is a consequence of its ceaseless process. Insofar as it transcends the present, creativity has the modal and ontological properties of the future. It can function as a pure potentiality that is "nothing in itself" and out of which everything novel actuates.

The most fundamental novelty envisioned by this scheme is not, however, something qualitatively new, but sameness—the purely numerical novelty of repetition. Because creativity transcends the present and "occupies" the imminent future, it can, at the "same time" as it were, inherit the present as something just past.[87] And because the imminent future, in which creativity begins its activity, is *nothing in itself*, it can behave like a receptacle with no positive nature of its own, receiving the transcended present (as just past) into itself *without altering it*. In this way Whitehead preserves intact the Platonic-Aristotelian idea of unresisting accommodation of the faculty to the object, and this becomes the basis not only of his theory of efficient causation, but also of his epistemology and theory of experience.[88] Above all, creativity explains the baseline continuity that characterizes everything existing in time. Nothing can exist for an instant only, and nothing can change abruptly that has not existed continuously for some time, however small. Continuity is therefore the condition of the possibility of existence in time. Materialism takes this continuity for granted as a kind of ontological inertia, but later finds it has no explanation for diachronic regularity of any kind (see chapter 4). Persistence and continuity are the simplest forms of regularity demanding explanation. In Whitehead's scheme, re-creation of the just-past guarantees that the present, however different or novel it may turn out to be, will nevertheless always be a continuation of the past. The dynamic in brief: Because the imminent future is nothing in itself, creativity is a pure potentiality with no actual nature of its own. Because imminence of the immediate future is simultaneously the unobstructed prominence of the just-past, the first act of creativity is literally to become everything that is—just as the potential intellect "becomes all things."

It is therefore creativity that satisfies Aristotle's definition of passive mind in Whitehead's scheme: "Creativity is *without character of its own* in exactly the same sense in which the Aristotelian 'matter' is without a character of its own. It is that ultimate notion of the highest generality at the base of actuality. It cannot be characterized, because all characters are more special than it" (PR 31, emphasis added). In light of this passage from PR it is no surprise that Whitehead later (AI 187) adapts Plato's description of the Receptacle the same way Aristotle did—to explain the possibility of veridical experience. What Whitehead has done is to fuse Aristotle's notions of prime matter and passive mind into one so that the possibility of experience is also the possibility of becoming in the physical world. This yields exactly what Whitehead wanted: the promise of a fully naturalized epistemology that need not capitulate to reductionist materialism. We needn't lose our skepticism to appreciate the value of the thought experiment.

Notes

1. *Stoicorum Veterum Fragmenta* [hereafter: SVF] vol. 1, fr. 197, vol. 2, fr. 724, vol. 3, fr. 178, Long and Sedley 1987, § 57, 346–350; *Enneads* 1.4.9–10, 2.9.1, 3.9.6, 4.3.26, 5.1.12.

2. Stelzenberger 1963.

3. M. Aurel. 7.24; Epict., *Dissertationes* 1.2.30, 2.11.1, 2.12.6, 2.12.12, 2.14.29, 2.17.27–28, 3.22.109.

4. Epict., *Dissertationes* 3.22.94, 3.23.15, *Encheiridion* 34.

5. This meaning is not only clear from contexts (M. Aurel. 3.1, 5.1–2, 5.9; Epict., *Dissertationes* 1.6.13, 1.14.11, 1.28.20, 2.6.14, 2.8.6, 2.8.8, 2.14.14, 3.24.110, 4.7.32), but also from the expansion we find in Galen: *parakolouthein tēi dianoiai* (Kühn 2001, vol. 4, 444). *Consciousness* is also the meaning of *synaisthēsis* and *parakolouthein* in Plotinus (*Enneads* 1.4.9 and 4.3.26), who more than any other ancient writer seems to anticipate at times the modern concept of consciousness. What seems to be missing in Plotinus' understanding of consciousness is the modern stress on its *subjectivity*.

6. *Pyrrhoneae Hypotyposes* 3.108; *Adversus Mathematicos* 7.279, 9.353–355, 10.64, 10.176.

7. Presumably for the Stoics all the modalities of consciousness mentioned are forms of *phantasia*, raising the question whether the Stoics' *phantasia* does not approach our concept of consciousness. How and why *phantasia* differs from consciousness will concern us later in this chapter.

8. The verb *conscire* is extremely rare. In its place we find *conscius esse* (literally, *to be* conscious) and other kinds of periphrasis employing the noun *conscientia*.

9. *Ge*, besides being intensive (as in *gewiss*), collective (as in *Geäst*), or resultative (as in *Gefüge*), can also express belonging or being along with (as in *Gevatter*).

10. In the dramatist Massinger's *Maid of Honour* (1632), *consciousness* functions as a mass noun meaning the state or condition of being aware: "The consciousness of mine own wants" (OED 1989, "consciousness").

11. Wolff 1983b, §§ 727–736. See entries on *"Bewusstsein"* in Goetze 1939–1957 and Ritter 1971.

12. Cudworth 1678, 800; Wolff 1976, Pt. 1, ch. 2, *"Von dem Gewissen,"* §§ 73–138.

13. Cudworth 1678, *inter alia*: 27, 39, 44, 136, 143, 190, 754, 763, 829, 840, 846.

14. Wolff 1972/1734, §§ 10–28; 1968/1732, §§ 23–28.

15. Wolff 1972/1734, §§ 10–31; 1968/1732, §§ 23–25; 1983a /1730, § 1.

16. Similarly, we can understand why Wolff did not give *apperceptio* or *cogitatio* as the glossary equivalents of *Bewusstsein*: neologisms and peculiar usages are of no use in clarifying neologisms and peculiar usages.

17. Noted by Jung 1933, 536, and by Goetze 1939–1957, entry for *"Bewusstsein."*

18. Malebranche 1997, 198, 202, 236, 238, 239, 625, 633, 635, 636; 1979, 1:294, 300, 347, 350–351, 922, 933, 937, 939.

19. In Cudworth's case what is flagged by the pairing is the meaning of a neologism cognate with *conscience* and derived from *conscious*, but narrowed in scope to exclude ethical consciousness. In Malebranche's case what is flagged by the pairing is the substitution of a cognitive for an ethical meaning of an otherwise familiar word.

20. Coste 1758/1700. Most occurrences of "consciousness" are to be found in the chapter on identity (ch. 27).

21. Leibniz 1962, 53–59, 76–78, 115–118, 134, 239 (*apperception*); 235–236 and 245 (*consciosité*); Leibniz 1981 (trans.), pagination identical to Leibniz 1962.

22. Gerhardt 1961, 608–609 (*Monadology* § 14).

23. Gerhardt 1961, 600 (*Principes de la Nature et de la Grâce, fondés en raison* § 4).

24. For the semantic, grammatical, and morphological evolution of the *syneidēsis/conscientia* word groups in antiquity, the following analysis draws on: TLL 1906–1609, Bölig 1914, Bosman 2003, Eckstein 1983, Jung 1933, Kähler 1967, Rudberg 1955, Schönlein 1965, Schönlein 1969, and Zucker 1963. For extreme skepticism about developmental chronology, see Seel 1953.

25. Goetze 1939–1957, entry for "*Gewissen.*" See also Ritter 1971, entry for "*Gewissen.*"

26. OED 1989, entries for "Conscience," "Conscious," and "Consciousness."

27. Roughly the same pattern of development is adduced by Hobbes in his *Leviathan* (1651): "When two, or more men, know of one and the same fact, they are said to be Conscious of it one to another; which is as much as to know it together. And because such are fittest witnesses of the facts of one another, or of a third; it was, and ever will be reputed a very Evill act, for any man to speak against his *Conscience*; or to corrupt or force another so to do: Insomuch that the plea of Conscience, has been always hearkened unto very diligently in all times. Afterwards, men made use of the same word metaphorically, for the knowledge of their own secret facts, and secret thoughts; and therefore it is Rhetorically said, that the Conscience is a thousand witnesses. And last of all, men, vehemently in love with their own opinions, (though never so absurd,) and obstinately bent to maintain them, gave those their opinions also that reverenced name of Conscience, as if they would have it seem unlawfull, to change or speak against them; and so pretend to know they are true, when they know at most, but that they think so" (Hobbes 1968, 131–132).

28. Old High German dates approximately from 500 to 1000 CE.

29. Hennig 2006 and Ross 1988. The revisionism of both authors is unconvincingly radical.

30. Descartes 1964–1976, 9A:124 (Fr.) [=7:160 (L.)].

31. Descartes 1964–1976, 9B:28 (Fr.) [=8A:7 (L.)]. Picot's periphrasis of *conscientia* as "*se appercevoir*" is the likely inspiration for Leibniz's attempt to create a French noun meaning *consciousness* by concocting the substantive *apperception*.

32. Descartes 1964–1976, 9A:137 (Fr.) [=7:176 (L.)]. Descartes' "*qui omnes sub ratione communi cogitationis, sive perceptionis, sive conscientiae, conveniunt*" becomes "tout lesquels conuiennent entr'eux en ce qu'ils ne peuuent estre sans pensée, ou perception, ou conscience and connoissance [. . .]." As noted above, restrictive pairing was also employed by both Malebranche and Cudworth to help dissociate the terms *conscience* and *conscious[ness]* from their usual or frequent ethical connotations.

33. This is a logical inevitability, the inevitability of implied consequences being explicitly drawn in the subsequent elaboration of an influential doctrine. This is all that is meant here by *inevitable*. But as the following sections make clear, this development was also *historically* inevitable because the reification of consciousness

implicit in Cartesian philosophy reflected major social-historical changes in the way individuals actually experienced themselves.

34. Other common locutions are: [something] begets consciousness; [something] is devoid of consciousness; [someone] does/does not attribute consciousness to [something]; etc. "Consciousness" does not appear as the subject of active verbs unless they have a passive meaning, as in *consciousness results from [something]*. It rarely appears in the nominative except in locutions such as *the consciousness of [something]*. An interesting exception: Cudworth assails the proposition "that *Life* and *Cogitation, Sense* and *Consciousness, Reason* and *Understanding*, all our own *Minds*, and *Personalities*, are no *Real Entities* [. . .]" (Cudworth 1678, 754).

35. Note the conspicuous role responsibility plays in Locke's justification for an entified concept of consciousness.

36. See Harold Bloom's edited anthology *Romanticism and Consciousness* (1970).

37. The political and ethical problems of relativity were among the first outcroppings of the fifth century turn from the objective world and speculations about nature to the subjective world and speculations about the human being and society. Highlighting an almost psychotherapeutic orientation of the latter, one of us has described it as a turn to "hygiology" (we could say: the study of the health or wholeness of the soul) (Weber 2003). Interestingly, this reorientation coincides with the advent of medicine as the science of (bodily) human nature and the treatment of its diseases. Medicine is of course an indispensable metaphor for philosophy in Socratic discourse as represented by Plato. The emergence of a new philosophical orientation bringing the inner dynamics of human subjectivity into view also coincides with a shift in legal thinking to a concern with the determination of guilt based on the intent rather than the consequences of an action. This is, understandably, the broader historical context in which we find the earliest attestations of the verb *syneidenai* (Kähler 1967, 74; Zucker 1963, 104–106). Recall that it originally means personal knowledge of (consciousness of) guilt or complicity. It is noteworthy that the afflictions of a guilty conscience were seen in antiquity as a kind of disease of the soul (Euripides, *Orestes* 396), bringing the new art of medicine and the new concepts of legal responsibility together in the emerging concept of an episodically occurring *conscience*. The context in which we find the earliest attestations of *conscientia* in Latin (early first century CE: Pseudo-Cicero, *Rhetorica ad Herennium*, II v 8) are explicitly juridical (Schönlein 1969), evoking an interesting parallel with the earlier emergence of the Greek word group.

38. A comparison of Descartes' *Meditations* with the section of al-Ghazālī's autobiography entitled "The Avenues to Sophistry and Skepticism" (Ghazali 2000, 21–24) is startling.

39. Khan 1965, Weinberg 1969 and 1977, Gyeke 1973, Lennon 1985.

40. Premodern precedents for a developed sense of an individual's private interior life are not impossible to find, but not easy to find either. Hennig (2006) has drawn attention to Augustine's novel confinement of moral conscience to something no longer outwardly manifest or publicly available in his *Contra Cresconium*, and Harper (1997) has drawn attention to Thomas Hoccleve's *Complaint* (ca. 1421), which attests

to the outward invisibility of sanity and madness: "By cowntynaunce it is not wist," says Hoccleve (i.e., you can't tell from someone's looks if he is mad).

41. For Zeno, see Aristotle's *Physics* 239b34–240a18; for Democritus, see Kranz's 6th ed. of the *Fragmente der Vorsokratiker*, ch. 68, Frgs. 6–11 (Kranz 1985, 2:13840).

42. Respectively: *"le sensate esperienze," "esperienze manifeste," "esperienze," "il senso manifesto,"* Galilei 1998 (Critical Edition), 35, 36, 137, 184; 1897 (National Edition), 57, 58, 153, 197; 1967 (Drake), 32, 34, 127, 171.

43. The *Letters on Sunspots* (1613) states this unequivocally (Galilei 1957, 118).

44. Drake's etymological rendering of *esperienze manifeste* as "palpable experience" (1967, 34) is unfortunate inasmuch as it appears to be the *terminus technicus* around whose meaning the other terms cluster. By showing how important *refuting* the doctrine of "manifest experience" was to the new science of the seventeenth century, Tamny (1980) makes a convincing case that it must indeed have had something like the status of a recognized doctrine among Renaissance Peripatetics. He is, however, familiar with the doctrine only through its caricature and refutation by Galileo and later by Robert Boyle. Who were the real proponents of this doctrine and what is its provenance? The occurrence of this term in the *Dialogues* goes unremarked in the otherwise heavily annotated critical edition of 1998. It also does not appear to be discussed anywhere in the literature (except by Tamny). Its authenticity as a Scholastic doctrine already in the Middle Ages can be documented in Buridan (ca. 1300–1358), who makes use of it in refuting Scholastic theories of free fall that attribute the body's acceleration to the increased power of final causation as it nears its natural place (Buridan 1942, Grant 1974, 281). Buridan's Latin is *experentia manifesta*—the same phase used to render Galileo's Italian back into Latin in the 1641 translation of the *Dialogues* (Galileo 1641, 20). The fact that Buridan's appeal to manifest experience strikes us as a methodologically unexceptional example of empirical falsification, while the Renaissance appeal is clearly specious, underscores how difficult it is to give the idea of empirical verification an epistemologically tenable interpretation. The fact that all sides—Buridan, Galileo's contemporaries, and Galileo himself in 1610—think that their way of appealing to experience is endorsed by Aristotle reminds us that the evidentiary role ascribed to experience in Aristotle is equally fraught with difficulties of interpretation. Indeed, this is highlighted by the fact that Aristotle has been alternately championed for his hard-nosed empiricism, pilloried for his naive empiricism, championed for rising above mere empiricism, and pilloried for trying to rise above empiricism. In light of these competing clichés it is instructive to pose the question where the idea of *manifest experience* actually comes from and whether it is ever attested in the texts of Aristotle. While it is not hard to see how such a doctrine could be *derived* from Aristotle, it is very hard to imagine what Greek vocabulary the phrase could possibly be translating. The terminology is simply not Aristotelian. The closest approximation in Aristotle would be phrasings such as *ek tēs aisthēseōs phaneron* (*De Sensu* 445a30), while *experientia manifesta* looks suspiciously like a Latin rendering of the Stoic *periptōsis enargēs* (Sextus Empiricus, *Adversus Mathematicos*, 3.40), which designates the primary impingement of sensible things on the soul and is, according to the Stoics, the epistemologically certain basis

of all knowledge. This might lead one to suspect that "manifest experience" answers the needs of a Peripateticism already disrupted by the Hellenistic imagination.

45. "[I]t is to be a history not only of nature free and at large (when she is left to her own course and does her work her own way [...] but much more of a nature under constraint and vexed; that is to say, when by art and the hand of man she is forced out of her natural state, and squeezed and moulded" (Bacon 1960, 25).

46. *Discourse on Method*, Part 1 and 2 (Descartes 1964–1976, 6:1–22; 1984, 1:111–122). In what appears to be a deliberate reference to Cervantes' sardonic masterpiece, Descartes insinuates that those who try to learn from their intellectual patrimony—studying, for example, the "literature of the ancients"—are "liable to fall into the excesses of the knights-errant in our tales of chivalry, and conceive plans beyond their powers" (1964–1976, 6:7; 1984, 1:114).

47. *Discourse on Method*, Part 4 (1964–1976, 6:31–30; 1984, 1:126–131).

48. "the greatest part of the questions and controversies that perplex mankind depending on the doubtful and uncertain use of words, or (which is the same) indetermined ideas, which they are made to stand for" (Locke 1959, 1:23). See the chapters on "Clear and Obscure, Distinct and Confused Ideas," "Real and Fantastical Ideas," "Adequate and Inadequate Ideas," "True and False Ideas" (1959, 1:486–526), and on the "Imperfections of Words," the "Abuse of Words," and the "Remedies of the Abuse of Words" (1959, 2:104–164). The same concern afflicts Bacon (1960, 19–20).

49. This passage is also discussed by Xavier Verley in his contribution to this volume.

50. Hume 1978, xv–xvi; Locke 1959, 1:9, 14, 25–32; Descartes 1964–1976, 10:371–373; 1984, 1:15–17; Descartes 1964, 6:4–6; 1984, 1:113–115.

51. A phenomenon often alluded to by Nietzsche; see, for striking examples, *Beyond Good and Evil*, Aphorisms 10, 15–17, 29, 31, and the *Gay Science*, Aphorism 335, where he asks how one knows that a judgment of conscience, which declares that some behavior is *right*, is *true* and what *right* one has to think it is true (1969, 3:19–20, 25–27, 40–42; 2:468–470).

52. SVF 1986, vol. 2, frs. 53, 70, 90, 91 (2:21, lns. 12–21, 26, lns. 30–33, 29, lns. 37–38, 30, lns. 6–7); Long and Sedley 1987, 1:242 and 254.

53. SVF 1986, vol. 1, fr. 61 (1:19, lns. 1–3); Long and Sedley 1986, 1:242; compare with Descartes' "Meditation IV" and his Letter to Mesland of 2 May 1644 (Descartes 1964–1976, 7:52–43, 4:111–123; 1984, 2:37–43, 3:231–237).

54. See Xavier Verley's contribution to this volume.

55. See Plutarch, *On Stoic Self-Contradictions* and *Against the Stoics on Common Conceptions* (*Moralia* 13), 1036A, 1036B, 1048A, 1059B, 1063D, 1073C–F.

56. We can find testimony to support this interpretation of consciousness as a kind of "theoretical conscience" from two very different sources: Peirce, for whom the impossibility of theoretical conscience is reason to reject entirely this modern concept of consciousness, and Husserl, for whom theoretical conscience represents the possibility of philosophy reaching its ultimate fulfillment. What they agree on is the peculiar interpenetration of theory and practice in the modern self-understanding of consciousness. We find that Peirce (1955, 46–48, 228–230, and note on 15–17) disavows the modern concept of consciousness as a private source of immediate intuitive knowledge precisely on the grounds that it represents a monstrous conflation

of *a priori* reason and conscience. According to Peirce, theoretical knowledge never possesses the intuitive immediacy characteristic of ethical conscience. Any attempt to arrive at knowledge through pure "self-consciousness" (the reflective examination of consciousness) is therefore misguided. He makes this judgment specifically in relation to Descartes, but obviously it applies not just to Descartes' *inspectio mentis*, but also to Cherbury's inner reason, Locke's reflection, Spinoza's *reflectio*, Kant's critique of pure reason, and, finally, even Husserl's phenomenology. Peirce in effect believes that modern subjectivity, with its characteristic demand for a private certainty based on immediate intuition, results from a kind of overreaching of conscience into theory or, conversely, a perversion of reason that makes it jealous of conscience. We find, on the other hand, that Husserl (1984 [Husserliana 24], Abschnitt 2, 116–242) views cognition as a kind of interior praxis in need of a "jurisprudence of knowledge" (132: *Rechtswissenschaft der Erkenntnis*) or "cognitive theory of right" (116: *Rechtslehre der Erkenntnis*) in order to achieve its goal, which he explicitly identifies as cognition with an "absolutely good noetic conscience" (139: *absolut gutes noeticshes Gewissen*). For Husserl, of course, it is Phenomenology that ultimately satisfies this need, the inescapability of which defines the very being of consciousness. A final piece of testimony deserves extended quotation:

> When the epistemologists' concept of consciousness first become popular, it seems to have been in part a transformed application of the Protestant notion of conscience. The Protestants had to hold that a man could know the moral state of his soul and the wishes of God without the aid of confessors and scholars; they spoke therefore of the God-given "light" of private conscience. When Galileo's and Descartes' representations of the mechanical world seemed to require that the minds should be salved from mechanism by being represented as constituting a duplicate world, the need was felt to explain how the contents of this ghostly world could be ascertained, again without the help of schooling, but also without the help of sense perception. The metaphor of "light" seemed peculiarly appropriate, since Galilean science dealt so largely with the optically discovered world. "Consciousness" was imported to play in the mental world the part played by light in the mechanical world. In this metaphorical sense, the contents of the mental world were thought of as being self-luminous or refulgent.
>
> This model was employed again by Locke when he described the deliberate observational scrutiny which a mind can from time to time turn upon its current states and processes. He called this supposed inner perception "reflexion" (our "introspection"), borrowing the word "reflexion" from the familiar optical phenomenon of the reflections of faces in mirrors. The mind can "see" or "look at" its own operations in the "light" given off by themselves. The myth of consciousness is a piece of para-optics. (Ryle 1984, 159)

Ryle does not know that "para-optics" goes back to the Stoic definition of representation: "He [Chrysippus] says that presentation [*phantasia*] comes from light [*phōs*]. For just as light reveals itself and the other things that it encloses in itself, so presentation reveals both itself and what has caused it" (SVF 1986, vol. 2, fr. 54, [p. 21, ln. 28–p. 22, ln. 2]; Long and Sedley 1987, 1:237).

57. Locke 1959, 1:130, 138, 448–451,458–459, 456.

58. This is the sense of consciousness that the French denote with *connaissance*, rather than *conscience*.

59. See note 10 of this chapter.

60. In Locke's definition of *consciousness* as "the perception of what passes in a man's own mind" (1959, 1:138), it is the *own* we must pay special attention to because this implies self-consciousness, which implies self. It therefore leads, via self-consciousness, to the idea of the *self* as an entity: "*Self* is that conscious thinking thing [. . .]" (1959, 1:458). Compare Samuel Clarke, "Consciousness [. . .] signifies [. . .] the Reflex Act by which I know that I think, and that my Thoughts and Actions are my own and not Anothers" (1707, 4), or David Hartley, "Mad persons [. . .] lose, in great measure, that connecting Consciousness which accompanies our Thoughts and Actions, and by which we connect ourselves with ourselves from time to time" (1976/1749, 390). Hartley attributes the "Erroneousness of the Judgment in Children and Idiots" to the imperfection of "the connecting Consciousness," which lacks in their case the "usual Permanency" (391).

61. "For indeed the latter [Democritus] taught that the soul [conceived as the totality of *organic* functions] and the mind are simply identical. For he thought truth to be appearance. [. . .] He thus does not use [the term] 'mind' as [denoting] some kind of faculty concerned with truth, but rather he says soul and mind are the same" (*De Anima* 404a27–28). "The Ancients said that thinking and perceiving are the same thing. [. . .] All these [Empedocles and Homer] take intellection to be something corporeal, like perceiving [. . .] so it follows of necessity that, as some say, all appearances are true, or error is [some kind of physical process]" (*De Anima* 427a22–427b5). Thus, Aristotle asks rhetorically "whether the concern of physics is with the whole of the soul [inclusive of mind] or part of it [everything but mind]. For if [its concern is] with the whole of it, nothing will be left of philosophy apart from physical science. For mind is [the faculty] of the intelligible objects. So physical knowledge would be of all things. For consider [that knowledge] about mind and the intelligible objects belongs to the same [science], if indeed [they are] correlatives, and all correlatives are objects of the same study" (*De Partibus Animalium* 641a34–6). Aristotle's answer is clear: "Not all of the soul is nature" (*ibid.*). "If there were no other substance apart from the ones formed by nature, then physics would be the primary science" (*Metaphysica* 1026a27–29), and truth would be appearance, just as Protagoras claimed (interpreting the *homo-mensura* dictum, as did Plato and Aristotle, to mean: what *seems to me now* is the measure of all things). Cast in their logical order, the steps of Aristotle's argument are as follows: (1) A faculty is correlative with its objects. (2) The intellect is a faculty, so from (1) it follows that it is correlative with the intelligible objects it knows. (3) If A is correlative with B, then the same science that knows the nature of A knows the nature of B. (4) If the intellect is simply (a part of) the organically embodied soul, it will belong to a physical science to know its nature. (5) From (2), (3), and (4) we can infer that intelligible objects will be known by a physical science, which is the same as saying that there are no

objects besides corporeal ones. (6) From (5) Aristotle infers that cognition would not be the manifestation of an objective truth (because this presupposes the unresisting accommodation of the faculty to its object), but only a relative manifestation resulting from a physical interaction. In short, the identification of intellect with (a part of) the soul implies the reductive identification of truth with subjective appearances. While the terms in which Aristotle's argument is couched seem quaint, in essence it is valid and remains the focus of discussions of consciousness. Reductive materialism is the doctrine that "physics is the primary science" and hence concerned with "the whole of the soul" with the implication that "soul and the mind are the same thing" and "thinking is just [like] perceiving," namely, an organic process with a physical cause as its only objective correlative. Aristotle's claim that this leads directly to the problem of relativism, that is, the problem of accounting for knowledge of truths that are necessary, universal, or normative, is borne out by the history of philosophy in the twentieth century and its many attempts to make peace with the consequences of positivism. As David Griffin argues below, allowing for the possibility of nonsensory knowledge (a truth that is more than the shifting relativity of "appearances") is a main selling point of dualist theories of mind.

62. Caterus, author of the "First Set of Objections" to the *Meditations*, in response to Descartes (Descartes 1964–1976, 7:92–94; 1984, 2:66–68), Sergeant, author of the polemic *Solid Philosophy asserted, against the fancies of the Ideists*, in response to Locke (Sergeant 1697, 24, 27); see also Locke's reference to Sergeant's critique in his correspondence with Stillingfleet (Locke 1963, 4:390–391).

63. This position is rehabilitated by Bergson and James and embraced by Whitehead (see Weekes 2004, 254–262).

64. "Things do not lodge in us with their form and their essence; they do not come in by the force of their own authority. [. . .] [I]f [. . .] we could receive anything without changing it [. . .] then truth could be passed on from hand to hand [. . .]. Nobody claims that the essence of anything relates only to its effect on Man [. . .]. [S]ince our state makes things correspond to itself and transforms them in conformity with itself, we can no longer claim to know what anything truly is: nothing reaches us except as altered and falsified by our senses. [. . .] [W]ho will be a proper judge [. . .] ? [. . .] We would need a man exempt from all [. . .] qualities, so that, without preconception, he could judge [. . .] propositions as matters indifferent to him" (Montaigne 1987, 141, 184–185). The reference to *absence of intrinsic qualities* as a precondition of adequation betrays familiarity with the logic if not also the language of *Timaeus* and *De Anima*. Compare PR 31: "Creativity is without character of its own [. . .]."

65. Book 1, Aphorism 41; (Bacon 1960, 48; see also 22). A similar passage appears in the *Advancement of Learning*: "For the mind of man is far from the nature of a clear and equal glass, wherein the beams of things should reflect according to their true incidence; nay, it is, rather like an enchanted glass, full of superstition and imposture, if it be not delivered and reduced" (Bacon 1973, 132).

66. "That as in *vision*, so also in conceptions that arise from the *other senses*, the subject of their *inherence* is not the *object*, but the *sentient*" (Hobbes 1994, 4; emphasis in original).

67. "Meditation 2" (Descartes 1964–1976, 7:26–29; 1984, 2:18–19). In fact, it can be demonstrated that the designation of the experient as "subject" originates with Hobbes and finds its way into Cartesian philosophy through Descartes' interchange with Hobbes in the *Objections and Replies*. The *res cogitans* is *never* designated "*subjectum*" in the *Meditations*. On the contrary, the "subjectum meae cogitationis" (1964–1976, 7:37) is the *subject-matter* of my thought and rightly rendered by Cottingham et al. as "object of my thought" (1984, 2:26). And yet, strangely enough, the inevitability of calling the *res cogitans* a subject is only a syllogism away from Descartes' own definitions in the "Arguments [...] arranged in geometrical fashion" appended to the "Second Set of Replies." To wit, Definition 5: "*Substance* [...] applies to every thing in which whatever we perceive immediately resides, as in a subject [...]." and Definition 6: "The substance in which thought immediately resides is called *mind*" (Descartes 1964–1976, 7:161; 1984, 2:114). It is not clear why Descartes doesn't just say "substance is the *subject* in which whatever we perceive inheres" unless he wants to circumlocute his way around having to call the mind a subject when he gets to Definition 6. But whether he likes it or not, the mind as "subject" is forced on him by Hobbes, author of the "Third Set of Objections": "How do we know the proposition 'I am thinking'? It can only be from our inability to conceive an act without its subject" (1964–1976, 7:173; 1984, 2:122). Hobbes' objection contains a critical element that Descartes allows to go unchallenged: thinking is not, as it was for Aristotle and Scholasticism, an action of the thing known that the mind under appropriate circumstances suffers, but an act of the mind. This implies that "I know..." is no longer an abbreviation of "it manifests itself to me." We should not be surprised, then, that Descartes' "Reply" to Hobbes contains his first real concessions to this usage: "He is quite right saying that 'we cannot conceive of an act without its subject'. We cannot conceive of thought without a thinking thing, since that which thinks is not nothing. But he then goes on to say, quite without any reason, and in violation of all usage and all logic: 'It seems to follow from this that a thinking thing is something corporeal.' *It may be that the subject of any act can be understood only in terms of a substance* [...] but it does not follow that it must be understood in terms of a body" (1964–1976, 7:175–176; 1984, 2:123–124; emphasis added). Hobbes identifies subject of action and subject of inherence; Descartes feels compelled to accept their identity, but not their materiality. Thus we have the incorporeal subject of experience.

68. "the expurgation of the intellect" (Bacon 1960, 23).

69. "and the understanding thoroughly freed and cleansed; the entrance into the kingdom of man, founded on the sciences, being not much other than the entrance into the kingdom of heaven, whereinto none may enter except as a little child" (Bacon 1960, 66).

70. Descartes devotes the whole of Part III of his *Discourse on Method* to this important prerequisite (Descartes 1964–1976, 6:22–31; 1984, 1:122–126).

71. Montaigne even alludes to the old image of the mind as a *tabula rasa*, which has it source in Aristotle's description of passive mind (*De Anima* 430a1–2): "No system discovered by Man has greater usefulness nor a greater appearance of truth [than Pyrrhonism] which shows us Man naked, empty, aware of his natural weakness, fit to accept outside help from on high: Man, stripped of all human learning

and so all the more able to lodge the divine within him, annihilating his intellect to make room for faith; [. . .] he holds no doctrine contrary to established custom; he is humble, obedient, teachable, keen to learn [. . .] a sworn enemy of heresy. [. . .] He is a blank writing-tablet, made ready for the finger of God to carve such letters on him as he pleases." (1987, 74)

72. "Now philosophy has always proceeded on the sound principle that its generalizations must be based upon the primary elements in actual experience as starting-points. Greek philosophy had recourse to the common forms of language to suggest its generalizations. It found the typical statement, "That stone is grey," and it evolved the generalization that the actual world can be conceived as a collection of primary substances qualified by universal qualities" (PR 158). The generalization made by the Greeks was erroneous because it neglected the important fact that this stone is gray only *for* a subject perceiving it. Put forth as an example of a primary metaphysical fact with the universal form *S is P*, it thus constitutes what Whitehead calls the fallacy of misplaced concreteness. *This stone is gray* is really an abstraction that can be got only by mentally detaching from the wholeness of concrete experience a part that is not actually separable. It is as though the stone's being gray has been artificially treated with a fixative agent and chipped out of its natural organic context. It is then misleadingly offered as a self-sustaining piece of reality that could and does exist independently of experience.

73. Whitehead likes to give names to ideas, both the ones he likes and the ones he dislikes. Unfortunately he fails to use his own labels consistently. The result is a disorienting swirl of nomenclature. Besides the (version of the) Subjectivist Principle that Whitehead accepts, for example, there is also a (version of the) Subjectivist Principle he rejects. Whether the former is the same as or different from his Reformed Subjectivist Principle and how it relates to the Subjectivist Doctrine and the Subjectivist Bias are questions that we happily do not have to answer. See Lindsey 1976 and Griffin 1977.

74. "[Descartes] laid down the principle, that those substances which are the subjects of enjoying conscious experiences provide the primary data for philosophy, namely, themselves as in the enjoyment of such experience. This is the famous subjectivist bias which entered into modern philosophy through Descartes. In this doctrine Descartes undoubtedly made the greatest philosophical discovery since the age of Plato and Aristotle. For his doctrine directly traversed the notion that the proposition, 'This stone is grey,' expresses a primary form of known fact from which metaphysics can start its generalizations. If we are to go back to the subjective enjoyment of experience, the type of primary starting-point is 'my perception of the stone as grey'" (PR 159).

75. "The difficulties of all schools of modern philosophy lie in the fact that, having accepted the subjectivist principle, they continue to use philosophical categories derived from another point of view" (PR 167).

76. The conservative cast of Whitehead's thought comes to light here. On Whitehead's interpretation, the fundamental mistake of the early modern philosophers was their relinquishment of the Aristotelian concept of passive mind (although it is not clear to what extent he realized this concept was Aristotle's). A different interpretation—one more agreeable to contemporary sensibilities—is obviously possible:

the problem is not so much that early modern philosophers gave up the concept of passive mind by recognizing the mind to be a thing, but rather that they *refused* to give up the concept of passive mind *despite* recognizing the mind to be a thing. As a normative model, passive mind obviously remains intact, so philosophy becomes a remedial or therapeutic practice the purpose of which is to super-induce pure passivity on the mind despite its being a thing. Giving up passive mind entirely, even as a normative model, is what Richard Rorty has been agitating for. Whitehead, unwilling to accept such apparent consequences as relativism, solipsism, or positivism, wants to explore ways that it might, conceivably, still be possible to trade thinghood for passivity. What makes Whitehead's philosophy exciting and novel despite its conservative orientation is the radical proposal that thinghood may not be at the heart of anything—neither mind nor being is made of things.

77. For discussion, see Verley's contribution to this volume. The Aristotelian principle is: "The actuality of what is sensed and of sensation are one and the same [numerically], but [what it is] to be each of these is not the same" (*De Anima*, 425b27). The example is sound and hearing: an actual sound is a heard sound, and actual hearing is a sound heard. Let it be noted that sound and hearing are *distinct sorts of things* but *actually inseparable*, so that their unity is synthetic, but necessary. A description of the causal nexus occurring in the act of perception therefore constitutes a *necessary synthetic proposition* (and thus *a priori* in the Kantian sense). "I hear a sound" means, *pace* Husserl, "I am one with (but not indistinguishable from) a transcendent entity" or "A transcendent entity is one with (but not indistinguishable from) me." In his contribution to this volume, Gregg Rosenberg gives a similar analysis of the relationship between the act of experiencing and the object experienced: "phenomenal qualities could not exist unless some subject was experiencing them, and experiences could not exist unless they were experiences of phenomenal qualities. Yet, despite this mutual participation in one another's natures, they are distinct essences. A phenomenal quality is an *object* of experience, and should not be identified with the experiencing of it. And an individual experiencer is a subject of qualitative experience, and should not be identified with its objects." This becomes the basis for his argument for panexperientialism. Causation is possible only if there exist "carriers" that do in fact satisfy the seemingly perverse logical requirements of a causal nexus: "each of the receptive and effective carriers must have a nature that is dependent on the nature of something distinct from it in the compositionally circular way that effective and receptive properties are dependent on one another." The logical structure of a true causal nexus is notoriously difficult to make sense of precisely because it involves the necessary connection (interdependence) of distinct things. Panexperientialism is thus uniquely qualified to meet the classical Humean objections to the possibility of causation as a real physical operation involving some kind of nontautological necessity. The relation between act and object of experience meets the criteria for being a "carrier" of causation and provides a perspicuous paradigm of how distinct things can be interdependent. Therefore, after examining a number of arresting homologies between experience and causation, he concludes that causation is most plausibly explained as a kind of experience. "The ontological relation between phenomenal qualities and their participation in the experiencings of subjects matches this crucial logical structure of the relationship between effective properties and their shared receptivity. . . . [J]ust

like effective and receptive properties, the experiencer and the experienced qualities are distinct yet interdependent properties of the total individual." See as well Weekes' contribution to Part V of this volume.

78. "[W]e must remember and acknowledge that there be in our minds continually certain *images* or conceptions of the things without us, insomuch that if a man could be alive, and all the rest of the world annihilated, he should nevertheless retain the *image* thereof, and all those things which he had before seen or perceived in it; every one by his own experience knowing, that the *absence* or *destruction* of things once imagined doth not cause the *absence* or *destruction* of the imagination itself. This *imagery* and *representations* of the qualities of the thing without, is that we call our *conception, imagination, ideas, notice* or *knowledge* of them; and the *faculty* or power by which we are capable of such knowledge, is that I here call *cognitive power*, or *conceptive*, the power of knowing or conceiving" (Hobbes 1994, 2–3).

79. Whitehead notes that neither Descartes (SMW 73–74; PR 49, 76, 122, 158) nor Locke (PR 51–60, 113, 122–123, 138, 146–147, 149, 152, 157) are entirely of one mind on the question of the reality or ideality of the subject's relation to things in the world. On the one hand, their sometime emphasis on judgment as what *gives* existential import to ideas implies that this is something ideas lack intrinsically and acquire only as a sort of extrinsic denomination if they pass mental inspection. This suggests the disconnection of the subject from reality and its ontological isolation due to the ideality of the world it actually experiences. On the other hand, their sometime emphasis on some version of the Scholastic doctrine of objective reality, according to which real things "object" themselves into the mind, suggests the connectedness of the subject and the reality of the world it actually experiences. As with Descartes and Locke, so too with Hobbes. Contrast the passage quoted in the previous footnote, which suggests isolation and ideality, with Hobbes' comments on perception in *On Body*, which seem to be a materialistic take on the doctrine of objective reality and thus sound particularly Whiteheadian: "The subject of sense is the sentient itself, namely, some living creature; and we speak more correctly, when we say a living creature seeth, than when we say the eye seeth. *The object is the thing received*; and it is more accurately said, that we see the sun, than that we see the light" (Hobbes 1989, 117, emphasis added).

80. The necessity that God's *Logos* be at once eternal and a blueprint for the temporal unfolding of things led to the idea that everything temporal has its perfect, adequate representation in eternity. This *Logos* is wholly unlike Plato's eternal forms, because it leaves out no features of the imaging reality. Plato's forms represent the ideal (static) states that changing things are trying to be, leaving out the specific temporality of things, which is, as in Aristotle, an effect of the imperfect medium in which the forms are being realized. The *Logos*, by contrast, is a timeless encoding of the temporal process itself. This would appear to be the origin of our concept of a "law of nature." It seems to be original to Philo, but Augustine takes it an important step further, arguing that the *Ratio*, in addition to its godly form as Uncreated Light, gets naturalized at creation as a timelessly immanent order of nature. See Philo, *On the Creation of the Cosmos according to Moses* (*De Opificio Mundi*) §§ 13, 24, 26, 27, 67; Augustine, *The Literal Meaning of Genesis* (*De Genesi ad litteram*) bk. 1 §§ 4, 9, 15; bk. 4 §§ 1, 22–23, 43–56, bk. 6 §§ 17–19, 25–29, bk. 8 § 48, bk. 9 § 32 (Philo

2001, 49, 51–52, 63; Augustine 2002, 169, 171–172, 174, 241, 253–254, 266–275, 310–312, 315–317, 373–374, 394–395).

81. Galilei 1967, 102–105; see Cassirer 1942/1969, 115–131; Blumenberg 1981, 489–502.

82. We should remember at this juncture the bold and formidable attempt made early in the twentieth century by the German mathematician and philosopher Edmund Husserl to develop a subjective methodology that was rigorous and every bit as scientific as the experimental method, which he called Phenomenology. Needless to say, for this perspective, consciousness not only did not become taboo, but also continued to be the principle object of investigation. However, the European and Anglo-American intellectual communities remained almost completely isolated from one another until the last few decades of the century, and each evolved with little interference from the other.

83. "Really distinct" is Scholastic for "externally related."

84. Similarly for Aristotle, appearing does not testify to the weakness of a subject that cannot swallow the object itself, but to the eminence of things and their power to disseminate themselves.

85. Only because inter-subjectivity is always also intercorporeity does the interlocking of perspectives finds itself subtended by a formal system of extensive relationships. In this way, the applicability of mathematics in a formal ontology of nature receives its due. But the unit and ground of being is not such a formal fact. Rather, it is the subjective experience shaped by such facts.

86. *De Rerum Natura* 1, lns. 958–983 (Mantinband 1972, 28–29).

87. How creativity can be "literally" present and past at the same time is the topic of chapter 15 below.

88. It bears repeating, however, that for Whitehead this is not the whole of the story. For just as there is no subjectivity that does not have objectivity as its foundational ingredient (no present that does not contain the past), which preserves a classical meaning of truth, there is no objectivity that is not already ingredient in subjectivity (no past that is not already part of a novel present), which preserves appearance and perspective as means rather than obstacles to knowledge. It is not subjectivity, but its alienating potentiation as consciousness that needs to be overcome.

References

Augustine. 2002. *The Works of Saint Augustine.* A Translation for the 21st Century. Pt. 1, vol. 13. *On Genesis*: [1] *On Genesis: A Refutation of the Manichees.* [2] *Unfinished Literal Commentary on Genesis.* [3] *The Literal Meaning of Genesis*; introduction, translation and notes by Edmund Hill, O.P.; editor, John Rotelle, O.S.A. Hyde Park, NY: New City Press.

Bacon, Francis. 1960. *The New Organon.* Fulton H. Anderson, ed. Indianapolis: Bobbs-Merrill.

Bacon, Francis. 1973. *The Advancement of Learning.* G.W. Kitchin, ed. London: J.M. Dent and Sons.

Bloom, Harold, ed. 1970. *Romanticism and Consciousness: Essays in Criticism*. New York: W.W. Norton.

Blumenberg, Hans. 1965. "Das Fernrohr und die Ohnmacht der Wahrheit." In Galilei 1965, 1–75.

Blumenberg, Hans. 1981. *Die Genesis der kopernikanischen Welt*. 3 vols. Frankfurt am Main: Suhrkamp-Taschenbuch Wissenschaft.

Bölig, H. 1914. "Das Gewissen bei Seneca und Paulus." *Theologische Studien und Kritiken. Eine Zeitschrift für das gesamte Gebiet der Theologie*, 1:1–24.

Bosman, Philip. 2003. *Conscience in Philo and Paul. A Conceptual History of the Synoida Word Group*. Tübingen: Mohr Siebeck.

Buridan, Jean. 1942. *Quaestiones super libris quattuor de caelo et mundo*. Ernest Addison Moody, ed. Cambridge, MA: Mediaeval Academy of America.

Burnyeat, Miles, ed. 1983. *The Skeptical Tradition*. Berkeley: University of California Press.

Cassirer, Ernst. 1942. "Galilei: A New Science and a New Spirit." *American Scholar* 12:5–19. Reprinted in German translation in Cassirer 1969, 115–131.

Cassirer, Ernst. 1969. *Philosophie und Exakte Wissenschaft*. Kleine Schriften. Eingeleiter und erläutert von Wilhelm Krampf. Frankfurt am Main: Vittorio Klostermann.

Clarke, Samuel. 1706. *Letter to Mr. Dodwell; wherein all the arguments in his Epistolary discourse against the immortality of the soul are particularly answered*. London: W. Botham.

Clarke, Samuel. 1707. *A Second Defense of an Argument Made Use of in a Letter to Mr. Dodwell, to Prove the Immateriality and Natural Immortality of the Soul*. London: James Knapton.

Coste, Pierre, trans. 1758/1700. *Essai philosophique concernant l'entendement humain, où l'on montre quelle est l'étendue de nos connoissances certaines, et la maniere dont nous y parvenons*. Par M. Locke. Traduit de l'anglois. Amsterdam: Aux dépens de la Compagnie.

Cudworth, Ralph. 1678. *The True Intellectual System of the Universe*. London: Richard Royston.

Descartes, René. 1964–1976. *Œuvres de Descartes*. Ed. by Ch. Adam and P. Tannery. Revised ed. Paris: Vrin/C.N.R.S.

Descartes, René. 1984. *The Philosophical Writings of Descartes*. 3 vols. Trans. John Cottingham, Robert Stoothoff, Dugald Murdoch. Cambridge: Cambridge University Press.

Eckstein, Hans-Joachim. 1983. *Der Begriff Syneidesis bei Paulus: eine neutestamentlich-exegetische Untersuchung zum "Gewissensbegriff."* Wissenschaftliche Untersuchungen zum Neuen Testament. Series 2, vol. 10. Tuübingen: Mohr.

Favaro, Antonio. 1890–1909. *Le opere di Galileo Galilei*. Edizione nazionale, direttore: Antonio Favaro. Firenze: Tipografia di G. Barbèra.

Galilei, Galileo. 1641. *Systema cosmicum: In quo dialogis IV de duobus maximis mundi systematibus, ptolemaico and copernicano, rationibus utrinque propositis indefinitè disseritur*. Lugduni, Sumptibus I.A. Huguetan.

Galilei, Galileo. 1897. *I due massimi sistemi del mondo*. Vol. 7 in Favaro 1890–1909.

Galilei, Galileo. 1957. *Discoveries and Opinions of Galileo*. Trans. with an introduction and notes by Stillman Drake. Garden City: Doubleday Anchor Books.

Galilei, Galileo. 1965. *Siderius Nuncius* [et al.]. Herausgegeben und eingeleiter von Hans Blumenberg. Frankfurt am Main: Insel Verlag.

Galilei, Galileo. 1967. *Dialogue Concerning the Two Chief World Systems—Ptolemaic and Copernican*. Stillman Drake, trans. 2nd ed. Berkeley: University of California Press.

Galilei, Galileo. 1998. *Dialogo sopra i due massimi sistemi del mondo, Tolemaico e Copernicano*. Edizione critica e commento a cura di Ottavio Besomi e Mario Helbing. Padova: Antenore.

Gerhardt, C.J., ed. 1961. *Die Philosophischen Schriften von Gottfried Willhelm Leibniz*. Hildesheim: Georg Olms Verlagsbuchhandlung.

Ghazali (al-Ghazālī), Muhammud. 2000. *Al-Ghazali's Path to Sufism, his Deliverance from Error (al-Munqidh min al-Dalal)*. Trans. from the Arabic by R.J. McCarthy, S.J. Preface by David Burrell, C.S.C. Louisville: Fons Vitae.

Goetze, Alfred, ed. 1939–1957. *Trübners deutsches Wörterbuch*. Im Auftrag der Arbeitsgemeinschaft für deutsche Wortforschung. Berlin: W. de Grunter.

Grant, Edward. 1974. *A Source Book in Medieval Science*. Cambridge, MA: Harvard University Press.

Griffin, David Ray. 1977. "The Subjectivist Principle and Its Reformed and Unreformed Versions." *Process Studies* 7 (1): 27–36.

Groarke, Leo. 1990. *Greek Skepticism: Anti-Realist Trends in Ancient Thought*. Montreal and Kingston: McGill-Queen's University Press.

Gyeke, Kwame. 1973. "Al-Ghazali on Causation." *Second Order. An African Journal of Philosophy* 2 (1): 31–39.

Hamanaka, Toshihiko. 1997. "The Concept of Consciousness in the History of Neuropsychiatry." *History of Psychiatry* 8:361–373.

Harper, Stephen. 1997. "'By cowntynaunce it is not wist': Thomas Hoccleve's Complaint and the Spectacularity of Madness in the Middle Ages." *History of Psychiatry* 8, pt. 3, no. 31: 387–394.

Hartley, David. 1978/1749. *Observations on Man, His Frame, His Duty, and His Expectations*. 2 vols. in 1. Facsimile reproduction with an introduction by Theodore L. Huguelet. Delmar: Scholars' Facsimiles and Reprints.

Hennig, Boris. 2006. "*Conscientia* bei Descartes." *Zeitschrift für Philosophische Forschung* 60 (1): 21–36.

Henrich, Dieter. 1989. "Kant's Notion of a Deduction and the Methodological Background of the first *Critique*." In Förster, Eckhart, ed. 1989. *Kant's Transcendental Deductions. The Three Critiques and the Opus postumum*. Stanford: Stanford University Press.

Herbert of Cherbury (Edward Herbert, Baron). 1937/1624. *De Veritate*. Meyrick H. Carré, trans. Bristol: University of Bristol.

Hobbes, Thomas. 1968. *Leviathan*. Ed. with an introduction by C.B. MacPherson. Harmondsworth: Penguin Books.

Hobbes, Thomas. 1989. *Metaphysical Writings*. Ed. by Mary Whiton Calkins. La Salle: Open Court.

Hobbes, Thomas. 1994. *Human Nature or the Fundamental Elements of Policy* and *De Corpore Politico: Or the Elements of Law*. Bristol: Thoemmes Press.

Huguet, Edmond. ed. 1977/1863–1948. *Dictionnaire de la langue française du seizième siècle*. Paris: Didier.

Hume, David. 1978. *A Treatise of Human Nature*. 2nd edition with text revised and notes by P.H. Nidditch. Oxford: Clarendon Press.

Husserl, Edmund. 1984. *Einleitung in die Logik und Erkenntnistheorie. Vorlesungen 1906/7*. Herausgegeben von Ullrich Melle. Husserliana 24. Dordrecht: Martnus Nijhoff.

Husserl, Edmund. 1969. *Die Krisis der europäischen Wissenschaften und die transzendentalen Phanomenologie: Eine Einleitung in die phänomenologische Philosophie*. Husserliana Band 6. Herausgegeben von Walter Biemel. Haag: Martinus Nijhoff.

Jung, Gertrud. 1933. "ΣΥΝΕΙΔΗΣΙΣ, Conscientia, Bewusstsein." *Archiv für die gesamte Psychologie* 89 (3–4): 525–540.

Kähler, Martin. 1967/1878. *Das Gesissen. Ethische Untersuchung. Die Entwicklung seiner Namen und seines Begriffes. Erster, geschichtlicher Teil. Geschichtliche Untersuchung zur Lehre von der Begründung der sittlichen Erkenntnis. Erste Hälfte. Altertum und Neues Testament*. Darmstadt: Wissenschaftliche Buchgesellschaft.

Khan, Qamaruddin. 1965. "Ghazali and Descartes." Twelfth Session of the *Pakistan Philosophical Congress*, Lahore 1965. Part 2, 389–393.

Kranz, Walther. 1985. *Die Fragmente der Vorsakratiker*. Griechisch und Deutsch von Hermann Diels. 3 vols. Zürich/Hildesheim: Weidmann.

Kühn, C.G., ed. 2001/1821. *Claudii Galeni Opera Omnia*. 20 vols. Hildesheim: Georg Olms Verlag.

Kusch, Horst. 1953. *Festschrift Franz Dornseiff zum 65. Geburtstag*. Leipzig: Veb Bibliographisches Institut.

Leibniz, G.W. 1981. *New Essays on Human Understanding*. Trans. and ed. by Peter Remnant and Jonathan Bennett. Cambridge: Cambridge University Press.

Leibniz, Gottfried Wilhelm. 1962/1765. *Philosophische Schriften*. Herausgegeben von der Leibniz-Forschungsstelle der Universität Münster. Sechster Band. *Nouveaux Essais*. Berlin: Akademie-Verlag.

Lennon. 1985. "Veritas Filia Temporis: Hume on Time and Causation." *History of Philosophy Quarterly* 2 (3): 275–290.

Lindsey, James E. 1976. "The Subjectivist Principle and the Linguistic Turn Revisited." *Process Studies* 6 (2): 97–102.

Locke, John. 1959/1690. *An Essay Concerning Human Understanding*. Complete and unabridged. Collated and annotated by Alexander Campbell Fraser. 2 vols. New York: Dover Publications.

Locke, John 1963/1823. *The Works of John Locke*. A New Edition, corrected. In 10 vols. Vol. 4. Aalen: Scientia Verlag.

Long, A.A., and D.N. Sedley. 1987. *The Hellenistic Philosophers*. Vol. 1. Trans. of the principal sources with philosophical commentary. Cambridge: Cambridge University Press.

Malebranche, Nicholas. 1979. *Œuvres*. Édition établie par Genevière Rodis-Lewis avec la collaboration de Germain Malbreil. 2 vols. Paris: Gallimard.

Malebranche, Nicholas. 1997. *The Search after Truth*. Trans. and ed. by Thomas M. Lennon and Paul J. Olscamp, and *Elucidation of the Search after Truth*, trans. and ed. by Thomas M. Lennon, in 1 vol. Cambridge: Cambridge University Press.

Mantinband, James, trans. 1972. *On the Nature of the Universe (De Rerum Natura)*. New York, Fredrick Ungar.

Montaigne, Michel de, 1987. *An Apology for Raymond Sebond*. Trans. and ed. with an introduction and notes by M.A. Screech (London: Penguin Books).

Nietzsche, Friedrich. 1969. *Werke*. Herausgegeben von Karl Schlechte. 5 vols. Frankfurt am Main: Ullstein Materialien.

OED. 1989. *Oxford English Dictionary*. 2nd ed. Oxford: Oxford University Press.

Peirce, Charles Sanders. 1955. *Philosophical Writings of Peirce*. Ed. by Justus Buchler. New York: Dover Publications.

Philo of Alexandria (Philo Judea). 2001. *On the Creation of the Cosmos according to Moses*. Introduction, translation, and commentary by David T. Runia. Leiden: Brill.

Psuedo-Mayne. 1983/1728. *Über das Bewusstsein*. Übersetzt und mit Einleitung und Anmerkungen herausgegeben von Reinhard Brandt. English-Deutsch. Hamburg: Felix Meiner Verlag.

Putnam, Hilary. 1960. "Minds and Machines." In Putnam 1975, 362–386.

Putnam, Hilary. 1975. *Mind, Language and Reality. Philosophical Papers*. Vol. 2. Cambridge: Cambridge University Press.

Rey, Alain, ed. 1992. *Dictionnaire Historique de la Langue Française*. Paris: Robert.

Riffert, Franz G., and Michel Weber, eds. 2003. *Searching for New Contrasts: Whiteheadian Contributions to Contemporary Challenges in Neurophysiology, Psychology, Psychotherapy and the Philosophy of Mind*. Frankfurt am Main: Peter Lang.

Ritter, Jaochim, ed. 1971–. *Historisches Wörterbuch der Philosophie*. Unter Mitwirkung von mehr als 700 Fachgelehrten in Verbindung mit Günther Bien et al. Basel/Stuttgart : Schwabe and Co.

Ross, George MacDonald. 1988. "Hobbes and Descartes on the Relation between Language and Consciousness." *Synthese* 75, 217–229.

Rudberg, Gunnar. 1955. "Cicero und das Gewissen." Symbolae Osloenses 1:96–104.

Ryle, Gilbert. 1984/1949. *The Concept of Mind*. Chicago: University of Chicago Press.

Schmitt, C.B. 1983. "The Rediscovery of Ancient Skepticism in Modern Times." In Burnyeat 1983, 225–252.

Schönlein, Peter. 1965. *Sittliches Bewusstsein als Handlungsmotive bei römischen Historikern*. Inaugural-Dissertation der Philosophischen Fakultät der Friedrich-Alexander-Universität zu Erlangen-Nürnberg.

Schönlein, Peter. 1969. "Zur Entstehung eines Gewissensbegriffes bei Griechen und Römern." *Rheinisches Museum für Philologie*. Neue Folge 112 (4): 289–305.

Seel, Otto. 1953. "Zur Vorgeschichte des Gewissen-Begriffes im Altgriechischen Denken." In Kusch 1953, 290–319.

Sergeant, John. 1697. *Solid Philosophy Asserted, Against the Fancies of the Ideists: or, The Method to Science Farther Illustrated with Reflexions on Mr. Locke's Essay concerning Human Understanding*. London: Roger Clavil.

Siebeck, Hermann. 1882. "Der Begriff des Bewusstseyns in der alten Philosophie." *Zeitschrift für Philosophie und philosophische Kritik* 80:213–239.

Sorabji, Richard. 1983. *Time, Creation and the Continuum: Theories in Antiquity and the Early Middle Ages.* London: Duckworth.

Stelzenberger, Johannes. 1963. *Syneidesis, conscientia, Gewissen. Studie zum Bedeutungswandel eines moraltheologischen Begriffes.* Paderborn: Ferdanand Schöningh.

SVF. 1986. *Stoicorum Veterum Fragmenta.* Collegit Ioannes ab Arnim. 4 vols. in 2. New York: Irvington.

Tamny, Martin, 1980. "Boyle, Galileo, and Manifest Experience." *The College. The St. John's Review* 31 (2): 46–55.

TLL. 1906–1909. *Thesaurus Linguae Latinae.* Lipsiae in aedibus B.G. Teubneri.

Weber, Michel. 2003. "The Art of Epochal Change." In Riffert and Weber 2003, 243–267.

Weekes, Anderson. 2004. "Process Philosophy: *Via Idearum or Via Negativa?*" In *After Whitehead: Rescher on Process Metaphysics*, Michel Weber, ed., 222–266. Frankfurt/Lancaster: Ontos Verlag.

Weekes, Anderson. 2007. "Abstraction and Individuation in Whitehead and Wiehl: A Comparative Historical Approach." In *Subjectivity, Process, and Rationality*, Michel Weber, ed., 39–119. Frankfurt/Lancaster: Ontos Verlag.

Weinberg, Julius R. 1969/1948. *Nicolaus of Autrecourt. A Study in 14th Century Thought.* With a preface to the Greenwood reprint by the author. New York: Greenwood Press.

Weinberg, Julius R. 1977. *Ockham, Descartes, and Hume: Self-knowledge, Substance, and Causality.* Madison: University of Wisconsin Press.

Wilkes, Kathleen. 1988. "—, yìshìi, duh, um, and consciousness." In *Consciousness in Contemporary Science*, A.J. Marcel and E. Brisiach, eds., 16–41. Oxford: Clarendon Press.

Wolff, Christian. 1968/1732. *Gesammelte Werke.* Herausgegeben und bearbeitet von J. École, J.E. Hofmann, M. Thomann, and H.W. Arndt. Abteilung 2: Band 3, *Psychologia Empirica* (reproduction of 3rd ed., 1738). Hildesheim: Georg Olms Verlag.

Wolff, Christian. 1972/1734. *Gesammelte Werke.* Herausgegeben und bearbeitet von J. École, J.E. Hofmann, M. Thomann, and H.W. Arndt. Abteilung 2: Band 6, *Psychologia Rationalis* (reproduction of 3rd ed., 1740). Hildesheim: Georg Olms Verlag.

Wolff, Christian. 1976/1720. *Gesammelte Werke.* Herausgegeben und bearbeitet von J. École, J.E. Hofmann, M. Thomann, and H.W. Arndt. Abteilung 1: Band 4, *Vernünftige Gedancken von der Menschen Thun und Lassen, zu Beförderung ihrer Glückseeligkeit* (reproduction of 4th ed., 1733). Hildesheim: Georg Olms Verlag.

Wolff, Christian. 1983a/1730. *Gesammelte Werke.* Herausgegeben und bearbeitet von J. École, J.E. Hofmann, M. Thomann, and H.W. Arndt. Abteilung 2: Band 2, *Cogitationes Rationales de Viribus Intellectus Humani* (reproduction of 3rd ed., 1740). Hildesheim: Georg Olms Verlag.

Wolff, Christian. 1983b/1720. *Gesammelte Werke.* Herausgegeben und bearbeitet von J. École, J.E. Hofmann, M. Thomann, and H.W. Arndt. Abteilung 1: Band

1, *Vernüngtige Gedancken von GOTT, der Welt und der Seele des Menschen, auch allen Dingen überhaupt* (reproduction of 11th ed., 1751). Hildesheim: Georg Olms Verlag.

Zeman, Adam. 2002. *Consciousness: A User's Guide.* New Haven and London: Yale University Press.

Zucker, Friedrich. 1963/1928. "Syneidesis–Conscientia. Ein Versuch zur Geschichte des sittlichen Bewusstseins im griechischen un im griech-römischen Altertum." In Zucke, Friedrich, *Semantica, Rhetorica, Ethica,* 96–117. Berlin: Akademie-Verlag, 1963.

4

Whitehead's Unique Approach to the Topic of Consciousness

Anderson Weekes

Granting the reader a foretaste of his "cosmological scheme," Whitehead announces at the end of Part I of *Process and Reality* that

> one implicit assumption of the philosophical tradition is repudi-
> ated. The assumption is that the basic elements of experience are
> to be described in terms of one, or all, of the three ingredients,
> consciousness, thought, sense-perception. The last term is used in
> the sense of "conscious perception in the mode of presentational
> immediacy." (PR 36)

Just as sense perception here means conscious sense perception, thought means conscious thought.[1] Thought and sense perception name two of the three traditionally recognized parts of conscious mental activity: sensitive, intellective, and affective. Whitehead's list is significant for what it leaves out. By expressly repudiating the relevance of sense perception and thought, he implies that he is interested in the remaining type of mental activity, which is feeling. By repudiating the relevance of consciousness he implies that his focus will be feelings of a nonconscious variety.

Whitehead presents most of his philosophical ideas in the form of a critique of the modern philosophical tradition. In the main his critique presupposes an interpretation of the modern tradition that is not controversial. It is undeniable that modern philosophy was preoccupied with thought and sense perception, assumed that they were the fundamental modalities of consciousness, and usually assumed that consciousness exhausted mental activity. Whitehead, who proposed *Critique of Pure Feeling* as an alternate title for his own philosophical endeavor (PR 113), faults modern philosophy on all these counts.

Whitehead thinks that the overvaluation of consciousness is what generates many of the most famous problems of modern philosophy. According to Whitehead's analysis, consciousness by its very nature tends to obscure the reality of process. But many salient phenomena are process-dependent. Emphasizing consciousness therefore makes them impossible to understand. This includes such notorious philosophical vexations as time, causality, the reality of the external world, and finally consciousness itself.

Just as documenting the unhappy consequences of overvaluing consciousness is the main thrust of Whitehead's critique of modern philosophy, its devaluation and displacement are central to his own approach. So the first important thing to stress about Whitehead's theory of consciousness is that all in all it accords consciousness relatively little importance. This will come as a surprise to those who associate Whitehead's name with an implausible metaphysics of panpsychism that attributes consciousness to just about everything. It also makes a volume devoted to the exploration of consciousness from a Whiteheadian process perspective seem paradox. But Whitehead never suggested consciousness was unworthy of philosophical consideration—any more than he attributed it to everything—and some of his most fertile ideas emerge from his detailed analysis of consciousness and the highly specialized conditions under which something so sophisticated and comparatively rare could take its place in nature as the fruition of physical processes (PR 157–199, 219–280).

Understanding consciousness as the fruition of physical processes is a goal Whitehead shares with a great many contemporary researchers. Nevertheless, conventional wisdom finds little ground for comparison between Whitehead and mainstream research. What sets Whitehead apart can be summed up in terms of starting points and heuristic goals. In the common topic "emergence of consciousness from nature" mainstream research hopes to use what it knows about nature to learn something about consciousness, while Whitehead hopes to use what everyone knows about consciousness to learn something about nature. Because (for reasons discussed later in this chapter) the tendency for mainstream research is still to construe nature mechanistically, its order of proceeding indicates a similar interpretation of consciousness. In this way a naturalistic explanation of consciousness comes to be narrowly identified with a mechanistic explanation of consciousness. Algorithmic predictability assumes the role of a legitimate desideratum of psychology, to which Cognitive Science, like Behaviorism before it, is a tailored response. We wish to stress that the legitimacy of such a heuristic goal is not self-evident, but dependent on the legitimacy of the starting point it presupposes. In what follows we shall question the legitimacy of this starting point on the Whiteheadian grounds that *it overrates the epistemological value of consciousness*. Whitehead's starting point, by contrast, is not a particular representation of nature vouchsafed by consciousness, but rather what everyone implicitly knows that consciousness is by virtue of being conscious. The value of this self-understanding of ordinary consciousness is much debated and often denigrated as "folk psychology." By no coincidence Whitehead takes his start from these very features of conscious experience that a mechanistic explanation of consciousness rules out. From this starting point, the heuristic goal becomes an interpretation of nature that does not preclude the emergence and existence of consciousness as we actually know it, moment by moment, in ourselves. As Bergson's close psychological description of experience brought out, one of the things we implicitly know about consciousness is that it has an organic rather than aggregational or mechanical coherence. Whitehead takes this to be the critical clue. Accordingly, with embodied experience as its starting point and the thing to be ultimately explained, Whitehead's order of proceeding invites an organic interpretation of nature that makes it possible to understand how nonconscious nature could give rise to a consciousness that experiences itself as an organic unity.

In light of these observations it can be said that indirectly consciousness does acquire considerable importance for Whitehead. Because it offers a singularly important clue to the nature of the nature that produced it, it has exceptional heuristic value for metaphysics. This contrasts sharply with the unqualified methodological and epistemological importance consciousness enjoys in mainstream research, where it is assumed that consciousness will tell us what we want to know about nature—not indirectly, by an inference from what consciousness is to the nature that was able to produce it, but directly, by taking cognizance of what consciousness delivers up under well-designed experimental constraints as it objective content. To this disparity in their respective ways of valuing consciousness corresponds a disparity in their understandings of physical process. We will now examine these disparities in greater detail. We will examine first the default assumptions of the mainstream position, and then contrast Whitehead with the mainstream, noting first the respects in which consciousness for Whitehead is less important than for traditional approaches, and then the respects in which it becomes more important.

Conventional Wisdom and the Mystery of Consciousness

As Michael Katzko observes in his contribution to this volume, it is assumed in the mainstream—almost universally—that we know more or less what a physical process is, and this is the starting point taken for granted in the

naturalism of common sense and in the naturalism of science.[2] The mystery
is consciousness. So what makes consciousness mysterious? Some philosophers seem to have accustomed themselves to the idea that consciousness
is something inherently or necessarily mysterious,[3] but this just shows that
their metaphysical presuppositions are invisible to them, or that they take
their presuppositions dogmatically to be absolutes. It is not hard to find
examples of a very different perspective for which matter or physical process
seems mysterious, while consciousness sets the standard for what it's like to
be unproblematic, self-evident, always already understood. Certain schools
of medieval Buddhism come to mind, as well as the Phenomenology of
Edmund Husserl.

So what are the specific presuppositions that make consciousness
mysterious in mainstream consciousness studies? The leading presupposition
is one that has come to seem perfectly natural to the modern world—so
much so that even Husserl, one of its most principled dissenters, associates it with what he calls the "natural" attitude.[4] The assumption is that
the world or reality consists of physical processes or at least that it consists
"fundamentally" of physical processes, while what is not "fundamental" consists "ultimately" of physical processes. Attempting to specify the identity
conditions of a "physical process" can spark disagreements, as the history of
modern science shows. The initial Cartesian conditions, which allowed only
percussive interactions among noncompressible volumes, were progressively
relaxed to allow for mass and void, *vis viva*, action at a distance, and by the
mid-nineteenth century, energy and fields of force. Similarly, strictly deterministic constraints gave way to include probabilistic ones in the nineteenth
century. The relaxed criteria remained true to Descartes, however, in that
all the additional phenomena can be defined operationally in terms of the
two parameters of space and time; that is, in terms of the sort of extensive
quantities Descartes' metaphysics of nature found unproblematic. What
this implies is that information about the physical world, to be objectively
valid, must come in the form of measurements and that physical processes
can be represented as the transformation of one set of measurement values
into another. An explanation is a calculus that accurately represents such
transformations. In a familiar parlance, the initial measurement values are
the boundary conditions; the calculus is the covering law; and the derived
set of values is the explanandum. This particular specification of what counts
as a physical process (its "identity conditions") is a secondary presupposition
that, together with the first, makes consciousness mysterious.

It might seem more to the point in this context to say what this understanding of nature implies that a physical process is not. A physical process,
on this understanding, is not teleological. Consequently, an adequate model
of a physical process must be one that achieves its desired result without

presupposing any information about the result ahead of time. This is the reason processes of physical nature are usually described as "blind" and why they are thought to be ideally represented by a mechanically computable procedure. Because this understanding of physical process is felt so strongly to be natural and beyond question, it sets an implicit standard for what it means to understand something and thus cannot help but cast its shadow on efforts to understand consciousness. Consequently, the holistically purposive character of consciousness that appears to result from self-regulatory processes structuring personality, perception, and cognition becomes a target for reduction. Just as biology achieved recognition as a "harder" science when it succeeded in reducing the appearance of self-regulation (both in the species and in the individual) to deterministic mechanism, so psychology strives for a similar outcome. In the end, however, this seems to make consciousness more rather than less mysterious.

Consciousness becomes mysterious because it has phenomenological properties that seem *prima facie* impossible or incomprehensible in a world consisting of physical processes *so understood*. There do not seem to be any measurements that can make sense of such things as intentionality, reflexivity, the unity of consciousness, the qualitative feel of experience, or its being centered on a first-person perspective. Nevertheless, *given the stated presuppositions*, we can say what it would mean conceptually to understand consciousness as the fruition of physical processes (that is, naturalistically).

Understanding consciousness naturalistically under the stated presuppositions means eliminating its mystery by showing how specific physical processes under nothing more than quantitatively defined physical constraints are constitutive of consciousness. What is to be constituted are the familiar phenomenological properties of consciousness just listed (intentionality, reflexivity, unity, qualitativeness, first-person perspective), to which we could add such things as free will, valuation, perception, and recollection as specific forms of intentionality that appear to be ubiquitous features of consciousness.

Understanding how physical processes (so construed) could constitute these features of consciousness is the challenging mandate to which reductive materialism and functionalism are responses. We must note that reductive materialism and functionalism begin by weakening the mandate: they concede that measurements will never "make sense" of consciousness. But despite the phenomenological disparity between consciousness lived in the first person and the kind of explanation sought, they postulate an equivalence that would be necessary even if it cannot be transparent. But precisely because of the conceded phenomenological disparity it remains unclear how any set of physical process, whether defined materially or functionally, could constitute consciousness; that is, be identical with consciousness *in all possible worlds*. Even if we discover processes that are always or typically associated with consciousness, it seems impossible to understand why they could not just as well obtain without associated consciousness. Following David Chalmers, this is now usually referred to as the "hard problem" (Chalmers 1995).

The persistence of the hard problem explains the persistence of several permutations of explanatory approach that essentially redefine the mandate. Eliminative materialism holds that the mystery is an illusion that will vanish when we finally understand the identity of physical processes and consciousness. Ironically, the social constructionist agenda of post-structuralism, hermeneutic phenomenology, and the "strong program" in the sociology of knowledge agrees that the mystery would vanish if we understood the identity of physical processes and consciousness. Not entirely without justification we could call this project eliminative idealism.

We have identified two presuppositions that together make consciousness mysterious in mainstream thinking. It is entirely possible to agree with the first presupposition, the metaphysical principle that the world consists of physical processes, but to disagree with the second, the specification of what constitutes a physical process that says it is defined exclusively by a quantitative calculus. This is the position Whitehead takes. The fact that the purely quantitative interpretation of physical process makes consciousness impossible to understand naturalistically is, according to Whitehead, *prima facie* evidence that such an interpretation is wrong or at least incomplete.[5] Thus, the mystery for Whitehead is not what consciousness must be, assuming it is the product of a nature already understood, but what nature must be, assuming it can produce consciousness. The unknown in the equation is not consciousness with its familiar phenomenological properties, but the physical processes able to produce it. In short, it is not consciousness, but process that we must go out of our way to understand, especially the process by which consciousness itself comes to be. Already in SMW, Whitehead pointedly expresses this view, announcing the philosophical project that will occupy him for the next two decades:

> [A] thoroughgoing evolutionary philosophy is inconsistent with materialism. The aboriginal stuff, or material, from which a materialistic philosophy starts is incapable of evolution. This material is in itself the ultimate substance. Evolution, on the materialistic theory, is reduced to the role of being another word for the description of the changes of the external relations between portions of matter. There is nothing to evolve, because one set of external relations is as good as any other set of external relations. There can merely be change, purposeless and unprogressive. But the whole point of the modern doctrine is the evolution of the complex organism from antecedent states of less complex organ-

isms. The doctrine thus cries aloud for a conception of organism as fundamental for nature. It also requires an underlying activity—a substantial activity—expressing itself in individual embodiments, and evolving in achievements of organism. (SMW 107)

In this passage, Whitehead identifies two cardinal elements missing from materialism: the neglect of which he (in agreement with other evolutionary philosophers of the early twentieth century) believes makes a process such as evolutionary development impossible to understand: *internal relations* and *substantial activity*. By substantial activity he means an activity that is intrinsically active (or originative) rather than passively reactive. If we bear in mind Whitehead's conviction that our own experience as it is lived in the first person provides us with a paradigm of substantial activity, then we can capture the sweep of Whitehead's metaphysics in a short span. In brief, Whitehead's argument is this: from what everyone implicitly knows about consciousness (their own, that is), we can infer that nonconscious, even so-called "inanimate" nature must harbor some kind of substantial activity and be able to accumulate a plethora of internal relations if something like consciousness is ever to evolve from it (diachronically) or emerge from it (synchronically) moment by moment.[6] There can be no denying that Whitehead's mistrust of materialism sounds quaint. But we should bear in mind that materialism itself is a view that has, remarkably enough, now passed for "modern" for more than three hundred years.

This brings us to Whitehead's very different approach to a naturalistic explanation of consciousness and the unconventional respects in which he thinks consciousness is and is not cognitively valuable. Let's look at the different ways that consciousness is and is not important for Whitehead.

Two Ways Consciousness Is Unimportant for Whitehead: Metaphysical Derivativeness and Epistemological Barrenness

One aspect of the *unimportance* of consciousness is metaphysical and has to do with its rarity in nature and its highly derivative ontological status. To a certain extent this is just a corollary of the biological and the evolutionary accounts of *homo sapiens*, for both of which consciousness must count as a highly derivative end-stage of process and organization. As such, it is ingredient in a vanishingly small number of events in the spatio-temporal expanse of the universe and least fundamental in the order of things.

The other aspect of the unimportance of consciousness for Whitehead is epistemological and presents us with a distinctively Whiteheadian thesis. It has to do with the sort of evidence consciousness provides about the world and more specifically about nature. If consciousness itself is a fruition of nature, what can we say about it as a window on nature?

It is commonly assumed that this unique fruition of nature is the appropriate vantage—or perhaps the only possible vantage—from which to understand nature and the place of consciousness in it. This is an assumption Whitehead rejects, putting him at odds with any methodology that ascribes special or exclusive cognitive value to the deliverances of consciousness. Instead, Whitehead wants to recover what the organism knows about its world *without being conscious*. One will rightly ask: *if this is even possible, why do we need to be so roundabout?*

Is it possible for the organism to have unconscious knowledge of its environment? Certainly—it's even necessary. The survival of the individual, just like the survival of the species, requires ongoing alterations in the organism to compensate for alterations in the environment—alterations that would otherwise terminate its survival. These adjustments occur at multiple levels and constitute several distinguishable (but not independent) systems of compensation. These adjustments obviously "reflect" the environment. However, they are not just reactions and do not reflect the environment simply in the way an effect can be said to reflect its cause. They are facultative adjustments—changes in what the organism or species can endure. In a weak but meaningful sense they are *self*-adjustments (hence the term "autopoiesis" used by Schweiger et al. in their contribution below) in that they facilitate tolerance to highly specific changes in the environment *without being caused by them*: without being caused by them at all in the case of the survival of the species and without being caused by them *exclusively* in the case of the survival of the individual. Because of the element of self-regulation in the individual and the pseudo-self-regulation of the species in the process of natural selection, we are beyond a simple correlation of cause and effect—beyond Peirce's category of Secondness. Self-adjustment with an objective correlative gives us three terms and allows us, invoking Peirce's category of Thirdness, to speak, however minimally, of representation. *Stabilized patterns of compensation reflect the environment without simply being caused by it.* Thus, without "picturing" the environment, these patterns can be said, each in their own way, to constitute a "representation" of the environment that is in some sense "true."

The idea that the organism embodies a kind of knowledge of its environment independent of consciousness is therefore a basic truism of biology and evolutionary theory.[7] Adaptation, after all, is a kind of *adequatio ad rem*. Just as the surviving species adapts to its niche, the surviving organism adapts itself moment by moment to ambient influences from its immediate environment. This happens in internal processes of homeostasis that continually compensate for fluctuations in critical parameters of the organism's milieu, as well as in reflex movement and the many forms of arousal and affectivity that are elicited biochemically and do not depend on conscious mediation. In all of these self-adjustments the organism is representing its environment. Without this unconscious level of representation, incomparably rich in information about the organism's surroundings, conscious representation would never be possible. Exploiting the language used by Schweiger et al. in their contribution to this volume, we could say that, for Whitehead, the original locus of perception is not in consciousness, but in the organism's manifold forms of autopoiesis insofar as this autopoiesis is necessarily congruent with the environment in which it manages to survive.

Granting that the organism has unconscious knowledge of its environment, why do we, as philosophers, need to be so roundabout? We do, after all, have consciousness at our disposal. Can't we use it to gain direct knowledge of the world, and don't we need it even if we are to take the biological detour just described? The danger Whitehead sees lies in using consciousness uncritically—indeed, in assuming that acute consciousness is the essence of criticism and hence that the "uncritical use of consciousness" is an impossibility, a contradiction in terms. From a biological standpoint, one assumes that the evolution of consciousness is—perhaps necessarily—the evolution of the organism's faculty of experience from an inferior capacity to function cognitively to a superior capacity to function cognitively. If consciousness does not, for example, provide more information than unconscious experience, then it provides a representation of greater cognitive fidelity. (The reader still skeptical of unconscious experience may substitute "reflective experience" for "consciousness" and "unreflective experience" for "unconscious experience" in the preceding sentence.) Whitehead disagrees. He thinks the uniqueness of consciousness as a function of highly evolved higher-order processes does not increase, but rather diminishes its value as a perspective on the physical world from which it emerged. It emerged from this world very late in the course of evolution, and it continues to emerge from it, moment by moment, as an organic function of peculiar, possibly unparalleled complexity. It may seem self-evident that the more sophisticated fruition can explain or understand its less sophisticated antecedents without having to control for a difference of perspective, but this *assumes that the world as it is present to consciousness actually contains (or could actually contain) the sorts of things that are the antecedents of consciousness.* But what if the objects of consciousness are not an all-inclusive set of all sets? What if consciousness tends to picture the world in a way that leaves out the conditions of its own possibility? This is the conclusion to which Whitehead's analysis leads him.[8]

The world *as presented objectively to consciousness* does not according to Whitehead give clear and distinct evidence of any process. This point, mentioned at the beginning of this chapter, must now be explained. The problem arises from the unique way that consciousness objectifies time, which

makes it difficult for consciousness to verify its naive first impression of a
world full of process. Whitehead gives a sophisticated analysis (PR 61–70,
112–127, 160–162, 171–183, 311–333) of why consciousness tends to be
peculiarly invested in the present moment and disconnected from the past
and future (in a way, for example, that bodily affect and urge are not). The
result is that reflective consciousness arrives at a fragmented experience of
time that makes diachronic order, purposiveness, and cumulative development rationally impossible to understand, although it naturally feels them
all the time. Whitehead's analysis employs three distinctively Whiteheadian
ideas. The first has to do with the differently structured temporality of the
two primary modes of perception that Whitehead identifies: presentational
immediacy and causal efficacy. Presentational immediacy foregrounds an
isolated present, while causal efficacy involves influence from the past and
on the future. The second idea understands consciousness as the final modification of an initially nonconscious experience and hence as the retrospective illumination of the latter phases of its own genesis. Tying these theses
together, the third idea has to do with the genetic ordering of experience
according to which presentational immediacy succeeds causal efficacy and
consciousness succeeds presentational immediacy, making the temporality
of presentational immediacy the proximate substrate of consciousness. The
temporality of causal efficacy is therefore foundational, but it is a distal
foundation, present in clear consciousness only vestigially. It must remain
for reflective consciousness a kind of vague and archaic undercurrent. The
conclusion: to the extent that consciousness achieves a focus that is explicit,
clear, and distinct, it tends to experience the world in a discrete sequence
of "private presents."[9] To the extent that it experiences temporal continuity,
it tends to be diffuse, raw, and emotive.

Luckily, we can avoid the complications of Whitehead's analysis and
still reach the same conclusion by considering the problem in a simpler way.
What looks to consciousness like manifestations of process—we know all too
well from motion recording technology—can always be broken down into
a multiplicity of things of which motion is never a part. Thinking that this
is the very nature of all motion is what Bergson—in passages Whitehead
knew well—called the "cinematographical illusion."[10] The problem is that
consciousness has an inherent tendency to succumb to this illusion. In seeking
to document the reality of process, analytic consciousness verifies a succession
of discrete facts, each of which is contemporaneous with consciousness for
an instant, but none of which will involve any process of becoming. The
Nominalist account of motion offers a striking illustration of this tendency.
Long before there was cinema, the cinematographical illusion was embraced
as reality. It is, after all, the position famously propounded by William of
Ockham and his school (Ockham 1944; for partial translation see Grant

1974, 228–234). According to the fourteenth-century Nominalists, "motion" is a name, not a thing named. There is no such thing as motion, so the word motion is a kind of syncategorema, like the word "and" when I say "Joe and John are in the room." Obviously "and" does not name a thing, and so there are only two, not three things in the room. "Motion" is correctly attached to sets of things bearing certain relationships of similarity and being present at contiguous locations of space at immediately successive times.

How close this analysis comes to Whitehead's own view is astonishing—motion as the apparent difference between successive events—and yet it could not be more antithetical. For Ockham, *nothing happens* at the successive moments and places where the apparent moveable finds itself. What Aristotle called *kinēsis*—a process that takes time and comes to be only by anticipating a conclusion that is presupposed without being wholly predetermined—this vanishes entirely from Ockham's world. Whitehead, by contrast, restores it as the inner process by means of which each event (including the event called consciousness) creates coherence with the other events in the series.[11] Whitehead proposes that apparent continuity of becoming results in this way from a moment-by-moment becoming of continuity. Each present moment involves a "subjective" durational spread within which an actuality-in-the-making appropriates its predecessors before it bleeds into its successors. According to Whitehead, the evidence for such a "subjective" process, indeed, its paradigm example, is consciousness itself. At each moment of its existence, consciousness is in fact enacting just such a process of creative continuation (a) of its own immediately preceding experience and (b) of ambient events in or in close causal relation to the animal body. But this fact about itself, while always implicitly presupposed in its experience, does not enter into its objective representation of the world. On the contrary, consciousness is *naturally* preoccupied with the world as objectified in presentational immediacy.[12] Why? Because the role played by causal efficacy in defining the location of events in and around the animal body remains unthematic and obscure. The crucial utilitarian benefits of such localization appear therefore to derive from the precise demarcation of presentational immediacy alone. A consciousness invested in achieving ever-greater clarity vis-à-vis objects and environment thus tends to obscure from itself the reality of process.

In general, consciousness of perception in the mode of causal efficacy functions as the unobjectified background of consciousness in the mode of presentational immediacy. We mentioned above (chapter 1) one function of art (and possibly religion): to objectify and represent as if presentationally immediate what can really only be causally efficacious. We now note another characteristic function of aesthetic and religious experience: instead of a make-belief objectification of what cannot be objectified, they can also effect a foreground-background reversal and bring an unobjectified feeling of causal efficacy into conscious relief. This is the intention behind symbolist and surrealist artwork as well as the claim made by confessors of religious ecstasy. The point to emphasize is the seemingly extraordinary nature of such a reversal. Human consciousness functions "normally" when it is most utilitarian, and that means when consciousness of causal efficacy operates unobtrusively.

The result of this necessary unobtrusiveness is that consciousness is easily seduced into disregarding the philosophical value of its own example, and it attempts to understand the world in terms of a static morphology alien to its own fundamental manner of existing. In fact, Whitehead thinks it is alien to the very nature of existence:

> The nature of *any* type of existence can only be explained by reference to its implication in creative activity, essentially involving three factors: namely, data, process with its form relevant to these data, and issue into datum for further process—data, process, issue. The alternative is the reduction of the universe to a barren tautological absolute, with a dream of life and motion. (MT 93, emphasis added)

One version of the "barren tautological absolute" that Whitehead has in mind is, of course, Bradley's idealism. But another one, which the co-author of *Principia Mathematica* knew well, is mathematics. The passage continues: "The discovery of mathematics, like all discoveries, both advanced human understanding, and also produced novel modes of error. Its error was the introduction of the doctrine of form, devoid of life and motion" (MT 93). By "the doctrine of form, devoid of life and motion" Whitehead means what in PR he called "morphology." It designates any theory of order whose generative grammar is formal logical tautology—any theory of order, that is, that can be expressed in the language of *Principia Mathematica*. The morphological view of the world is necessarily static because there can be no real progress to something new in such a view, only repetition of something implicitly already given. Everything is assumed to be generable by algorithm and hence always already "computable."

This static view of the world prevents consciousness from recognizing that it is indeed a creative continuation of the antecedent word. Instead of valorizing its vague but inescapable sense of kinship and continuity with the world it appropriates, thematic self-consciousness polarizes itself against the world it experiences, depriving itself of its most relevant and accessible paradigm for understanding the world in terms of dynamic events. This is the circumstance in which we have to understand the argument well known to philosophers from Hume's *Treatise* that consciousness cannot find any necessary connections between events happening at different times. Together with the morphological suppression of process, the impossibility of reducing development and diachrony to tautology forces the counter-intuitive conclusion on consciousness that there are no real connections between events at all. This renders causation unintelligible:

> How can one event be the cause of another? [...] The mere notion of transferring a quality is entirely unintelligible. Suppose that two occurrences may be in fact detached so that one of them is comprehensible without reference to the other. Then all notion of causation between them, or of conditioning, becomes unintelligible. (MT 164)

Here we see from where the regularity theory of causation draws its unlikely stamina: because real becoming cannot be generated by the iteration of logical tautology, ordered diachrony becomes an explanatory problem. It follows that events seemingly ordered in time must, appearances to the contrary, not really be ordered at all. An interesting alternative explored by the "block universe" theory is that events seemingly ordered in time are indeed ordered, but—appearances to the contrary—are not really *in time*. In this way their appearance of ordering is preserved and validated under a strictly morphological interpretation. *Ordered but not in time* or *in time but not ordered*. By eliding process in its creative mediating role between data and issue, the philosophy of consciousness creates the famous dilemma of modern thought, which Whitehead sees as a false dilemma: that data and issue are either connected by formal logical tautology or not connected at all. Either way, their relationship is purely morphological. *Being a tautology* and *not being a tautology* are the two basic morphological relationships, whose presumed exhaustiveness (*tertium non datur*) and mutual exclusiveness (*contradictio non est*) makes process impossible (and impossible to understand if it does exist). These are the terms in which Whitehead diagnoses the cause of Hume's crisis:

> Hume's train of thought unwittingly emphasizes "process." His very scepticism is nothing but the discovery that there is something in the world which cannot be expressed in analytic propositions. [...] Hume proclaimed the bankruptcy of morphology. (PR 140)

The alternative Whitehead proposes is that data and issue are related by the logical ambiguity of a becoming that involves both continuity and novelty.[13] Such a process defies understanding in the sense of clear and distinct consciousness because it is not purely tautological: "When there is full understanding, any particular item belongs to what is already clear. Thus it is merely a repetition of the known. In that sense, there is tautology" (MT 57). It is only by valorizing the vague, dynamic undercurrent (or background or fringe) of experience that consciousness can begin to understand such things as causation, time, or the existence of consciousness in a physical universe.

The critical and distinctively Whiteheadian idea in this is that the actuality of present experience, taken in its full concreteness, reveals the temporal structure of all actuality (whether conscious or unconscious, organic or inorganic). The problem with consciousness is that it can never clearly represent to itself the very type of process that it actually instantiates. What disappears from the world as present to consciousness is therefore the world's actual (as opposed to cinematographically represented) becoming and the internal coherence that can be revealed only as an achievement of real becoming:

> Hume's polemic respecting causation is, in fact, one prolonged, convincing argument that pure presentational immediacy does not disclose any causal influence, either whereby one actual entity is constitutive of the percipient actual entity, or whereby one perceived actual entity is constitutive of another perceived actual entity. The conclusion is that in so far as concerns their disclosure by presentational immediacy, actual entities in the contemporary universe are causally independent. (PR 123)

The connectedness of things remains invisible to the clear and distinct consciousness of presentational immediacy, as does the possibility of real (i.e., internal) connectedness of consciousness to the world it is conscious of. In short, if reality is the world as revealed when it is the object of explicitly focused consciousness, then there is no real process. Consequently, consciousness must find itself irredeemably disconnected from its own world. In this case, consciousness does indeed become inherently mysterious and the mind-body problem impossible to solve.

The Defects of Methods Granting Epistemological Primacy to Consciousness

Whitehead's mistrust of consciousness as an epistemological tool puts him at odds with a number of intellectual disciplines that seem at first to have little in common. But what they have in common is the primacy they ascribe to consciousness. The methodological primacy of consciousness defines Continental Phenomenology, for example. Husserl's phenomenological reduction, like Merleau-Ponty's methodological suspension of the "constancy hypothesis," is an artifice meant to guarantee that nothing slips into the descriptive ontology that is merely assumed or taken for granted and not actually "given"—and given means given to consciousness (Husserl 1980, 48–57; Merleau-Ponty 1962, 3–63). The methodological (and sometimes ontological) primacy of consciousness is something Phenomenology shares with the great tradition of modern European philosophy. Whitehead often draws attention to the privileged role accorded to consciousness in modern philosophy.

The primacy of consciousness is also a postulate of Logical Positivism inasmuch as its basic observation (or "protocol") sentences were allowed to record nothing more than the present content of conscious experiences. Karl Popper was sufficiently clearheaded about this that he accused Positivism of "psychologism"—confusing objective truths about facts with subjective psychological states (such as private perceptual experiences or beliefs about private perceptual experiences or feelings of certainty) (Popper 1968, 93–111). Indeed, the best candidates for protocol sentences turned out to be things like (the oddly Hegelian sounding) "Here now red," although this sort of example was facetiously standing in for what was really at issue, namely, sentences such as "Pointer now at degree x"—in other words, measurement (Schlick 1934). This brings us to the other important methodology premised on the primacy of consciousness, which is measurement and quantitative analysis of all sorts.

Whitehead believes that the exact sciences, precisely because their mathematical interpretation of nature relies on measurement, are predicated on a dubious assumption. The assumption is that consciousness is the Philosopher's Stone that transmutes being into cognition of being. The epoch-making success of the exact sciences cannot be denied and should not be slighted. They have allowed us to predict and control the course of nature to an extent that still staggers the imagination. But this, too, is a datum for philosophical reflection, and to infer from their efficacy that they deserve the last word on metaphysics is a perilous leap. According to Whitehead the mathematically interpreted sciences of nature cannot have the last word on metaphysics because they rest on an aggregation of measurements each one of which is a snapshot of a piece of the world as depicted by consciousness, the result being the "cinematographical illusion" just discussed. The mathematical science of nature accepts this picture of the world uncritically, without questioning its hidden premises or addressing its troublesome consequences. It is now incumbent on us to prove what we have alleged in the previous part of this chapter: that such a picture of the world does indeed lead to incoherence in metaphysics and epistemology. We contend that it has at least two signal defects. It renders two things impossible to grasp: (1) the existence of consciousness within the world as interpreted scientifically (interpreted, that is, according to pure "morphology"), and (2) the possession of scientific knowledge by consciousness. We will see that because consciousness is a process, it cannot inhabit a world of pure structure, and because there is no way to construe the relation of consciousness to what it knows as purely "morphological" even the possession of morphological knowledge cannot be a morphological fact. We turn to the arguments.

Our starting point is Hume's conclusion: that there are no necessary connections between events happening at different times.[14] It follows that the values of measurements taken at different times must constitute an entirely contingent series in which no member implies any other. Logically they are wholly independent of one another. This is the thrust of Hume's argument. Descartes makes the same point when he claims that the moments of time are "really distinct"—that is, they are separated from one another by a distinctio realis. Whitehead in fact agrees with Hume and Descartes about this. But Hume in particular follows his argument to a different place than Whitehead. Hume and the philosophy of science influenced by him conclude that because consciousness cannot find them, necessary connections across time do not exist. Whitehead, on the other hand, thinks this is an artifact of the way consciousness samples the world.

The critical problem that casts doubt on the finality of the perspective offered by consciousness arises when we ask about a particular sequence of events, namely, the one commencing with the measurements and concluding with the interpretation of them by consciousness. When the measurements are being interpreted, obviously they are no longer being taken, but being remembered. If the relationship between the act of recollection and what is recollected is like the relationship assumed to exist among the values, that is, external, then there is no necessary connection between them. But if consciousness is externally related to its own past—that is, separated from it by a real distinction—then in no meaningful sense is the recollection about actually past events. For in that case either term in the relation could change arbitrarily or even cease to exist without entailing any change in the other. We conclude: an internal relation between the present and the past is the condition of possibility of the representation of the past, even when time itself is being represented (imagined?) in such a way as to make such a relation impossible. This is the first problem.

A second problem comes into play whenever the object of measurement is a process taking place over time.[15] In this case, it is strictly impossible for the measurements to take place at the same time. Hence, in addition to the temporality of the measuring we now have the temporality of the measured as well. In other words, the temporality of the measuring is no longer accidental, but essential. Consider the case where we are determining a trajectory. While it is impossible for the measurements to take place at the same time, we nevertheless must juxtapose the values in order to make our determination.

We must form a representation of the temporal series in which the values are simultaneous, while nevertheless preserving their order. This is what Bergson meant by the spatialization of time. It requires that we cast the values in the form of what McTaggart called an "A-series"—an order of earlier and later, but not of past, present, and future (what he called a "B-series"). The members of such a series have ordinality in a timeless present. One value *is* first; another *is* second; another *is* third—all "at the same time." Bergson was focused on the disastrous consequences to philosophy of spatially hypostasizing time, although he did not deny its great scientific utility. Here our question concerns the conditions of getting to such a useful construct in the first place. The fact is that timeless ordinality eliminates from the representation of the temporal series the very thing that makes it possible. Because the object is, by hypothesis, a temporal phenomenon, the process by which we arrive at our series of values necessarily involves as many distinct moments and hence *as many stages of synthesis* as there are values. This should be clear from the following considerations. Suppose at time t we establish that the pointer is at x. Then at time $t + 1$ we establish that the pointer is at y and at time $t + 2$ at z, and so on to $t + n$. In all there will be $1 + n$ values spread over $1 + n$ moments in which measurements were taken. Now it is true that at time $t + n + 1$ we have before us $1 + n$ values whose interpretation requires their synthesis. But this assumes that all the values are already available to us in simultaneous juxtaposition. This doesn't seem to be a problem as long as we "haven't forgotten them." But this is possible only because there have already been n acts of synthesis—one for each measurement subsequent to the first. For in order to arrive at our series we must know at time $t + 1$ that the pointer *was* at x at time t, and at time $t + 2$ that it *was* at x at time t and *was* at y at time $t + 1$, etc. But this, clearly, is a B-series, and what we have shown is that there is no way to generate the A-series without passing through a B-series. There is no way to get from the protocol sentence "the pointer is at x" established at time t to the recorded protocol asserted at time $t + 1$ "the pointer *was* at x at time t" unless the time sequence t, $t + 1$, $t + 2$, $t + n$, $t + n + 1$ is a B-series. The B-series is a condition of the possibility of representing a chronology as an A-series.

Both these problems drive us to the same conclusion. Consciousness *enacts* time as a B-series in which it is internally related to past events, even if it likes to *represent* time as a quasi-spatial A-series; that is, in a way that is incompatible with the very existence of consciousness. Consciousness therefore finds that it cannot inhabit, cannot belong to or be part of, the world it represents to itself. This is not just the genesis of the mind-body problem, but also of the problem of idealism and the "external world." In this way we can say that the epistemological hypervaluation of consciousness (which Descartes and his posterity offered as a cure for the problem of subjectivity) generates the classical problems of modern philosophy. We turn now to the ways in which consciousness *does* assume philosophical importance for Whitehead.

The Heuristic Importance of Consciousness as a Metaphysical Clue

As noted above, the unimportance of consciousness must be strongly qualified insofar as consciousness offers a singularly important clue to the nature that is able to evolve it and sustain it organically: preconscious processes must be of such a kind that consciousness can evolve and emerge from them. Thus, despite its rarity and derivativeness, it has exceptional heuristic value for a metaphysics of nature. Darwin's own theory of evolution employed this sort of heuristic strategy. When, for example, he used the distribution of phenotypes to draw inferences about their origins he was viewing end-points as clues to genesis. Of course, Whitehead's argument differs from Darwin's in a very fundamental respect. Whitehead's argument is not empirical, but transcendental in the sense defined by Kant: arguing from the fact of something to the conditions of its possibility. But it also differs in a striking way from Kant's classic use of this form of argument. Kant sought the conditions under which nature could appear to and be known by consciousness. Whitehead seeks the conditions under which consciousness could evolve and emerge from nature. One consequence of this inversion is the epistemological devaluation of consciousness just discussed. The phenomenology of the objects of consciousness is the starting point of Kant's transcendental argument. The world as it appears is described, and the question is then raised: what are the subjective conditions of such a world appearing to consciousness? Like Descartes, Kant wants to know the specific conditions under which the phenomenology of the objects of consciousness can be taken as evidence of the nature of the things experienced and, more important to philosophy, why and how such a reliance of knowledge on appearance is possible. For Whitehead, however, the phenomenology of consciousness is much less important as evidence of the nature of *things experienced*, whose peculiar knowability would then call out for explanation, than as evidence of the nature of the *thing experiencing*, whose possibility as a fruition of nature is what demands explanation. Kant's epistemological orientation drove him in the opposite direction—to the conclusion that consciousness could not possibly be the fruition of natural processes. On the contrary, nature had to be understood as the fruition of conscious and unconscious mental processes if its knowability was a condition of its possibility.

We find as a result of this shift in orientation that the phenomenology of consciousness, while epistemologically less important for Whitehead than for more mainstream thinkers, is oftentimes metaphysically more important. The reason is that many philosophers think that consciousness does or at least under optimal circumstances can deliver a representation of the world "as it really is." Rather than experience a reality cofabricated by consciousness, consciousness, they believe, finds a prefabricated one.[16] This gives consciousness enormous epistemological value. It is the "mirror of nature" rather than a participant in its creation. But this approach generates the paradox whose diagnosis remains one of the singular achievements of Whitehead's philosophical activity: as elucidated above, the world as it is disclosed to consciousness has no place for and is even incompatible with anything having the peculiar phenomenological properties of consciousness. To solve this problem, not a few philosophers are willing to explain consciousness in a way that "eliminates" its problematic phenomenological properties so that its ontological membership in the sort of world consciousness pictures becomes unproblematic. For these thinkers, then, the phenomenology of consciousness is epistemologically valid and therefore metaphysically suspect. Whitehead, on the other hand, insists that however rare and unusual, however unimportant in the larger scheme of things consciousness may be, it nevertheless exists and has the phenomenological properties it has, and whatever else the world of preconscious nature may or may not be, it must be the sort of thing that can, at least sometimes, produce something with the familiar phenomenological properties of consciousness. For Whitehead the phenomenology of consciousness is metaphysically valid and therefore epistemologically suspect.

We can see how a debate on this topic would reach a stalemate. Both sides take the phenomenology of consciousness at face value. The more mainstream and traditional view tends to take the phenomenology of consciousness at face value objectively—insofar as it manifests the natural world it supposedly represents. Here, what the world looks like takes precedence. We don't see or experience inanimate things as having an interior or subjective life, so they don't have one. If this ends up making the existence of such an interior life hard to explain in our own case, then maybe we don't really have one either. Whitehead, on the other hand, takes the phenomenology of consciousness at face value subjectively—insofar as it reveals the nature of a peculiar type of entity within the world, the entity that is conscious. Assuming that this entity arose in and from processes in this world that are themselves not yet consciousness, Whitehead believes he can make a legitimate transcendental genetic inference.[17] This sounds of course like the "dormative power" of opium: to say that preconscious processes must harbor—somehow proleptically—whatever capacities are necessary to produce and sustain consciousness is to say that consciousness is produced by matter's innate ability to produce consciousness. Even Plato, who first used this kind of argument (transcendental argument) noted—in passages well know to Whitehead—that it employs a "bastard reasoning" (*Timaeus* 52b1–3; see AI 122, 134–135, 150, 187–188, 275). To critics, Whitehead's project looks like an attempt to vindicate a folk-psychological understanding of consciousness by retrofitting matter with its canonical hallmarks. They object that Whitehead, in order to make subjective properties of the phenomenology of consciousness possible in the context of a naturalistic metaphysics, was forced to undertake deep revisions in the usual view of physical nature and to attribute to elementary physical constituents what any good Cartesian would consider "occult" qualities, which, moreover, seem to be fully corroborated only by the peculiar first-person evidence they were designed to explain in the first place. There is no denying that these considerations militate strongly against the plausibility of Whitehead's project. It is nevertheless instructive to see why Whitehead did not demur—and that the prescience of his rationale has been to some extent vindicated by recent turns in the debate about consciousness. For, as noted above, it seems that in order to avoid attributing previously unsuspected properties to preconscious nature we must deny that these or similar properties are truly attested even in the case of our own consciousness. Whitehead's explanation seems to add something to our ontology, while his critics subtract something their theory can't explain. It is hard to say which option is more brash. Whitehead's temerity is at least partly mitigated because he is operating with a redefinition of subjectivity that has almost nothing in common with the consciousness-centered subjectivity of modern philosophy. As we will elaborate below, the subjectivity Whitehead attributes to nature is so attenuated that it implies only modest revision in our ontology, while eliminating a number of onerous problems.

Whitehead's diagnosis of the mind-body problem as a symptom of the overvaluation of consciousness allows us to look at the usual array of attempted solutions in a new light. There are those who are unwilling to relinquish either the putative epistemological or the putative metaphysical value of consciousness, and in order to reconcile the resulting conflict are forced to a position of dualism: the world is inhabited both by the sort of thing disclosed as the object of consciousness and the sort of thing disclosed as the subject of consciousness. How they can be related then becomes the great metaphysical "world-knot." Then there are those, dissatisfied with the incoherence of dualism, who seek monistic solutions. This is the point at which Whitehead's analysis bears unexpected fruit. Materialism and idealism, usually seen as the two possible monistic alternatives, emerge from this schematic as being more alike than different. They are both predicated on a commitment to the epistemological importance of consciousness. Materialism is willing to jettison the metaphysical importance of consciousness in order to preserve its epistemological importance: because the world is assumed to be essentially as it is for consciousness, consciousness, which can have no real place in this world, must be somehow unreal. But idealism starts with the same commitment. Because the world is essentially as it is for consciousness and has no place for consciousness, it concludes that the world must somehow be unreal (thus Kant: the world is "transcendentally ideal"). Idealism is a nondualistic attempt to preserve both the epistemological and the metaphysical importance of consciousness by redefining reality as a special kind of ideality. Insofar as they are all committed to the epistemological importance of consciousness, dualism, idealism, and materialism are variations on a theme and do not represent radical alternatives. Whitehead, by contrast, proposes that we preserve the (heuristic) metaphysical importance of consciousness by relinquishing its presumed epistemological importance. What this means in particular is that we stop taking for granted the modernist concept of nature and reopen discussion of what constitutes a physical process.[18] Vague feelings and organic events at the fringes of consciousness (such as visceral innervations) may tell us more about what a physical process is than the differential calculus: the former discloses the operative temporality that the latter conceals under a static representation. If we want to know what nature is like "in itself" we should pay much less attention to its clear and distinct representation in consciousness and much more attention to its instantiation in the vague and emotional viscerality that consciousness likes to ignore. This explains Whitehead's otherwise strange sounding claim that the key to understanding the physical concept of energy is the psychological experience of emotional affect and that an adequate cosmology must commence with this psychological insight into physics (MT 168).

This brings us back to something we must not lose sight of. The "metaphysical" importance of consciousness is not absolute, but heuristic and depends on its being a clue to something much more important and fundamental. "Consciousness studies from a Whiteheadian process perspective" must indeed be committed to a certain self-effacement. As the following chapters will show again and again, the best way to begin talking about consciousness is—to change the subject! To understand consciousness, we must first understand subjectivity and understand that consciousness and subjectivity are not the same thing.

Whitehead's Nonconscious Subjectivity, Renaissance Animism, and Cartesian Mechanicism

Contemporary consciousness studies tend to share with the modern tradition a sense that consciousness is something experientially primitive. Its feel—what it's like to be conscious—is absolute, unlike anything else, phenomenologically basic. What this view shares with the early modern tradition is the identifica-tion of consciousness and subjectivity. Whitehead, on the other hand, wants to distinguish consciousness and subjectivity. Consciousness is a specific kind of subjectivity—a refinement always belonging to a richer subjectivity that is necessarily much more than just conscious. Conscious experience is only a sliver of the experience any subject enjoys.

What is such nonconscious subjectivity supposed to be like? According to Whitehead it is an unconscious experience of feelings—an unreflective experience subject to the content of feelings but not to the reflective disclosure that it is having them or that they are of such and such a description. Even apart from Whitehead's speculations we have the means to understand such a notion and appreciate its importance. That our feelings about the world and that our being affected by it far outstrip the content of what we are at any time consciously aware of are things we all understand intuitively, but often forget when we begin to do philosophy. Nevertheless, we *can* find the philosophical concepts needed to understand this important phenomenon without having to resort to Whitehead's complicated schematics. In discussing the nature of intentionality, the nineteenth-century philosopher who revived interest in this Scholastic concept, Franz Brentano, raised an important ques-tion (Brentano 1973, 1:141–194, bk. 2, ch. 2). Is every intentional act (*ein Bewusstsein von etwas*—"a consciousness of something") itself the object of an intentional act (*etwas Bewusstes*—"something conscious"), or can there be an intentional act that is not itself the object of an intentional act (*gibt es unbewusstes Bewusstsein*—"is there unconscious consciousness")?[19] Although it led to dizzying complications in his theory, Brentano's answer was *no*: we can never experience something or have it "in mind" without being aware that we are experiencing it or have it in mind. The mind has no blind spots. It is wholly self-conscious, through and through. Its self-disclosure is ple-nary, involuntary, and instantaneous. Every act of mind targeting an object is therefore itself always already the object of a disclosive act of mind. Not all his auditors were convinced, however, and among them was a student named Sigmund Freud, who went on to develop the psychoanalytic theory of the Unconscious nowadays familiar to everyone (Merlan 1945 and 1949, Barclay 1964, Bergo 2004, 340–341). What Freud calls the Unconscious is an "unconscious consciousness" in the very sense that Brentano, in order to deny its existence, defined and conceptualized.[20] But Freud also rebelled against Brentano's overly cognitive theory of mind. His Unconscious is therefore less an *unconscious consciousness* than an *unconscious subjectivity*: it is subject primarily to nonconscious feelings. More recently, work in experimental psychology has found even greater latitude for the idea non-conscious experience. It turns out that the greatest part of thought and sense perception—the two bastions of the classical focus on consciousness—takes place unconsciously as well.[21]

These discoveries create a wide opening for Whiteheadian analysis and even vindicate to some extent Whitehead's "pansubjectivism" (or "panmentalism" or "panexperientialism").

When Whiteheadians speaks of panexperientialism, what they have in mind is not a universality of consciousness, but of nonconscious subjectivity. Whatever good reason there may be for denying consciousness (in the sense of *bewusstes Bewusstsein*) to lower life forms, there seems to be no good reasons to deny unconscious feeling to anything with a nervous system. The distinction between consciousness and subjectivity thus liberates human beings from the burden of singularity and allows for a reintegration the cosmos. It may be difficult to see how other, especially lower, life forms can be conscious in the same way that we are, but it is not so difficult to see how they can be subjects of feeling and affect. It may be impossible to see how inorganic matter could be conscious, but—however difficult—it may not be impossible to see it as an aggregation of elements individuated by an extremely rudimentary form of unconscious subjectivity.

The distinction between consciousness and subjectivity also allows Whitehead to overcome one of the built-in limitations of the absolute view of consciousness, namely, the notorious difficulty of deriving it from anything that is not already conscious. It seems impossible to understand how intentionality, the unity and qualitative feel of experience, or its being centered on a first-person perspective could be derived from or built up out of elements or factors that—just because they are taken from the objective content of a third-person perspective—lack these properties. For this reason it may indeed be impossible to show how subjectivity could result (evolve or emerge) from nonsubjectivity. But it need not be impossible to see how consciousness could result from a nonconscious subjectivity that already possesses these fundamentals.

The provocative—not to say scandalous—proposal of Whitehead's metaphysics is that physical process at its most elementary level is a faint wisp of affective experience "enjoyed" by an extremely rudimentary nonconscious subjectivity. It must be conceded that this is a view considered by many to be self-evidently absurd—which brings us back to the question of "self-evidence" and its latent assumptions. We raised the question why consciousness seems mysterious to modern scientific thought, and the answer had to do with the self-evidence and naturalness of certain essentially Cartesian assumptions about nature and physical process. However, we did not ask why this Cartesian viewpoint itself seems self-evident. We now pose this question.

In the global history of human experience, the Cartesian view of nature is clearly the odd man out. The anthropological evidence tells us that only a small minority of human beings have found such a view "self-evident," so "self-evident" seems to be the wrong concept. Perhaps it's right, but given the anthropological evidence, "self-evident" would be question-begging. This assessment may be unwelcome since it questions the prerogatives of modern European civilization, or at least its current scientific establishment,[22] and imposes a responsibility on the proponents of the Cartesian view to show why it's right. The argument advanced by Descartes that still seems to play an unacknowledged role in both philosophical and everyday attitudes is that it's right because it's self-evident (primitive anthropology notwithstanding). The presumption seems to be that no argument is necessary. We can see here one of those archetypal controversies that punctuate the history of thought. Descartes was explicitly rejecting the rich Renaissance concept of nature for which even supposedly inanimate matter was thought to have a kind of inner life and thus to possess some degree of reactive sensitivity to its environment. All things are involved in a dramatic interplay of vital forces whose mutual expression and interference is the course of nature as we know it. In the book that marks his turn from a philosophy of nature to metaphysics, *Science and the Modern World*, Whitehead quotes from Bacon a passage typical of this Renaissance view (SMW 41–42). He makes it clear that he thinks it is time for modern science to renege on the Cartesian repudiation of this view. Before we know what to make of this, we must continue our dialogue with Descartes in order to come to terms with the novelty of his view and why it has come to enjoy the presumption of self-evidence.

Descartes' idea was that nature is precisely that sort of thing that can be understood entirely—without any mystery or unexplained residue and thus leaving no excuse for uncertainty. Nature is defined by its difference from mind in this respect. The problem of subjectivity discussed in the previous chapter is therefore a problem of mind, not a problem of nature. In terms of ontological classification what this meant *in practice* was that everything uncertain, mysterious, or somehow opaque or otherwise inscrutable to cognition—like appearance—was simply shifted over to the region of mind. Besides appearances ("secondary qualities"), causality poses an interesting example of this kind of convenient reassignment.

For modern thought causality has always been the great stumbling block, and its response has usually been the premeditated one dictated by its overall agenda: *Anything that is not intellectually transparent is an artifact of subjectivity. Causality is not intellectually transparent, therefore it is an artifact of subjectivity.* Hume's relegation of causality to the mind as an expectation based on habitual association can thus be seen as an inevitable consequence of the Cartesian view of nature. Many philosophers have sought to make their peace with this consequence. Comte, Mach, and Russell all thought causation was a relic of animist and metaphysical thought that had no place in a positive science of nature (Comte 1988, 9; Mach 1985, 69–83; Russell 1957, 174–201). Russell argued that it had rightly been superseded by the entirely mathematical notion of the function. One thing is certain. A world without agency has no place for human beings. It is very significant indeed that the idea of an actionless universe, describable mathematically and containing no agency, received unexpected support from interpretations of Relativity Theory that see the universe as a timeless block of mathematical structure. The lesson to draw from this development is harsh. It suggests that to preserve the Cartesian thesis of the absolute objective intelligibility of nature not just causal agency, but time itself might need to be reassigned to the domain of the mind's subjectivity as a sort of false appearance.

Why is a view with so many onerous consequences perceived as self-evident—unless perhaps it is? In the Cartesian definition, nature is the definiendum, and self-evidence features in the definiens. We must not confuse self-evidence as a putative *definiens* with self-evidence *of the definition*. Is the definition of nature as that region of reality that can be understood with self-evidence itself self-evident? Certainly not if it is wrong, but notice the peculiar logical consequence of using self-evidence in the definiens. If the definition *is* right, then it would *have to be* self-evident (and not just true "assertorically"). Thus, to the extent that the definition seems to be right, it will seem to be self-evident. To the extent that processes of nature can be explained with apparent self-evidence, it will seem that the Cartesian definition of nature itself is not just true, but self-evident. However, once we proceed to embrace the definition as self-evident, its truth ceases to be provisional. We then feel entitled to reject whatever cannot be explained with self-evidence as outside the realm of nature, making the Cartesian view of nature self-fulfilling. Now what does it mean for something to be capable of being understood with self-evidence except that it can be explained mathematically? The extraordinary success of mathematics in explaining natural processes has inured us to the idea that nature can be understood with self-evidence and lent credence to the Cartesian idea that self-evident intelligibility defines what it means to be natural. Whitehead, of course, thinks that what we are really dealing with in this case is not nature, but an abstraction.

To sum up: According to the Cartesian definition, nature is that region of real being capable of being explained mathematically through and through, and with mathematical certainty. In light of the overwhelming achievements of the mathematical science of nature, the Cartesian view of nature seems right and therefore (because of the peculiarity of its definiens) self-evident. But the Cartesian doctrine of nature is found to be unexceptionable only because anything refractory to mathematical analysis is seen not as a counter-example to the doctrine, but—by definition—as an artifact of subjectivity.

There are two fundamental problems with the Cartesian view. We have already dwelt at some length on the first of these problems: how the mathematical ontology of nature creates the mind-body problem and makes

(a) the existence of consciousness and (b) the possibility of something like a science of nature impossible to understand. (The science of nature fails to notice this incoherence because it is concerned with nature, not with its own possibility as a science.) The first problem, then, is that the Cartesian idea of *subjectivity* is incoherent. Specifically, Cartesian subjectivity presupposes a kind of temporality that its own manner of representing the world leads it to deny. But the second problem is that the Cartesian idea of *objectivity* is *also* incoherent. It implies what Thomas Nagel calls the view from nowhere—a description of the world that presupposes no standpoint and is somehow free of all perspective.[23] Accordingly, it seems to imply that scientific descriptions can and ultimately should dispense with all indexical words—what Husserl called "essentially occasional expressions" (Husserl 1984, I 85–92) and Analytic philosophy calls "token reflexive terms" (Rorty 1989, 154, n. 4). The task of science would then be to explain the content of acquaintance (in Russell's sense) through knowledge by description that presupposes no acquaintance at all (Weekes 2007, 69–74). In the course of the last century philosophers have become more comfortable with the realization that such a description is impossible and the ideal absurd (Weekes 2007, 74–78). The question is whether we shall continue to blame the problem on the inadequacies of consciousness or see it as a necessary feature of concreteness and temporal- ity—an ontological fact built in to the texture of the world.

These two problems are closely related, of course. If the world as it really is "in itself" contains no perspective, no subjectivity, no token reflexiv- ity, then consciousness, which depends on all these things, cannot be part of the world it knows (first problem). By the same token, if these hallmarks of consciousness are completely alien to the world, then knowing the world "as it really is" would have to mean transcending subjectivity and perspec- tive, and achieving a cognition that presupposes no token reflexivity (second problem).[24] It's not at all clear what would satisfy such a requirement, unless it's the *magisteria* of concepts like Newton's absolute space, which, as God's sensorium, somehow comprehends all things without occupying any standpoint within space, or Augustine's eternal Word, which comprehends all time in its ordered sequence (i.e., as an A-series), without having any standpoint in time. It is difficult, if not impossible to wrap one's head around these extreme metaphysical concepts of objectivity. And yet, substituting positive science for metaphysics in an attempt to avoid metaphysics altogether fails, for science so conceived presupposes nothing less than the validity of such extreme metaphysical concepts. Simply removing the theological descriptors does not transform these mysteries into concepts of "hard-nosed common sense." Comparatively speaking, Whitehead's proposal may not after all be so incredible. As a remedy to both problems (the incoherence of the Car- tesian concept of subjectivity and the incoherence of the Cartesian concept of objectivity), Whitehead proposes to rehabilitate a Renaissance concept of nature, albeit in a highly attenuated form. Just how attenuated it is can be better appreciated if we introduce the language of intensionality and extensionality, and reformulate some of our contrasts and alternatives in terms of these logical concepts.

Descartes' dualism postulates that an adequate ontology of the sort of thing that thinks must employ in part an intensional language, but that an adequate ontology of the sort of thing that is extended in space must employ an extensional language and *only* an extensional language. Descartes understood that referential opacity is a function of intensional abstraction[25] and that to be at least in part intensionally abstract is constitutive of experience. That's why he needed a rigorous procedure to determine when it would be licit to quantify over objects of belief. A complete description of a mind requires statements about what that mind is thinking about, but whether those things exist will be *prima facie* uncertain. However, a complete description of a body (as opposed to a description of someone's beliefs about a body), should involve nothing that cannot be *prima facie* certain. Opacity in the sense understood here becomes a distinctive and even defining feature of mind because its absence becomes a distinctive and defining feature of bodies.

The Cartesian concept of nature is therefore committed at the deepest level to the modern idea of absolute objectivity. Nature is a domain that can in principle be described exhaustively in an entirely extensional language, with complete determinacy and certainty. Our science of nature is successful to the extent that it approximates to this ideal. One major problem with this view is the one that we have so far focused on in this chapter: that once intensional abstraction has been excised from the "objective" description of the world, it is impossible to put it back in. This explains Whitehead's unconventional proposal, which is simply that some degree of intensional abstraction is constitutive of everything from the outset. "To be" means, first and foremost, to be a subject of experience so that each actual entity is a unique intensional abstraction of the world. At its most rudimentary level, this intensional abstraction is simply "what it's like to be a such and such." Whitehead's thesis is that *to be* in its primary meaning is always in part to experience *what it's like to be*, and *what it's like to be* is always *what it's like to be in (to experience) such and such a world*.

We qualify this as the "primary" meaning of being because there is also a secondary meaning, which is not to be the *subject* of experience, but to be the object of experience. This latter constitutes a meaning derivative from rather than coordinate with the former because the object in all cases is simply a subject that has terminated its process of becoming (which is its "experience"). Whitehead thinks that Zeno's paradox of the arrow proves that all becoming must be terminal and therefore happen in finitely achieved episodes. Thus, the being that is the actuality of becoming always issues in a being that becoming has finally become. Whitehead calls the former the subject, the latter the superject of experience. It is only the superject that is available to become the object of another subject's experience.

Besides the central claim that *to be* in the primary sense involves a feeling of *what it's like to be*, there are three unusual contentions that need to be stressed here: (1) that *what it's like to be such-and-such* is an intentional state, (2) that it has a kind of rudimentary truth-value, and (3) that it is intensionally abstract (or referentially opaque). Let's take the famous example of "what it's like to be a bat." After some initial terminology, the Whiteheadian analysis will be straightforward. The ultimate constituents of all things, which Whitehead calls "actual entities" or "actual occasions," are Planck-scale units of nature—brief, microscopic events organized into societies of events and influenced by the societies into which they are organized. A bat is such a society, organized in such a way that a more or less stable structure endures over time. *All* occasions are, in the most rudimentary sense, occasions of experience, but some occasions, because they benefit from the massive organization of the "social order" to which they belong, enjoy a richer and more intense experience of their environment. This analysis makes it fairly easy to explicate what it means for it to be *like something* to be a bat.[26] Something is a bat, and in order for it to be like something to be this bat, that something must experience being this bat. This may look like a vicious circle: if "to be" depends on "what it's like to be," then we cannot turn around and explain "what it's like to be" by reference to "to be." But here is where the two distinct senses of being in Whitehead prove their usefulness. Something is a bat "superjectively," and a novel occasion feels what it's like subjectively to inherit the order preserved in this objective bat-environment. So being in its primary sense involves a feeling of what it's like to be something in the secondary sense. (From this we can see that the primary sense depends on the secondary sense as much as the secondary sense depends on the primary one, even though the two meanings are not metaphysically coordinate.) So for Whitehead, to experience being a bat will simply mean that one or more occasions within the bat's central nervous system are feeling their immediate environment, which, because it happens to be a bat-body, means feeling what it's like to be a bat. What it's like to be a bat is not, therefore, logically different from what it's like to inhabit the wider world. It involves a feeling that the more or less proximate environment is of a certain quality, which is as much an intentional attitude as a belief state. Furthermore, there is a rudimentary kind of truth-value here because the felt environment is also constituted by similar rudimentary feelings, and the feeling in the act of feeling either conforms to the tenor of the feelings being felt or it does not. The fact that more or less conformity is possible underscores the uniqueness of this kind of truth-value but does not militate against it. Finally, the experience of what it's like to feel such an environment lifts into relevance limited aspects of that environment such that extensionally equivalent substitutions will not preserve the truth-value of statements describing what is being felt.

The upshot, in other words, is that it is impossible to eliminate from what an entity is its perspective on the world, and it is impossible to reduce its perspective on the world completely to when and where it is in the world. This not only puts mind back into nature, it also liberates us from the false ideal of absolute objectivity. By and large the subjective uniqueness of an event in nature is marginal, so that quantitative analysis and extensional logic (rather than empathy) will still be the most informative cognitive approach. But its subjective uniqueness will never be completely null. There is always some residual "feel," which has an objective referent, but is nevertheless intensionally abstract—with the result that it would be false to say the feeler is influenced by the felt entity under all extensionally equivalent descriptions of that entity. Embedding this truism of social life into the working of nature is the goal of Whitehead's attenuated Renaissance "animism." It guarantees, on the one hand, a residual margin of privacy to the being of all things. But, on the other hand, the being that it's like something to be is always ultimately *being in the world* so that internal relatedness to the world is equally constitutive of what it means to be.

According to Whitehead's view, then, the basic meaning of physical process is experience. His concept of process has two critical components, each of which is denied by consciousness-centered philosophy. The one component is the internal relatedness of process to the antecedents from which it is emerging. This was discussed in chapter 3 in terms of the subject of experience being internally related to the world it experiences and in the present essay in terms of the processual nature of time as a moment-by-moment synthesis resulting in continuity. The other component is an element of intensional abstraction, by dint of which all process can be described as experience. Integrating these two components coherently is the goal Whitehead set for his metaphysics. By way of conclusion we can now state in briefest outline how Whitehead proposes to unite these two components.

Each actual occasion is a process that begins as an internal relation with the world from the perspective of its space-time locus.[27] At the moment of inception, it is already an internal relation, but not yet *for itself* an internal relation. Because it is really a multiplicity of relations, it cannot be for itself such a relation without integrating them into a single coherent set of relations with itself as the common relatum. Process is governed by an internal dynamic by means of which the actual occasion, emerging as such a common relatum, becomes unified and hence fully individuated. As this process continues, it becomes more "intensionally abstract." As its own reality becomes more concrete, its world-reference becomes more opaque, until at last it ceases to be internally related to the world at all. At this point it is fully individuated and concrete, but by the same token it is no longer a subject. It has become what Whitehead calls a "superject"—a thing, related only externally to the rest of the world of which it is now an inert piece.

In order to approach Whitehead's theory of consciousness with an open mind it is not necessary to embrace the details of his metaphysics. As the chapters that follow will show, it is enough if we understand their motivation. One important point to keep in mind is that consciousness for Whitehead is the last stage in the process described above, which allows us to understand why he describes philosophy as the self-correction by consciousness of its excess of subjectivity. Whitehead wants to recover in philosophical analysis a stage of experience in which nature is more accessible because the individuality of the subject less developed. In this respect, Whitehead's philosophy is indeed wholly modern. He wants to recover our lost place in the nature we have objectified. But he thinks we are more likely to succeed at this by enriching our concept of nature than by impoverishing our concept of consciousness.

Notes

1. We are deeply indebted to Michael Katzko's clarity of insight in the way we structure and present the following arguments. See his contribution to this volume.

2. But, as George W. Shields notes in his contribution, this attitude is not characteristic of physics at the frontiers of research. Rather, it characterizes the wider cultural perception of physics and of what constitutes the naturalism of natural science. Shields speaks therefore of a "cultural lag" between research in physics and its dissemination among scholars and scientists in other fields.

3. A recent example would be Colin McGinn (1991 and 1995).

4. Husserl 1980 [1913], 48–87; when Husserl later discovers the "life-world" as the appropriate object of Transcendental Phenomenology, he re-christens this presupposition "naturalistic," reserving "natural" for the everyday, prereflective attitude of "naive" consciousness vis-à-vis the life-world (Husserl 1969, 294–313).

5. In his contribution to this volume, Gregg Rosenberg gives fresh and compelling arguments why such an understanding of physical processes is fundamentally incomplete, and in his book, *A Place for Consciousness* (2004), he gives strong independent support for the Whiteheadian thesis that understanding consciousness is impossible without understanding the nonquantitative aspect of physical process.

6. The similarity here to the arguments of Cudworth refereed in the previous chapter cannot be missed and are not accidental. One inspiration for Whitehead is Bergson, who, like Cudworth, had learned something from Plotinus.

7. Schweiger et al. discuss this kind of "knowledge" in their contribution to this volume.

8. Gregg Rosenberg draws a similar conclusion; see his contribution to this volume and Rosenberg 2004.

9. We do not wish to convey the impression that presentational immediacy is simply the "bad guy" and causal efficacy the "underdog." The privacy of presentational immediacy and its discontinuity with the external world are aspects of the same autonomy that makes freedom and self-determination possible in high-grade occasions. But for the same reason that presentational immediacy reflects to some extent the individual occasion's creative self-determination (insofar as it creates for itself a privately enjoyed and causally insulated representation of the world) it is also bad at disclosing the causal continuity of things and especially its own hetero-determination by the world without.

10. The fourth chapter of Bergson's *Creative Evolution* (1907) is entitled "The Cinematographical Mechanism of Thought and the Mechanistic Illusion"; see Bergson 1944, 296–402/1907, 272–369/1959, 725–807.

11. Some caveats: *Kinēsis* in Aristotle is not to be identified with translation in space (locomotion). *Kinēsis* is the "actuality of the potential qua potential," and the analysis of this definition reveals that *kinēsis* is a unique kind of being-in-the-making, something inherently processual and incomplete, infected with potentiality, at the mercy of contingency, but necessarily teleological and structured by an order not rooted in phenomenal chronology. In all *these* respects it resembles concrescence. *Kinēsis*, according to Aristotle, is a kind of change (*metabolē*). Change is always the change from privation to possession (or vice versa) of a predicate in a given category of being. When the change is between contraries rather than contradictories, the change is a motion in the specific sense of *kinēsis*. By the process of elimination so dear to Aristotle, we find only three categories in which contrariety is possible, yielding three possible kinds of motion: with respect to quality (e.g., hot-cold), quantity (e.g., big-small), and place (e.g., up-down). Locomotion is therefore only one of three kinds of motion, along with alteration and diminution/growth. Actual entities for Whitehead do not, of course, move in space any more than they change their qualities or sizes. For Whitehead, these sorts of phenomenal changes are not changes at all, but the apparent differences between successive and otherwise similar occasions. In *these* respects *kinēsis* does *not* resemble concrescence. *Kinēsis* belongs to an enduring subject (the substance), envisioned as undergoing a series of adventures (liaisons with various predicates) one after another in time. It is this derogation of motion to an "accident" that separates Aristotle from Whitehead. Notice how this view of motion presupposes the Aristotelian distinction between essential and accidental predicates. We can say that something moved only because it is the same thing first in one and then in another state. It is the "same thing" only because its essential (identifying) properties have remained the same, sustaining its self-identity while it runs through a series of consecutive accidental states. For Whitehead, on the other hand, *all* predicates are essential, making change or motion in this sense impossible. The *same* subject could never have a *different* predicate. It would be *ipso facto* a different subject! In this respect, the similarity of *kinēsis* and concrescence must

be denied. Concresence represents a recurrence to the Aristotelian idea of *kinēsis* in its *internal* structure, not its external relations—the way it is impregnated with efficacious possibility and final causation in an internal dynamic so that the parts of the process presuppose the whole process. Concresence needs to be thought of as a kind of Aristotelian *kinēsis* with respect to the category of substance, with potentiality and actuality as ontological contraries between which process takes place.

12. This explains to some extent the development that so exercised Heidegger and the later Husserl: why the *natural* attitude of everyday existence tends to become the *naturalistic* attitude of modern science.

13. These issues are discussed by Weekes in his contribution to this volume (ch. 15).

14. The following argument, derived from Whitehead, figures importantly in three of the contributions to this volume. Verley adverts to it in refereeing Whitehead's critique of Descartes; Shields advances it against Russell; and Weekes advances it against Husserl.

15. Unless we are mistaken there is nothing original in the following argument. Of course, the thinkers to whom we are indebted should not be blamed for the use to which we have put their ideas. See Dummet 1978/1960, 350–357; Sellars 1962; Rorty 1989/1963.

16. This point is made by Schweiger et al. in their contribution to this volume. Whitehead's position is a midpoint between those who think consciousness emerges from nature but does not contribute to what it experiences *as* nature and those who think it contributes to what it experiences *as* nature but does not emerge from nature.

17. Needless to say, in these pages the word *genetic* has nothing to do with the science of genes, but refers to the *genesis* of something, its process of coming to be.

18. As Gregg Rosenberg argues in his contribution below, the modernist concept of nature is still very much alive in the information-theoretic "It from bit" view for understanding the essential nature of the physical world. According to this view, the fundamental entities of physics are "mere dynamic quantities, mere information structures in a vacuum" so that "fundamental reality . . . is purely structural and quantifiable, with no intrinsic nature of its own that escapes the formal description of a pattern." Rosenberg deploys a wholly original argument to demonstrate that this doctrine is incoherent, but he also adverts to the notorious problem of "qualia," which proves that such a doctrine is, at the very least, incomplete: since Locke philosophers have acknowledged the impossibility of accounting for qualia through morphology alone, of "reducing" them to primary qualities. Whitehead's point is that "passage" is a qualium *sui generis* whose omission is fatal to any account of nature.

19. Obviously the German adjective *bewusst* behaves somewhat differently than the English *conscious*. While the German word includes in its scope the familiar meanings of the English one, it also possesses a meaning that does not correspond to anything in the English usage of *conscious*, and this in fact is the meaning in question when Brentano asks if there can be "unconscious consciousness." In this sense something is *bewusst* if it is the *object* of consciousness, just as in English something is *known* if it is the object of knowledge. Brentano's question is therefore whether

we can ever be conscious of something without simultaneously being conscious of this consciousness.

20. Pachalska and MacQueen, in their contribution below, advance a similar interpretation of consciousness and the Unconscious in Freud.

21. This has been a particular focus of investigation for Velmans; see his contribution to this volume and Velmans 1991a, 1991b, 1993, 1996, 2000, 2002a, 2002b, 2003.

22. David Skrbina (2005) provides ample documentation that in some form "panpsychism" was never the fringe minority view that it is now made out to be. On the contrary, into the twentieth century it continued to be a prevalent view among natural scientists, many of whom are still lionized for their contributions to the scientific worldview.

23. Nagel 1986. At times it almost seems as if Nagel is employing the technique of "double writing" that the Straussians seem to find so much of. His style and tone seems designed to be nonthreatening to the establishment, but like Maimonides slipping in his unreconstructed Aristotelianism, Nagel slips in some fairly strong arguments for pansubjectivism. The casual Analytic reader is likely to fault Nagel for little more than an excessively open mind, but not everyone will miss the oblique response to Rorty's famously damning critique of Whitehead. Rorty: "one cannot satisfy the methodological form of the subjectivist principle simply by borrowing the primitive predicates of the vocabulary in which one will phrase one's philosophical explanations from the ordinary reports of mental states (rather than from the ordinary vocabulary of reports of events in the physical world), unless one can supply criteria for applying these terms, in their extended meanings, to particular cases—instructions which have the same degree of specificity as the criteria which we use in applying these terms to particular cases in their unextended meanings" (Rorty 1989). Nagel: "Does the general concept of experience really lose all content if an attempt is made to use it to think about cases in which we cannot now and perhaps even never could apply it more specifically? I think not. [. . .] [T]he generalization of the concept of experience beyond our capacity to apply it doesn't *contradict* the condition of application that it tries to transcend, even if some examples, like the ascription of pain to a stove, do pass the limits of intelligibility" (23, emphasis in original). This should be read in tandem with the chapter on "Panpsychism and Mental Unity," which concludes: the possibility of panpsychism "seems to me, *precisely because of its impossibility,* one of the most promising questions to concentrate on if we wish to generate new ideas about the mind-body problem" (1986, 49–51, emphasis added—imagine the very different reception this book would have gotten without that odd qualification!). See also "Panpsychism" (Nagel 1979, 180–195).

24. It turns out that the old Scholastic controversy about the *principium individuationis* is alive and kicking: the idea of purely objective knowledge is intrinsically bound up with the idea that every individual thing can be completely specified with concepts—without recourse to acquaintance (in Russell's sense) or anything else that would involve indexical or token-reflexive reference. Purely objective knowledge thus presupposes that individuality is just typological uniqueness, for otherwise it would not be possible to exhaustively describe the individual using universals alone. The role played by the idea of purely objective knowledge in the history of western thought

and its veiled connection with an "essentialist" or "logicist" theory of individuation is examined by Weekes (2007, 64–80).

25. For an account of the original *raison d'être* of this very useful concept (and of *intensionality* in general) see Kneale 1962, 601–618.

26. The example is from Thomas Nagel's famous article (Nagel 1979, 164–180), but see Whitehead: "he [Leibniz] approached the problem of cosmology from the subjective side, whereas Lucretius and Newton approach it form the objective point of view. They implicitly ask the question, What does the world of atoms look like to an intellect surveying it? [. . .] But Leibniz answered another question. He explained what it must be like to be an atom" (AI 132).

27. To keep the record straight, it is important to underline that the space-time continuum is, so to speak, the surface effect of a deeper matrix of solidarity, which Whitehead calls the "extensive continuum."

References

Barclay, James R. 1964. "Franz Brentano and Sigmund Freud." *Journal of Existentialism* 5 (17): 1–36.

Bergo, Bettina. 2004. "Freud's Debt to Philosophy and His Copernican Revolution" In *The Philosophy of Psychiatry: A Companion*, ed. by Jennifer Radden, 338–350. Oxford: Oxford University Press.

Bergson, Henri. 1907. *L'Évolution créatrice*. Paris: Félix Alcan.

Bergson, Henri. 1944. *Creative Evolution*. Trans. by Arthur Mitchell. New York: Modern Library.

Bergson, Henri. 1959. *Œuvres*. Édition du centenaire. Textes annotés par André Robinet. Introduction par Henri Gouhier. Paris: Presses Universitaires de France.

Brentano, Franz.1973/1874. *Die Psychologie vom empirischen Standpunkt*. 3 vols., rd. by Oskar Kraus. Hamburg: Felix Meiner Verlag.

Chalmers, David. 1995. "Facing up to the Problem of Consciousness." *Journal of Consciousness Studies* 3:200–219. Reprinted in Shear 1998, 9–30.

Comte, Auguste. 1988. *Introduction to Positive Philosophy*. Ed. with revised trans. by Frederick Ferré (Indianapolis: Hackett Publishing).

Dummet, Michael. 1978/1960. "A Defence of McTaggart's Proof of the Unreality of Time." In *Truth and Other Enigmas*. Cambridge, MA: Harvard University Press.

Grant, Edward. 1974. *A Source Book in Medieval Science*. Cambridge, MA: Harvard University Press.

Husserl, Edmund. 1969. *Die Krisis der europäischen Wissenschaften und die Transzendentale Phänomenologie: Eine Einleitung in die phänomenologische Philosophie*. 2. Auflage. Haag: Martinus Nijhoff.

Husserl, Edmund. 1984. *Logische Untersuchungen*. Zweiter Band. Erster Teil. *Untersuchungen zur Phänomenologie und Theorie der Erkenntnis*. Herausgegeben von Ursula Panzer. Husserliana 19/1. The Hague: Martinus Nijhoff Publishers.

Husserl, Edmund. 1980/1913. *Ideen zu einer reinen Phänomenologie und phänomenologischen Philosophie: Allgemeine Einführung in die reine Phänomenologie.* Tübingen: Max Niemeyer Verlag.

Kneale, William and Martha. 1962. *The Development of Logic.* London: Oxford University Press.

Mach, Ernst. 1985/1885. *Die Analyse der Empfindungen und das Verhältnis des Physischen zum Psychischen.* Mit einem Vorwort zum Neudruck von Gereon Wolters. Darmstadt: Wissenschaftliche Buchgesellschaft.

McGinn, Colin. 1991. *The Problem of Consciousness.* Oxford: Oxford University Press.

McGinn, Colin. 1995. "Consciousness and Space." In Shear 1998, 97–108.

Merlan, Philip. 1945. "Brentano and Freud." *Journal of the History of Ideas* 6:375–377.

Merlan, Philip. 1949. "Brentano and Freud—A Sequel." *Journal of the History of Ideas* 10:451.

Merleau-Ponty, Maurice. 1962. *Phenomenology of Perception.* Trans. by Colin Smith. London: Routledge.

Nagel, Thomas, 1979. *Mortal Questions.* Cambridge: Cambridge University Press.

Nagel, Thomas. 1986. *The View from Nowhere.* New York/Oxford: Oxford University Press.

Ockham, William of. 1944. *Tractatus de successivis.* Attributed to William Ockham, ed. with a study on the life and works of Ockham by Philotheus Boehner, O.F.M. St. Bonaventure: The Franciscan Institute, St. Bonaventure College.

Popper, Karl. 1968. *The Logic of Scientific Discovery.* New York: Harper & Row.

Rorty, Richard. 1989/1963. "The Subjectivist Principle and the Linguistic Turn." In *Alfred North Whitehead: Essays on His Philosophy,* ed. by George Kline, 134–157. Lanham: University Press of America.

Rosenberg, Gregg H. 2004. *A Place for Consciousness: The Theory of Natural Individuals.* Oxford: Oxford University Press.

Russell, Bertrand. 1957. *Mysticism and Logic.* Garden City: Doubleday and Company.

Schlick, Moritz. 1934. "Über das Fundament der Erkenntnis." *Erkenntnis* 4:79–97.

Sellars, Wilfred. 1962. "Time and the World Order." In *Minnesota Studies in the Philosophy of Science III,* 527–616. Minneapolis: University of Minnesota Press.

Shear, Jonathan. 1998. *Explaining Consciousness—The Hard Problem.* Ed. by Jonathan Shear. Cambridge, MA/London: MIT Press.

Skrbina, David. 2005. *Panpsychism in the West.* Cambridge, MA: MIT Press

Velmans, Max. 1991a. "Is Human Information Processing Conscious?" *Behavioral and Brain Sciences* 14 (4): 651–669; http://cogprints.ecs.soton.ac.uk/archive/00000593/.

Velmans, Max. 1991b. "Consciousness from a First-Person Perspective." *Behavioral and Brain Sciences* 14 (4): 702–726; http://cogprints.ecs.soton.ac.uk/archive/00000594/.

Velmans, Max. 1993. "Consciousness, Causality and Complementarity." *Behavioral and Brain Sciences* 16 (2): 409–416; http://cogprints.ecs.soton.ac.uk/archive/00000595/.

Velmans, Max. 1996. "Consciousness and the 'Causal Paradox.'" *Behavioral and Brain Sciences* 19 (3): 538–542; http://cogprints.ecs.soton.ac.uk/archive/00000596/.

Velmans, Max. 2000. *Understanding Consciousness.* London: Routledge/Psychology Press.

Velmans, Max. 2002a. "How Could Conscious Experiences Affect Brains?" Target article for Special Issue, *Journal of Consciousness Studies* 9 (11): 3–29; http://cogprints.ecs.soton.ac.uk/archive/00002750/.

Velmans, Max. 2002b. "Making Sense of the Causal Interactions between Consciousness and Brain, a Reply to Commentaries." *Journal of Consciousness Studies* 9 (11): 69–95; http://cogprints.ecs.soton.ac.uk/archive/00002751/.

Velmans, Max. 2003. "How Could Conscious Experiences Affect Brains?" Exeter: Academic.

Weekes, Anderson. 2007. "Abstraction and Individuation in Whitehead and Wiehl: A Comparative Historical Approach." In *Subjectivity, Process, and Rationality*, Michel Weber, ed., 39–119. Frankfurt/Lancaster: Ontos Verlag.

Part II

Psychology and Philosophy of Mind

5

Consciousness as Subjective Form

Whitehead's Nonreductionist Naturalism

David Griffin

Whitehead's position on consciousness differs radically from that of the hitherto dominant approaches, Cartesian dualism and reductionist materialism, but it does share aspects of these two positions. Part of its novelty, in fact, is that it can combine ideas that had previously seemed irreconcilable. With dualists, Whitehead agrees that consciousness belongs to an entity—a mind or psyche—that is distinct from the brain, and that genuine freedom can, partly for this reason, be attributed to conscious experience. With materialists, Whitehead shares a naturalistic sensibility, thereby eschewing any even implicitly supernaturalistic solution to philosophical problems, and, partly for this reason, rejects any dualism between two kinds of actualities. Like materialists, in other words, he affirms a pluralistic monism. He thereby regards consciousness as a function of something more fundamental. And yet he, like dualists, rejects the reductionism involved in functionalism as understood by materialists. All of these features of Whitehead's position are implicit in his doctrine that *consciousness is the subjective form of an intellectual feeling, which arises, if at all, only in a late phase of a moment of experience.* It will be the purpose of this chapter to explain this idea and show how it enables us to solve a number of philosophical problems associated with consciousness.

Some Criteria for an Adequate Doctrine of Consciousness

In listing the criteria by which to judge the success of any metaphysical theory, Whitehead includes "adequacy" as well as self-consistency and coherence (PR 3). Although it is now fashionable in some philosophical circles to argue that there can be no universal, tradition-transcendent criteria in terms of which to judge the adequacy of theories, Whitehead disagreed. The "metaphysical rule of evidence," he said, is "that we must bow to those presumptions which, in despite of criticism, we still employ for the regulation of our lives" (PR 151). In affirming this view, Whitehead was explicitly rejecting Hume's dualism between theory and practice, according to which we have various "natural beliefs," such as the belief in an external world, which we necessarily presuppose in practice but cannot affirm in philosophical theory. Whitehead, in response, said:

> Whatever is found in "practice" must lie within the scope of the metaphysical description. When the description fails to include the "practice," the metaphysics is inadequate and requires revision. There can be no appeal to practice to supplement metaphysics. (PR 13)

Some advocates of deconstruction, using a Kantian description, refer to ideas that we cannot help presupposing, but that we must nevertheless consider false, as "transcendental illusions" (see McCarthy 1993, 102–103). However, to say that an idea is false, even though one cannot help presupposing this idea, is to violate the law of noncontradiction, usually considered the first rule of reason, because one is both (implicitly) affirming and (explicitly) denying one and the same proposition. Such a self-contradiction is "absolutely self-refuting" in the sense clarified by John Passmore: "The proposition p is absolutely self-refuting, if to assert p is equivalent to asserting *both p and not-p*" (Passmore 1969, 60). Jürgen Habermas and Karl-Otto Apel call such a self-contradiction a "performative contradiction," because the performance of making the statement contradicts the statement's meaning (see Jay 1993, 25–37). For example, if I say that I doubt your existence, the fact that I am addressing you contradicts my professed doubt. Whitehead agrees with Passmore, Habermas, and Apel that our theories must seek to avoid such self-contradictions by avoiding "negations of what in practice is presupposed" (PR 13).

In enunciating this criterion, Whitehead thereby stood in the tradition of "commonsense" philosophy. The term "common sense," however, is now often used quite differently, to refer to ideas that, although widely held at a certain time and place, are false. Science, in fact, is often described as a systematic assault on common sense, undermining such "commonsense" ideas as the flatness of the Earth, its centrality in the universe, and the solidity of matter. I distinguish between these two meanings, accordingly, by referring to common sense in the latter sense as soft-core common sense, while referring to those ideas that we all inevitably presuppose as hard-core commonsense ideas. It was common sense in the hard-core sense that Whitehead had in mind in referring to his "endeavor to interpret experience in accordance with the overpowering deliverance of common sense" (PR 50). Commonsense notions of this hard-core type are "overpowering" because we cannot help presupposing them, even in the act of verbally denying them.

With regard to conscious experience, four of these overpowering notions are that conscious experience exists, that it exerts influence upon the body, that it has a degree of self-determining freedom, and that it can act in accord with various norms. The fact that all four of these notions are inevitably presupposed in practice is widely recognized by contemporary philosophers.

1. The impossibility of doubting the existence of one's own conscious experience was famously emphasized by Descartes. Now Jaakko Hintikka, in an essay titled "Cogito, Ergo Sum," has shown that Descartes' argument involved the notion of a performative self-contradiction. If I say, "I doubt herewith, now, that I exist," then, explains Hintikka, "the propositional component contradicts the performative component of the speech act expressed by that self-referential sentence" (Hintikka 1962, 32). Insofar as the extreme version of materialism known as "eliminative materialism" seeks to eliminate all references to conscious experience, it is involved in this kind of self-refuting contradiction.

2. With regard to our second notion, the efficacy of conscious experience for bodily behavior, William Seager observes that "it presents the aspect of a datum rather than a disputable hypothesis" (Seager 1991, 188). Ted Honderich, explicitly bringing out the hard-core commonsense status of this belief, says that its main recommendation is "the futility of contemplating its denial." With regard to epiphenomenalism, which is the doctrine that conscious experience does not exert causal efficacy on the body, Honderich says: "Off the page, no one believes it" (Honderich 1987, 447). Suggesting a reductio ad absurdum of epiphenomenalism, Jaegwon Kim says: "If our reasons and desires have no causal efficacy at all in influencing our bodily actions, then perhaps no one has ever performed a single intentional action!" (Kim 1993, 104). One's theory, Kim insists, must have room for the reality of psychophysical causation, as when, feeling a pain, one's decision to call the doctor leads one to walk to the telephone and dial it (286). John Searle, in a similar vein, includes "the reality and causal efficacy of consciousness" among the "obvious facts" about our minds and endorses the "commonsense objection to 'eliminative materialism' that it is 'crazy to say that . . . my beliefs and desires don't play any role in my behavior'" (Searle 1992, 54, 48).

3. The third idea, that such actions are based on a degree of self-determining freedom, is equally recognized to be an inevitable presupposition. Searle, pointing out that people have been able to give up some commonsense beliefs, such as the beliefs in a flat Earth and literal "sunsets," says that

> we can't similarly give up the conviction of freedom because
> that conviction is built into every normal, conscious intentional
> action . . . . [W]e can't act otherwise than on the assumption of
> freedom, no matter how much we learn about how the world
> works as a determined physical system. (Searle 1984, 97)

Similarly, Thomas Nagel, in spite of seeing no way to give a coherent account
of freedom, says: "I can no more help holding myself and others responsible
in ordinary life than I can help feeling that my actions originate with me
(Nagel 1986, 110–117, 123). To be sure, some philosophers, such as William Lycan, try to make this feeling of freedom compatible with complete
determinism by redefining freedom. According to this compatibilist definition, to say I did X freely is not to say that I could have acted otherwise
(Lycan 1987, 113–114). But to speak of freedom only in this compatibilist,
Pickwickian sense, both Nagel and Searle see, is not to speak of freedom as
we presuppose it (Nagel 1986, 110–117; Searle 1984, 87, 92, 95).

 4. It is also widely recognized that we presuppose that our actions can
be shaped by various norms. Kim, in emphasizing the importance of affirming
the efficacy of our decisions for our bodily actions, says that otherwise we
"would render our moral and cognitive life wholly unintelligible" because we
could no longer affirm that "our norms and beliefs regulate our deliberations
and decisions" (Kim 1993, xv). Charles Larmore likewise recognizes that both
moral and cognitive norms somehow exercise authority over our conscious
experience. He says, for example, that it would be ridiculous to suggest "that
even so basic a rule of reasoning as the avoidance of contradiction has no
more authority than what we choose to give it" (Searle 1984, 87).

Inadequacies of Dualism and Materialism

It would seem to be widely agreed, therefore, that for any theory of conscious experience to be deemed even minimally adequate, it would have to
do justice to these four notions. But both dualism and materialism have
difficulty affirming these notions in a self-consistent way, at least without
appealing to supernatural assistance. I will discuss their difficulties with these
four notions in order.

 1. For Descartes, there was no problem in asserting *the existence of
consciousness*, as he simply assumed that God, in creating the world, had
created minds as well as bodies *ex nihilo*. But philosophers today presuppose a naturalistic, evolutionary worldview. Materialists and dualists, both
presupposing a materialistic view of the ultimate units of nature, must affirm
that conscious experience somehow emerged out of entities wholly devoid

of experience. For dualists, this means the emergence of minds, as a new kind of actuality (or substance); for materialists, this means the emergence of consciousness as a new property of matter. In either case, this kind of emergence is hard to make intelligible.

From the side of dualism, Karl Popper and H.D. Lewis have implicitly admitted that they cannot explain it (see Popper and Eccles 1977, 105; Lewis 1969, 26). Geoffrey Madell, more candidly, has explicitly admitted that "the appearance of consciousness in the course of evolution must appear for the dualist to be an utterly inexplicable emergence of something entirely new, an emergence which must appear quite bizarre" (Madell 1988, 140–141). Some materialists think that this problem uniquely exists for dualism. J.J.C. Smart, for example, said:

> How could a nonphysical property or entity suddenly arise in the course of animal evolution? . . . [W]hat sort of chemical process could lead to the springing into existence of something nonphysical? No enzyme can catalyze the production of a spook! (Smart 1979, 165, 168–169)

Smart failed to see, however, that the idea that an apparent spook is produced out of wholly insentient stuff creates an equal difficulty. But Colin McGinn, another materialist, does see this, saying that we do not know how consciousness might have arisen by natural processes from antecedently existing material things. Somehow or other sentience sprang from pulpy matter, giving matter an inner aspect, but we have no idea how this leap was propelled.

McGinn's reference to natural processes is essential to his point. "One is tempted," he says, to turn to divine assistance: for only a kind of miracle could produce *this* from *that*.

> It would take a supernatural magician to extract consciousness from matter. Consciousness appears to introduce a sharp break in the natural order—a point at which scientific naturalism runs out of steam. (McGinn 1991, 45)

At least one contemporary philosopher, Richard Swinburne, succumbs to this temptation, arguing thus:

> [S]cience cannot explain the evolution of a mental life. That is to say, . . . there is nothing in the nature of certain physical events . . . to give rise to connections to [mental events] . . . .

God, being omnipotent, would have the power to produce a soul.
(Swinburne 1986, 198–199)[1]

But McGinn, speaking for most contemporary philosophers by insisting
that naturalism must be presupposed, cannot countenance such an answer
(McGinn 1991, 47).

McGinn is far from the only materialist to see the difficulty of how, as
McGinn puts it, "the aggregation of millions of individually insentient neurons
[constituting the brain could] generate subjective awareness" (McGinn 1991,
1). Thomas Nagel, using *en soi* for a being that exists merely "in itself" and
pour soi for one that exists "for itself," has said:

> One cannot derive a *pour soi* from an *en soi*. . . . This gap is logi-
> cally unbridgeable. If a bodiless god wanted to create a conscious
> being, he could not expect to do it by combining together in
> organic form a lot of particles with none but physical properties.
> (Nagel 1979, 188–189)

The problem here for both dualists and materialists is not that they
deny the existence of consciousness. It is that their positions cannot account
for this existence.

2. A similar problem obtains with our hard-core commonsense presupposition that *our conscious experience exerts causal efficacy upon our bodies*, thus
directing our bodily actions. Although dualists and materialists inevitably
presuppose that such efficacy occurs, as we have seen, they cannot explain
how. For dualists, one reason for this difficulty is simply the problem of
understanding how a mental or spiritual entity could influence physical entities, understood to be completely different in kind. As Madell admits, "the
nature of the causal connection between the mental and the physical, as the
Cartesian conceives of it, is utterly mysterious" (Madell 1988, 2). Descartes
himself was not embarrassed by this mysteriousness, because for him the
problem was solved by appeal to divine omnipotence, an appeal that was
brought out more explicitly in the doctrine of "occasionalism" enunciated by
his followers Nicolas Malebranche and Arnold Geulincx.[2] As William James
said, "For thinkers of that age, 'God' was the great solvent of all absurdities"
(James 1911, 194). Aside from a few throwbacks to that age such as Richard
Swinburne, dualists today cannot employ this solvent, so they cannot explain
our conviction that the mind affects the body.

Epiphenomenalists, like dualists, think of the mind as a mental or
spiritual entity, distinct from the brain, but they use the impossibility of
understanding how it *could* affect the brain as a basis for denying that it

does. This denial, however, involves arbitrariness. At least one advocate of epiphenomenalism, Keith Campbell, admits that it is arbitrary, because it "rejects only one half of the interaction of matter and spirit." That is, epiphenomenalism denies "the action of spirit on matter" while accepting the idea that the spiritual mind emerged out of a wholly materialistic universe, thereby affirming "the action of the material on the spiritual" (132, 131). Campbell's twofold motive for this arbitrariness, he says, is that it allows him, on the one hand, to admit that the mind exists, so that he need not, with materialists, think of psychological states, such as pains, as simply properties of the brain (38, 48, 105–109), and yet, on the other hand, to "preserve the completeness of the physical accounts of human action" (125).

This latter part of Campbell's motive reflects a widespread conviction held by materialists as well as epiphenomenalists, the conviction that, as Jaegwon Kim puts it, the bottom layer of nature is controlled by the laws of physics and chemistry, so that it cannot be influenced by higher levels of nature. Given this conviction, our thoughts cannot influence our bodily behavior, because the latter must in principle be fully understandable in terms of the laws of physics and chemistry. But this view rules out Kim's affirmation, which he had made in opposition to epiphenomenalism, that we walk to the telephone *because* we have decided to make a call. Upon seeing this contradiction, Kim admitted that materialism seems "to be up against a dead end" (Kim 1993, 367).

3. Materialists have even greater difficulty with freedom than with downward causation. Searle, for example, believes that science "allows no place for freedom of the will" (Searle 1984, 92). This denial follows from Searle's materialistic assumptions, which he summarizes thus:

> Since nature consists of particles and their relations with each other, and since everything can be accounted for in terms of those particles and their relations, there is simply no room for freedom of the will. (86)

Scientific explanation, Searle further elaborates, is bottom-up explanation, which explains the behavior of all complex things in terms of their most elementary constituents (93). The idea of statistical indeterminacy at the quantum level provides no basis for affirming freedom, Searle adds, because all such indeterminacy is canceled out in macro-objects, such as billiard balls and human bodies (87). So, although Searle admits that we cannot help presupposing that we and others act freely, the fact that freedom is not reconcilable with scientific materialism means that our feeling of freedom must be an illusion built into the structure of human experience by evolution (5, 94, 98). Searle explicitly admits his failure, saying that although

ideally, I would like to be able to keep both my commonsense
conceptions and my scientific beliefs . . . [,] when it comes to
the question of freedom and determinism, I am . . . unable
to reconcile the two. (86)

Searle's inability to affirm genuine freedom is echoed by many other
materialists, such as Colin McGinn, Thomas Nagel, and Daniel Dennett
(see McGinn 1991, 17n; Nagel 1986, 110–123; Dennett 1984).

This inability to affirm freedom, furthermore, undermines the claim by
materialists to have endorsed our second notion, downward causation from
conscious experience to the body. This is at least the case if we accept, as
I do, Mortimer Taube's careful definition of an efficient cause: "An event
A causes event B, when B results partly from some activity or influence
originating in A" (Taube 1936, 17). In other words, if an event in the life of
my mind helps bring about an event in my body, I can rightly refer to my
mind as a cause upon my body only if the bodily event resulted partly from
some activity that originated in the mind-event itself. Materialists cannot
say this because for them the mind, not being an entity distinct from the
brain, cannot be a locus of power.

Searle is explicit about the fact that his denial of human freedom
depends on this assumption that we do not have a mind that could, as he
puts it, force the particles of the brain to "swerve from their paths" (Searle
1984, 87).[3] Because consciousness is merely an emergent property of the
brain, it cannot "cause things that could not be explained by the causal
behavior of the neurons" (Searle 1992, 63). Dualists, by contrast, do affirm
the existence of a mind that, being distinct from the brain, can be affirmed
as the locus of self-determining freedom. Dualists, however, cannot explain
how the mind, being different in kind from the neurons of the brain, can
influence them. Searle, driving home this problem, says:

How could something mental make a physical difference? Are we
supposed to think that our thoughts and feelings can somehow
produce chemical effects on our brains . . . ? How could such a
thing occur? Are we supposed to think that thoughts can wrap
themselves around the axons or shake the dendrites or sneak inside
the cell wall and attack the cell nucleus? (Searle 1984, 117)

Dualists, not being able to answer this question—as Madell and others
admit—can, therefore, really do little more justice than can materialists to our
inescapable assumption that our bodily actions reflect a degree of freedom.

4. The same inability obtains with regard to our presupposition that
we can *consciously act in terms of norms*. McGinn points to the difficulty of
this problem for his materialist position by asking "how a physical organ-

ism can be subject to the norms of rationality. How, for example, does *modus ponens* get its grip on the causal transitions between mental states" (McGinn 1991, 23n.). The problem is that causation involving norms, which are *abstract* (rather than physical) entities, would be wholly different from billiard-ball causation, which McGinn, in line with his materialism, takes to be paradigmatic for causation in general (55). "[C]ausal relations between . . . abstract entities and human minds," says McGinn, would be "funny kinds of causation" (55, 53). Another way to state the problem is to point out that if norms—whether cognitive, moral, or aesthetic—are to have some authority over our experience, there must be some way for us to apprehend these norms. But materialists, equating the mind with the brain, hold that all perception is through the body's physical senses, which cannot be activated by nonphysical things such as norms.

Again, dualists, by virtue of distinguishing between the mind and the brain, are able in principle to affirm the reality of nonsensory perception, through which norms could be apprehended, and some dualists do make this affirmation (see, for example, Beloff 1962). But they still have the problem of being unable to explain how a nonphysical mind can affect the physical body, so dualists cannot really explain how norm-guided behavior is possible.

Dualism and materialism, in sum, are complete failures with regard to our hard-core commonsense assumptions about our own conscious experience. They, accordingly, must be regarded as woefully inadequate. This woeful inadequacy suggests that the world must in reality be radically different from the world as portrayed by both dualists and materialists.

Whitehead's Panexperientialism

Such a radically different worldview was proffered by Whitehead. Part of this difference involves the fact that Whitehead became a theist of sorts, in order to explain various features of our world that seemed otherwise inexplicable. But this adoption of a theistic perspective did not involve any recursion to supernaturalism. He rejected the earlier "appeal to a *deus ex machina* who was capable of rising superior to the difficulties of metaphysics" (SMW 156). In line with his complete eschewal of supernaturalism, he rejected any doctrine that implied a dualism between two types of actualities.[4] Positively, this rejection took the form of the acceptance of panexperientialism, according to which all actualities have experience. Accepting this view implied the rejection of what he called "vacuous actualities," meaning things that are fully actual and yet wholly devoid of experience (PR 29, 167).

Panexperientialism is, to be sure, still thought in many circles to be self-evidently absurd. But this is partly because the "pan" in panexperientialism is often taken to mean that literally *all* things, including aggregations such as sticks and stones, have experience. Whitehead's doctrine, however, is only that all *genuine individuals* have experience. Genuine individuals are of two types. There are simple individuals, which are the most elementary units of nature (whether these are thought to be quarks or even simpler units). And there are what Charles Hartshorne, in developing Whitehead's panexperientialism more fully, called "compound individuals" (Hartshorne 1972), which are compounded out of simpler individuals, as when atoms are compounded out of subatomic particles, molecules out of atoms, living cells out of macromolecules, and animals out of cells. These compound individuals are true individuals because the experience of their members gives birth to a highest-level experience, which is the "dominant" member of the organism as a whole. This dominant member gives the compound individual a unity of experience and a unity of action, so that it can act purposively with a degree of freedom. These compound individuals hence *differ in kind* from mere aggregations of individuals, such as rocks and telephones, in which the experiences of the individual molecules do *not* give rise to a higher-level, inclusive experience. For this reason, I emphasize that Whitehead's doctrine should be called not simply "panexperientialism," but "panexperientialism with organizational duality."[5]

A second reason for considering doctrines of this type absurd is the assumption that they attribute not just experience, but conscious experience, to all things, or at least all individuals. This assumption has been based partly on the older term for such doctrines, "panpsychism," which, by implying that all things are psyches, suggests that they all have high-grade, conscious mentality. Whitehead himself evidently rejected the term "panpsychism" for this reason (Johnson 1969, 354). Although he did not propose the term "panexperientialism" as an alternative, it is suggested by many of his statements, such as his rejection of the concept of an actuality "void of subjective experience," his statement that "apart from the experiences of subjects there is nothing," and his denial that there is any meaning of "togetherness" other than "experiential togetherness" (PR 167, 189).[6] Whitehead's panexperientialism, in any case, holds that all individuals have experience, but that consciousness is a very high-level form of experience, enjoyed by relatively few individuals. With these clarifications, we can see that the standard rejections of panexperientialism as absurd—such as McGinn's claim that it attributes thoughts to rocks (McGinn 1982, 32)—do not apply to Whitehead's version of it.[7]

There are still, to be sure, other reasons for resisting the doctrine, chief among which is probably pointed to by Nagel's statement that "if one travels too far down the phylogenetic tree, people gradually shed their faith that there is experience there at all" (Nagel 1979, 168). This reason, how-ever, is an example of *soft-core* common sense, which science has repeatedly undermined. And the scientific undermining of this particular assumption, that experience could not go all the way down, is already well advanced. Whereas Descartes denied experience to all earthly creatures except humans, some leading ethologists now posit experience at least as far down as bees (Griffin 1992). Going much further down, there is now a wide range of evidence suggestive of the idea that single-cell organisms, such as amoebae and paramecia, have a primitive type of experience (Hameroff 1994, 97–99). Going still further, to the prokaryotic level, some biologists have provided evidence for a rudimentary form of decision making, based on a rudimentary form of memory, in bacteria (Adler and Tse 1974; Goldbetter and Koshland 1982). Furthermore, although DNA molecules were originally pictured in mechanistic terms, later studies suggested a more organismic understanding (Keller 1983). Going all the way down, quantum physics has shown entities at this level not to be analogous to billiard balls (see Capek 1991, 54, 135, 205, 211), and, as physicist David Bohm and philosopher William Seager have said, quantum theory implies that the behavior of the elementary units of nature can be explained only by attributing to them something analogous to our own mentality (Bohm and Hiley 1993, 384–387; Seager 1995, 282–283). Accordingly, the prejudice that experience cannot go all the way down, far from being supported by any scientific evidence, is being increasingly undermined by the relevant evidence.

I have, in any case, argued elsewhere that this empirical support for panexperientialism is only one of many lines of argument pointing toward its truth (Griffin 1997, 251–261; 1998, 89–92; 2001, 97–109). One of those lines of arguments is that panexperientialism, and apparently *only* panexperientialism, does justice to the four hard-core commonsense assumptions about conscious experience examined earlier. A basis for this argument can be provided by spelling out Whitehead's panexperientialism as the doctrine that the actual world is comprised of *creative, experiential, physical-mental events*. I will deal with each of these terms in reverse order, beginning with the fourth term, "events."

All the world's actual entities in the fullest sense are momentary events. These are all spatiotemporal events with a finite inner duration, ranging perhaps from less than a billionth of a second at the subatomic level to a tenth or twentieth of a second at the level of human experience. All enduring individuals, such as electrons and minds, are temporal societies of such events. This feature provides another reason why "panexperientialism" is a better term for this doctrine than "panpsychism." The latter term, being based on the word "psyche," suggests that the ultimate units of the world are enduring individuals, whereas the term "panexperientialism" suggests that they are experiences, which are momentary.

In any case, each such event has both physical and mental aspects, with the physical aspect always being prior. The physical aspect is the event's reception of the efficient causation of prior events into itself. This receptivity is called "physical prehension," or "physical feeling," which is a mode of perception more basic than sensory perception. An event originates with a multiplicity of physical prehensions, each of which has two aspects: an *objective datum*, which is what is felt, and a *subjective form*, which is how that datum is felt. To say that every unit-event (in distinction from an aggregational event[8]) has a mental aspect means that it has a degree—however slight in the most elementary events—of spontaneity or self-determination. Although the event's physical pole is given to it, its mentality is its capacity to decide precisely what to make of its given foundation. Its physicality is its relation to past actuality; its mentality involves its prehension of ideality or possibility, through which it escapes total determination by the past.

Each event, the second of our terms indicates, is experiential from beginning to end, which means that, in distinction from usage reflecting dualism, the "physical" aspect of the event is not devoid of experience, hence the "mental" aspect is not uniquely associated with experience. An event's mentality is simply its experience insofar as it is self-determining. Whitehead emphasizes the experiential nature of unit-events by calling them "occasions of experience."

With regard to the first term, *creative*, I have already stated that each event is, in its mental pole, *self*-creative, deciding precisely how to respond to the efficient causation exerted upon it. A second dimension of an experience's creativity, which comes after its self-determination, is its efficient causation on subsequent events, through which it shares in the creation of the future. This transition from self-creation to efficient causation betokens another distinction to be made with regard to each unit-event. Each occasion of experience exists first as a subject of experience, with its physical and mental poles. But then its subjectivity perishes and it becomes an object for subsequent subjects. In each enduring individual, accordingly, there is a perpetual oscillation between two modes of existence: subjectivity and objectivity.[9] Put in causal language, there is a perpetual oscillation between final causation (in the sense of self-determination) and efficient causation.

Whitehead's solution to the mind-body problem depends partly on this doctrine of creative, experiential, physical-mental events and partly on the idea of compound individuals, one crucial point of which is that the dominant members of increasingly complex compound individuals have an increasing degree of mentality and thereby an increasingly greater capacity for both richness of experience and self-determination. The occasions of experience constituting a squirrel's psyche, for example, enjoy a much more complex, sophisticated mode of experience, and far more power for self-determination, than the occasions of experience constituting any of the cells in its body.

Whitehead's Explanation of Our Hard-Core Commonsense Assumptions about Consciousness

I will now explain how Whitehead's panexperientialism can do justice to our hard-core commonsense assumptions about conscious experience.

With regard to the existence of consciousness, we can begin with Whitehead's discussion of William James's essay "Does Consciousness Exist?" (James 1904). Whitehead accepts James's rejection of the existence of consciousness in the sense of an "entity" or an "aboriginal stuff..., contrasted with that of which material objects are made, out of which our thoughts of them are made" (SMW 144). Whitehead also accepts James's contention that consciousness is a particular function of experience. To understand James and Whitehead correctly here, it is important to see that they are not saying that consciousness is a function of the brain, or of nonexperiencing "material objects." Rather, consciousness is a function of experience. It is also important not to take the denial that consciousness is an "aboriginal stuff" to mean that experience is not. Experience is an aboriginal stuff—for James, who affirmed panpsychism,[10] and for Whitehead. But it is not, of course, an aboriginal stuff different from the stuff out of which material things are made. The whole point of panexperientialism is that creative experience is the aboriginal stuff out of which human experience and what we call material objects are both made. However, in human beings and other highly complex compound individuals, experience can give rise to conscious thoughts, which have a function that is not enjoyed in the experience of low-grade individuals. This function, said James, is "*knowing*." Whitehead agreed, saying that consciousness is "the function of knowing" (SMW 144, 151).

Given Whitehead's panexperientialist ontology, the main reasons for denying the full-fledged reality of conscious experience disappear. If we hold that neurons are sentient, the insoluble problem of how conscious experience could emerge out of insentient neurons does not arise. Even McGinn grants this point, saying that if we could suppose neurons to have "proto-conscious states," it would be "easy enough to see how neurons could generate consciousness" (McGinn 1991, 28n.).[11]

The problem of mental or downward causation—how one's decisions can affect one's brain and thereby one's bodily behavior—is overcome for the same reason. Hartshorne explains panexperientialism's solution to both sides of the problem of interaction thus:

> cells can influence our human experiences because they have feelings that we can feel. To deal with the influences of human

experiences upon cells, one turns this around. *We* have feelings
that *cells* can feel. (Hartshorne 1962, 229)

As this statement shows, panexperientialism involves a radically new
conception of causation. Rather than, with materialists, thinking of billiard-
ball collisions as paradigmatic or, with dualists, thinking in terms of two
radically different kinds of causation—that between minds, and that between
bodies—and then wondering how minds and bodies can interact, panexperientialism conceives of all causation as involving causation that is analogous
to the transference of feeling between two moments of our own experience.[12]
Accordingly, to hold that "our thoughts and feelings can somehow produce
chemical effects on our brains," we do not have to imagine, as Searle suggests, thoughts "wrap[ping] themselves around the axons or shak[ing] the
dendrites [of the brain's neurons]."

The other standard reason for denying downward causation from
conscious experience to the body—the idea that the behavior of things in
the physical world is determined by laws of nature—also does not apply. For
Whitehead's panexperientialism, like that of James and Peirce before him,
the so-called laws of nature are not to be thought of as prescriptive, but as
descriptive of the widespread habits of nature (MT 154–155; on James and
Peirce, see Ochs 1993, 67–68). And, just as we feel and act differently in
different environments, so do cells, molecules, and electrons. After a molecule
migrates from the soil through a carrot to a human body, it is subject to
different influences—including influences from the body's living cells and its
dominant member, the mind—and hence behaves differently (SMW 78–80).
This fact is one of the "laws of nature." Holding that our conscious experiences, with their degree of freedom, guide our bodies, therefore, does not
violate any laws of nature.

I have just mentioned our third hard-core commonsense assumption
about our own experience, namely, that we act with a degree of freedom.
One dimension of Whitehead's explanation of this assumption is the idea
that all individual events are creative events, exercising at least some slight
iota of self-determination. Besides not having to explain how conscious
experience could have arisen out of wholly insentient entities, therefore,
he also did not have to explain how our experience, with its great capacity
for self-determination, could have arisen out of entities that interacted in a
wholly deterministic way. Freedom did not suddenly appear at some point
in the evolutionary process. Rather, compound individuals with increasingly
more mentality emerged out of ones with less.

It is, of course, one thing to assert that all individuals have a degree
of freedom; it is another thing to *explain how* freedom is conceivable in a

world in which all events are enmeshed in a universal nexus of efficient causation. The key to this explanation is the idea, discussed above, that every enduring individual, such as a molecule or a human psyche, perpetually oscillates between subjectivity and objectivity. Each occasion of experience in an enduring individual exists first as a subject. In this mode, it begins as an effect of prior events, receiving efficient causation from them. This is the subject's physical pole. Then the event exercises its self-determination, deciding precisely how to respond to the various causal influences upon it. This is the subject's mental pole, during which it exercises final causation. But then the event becomes an object, at which time it exerts efficient causation on future subjects. This efficient causation is based upon the event's final causation, its self-determination. The event's freedom, in other words, is exercised between its reception of efficient causation from the past and its exertion of efficient causation on the future. In Whitehead's words, each "occasion arises as an effect facing its past and ends as a cause facing its future. In between there lies the teleology of the universe" (AI 194).

We need only apply this idea to the human mind or psyche, understood as a temporal society of dominant occasions of experience, to understand its freedom in relation to its body. In each moment, the dominant occasion arises out of causal influences from the past world—most immediately its own past experiences and its bodily parts, as mediated through its brain. It then exercises its self-determination in deciding how to respond to these influences. This decision then influences its future experiences and its brain cells, which then transmit the decisions to the relevant parts of the body. Therefore, our bodily action does, as we assume, reflect our free choices.

Implicit in this discussion of the psyche—as a temporal series of dominant occasions of experience—is the major way in which Whiteheadian panexperientialism agrees with dualism. Materialists cannot even begin to do justice to our freedom because of their view that the mind is numerically identical with the brain. As I emphasized earlier, this identification entails the denial that the mind is a locus of power that could exercise self-determination. Structurally, therefore, a human being or a dog is not different in kind from a toaster or a computer. Searle brings out this fact by saying that human and canine behavior must be explained in terms of bottom-up causation just as it is in those other things, because there is nothing in a human being or a dog to exert any top-down causation, at least not causation that reflects self-determination. Dualists have always rejected this account, insisting that the human mind, being a numerically distinct entity, is a locus of self-determining power. Structurally, therefore, humans are different in kind from rocks, toasters, and computers. Whiteheadian panexperientialism, with its distinction between compound individuals and nonindividualized aggregational societies, agrees with dualists on this score. Both views affirm human freedom, and both views, thereby, affirm the mind's efficient causation on the body in Taube's sense. Both views, more generally, endorse interactionism—that the mind and the brain, being numerically distinct, interact, with each exerting causal efficacy on the other.[13]

The only difference is that dualism, in addition to affirming this numerical distinctness, affirms that the mind is ontologically different in kind from the brain's components, being composed of different stuff. So, although dualism's numerical thesis provides a necessary condition for making interaction intelligible, its ontological thesis makes this interaction *un*intelligible. Whiteheadian panexperientialism keeps the numerical thesis while rejecting the ontological thesis. And it is the ontological thesis, not the numerical thesis by itself, that makes the position dualistic and hence problematic.[14] Whitehead's position, therefore, can be called *nondualistic interactionism*.[15] This doctrine is essential to his defense of human freedom.

Our fourth hard-core assumption is that our action, besides embodying freedom, also involves acting in accord with norms. Part of the Whiteheadian vindication of this assumption has already been given—namely, that in exercising final causation, we are aiming at a goal, and this goal can well involve some ideal, such as the ideal to be moral or self-consistent. Implicit in this position, however, is the idea that we can be *aware* of norms. Whitehead's panexperientialism speaks to this issue as well. The modern belief that we could not perceive cognitive, moral, and aesthetic norms, even if such norms exist, is based on the belief that we experience things beyond ourselves only by means of our sensory organs. However, the idea that perceptual experience is enjoyed by all individuals, including all individuals without sense-organs, implies that there is a mode of perception more basic than sensory perception. And this is Whitehead's doctrine—that sensory perception is a high-level form of perception, derivative from a more primitive, nonsensory mode of perception, which he calls "prehension" or "feeling." It is through this nonsensory prehension that we apprehend norms.[16]

I have been explaining how Whitehead's panexperientialism, with its nonreductionistic naturalism, allows us to do justice to four of our hard-core commonsense assumptions about conscious experience that have been problematic for both dualists and materialists. One ingredient in this explanation is the Jamesian demotion of consciousness from the status of an entity or a stuff[17] to that an emergent function. In the final section, I will explain Whitehead's development of this Jamesian notion into the doctrine that consciousness is the subjective form of a feeling of a certain type. I will also point out some other ways, in addition to its being a necessary ingredient in Whitehead's solution to the mind-body problem, that this doctrine is important.

The Doctrine of Consciousness as a Subjective Form: Its Meaning and Importance

Consciousness for Whitehead, to recall, is the subjective form of an intellectual feeling, which arises, if at all, only in a *late phase* of an occasion of experience. Thus far the discussion of different phases of experience has been limited to two: the physical and the mental poles. In an occasion of experience that attains consciousness, however, the mental pole itself has phases. According to Whitehead's more detailed analysis of a conscious occasion of experience, there are four phases altogether. The first phase is the physical phase, which feels past actual occasions. In the second phase, various pure possibilities (eternal objects) are felt conceptually or appetitively. In the third phase, these possibilities are conjoined with the actualities felt in the physical pole, resulting in the feeling of propositions. In the fourth phase, these propositions are compared with the original physical feelings, resulting in "intellectual feelings" (PR 241, 266, 277, 344). What is unique about an intellectual feeling is that it involves a contrast between a fact and a proposition (or theory)—between what is and what might be. This is called the "affirmation-negation contrast."

Like all other feelings, intellectual feelings have, besides an objective datum, also a subjective form, which is how that datum is felt. The objective datum of an intellectual feeling is an affirmation-negation contrast; the subjective form is consciousness. Consciousness, in other words, involves awareness both of something definite and of potentialities that

> illustrate *either* what it is and might not be, or what it is not
> and might be. In other words, there is no consciousness without
> reference to definiteness, affirmation, and negation. Consciousness
> is how we feel the affirmation-negation contrast. (PR 243)

To explain more fully the difference between experience that is and is not conscious: Experience is present whenever there is any awareness of what is; but we should not speak of *conscious* experience, Whitehead proposes, except where there is also an awareness of *what is not.*

> Consciousness is the feeling of negation: in the perception of "the
> stone as grey," such feeling is in barest germ; in the perception
> of "the stone as not grey," such feeling is in full development.
> Thus the negative perception is the triumph of consciousness.
> (PR 161)

Consciousness, according to this analysis, is provoked into existence by, and only by, the right type of datum, this being an affirmation-negation contrast. Without this datum, there can be no consciousness. This explains why consciousness can appear only in a late phase of experience: An intellectual feeling is a complex feeling, involving the integration of feelings arising in earlier phases, so it can arise only in a late phase. This idea lies behind Whitehead's well-known statement that "consciousness presupposes experience, and not experience consciousness" (PR 53). Consciousness, if it occurs, lights up experience that preceded it, a level of experience that can exist without consciousness. Whitehead says, accordingly, that "consciousness is the crown of experience, only occasionally attained, not its necessary base" (PR 267).

In saying that consciousness is only occasionally attained, Whitehead means partly that those enduring individuals that are capable of attaining consciousness do not do so in every occasion of their experience (as in dreamless sleep). But he is mainly referring to the fact that most of the occasions of experience in the universe are too simple to go beyond the third phase. They are hence incapable of creating any full-fledged propositions, which are necessary conditions for intellectual feelings. Whitehead thereby explains how there can be experience without consciousness, and also how compound individuals capable of consciousness could have emerged out of ones without this capacity.

An explanation of how consciousness could have emerged is an essential component in the theory's adequacy. Panexperientialism, as we saw earlier, avoids what has rightly been seen as an insoluble problem: how conscious experience could have emerged out of entities wholly devoid of experience. But one could accept panexperientialism and still not find it self-evident how experience of our type could have emerged out of entities such as quarks and photons. Whitehead's account of the phases of concrescence provides an abstract scheme that shows what kind of experiences the intervening steps might have had. This scheme can be described in terms of the language of "intentionality," which many philosophers of mind have used to express the problem of how consciousness could have emerged. That is, consciousness involves "intentionality" in the sense of "aboutness"; it has "intentional objects." These intended objects may be actual things, such as food, or ideal things, such as numbers or propositions. In any case, the puzzle is how beings such as us, with our intentionality, could have emerged out of things such as quarks and photons, which, even if we grant them some type of experience, cannot be supposed to have anything approaching the intentionality that we enjoy.

The abstract line of development suggested by Whitehead's analysis goes like this: Very elementary occasions of experience are not able to synthesize physical and conceptual feelings into propositional feelings, but they do syn-thesize them into rudimentary analogues, which Whitehead calls "physical purposes" (PR 267, 276). These experiences, not being able to focus on a pos-sibility *qua* possibility, have only, we can say, incipient intentionality. Somewhat higher-level occasions of experience, complex enough to have propositional (but not intellectual) feelings, have, we can say, *proto*-intentionality. Only very high-level experiences have full-fledged, conscious intentionality, because only they are sophisticated enough to contrast propositions, as possibilities, with the perceived facts. Given the idea of evolution as involving increasingly complex compound individuals, which can provide their dominant occasions with increasingly complex data, we can see how experiences of our type could have gradually arisen out of extremely trivial experiences.

Whitehead's analysis of consciousness, I have shown, is part and parcel of his explanation of how conscious beings could have emerged evolutionarily and of his justification of our hard-core commonsense assumptions about our experience. I will conclude by pointing out how it also lies behind Whitehead's explanation of why, although our hard-core commonsense beliefs have an empirical basis, philosophers have tended to overlook this basis.

The main idea in this explanation is that consciousness, arising only near the conclusion of an occasion of experience, fails to shed its light upon the origins of that experience and thereby its most basic ingredients. In Whitehead's words: "Consciousness only arises in a late derivative phase of complex integrations" and "primarily illuminates the higher phase in which it arises." Accordingly, "consciousness only dimly illuminates the . . . prim-itive elements in our experience." Whitehead even refers to this point as a "law"—"that the late derivative elements are more clearly illuminated by consciousness than the primitive elements" (PR 162). We can call this "Whitehead's perceptual law."

On the basis of this law, we can understand why philosophers, at least since the time of Hume, have worried about the empirical basis of our beliefs about causation and the "external world." We do, Whitehead says, directly perceive the existence of actual things beyond ourselves and also their causal efficacy on us. Whitehead, in fact, refers to this as a distinct mode of percep-tion, which he calls "perception in the mode of causal efficacy" (this being a synonym for "physical prehension"). This mode stands in contrast with another mode, which he calls "perception in the mode of presentational immediacy," because in this latter mode various data are immediately present to our con-sciousness. The perception of sense-data, such as colored shapes, is the most obvious example of perception in this mode. *Full-fledged sense-perception* always involves a synthesis of these two modes, which Whitehead calls "perception in the mode of symbolic reference."[18] In our conscious experience, however, the data of perception in the mode of causal efficacy tend to drop out, so that sensory perception gets virtually equated with perception in the mode of presentational immediacy. This is especially the case with philosophers insofar as they focus on the "clear and distinct" data of perception, presuming them to be basic. Accordingly, Hume, while admitting that in "practice" he could not help presupposing a real world and causation as real influence, said that in his philosophical "theory," which was to be based rigidly on perceptual experience, he could not refute solipsism and could define causation only as the "constant conjunction" of two types of phenomena.

Whitehead's perceptual law—"that the late derivative elements [in an occasion of experience] are more clearly illuminated by consciousness than the primitive elements"—explains why Hume, focusing on the clear and distinct elements in perceptual experience, came to that conclusion. "[C]onsciousness only dimly illuminates the prehensions in the mode of causal efficacy," says Whitehead, "because these prehensions are primitive elements in our experience." By contrast, "prehensions in the mode of presentational immediacy . . . are late derivatives"; they, accordingly, "are among those prehensions which we enjoy with the most vivid consciousness" (PR 162).

Whitehead's perceptual law presupposes his idea that the mind or psyche is not an enduring substance, or even stream, numerically one through time, with consciousness as the stuff of which it consists. *Consciousness is not, accordingly, simply waiting there, as it were, to be filled by this or that content.* If it were, we would expect it to light up early arrivals as clearly as, or even more clearly than, late-comers. This seemed to be Hume's assumption. But the mind or psyche is, instead, a serially ordered society of distinct (albeit intimately interconnected) occasions of experience, and consciousness is a subjective form that arises, if at all, only in a late phase of these occasions. *It is not lying in waiting, but must be provoked into existence.* And this provocation, as we have seen, can occur only in a late phase. Consciousness, accordingly, primarily illuminates the latecomers, which have been constructed by the occasion of experience itself, rather than the early arrivals, which were given to the occasion of experience from beyond itself.

If this were the only implication of Whitehead's perceptual law, it would be of importance only to philosophers, who seem to be the only ones tempted to solipsism and phenomenalist definitions of causality. A more general cultural problem of modernity, however, is the widespread doubt that normative ideals are given to our experience. Max Weber called modernity's transition to seeing the world as not embodying such ideals "the disenchantment of the world." The existential implication of this disenchantment is the relativistic belief that ideals are invented, not discovered (see Mackie 1977, the subtitle of which is *Inventing Right and Wrong*). The political implication is that "might makes right" (see Griffin 1988, 9–10; 2001, 285–287).

The denial that we perceive normative ideals is closely related to the equation of perception with sensory perception. Because ideals are not the kinds of things that can be detected by means of our physical sense organs, the belief that we can perceive only by means of our senses can persuade us that we do not perceive ideals. But this denial is also due in part to the fact that this perception is generally at the fringes of the conscious portion of our experience. This fringiness of ideals does not mean that they are absent or secondary in our experience. The exact contrary is the case: They are secondary or even tertiary in consciousness because they are primary in experience.

To explain this point more fully would require a discussion of White-head's theism, God's provision of an "initial aim" for each finite occasion of experience, and our direct perception of God (in whom, by the "ontological principle," the normative ideals must subsist if they are to exist and be per-ceivable). A complete account of Whitehead's psychology, in other words, is not possible in abstraction from his theology. I have discussed this connection elsewhere (see Griffin 2001, ch. 8; 2003). For now I simply repeat the main points of the present account—that Whitehead defines consciousness as the subjective form of an intellectual feeling; that this conception of conscious-ness is part and parcel of Whitehead's panexperientialist worldview; that this worldview, with its nonreductionistic naturalism, is far more adequate to our inevitable presuppositions than are both dualism and materialism; and that this conception of consciousness can help us understand that our inevitable presuppositions have a basis in our perceptual experience even though modern philosophers, and our conscious experience more generally, tend to overlook this basis.

I close by noting that one of the central tasks of philosophy, in Whitehead's view, involves overcoming the illusions produced by the fact that consciousness tends to leave the most fundamental elements of our experience in the dark. In his words:

> Philosophy is the self-correction by consciousness of its own initial excess of subjectivity. Each actual occasion contributes to the circumstances of its origin additional formative elements . . . . Consciousness is only the last and greatest of such elements by which the selective character of the individual obscures the external totality, from which it originates and which it embodies. An actual individual, of such higher grade, has truck with the totality of things . . . ; but it has attained its individual depth of being by a selective emphasis . . . . The task of philosophy is to recover the totality obscured by the selection. (PR 15)

Calling this task "the metaphysical correction" (PR xvii), Whitehead shows that metaphysics can be relevant to psychology, even to its existential dimensions.

Notes

1. Although Swinburne is a dualist, he sees that this problem is the same whether one is a dualist or a materialist.

2. For the interpretation of Descartes as an occasionalist, see Baker and Morris 1996, 153–154, 167–170. On Malebranche and Geulincx, see Copleston 1960, 117–119, 188–190.

3. Explicitly denying that we have a mind that is distinct from the brain, Searle says, referring to the human head, that "the brain is the only thing in there" (1992, 248).

4. For example, he rejected vitalism, pointing out that it "involves an essential dualism somewhere" (SMW 79).

5. I have included this doctrine in a list of ten core doctrines of process philosophy (2001, 6).

6. The term "panexperientialism" was coined after Whitehead's time. As far as I know, I coined it and first used it in print in Cobb and Griffin 1977, 98. But Charles Hartshorne commented favorably on it, saying that this term had advantages over both "panpsychism" and the alternative he had proposed, "psychicalism" (1989, 181).

7. This fact does not, to be sure, deter some hostile critics, determined to portray all versions of panexperientialism as unintelligible. For example, Paul Edwards, in an encyclopedia article on panpsychism, criticizes the doctrine as unintelligible for attributing experience to stars and stones, even while pointing out that Whitehead, the twentieth-century's "most distinguished champion of panpsychism," held the experiencing units to be "not stars and stones but the events out of which stars and stones are constituted" (Edwards 197, 31). I have criticized Edwards for this treatment in Griffin 1998, 96–97.

8. By an "aggregational event" I mean simply the occurrence of something such as a rock at a particular moment—that is, the occurrence of all the molecular events that constitute the rock at that moment.

9. The term "perpetual oscillation," I have suggested (Griffin 2001, 115–116), is more helpful than Whitehead's term "perpetual perishing," which has proved to be perpetually confusing. (Many interpreters have taken the statement that an actual entity "perishes" after it reaches satisfaction to mean that it is no longer actual—which would mean that, by the ontological principle that only actualities can act, it would not be able to exert causation. But this is the exact opposite of Whitehead's meaning, as the following quotation makes clear: "actual entities 'perpetually perish' subjectively, but are immortal objectively. Actuality in perishing acquires objectivity, while it loses subjective immediacy. It loses the final causation . . . and it acquires efficient causation" [PR 29].)

10. This has been conclusively shown in Ford 1982 and 1993.

11. McGinn even quotes a passage showing that Kant realized that panexperientialism, which he knew in its Leibnizian-Wolffian form, could overcome the chief difficulty in understanding the communion of body and soul. "The difficulty peculiar to the problem consists," suggested Kant, "in the assumed heterogeneity of the object of inner sense (the soul) and the objects of the outer senses . . . . But if we consider that the two kinds of objects thus differ from each other, not inwardly but only in so far as one appears outwardly to another, and that what, as thing in itself, underlies the appearances of matter, perhaps after all may not be so heterogeneous in character, this difficulty vanishes" (Kant 1965, 381 [B428]; quoted in McGinn 1991, 81). McGinn, however, is unable to incorporate this solution because of his conviction that panexperientialism is absurd.

12. "[I]f we hold," said Whitehead, "that all final individual actualities have the metaphysical character of occasions of experience, then . . . the connectedness of one's immediate present occasion of experience with one's immediately past occasions, can be validly used to suggest categories applying to the connectedness of all occasions in nature" (AI 221). Indeed, he argued, we *must* do this if we are to use the notion of "causation" meaningfully. Since "we can only understand causation in terms of our observations of [our own occasions of experience]," then "in so far as we apply notions of causation to the understanding of events in nature, we must conceive these events under the general notions which apply to occasions of experience" (AI 184).

13. In this statement of the way in which Whiteheadian panexperientialism agrees with dualism, I have restricted the discussion to *human* minds, because some dualists, including Descartes himself, do not attribute minds to nonhuman animals.

14. There has been a pervasive tendency, among both dualists and materialists, to conflate the two theses, as if affirming numerical distinctness were *ipso facto* to affirm ontological difference. I have discussed this tendency in Griffin 2000, 173–175.

15. On this view, the mind or soul is not, in Gilbert Ryle's pejorative phrase, a "ghost in the machine" because the body is no machine but a vast society of less sophisticated experiences.

16. These norms can be understood, in Whitehead's technical language, as either "eternal objects" or "propositions." In either case, they exist in God—in what Whitehead calls "the primordial nature of God," which is God's primordial envisagement of all pure possibilities, or eternal objects, with the appetition that they be realized in due season. Understanding Whitehead's psychology, accordingly, finally requires an understanding of his theology. But this dimension of this thought lies beyond the scope of the present chapter. It suffices here to point out that we apprehend norms by apprehending God, in whom they exist. By virtue of this doctrine, Whitehead avoids McGinn's criticism that the causal effect of norms on our conscious experience would be a "funny" kind of causation, because it would involve the exercise of efficient causation on the mind by an abstract (nonactual) entity. In Whitehead's views, because the norms are in God, understood as the dominant member of the universe as a whole, our normative experience can be understood by analogy with the relation between our minds and our bodily cells.

17. It is, incidentally, not only dualists who have thought of consciousness as the stuff of the mind. Colin McGinn has said: "Logically, 'consciousness' is a stuff

term, as 'matter' is; and I see nothing wrong, metaphysically, with recognizing that consciousness *is* a kind of stuff" (1991, 60n).

18. Insofar as Whitehead equates sense-perception with perception in the mode of causal efficacy, he agrees with those "direct realists" who maintain, contrary to Hume, that sensory perception is not solipsistic but gives us direct knowledge of the existence of an external world. Whitehead differs from them, however, insofar as they fail to regard sense-perception as a mixed mode of perception involving a nonsensory mode.

References

Adler, Julius, and Wing-Wai Tse. 1974. "Decision-Making in Bacteria." *Science* 184 (June 21): 1292–1294.

Baker, Gordon, and Katherine J. Morris. 1996. *Descartes' Dualism*. London and New York: Routledge.

Beloff, John. 1962. *The Existence of Mind*. London: MacGibbon and Kee.

Bohm, David, and B.J. Hiley. 1993. *The Undivided Universe: An Ontological Interpretation of Quantum Theory*. London and New York: Routledge.

Campbell, Keith. 1984. *Body and Mind*. 2nd ed. Notre Dame: University of Notre Dame Press.

Capek, Milic. 1991. *The New Aspects of Time: Its Continuity and Novelties: Selected Papers in the Philosophy of Science*. Ed. Robert S. Cohen. Boston: Kluwer Academic Publishers.

Cobb, John B. Jr., and David Ray Griffin, eds. 1977. *Mind in Nature: Essays on the Interface of Science and Philosophy*. Washington, DC: University Press of America.

Copleston, F.C. 1960. *A History of Philosophy*, vol. 4: *Descartes to Leibniz*. London: Burns Oates.

Dennett, Daniel E. 1984. *Elbow Room: The Varieties of Free Will Worth Wanting*. Cambridge, MA: MIT Press.

Edwards, Paul. 1972. "Panpsychism." In *Encyclopedia of Philosophy*, editor-in-chief Paul Edwards, 6:23–31. New York: Macmillan.

Ford, Marcus P. 1982. *William James's Philosophy: A New Perspective*. Amherst: University of Massachusetts Press.

Ford, Marcus P. 1993. "William James." In David Griffin et al. 1993, 89–132.

Goldbetter, A., and D.E. Koshland Jr. 1982. "Simple Molecular Model for Sensing and Adaptation Based on Receptor Modification with Application to Bacterial Chemotaxis." *Journal of Molecular Biology* 161 (3): 395–416.

Griffin, David Ray, ed. 1988. *Spirituality and Society: Postmodern Visions*. Albany: State University of New York Press.

Griffin, David Ray et al. 1993. *Founders of Constructive Postmodern Philosophy: Peirce, James, Bergson, Whitehead, and Hartshorne*. Albany: State University of New York Press.

Griffin, David Ray. 1997. "Panexperientialist Physicalism and the Mind-Body Problem." *Journal of Consciousness Studies* 4 (3): 248–268.

Griffin, David Ray. 1998. *Unsnarling the World-Knot: Consciousness, Freedom, and the Mind-Body Problem.* Berkeley and Los Angeles: University of California Press (repr. 2008. Eugene, Oregon: Wipf and Stock).

Griffin, David Ray. 2000. *Religion and Scientific Naturalism: Overcoming the Conflicts.* Albany: State University of New York Press.

Griffin, David Ray. 2001. *Reenchantment without Supernaturalism: A Process Philosophy of Religion.* Ithaca: Cornell University Press.

Griffin, David Ray. 2003. "Morality and Scientific Naturalism: Overcoming the Conflicts." In *Philosophy of Religion for a New Century,* ed. Jerald T. Wallulis and Jeremiah Hackett, 81–104. Dordrecht: Kluwer.

Griffin, Donald R. 1992. *Animal Minds.* Chicago: University of Chicago Press.

Hartshorne, Charles. 1962. *The Logic of Perfection and Other Essays in Neoclassical Metaphysics.* LaSalle: Open Court.

Hartshorne, Charles. 1972. "The Compound Individual." In Hartshorne, *Whitehead's Philosophy: Selected Essays 1935–1970,* 41–61. Lincoln: University of Nebraska Press.

Hartshorne, Charles. 1989. "General Remarks." *Hartshorne, Process Philosophy, and Theology.* Ed. Robert Kane and Stephen H. Phillips. Albany: State University of New York Press, 181–196.

Hintikka, Jaakko. 1962. "Cogito, Ergo Sum: Inference or Performance." *Philosophical Review* 71:3–32.

Hameroff, Stuart R. 1994. "Quantum Coherence in Microtubules: A Neural Basis for Emergent Consciousness?" *Journal of Consciousness Studies* 1:91–118.

Honderich, Ted. 1987. "Mind, Brain, and Self-Conscious Mind." *Mindwaves: Thoughts on Intelligence, Identity, and Consciousness.* Eds. Colin Blakemore and Susan Greenfield. Oxford: Basil Blackwell, 445–458.

James, William. 1904. "Does Consciousness Exist?" *Journal of Philosophy, Psychology and Scientific Methods* 1 (18 [September 1]). Reprinted in James, *Essays in Radical Empiricism,* ed. Ralph Barton Perry (1912), republished in a volume also containing James's *A Pluralistic Universe* by E.P. Dutton, 1971.

James, William. 1911. *Some Problems of Philosophy.* London: Longman and Green.

Jay, Martin. 1993. "The Debate over Performative Contradiction: Habermas versus the Poststructuralists." In Martin Jay, *Force Fields: Between Intellectual History and Cultural Critique,* 25–37. New York and London: Routledge.

Johnson, A.H. 1969. "Whitehead as Teacher and Philosopher." *Philosophy and Phenomenological Research* 29:351–376.

Kant, Immanuel. 1965. *Critique of Pure Reason.* Trans. Norman Kemp Smith. New York: St. Martin's.

Keller, Evelyn Fox. 1983. *A Feeling for the Organism: The Life and Work of Barbara McClintock.* New York: Freeman.

Kim, Jaegwon. 1993. *Supervenience and Mind: Selected Philosophical Essays.* Cambridge: Cambridge University Press.

Lewis, H.D. 1969. *The Elusive Mind.* London: George Allen and Unwin.

Lycan, William G. 1987. *Consciousness.* Cambridge, MA: MIT Press.

Mackie, John. 1977. *Ethics: Inventing Right and Wrong.* New York: Penguin.

Madell, Geoffrey. 1988. *Mind and Materialism.* Edinburgh: University Press.

McCarthy, Thomas. 1993. *Ideals and Illusions: On Reconstruction and Deconstruction in Contemporary Critical Theory*. Cambridge, MA: MIT Press.

McGinn, Colin. 1982. *The Character of Mind*. Oxford: Oxford University Press.

McGinn, Colin. 1991. *The Problem of Consciousness: Essays Toward a Resolution*. Oxford: Basil Blackwell.

Nagel, Thomas. 1979. *Mortal Questions*. London: Cambridge University Press.

Nagel, Thomas. 1986. *The View from Nowhere*. New York: Oxford University Press.

Ochs, Peter. 1993. "Charles Sanders Pierce." In Griffin 1993, 43–87.

Passmore, John. 1961. *Philosophical Reasoning*. New York: Basic Books.

Popper, Karl R., and John C. Eccles. 1977. *The Self and Its Brain: An Argument for Interactionism*. Heidelberg: Springer-Verlag.

Seager, William. 1991. *Metaphysics of Consciousness*. London and New York: Routledge.

Seager, William. 1995. "Consciousness, Information, and Panpsychism." *Journal of Consciousness Studies* 2:272–288.

Searle, John R. 1984. *Minds, Brains, and Science: The 1984 Reith Lectures*. London: British Broadcasting Corporation.

Searle, John R. 1992. *The Rediscovery of the Mind*. Cambridge, MA: MIT Press.

Smart, J.J.C. 1979. "Materialism." In *The Mind-Brain Identity Theory*, ed. C.V. Borst, 159–170. London: Macmillan.

Swinburne, Richard. 1986. *The Evolution of the Soul*. Oxford: Clarendon.

Taube, Mortimer. 1936. *Causation, Freedom and Determinism*. London: George Allen and Unwin.

6

The Interpretation and Integration of the Literature on Consciousness from a Process Perspective

Michael Katzko

Psychology has lacked a good general perspective on how to think about mental experience. Over the past hundred years the topic has been largely ignored in most areas of the mainstream. Only recently has the topic resurfaced as a legitimate concern for psychologists. One area of study has been the nature of "self," in the first instance as a revolt against a Cartesian notion of a single self in favor of a more complex multiplicity. However, the arguments of this revolt are only crudely empirical, pointing to a phenomenon not yet interpreted into a theory that accommodates both the apparent subjective unity of experience and the empirical notion of multiplicity.[1]

The writings of A.N. Whitehead, culminating in *Process and Reality* (PR), exemplify an intuition of mental experience that offers a perspective that psychology requires. A clue to the nature of his intuition—his "vision," perhaps—comes early in PR where he is discussing philosophical method and uses the term "consciousness" nontechnically:

Philosophy is the self-correction by consciousness of its own initial excess of subjectivity. The methodology of rational interpretation is the product of the fitful vagueness of consciousness. Each actual occasion contributes to the circumstances of its origin additional formative elements deepening its own peculiar individuality. Consciousness is only the last and greatest of such elements by which the selective character of the individual obscures the external totality from which it originates and which it embodies. . . . Elements which shine with immediate distinctness, in some occasions, retire into penumbral shadow in other circumstances, and into black darkness on other occasions. (PR 15)

What Whitehead means by "external totality" is the "initial data" that are formative of an actual occasion. Countless strands of multiplicity can combine and recombine in patterns of emphasis in terminal occasions we call conscious experience. When Whitehead asserts that "the task of philosophy is to recover the totality obscured by the selection" (PR 15) he also provides psychology with an image of the problem that any conscious entity confronts, be that entity a professional philosopher or a shopkeeper.

The second main area of psychology within which the topic of consciousness has recently been discussed is the broadly conceived program of cognitive neuroscience. However, one can reasonably doubt that this literature has as yet made constructive headway in understanding the nature of conscious experience. An editor of a recent anthology on the consciousness debate felt obliged to address a possible reaction to the book's contents: "An unsympathetic observer leafing through the family album of this debate might cast the participants in the role of alchemists arguing over whether lead can be transmuted into gold . . . a squabble among possibly helpful underlaborers hoping to prepare the way for a future serious science" (Warner 1994, 7–8). Collectively, this literature appears to do little more than reconstruct doctrines from the seventeenth century. There is almost an obsessiveness that grips the debate, with articles written, and commented on, and the comments replied to. At times, the discussants appear preoccupied with the debate as an intellectual end in itself, with the substantive topic only a subsidiary concern.

The purpose of this article is to use this literature as a case study in the applicability of Whitehead's process perspective on consciousness generally. In short, it is the character of daily conscious existence that it is a process of selection and emphasis. Historically, it is precisely this process of selection that has masked the true nature of conscious experience, the result being that the literature has only been a multiplicity of unintegrated patterns of emphasis of diverse individual thinkers.

However, rather than confronting the current literature directly with details of Whitehead's philosophy, the literature will be assessed from the standpoint of Whitehead's intellectual motives. A key to understanding Whitehead is to understand how he evaluated the context for his intellectual work. One of the beliefs that shaped Whitehead's intellectual activity was that "the movement of historical, and philosophical, criticism of detached questions, which on the whole has dominated the last two centuries, has done its work" (PR xiv). The mistakes, shortcomings, inconsistencies and also the positive contributions of the philosophical and scientific tradition are now understood, and it is time for "a more sustained effort of constructive thought." I suggest that the literature on consciousness fails to heed the lessons of history. In fact, a strong case can be made that this is true of much of twentieth-century philosophy (see, for example, Lagerspetz 2002, Weekes, 2003). I will first summarize some of Whitehead's motivations, their origins and how they influenced his choices in developing his philosophical doctrine. I will then use this account to critically evaluate some recent literature that addresses the problem of consciousness. Third, I will turn to some substantive details of Whitehead's doctrine, to illustrate how his overall aims and his recognition of philosophical flaws shape his philosophy and thereby integrate a variety of topics that are unintegrated in contemporary literature. I will close with some remarks about constructive routes of development in psychology and philosophy that Whitehead's metaphysics imply.

Whitehead's Methodological Concerns

A recurring aspect of Whitehead's writings is his concern for the way in which he defines his intellectual task. This can be seen as early as his *Concept of Nature* (CN). Here, the intellectual ideal "is the attainment of some unifying concept, which will set in assigned relationships within itself *all that there is* for knowledge, for feeling, and for emotion" (CN 2, emphasis added). When translated into a substantive issue this means that "the immediate fact of awareness is the *whole* occurrence of nature. It is nature as an event present for sense-awareness, and essentially passing" (CN 14, emphasis added).

By the time he came to write PR this theme was formalized as complementary ideals of adequacy and coherence. Adequacy represents the scope of the empirical domain to which some doctrine is to be applied, while coherence represents the relations of concepts in the doctrine to each other. For a complete metaphysics the ideals of adequacy and coherence must be comprehensive. Practically, however, the historical development of science and philosophy illustrates the rhythmic swing between these ideals: from a partial selection of data to a provisional theoretical generalization, then to the application of the generalization to a broader empirical domain, and finally readjustment of the theory as required.

In this historical process the ideals of adequacy and coherence are complementary and mutually constraining. Yet Whitehead's concern is not merely a methodological formality. His concern has its origins in real difficulties in the philosophical literature. For example, he asserted that "for natural philosophy everything perceived is in nature. We may not pick and choose" (CN 29). Either reasons must be found for this "picking and choosing" or—and this is what he believed to be the proper approach of intellectual inquiry—"so far as reality is concerned all our sense-perceptions are in the same boat, and must be treated on the *same principle*" (CN 44, emphasis added). The consequence of an arbitrary empirical picking and choosing resulted in a doctrinal incoherence that he termed the bifurcation of nature "into two systems of reality, which, insofar as they are real, are real in different senses" (CN 30), or, "into the nature apprehended in awareness and the nature which is the cause of awareness" (CN 31). Bifurcation reflects an arbitrariness in selecting from the data within a given domain of study.

In *Science and the Modern World* (SMW) he offered a reason for how and why bifurcation takes place. This is his principle of misplaced concreteness, a confusion of the abstract with the concrete. "Nature" is the totality given, and this totality entails events with an internal relational structure. The intellectual analysis of these relations by scientists or philosophers delivers abstractions as products. These abstractions have been incorrectly conceived as the proper generalizations of the most basic or concrete descriptions of the reality within which the events of nature take place.

It cannot be stressed too much that the impetus for Whitehead's analysis came from contemporary discoveries in the natural sciences. SMW is one extended demonstration of how his doctrinal choices emerged from empirical developments in physics. The essential implication of these developments was that they required a modification of the basic physical concepts formulated within Newtonian cosmology. In the first place, they exposed the fallacy of "simple location." This is the conception of absolute space and time within which unchanging bits of matter live out their lives.[2] Furthermore, the fallacy of misplaced concreteness is reflected in other concepts such as substance and quality. This leads to the doctrine of primary and secondary qualities, which is another guise for bifurcation. Finally, in PR the fallacy of misplaced concreteness reemerges as an explicitly repudiated assumption in the philosophical tradition that "the basic elements of experience are to be described in terms of one, or all, of the three ingredients, consciousness, thought, sense-perception . . . these three components are unessential elements in experience" (PR 36). "Mind" in a Cartesian sense exhibits the same fallacy as does the conceptualization of matter in Newtonian space-time.

PR broadens the scope of his argument. Mere abstractions such as *space* or *time* or *consciousness* all have in common the fact that they are found at a terminus of intellectual experience. As usual, Whitehead places great store in the adequacy of a metaphysical scheme, that "everything of which we are conscious, as enjoyed, perceived, willed, or thought, shall have the character of a particular instance of the general scheme . . . all related experience must exhibit the same texture" (PR 3–4). As he elaborates in the well-known passage in *Adventures of Ideas*, given this goal of finding the metaphysical generalities "we must appeal to evidence relating to every variety of occasion.

Nothing can be omitted, experience drunk, experience sober, experience sleeping and experience waking . . ." (AI 290). He means *everything*, including the capacity to abstract and create philosophical systems. The true business of philosophy "is to explain the emergence of the more abstract things from the more concrete things" (PR 20). The business of scientists and philosophers is to take account of *their own intellectual activity* as the process by which the intellectual accounts of some domain of study are produced.

This observation has a fundamental influence on the doctrinal content of PR. The other face of adequacy is coherence, that "the fundamental ideas . . . presuppose each other so that in isolation they are meaningless" (PR 3). This implies that the philosophical scheme itself has to be part of the broader scheme of things, that it "should be 'necessary,' in the sense of bearing in itself its own warrant of universality throughout all experience" (PR 4). Thus, the demand for doctrinal coherence is nothing other than a reflection of the metaphysical ideal that the universe is essentially relational, that "no entity can be conceived in complete isolation from the system of the universe" (PR 3).

Whitehead is responding to a professional "habit of thought" of scientists or philosophers to abstract themselves from their own intellectual activity. If, in the course of developing an explanatory framework for some domain of study an explanation is offered for some items of that domain, then the reason offered must also be included within the scope of that domain of study. It is the habit of not doing this that creates the incoherence in philosophical systems. Something is added to the philosophical discourse to make the doctrine work, without adding it either to the doctrine or to the reality being explained. An example is the notion of "in practice," an appeal to common sense employed by some philosophers—admitting the "data" but not adjusting the doctrine to cover it. It is for this reason that he asserts "whatever is found in 'practice' must lie within the scope of the metaphysical description" (PR 13). This is an appeal to both doctrinal adequacy and coherence. He had in mind an explicit charge against arguments in Hume and Russell.[3]

In summary, Whitehead was concerned both with the obvious shortcomings of existing philosophical doctrines and with the doctrinal changes implied in the advances of twentieth-century physics. He analyzed the shortcomings in terms of "habits of thought," that is, in terms of the intellectual operations of the philosophers themselves. These operations became part of the comprehensive data of experience, which a complete doctrine must explain. The coherence of the universe must be reflected in the coherence of the doctrine: "vacuous actuality" is the final result of habits of thought that permit concepts to be treated in isolation from one another.

The Dualist Character Contemporary Literature

It is characteristic of the recent literature on consciousness that a conceptual bifurcation is presupposed in how the problem of consciousness is defined, even while authors may be denying a metaphysics of dualism. For example, in one anthology the root question is phrased as follows: "the contributions . . . [concern] the basic question 'Is the mental just the physical?'" (Warner 1994, 1). In another anthology the bifurcation is explicit in the book's first sentence: "How can consciousness arise in a physical universe?" (Metzinger 1995, 3). Lower on the same page it is claimed that "it has become obvious that . . . we have been reaching for a new theory of mind." Contrast this claim with Whitehead's argument that early twentieth-century developments in physics force us toward a new theory of the physical! Whitehead's own question was: How does the abstract notion of "physical" arise?

In this section I will give some illustrations of how philosophers sharing presuppositions about how to define the "problem" nonetheless diverge in their beliefs about and explanations of consciousness. This divergence ultimately reflects the inherent incoherence of the presuppositions. In the subsequent section I will discuss how this is related to the inadequacy with which they have selected the data for explanation.

Consider Chalmers' oft-discussed distinction between the "easy" and the "hard" problem(s) of consciousness. There are two difficulties with his presentation. The first difficulty arises directly from an explicit bifurcation of his subject matter. Chalmers defines the so-called easy problems as those where functions or processes are explained through the use of "the methods of cognitive science and neuroscience" (Chalmers 1995, 201). Thus, "to explain a cognitive function, we need only specify a mechanism that can perform the function" (201). This argument is tautological. In effect, he's saying that a theory of type X (a neurocognitive theory) can explain whatever it is which that sort of theory is capable of explaining. He then, perhaps inadvertently, slips in a shift of terminology. He identifies a *neurocognitive* explanation with a *physical* explanation. This logically forces him to phrase the hard problem as: "why should physical processing give rise to a rich inner life at all?" (201).

The second difficulty emerges from his attempt to characterize the meaning of the phrase "rich inner life," a difficulty shared by writers attempting to describe the phenomena to which the term "consciousness" refers. "The really hard problem of consciousness is the problem of *experience* . . . when we think and perceive . . . there is a *subjective* aspect . . . this *subjective* aspect is experience" (201). Here, he is introducing several ideas in an effort to cash in on the reader's intuitions regarding the diverse meanings of words such as consciousness, experience, perceive, or subjective. However, he then asserts implicitly an equivalence among these terms. For example, "I find it more natural to speak of 'conscious experience' or simply 'experience'" (201). Compare this with Whitehead's explicit denial of the equivalence of these terms. Chalmers then provides several examples of what he is referring to, such as "the felt quality of redness," the "sound of a clarinet," or the "smell of mothballs." Notice how Chalmers reduces his hard problem to the issue of qualia. He collapses meanings into a single category and thereby eliminates potentially relevant discriminations he initially introduced. There is a potential *loss of meaning*. Ultimately, this results in a failure of adequacy since the meanings of the words limit the selection of topics for analysis. His analysis fails to properly interconnect a range of concepts into a coherent scheme.

Chalmers' analysis begins with an implicit bifurcation, since he accepts the "physical" as the given frame of reference. Thus, the hard problem becomes one of accounting for a residual, given this frame of reference. In defining the hard problem in this way, Chalmers and others re-create a metaphysics in the style of Descartes or Hume, with all the inherent flaws. This can be seen in Chalmers' solution to the hard problem. He summarizes and dismisses as inadequate several functionalist variants of a physical monism, and then concludes: "to account for conscious experience we need *an extra ingredient* in the explanation" (207, emphasis added), and "the emergence of experience goes beyond what can be derived from physical theory" (208). This entails a supplementation of the given physical theory, rather than a modification of it to accommodate a wider range of phenomena.

The same rationale is used by Dennett in *Consciousness Explained*. Dennett believes that consciousness is "the last surviving mystery" and that "if dualism is the best we can do, then we can't understand human consciousness" (Dennett 1991, 21, 39). At the same time he wants to assert that "consciousness" is something that can be explained scientifically. Thus, we must accept as given the obviousness that each of us is an "enjoyer of perceptions and sensations, a sufferer of pain, an entertainer of ideas . . ." So, what is the mystery? Dennett: "How can living physical bodies in the physical world produce such phenomena? That is the mystery" (25). Once again, the "physical" is the reference frame against which the phenomenal is to be explained. His perspective is essentially reductionistic. Given the "physical" and given the "phenomenal," if we can establish some sort of correlation between the two then we do not need to worry about the phenomenal. In fact, in spite of Dennett's own assertion that the phenomenal is to be explained, much of his effort is to explain away. For example: "When we learn that the only difference between gold and silver is the number of subatomic particles in their atoms, we may feel cheated or angry—those physicists have explained something away: The goldness is gone from gold . . . leaving something out is not a feature of failed explanations, but of successful explanation" (454).

He then concludes that "some of the 'obvious' features of phenomenology are not real at all," and "a few of the [amazing phenomena] just don't exist at all, and hence require no explanation" (434). In this way his analysis still exemplifies a bifurcation of the subject matter. He implicitly accepts the basis for the dichotomy, then dismisses one part of it without altering the other. Thus, what remains is inadequate—his exposition reduces to dismissing as irrelevant whatever cannot be accommodated within that part of the bifurcation that he does accept.

It will be noted that recognizing the latent dualism in physicalist/functionalist theories does not guarantee escape from this difficulty. For example, Searle's aim is "to criticize and overcome the dominant traditions in the study of mind, both 'materialist' and 'dualist'" (Searle 1994, xi). He also appears to have Dennett in mind when he asserts that some materialists/functionalists "share . . . a hostility toward the existence and mental character of our ordinary mental life" (5). Yet, his own account of the "problem" is strangely similar to Dennett's. Searle also claims it is obvious "consciousness . . . is a biological feature of human and certain animal brains" (90). For Searle, the only reason why there is a "problem" of consciousness at all is because some analysts fail to recognize this obvious fact, and this failure is due to an implicit adherence to outmoded Cartesian thought. He is quick to assert unambiguously his own proposal: "Mental phenomena are caused by neurophysical processes in the brain and are themselves features of the brain" (1). Like Dennett, Searle accepts the correlation between the physical and phenomenal. Unlike Dennett he asserts both that the correlation is causal, and that the caused phenomenal elements have their own ontological status. We again see how Searle's analysis ultimately makes the notion of consciousness subservient to the *a priori* biological mechanism, thus retaining the dualism he rejects.

The debate as a whole, which pits one partial interpretation against the other, lacks coherence. The reason is that the participants share an initial partition of the problem space into a physical and a phenomenal component. But, given the shared start-point none can demonstrate in coherent terms the reason for their personal doctrinal preference. Thus, Chalmers recognizes that Dennett's so-called solution involves accepting half the bifurcation on blind faith, and rejecting or denying the rest. Dennett recognizes that Chalmers' add-on solution is *ad hoc* and implicitly dualistic. Searle accepts both halves of the bifurcation and asserts a blind faith that with the advance of science the phenomenal will somehow be absorbed into the physical. None of them recognizes that the outcome of their efforts is limited before they start by virtue of how they set up the problem. Their options are reduced to either a denial of the phenomenal or a search for a defining feature of "consciousness" to set it apart from the physical. It is the latter option, and its essential inadequacy, which I will examine in the next section.

Whitehead's Partition of the Data of Experience

Whitehead not only diagnosed the errors of history; his philosophical aim was to provide an account of how such errors could occur in the first place. In this section I will illustrate the utility of Whitehead's procedural insistence on adequacy and coherence, in particular on the criterion that requires the meanings of terms necessarily limit and supplement each other. I will briefly summarize how topics are ordered radically differently in Whitehead's system from their conventional treatment in the literature and indicate briefly some of the implications of this alternative ordering. The first two topics are intentionality and qualia. This choice is motivated by a major misconception in the literature that the residual problems of consciousness, once the presumed gains of physicalism/functionalism have been taken account of, "fall into two main categories, respectively headed, by philosophers, 'qualia' and 'intentionality'" (Lycan 1999, 10). For example, while Chalmers and Dennett focus on consciousness as phenomenal qualia, Searle treats "consciousness" as approximately synonymous with "awareness" (Searle 1994, 84) and this meaning is expanded in a conventional manner to include subjective perspective, the notion of "privacy" and intentionality. Finally, the third topic to be discussed is Whitehead's notions of actual entity and subjective form, in order to illustrate how his insistence on a rigorous terminological coherence places "consciousness" within a more integrated conceptual framework.

Intentionality

One "habit of thought" in the philosophical tradition that Whitehead rejects is "the doctrine of vacuous actuality" (PR xiii), the notion of a thing without any internal activity of synthesis, which goes hand in hand with the idea that all relations are external. This implies a self-contained individuality in a universe of elements completely distinct and independent of each other. Such a notion can be seen as a particular instance of misplaced concreteness when applied to the notion of substance. As an isolated doctrinal claim "vacuous actuality" is completely neutral. Whitehead's alternative of stressing "relatedness" might also be entirely neutral if it were not for an appeal to the facts, both of science and of common intuition. Whitehead invokes the adequacy criterion and asks: why exclude from the data for philosophy the sense of "otherness" that pervades experience? The notion of unattached entities implied in the assumption of "vacuous actuality" directly transgresses this intuition.

Given the intuition of our experience of connectedness, and accepting dualism as a starting point for analysis, has had the result in some quarters of identifying this "aboutness" character with the notion of mind. Thus, "aboutness," "intentionality," or "reference" are introduced as somehow uniquely qualifying mind. This claim only admits to the intuition, and is a fallacy of misplaced concreteness when the intuition is predicated of a self-contained abstraction called "mind." In particular, it entrenches an epistemological gap between mind and nature that is both fundamental and unbridgeable. This doctrine is incoherent because the intuition is added to a dualism predicated on its denial, in other words, the assumption of vacuous actuality.[4] Even Searle, who disavows both dualism and materialism, still claims that "a complete theory of intentionality requires an account of consciousness" (Searle 1994, 132), which inverts the order of requirement.

Either the events of the universe are related or they are not. If relatedness is a fundamental principle then it holds for all entities. Thus, the working hypothesis that Whitehead adopts is that entities *are* related, that entities *do* enter into the constitution of other entities. This fairly straightforward claim has, unfortunately in my view, been linked to panpsychism—unfortunate if only because it is left too easily open to misinterpretation from an implicitly Cartesian perspective, which would embrace idealism only because it had tacitly presupposed dualism in setting up the initial contrast for selection. The erroneous extrapolation is that all entities have a mind or that all things have consciousness, if the terms are understood in their conventional Cartesian sense. But, this is incorrect and misses what ought to be a very simple working hypothesis. To assert that any actual occasion is a drop of experience, is not to use "experience" as a compression of "conscious experience" (e.g., as Chalmers does). It is simply a way of indicating that relatedness is fundamental, to make "aboutness" intrinsic to the nature of any entity. What makes Whitehead's system "monistic" is the aim to provide one coherent scheme of explanation. In this sense it is neither physicalist/materialist on the one hand nor idealistic/panpsychic on the other.

In turning to the scientific evidence Whitehead repeatedly refers to vector quantities as a manifestation of this "aboutness" character. The twentieth-century notion of the physical universe is not a static distribution of independent objects. The physics of the universe has become vector transitions and this includes two related notions. First, the "referring" or "aboutness" as such: the vector elements of any event refer to both their origins and future. The vector character of an object in motion says something where it came from and where it will go. Second, that in this transition there is a real transference of energy, not simply an abstract account of cause and effect. The energy in the "cause" is constituted directly as an "effect" in the novel entity. Thus, the relational or constitutive character is universal; it constitutes an entity and is independent of consciousness or mind in a Cartesian sense. Third, Whitehead stresses that "appetition" is fundamental to the notion of transition. The so-called mental pole of any entity (PR 33) can be described in several ways, but it essentially reduces to a notion of appetition, and appetition entails a conceptual prehension of an eternal object functioning as a potential, as a "lure," as a vectored character of transition.

We thus see certain correspondences between Whitehead and contemporary literature insofar as attention is directed at similar phenomena, such as the intuition of "aboutness." However, Whitehead always refers such intuitions back to the root problems and not to a derivation that emerges after an *a priori* (Cartesian) theory has been implicitly accepted. Whitehead attempts to eliminate the incoherence that results from attempts to reintroduce the intuition of connectedness into a philosophical scheme that has excluded it from its fundamental notions.

Qualia

The notion of "qualia" has sometimes been used discursively to circumscribe the topic domain of consciousness (for example, Chalmers 1995, Tye 1995). The implication is that qualia are somehow left over from the physical analysis of an external world, thus to be ascribed by default to some nonphysical event. But this sort of analysis is only a regression to the distinction between primary and secondary qualities.

First, many discussions of qualia are highly limited in their chosen subject matter, violating the adequacy criterion. Whitehead argues that the so-called "physical world" is an abstraction, a reduction from nature. In the process of this reduction scientists have been arbitrary in their "picking and choosing" the qualia that are indicative of a mental in contrast to a physical event. This limitation is typically to only some aspects of some senses, for example, sounds, tastes, or colors. In pointing to this arbitrariness, Whitehead gives the example of the sense of touch, which *was* abstracted to the concept of material "inertia," while other sensa were left as properties of "mind" (CN 43). A failure of adequacy thus leads to arbitrary doctrinal incoherence.

Contemporary research in psychology provides an even better example. Consider the sense of motion. Discrete objects move in space: it would seem obvious, and for that reason "motion" is not on anyone's list of "qualia" or "sensa." Yet one need go no further than the most primitive form of visual recording technology for a demonstration of how "motion" counts as a sensum of prehended discrepancy. In fact, there is now a substantial history of research on subjective or "apparent motion." It is even possible to demonstrate that if the two discrete events are themselves of short enough duration, then the events will not be experienced but only the sensum of "motion" (Kolers 1972).

Thus, theory has been arbitrary in extrapolating from qualia to the abstracted physical reality. Whitehead asserts that for the sake of adequacy, all should be included on equal footing.

To understand the generic character of "qualia" one needs to understand their place in the metaphysical category of which they are examples. Thus, Whitehead places sensa in the general category of eternal objects: "those . . . which will be classified under the name 'sensa' constitute the lowest category" (PR 114). Even when restricted to complex human experience, the conventional notion of sensa is too limited, and Whitehead adds "pattern" and "contrasts" to his list. Interestingly enough, at least one psychologist, James Gibson, has argued for extending the notion of what counts as a sensum, and that structure or pattern is just as much a perceived quality of the environment as the more limited list of items such as color or taste or sound (Gibson 1966).

But the survey of what counts as qualia does not end here. Whitehead generalizes a notion of perception "wider than the narrow definition based on . . . sensa" (AI, ch. 9, sec. 2, 231). He develops a so-called "physical" conception of perception where the conventional notion of efficient cause can be interpreted as a simple act of "perception" in the more general sense he develops. Sensa, properly generalized and applicable to all entities, include the forms of energy (PR 116) by which entities affect one another. As another example of nonsensuous perception he points to "our knowledge of our own immediate past" (AI 233). This is a generic awareness of continuity, which is essentially relatedness, "non-sensuous perception is one aspect of the continuity of nature" (AI 236). This topic concerns how "otherness" as a vector transmission is intrinsic to any entity. This is discussed in PR as perception in the mode of causal efficacy, and this is precisely that "intuition" that underlies the notion of "reference" or "intentionality" discussed in the previous section.

It will be noted that Whitehead's category of eternal objects is nowhere dependent on consciousness. A discussion of qualia-cum-consciousness in Chalmers' sense would be neither a discussion of "eternal objects" nor of "consciousness" in Whitehead's sense. Chalmers effectively blurs the distinction to the point of incomprehensibility. Whitehead's insistence on coherence—the adjustment of the meanings of terms relative to each other—guarantees that his use of the category of eternal object is *already* adjusted to the other categories of his complete doctrine.

The "Coherence" of Actual Entities

To situate Whitehead's use of the term "consciousness" within his metaphysical scheme we need to take full account of the manner in which he integrates several distinctions into one descriptive framework. To recapitulate: in CN he talks of nature given in sense awareness *for* intellectual analysis. In PR he has expanded this second phrase: "this higher grade of mental activity is the intellectual self-analysis of the entity in an earlier stage of incompletion, effected by intellectual feelings produced in a later stage of concresence" (PR 56). Here is where we find the inquiring minds of philosophers and scientists. This higher grade of analysis delivers abstractions from the concrete. A failure to explicitly take this into account can result in confusing the abstract with the concrete. This is the fallacy of misplaced concreteness. Thus, we have to understand the "order" of complexity of this process. Intellectual analysis is a high-grade "terminus" of a complex process. Consonant with the bifurcation of nature this terminus has been interpreted as something simple, as a categorical polarity of mind against inert matter-in-space-time (the physical).

Those inquiring philosophers at the terminus of this sequence have the intellectual task of "partitioning" the received data of their experience into a coherent scheme. With respect to this terminus for experience, everyone is in the same position: Descartes, Chalmers, Dennett, Searle, Whitehead. The question is: how do they deal with the nexus of presented data? Some partition the initial data conformal to a "received" theory, such as dualism, thereby eliminating from consideration some of the initial data. They have the received totality as a complex unit (the unity of experience) but have interpreted it as a primitive. Thus, they have no doctrine that allows them to identify any part with any grade or phase of the complex process that delivers the "conscious" event as a terminal concresence. They may "partition" it into several parts ("self," "sensa," "intentionality," "matter," "space," "agency," etc.), but what they lacked is a coherent scheme that presents those parts in proper relation to each other.

Others may explicitly eliminate the "received" theory and accept more of the data. However, from this rich nexus of data they work on the presupposition that some factor can be easily associated with a given concept, such as "consciousness," which can then be examined in structural isolation from the complex data from which it has been abstracted. This manner of thought reintroduces the implicit "vacuous actuality" that was the reason why the Cartesian theory was rejected in the first place. The result, given the richness of the initial data, is an indeterminately large number of "partitions" or theories of consciousness, determined partly by what was eliminated, partly by the particular pattern of emphasis in any one analysis.

Thus, Whitehead's doctrine can account for the incoherent character of the literature. But, for the sake of argument, let's assume that the current literature on consciousness, taken as a whole, meets the adequacy criterion. Let's suppose that all the pieces of the puzzle are there but that they have not yet been assembled into a coherent design. Whitehead's goal is to place those parts in proper relation to each other. An application of Whitehead's philosophy here serves the double purpose of integrating those pieces and, derivatively, of allowing us to understand the literature insofar as it has at least identified the pieces.

Whitehead's analysis is here summarized only in synoptic form, and only to identify those places where distinctions in the literature "fit" the integrated scheme that he developed. Whitehead identifies the terminus as complex, as a concrescence of several phases, which are not physically "causing" the mental reaction because he does not distinguish entities into mental and physical "types" in the first place. Rather, the process is cumulative/additive where prior occasions are incorporated into the structure of a new occasion. This means that an arbitrarily complex terminal occasion will contain *all* components of all occasions absorbed into it. Among his categories, the notion of an actual entity (or actual occasion) is intended to function in this way. An actual entity has, as factors in its internal constitution, objective data, a "subject," and a subjective form. The term "consciousness" refers to just one type of subjective form.

Sensa are only one sort of what Whitehead calls an "eternal object," a category of existence other than an actual entity. Thus, sensa or qualia have nothing uniquely to do with defining or even identifying "consciousness."

"Intentionality" in the sense of "aboutness" is treated as intrinsic to the concrescent process that defines *any* actual entity, which is necessary to evade the doctrine of vacuous actuality. It has nothing uniquely to do with defining or even identifying consciousness.

The notion of subject is not to be equated with a notion of "self." In the first place the latter term is simply too ambiguous to be of technical value (Katzko 2003). Second, it implies a Cartesian mind or agent as substance that has properties, such as "experience." In Whitehead's scheme, a subject is not a substance with experience predicated of it. A subject is constituted within the process of concrescence of an actual entity. It is both the final perspective on the data as well as the subjective aim (the final cause) that determines the way in which the data are integrated into the final unity of the actual entity. The "subject" has nothing uniquely to do with defining or even identifying consciousness.

The closest that existing literature comes to Whitehead's technical definition of consciousness is the notion that it is in some sense "higher-order" (perception, thinking, etc.). This is phrased in terms of a reflexivity, such as awareness of awareness, or awareness of mental activity. But any variant of this notion that consciousness is an act of self-reflection or introspection, or awareness of "internal" or "mental" states, implicitly assumes a separate internal mind in contrast to an "external" physical world. Several variants of this idea[5] only equate consciousness with awareness and then posit a distinction based on the content of awareness, that is, on what Whitehead would call the data of the actual entity. This is a category error in Whitehead's scheme.

Moreover, Whitehead does not make this distinction between "internal" and "external" occasions. Any actual entity always absorbs the data constituting its own past. Finally, the coherent aspect of Whitehead's treatment is that "consciousness" is only one type of subjective form. Thus, factors of consciousness that identify it as a subjective form will be constitutive of *any* subjective form, and so have nothing uniquely to do with defining or even identifying consciousness.

Conclusions

The process of conscious experience is one of simplification and abstraction. The analysis in this chapter is a case study of some philosophical/scientific literature that illustrates this proposition. Stated more generally, the analysis illustrates the utility of Whitehead's doctrine for understanding any higher grade of conscious intellectual activity of any type in any context. Professional philosophers have yet to grasp the nature of this process, and their own writings illustrate the selective emphasis that their own experience imposes on the data. Whitehead's perspective on conscious experience (1) allows us to understand the incoherence of the literature as due to a partial analysis guided by flawed philosophical assumptions uncorrected by a consideration of historical developments in science and philosophy; and (2) provides a unifying "coherent" framework within which it may still be possible to place some of that literature, if interpreted as a focus on specialized topics.

It follows that if professional intellectuals have yet to fully grasp the process character of their own intellect, then little else can be expected from the average person. In this regard, Whitehead anticipated the problem of multiplicity as discussed in the psychological literature on the "self" by well over half a century. Within his doctrine "what needs to be explained is not the dissociation of personality but unifying control, by reason of which we not only have unified behavior, which can be observed by others, but also consciousness of a unified experience" (PR 108). What is delivered for those higher-grade occasions qualified as "conscious" is every grade of concresent activity in experience, selected, emphasized, contrasted, or ignored. In conventional psychological terms, how this partition is effected—how the person assigns the influences of received data to the environment or to his own cognitive activity, and how this may be achieved willfully or not—ultimately determines the character of all human behavior ranging from normal to deviant. Thus, what I alluded to as the terminal occasion, that is, "the presiding occasion, if there be one, is the final node, or intersection, of a complex structure of many enduring objects. . . . The harmonized relations of the parts of the body constitute this wealth of inheritance into a harmony of contrasts, issuing into intensity of experience" (PR 109). This account provides a standard for an ideal of psychological health. However, such a description is not always exemplified, and so his account also holds for determining the actual psychological processes of daily experience. The full nexus of occasions creative of a terminal conscious experience includes a bewildering array of hopes, desires, memories, imaginings, perceptions. Only some in any one unifying moment may be accentuated, and on another occasion some other pattern may emerge. As Whitehead concludes, "central personal dominance is only partial, and in pathological cases is apt to vanish" (PR 109).

Notes

1. See Katzko 2003 for a review and critical analysis of this literature.
2. The argument can be found in SMW chapter 3 and PR 77–79.
3. See, for example, the essay "Uniformity and Contingency" in ESP and PR on "Symbolic Reference," part 2, chapter 8, section 3.
4. Compare with the discussion in the chapter "Subjects and Objects" in AI.
5. See Güzeldere 1995 for a review. This chapter is also reprinted in Block et al. 1997.

References

Block, N., O. Flanagan, and G. Güzeldere, eds. 1997. *The Nature of Consciousness. Philosophical Debates*. Cambridge, MA: MIT Press.

Chalmers, D.J. 1995. "Facing up to the Problem of Consciousness." *Journal of Consciousness Studies* 3:200–219.

Dennett, D.C. 1991. *Consciousness Explained*. Boston: Little, Brown, and Company.

Gibson, J.J. 1966. *The Senses Considered as Perceptual Systems*. Boston: Houghton Mifflin.

Güzeldere, G. 1995. "Is Consciousness the Perception of What Passes in One's Own Mind?" In Metzinger 1995.

Katzko, M.W. 2003. "Unity vs. Multiplicity: A Conceptual Analysis of the Term 'Self' and Its Use in Personality Theories." *Journal of Personality* 71:83–114.

Kolers, P.A. 1972. *Aspects of Motion Perception*. New York: Pergamon Press.

Lagerspetz, O. 2002. "Experience and Consciousness in the Shadow of Descartes." *Philosophical Psychology* 15:5–18.

Lycan, W.G. 1999. *Mind and Cognition. An Anthology*. 2nd ed. Oxford: Blackwell.

Metzinger. T., ed. 1995. *Conscious Experience*. Schöningh: Imprint Academic.

Riffert, F.G., and Michel Weber, eds. 2003. *Searching for New Contrasts: Whiteheadian Contributions to Contemporary Challenges in Neurophysiology, Psychology, Psychotherapy and the Philosophy of Mind*. Frankfurt am Main: Peter Lang.

Searle, J.R. 1994. *The Rediscovery of the Mind*. Cambridge, MA: MIT Press.

Tye, M. 1995. *Ten Problems of Consciousness. A Representational Theory of the Phenomenal Mind*. Cambridge, MA: MIT Press.

Warner, R. 1994. "Introduction. The Mind–Body Debate." In Warner and Szubka 1994.

Warner, R., and T. Szubka, eds. 1994. *The Mind–Body Problem. A Guide to the Current Debate*. Oxford: Blackwell.

Weekes, A. 2003. "Psychology and Physics Reconciled: Whitehead's Vision of Metaphysics." In Riffert and Weber 2003.

7

Windows on Nonhuman Minds

Donald Redfield Griffin

The existence and nature of nonhuman minds are significant aspects of the philosophers' Problem of Other Minds. In this chapter I will use the term *conscious* to mean subjectively experiencing feelings or thoughts, however simple and basic or elaborate and subtle they may be. We all know that we experience thoughts and feelings, even though their full content cannot be conveyed precisely to others. The central question I will consider is to what extent other animals experience anything comparable, and if so what their experiences are likely to be, recognizing that they are doubtless very limited compared to human consciousness. Whitehead had no doubt that "the higher animals entertain notions, hopes, and fears;" and that the "difference between men and animals is in one sense only a difference in degree. But the extent of the degree makes all the difference. The Rubicon has been crossed" (MT 3–4, 27).

As a biologist I would like to review scientific evidence in favor of two propositions: (1) Many animals engage in simple but conscious and rational thinking, and (2) such thinking confers a significant advantage by enabling them to think about various actions of which they are capable and to select those they believe will get what they want or avoid what they fear. As Karl Popper might have put it, conscious animals can try out various actions in their heads without the considerable risk, under natural conditions, of actually performing them in trial and error fashion to learn what gets you fed and what gets you eaten (Popper 1987). Since the 1930s we have learned that animal behavior is much more versatile and adapted to the animal's needs than we used to believe. If Whitehead had known of these discoveries I think he would have recognized that the extent of the degree has been significantly reduced.

Some scientists have tended to redefine mind by limiting it to information processing in nervous systems; and students of animal behavior have paid very little attention to the possible existence of conscious experiences in the animals they study. This aversion stems from a perceived epistemological impasse. This is the conviction that there is no conceivable way in which valid, objective evidence about conscious experiences of other species can ever be obtained. This claim is accepted so widely, and so strongly that it has become a pervasive taboo against scientific consideration of what life may be like for animals. The result has been that when philosophers consider the possibility of nonhuman minds they have been forced to rely on casual observations of familiar animals, or television programs, without much opportunity to appreciate how much behavioral versatility has been discovered by scientific students of animal behavior.

Although many behavior patterns exhibited by animals are suggestive of conscious experience, as I have reviewed elsewhere (Griffin 2001), two general categories of scientific evidence have been especially telling in challenging this epistemological taboo: (1) The close similarity of basic neural structure and function between human and animal nervous systems means that there is no inherent reason why animal brains cannot produce conscious experiences, and (2) animal communication sometimes appears to be an expression of subjective experiences and therefore it provides evidence about such experiences.

A few specific examples may be helpful to indicate the rich body of evidence of animal consciousness that is becoming available. No single piece of evidence provides a "smoking gun" of totally perfect proof of consciousness; and many scientists therefore prefer to interpret all animal behavior as the result of nonconscious neural events. But the cumulative weight of suggestive evidence has made it more and more likely that nonhuman conscious experiences exist and furthermore that they can be investigated by scientific methods with significant results.

The Neural Correlates of Consciousness

Neuroscientists have made substantial progress in identifying activities of human brains that accompany and seem to be responsible for feelings or thoughts, which human subjects can report verbally. These processes are detected by electrical potentials recorded from the scalp or by newly developed noninvasive methods of imaging metabolic activity of neurons in the brain (positron emission tomography, PET, and functional magnetic resonance imagery, fMRI). Additional evidence has been obtained from more direct and invasive observations and experiments on the brains of monkeys when these animals appear to have some sort of conscious experience. Three examples of this type of evidence will be briefly described below: blind sight, mirror neurons, and evidence that monkeys know that they know.

First, however, it is important to recognize that the most promising candidates for neural correlates of consciousness are considered by neuroscientists to be widely distributed but coordinated activity engaging large areas of the brain. None of the contemporary ideas about the differences between human brain activity that does and does not involve consciousness require any consciousness generating structure or process that is limited to human brains and absent in all others.

One neuroscientist puts it this way: "I speculate that in order for a focal neural representation to reach awareness it may have to be accessible to other parts of the brain .... I suggest that a conscious percept is not simply a disorganized soup of activated neural attributes, but rather a spatio-temporally structured representation in which visual attributes are associated with particular objects and events." (Kanwisher 2001, 109). Crick and Koch (1998), Tononi and Edelman (1998) and Dehaene and Naccache (2001) have expressed quite similar general conclusions about the neural correlates of consciousness.

The evidence on which these ideas are based has been obtained from studies of human or monkey brains; there is every reason to expect that when it becomes possible to study other brains by comparable methods, they will show "spatiotemporally structured representations . . . associated with particular objects and events" that are important to the animal.

Blindsight

Discrimination between different visual stimuli is possible for human patients with extensive damage to the visual cortex that renders them blind by ordinary criteria in large areas of their visual fields. Yet if obliged in a test situation to guess about something they say they cannot see, they are surprised when later told that their guesses were correct far more often than expected by chance. Blindsight is greatly inferior to normal vision, however, and these results are obtained only with quite conspicuous stimuli having high contrast.

Monkeys whose visual cortex has been partly destroyed can be trained to respond correctly to objects that are located in parts of the visual field corresponding to the missing portion of the visual cortex. Ingenious experiments devised by Cowey and Stoerig (1995) allowed such monkeys to signal by pressing appropriate patterns on a touch-sensitive computer screen whether they did or did not see a particular visual stimulus. These monkeys were also trained to touch a different bright spot on the screen in order to obtain favorite foods; and they could do this even when the spot was located in the blind area. In other words in one test the monkey signaled that it could see nothing; but in another experiment, when a conspicuous pattern was shown to its blind field, the same animal touched this pattern in order to obtain food.

The importance of these experiments is that through this experimentally contrived form of communication these monkeys were telling the experimenters something about their conscious perception, namely whether they did, or did not, see a visual stimulus. The fact that monkeys seem to perform similarly to human blindsight patients does not rigorously prove that the monkeys were conscious before having roughly half of their visual cortices removed, but it does provide strong evidence of a comparable relationship between brain function and simple levels of consciousness in human and simian brains.

Mirror Neurons

Another significant recent advance in neuroscience is the discovery of what are called "mirror neurons" in the ventral premotor cerebral cortex of monkeys (reviewed by Gallese and Goldman 1998). Action potentials recorded from microelectrodes inserted into this area of a monkey brain showed that these neurons are active in two different but significantly related situations: (1) When the monkey performs a particular action, and (2) when it sees either a human or another monkey do the same thing. For example, mirror neurons discharge nerve impulses when the monkey sees a human experimenter pick up a piece of food between his fingers; but they stop discharging as he moves the food to a position where the monkey can reach it. If the monkey then grasps the food with its own hand, the mirror neuron becomes active again. Indirect evidence from imaging and localized magnetic stimulation of human brains indicates that similar cells are present.

The activities of these mirror neurons might take place in the brain of a monkey who is not consciously thinking about grasping with its fingers. But it is suggestive that the same cells in monkey brains are activated either by performing a grasping action or by seeing someone else do so.

Monkeys Who Know Whether They Know

In a third recent experiment Hampton (2001) first trained monkeys to respond to two types of visual pattern displayed on a touch-sensitive computer screen. In one case they were first shown four pictures, conveniently designated A, B, C, and D. Then these were turned off and four more pictures, E, F, C, and G appeared. The monkey's task was to touch C, the one of the new four that had also been in the previous set. For convenience I will in all cases term this duplicated picture C; but all the actual pictures (A through G) were varied between experiments, so that the monkey could not solve the problem by remembering particular images or their positions. Touching C, the picture that had been in the previous set of four, caused the apparatus to make available a favorite type of food.

A second problem presented to these monkeys employed a display of two quite different pictures, H and I, after they had seen the first set of four but before the second set was shown. If the monkey now touched H, it always received a less-preferred food; but if it touched I, pictures E, F, C and G were displayed and the favorite food could be obtained by touching C. But if it touched any of the other three it received no food at all.

A rational monkey would be expected to press I provided it was sure it remembered which of the four pictures had been in the first set; but it should choose H if it did not remember. The result was that when H and I were shown only 30 seconds or less after A, B, C, and D the monkeys almost always touched I, causing the second set of four pictures to appear, then touched C and received their favorite food. But when the interval was two or four minutes they usually avoided the test by pressing H and settled for the less-preferred food.

This experiment is especially significant because many students of monkey behavior have claimed that although they know many facts that are important in their lives, especially their social relationships with other monkeys, they do not know that they know. In this special experimental situation Hampton's monkeys clearly did know whether they remembered the first set of pictures.

Communication of Subjective Experiences

Many animals communicate to others what seem to be expressions of emotional feelings or simple conscious thoughts; and in doing so they may be literally telling us at least part of what they are feeling or thinking. Interpreting the communicative signals of animals as indications of their feelings and thoughts is comparable to the way in which we make inferences about the subjective feelings and thoughts of our human companions on the basis of what they tell us. They tell us both by means of our supremely versatile language and also by nonverbal communication or body language. So much human behavior occurs without our conscious awareness that to ascertain what another person is consciously feeling or thinking we ordinarily rely primarily on communication.

Communicative behavior opens a figurative window on both human and animal minds, once we are prepared to open our own minds to this possibility. Once particular communications have been linked to patterns of overt behavior, the latter are often used with reasonable confidence to infer subjective experiences. Of course neither human nor animal communication tells us everything the communicator is thinking and feeling. But this figurative window does provide some significant information. In the case of animals it breaks through the epistemological barrier alleged to render animal experiences hopelessly inaccessible.

This idea that we can obtain objective information about animal experiences from their communicative exchanges is out of step with contemporary scientific approaches to animal behavior. But no compelling reasons have been advanced to explain why this evidence is not valid and helpful. To most scientists interested in animal behavior it seems to be such an unwelcome idea that it has simply been ignored. One objection has been that human speech is an unreliable source of information about the causes of our thoughts or our behavior. But it is our best evidence about their content.

Alarm Calls that Convey Semantic Information

Many animals make characteristic alarm calls when frightened by dangerous predators; but in most cases we have no evidence that any information other than the intensity of alarm is conveyed. Vervet monkeys and some other primates, however, use alarm calls that differ according to the type of danger and the most effective way to escape from it. The three most dangerous predators of vervet monkeys are leopards, martial eagles, and large boa constrictors. For leopards an effective escape tactic is to climb out on small limbs where the heavier leopard cannot reach them. But this is just the wrong thing to do if the danger is from an eagle swooping down from the sky. By retreating into thick underbrush a monkey can avoid the eagle, but this would make it easy prey for a leopard. For a snake it is only necessary to see it, because monkeys can easily avoid capture by simply moving away, although boas do take vervet monkeys by surprise.

Vervet monkeys ordinarily escape in appropriately different ways when they hear one of the three types of alarm call. And when recorded alarm calls were played back in the absence of real predators most of the monkeys climbed trees when they heard leopard alarm calls, dove into underbrush for eagle alarm calls, and in response to the snake alarm call stood on their hind legs looking around for the nonexistent snake (Seyfarth et al. 1980, Cheney and Seyfarth 1990).

In most other cases where animals give alarm calls it is much less clear whether anything other than intensity of alarm is conveyed, because there are not such obvious differences in responses of hearers. But the fact that under natural conditions some monkeys convey information about the type of danger or the appropriate way of escaping it tells us that animal communication can convey semantic information as well as emotional arousal.

Ape "Language"

One of the most surprising twentieth-century discoveries about the behavioral capabilities of animals began when the Gardners taught a young chimpanzee named Washoe to communicate by simple gestures modeled after the manual signing used by the deaf (Gardner and Gardner 1969, Fouts 1997). Washoe and other chimpanzees have learned several dozen such gestures, use them to ask for desired objects and activities, and give the appropriate signs for familiar objects when shown pictures of them. They also sign to each other. These discoveries were severely criticized when it was suggested that this gestural signing was remotely comparable to human language; and there were also uncertainties in interpreting the gestures.

Savage-Rumbaugh and her colleagues later developed modified computer keyboards that apes have learned to use. Arbitrary symbols on the keys represent objects and actions, and some apes have learned to press the appropriate keys to request desired objects, to tell their human companions what they wish to do, and when shown pictures of familiar objects to press the appropriate key representing that object. This use of a keyboard greatly reduces any uncertainty in judging what information the ape conveys (reviewed by Savage-Rumbaugh and Lewin 1994 and Savage-Rumbaugh, Shanker and Taylor 1998). Abundant nonverbal communication is also displayed by apes in addition to these artificial human communication systems they have learned to use.

Intense controversy still rages around these discoveries, because many scientists and others are reluctant to believe that any nonhuman animal can communicate in ways that even remotely resemble our magnificent language. And of course the scope and versatility of the communication systems that apes have learned to use fall astronomically short of the enormous capabilities of human language. But gestural signs and use of the keyboard do serve to express simple thoughts about what a given picture shows or what the ape wants to do.

Parrots Who Mean What They Say

Apes communicating simple thoughts by means of gestures or keyboards were surprising enough, but our gut feeling of human uniqueness with respect to language and thought could be buttressed by the realization that apes are our closest biological relatives. But then Irene Pepperberg trained first one African grey parrot named Alex, and later others of the same species to use their imitations of spoken words in a meaningful fashion (Pepperberg 1999). Although "parroting" has come to mean imitation without understanding, these parrots learned to ask for things they wanted to play with, to report the color, shape or material of objects presented to them, and to say what was the same or different about such objects. For example Alex can answer the question "What different?" when shown two objects by saying "shape" or "color" when that is what actually differs. Thus at least one species of bird can learn to express simple thoughts. And many natural forms of vocal communication and body language are often combined with this newly acquired system.

Dolphins have also been trained to understand moderately complex human gestures, so that this general ability is not limited to Great Apes or African grey parrots. There is thus no escaping the fact that certain animals have been trained to convey basic information about objects and actions by methods of communication that we can easily understand. To what extent other animal communication may turn out to reveal evidence of simple thoughts remains to be determined, once appropriate investigations are undertaken.

Symbolic Communication Leading to Group Decision

There is one important limitation to the examples of animal communication mentioned so far. All are direct reactions to the current situation in which the animal finds itself. Human thinking and communication have of course the important additional attribute that we often think and communicate about past occurrences or what may happen in the future. It is therefore appropriate to inquire whether any forms of animal communication express thoughts about previous events or what the animal expects in the future. The answer is yes, but the animal and the communication system are so far removed from customary expectations that scientists have been most reluctant to view them in this light. These animals are worker honeybees and the communication system employs symbolic gestures.

Karl von Frisch who discovered the meaning of these gestures called them *Schwänzeltänze*, usually translated as waggle dances (Frisch 1967). They are used to inform the dancer's sisters about the distance, direction, and desirability of food sources. This information is critically important to the mutually interdependent colony of bees, because they need large amounts of nectar and pollen from flowers that usually make them available at distant locations and for brief periods of time. The nectar and pollen are also gathered avidly by other insects so that when one scout bee discovers a new source of nectar or pollen it is critically important that as many other workers as possible reach it before it is depleted.

The waggle dance is a movement in a straight line, ordinarily on a vertical surface of honeycomb, while the body oscillates from side to side. Distance is communicated by the duration of the dance, and direction by its orientation relative to gravity within the dark hive. The "code" for direction is that straight up means fly toward the sun, and other angles of dance direction have comparable meaning; for instance 90 degrees to the right means fly at about that angle to the sun's horizontal direction. By means of this symbolism direction of movement in a dark hive stands for direction of flight relative to the sun out in the open. The system thus has what linguists have called displacement, because it conveys information about something displaced in space or time from the situation where the communication takes place.

Desirability is communicated by the number of times the dance is repeated, and by the time devoted to circling back after a waggle run before starting another cycle. When the food is very desirable the bee, so to speak, hurries around to repeat the waggle run, but with less desirable food there is a longer time lag between repetitions of the waggle dance (Seeley 1995, Seeley and Buhrman 1999).

Von Frisch called this system *Tanzsprache*, literally dance speech; but many have objected to calling it language. Jonathan Bennett (1964) discussed in detail why he felt that these dances do not qualify as a language. His principal reasons were that their use appeared to be limited to the specific situation of food gathering and that it was not remotely as flexible and versatile as human language which we use to describe an enormous variety of subject matter.

Bennett and many others who have dismissed the waggle dances as rigid instinctive behavior have not given adequate consideration to their use in several other situations such as in announcing the location of water and of waxy material used to build and repair the hive itself when these are urgently needed. The most significant extension of usage of the dance communication was discovered by Martin Lindauer (1955, 1971). At the time of swarming roughly half of a large colony of bees move out of the cavity where they have lived for months; and they must find a new cavity as quickly as possible if they are to survive. Swarming usually occurs only at intervals longer than the life span of a worker bee, so that for them this is a totally new situation without precedent in their individual experience.

Worker bees that would ordinarily fly out in search of flowers now search for cavities, crawl into any they find, seeming to evaluate them, then return to the swarm and perform dances that indicate by the same code their distance, direction, and desirability. Desirability in this case means dryness, darkness inside of a small opening, and freedom from ants, along with other attributes that are important for the survival of the new colony. Suitable cavities are often rare and individual scouts usually find them in widely different directions and at distances from a few hundred meters to as much as three kilometers. The result is that a dozen or more dances come to be performed over the surface of the swarm, each reporting a different cavity. It is then crucially important for the swarm to select the most suitable of these, and usually this happens after a few days when the entire swarm of thousands of bees, including the queen, fly off together to one particular cavity a considerable distance away.

A highly important group decision is thus reached, and the process of reaching it depends in large measure on the differing dance messages. Many bees that have visited a poor or mediocre cavity simply stop dancing; others that are highly motivated continue to dance for longer periods of time. One might expect that this process alone would eventually lead to a situation in which only the best cavity was being reported. But this is not all that happens. In many cases a dancer also follows dances of one or more of her sisters, and if these report a better cavity than the one she has herself visited she may change her behavior in one of at least three ways. She may simply stop dancing; she may fly out to the location that she has learned about as a dance follower, visit that cavity, return to the hive and dance about it. Or in a few cases such bees have been observed to change their dance pattern and repeat the message reporting the superior cavities even without visiting them.

There is thus an extensive exchange of information by dancers reporting on a swarm about the cavities they have visited and evaluated or those they have learned about by following dances. These exchanges ordinarily continue for many hours or a few days until gradually more and more of the dances come to report the distance and direction of one cavity. Then after this process has been under way for some time, and after other types of communication that serve to activate many bees whose body temperature was too low for active flight, the whole swarm takes wing and flies to the cavity about which the recent dancing has been confined. Thus by an exchange of symbolic gestures the bees reach a vitally important group decision. No other system of animal communication has yet been discovered that reports so clearly about important objects that are far removed in space and time from the situation in which the communication takes place.

It is of course somewhat embarrassing, to some even shocking, to learn that it is a social insect, rather than a primate, a mammal, or even a vertebrate, which provides us with such telling evidence of communication that gives every sign of being the expression of simple but important thoughts. One may feel so strongly that a mere insect could not possibly think or communicate symbolically, that one therefore rejects communication of any kind as evidence of conscious thinking. But if we are consistent this would require also rejecting communication as evidence of human thoughts. To a scientist evidence is evidence.

The brains of honeybees are of course small, weighing roughly one milligram, and they contain about 900,000 neurons (Menzel and Giurfa 2001). At present it is not possible to apply the most advanced methods of imaging brain activity to small animals. The resolution is far too limited to distinguish different parts of a honeybee brain, and it is even very difficult to apply these methods to monkeys. The animal must remain motionless, which animals are not inclined to do unless firmly restrained or anesthetized. Furthermore one would need to have the animal engage in cognitive activity while the imaging procedure takes place, which is so far quite impractical for small animals.

We are thus constrained by the limitations of current methodology. But as pointed out above none of the current ideas about neural correlates of consciousness that neuroscientists have formulated require any structure or process that is definitely known to be limited to human brains. Honeybee and other insect brains contain structures called mushroom bodies that are involved in learning and other complex cognitive processes; and there is no reason why they cannot engage in what Kanwisher terms "spatiotemporally structured representations ... associated with particular objects." The brains of bees are tiny compared to parrot, monkey or human brains, but we are considering the basic question whether honeybees have any conscious experience, not how complex it may be. On balance, the weight of evidence seems sufficient to warrant keeping our minds open to this possibility.

Conclusion

As discussed above, the principal evidence that our human companions experience conscious feelings and thoughts stems from their communication, verbal and nonverbal. Without any communication at all we would be hard pressed to tell what they feel or think, if anything. We can now gather comparable evidence from the communicative exchanges of some animals. Ordinarily we make inferences about the subjective experiences of animals from their overt behavior; but behavioral scientists have been busy warning us that behavior alone does not conclusively demonstrate what conscious experience, if any, accompanies the behavior we may observe. One basis for this warning is the fact that much human behavior occurs without conscious awareness. In the human case we assume that verbal or nonverbal reports of feelings and thoughts are stronger evidence than overt behavior. With other species we now have a few examples where we can do the same.

Of course communication is not perfect or infallible evidence. We, and probably other animals, can deceive or withhold information about subjective experiences. But imperfect evidence is better than none, and our understanding of the meanings conveyed by animal communication is still rudimentary. As cognitive ethologists learn more about it, we may find that what Whitehead called "the extent of the degree" of differences between animal and human thinking and emotional experiences is significantly less than we have been accustomed to assume.

Biologists often weigh significant but incomplete and seldom wholly satisfactory evidence, striving to discern what interpretation is most likely to be correct. I have therefore been surprised that many philosophical discussions appear to be seeking absolutely perfect answers to the deepest and most difficult questions. Perhaps efforts to clarify the mind-body problem would make more substantial progress by seeking to evaluate probabilities that particular interpretations are sound, rather than what may be premature efforts to achieve totally conclusive evidence.

Philosophers can contribute to the challenging investigation of animal minds by helping to clarify our thinking about the kinds of evidence that can reasonably be expected to increase or decrease the likelihood of various kinds of conscious experience in animals. Was Dennett (1989, 446) right to suggest that cognitive ethology is a wild goose chase? How sound is David Griffin's (1998) extension of Whitehead's ideas in advocating "panexperientialism"? What can we reasonably infer about subjective, conscious experiences from versatility of behavior and from communicative exchanges? Is only human language adequate to convey conscious experiences, or can nonverbal communication, and animal communication, serve the same function? Is it reasonable to place greater reliance on adaptive coping with novel challenges for which the animal is unlikely to have been prepared by evolution or individual learning? And, in general, what sorts of behavior or communication provide the most convincing evidence of conscious experiences?

References

Bennett, J. 1964. *Rationality: An Essay towards an Analysis*. London: Routledge and Kegan Paul.

Cheney, D.L., and R.M. Seyfarth. 1990. *How Monkeys See the World: Inside the Mind of Another Species*. Chicago: University of Chicago Press.

Cowey, A., and P. Stoerig. 1995. "Blindsight in Monkeys." *Nature* 373:247–249.

Crick, F., and C. Koch. 1998. "Consciousness and Neuroscience." *Cerebral Cortex* 8:97–107.

Dehaene, S., and L. Naccache. 2001. "Towards a Cognitive Neuroscience of Consciousness: Basic Evidence and a Workspace Framework." *Cognition* 79:1–37.

Dennett, D.C. 1989. "Cognitive Ethology: Hunting for Bargains or a Wild Goose Chase?" In *Goals, No-goals, and Own Goals: A Debate on Goal-oriented and Intentional Behaviour*. Ed. A. Montefiore and D. Noble. London: Unwin Hyman.

Fouts, R.S. 1997. *Next of Kin: What Chimpanzees Have Taught Me about Who We Are*. New York: William Morrow.

Frisch, K. von. 1967. *The Dance Language and Orientation of Bees*. Cambridge, MA: Harvard University Press.

Gallese, V., and A. Goldman. 1998. "Mirror Neurons and the Simulation Theory of Mind Reading." *Trends in Neurosciences* 2:493–501.

Gardner, R.A., and B.T. Gardner. 1969. "Teaching Sign Language to a Chimpanzee." *Science* 165:664–672.

Griffin, D. 1998. *Unsnarling the World-Knot: Consciousness, Freedom, and the Mind-Body Problem*. Berkeley and Los Angeles: University of California Press (repr. 2008. Eugene, Oregon: Wipf and Stock).

Griffin, D.R. 2001. *Animal Minds, Beyond Cognition to Consciousness*. Chicago: University of Chicago Press.

Hampton, R.R. 2001. "Rhesus Monkeys Know When They Know." *Proceedings of the National Academy of Sciences* 98:5359-62; see also comments 4833–4834 (ibid.).

Kanwisher, N. 2001. "Neural Events and Perceptual Awareness." *Cognition* 79:80–113.

Lindauer, M. 1955. "Schwarmbeinen auf Wohnungssuche." *Zeitschrift fuer vergleichende Physiologie* 37:263–324.

Lindauer, M. 1971. *Communication among Social Bees*. 2nd ed. Cambridge, MA: Harvard University Press.

Menzel, R., and M. Giurfa 2001. "Cognitive Architecture of a Mini-brain: The Honeybee." *Trends in Cognitive Science* 5:62–71.

Pepperberg, I.M. 1999. *The Alex Studies: Cognitive and Communicative Abilities of Grey Parrots*. Cambridge, MA: Harvard University Press.

Popper, K. 1987. "Natural Selection and the Emergance of Mind." In *Evolutionary Epistemology, Rationality, and the Sociology of Knowledge*, G. Radnitzky and W.W. Bartley III, eds. La Salle: Open Court, 139–153.

Savage-Rumbaugh, S., and R. Lewin. 1994. *Kanzi: An Ape at the Brink of Human Mind*. New York: John Wiley & Sons.

Savage-Rumbaugh, S., S. Shanker, and T. Taylor. 1998. *Ape Language and the Human Mind*. Oxford: Oxford University Press.

Seeley, T.D. 1995. *The Wisdom of the Hive: The Social Physiology of Honey Bee Colonies*. Cambridge, MA: Harvard University Press.

Seeley, T.D., and S.C. Buhrman. 1999. "Group Decision Making in Swarms of Honey Bees." *Behavioral Ecology and Sociobiology* 45:19–31.

Seyfarth, R.M., D.L. Cheney, and P. Marler. 1980. "Vervet Monkey Alarm Calls: Evidence for Predator Classification and Semantic Communication." *Animal Behaviour* 28:1070–1094.

Tononi, G., and G.M. Edelman. 1998. "Consciousnes and Complexity." *Science* 282:1846–1851.

Part III

From Metaphysics to (Neuro)Science (and Back Again)

8

Panexperientialism, Quantum Theory, and Neuroplasticity

George W. Shields

In this chapter I will attempt to defend the panexperientialist position of A.N. Whitehead and his close intellectual compatriot, Charles Hartshorne, on both logico-philosophical and empirical scientific grounds. Panexperientialism is a point of view still much resisted by many philosophers of a self-described "naturalist" bent, by many scientists interested in fundamental questions of the philosophy of nature, and by theologians influenced by these thinkers. Witness the following anecdote told by neo-Whiteheadian theologian and science-religion writer John F. Haught (2000, 166):

> Even to many theologians, Whitehead's panpsychist (or panexperientialist) solution is simply unbelievable. At a recent conference of scientists and theologians, I was reminded once again of how much resistance there is to Whitehead's attributing "subjectivity" to nonliving nature.

I will argue that this reaction to Haught's panexperientialist suggestion expresses a certain "cultural lag," and that, quite to the contrary, the expressed disdain is a much more fitting posture for reductionist-materialism; this is especially so given the recent phenomena of quantum entanglement and neuroplasticity, the main foci of the "empirical" portions of this paper.

In the first section on "Philosophical Arguments," I shall provide a synopsis of a number of powerful arguments, and powerful counter-objections to objections, which support Whiteheadian panexperientialism. Much of the direct inspiration for these arguments is provided by Charles Hartshorne, David Griffin, and philosopher of science Milic Capek, although my way of framing the arguments is perhaps (at least sometimes) more recognizably "analytic" in style (and thus perhaps more "mainstream" at least from an Anglo-American perspective). In the course of responding to Karl Popper in this section, I will also provide a brief exposition of the "argument from quantum entanglement." The purported net result will be that panexperientialism has strong funda-mental philosophical appeal in (1) its theoretical parsimony vis-à-vis Cartesian dualist and reductionist-materialist ontologies, (2) its fit with entanglement phenomena, and (3) its basic phenomenological adequacy.

In the second section, perhaps of more direct interest to psychologists, I will briefly develop the work of Jeffrey M. Schwartz, a leading researcher in the field of neuroplasticity at UCLA's School of Medicine. Schwartz's 2002 treatise (co-authored with researcher Sharon Begley) entitled *The Mind and the Brain: Neuroplasticity and the Power of Mental Force* is clearly an extended empirical argument for a process panexperientialist perspective. Although he devotes only one brief sympathetic paragraph to the topic of A.N. Whitehead and process philosophy (45), his admitted "tacit" third co-author is none other than Berkeley physicist Henry P. Stapp, long an important advocate of Whitehead's ontology as a foundational framework for making sense of quantum phenomena. To my knowledge, no one has yet juxtaposed the philosophical arguments of the first section and the empirical argument from neuroplasticity to make the particularly ample "cumulative" case for process panexperientialism I attempt to make here. Of course, no discussion of Schwartz and Begley's work on neuroplasticity could avoid showing its direct implications for clinical psychiatric treatment of obses-sive-compulsive disorder. Importantly, since process philosophy undergirds neuroplastic phenomena, it follows that process philosophy undergirds the clinical ramifications of neuroplasticity.

Philosophical Arguments

Following A.N. Whitehead and C.S. Peirce, Charles Hartshorne has long championed the view he termed "panpsychism" earlier in his career and later "psychicalism." This shift in vocabulary was occasioned by his realization that the continued use of "panpsychism" was much too often causing his position to be associated with the metaphysics of German idealists such as Lotze and Paulsen, who held that any macroscopic entity you please has psychologi-cal properties—a point of view expressly rejected by both Whitehead and Hartshorne. More recently, David Griffin has introduced the terminology "panexperientialism," and more specifically "panexperientialist physicalism," as a label for the Whitehead-Hartshorne position, the latter expression (physicalism) being employed in order to underscore the agreement with physicalist ontologies in their assertion that all genuine individuals have a physical aspect or aspect of space-time extension (Griffin 1998, 3, 78). I will follow Griffin's usage here and shall abbreviate it as *PPE*.

What *is* PPE? Briefly and roughly stated, PPE is the view that each genuine active individual (1) has extension in space-time (this holds surely for all Whiteheadian actual occasions when taken as transitional) and (2) grasps or takes account of or prehends data in its past environment (as Whitehead says explicitly, each actual occasion has a "mental pole" as well as a "physical pole"). PPE observes the fundamental logical distinction made by Leibniz between genuine active individuals or singulars and aggregates or swarms of such active singulars. Thus, rocks and pens are aggregates of atomic singulars and as such are no more centers for or subjects of experience than a flock of geese. Another way of expressing the essence of this position is to say that each genuine individual has at the very least internal relations with its past environment. For Whitehead and Hartshorne, this holds from electrons to God.

Now, in the proceeding section I want to present two positive strands of argument for this position, based on or suggested by Whitehead's and Hartshorne's writings, which I think are extremely powerful and insufficiently appreciated. The first strand of argument follows a kind of reduction to absurdity strategy (more precisely, it is a reduction to "pragmatic absurdity" strategy): If we assume the denial of PPE, in effect, if we posit the existence of genuine individuals that have only external relations with their environment,[1] we must settle for a point of view that denies certain "deep protocols of common sense" (by "deep protocols of common sense" I mean assumptions that we presume *in our practice* universally or nearly universally). Such denials are strongly paradoxical and thus high in cognitive cost. While there are philosophers who may be willing to embrace these paradoxes and pay the cognitive costs, I simply cannot be counted among them. The particular "deep protocols" to which I refer are the assumptions that (1) our experience as temporally conceptualized into past, present, and future is coherent; (2) the act of remembering is in principle not the same as the act of imagining; (3) causal influence is objectively real; and (4) a "skeptical solipsism of the present" is false. The second strand of argument contends that PPE neatly and economically avoids the major paradoxes of the two mind-brain relation theories (or groups of theories) that receive most of the attention from contemporary philosophers of mind: reductionist-materialist physicalism (in all its variations from central state to eliminative to functionalist versions) and dualistic interactionism.

Then I proceed to show that six major challenges to PPE found in the critical literature are rife with difficulties. PPE can thus claim powerful, systematic responses to each. It seems to me that such responses have not been sufficiently appreciated by either the theory's specific critics or the community of philosophers generally.

Two Strands of Argument for PPE

First, let me begin by explicating with some precision the ramifications of the denial of PPE, that is, the ramifications of a pure external relations ontology. I will do this by undertaking a brief thought-experiment set out in terms of (quasi-formal) possible worlds semantics.

Let us stipulate a possible world W such that there is at least one entity x that is "externally related" to all other entities in W (entities-other-than-x in W can be regarded as the set-complement of x). By parity of reasoning, the results we get concerning x of W could be applied to any other entity of W stipulated to be externally related to the members of W. Now, to say that x is externally related to its set-complement in W is to say that x would have all of its properties P whether any member of the set-complement of x in W existed or not. As such x could not genuinely be a "part" of W, since, by definition of "externally related," x is logically self-subsistent or could exist even if the entire set-complement of x did not exist; so to speak, x is W-context-independent. However, there should be nothing modally privileged about W (it is just an arbitrary possible world), and so long as x is regarded as externally related to its set-complement in some distinctive possible world W^1, x would be W^1-context-independent, and so for W^2, W^3, and on and on *ad infinitum*. To make x context dependent, we would have to stipulate that x is internally related to members of its set-complement in some possible world. As such only then does x properly "belong" to a possible world. Of course, however, this would be just to deny the assumption with which we started, namely, the assumption of a purely externally related, logically self-subsistent entity. This context independence could be removed in only one other way, which would be by stipulation of the special case of a world W^u where x comprises its sole member. However, in such case, the properties P of x would be strictly indefinable, since they could not be contextualized by any properties of any entities in W^u other than x (by definition of the domain of W^u), and any other possible worlds by virtue of the possible world-context-independence of x. In effect, using Hartshorne's felicitous phrase, a purely externally related entity x would be a "*sheer* addition to reality as a whole."[2]

What the above reflections show is that a purely externally related entity is completely arbitrary. Because it entails complete independence and lack of intrinsic connection or relation to anything else, such a conception allows for temporal arbitrariness, lack of all causal connection, and what Andrew Bjelland (following Santayana) has aptly called "the skeptical solipsism of the present moment" (Bjelland 1986, 65).

These implications become clear when we examine historical representations of pure external relations doctrines in the atomist tradition from

Hume to Russell. Thus, consider Hume's celebrated passage in *A Treatise of Human Nature*:

> Whatever is distinct, is distinguishable; and whatever is distinguishable, is separable by the thought or imagination. All perceptions are distinct. They are, therefore, distinguishable, and separable, and may be conceived as separately existent, and may exist separately, without any contradiction or absurdity. (Hume 1868, 634)

In light of this, it follows that percepts or events can logically come in any sequence whatsoever. It is as if the conjunction sign is logically primitive and sequence is irrelevant as in the familiar law of commutation where the compound proposition $((x \cdot y) \cdot z)$ is logically equivalent to $((z \cdot y) \cdot x)$ or $(z \cdot x) \cdot y)$ or $((y \cdot x) \cdot z)$ and so on. Thus, Hume's rejection of any "rational" case for causal connection is, of course, no accident. It is not without interest in this context that Hartshorne and Peirce, both panexperientialists and advocates of the concomitant doctrines of *de re* causal connection and *de re* temporal asymmetry, argue that entailment or "illation" is logically primitive and thus that asymmetry and sequence are fundamental. Thus, we have Peirce's proofs (prior to Sheffer) of the truth-functional completeness of negation-disjunction and negation-conjunction, which collapse into Sheffer's unitary stroke operators. As Hartshorne argues in his "The Prejudice in Favor of Symmetry," the defining power of logical operators varies inversely with their degree of asymmetry (1970, ch. 10). Thus, Sheffer's stroke and dagger—the most asymmetrical of operators—can be employed to define any well-formed formula of propositional logic, while equivalence—the most symmetrical of operators—cannot be. Why should we get this result if Hume's "contingent conjunctions" model is in fact taken as logically fundamental? This result indicates that Hume's model is not logically fundamental.

But Russell brings out the full flavor of the arbitrariness of external relations ontology with his notion that the hypothesis that the cosmos began five minutes ago is not logically impossible on atomist principles:

> There is no logically necessary connection between events at different times; therefore nothing that is happening now or will happen in the future can disprove the hypothesis that the world began five minutes ago. Hence the occurrences that are *called* knowledge of the past are logically independent of the past; they are wholly analyzable into present contents, which might, theoretically, be just what they are even if no past had existed. Thus,

what we call "the past" may well be an imaginary projection out of the present moment only. (Russell 1921, 159–160)

This undercuts any clear, principled distinction between past and present, and between the intentional acts of remembering and imagining, in a radical way. On Russell's Humean view, it is theoretically possible that every alleged case of memory is in fact not an act of memory, but of feigning. Indeed, what Russell doesn't go on to say, but his principles allow nonetheless, is that every present moment could represent an entirely novel universe from the perspective of each "present" knower. Thus, at one moment, I believe myself to be a college professor who attended graduate school at the University of Chicago; at the next moment, I am a professional football player who was tight end on my college team, and so on and on, each moment being "loaded," as it were, with a detailed false "memory."

Bjelland nicely summarizes the result of these reflections as follows:

The logic of external relations wreaks havoc with our temporal categories and renders our temporal concepts incoherent. In the end the logic of external relations, if consistently pursued, would issue first in a doctrine of sheer causal contingentism and ultimately in the skeptical solipsism of the present moment [illustrated above]. (Bjelland 1986, 65)

Now, Hartshorne wants to make the strong claim that a pure external relations ontology is logically incoherent in the strong sense that no possible world could contain purely externally related entities. He may well make the case for this on grounds that such entities are surds and are unknowable even in principle. However, the Hartshorne-inspired argument I am presenting here makes the different claim that such a doctrine is "pragmatically impossible," that is, it maintains that the doctrine undercuts notions we constantly assume in practice willy-nilly, come what may. However, in my view (as well as Hartshorne's[3]), pragmatic considerations provide genuine evidence in adjudicating opposing philosophical contentions. Hartshorne's view that all genuine individuals have internal relations (or obversely that no genuine individuals have only external relations) makes possible all of the mentioned common sense protocols. But why should we *rationally prefer* a doctrine, even if it is logically possible, that undercuts such protocols?

Now, there is another fundamental position to which PPE is opposed. This is the opposite of logical atomism, namely, monism. Here it is the reference to "genuine individuals" (plural) in the above definition of PPE that is denied. Mind-body monism comes in both idealist and physicalist forms. In its idealist version, say, à la Bradley, Green, or Bosanquet, the idea is that there is one genuine individual, not many, and this one or absolute is an unbroken continuum of experience. The whole universe is thus a tight chain of internal relations (although Bradley would qualify "in so far as internal relatives are real"). In its physicalist version, say, à la Grünbaum, the world exists as a tenseless, four-dimensional space-time continuum with events as world-tubes already mapped, so to speak, on the continuum. Our temporal experience is an illusion created by consciousness "crawling upon the [already given] world-lines," to use Herman Weyl's apt expression (Weyl 1949, 166).

Hartshorne has attacked the idealist version in numerous ways, for example:[4] (1) by pointing out that a pure internal relations ontology is as extreme as a pure external relations ontology and will die the death of other such extremes; (2) that, *contra* Bradley, our discourse about relations does seem to invoke a legitimate role for external relations, particularly when making sense out of temporal succession where past events are externally related to the present event (although the present event is internally related to the past); and (3) that McTaggart's famous reduction of A-Series concepts to absurdity begs the question by tacitly presupposing that the future events to which his proof refers are as determinate and concrete as the past. Also, in light of the above logical syntax analogies, (4) Bradley seems to take equivalence as most primitive as in his express notion that every entity is ground and consequence for every other and thus **[(xRy)** *iff* **(yRx)]**. Again, why should we get the result that asymmetrical operators have greater defining power if Bradley's equivalence relation model is taken as fundamental?

But the "knock out blow" against both[5] versions of monism comes by way of an argument suggested by Milic Capek, an argument at least implied by Hartshorne in his assertion in *Creative Synthesis* that a temporalistic and prehensive model of mind-brain interaction is "most economical" in comparison with the alternatives of Cartesian dualism, parallelism, epiphenomenalism, etc. (Hartshorne 1970, 107). I expand upon Capek (somewhat liberally) to give the following argument (see Capek 1978, 57–58):

> P1—All partisans accept the notion of temporal experience as a phenomenological given. The words "past," "present," and "future" are communicable and intelligible, because we remember the past, experience the present, and anticipate the future.

> P2—Parallelism, which denies mind-brain causal influence of any sort, is inherently mysterious and arbitrary; it is an *ad hoc* solution to the paradoxes of Cartesian interaction.

> P3—All other models of the mind-brain relation posit at least *sine qua non* causal influence (and at least in the direction of brain to mind).

P4—If a tenseless monistic ontology holds, then brain events are tenseless and are already present simultaneously somewhere on a continuum of being.

P5—If brain events are at least *sine qua non* causal influences upon conscious states, then conscious states should be tenseless, because brain events are.

∴ Either we must embrace parallelism (with all of its mystery) or we must reject the phenomenological givenness of temporalized experience.

In other words, we cannot comprehend the "*crawling* of consciousness along world-lines," or in effect, understand how even the *illusion* of temporal experience could occur if we adopt a tenseless "block of being" ontology.

The second set of arguments picks up again on Hartshorne's theme of the theoretical economy of PPE. One of the strongest positive arguments for PPE is that it simply does not raise the persistent problems of the two major competitors among theories of mind-brain relation, that is, Cartesian interactionistic dualism and materialistic monism. Indeed, the current situation in analytic philosophy of mind seems to be one of increasing recognition that current research programs have reached a dead end. To put it quite tersely, materialist programs have struggled especially with the issue of the emergence of consciousness, while dualist programs have struggled especially with the problems of mental influences upon the physical. Without a viable alternative in sight, Colin McGinn has thus summarily argued that "we will *never* resolve the mind-brain conundrum"(1982; see especially ch. 1). And John Searle has regarded the attempts of materialist philosophers to save the materialist hypothesis as almost neurotically desperate:

> Criticisms of the materialist theory usually take a more or less technical form, but in fact, underlying the technical objections is a much deeper objection . . . : The theory in question has left out . . . some essential feature of the mind, such as consciousness or "qualia" or semantic content . . . . And this leads to ever more frenzied efforts to stick with the materialist thesis and try to defeat the arguments put forward by those who insist on preserving the facts. After some years of desperate maneuvers to account for the difficulties, some new development is put forward that allegedly solves the difficulties, but then we find that it encounters . . . the same old difficulties. (Searle 1994, 3)

What is called for, writes Galen Strawson, is some novel "radical alternative" that is geared to providing "an adequate grasp of the fundamental nature of matter at some crucial *general* level of understanding" (1994, 92).

It seems to me that PPE offers that "radical alternative" with least paradox. I will try to show this by selecting a major problem with each mentioned competing theory that seems to be intractable, and then by showing how PPE circumvents those problems.

A great trouble with any materialist theory of consciousness, long noticed in one manner or another by commentators on the Greek atomists, by John Locke in his *An Essay Concerning Human Understanding* (bk. 4, ch. 10), and by contemporary philosophers such as Thomas Nagel and John Searle (see especially Nagel 1979 and Searle 1994), is the problem of how subjective, phenomenally qualitative states of consciousness could ever arise from material states that are by definition devoid of subjective, phenomenally qualitative properties. Reductionist identity materialists indeed hold that all mental states are "reducible" to physical brain states, which are in turn "reducible" to microphysical states or constellations of carbon, hydrogen, oxygen and other atoms and their subatomic constituents. This means that under materialist descriptions of atomic entities, our conscious states *are* merely structural-quantitative states, a special positioning or location of bits of stuff having merely quantitative properties such as mass, charge, and spin. This seems completely absurd. In the last analysis, my experience of a patch of blue *is* qualitative and not merely quantitative or structural. As Hartshorne has put it (1977a, 89), how can (reductionist) materialism ever bridge "the logical gap" between qualitative and quantitative-structural properties? Indeed, this so-called "problem of phenomenal qualia" and the apparent impossibility of physicalist reduction of qualia has moved some materialists to an even more radically absurd position, which is to eliminate consciousness, subjectivity, phenomenal qualia altogether. Says Paul Churchland, "If we do give up hope of reduction, then elimination emerges as the only coherent alternative" (cited by Griffin 1998, 54). But this is hard to take seriously. If there are any facts, it *is* a fact that I experience blue and sweet and pains and tickles, etc.

No such problem arises for PPE, because, by definition, it attributes subjectivity or interiority to atomic entities, or more precisely, to the actual occasions that constitute atomic entities. Indeed, the following are fundamental contentions of Whitehead's and Hartshorne's philosophy (cf. Hartshorne 1964b, ch. 8): (1) There are no "vacuous actualities," no "bits of *mere* stuff"; (2) the content of actualities is describable as a certain organization, contextualization, or synthesis of aesthetic qualia; and, (3) from this qualitative content, quantitative descriptions are made possible. Thus, subjectivity and quality do not somehow "emerge" as properties of conscious states, they are already present in the very building blocks of conscious states, which are the billions of actual occasions constituting the atoms that in turn constitute the neural occasions that in turn give out their prehensive data for the large-scale or dominant actual occasions constituting our moments of consciousness.

It might be objected that this still evades the problem at hand, because bits of subjectivity and qualia can no more give you a new whole of subjectivity than can bits of vacuous stuff. To use (partially) William James' classic analogy in *The Principles of Psychology* (James probably was aiming this at pantheistic experientialists like Royce, not "panpsychism" as such),[6] if you take a dozen men and/or women and give them each a word of a coherent sentence and have them think the word intently, you get no emergent consciousness of the whole sentence. But this objection would entirely miss the point of the doctrine of *compound* actual occasions. The large-scale or "regnant" actual occasions that constitute a series of human conscious states are precisely new, sequentially distinct entities that compound many antecedent entities of qualia. This compounding necessarily involves a qualitative intensification sheerly by virtue of the *many* that are prehended and also by the creative reaction of the new occasion to its prehended data (that is to say, every actual occasion is a synthetic contextualization of its prehended data by virtue of which it is a novel, distinct occasion discernible from others). In terms of James' analogy, PPE would require alterations in it such that a thirteenth person (analogous to a new regnant occasion) would be posited whose conscious experience was given content by the discrete words of each of the twelve to which the thirteenth person has access (analogous to the prehensions of the new regnant occasion). We would indeed then have a new consciousness of the whole sentence.

Cartesian dualist interaction theories can avoid the problem of ontological reduction of the mental to the physical-extensional; indeed, by definition, they ontologically separate the mental and physical. But in doing this they create the intractable problem of making sense out of an entirely nonphysical mode of causation. For dualism, while brain states causally influence mental states, the converse is also the case, mental states causally influence brain states. A severe problem arises here when we see that, for Cartesian theory, mental states are taken as the contradictories of physical-extensional states. The mental is precisely that which lacks extensional properties of mass, length, shape, etc. Mental entities are thus "abstract" entities. But then how can such entities cause physical alterations? To use Jeffry Olen's apt analogy (1983, 216), we can no more make sense of how Cartesian mental states can causally influence brain states, than we can understand how the square root of two could push a book (or even molecules of a book).

PPE has no such difficulty, because, by definition, it *is* a physicalist ontology—for it, all occasions have extension in space-time. Indeed, Hartshorne makes much of the inadequate phenomenology of experience involved in the anti-physicalism of Cartesian theories (for sources, see footnote 28). It is simply erroneous, Hartshorne observes, to claim categorically that all mental states have no extension: pains, tickles, sexual sensations, warmth, tastes, smells, and other mental qualia have approximate extensions measured along the sites of their sensory receptors. Thus, I do not regard my toes as the place where I am smelling the aroma of dinner, and a pain can extend for two inches on my arm.

But surely at least thoughts *do* have abstract, nonextensional properties. Consider the following example: the sentential schema "**x** is round and weighs twelve pounds" makes clear sense when the value for **x** is "my bowling ball," but does not make sense when the value for **x** is "my thought." (The sense of absurdity would not change if the extensional predicates I provide accord with neo-cortex measurements of brain sites for thought and language processing.) The root of the nonextensional aspect of thought comes in to clearer view when we consider that thought has the property of intentionality. "My thought" in question *is* not itself something round that weighs twelve pounds, but rather is *of* something round that weighs twelve pounds. As such, conscious thoughts are states that have, in Sartrean phrase, being *for* themselves. But this is precisely what an actual occasion *is*, in a manner of speaking, that is, an occasion is an actuality that becomes so because it has others for its very fabric; every occasion is *l' être pour soi*. Thus, regnant actual occasions constituting my moments of conscious thought already contain a social intentionality that transcends the mere physical location of acts of thinking. PPE then seems to be basically phenomenologically adequate. It embraces both the extensionality of feeling states and the intentionality of thinking states.

Hartshorne argues this latter point with particular effectiveness in two essays on Husserl (1968 and 1984, ch. 23). The way out of Husserl's Cartesian solipsism as developed in *Ideen I* and the *Cartesian Meditations*, which yet at once fully captures the evident intentionality of consciousness, is to see that a full account of "experience of" requires the positing of a *content* of the experience that is really independent of the experience. For, "no experience is merely 'of' that very experience, nor even merely of an earlier moment in the same stream of experiences [if it were experience merely 'of' an earlier moment of experience, it would have the exact content of the earlier experience], nor can merely 'intending' an object that may not exist constitute the 'of' in 'experience of' [because the projection of possibilities is grounded *somehow* in *actual* objects of experience]" (1984, 275). For PPE, the whole move to *epoché* is entirely unnecessary as any dominant actual occasion involves the prehension of physical states, that is, the feeling content of the neuronic occasions. *Contra* Descartes and Husserl, any experience whatsoever is already an instance of contact with physical reality.

Some Objections Considered

I now turn to the consideration of six objections to PPE that have been issued by the minority of analytic philosophers of mind who have commented on the theory. My discussion of three of these objections is indebted, as mentioned earlier, to Griffin's analysis (namely, the first, second, fifth, and sixth). I have added to the discussion by treating what might be called the "Ordinary Language Objection" and "Popper's Objection."

First, panexperientialism is for some philosophers simply to be *equated* with the "classical panpsychism" of such post-Kantian German idealists as Herman Lotze and Frederick Paulsen wherein any macroscopic "thing" or "individual" is possessed of consciousness, is a center of experience. As Colin McGinn has put it, "panpsychism" entails the "scientifically and metaphysically outrageous" assertion that "rocks actually have thoughts" (1982a, 31). But this objection is especially weak as it simply has no application to the panexperientialist theory advocated by contemporary process philosophers, and on two basic counts. To begin with, the Whiteheadian-Hartshornean version holds that not all experience is *conscious* experience. On panexperientialism, there can be low-grade sentience that is profoundly different in complexity from full-bodied consciousness (e.g., the posited sentience of neuronal occasions constituting a particular brain cell). Moreover, as Hartshorne has emphasized *ad nauseum* (but apparently to little avail), Leibniz had long ago introduced the proper distinction between genuine individuals and aggregates or swarms. Thus, rocks are aggregates of atoms and *qua* aggregates are insufficiently organized to have *any* sort of sentient or subjective states, much less "thoughts." However, the atomic entities that constitute rocks may be said to be constituted by occasions that have some extremely low degree of "sentience" or "openness to the environment."

Second, philosophers such as McGinn have asserted that "panpsychism" is absurd, because it entails that the behavior of atoms and subatomic particles would not be predictable through "their physical properties alone," something that McGinn claims "we know . . . not to be the case" (1982a, 32). But this is at best a dangerously problematic assertion, if not altogether totally implausible in the light of quantum theory. Quantum mechanics suggests just the opposite, namely, that physical information has intrinsic limits such that prediction of behavior can be determined only in the case of large statistical generalizations of elementary particles, not individual particles. This, of course, leaves room for the notion of elementary particles as partially self-determinant. Thus, PPE is at the very least compatible with quantum theory. Moreover, current information-theoretic models of quantum mechanics directly imply that elementary particles process something more akin to semantic information than mere syntactical-bit information, and are thus strongly suggestive of protomental capacities of elementary particles.[7] This suggestion holds for both the orthodox and revisionary Bohm-Hiley interpretations of quantum mechanics according to which "active information" must be posited for subatomic particles (Bohm and Hiley 1993, especially 387). In fact, the notion of "protomental matter" has become commonplace vocabulary of quantum physicists from Bohm to Wheeler to Wigner.

Third, the response to McGinn above connects with Karl Popper's main objection to "panpsychist" and/or "protomentalist" theories of elementary particles. In his classic *The Self and Its Brain* (Eccles and Popper 1977), co-authored with John Eccles, Popper objects that elementary particles are "completely identical whatever their past histories" and thus they could not have any "interior" states. Consequently, panpsychist and/or protomentalist concepts of elemental entities have no discernible empirical content and are "metaphysical (in the bad sense)" as they thus have no discernible "explanatory power" (71).

However, this objection is riddled with difficulties. First of all, Popper has a very narrow conception of the "empirical content" of protomentalist notions of elemental entities. True, say, protons are not distinguishable in terms of direct experimental inspection of their physical properties. Any arbitrary proton P has the same mass (938 MeV/c^2), charge (+1), and spin (½) as any other proton P^1. But it isn't true that protons just remain static in terms of their empirically discernible behavior over periods of time. For example, the proton P in a tritium nucleus of hydrogen has a rate of radiation decay as compared to a proton P^1 in a lead-206 nucleus (which has no decay) as is now familiar to us through the "half life radiation law." Using Hartshorne's helpful notion of "dipolarity," we might say that Popper is here conflating the gen-identity description of protonic occasions with their strict identity description, that is, the description that would demarcate just this sequence of protonic occasions P with its particular features of radiation decay as opposed to some other sequence P^1 with its particular stability or decay. Moreover, notice that the behavioral differences between P and P^1 are *dependent on their physical contexts*. Why should context matter for entities that are utterly closed to their environments (given Popper's view)?

Perhaps more important (and Popper could not have known about any of this when writing *The Self and Its Brain*), the protomentalist concept has indirect empirical content by virtue of the phenomena of quantum holism or entanglement and the result of the various EPR experiments undertaken since the 1980s (I assume an information-theoretic interpretation here). That is to say, if we assume that elementary particles are "open" to the influences of information transfer, and not merely so by virtue of light-cone propagation, we can more plausibly explain nonlocal data correlations of projected photons, correlations that can be altered by alterations in initial experimental designs (e.g., changes in polarization orientations). Whatever controversies may be involved with the interpretation of these phenomena (e.g., whether they confirm the notion of instantaneous information transfer), it seems clear that they strongly favor a social and interactive interpretation of elemental entities very much in the spirit of Whitehead's denial of simple location. Indeed, mathematical physicists Robert Valenza and Granville Henry have recently proposed an (I think) effective solution to Young's two-slit photon experiment paradox, which is based precisely on Whiteheadian assumptions of prehensive events and rejection of simple location (Valenza and Henry 1997). So much then, it seems to me, for Popper's claim of protomentalism's lack of empirical explanatory power.

Fourth, some analytic philosophers have rejected panexperientialism on the grounds that such Whiteheadian constructions as "feeling-tones" of atoms (and so forth) stretch language beyond its sensible limits. Indeed, if process thinkers reject the notion that "atoms think," then why not reject "atoms feel"? At least one philosopher has offered a "Wittgensteinian" critique of Hartshorne's panexperientialism precisely on this basis—a set of considerations that is close to Nagel's worry about "panpsychism": "if one travels too far down the phylogenetic tree, people gradually shed their faith that there is experience there at all" (1979, 168).

Bryant Keeling argues that Hartshorne's use of the term "feeling" when speaking of atoms is out of accord with the use of that term in its ordinary contexts and thus constitutes a serious misuse of words. Specifically, "the thing which is said to feel must be capable of observable behavior which is very similar to human behavior"(1976, 63). Thus, I can licitly say that, for example, "my dog feels happy," because my dog dances about excitedly when I bring out her fetching ball, just as I might say that a human being is feeling happy when dancing about in an expression of glee. But what observable behavior does an atom or electron display that gives us an observational analogue for attributing feeling to it?

Hartshorne and proponents of PPE have several ready and effective responses to this sort of criticism. First of all, thinking and feeling are very different sorts of mental states, and thus the denial of atomic thinking states along with the acceptance of atomic feeling-tones is in so far intelligible. Again, notice that PPE is not the view that higher order conscious states are to be generalized to all genuine individuals. Indeed, there are numerous commonplace examples of the distinction; for example, plants (or at least plant cells) are living and sentient, but human beings (not apparently plants) think in the sense of deliberating by means of symbolic systems possessing semantic content. Feeling or sentient states are thus more elemental and generalizable than thinking states. Moreover, Hartshorne has responded to Keeling directly with an all-important clarification: Says Hartshorne, "the [behavioral] criteria are generalized, not just the concept [of feeling]" (1976, 67). For Hartshorne, the behavioral criteria need not be "very similar to restrictively human behavior." (Ironically [in the context of Keeling's criticisms], the acceptance of such restrictive criteria would indeed represent a much too anthropomorphic procedure in metaphysical thinking.) The behavioral criteria to be generalized are such items as "self-initiated activity" and having "influences of the past and the environment," in effect, the most *abstract* features of human experience. Thus, observational analogues for attributing sentience or feeling-tones to, for example, electrons, are to be found in, say, their bonding behavior. Plato had the criteriological matter essentially right, then, when he said that anima or soul is to be attributed wherever we detect genuine self-motion.

But suppose we grant Keeling's critique of PPE's specific use of the term "feeling." I still do not agree that such a critique would cut very deeply. If the use of such language as "feeling" in talk about elementary particles is to be deemed inappropriately anthropomorphic (or biomorphic)—or is otherwise a misuse of the term "feeling"—it can be replaced by more abstract philosophical language that expresses the position of PPE in a way that still suggests "psychological" predication in the description of all actual occasions. For example, to assert that an "electron has *internal relations* with its environment" is to assert a characterization of electrons in direct contradistinction to their reductionistic physicalist characterization. Inert, contextless, externally related electrons *are* fundamentally different entities from electrons with "windows," and this difference cannot be ignored no matter what the outcome of any debate on the appropriateness of such decriptors as "feeling."

Fifth, another objection from analytic quarters is based on the notion of supervenience as developed in the philosophy of Jaegwon Kim (see Kim 1992). Kim wants to preserve both physicalism and the common sense notion of mental causation. In order to achieve this he has proposed a "mereological supervenience" model of the mind-body relation in which mental causation is viewed as a kind of supervenient causation. In Kim's analysis, mental phenomena do not directly cause other mental phenomena to occur; rather, they do so only in the sense of being supervenient upon a physical state that in turn causes another physical state upon which a mental state supervenes. Thus, the mind-body relation is roughly analyzed as follows (106):

A: "when a mental event **M** causes a physical event **P**, this is so because **M** is supervenient upon a physical event, **P***, and **P*** causes **P**"

A¹: "when a mental event **M** causes another mental event **M***, this is so because **M** supervenes on a physical state **P**, and similarly **M*** on **P***, and **P** causes **P***"

The analyses **A** and **A¹** make it clear that the exercise of casual agency really takes place at the physical level (in **A**, **P*** causes **P**, and in **A¹**, **P** causes **P***), while the mental events function as macrolevel descriptions of whole sets of microphysical events, sets labeled collectively as **P** and **P*** (and this is just one way of defining "supervenience"). But, as Griffin (1998, 219–227) argues and as Kim himself has more recently suggested, this whole approach seems to dissolve into epiphenomenalism. Kim has changed the vocabulary of the epiphenomenalist model (i.e., Kim speaks of a mental event as being supervenient upon the physical event rather than of a physical event causing a mental event), but the point remains that there is no direct casual role played by mental events. Thus, in Kim's own words, "any 'physicalistically correct' account of mental causation must . . . expos[e] itself to the charge of epiphenomenalism" (360). This is a serious flaw as epiphenomenalism presents mental events as lacking causal efficacy and thus implies that our notion of intentional action is entirely illusory. Contrary to Kim's own desire to build our philosophical theories around the best of current scientific theory and practice, epiphenomenalism is an inherently anti-evolutionary perspective as it suggests that animals and humans evolved with persistent natural selection of entirely superfluous mental entities.

Sixth, one of the most common objections to PPE is to urge that its positing of subjective "building blocks" of consciousness is entirely unnecessary, for there is an argument from analogy that purportedly explains how consciousness emerges from "matter." Consider the case of liquidity. Consciousness is an emergent macro-level property of micro-level brain states in the same way that liquidity is a macro-level emergent property of micro-level H_2O molecules. This is one of John Searle's favorite analogies offered in support of his so-called "biological naturalist" view, and has figured prominently as well in Jaegwon Kim's reply to David Griffin in a *Process Studies* Forum Article (vol. 28, nos. 1–2). As Griffin points out, however, this "analogy" won't at all do, because in application to the mind-body case it is tantamount merely to what William Seager has aptly called a *correlative* analogy, not a *constitutive* one that does real explanatory work. Given what we know about the physical properties of hydrogen and oxygen and about how these molecules interact (the van de Waals molecular-interaction properties), we can get a very clear intuitive expectation of liquidity at the macro-level. Here we can understand how such interaction could *constitute* liquidity. But, as Griffin puts it, "nothing about the behavior and properties of the neurons as studied from without would lead us to expect some brain states to produce consciousness" (1998, 57). Measurements of synaptic firings or ionization features of brain cell walls, etc., etc., give us no intuitive clues whatsoever about expectations of consciousness as a macro-level property. Griffin here appropriately cites Galen Strawson as agreeing that any constitutive analogy between physical properties of neurons and consciousness is "impossible" to imagine. In effect, Searle's liquidity analogy merely correlates macro-level consciousness with micro-level neuronal activity and doesn't do any particular explanatory work. As Simon Blackburn has put it while discussing the related notion of supervenience of psychological states on physical states, philosophers are here simply stating the problem, not solving it (cited at Griffin 1998, 57).

An Empirical Argument from Neuroplasticity

CLA psychiatric neuroscientist Jeffrey Schwartz and his research colleague Sharon Begley have authored an impressive and quite readable treatise, *The Mind and The Brain* (2002), which narrates the history of empirical scientific research on the phenomena of neuroplasticity (i.e., roughly, alterations in the brain or neural system due to sensory and/or cognitional input or growth in the amount of neurotransmitters or neurotransmitter-related enzymes due to such input) and the clinical applications that flow from this research. Consider the following brief sketch (Schwartz and Begley 2002, 225–254):

Neuroplastic phenomena began to emerge in the early 1980s with neuroscientist Edward Taub's research on the so-called Silver Spring monkeys (impaired monkeys who could be trained to use formerly useless limbs by constraining usable limbs), and quickly moved on to a successful application of constraint-induced therapy in stroke patients. By the mid-1990s, Schwartz had developed a "mindful" or "attention" based approach to obsessive-compulsive patients that began to show behavioral results and corresponding alterations in PET brain scans; this led to a collaboration with Yale Tourett's Syndrome researcher Jim Leckman. This collaboration, along with UCLA's John Piacentini, led to a successful attention-based treatment of a biologically "hard wired" disorder, Tourette's, with changes as high as a "56 percent improvement in tic-related impairment." In 1997 at California's Salk Institute, actual "neurogenesis" (the production of new neurons, not just new neuronal connections or new axons and dendrites) had been established in experiments with adult mice by placing them in a more stimulating, complex environment. This was followed in 1998 by Swedish neuroscientist Peter Eriksson and Salk researcher Fred Gage's discovery of neurogenesis in the hippocampus of adult humans. By August 2000, an epoch-making paper on neuroplasticity was published by John Teasdale of Cambridge, England's Cognition and Brain Sciences Unit, where he showed that there was a significant (44%) improvement in depression relapses among patients receiving a Schwartz style regimen of attentional therapy as opposed to patients receiving a nonattentional therapy (Teasdale et al. 2000). (Attentional therapy here involved the exercise of "observing" thoughts and emotions in an impartial manner, examining them, and then focusing attention on alternative thoughts or emotions.) By the turn of the millennium, neuroplasticity—including the "top-down" variety involved in attentional therapy—had become rather firmly accepted in the neuroscience community and arguably the hottest research topic in the field. Neuroscience had come a long way in two decades or so from the old dogma that neuronal pathways are immutable and rigidly fixed to the following summary statement of Schwartz and Begley (224):

> The existence, and importance, of brain plasticity are no longer in doubt. "Some of the most remarkable observations made in recent neuroscience history have been on the capacity of . . . the cerebral cortex to reorganize [itself] in the face of reduced or enhanced afferent input," declared Edward Jones of the University of California, Davis, Center for Neuroscience, in 2000. What had been learned from the many experiments in which afferent input to the brain increased? Cortical representations are not immutable; they are, to the contrary, dynamic, continuously modified by the lives we lead.

Now, as we have just seen, the basic thesis of neuroplasticity (or NP-Thesis) is that sufficiently repeated acts of mental attention at the macro-level of conscious experiences can cause alterations at the micro-physical level of the brain, resulting in significant experiential and behavioral alterations. Not only is there compelling empirical evidence (as briefly sketched above) for the existence of neuroplasticity, but the phenomena have a nice theoretical fit with contemporary quantum theory and its observational credentials. In effect, the NP-Thesis can be coherently illustrated by employing basic rules of quantum mechanics as applied to the micro-physical constitution of the brain; no Cartesian assumption of a nonphysical mental state somehow mysteriously acting on this micro-physical constitution is required. As will also be argued, however, reductionist-materialism is strongly challenged by such phenomena. In nontechnical language, we can say the following:

Quantum mechanics makes it possible to understand how repeated acts of attention can causally influence brain activity. When neurotransmitters are released, calcium ions must pass through the extremely narrow, microscopic ion channels in a neuron. The narrowness is at such a microscopic level that quantum mechanical rules and Heisenberg's Uncertainty Principle can be applied to it. The vesicles of a neuron are triggered by calcium ions to release neurotransmitters, but the triggering is only probabilistic in nature. That is to say, the quantum wave functions of the neuronal vesicle exist as wave function superpositions—in effect, there is a wave function for "trigger the neurotransmitters" (label this $\Psi 1$) and a wave function for "do not trigger the neurotransmitters" (label this Ψg). Now, both Ψl and Ψg have a probability range of 0 to 1 for becoming actualized. Suppose that the brain we are considering is that of an obsessive-compulsive disorder (OCD) patient in a therapeutic situation. Also, suppose that the OCD patient is given to repeated thoughts verbalized as "turn the lights on and off eight times," while the therapist has suggested an alternative thought such as "go to your garden." Respectively, the physical infrastructure at the vesicle level or brain "circuit" for the OCD thought is represented by Ψl and the therapist's alternative thought and correlative physical infrastructure or brain "circuit" by Ψg. Early in the therapeutic process the probability for actualizing Ψl is much higher than for Ψg. However, as therapy continues and the patient concentrates on the therapist's alternative thought (in literally thousands of thought exercises), the probability of actualizing the calcium ionization in the brain circuit correlated with superposition Ψg increases. As the patient begins to act on the "go to the garden" thought, eventually on a regular basis, neuroplasticity firmly sets in, that is to say, the metabolism of the brain changes so that the brain circuit correlated with Ψg is greatly strengthened, and the relative probability of the quantum superpositions has in fact reversed:

$$P\ (\Psi g) > P\ (\Psi l).$$

One immediate objection to the NP-Thesis is to be anticipated as follows: If directed mental attention can alter brain circuitry metabolism in significant ways, then is the upshot that all patients with mental disorders such as OCD ought to be able to "will the disorders away" given enough "attention" therapy? Surely such a consequence would be absurd. Schwartz and Begley reply (320–321) that this poses a false dichotomy (or "fallacy of black and white thinking" as the logic textbooks might phrase it). The quantum brain picture painted above does seem to apply to the many of Dr. Schwartz's OCD patients who do in fact remarkably control their OCD urges and behavior through an extended regimen of directed attention therapy. But there are wide ranges of strength in the OCD brain circuitry (where neurons extending from the anterior cingulate gyrus and orbital frontal cortex to the caudate nucleus are metabolically "overheated" and issue in an intense sense of "error" calling out for a "corrective" response); some OCD patients have far more deeply pathological circuitry than others and are accordingly far more recalcitrant. Moreover, Schwartz's attention therapy has nuances (four major steps are involved—Reattribute, Refocus, Relabel, Revalue) and is oversimplified in the above quantum brain scenario; in effect, the therapy requires some practice and skill and accordingly the quality of attentional states will vary with individual practice and skill. Thus, neuroplastic phenomena will vary from individual to individual.

Schwartz and Begley add that the NP-Thesis as explicated in the scenario above is corroborated by an important empirically confirmed quantum phenomenon known as the "Quantum Zeno Effect" (QZE). QZE is the amazing phenomenon such that, the more frequently and rapidly you observe a physical system in a certain selected way, the more you "lock in" a certain physical state of the system. First introduced and promulgated by University of Texas-Austin physicist George Sudarshan and his colleagues in the late 1970s, the QZE has been tested and confirmed on numerous occasions. Write Schwartz and Begley (353):

> one of the neatest confirmations came in a 1990 study at the National Institute of Standards and Technology. There, researchers measured the probability that beryllium ions would decay from a high-energy to a low-energy state. As the number of measurements per unit time increased, the probability of that energy transition fell off; the beryllium atoms stayed in their initial, high-energy state because scientists kept asking them, "So, have you decayed yet?" The watched pot never boiled. As Sudarshan and Rothman conclude, "One really can stop an atomic transition by repeatedly looking at it."

As Schwartz and Begley also point out, neo-Whiteheadian physicist-philosopher H.P. Stapp was quick to notice the principled fit between QZE and the phenomenon of mental attention, so important in Schwartz's therapy regimen. For "attention" essentially involves the selective observation and sustaining of a thought over and against alternative potential thoughts that, on a quantum physical account of the brain, correlate with alternative quantum superpositions. Indeed, note that PET scans show that the same areas of the brain are activated whether one is perceiving an object with eyes open or is imagining the object with eyes closed. Further, the notion of experiencing a mental state or having "experience *of* an experience" is part and parcel of the Whiteheadian account of perceptual experience, since, given Whitehead's "perception in the mode of causal efficacy" and "perception in the mode of presentational immediacy" distinction, all perception and imagination is in fact an act of "immediate memory," which by phenomenological analysis is the "experience *of* an experience." So, clearly, Stapp's linkage between QZE and the notion of observation of mental states is perfectly consistent with a Whiteheadian phenomenology of experience. The QZE fits beautifully with and thus helps explain the results Dr. Schwartz has had with OCD patients, for there is a direct correlation between clinical results and brain scans and the *quality* of attention (Schwartz and Begley 2002, 355):

Both the PET scans and the clinical data suggest that the quality of the attentional state—that is, whether it is mindful or unmindful—influences the brain and affects how, and even whether, patients actively process or robotically experience sensory stimuli as well as emotions and thoughts.

Assuming Dr. Schwartz's clinical results and the reality of neuroplastic phenomena, the crucial question arises, "how could any of this be coherently accommodated on a classical reductionist-materialist ontology?" The Whiteheadian panexperientialist perspective has no difficulty with the "top-down" causal influence pattern exhibited by neuroplastic phenomena or the related QZE, because the atomic occasions constituting the brain circuitry are, on Whitehead's theory, "open" to information transfer. No redescription of the phenomenology of attention or quantum mechanics is necessary, given Whiteheadian actual occasions. But a reductionist-materialist must somehow dismiss or radically redescribe everything here, because of the nature of the theory's constitutive "material" atoms. By definition, they are "closed" to information transfer and can never internally change—in Popper's words, they are "completely identical whatever their past histories"; the materialist criterion for change thus must be entirely external, for example, a spear through the brain moving millions of atoms into radically different spatial configurations. The classical materialist is thereby strongly committed to determinism in order to explain (or explain away) neuroplasticity: there must be some inexorable "program" that causes the so-called "attention" states and correlated brain states to be as they are. The "attention" states are merely macro-level emergent properties of microphysical states and are supervenient upon those microphysical states. The attention states can only appear to be causing changes at the microphysical level, then; for the only causal mechanisms allowable on a materialist ontology are effects caused by the *spatial re-configuration* of material atoms—in good Hobbesian phrase, "the matter *in motion*." And the motion is caused by some deterministic program, since the material atoms *themselves* are not agents or initiators, but are patients to be acted upon. As Schwartz and Begley put it memorably, materialist determinism is committed to the view that (374):

Humans are essentially nothing more than fleshy computers spitting out the behavioral results of some inescapable neurogenetic program. "The brain is going to do what the brain was always going to do," say the materialists.

On such terms, there cannot be *really alternative* quantum superpositions attending ion channels in the brain, and no real probability or chance attending the superpositions, since the brain can only be *one way* as dictated by its "inescapable neurogenetic program"—in effect, the quantum wave function of the brain is always collapsed. So, not only attention states, but quantum theory must be ultimately discarded as appearance.

This raises not only the problem of squaring the otiosity of attention-intention mental states and evolutionary theory (see discussion of Kim's supervenience model above), but also brings the Capek Argument back into play. For to say that the quantum wave function is *always* collapsed is in effect to dismiss temporal becoming and to spatialize time, for in such case every actual event is connected to every other actual event in a continuum of being such that to ask "what is" is to ask "where is." Thus, again, we tacitly have Grünbaum's atemporalist view and its difficulty with the phenomenological fact of temporal awareness.

Conclusion

I conclude that Whiteheadian panexperientialist physicalism "saves" the phenomena, welcomes top-down neuroplasticity, QZE and quantum entanglement, and avoids the paradoxes of materialism and Cartesian dualism. At the very least, it is a serious contender in the debate over the mind-body relation, and, in the light of the cumulative sweep of all the above argumentation, hardly deserves the disdain issued by John Haught's conferees with which we began.

Notes

1. That "the existence of genuine individuals which have only external relations with their environment" is the contradictory of PPE follows directly from Hartshorne's notion of internal relations. Hartshorne gives an interesting technical explication of G.E. Moore's definition of external relations when he connects it with C.I. Lewis' system of "strict implication," where "P strictly implies Q" if and only if "necessarily, it is not the case that P and not-Q" (1948, 95): external is the negative of internal, and internal relations are ontological correlates of logical relations of "strict implication" or entailment. This seems to agree with Moore's definition. For that which the conception of a thing entails is that without which the entity could not be itself, the entity conceived. An internal relation then is the ontological correlate of a Lewisian strict implication, while an external relation is precisely *not* the ontological correlate of a Lewisian strict implication. This allows Hartshorne to see with great clarity that the logical notion of "independence" or "externality" can be modally construed as a relationship to *open* possibility, since internality or dependence is seen as *restriction* of possible alternatives—necessarily not, P without Q, if P is internally related to Q.

This insight undermines any absolute idealist's retort that an alleged "external relation to **P**" is itself a relation that necessarily involves **P** as a term of the conceived relation. As Hartshorne puts it (1948, 72): "the absoluteness [or externality] of [a] term . . . is not, strictly speaking with respect to relation to [**P**], but with respect to a *kind* of relation, which can be defined, as logicians say, intensionally, or without mentioning [**P**]. Thus arithmetic is independent, not merely of my awareness of it, but of any particular awareness. Nothing is added to this attribution of independence by saying, "and also arithmetic is independent of my awareness."

2. Hartshorne 1964b, 261. It might occur to some that an example of an entity **x,** which is logically self-subsistent would be God, and that the above Hartshornean thought-experiment shows only that, in a possible world where God existed and nothing else existed, God's properties would be independent of any possible worlds or world-states. Students of Hartshorne's writings know well what his response to this would be: Employing the dipolar distinction (or gen-identity/strict identity distinction), God's essential or gen-identity properties of omniscience, onmibenevolence, *necessary* existence, etc., are independent of possible worlds, but it doesn't follow from this that *all* of God's properties would be independent of the content of possible worlds or world states. For example, precisely *how* God's omniscience or perfect adequacy of knowledge is actualized depends on what possible world states to be known *are* actualized. Moreover, taking God as the value of **x** in **Wu** would constitute a contradiction. As Hartshorne points out famously in his paper on "Negative Facts and the Analogical Inference to Other Mind" (1964a), a God who is purportedly "omniscient," but has no *actual* objects of cognition, could not in fact be omniscient. This is because the very notion of *self*-knowledge logically implies knowledge of the contrast "not-self," and knowledge of merely potential objects of cognition would not sufficiently ground any actual knowledge of others and would in effect represent a clear inversion of the ontological principle (i.e., the principle that the potential is always potential *of* some actuality). I add that recent theological experiments with Social Trinitarianism, whatever else we may say about them, acknowledge implicitly Hartshorne's point about the necessarily *social* nature of any cognition.

3. See Hartshorne's comments on pragmatism in Hartshorne 1970, xvi. Also see Lee 1991 and Hartshorne's reply to Lee, ibid., 714–721.

4. Hartshorne 1970, 61, 118; 1948, 60–70; also see Hartshorne 1977b.

5. It may not be immediately clear how idealistic monism is undermined by the "Capek Argument," since such representatives as F.H. Bradley do not embrace the notion of causal influences between brain and mental events "when taken as real." However, the Capek Argument raises this issue for Bradley: how can the tenseless, static absolute experience give rise to even the illusion or appearance of "finite centers of experience"? This is much akin to the situation of classical Vedantic philosophy. Sankara regarded the question of the source of Brahman's "dreaming *maya*" to be forever rationally intractable.

6. James 1950, vol. 1, 160. My discussion here is indebted to Griffin 1998, 177–180. However, the counter-analogy is my own.

7. See William Seager's discussion of quantum mechanics in Seager 1995. Also see the two Special Focus issues of *Process Studies* on "Process Thought and Natural Science," edited by plasma physicist Timothy Eastman (1997 and 1998).

References

Barbour, Ian. 1986. "Bohm and Process Philosophy: A Response to Griffin and Cobb." In Griffin 1986: ch. 11.

Bjelland, Andrew. 1986. "Evolutionary Epistemology, Durational, Metaphysics, and Theoretical Physics: Capek and the Bergsonian Tradition." In Griffin 1986: ch. 2.

Bohm, D., and B.J. Hiley. 1993. *The Undivided Universe: An Ontological Interpretation of Quantum Theory*. London and New York: Routledge.

Capek, Milic. 1978. "Temporal Order and Spatial Order." In Cobb and Griffin 1977.

Cobb, John, and David R. Griffin, eds. 1977. *Mind in Nature: Essays on the Interface of Science and Philosophy*. Washington, DC: University Press of America.

Eastman, Timothy, ed. 1997–1998. "Process Thought and Natural Science." Special Focus Issue. *Process Studies* 26 (3–4) and 27 (3–4).

Eccles, John, and Karl Popper. 1977. *The Self and Its Brain*. New York: Springer-Verlag.

Griffin, David R. 1998. *Unsnarling the World-Knot: Consciousness, Freedom, and the Mind-Body Problem*. Berkeley: University of California Press. Reissued 2008 by Wipf and Stock Publishers, Eugene, Oregon.

Griffin, David R., ed. 1986. *Physics and the Ultimate Significance of Time*. Albany: State University of New York Press.

Hahn, Lewis, ed. 1991. *The Philosophy of Charles Hartshorne*. LaSalle, IL: Open Court.

Hartshorne, Charles. 1948. *The Divine Relativity: A Social Conception of God.* New Haven: Yale University Press.

Hartshorne, Charles. 1964. "Negative Facts and the Analogical Inference to 'Other Mind.'" In *The Radhakrishnan Souvenir Volume*. Darshana International.

Hartshorne, Charles. 1964. *Man's Vision of God and the Logic of Theism*. Reprint of 1934 original. Camden, CT: Archon Books.

Hartshorne, Charles. 1968. "Husserl and the Social Structure of Immediacy." In *Philosophical Essays in Memory of Edmund Husserl*. Ed. by Marvin Farber. Cambridge, MA: Harvard University Press.

Hartshorne, Charles. 1970. *Creative Synthesis and Philosophic Method*. LaSalle, IL: Open Court.

Hartshorne, Charles. 1976. "Why Psychicalism? A Response to Keeling's and Sheppard's Criticisms." *Process Studies* 6 (1): 67–72.

Hartshorne, Charles. 1977a. "Physics and Psychics: The Place of Mind in Nature." In Cobb and Griffin 1977, 89–96.

Hartshorne, Charles. 1977b. "The Neglect of Relative Predicates in Modern Philosophy." *American Philosophical Quarterly* 14 (4): 309–318.

Hartshorne, Charles. 1984. *Insights and Oversights of Great Thinkers: An Evaluation of Western Philosophy*. Albany: State University of New York Press.

Hartshorne, Charles. 1991. Reply to Lee 1991. In Hahn 1991, 714–721.

Haught, John F. 2000. *God After Darwin*. Boulder, CO: Westview Press.

Hume, David. 1868. *A Treatise of Human Nature.* Ed. by L. Selby-Bigge. Oxford: Oxford University Press.

James, William. 1950. *The Principles of Psychology.* New York: Dover Books (reprint of 1890, Henry Holt Co. original).

Keeling, L. Bryant. 1976. "Feeling as a Metaphysical Category: Hartshorne From an Analytical Point of View." *Process Studies* 6 (1).

Kim, Jaegwon. 1992. *Supervenience and Mind.* Cambridge: Cambridge University Press.

Lee, Donald S. 1991. "Hartshorne and Pragmatic Metaphysics." In Hahn 1991.

McGinn, Colin. 1982. *The Character of Mind.* Oxford: Oxford University Press.

McGinn, Colin. 1982. *The Problem of Consciousness.* Oxford: Oxford University Press.

Nagel, Thomas. 1979. *Mortal Questions.* Cambridge: Cambridge University Press.

Olen, J. 1983. *Persons and Their World.* New York: Random House.

Popper, Karl, and John. 1977. *The Self and Its Brain.* New York: Springer-Verlag.

Russell, Bertrand. 1921. *The Analysis of Mind.* London: Allen and Unwin.

Schwartz, Jeffrey M., and Sharon Begley. 2002. *The Mind and the Brain: Neuroplasticity and the Power of Mental Force.* New York: HarperCollins.

Seager, William. 1995. "Consciousness, Information, and Panpsychism." *The Journal of Consciousness Studies* 2 (3): 272–288.

Searle, John. 1994. *The Rediscovery of the Mind.* Cambridge, MA: MIT Press.

Strawson, Galen. 1994. *Mental Reality.* Cambridge, MA: MIT Press.

Teasdale, J., Z.V. Segal, J.M.G. Williams, et al. 2000. "Prevention of Relapse/Recurrence in Major Depression by Mindfulness-Based Cognitive Therapy." *The Journal of Consulting and Clinical Psychology* 33:25–39.

Valenza, R.J., and G. Henry. 1997. "The Preprojective and the Postprojective: A New Perspective on Causal Efficacy and Presentational Immediacy." *Process Studies* 26 (1–2): 33–56.

Weyl, H. 1949. *Philosophy of Mathematics and Natural Science.* Princeton: Princeton University Press.

9

The Evolution of Consciousness

Max Velmans

The Distribution of Consciousness

Theories about the evolution of consciousness are linked to theories about the distribution of consciousness.[1] Are we the only conscious beings? Or are other animals and other living systems also conscious and, if so, might consciousness extend to nonliving systems such as computers? Philosophers and scientists have expressed many different views on these matters. As the data needed to decide these matters is not currently available, all views are partly speculative. Why? Because we do not even know the necessary and sufficient conditions for consciousness in our own brains! As John (1976) points out we do not know the physical and chemical interactions involved, how big a neuronal system must be to sustain it, nor even whether it is confined to brains. Given this underdetermination by the data, opinions about the distribution of consciousness have ranged from the ultraconservative (only humans are conscious) to the extravagantly libertarian (everything that might possibly be construed as having consciousness *does* have consciousness).

The view that only humans have consciousness has a long history in theology, following naturally from the doctrine that only human beings have souls. Some philosophers and scientists have elaborated this doctrine into a philosophical position. According to Descartes only humans combine *res cogitans* (the stuff of consciousness) with *res extensa* (material stuff). Nonhuman animals, which he refers to as "brutes," are nothing more than nonconscious machines. Lacking consciousness, they do not have reason or language. Eccles (in Popper and Eccles 1976) adopted a similar dualist position—but argued that it is only through human language that one can communicate sufficiently well with another being to establish whether it is conscious. Without language, he suggests, the only defensible option is agnosticism or doubt. Jaynes

261

(1990) by contrast, argued that human language is a *necessary condition* for consciousness. And Humphrey (1983) adopted a similar view, arguing that consciousness emerged only when humans developed a "theory of mind." He accepts that we might find it useful for our own ethical purposes to treat other animals *as if* they were conscious, but without self-consciousness of the kind provided by a human "theory of mind" they really have no consciousness at all! There are other, modern variants of this position (e.g., Carruthers 1998) but we do not need an exhaustive survey. It is enough to note that thinkers of very different persuasions have held this view. Early versions of this position appear to be largely informed by theological doctrine; later versions are based on the supposition that higher mental processes of the kinds unique to humans are necessary for consciousness of any kind.

In my book *Understanding Consciousness*, I argue that this extreme position has little to recommend it *when applied to humans*, let alone other animals. Phenomenal consciousness in humans is constructed from different exteroceptive and interoceptive resources and is composed of different "experiential materials" (what we see, hear, touch, taste, smell, feel, and so on). It is true that our higher cognitive functions also have manifestations in experience, for example, in the form of verbal thoughts. Consequently, without language and the ability to reason, such thoughts would no longer be a part of what we experience (in the form of "inner speech"). But one can lose some sensory and even mental capacities while other capacities remain intact (in cases of sensory impairment, aphasia, agnosia, and so on). And there is *no* scientific evidence to support the view that language, the ability to reason and a theory of mind are *necessary conditions* for visual, auditory, and other sensory experiences. Applied to humans, this view is in any case highly counterintuitive. If true, we would have to believe that, prior to the development of language and other higher cognitive functions, babies experience neither pleasure nor pain, and that their cries and chuckles are just the nonconscious output of small biological machines. We would also have to accept that autistic children without a "theory of mind" never have any conscious experience! To any parent, such views are absurd.

Such views confuse the necessary conditions for the existence of consciousness with the added conditions required to support its many forms. Consciousness in humans appears to be regulated by global arousal systems, modulated by attentional systems that decide which representations (of the external world, body and mind/brain itself) are to receive focal attention. Neural representations, arousal systems, and mechanisms governing attention are found in many other animals (Jerison 1985). Other animals have sense organs that detect environmental information and perceptual and cognitive processes that analyze and organize that information. Many animals are also able to communicate and live in complex social worlds. Overall, the precise mix of sensory, perceptual, cognitive, and social processes found in each species is likely to be species-specific. Given this, it might be reasonable to suppose that only humans can have full human consciousness. But it is equally reasonable to suppose that some nonhuman animals have unique, nonhuman forms of consciousness.

Given the evidence for the gradual evolution of the human brain, it also seems unlikely that consciousness first emerged in the universe, fully formed, in *homo sapiens*. As the naturalist Thomas Huxley observed in 1874,

> The doctrine of continuity is too well established for it to be permissible to me to suppose that any complex natural phenomenon comes into existence suddenly, and without being preceded by simpler modifications; and very strong arguments would be needed to prove that such complex phenomena as those of consciousness, first make their appearance in man.

Is Consciousness Confined to Complex Brains?

One cannot be certain that other animals are conscious—or even that other people are conscious (the classical problem of "other minds"). However, the balance of evidence strongly supports it (Dawkins 1998). In cases where other animals have brain structures that are similar to humans, that support social behavior that is similar to humans (aggression, sexual activity, pair-bonding, and so on), it is difficult to believe that they experience nothing at all! But if one does not place the conscious/nonconscious boundary between humans and nonhumans where should one place it?

It might be that consciousness is confined to animals whose brains have achieved some (unknown) critical mass or critical complexity. The contents of human consciousness are constructed from different sense modalities, and within a given sense modality, experiences can be of unlimited variety and be exquisitely detailed. Where such conscious states are complex, the neural states that support them must have equivalent complexity. However it does not follow from this that *only* brains of similar complexity can support any experience. Complex, highly differentiated brains are likely to be needed to support complex, highly differentiated experiences. But it remains possible that relatively simple brains can support relatively simple experiences.

Given this, it is tempting to search for the conditions that distinguish conscious from nonconscious processing in our own brains irrespective of complexity—for example, to isolate neural changes produced by simple stimuli just above and below some threshold of awareness in different sense modalities. This is a sensible strategy that is widely pursued in psychology and associated brain sciences. In the human case, only representations at the focus of attention reach consciousness and then only in a sufficiently aroused state (an awake or dreaming state, but not coma or deep sleep), so it would be useful to learn what happens to such representations to make them conscious. Common suggestions are activation of neuronal activity above some critical threshold, the activation of specific consciousness-bearing circuitry, "neural binding" produced by relatively coherent, phase-locked activity of some neural subpopulations relative to the uncoordinated activity of other populations, and a transition from modular, restricted forms of information processing to widespread information dissemination throughout the brain.

Even if one of these or some combination of these conditions for consciousness turn out to be necessary for consciousness in the human mind/brain, we still need to be cautious about treating such conditions as universal. Under normal conditions, the human mind/brain receives simultaneous information from a range of sense organs that simultaneously monitor the external and internal environment and this information needs to be related to information in long-term memory, and assessed for importance in the light of ongoing needs and goals. In short, there are many things going on at once. But we cannot give everything our full, undivided attention. As Donald Broadbent pointed out in 1958, there is a "bottleneck" in human information processing. The human effector system is also limited—we only have two eyes, hands, legs, etc., and effective action in the world requires precise coordination of eye movements, limbs, and body posture. As a result, the mind/brain needs to select the most important information, to decide on best strategy, and to coordinate its activity sufficiently well to interact with the world in a coherent, integrated way.

To achieve this, it is as important to stop things happening in the brain as it is to make them happen. As William Uttal observed

> There is an a priori requirement that some substantial portion, perhaps a majority, of the synapses that occur at the terminals of the myriad synaptic contacts of the three-dimensional ... (neural) ... lattice must be inhibitory. Otherwise the system would be in a constant state of universal excitement after the very first input signal, and no coherent adaptive response to complex stimuli would be possible. (Uttal 1978, 192)

This opens up the possibility that selective attention doesn't so much add something special to neural representational states at the focus of attention to give them associated consciousness. Consciousness might be a "natural" accompaniment neural representation. If so, it may just be that for attended-to representational states, inhibitory processes don't prevent it. To prevent information overload, not to mention utter confusion, information and/or awareness of information outside the focus of attention is inhibited. Conversely, information that is integrated into a representation of the current, "psychological present" may be released from inhibition (Arbuthnott 1995).

If so, the mechanisms required to select, coordinate, integrate, and disseminate conscious information in the human brain may not be required for simpler creatures, with simpler brains. If consciousness is a natural accompaniment of neurally encoded information, such creatures might have a simple form of consciousness.

The visual system of the frog, for example, appears to be structured to respond to just four stimulus features: a sustained contrast in brightness between two portions of the visual field, the presence of moving edges, the presence of small moving spots and an overall dimming of the visual field. This is a far cry from the variety and detail provided by the human visual system. But there seems little reason to jump to the conclusion that the frog sees nothing. Rather, as Lettvin et al. (1959) propose, the frog may see just four things relating to its survival. A sudden dimming of the light or a moving edge may indicate the presence of a predator and is likely to initiate an escape response. Sustained differences in brightness may allow the frog to separate water from land and lily pad. And moving spot detectors may allow the frog to see (and catch) a moving fly at tongue's length.

As one continues to descend the evolutionary ladder, the plausibility of extrapolating from human to nonhuman animal consciousness becomes increasingly remote. There may, for example, be critical transition points in the development of consciousness that accompany critical transitions in functional organization (Sloman 1997). Self-awareness, for example, probably occurs only in creatures capable of self-representation. That said, phenomenal consciousness (of any kind) might only require representation. If so, even simple invertebrates might have some rudimentary awareness, in so far as they are able to represent and, indeed, respond to certain features of the world.

Planarians (flat worms) for example, can be taught to avoid a stimulus light if it has been previously associated with an electric shock (following a classical conditioning procedure). And simple mollusks such as the sea-hare Aplysia that withdraw into their shells when touched, respond to stimulus "novelty." For example, they may habituate (show diminished withdrawal) after repeated stimulation at a given site, but withdraw fully if the same stimulation is applied to another nearby site. Habituation in Aplysia appears to be mediated by events at just one centrally placed synapse between sensory and motor neurons. This is very simple learning, and it is very difficult to imagine what a mollusk might experience. But if the ability to learn and respond to the environment were the criterion for consciousness, there would be no principled grounds to rule this out. It might be, for example, that simple approach and avoidance are associated with rudimentary experiences of pleasure and pain.

Is Consciousness Confined to Brains?

It is commonly thought that the evolution of human consciousness is intimately linked to the evolution of the neocortex (e.g., Jerison 1985)—and it seems likely that cortical structures play a central role in determining the forms of consciousness that we experience. However, whether consciousness first emerged with the emergence of the neocortex or whether there is something special about the nature of cortical cells that somehow "produces" consciousness is less certain. As Charles Sherrington has pointed out, there appears to be nothing special about the internal structure of brain cells that might make them uniquely responsible for mind or consciousness. For,

> A brain-cell is not unalterably from birth a brain-cell. In the embryo-frog the cells destined to be brain can be replaced by cells from the skin of the back, the back even of another embryo; these after transplantation become in their new host brain-cells and seem to serve the brain's purpose duly. But cells of the skin it is difficult to suppose as having a special germ of mind. Moreover cells, like those of the brain in microscopic appearance, in chemical character, and in provenance, are elsewhere concerned with acts wholly devoid of mind, e.g. the knee-jerk, the light-reflex of the pupil. A knee-jerk "kick" and a mathematical problem employ similar-looking cells. With the spine broken and the spinal cords so torn across as to disconnect the body below from the brain above, although the former retains the unharmed remainder of the spinal cord consisting of masses of nervous cells, and retains a number of nervous reactions, it reveals no trace of recognizable mind. . . . Mind, as attaching to any unicellular life would seem to be unrecognizable to observation; but I would not feel that permits me to affirm that it is not there. Indeed, I would think, that since mind appears in the developing source that amounts to showing that it is potential in the ovum (and sperm) from which the source spring. The appearance of recognizable mind in the source would then be not a creation de novo but a development of mind from unrecognizable into recognizable. (Sherrington 1942)

Indeed, given our current, limited knowledge of the necessary and sufficient conditions for consciousness in humans, we cannot, as yet, rule out even more remote possibilities. If the ability to represent and respond to the world, or the ability to modify behavior consequent on interactions with the world are the criteria for consciousness then it may be that consciousness extends not just to simple invertebrates (such as Planaria) but also to unicellular organisms, fungi, and plants. For example, the leaflets of the Mimosa plant habituate to repeated stimulation, that is, the leaflets rapidly close when first touched, but after repeated stimulation they reopen fully and do not close again while the stimulus remains the same. Surprisingly, this habituation is stimulus-specific. For example, Holmes and Yost (1966) induced leaflet closure using either water droplets or brush strokes, and after repeated stimulation (with either stimulus) habituation occurred. But, if the stimulus was changed (from water drops to brush strokes or vice-versa) leaflet closure reoccurred.

For many who have thought about this matter, the transition from rudimentary consciousness in animal life to sentience in plants is one transition too far. Perhaps it is. It is important to note however that a criterion of consciousness based on the ability to respond to the world does not prevent it. Nor, on this criterion, can we rule out the possibility of consciousness in systems made of materials other than the carbon-based compounds that (on this planet) form the basis for organic life. Silicon-based computers can in principle carry out many functions that, in humans, we take to be evidence of conscious minds. So how can we be certain that they are not conscious?

One should recognize, too, that even a criterion for the existence of consciousness based on the ability to respond or adapt to the world is entirely arbitrary. It might, for example, be like something to *be* something irrespective of whether one does anything! Panpsychist such as Whitehead (SMW, PR, AI, MT) have suggested that there is no arbitrary line in the descent from macroscopic to microscopic matter at which consciousness suddenly appears out of nothing. Rather, elementary forms of matter may be associated with elementary forms of experience. And if they encode information they may be associated with rudimentary forms of mind (see also Griffin 1998).

Does Matter Matter?

Many would regard Whitehead's views as extreme (I give my own assessment below). But there is one position that is even more extreme—the view that the nature of matter doesn't matter to consciousness at all. At first glance, it might seem preposterous to claim that matter doesn't matter for consciousness. But, surprising as it might seem, it is a logical consequence of *computational functionalism*—one of the most widely adopted, current theories of mind. As John Searle (1997) has noted, it is important to distinguish this position from the view that *silicon robots* might be conscious. For him, human consciousness in spite of its subjectivity, intentionality, and qualia is an emergent *physical* property of the brain. If so, a silicon robot *might* have consciousness. But this would depend not on its programming, but on whether silicon just happens to have the same causal powers (to produce consciousness) as the carbon-based material of brains.

Computational functionalists such as Daniel Dennett (1991) take the further step that, apart from providing housing for functioning, material stuff is irrelevant. Any system that functions *as-if* it has consciousness and mind does have consciousness and mind. If a nonbiological system functions exactly like a human mind then it has a human mind, as the only thing that makes a system a "mind" is the way that it functions. In its usual reductionist versions, computational functionalism finesses questions about the distribution of first-person consciousness, routinely translating these into questions about how different systems function (see *Understanding Consciousness*, chapters 4 and 5).

Can One Draw a Line between Things that Have Consciousness and Those that Don't?

Where then should one draw the line between entities that are conscious and those that are not? Theories about the distribution of consciousness divide into continuity and discontinuity theories. Discontinuity theories all claim that consciousness emerged at a particular point in the evolution of the universe. They merely disagree about which point. Consequently, discontinuity theories all face the same problem. What switched the lights on? What is it about matter, at a particular stage of evolution, which suddenly gave it consciousness? As noted above, most try to define the point of transition in functional terms, although they disagree about the nature of the critical function. Some think consciousness "switched on" only in humans, for example, once they acquired language or a theory of mind. Some believe that consciousness emerged once brains reached a critical size or complexity. Others believe it co-emerged with the ability to learn, or to respond in an adaptive way to the environment.

In my view, such theories confuse the conditions for the existence of consciousness with the conditions that determine the many forms that it can take. Who can doubt that verbal thoughts require language, or that full human self-consciousness requires a theory of mind? Without internal representations of the world, how could consciousness be *of* anything? And without motility and the ability to approach or avoid, what point would there be to rudimentary pleasure or pain? However, none of these theories explains what it is about such biological functions that suddenly switch consciousness on.

Continuity theorists do not face this problem for the simple reason that they do not believe that consciousness suddenly emerged at any stage of evolution. Rather, as Sherrington suggests above, consciousness is a "development of mind from unrecognizable into recognizable." On this *panpsychist* view, all forms of matter have an associated form of consciousness, although in complex life forms such as ourselves, much of this consciousness is inhibited. In the cosmic explosion that gave birth to the universe, consciousness co-emerged with matter and co-evolves with it. As matter became more differentiated and developed in complexity, consciousness became correspondingly differentiated and complex. The emergence of carbon-based life forms developed into creatures with sensory systems that had associated sensory qualia. The development of representation was accompanied by the development of consciousness that is *of* something. The development of *self-representation* was accompanied by the dawn of differentiated self-consciousness and so on. On this view, evolution accounts for the different forms that consciousness takes. But, consciousness, in some primal form, did not emerge at any particular stage of evolution. Rather, it was there from the beginning. Its emergence, with the birth of the universe, is neither more nor less mysterious than the emergence of matter, energy, space, and time.

Most discontinuity theorists take it for granted that consciousness could only have appeared (out of nothing) through some random mutation in complex life forms that happened to confer a reproductive advantage (inclusive survival fitness) that can be specified in third-person functional terms. This deeply ingrained, pretheoretical assumption has set the agenda for what discontinuity theorists believe they need to explain. Within cognitive psychology, for example, consciousness has been thought by one or another theorist to be necessary for every major phase of human information processing, for example, in the analysis of complex or novel input, learning, memory, problem solving, planning, creativity, and the control and monitoring of complex, adaptive response. I have presented extensive analyses of the role of consciousness in human information processing that cast doubt on all these suggestions (Velmans 1991a,b, 1993, 1996, 2000, 2002a,b, 2003).

It should be apparent that continuity theory shifts this agenda. The persistence of different, emergent biological forms may be governed by reproductive advantage. If each of these biological forms has a unique, associated consciousness, then matter and consciousness co-evolve. However, conventional evolutionary theory does not claim that *matter itself* came into being, or persists through random mutation and reproductive advantage. According to continuity theory, neither does consciousness.

Which view is correct? One must choose for oneself. In the absence of anything other than arbitrary criteria for when consciousness suddenly emerged, I confess that I find continuity theory to be the more elegant. There may be critical transition points in the forms of consciousness associated with the development of life, representation, self-representation, and so on. However, continuity in the evolution of consciousness favors continuity in the distribution of consciousness.

Notes

1. This paper is adapted from parts of chapter 12 of Velmans 2000.

References

Arbuthnott, K.D. 1995. "Inhibitory Mechanisms in Cognition: Phenomena and Models." *Cahiers de Psychologie Cognitive* 14 (1): 3–45.

Broadbent, D. 1958. *Perception and Communication.* London: Pergamon Press.

Carruthers, P. 1998. "Natural Theories of Consciousness." *European Journal of Philosophy* 6 (2): 203–222.

Dawkins, M.S. 1998. *Through Our Eyes Only? The Search for Animal Consciousness.* Oxford: Oxford University Press.

Dennet, D. 1991. *Consciousness Explained.* London: Penguin.

Griffin, D. 1998. *Unsnarling the World-Knot: Consciousness, Freedom, and the Mind-Body Problem.* Berkeley and Los Angeles: University of California Press (repr. 2008. Eugene, Oregon: Wipf and Stock).

Holmes, E., and M. Yost. 1966. "Behavioral Studies in the Sensitive Plant." *Worm Runners Digest* 8:38.

Humphrey, N. 1983. *Consciousness Regained.* Oxford: Oxford University Press.

Jaynes, J. 1979. *The Origin of Consciousness in the Breakdown of the Bicameral Mind.* London: Allen Lane.

Jerison, H.J. 1985. "On the Evolution of Mind." In *Brain and mind*, D.A. Oakley, ed. London: Methuen.

John, E.R. 1976. "A Model of Consciousness." In *Consciousness and Self-Regulation*, G. Schwartz and D. Shapiro, eds. New York: Plenum Press.

Lettvin, J.Y., H.R. Maturana, W.S. McCulloch, and W.H. Pitts. 1959. "What the Frog's Eye Tells the Frog's Brain." *Institute of Radio Engineer's Proceedings* 47:1940–1951.

Popper, K.R., and J.C. Eccles. 1993/1976. *The Self and its Brain.* London: Routledge.

Searle, J. 1997. *The Mystery of Consciousness.* London: Granta Books.

Sherrington, C.S. 1942. *Man on His Nature.* Cambridge: Cambridge University Press.

Sloman, A. 1997b. "What Sorts of Machine Can Love? Architectural Requirements for Human-like Agents both Natural and Artificial." http://www.sbc.org.uk/literate.htm.

Uttal, W.R. 1978. *The Psychobiology of Mind*. Hillsdale, NJ: Lawrence Erlbaum.

Velmans, M. 1991a. "Is Human Information Processing Conscious?" *Behavioral and Brain Sciences* 14 (4): 651–669. http://cogprints.ecs.soton.ac.uk/archive/00000593/.

Velmans, M. 1991b. "Consciousness from a First-Person Perspective." *Behavioral and Brain Sciences* 14 (4): 702–726. http://cogprints.ecs.soton.ac.uk/archive/00000594/.

Velmans, M. 1993. "Consciousness, Causality and Complementarity." *Behavioral and Brain Sciences* 16 (2): 409–416. http://cogprints.ecs.soton.ac.uk/archive/00000595/.

Velmans, Max 1996. "Consciousness and the 'Causal Paradox.'" *Behavioral and Brain Sciences* 19 (3): 538–542. http://cogprints.ecs.soton.ac.uk/archive/00000596/.

Velmans, M. 2000. *Understanding Consciousness*. London: Routledge/Psychology Press.

Velmans, M. 2002a. "How Could Conscious Experiences Affect Brains?" (Target Article for Special Issue). *Journal of Consciousness Studies* 9 (11): 3–29. http://cogprints.ecs.soton.ac.uk/archive/00002750/.

Velmans, M. 2002b. "Making Sense of the Causal Interactions between Consciousness and Brain (A Reply to Commentaries)." *Journal of Consciousness Studies* 9 (11): 69–95. http://cogprints.ecs.soton.ac.uk/archive/00002751/.

Velmans, M. 2003. *How Could Conscious Experiences Affect Brains?* Exeter: Imprint Academic.

10

The Carrier Theory of Causation

Gregg Rosenberg

> Even if there is only one possible unified theory, it is just a set of rules and equations. What is it that breathes fire into the equations and makes a universe for them to describe?
>
> —Stephen Hawking, *A Brief History of Time*

Circularity in the Causal Mesh

Two cornerstones of Whitehead's process philosophy are his rejection of "vacuous actuality" and his acceptance of panexperientialism. *Vacuous Actuality* is Whitehead's complementary term, on the ontological side, for the epistemic fallacy of misplaced concreteness: the fallacy of taking theory to fully represent a reality. A Vacuous Actuality would be a fundamental reality that is purely structural and quantifiable, with no intrinsic nature of its own that escapes the formal description of a pattern. The rejection of Vacuous Actuality amounts to the assertion that the entities of fundamental physics, for instance, are more than mere dynamic quantities, mere information structures in the vacuum. It is the rejection of the now popular information-theoretic "It from bit" view for understanding the essential nature of the physical world.

Whitehead's panexperientialism was essentially a reaction to the void created by his rejection of Vacuous Actuality. *Panexperientialism* (Griffin 1997) is the view that experience and feeling are more primitive than cognition metaphysically as well as psychologically, and so the class of experiencing systems outruns the class of cognitive systems, reaching down even to the foundations of the world. Although these two views are deeply related, it is not clear on the surface just how deeply related because it is not clear, first, what the argument for the rejection of vacuous actuality is (Why *not* "It from bit"?), and it is not clear why the intrinsic nature of things should always be experiential (it is not even clear why things should *ever* be experiential). Panexperientialism, especially, can seem extravagant. On the surface, both cornerstones of the process philosophy view look like positions of insight, or even faith, not sufficiently motivated by argumentation. The purpose of this paper is to put more argumentation in place to support the rejection of Vacuous Actuality and the panexperientialist reaction to that rejection.

One can begin to see the problems that lead to the rejection of Vacuous Actuality through an analogy to *Life*, an artificial world (see Figure 10.1). The *Life* world is a two-dimensional world made up of cells we can visualize as squares. A *Life* world has three simple rules that fully describe its physical evolution:

1. If a cell has exactly two *on* neighbors it maintains its property, *on* or *off*, in the next time step.

2. If a cell has exactly three *on* neighbors it will be *on* in the next time step.

3. Otherwise the cell will be *off* in the next time step.

Consider the question: *What is it to be an "on" property within* Life? We only need to cite its distinctness from the "off" property, and that its

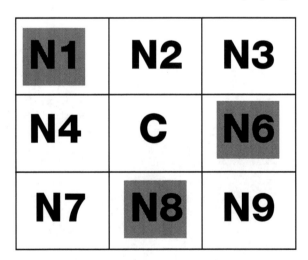

Figure 10.1. A depiction of a center cell, C, and its "neighborhood" on a Life world grid. Neighbors N1, N6, and N8 are depicted as "on."

patterns of instantiation exhibit the lawlike regularity prescribed by the rules. This schematic account entirely encompasses the categorical being of an "on" property within *Life*.

By themselves, *Life's* laws of nature represent a very minimalist view of causation in a world. It is possible to enrich the minimal view of causal content explicit in the bare physics of *Life* by proposing a theory of individual causation in addition to the three general laws describing the regularities in its dynamics. In *A Place for Consciousness* (Rosenberg 2004) I have done just this by arguing for effective and receptive faces to causation. There, I give a positive account of the relations between them and detail the distinct contributions they make to the causal character of a world. Still, with respect to full human consciousness, and panexperience generally, even the supplemented metaphysics remains limited because it still provides a merely schematic understanding of what it is to be a world with causal content.

For a real-world image think of the effective properties of billiard balls as the properties whose values we must know if we are going to be able to predict their responses when they collide. For example, in the view I propose we can adequately describe effective properties by (i) making names for the range of types; (ii) stipulating that the names designate distinct entities; (iii) defining a range of possible values for each type; and (iv) defining how the presence of each effective property contributes to the constraints on the overall state of a causal nexus. Descriptions meeting these conditions create identity conditions for each property and for the system of properties as a whole.

There is a kind of circularity involved in such stipulations, and I call the kind of circularity involved *contrastive circularity*. A contrastive circularity exists when we stipulate a set of distinct elements and we use the stipulated distinctness to create a relational story yielding the rest of each element's identity conditions. For any kind of element X, we may answer the question "What is it to be an X?" by citing its distinctness from the other elements of the system, and a (perhaps fuzzy) set of critical external relations to other elements within that system.

These property definitions are at least partially circular because the identity conditions for each property X within the theory include a statement to the effect that "X is a thing that is different from Y," where Y is another element of the theory, and when we inquire into what Y is, its identity conditions include a statement to the effect that "Y is a thing that is different from X." The rest of X and Y's identity conditions are then nothing more than a set of external relations between them. We can see this kind of contrastive circularity at work in the *Life* example. What is the "on" property? It is the property that is not the "off" property. This is helpful as long as we know what the "off" property is, but what is the "off" property? It is the property that is not the "on" property. That bare difference along with the external relations specified in *Life's* laws of evolution are all there is to know about those two properties (according to the toy physics). Contrastive circularity is enough to distinguish effective properties from one another, like "on" from "off," but in *A Place for Consciousness* I propose that a circularity of a different kind helps to distinguish receptive and effective properties. Think of receptive properties as distinct connective properties necessary for the billiard balls to absorb, and therefore respond, the forces transmitted when they collide. Receptive and effective properties together form a causal nexus. Here are the relevant definitions given in *A Place for Consciousness*:[1]

> **A causal nexus** (which, for convenience, I pluralize as causal nexii)—A receptive connection binding two or more determinable[2] individuals.
>
> **Effective properties**—Determinable properties that contribute to constraints on the determinate states of a causal nexus.
>
> **Receptive properties**—Connective properties enabling individuals to become members of causal nexii, and to be sensitive to constraints on the state of nexii where they are members.

Binding is an internal relation through which the effective and receptive properties may complete one another's inherently incomplete natures. Receptive and effective properties, therefore, do not relate categorically in a merely negative, contrastive way. Receptivity positively presupposes effectiveness, and vice versa. My name for this kind of circularity is *compositional circularity*. A circular relation is compositional when each element is partially defined by the way that it presupposes the other as a positive component in its own nature.

Of the two kinds of circularity the first kind in particular, contrastive circularity, is symptomatic of schematic thinking. Reflection on circular contrasts naturally raises questions about how these categories come to be in a world. After all, if **A** is defined as that which is distinct from **B**, **B** is defined as that which is distinct from **A**, and *no other* categorical facts are true of them other than external relations they share, it seems that the existence of each presupposes the existence of the other. The circularity has the logical feel of a vicious regress, and questions about how such properties get their footholds on existence in the first place forcefully present themselves. Understanding the ontological ground for the existence of these kinds of circularly interdependent properties is the chief task of this paper.

Circularity Instantiated

While puzzling, circularity is not deadly. The world is full of systems that realize circularly interlocking categories, and the *Life* world itself provides an example, as people implement finite *Life* worlds in a variety of ways. The original *Life* world was implemented on a checkerboard using checker pieces, and the implementations most familiar to people today are on computers. I think we can gain some insight by examining how a miniature checkerboard can become a *Life* world.

Actually existing *Life* worlds are parasitic on the presence of properties whose categorical natures[3] are *not* wholly defined by the *Life* schema but which already embody the distinctiveness needed to instantiate *Life* properties. For example, in a checkerboard implementation of *Life* the red and black checkers play the role of the "on" and "off" properties. The color distinction between them, a distinction that is not intrinsic to the conceptual schema that defines *Life*, is an extrinsic carrier of the needed distinctness between the "on" and "off" properties. The checkerboard carries the geometry of *Life*'s two-dimensional space, and allows us to create coordinate identities for the places in the world using the squares on the checkerboard. Finally, the intentions of the human beings manipulating the board guarantee the lawfully reliable patterns of instantiation between the properties (to the extent that human intentions are lawfully reliable). Once again, these human intentions have a nature that outruns the terms of the *Life* schema.

The form of the solution seems to be this. The circular properties of *Life* exist because we find elements with preexisting kinds of properties that, when put in the right combination, carry the relations the *Life* schema dictates. I call these elements *carriers*.

> **Carriers**—Objects or properties whose natures outrun the categories of a given schema, but which can enter into the appropriate relations with one another when put into the proper combinations.

Carriers are also present in computational implementations of *Life*. In those cases, the physical distinctness of the machine states carries the distinctness between the "on" and "off" properties. The major difference between the computational case and the checkerboard case is that the tokens in the computational case can directly carry the lawful reliability of the "on" and "off" properties, bypassing reliance on human intentions.

One naturally sees the carriers as having natures that are at least partially extrinsic to the *Life* world they are implementing. For instance, the specific distinction between the redness and blackness of the checkers goes beyond the requirement of generic distinctness for "on" and "off" properties. This observation applies to more than just the facts about their distinctness. The causal contents of the elements of the system transcend the causal powers attributable to them as "on" or "off" properties. This suggests a useful definition of what it is to be an extrinsic property, relative to a system the property occurs within.

P is an extrinsic property within a system **S IFF P** is instantiated within an instance of **S**, and **P** has a nature that is not exhausted by its relations to other elements as they are defined within **S**.

The idea of being an extrinsic property within the system **S** is different from the idea of being a property that is *intrinsic to* the system **S**. The properties intrinsic to a system are those whose identity conditions are grounded in relations between an object (or objects) in the system, and other elements of the system.

Thus, properties *intrinsic to* systems both constitute and presuppose the existence of the systems they exist within, which makes them unlike properties that are *extrinsic within* those systems. Stating the idea in another way, the properties intrinsic to a system have no nature entering into their categorical being except those defined by a system of the relevant type. In this sense, the categories of their systematic contexts exhaust their categorical natures.

For example, the properties of being "on" and "off" are properties intrinsic to the system of concepts defining *Life* because such properties both constitute and presuppose the existence of a *Life* world. In contrast, being a red checker is an extrinsic property within some implementations of the *Life* world. Redness, while present within some implementations of such worlds, is neither dependent upon, nor definable by, the system of concepts constitutive of *Life*. The categorical being of redness, unlike the being of "offness," is independent of the conceptual scheme demarcating *Life*.

Finally, a property being extrinsic within a system does not entail that it is extrinsic *tout court*, as it may be intrinsic to some other system. This is the case with computational states that may implement *Life*, as those states, qua computational states, are extrinsic within *Life* but intrinsic to the computational system they exist within.

> **Contrasts**—One particularly important feature of the examples is how extrinsic properties implement the stipulative contrasts within the system through what I call internal contrasts.

An *internal contrast* exists between **A** and **B** just in case there is a comparative relation **R** such that necessarily, if **A** exists and **B** exists then **R(A,B)**.

Internal contrasts are a kind of super-category here. They include the *stipulative contrasts* observed to exist within schemas and can include other kinds of contrasts too. Internal contrasts, rather than composing the involved properties the way that stipulative contrasts do, instead might be consequences of their natures. In fact, internal contrasts that are not themselves stipulative are good candidates to implement systems of stipulative contrasts: as long as both **A** and **B** are present within a world, the relation **R** that holds between them may carry a stipulative contrast. Thus, even though the entities composed by stipulative contrasts presuppose one another, they may come into existence within a system all at once by being a consequence of the nonstipulative internal contrasts of the carriers.

With red and black checkers, the redness and blackness constitute an internal contrast able to carry the stipulative contrast between "on" and "off" properties in a *Life* world. Although internal, the contrast between the colors is not stipulative because we cannot reduce the natures of the phenomenal colors to a structure of pure difference relations holding between them. Finally, it is worth anticipating that **R** may be a more complex kind of relation than mere distinctness, although I have not surveyed any such examples yet.

Reflection on the variety of circular systems that actually exist in the world strongly suggests that each exists in virtue of carriers that are extrinsic to the system. For example, a chess game consists of a circularly interdependent set of types: pawns, rooks, kings, queens, etc. Each type is defined by the set of allowable moves it may make within the game as a whole. Without the context of the game, no particular type could exist. The circularity between their categorical natures makes it look as if the existence of each part of the game presupposes the existence of the game as a whole, which, in turn, presupposes the existence of the parts (Sellars 1963, Haugeland 1993).

Why isn't the circularity of chess categories deadly? The reason chess games can actually exist is that each implementation takes advantage of external properties to introduce, piecemeal, the distinctions and dependencies that are defined whole cloth within the conceptual system. For instance, pieces that are recognizably physically distinct are used to stand in for tokens of distinct types. Board positions are defined relative to a physical space within which it has geometric relations to human players. These extrinsic distinctions and relations allow players to form intentions to move the pieces only in accord with the rules governing the types of which they will be tokens. When each of these extrinsic factors slips into place in a way that carries the circular relations of the system, a chess game exists.

Notice how the existence of a chess game seems essentially dependent on these extrinsic properties and relations: were it not for extrinsic factors that have internal relations able to carry the circular identity conditions, the game simply could not exist. If the pieces were not physically distinct, the players would soon lose track of which piece was standing in for each type, and could not form the proper intentions to play them according to chess rules. If the board did not exist in physical spatial relations to the players, the pieces could not be set up in accord with the rules, and the players could not decide the legality of moves. In other implementations, like computer implementations, some other set of extrinsic properties always performs the carrier role.

There are many more examples. A computer's logical components are circular because functional relations between the elements of a system are what define computational elements. As before, computer programs may exist by being carried by physical states that have natures extrinsic within the computational system. As we widen our view to other conceptual systems—economics, biology, and psychology are examples—we see the same pattern repeated.

In economics, what things count as goods and services? To a first approximation, goods and services are those things that consumers and producers barter. Who are the consumers and producers? Consumers and producers, in their turn, are people occupying distinct positions in the system of bartering for the goods and services.

In biology, organisms pass heritable characteristics through their genes. A heritable characteristic is one that parents pass from their generation to later generations. A parent, in its turn, is an organism that passes along its genes, or a significant portion of its genes, to the young.

In psychology, beliefs, desires, and perceptions are at least partially definable in terms of their functional role within the cognitive economy. An entity's functional role is its disposition to interact with other entities in the system.

In each case, a closed or semi-closed system of theoretical concepts, many of which are directly or indirectly circularly dependent on one another, exist. This circularity is hardly fatal, confusing or even objectionable. The reason the circularity is innocuous is that, in each case, extrinsic properties exist within the systems, and these properties have internal contrasts between them. These contrasts help carry the circular relations. In economics, we can appeal to the desires, needs, and opportunities of individuals in the wider social system of which the economy is part. In biology, we can appeal to the mechanics of molecular biochemistry. In psychology, we can appeal to computational or dynamical properties of neural systems and the way these properties help the organism survive in an ecological niche.

The Circularity of Physics

Reflections on examples like those above lead one inevitably to concepts with wider and wider spheres of application. In the case of the natural sciences, this expanding arena of circularly looping systems traces the same path as intuitive expectations of reduction. When we look at a circular system of concepts, we find that its instances are carried by objects with properties extrinsic within that system, but intrinsic to some other system. Inevitably, these other systems are themselves circular, partially or completely, and thus we find them carried by yet another set of objects with properties extrinsic within them. From economics we look to social relations of a broader sort, then from those to psychology, ecology and biology, then to chemistry, and finally to physics.

If this way of looking at these things is correct, these higher-level domains are not just *in fact* realized by the entities of some other domain, the domain of the carriers; in principle they need carriers to get their foothold on concreteness. The existence of carriers is an essential ingredient, a metaphysical presupposition, for the satisfaction of circularly interdependent systems of categories.

When we reach physics, we find the same kind of circularity as in other less fundamental sciences, and the pivotal, required role for carriers raises questions. We can easily see the circularity in physics by asking questions about the identity conditions on the basic physical entities. These conditions are broadly functional. What it is to be a photon, for instance, is to play the functional role in our environment that photons play in physics. What it is to be charge, mass, or spin is to be distinct from the other physical properties, and to nomically instantiate the pattern of regularities prescribed by the laws (again, in our environment). What it is to be gravity is to play the role gravity plays, and similarly for the other basic physical properties. As a result, physics incorporates the same kind of circularity all functional systems of concepts incorporate.[4]

The circularity of physical concepts leads to the question, *What is extrinsic within physics?* That is, what carries the contrasts and relations needed to satisfy our system of physical concepts? Taking a hard line here, insisting that nothing carries the physics, is unprecedented and problematic. It is unprecedented in that the extrinsic properties in other circular systems are not spandrels but elements required for the instantiation of those systems. It is problematic in that the resulting metaphysics seems unintelligible, if looked at too closely. The metaphysics requires a system of contrast, and relations between the contrasts, in which these contrasts have no carriers. Without carriers, it requires a notion of pure contrast, contrasts that seem not to be contrasts between anything. The idea seems to melt away before the mind's eye, like an echo issuing from no originating voice. The champion of such a metaphysic takes on a large unmet burden in trying to explain it. Unfortunately, the largeness of the circle in physics makes it easy to overlook the problem or feel it less vividly, and current philosophy tends not to press the issue. I think the *Life* world makes the strangeness clearer (it is, after all, just a toy physics). Enlarging the circle makes the carrier problem easier to ignore, but does not make it go away.

Taking the different tack of answering that physics has no ground level at all—it's turtles all the way down—is conceptually and logically a little less problematic. There perhaps could be such a world. The problem with the suggestion as an account of our world is empirical: Planck's constant seems to put a limit on how finely space, time, and matter can be divided. Below that level, there is no sense postulating further physical structure. Our world seems to have a fundamental physical floor.

If there is a physical floor, standards of intelligibility demand there must be a set of properties that are extrinsic within physics. To find these properties, it will not help to appeal to some wider system of properties or to circle back around in a constructivist way to society or to human psychology. Those maneuvers just enlarge the circle, presenting the same problem again. A proper solution will be one that short-circuits the puzzle, not one that moves it to a new arena. What the world needs from a carrier of physics are properties whose being would be extrinsic within every such system and yet which still have the requisite internal relations to one another. For physics, we need *ultimate carriers*.

The properties best answering to this description are best thought of as properties that are intrinsic *tout court*. A property whose categorical nature is extrinsic within every system of properties is simply one whose being is intrinsic at least partly to itself, rather than to its contextual relationships. That is, it is a property that we cannot understand in purely systematic terms without leaving something out. The least strained way of understanding the physics of the world is to suppose that some kind of intrinsic property carries each effective property, where we understand intrinsic as intrinsic *tout court*, rather than intrinsic to a system.[5] Having come to this end, perhaps it will help to summarize the kinds of properties I have discussed so far:

1. Property intrinsic *to* a system—A property whose identity conditions are given entirely by relations to other entities within some system to which it belongs (e.g., the "on-ness" of a *Life* cell).

2. Property that is intrinsic *tout court*—A property that is not intrinsic to any system (e.g., redness).

3. Property extrinsic *within* a system—A property that is present within an instance of a system, and that has a nature not exhausted by its relations to other elements as they are defined within that system (e.g., the redness of a checker used to instantiate the "on" property within a game of *Life*).

The carriers of physics will be intrinsic *tout court* and so extrinsic within the world as it is defined by physics. Additionally, to act as carriers of the effective properties described by physics, these intrinsic properties must have internal contrasts with one another that mirror the features and relations of physical properties: patterns of distinctness, variations in magnitude, and relations of compatibility, incompatibility, and requirement.

How many carrier candidates can there be? Upon reflection it seems the phenomenal qualities of phenomenal consciousness are the perfect candidates.

Phenomenal qualities are intrinsic *tout court*: one cannot understand what it is to be yellow in terms of a system of relations (that is one of the lessons of the anti-physicalist arguments such as Mary in Jackson's [1982] Knowledge Argument). Their intrinsicness is plausibly what makes qualia the funny things that they are, and what makes full knowledge of them attainable only by acquaintance with them. Formally, their natures are intrinsic in the sense that a phenomenal property is not categorically constituted by the structure of relations it enters into.[6]

The failure of facts about the phenomenal properties to be entailed by the facts of physics, even though they are part of the natural world, means they can plausibly meet the condition of being extrinsic within the physical world.

Phenomenal qualities also plausibly support the required kinds of non-stipulative internal contrasts. The differences between phenomenal qualities is grounded in the differences in their intrinsic natures so that, necessarily, if they exist then the differences obtain. For example, distinct sounds exist such that, if each exists, then they are necessarily distinct types of sound. It seems like a trivial point, but it is very important.

The internal contrasts between phenomenal properties are very important because phenomenal properties enter into much more complex internal relations than mere difference or distinctness. Of special importance is that they can possess internal *scalar* relations. Scalar comparisons within (but not necessarily between) phenomenal groups like colors, sounds, tastes and so forth come naturally to us. For example, some sounds are louder than others, some colors brighter than others, and some tastes are sourer than others. The most natural way to think of these groups is in terms of phenomenal spaces that they instantiate, with natural orderings of various types between the elements of these spaces.

These scalar relationships show that some kinds of phenomenal properties, when they exist, could carry the kinds of quantitative variations required by physics. With this in mind, the panexperientialist proposal is that, for given phenomenal qualities A and B, an internal contrast between phenomenal quality A and phenomenal quality B exists such that, when they both exist, necessarily $A > B$ is true along some natural metric. If that is so, then A and B (and presumably other members of the phenomenal group to which they belong) may carry the more complex kinds of quantitative contrasts required by physics.

Continuing this train of thought, a variety of compatibility and incompatibility relationships hold between phenomenal properties and possible phenomenal fields. A straightforward case is the postulated red/green incompatibility in our color space.[7] Much more subtle and sophisticated kinds of compatibility restrictions also show in experience, restrictions that apply to whole fields or subfields of a phenomenal manifold. For instance, it is not clear that one could simultaneously experience the Necker cube (shown below) as having face up and face down in the same visual manifold. If this restriction holds, then it is a very interesting kind of exclusion relation, one that incorporates the semantics of the conceptualization right inside the formation conditions on the qualitative experience. See Figure 10.2.

Also, certain properties might include others, thus necessitating their existence. For example, shapeless instantiations of color might be impossible, so the existence of a color property might necessitate the existence of a shape. Or, on an even finer grained level, one might postulate that the existence of a hue necessitates the existence of a brightness value (no hue without brightness). In the gap between simple red/green incompatibility and the very subtle Necker cube face up/face down incompatibility, there might be a whole host of subtle and interesting relations of exclusion, allowance, and necessitation between possible kinds of phenomenal properties. These kinds of relationships would be what are needed by a carrier that could drive the effective side of causation, as it is these relationships that would carry the natural possibilities, impossibilities, and necessities of physics.

A note of caution: the claim is not that the phenomenal qualities of human consciousness exist at the microphysical level, carrying the effective

Figure 10.2. The Necker Cube illustrates a purely qualitative incompatibility relation: the same linear pattern can be seen as a cube with its facing surface tilted down or tilted up, but not both at the same time.

dispositions of microphysical entities. The hypothesis here is like the pan-experientialist hypothesis: alien phenomenal (or maybe more appropriately, proto-phenomenal) intrinsic properties exist, properties in an abstract sense like the qualia of our own consciousness, which carry the effective dispositions of the world's basic natural individuals. Perhaps proto-phenomenal properties are to phenomenal properties as brightness, hue, and saturation are to a full-fledged color.

The abstract sense in which they are like the qualities of our consciousness comes to precisely this: they are intrinsic *tout court*, they are determinable, they share both simple and sophisticated internal contrasts with one another, and they have intrinsic relations of compatibility, incompatibility, and inclusion. The ways they are different from the qualities of our consciousness are this: their specific characters are presumably entirely different from those of our own qualia, and the internal contrasts that hold between them organize them into very different kinds of phenomenal subspaces.

But there remains one last foreboding question about the similarity of these proposed phenomenal qualities to the qualities of our own conscious experience. Are these alien qualities experiential, like the qualities of our own consciousness?

The Experiencing of Phenomenal Individuals

The physical properties are the effective properties, so by proposing carriers for the physical properties we have accounted for one half of the nomic content possessed by natural individuals. The other half of their nomic content is the irreducible receptivity in their nature, which binds effective individuals and creates a causal nexus. What carries receptivity?

In *A Place for Consciousness* I argue that physics suppresses the receptivity of the world in its theorizing, and thereby leaves out its receptive structure. The addition of receptivity to the effectiveness of physics brings a compositional circularity into the causal character of the world, magnifying the problems arising merely from the circular contrasts of the effective properties alone. An individual's nomic content as a whole, not just the effective aspect of it, needs to be carried, which means that receptivity needs a carrier as well. My fundamental proposal is that *experiencing itself carries receptivity*. This is the central thesis of the Carrier Theory of Causation:

> **The Central Thesis**—Things in the world are natural individuals
> if, and only if, they are experiencing phenomenal individuals.

The ontology implicit in the Central Thesis is a panexperientialist neutral monism. The fundamental kind is the causal nexus itself, and the nexus has multiple aspects: a phenomenal side consisting of intrinsic properties that carry the components of the world's effective constraints, and an experiential side to which the phenomenal natures are bound and through which they place their contribution to constraints. The Carrier Theory implies that neither experiencing nor phenomenal individuals are entirely physical because carriers are extrinsic within physics. They are nevertheless not epiphenomenal nor do they interact with the physical. The Central Thesis straightforwardly implies that some variety of panexperientialism holds in the world.

Why believe in the Central Thesis? Some strong reasons exist for adopting it. Whatever carries the nomic content of a natural individual must be something with properties that satisfy several constraints,

(i)   these properties must be intrinsic properties that are intrinsic *tout court*;

(ii)   they must have the structural characteristics needed to carry effective and receptive properties;

(iii) the effective carriers must be determinables with the right kinds of internal contrasts among them, along with relations of compatibility, incompatibility, and inclusion;

(iv)   the receptive carriers must have a kind of openness to their nature that can be filled by determinable properties; and

(v)   each of the receptive and effective carriers must have a nature that is dependent on the nature of something distinct from it in the compositionally circular way that effective and receptive properties are dependent on one another.

I have just been discussing how phenomenal properties are perfect carrier candidates for effective properties because they meet conditions (i)–(iii). What of conditions (iv) and (v)? The experiencing subject is a perfect candidate for a receptive carrier that meets condition (iv), and together phenomenal properties and the experiencing of them plausibly meet condition (v). Taking condition (iv) first: in its normal state, the experiencing subject shows itself to be intrinsically plastic, binding and rebinding a vast variety of phenomenal properties, opening itself to a carnival crowd of combinations and determinations of properties from the phenomenal world. Furthermore, the idea that experiencing is a kind of openness to phenomenal content coheres with common phenomenological reports about meditative states where people are denied normal sensory input. In a physical state of sensory isolation, these meditative experiencers consistently report achieving a mental state they identify as "pure" awareness in which consciousness is experienced as possessing a kind of contentless openness.

That leaves condition (v). Condition (v) is necessary because phenomenal properties, if they were just intrinsic *tout court*, lying next to one another in a Humean way, could not carry effective causation. The relationship between the effective and receptive aspects of an individual must be metaphysically intimate. For properties to be effective they must presuppose receptive connections as positive components in their own being and vice versa. In the relationship between effective and receptive causation, receptivity penetrates the being of effective properties, occurring as a presupposition in the very notion that they are effective. Furthermore, the logical intimacy between effective properties and receptivity plays an important metaphysical role. Through the intimacy of binding, the effective states of different individuals penetrate one another's being and present their constraints immediately. In a sense, having a shared receptivity provides a principle of substantial unity that activates the relations of compatibility and incompatibility between effective properties, making these internal constraints between them relevant in specific ways to specific cases.

The ontological relation between phenomenal qualities and their participation in the experiencings of subjects matches this crucial logical structure of the relationship between effective properties and their shared receptivity. Focusing first on the phenomenological side, the phenomenal qualities of our consciousness seem to depend for their existence on entering into the experiences of a subject. It is implausible, for example, that kinds of pain exist that could not be experienced. If this is right, its possible role in experiencings is essential to pain. As for experiencing, claiming that something is an experiencing subject implies that it can experience phenomenal qualities. That is, its capacity to host and experience phenomenal being is essential to it.

Questions about the relations between the experiencing subject and its experiences raise many complicated and controversial issues. I do not have space to go into much here, but I will go as far as proposing that phenomenal qualities could not exist unless some subject was experiencing them,[8] and experiences could not exist unless they were experiences of phenomenal qualities. Yet, despite this mutual participation in one another's natures, they are distinct essences. A phenomenal quality is an object of experience, and should not be identified with the experiencing of it. And an individual experiencer is a subject of qualitative experience, and should not be identified with its objects. So, just like effective and receptive properties, the experiencer and the experienced qualities are distinct yet interdependent properties of the total individual.

Together these observations form a striking tableau of support for the idea that experience acts as a carrier for causation. Table 10.1 below shows the requirements on the carrier role for natural individuals, and how the experiencing of phenomenal individuals fills the bill. *A Place for Consciousness* discusses a host of more detailed and striking parallels between the character of experience and what one would predict for the character of carriers. For now, the high-level mapping goes like this.

Table 10.1. How the Experiencing of Phenomenal Individuals Fills the Carrier Role

Phenomenal Properties	*Nomic Content*
1. The possibility of being experienced is essential to phenomenal qualities.	1. The possibility of being receptively bound is essential to effective properties.
2. Being an experiencing subject implies the experiencing of phenomenal qualities.	2. Being a receptive individual implies receiving the constraint of effective properties.
3. Phenomenal qualities are only potential unless actually being experienced.	3. Effective properties are only potential unless actually receptively bound.
4. Experience is only potential unless it is experiencing phenomenal quality.	4. A receptive connection is only potential unless it is binding effective properties.
5. Phenomenal properties are determinables.	5. Effective properties are determinables.
6. Phenomenological reports of the "pure" experiencing subject reveal a kind of contentless openness within pure consciousness.	6. Pure receptive connections are a kind of contentless openness.
7. Relations of inclusion, exclusion, compatibility and incompatibility exist between phenomenal properties.	7. Relations of inclusion, exclusion, compatibility and incompatibility exist between effective properties.
8. Scalar relations and relations of intrinsic difference exist between phenomenal properties.	8. Scalar relations and relations of stipulative difference exist between effective properties.
9. Despite mutually participating in one another's nature, phenomenal properties and the experiencing of them mark distinct essences.	9. Despite mutually participating in one another's nature, effective properties and the receptive binding of them mark distinct essences.

The Central Thesis solves the puzzle quite neatly and fruitfully, and that is its best defense. It turns out that the causal nexus has three aspects: the effective, the receptive, and the carriers of this nomic content. The effective and receptive properties are the two complementary aspects of causation that give natural individuals their nomic content, and these two aspects are carried, ultimately, by the experiencing of interlocked phenomenal qualities by subjects within the causal mesh.

Physical theory specifies only the constraints between the effective states of the basic natural individuals by describing the nomic regularities that hold between their instantiations. One might argue (e.g., Stoljar 2001) that physical specifications indirectly designate phenomenal or proto-phenomenal properties that carry these effective constraints. Combined with the Carrier Theory of Causation, it suggests the existence of experiencers at many levels of nature carrying the receptivity to the effective properties.

Physicalism is false because the facts about receptivity and the carriers are absent from physical explanation. These are two things about which there are further facts over and above those that physical science is committed to, and, fortunately, we can draft phenomenal individuals into duty to help with both. Because we already have independent reasons to believe in the existence and irreducibility of phenomenal individuals, the account is as ontologically parsimonious as one could possibly achieve.

The Central Thesis does have a price of admission, and that price is its implication that some kind of panexperientialism is true of our world. Just how widely spread experience is remains to be discovered, as the question of which individuals are the natural individuals is a substantial and important empirical question. However, panexperientialism is a *benign panpsychism* because experience is likely to be very simple in the vast majority of cases, to be restrained to highly specialized circumstances despite its outrunning cognition, and to be pure feeling or sensation unaccompanied by thought whenever it exists outside of cognitive contexts.

Notes

1. As this chapter progresses the meanings of these terms and definitions will be articulated further and more clearly.

2. An individual is determinable just in case one or more of its properties is determinable. A property is determinable just in case there are multiple values it may take on when exemplified.

3. When I speak of "categorical natures," I mean the kind of thing conveyed by an appropriate answer to the question, "What is it to be **X**?" for the property of being **X**, or "What is it to be an **X**?" for the property of being an **X**.

4. When making this claim, I do not wish to deny the importance of indexicality (i.e., designation) in fixing reference. Likely, physical concepts contain indexical

components, as "electron" may express a rigid designator. As Daniel Stoljar holds, electrons are arguably just the categorical natures that play the electron role in our world. The more important point is that, even if some categorical nature is picked out indexically by these concepts, the indexical place functions much like a variable in the conceptual structure. Even if the value of the index anchors the language system to categorical natures, and even if it does so in a way that depends on the deictic orientation of the concept user within its physical context, it is still functional roles that do the most essential work in fixing the *physical category* applied to that nature. The indexically designated nature is a nature that is otherwise *extrinsic* to these entities, relative to the system of physical concepts we employ in science. That is, these natures, if they exist, are extrinsic within the system of physical properties they are carrying.

5. Related arguments from the circularity/schematic nature of the physical to this conclusion are in Fales 1990, 219–220 and Chalmers 1996, 303–304.

6. Sometimes the *illusion* that colors (for instance) may be "defined" in terms of the relations between them is achieved by importing a color or hue into the system as a primitive, and using it as an anchor for the relational system. This sort of attempt is like importing zero into an axiom scheme as a primitive object, and then attempting to define the natural numbers through a system of relations to it and each other. Zero anchors the structural relations in number space just as a color may anchor structural relations in color space. The importation of an anchor in this way precludes reduction. For instance, when we consider applying the axiom system to sets like the supernatural numbers, the irreducible role that zero is playing in supplementing the structural story becomes apparent. The very need for such anchors shows that we are not reducing the elements in the space to their structural relations alone.

7. Kneale (1949) also uses red/green incompatibility as an example of a *de re* incompatibility between properties, proposing that it might serve as an analogical model for relations between physical properties. My suggestion in the text goes beyond Kneale in several ways, chiefly in taking the panexperientialist step of suggesting that they may serve as more than merely a model, and also by proposing the more subtle variety of relations I discuss in the text.

8. Not everyone agrees. See Lockwood (1989) for a different view.

References

Chalmers, David. 1996. *The Conscious Mind*. New York: Oxford University Press.

Fales, Evan. 1990. *Causation and Universals*. New York: Routledge.

Griffin, David Ray. 1997 "Panexperientialist Physicalism and The Mind-Body Problem." *Journal of Consciousness Studies* 4 (3): 248–268.

Haugeland, John. 1993. "Pattern and Being." In *Dennett and His Critics*, Bo Dahlbom, ed., 53–69. Cambridge, MA: Blackwell.

Jackson, Frank. 1982. "Epiphenomenal Qualia." *Philosophical Quarterly* 32 (127): 127–136.

Kneale, W.C. 1949. *Probability and Induction.* Oxford: Oxford University Press.

Lockwood, Michael. 1989. *Mind, Brain, and Quanta.* Cambridge, MA: Basil Blackwell.

Rosenberg, Gregg H. 2004. *A Place for Consciousness: The Theory of Natural Individuals.* Oxford: Oxford University Press.

Sellars, Wilfrid. 1963. "Some Reflections on Language Games." In *Science, Perception, and Reality.* New York: Humanities Press.

Stoljar, Daniel. 2001. "Two Conceptions of the Physical." *Philosophy and Phenomenological Research* 62 (2): 253–281.

Part IV

Clinical Applications

Consciousness as Process

11

The Microgenetic Revolution in Contemporary Neuropsychology and Neurolinguistics

Maria Pachalska and Bruce Duncan MacQueen

The terms *neuropsychology* and *neurolinguistics* emerged as the names of distinct branches of science after World War II, though both had appeared sporadically before, and the central issues of both disciplines also have a longer history. The postwar period was crucial, however, due to the confluence of a number of factors, ranging from theoretical (developments in neurology, psychology, and linguistics) to practical (the dramatic increase in the number of persons surviving gunshot wounds to the head during the war itself, with all the attendant symptoms and disabilities). Thus the Soviet neurologist Alexander Romanovich Luria, under the influence of the psychologists Pavlov and Vygotsky, and the linguists Jakobson and Leonteev, developed a body of systematic neuropsychological and neurolinguistic theory, supported by his own clinical practice with hundreds of World War II veterans. Although the claim that Luria "invented" neuropsychology and neurolinguistics is somehow redolent of Soviet propaganda, still, it is no easy task to find any earlier sources in Western literature for either term, used as the name of a putatively distinct science. The work of Hécaen in France, Goodglass in Boston, and Poeck in Germany, at about the same time as the publication of Luria's first books in English, all in the mid-1960s, suggests that (not for the first time in the history of science), many of the same ideas were emerging simultaneously in different places (Pachalska 1999). Thus establishing the priority of anyone's claim to authorship of the terms in question would seem to be at this point neither possible nor particularly important.

The founding premises and basic character of both neuropsychology and neurolinguistics are implicit in the very names, whose compound form reflects a compound origin. Neuropsychology was to consist in an interdisciplinary discourse between behavioral neurology (focused on the brain) and cognitive psychology (focused on the mind). Neurolinguistics was intended to bring linguists into a mutually enlightening dialogue with clinicians (especially speech pathologists), much as psycholinguistics was to be a bridge between psychology and linguistics, sociolinguistics between sociology and linguistics, and so on. Each of the new sciences, then, was conceived as a sort of bridge between two distinct bodies of knowledge with a common object of interest, but characterized by a different approach, and thus a different discourse. Knowledge about the brain, it was thought, would constrain the formation of theory in psychology and linguistics, while conversely, familiarity with psychological and linguistic principles would inform clinical practice in work with brain-damaged patients.

By the 1970s, both neuropsychology and neurolinguistics were well established as scientific disciplines, with clearly delimited fields of interest, generally accepted research methodologies, recognized academic centers, and official scientific journals. The "Decade of the Brain," which ended in the year 2001, markedly increased both the store of knowledge and the prestige of both these two fields, now clearly counted among the "neurosciences." To be sure, neurolinguistics remains a rather esoteric specialty, but neuropsychology has grown to such an extent that its major international conferences and congresses routinely number participants in the thousands.

All this has come at a certain cost, however. What has perhaps inevitably happened in the process of legitimating neuropsychology and neurolinguistics in the academic setting over the last 40 years is that the interdisciplinary discourse has turned inward, upon itself, and become a self-sufficient third discourse, no longer essentially in contact with either of the two disciplines whose dialectic was the rationale for its creation. Neuropsychologists and neurolinguists write books and articles for other neuropsychologists and neurolinguists to read, producing data and theory that motivate and inform further specialized research within the confines of the respective disciplines. Interdisciplinary dialogue with psychology, behavioral neurology, and linguistics has all but ceased.

What has been lost as a result of this inward turn, however, is more than just a potential new perspective on the founding assumptions of psychology and linguistics, important as that would be. The points at issue in both neuropsychology and neurolinguistics are also deeply and intrinsically philosophical problems. No philosophy of mind can be expounded today without at least addressing the mind-brain problem, and any philosophy of language that does not include a reasonable account of how a mental concept or intention becomes a speech act, and vice versa, is manifestly incomplete. These are precisely the issues that neuropsychology and neurolinguistics were intended to address, but the present authors are compelled to confess, not without chagrin, that these philosophical preoccupations have largely disappeared from the discourse of the neurosciences. Rather, simplifying assumptions are made at the starting point of research, and the territory that lies beyond them is labeled "Here be dragons" (read: "Here be philosophy") and carefully avoided. Thus the philosophy of mind is often done with a somewhat naive approach to the anatomical and physiological intricacies of brain work, while neuropsychology is typically done with a largely uncritical attitude toward the underlying concepts of cognition, perception, thinking, and so forth. Rather than a discourse unfolding at a meeting place where two roads intersect, we have built a cloverleaf exchange, with the mental vehicles whizzing past one another in opposite directions, meeting only with catastrophic consequences.

The absence of dialogue between the neurosciences and philosophy can be illustrated anecdotally. Several years ago, at very nearly the same time, Polish translations of Antonio Damasio's *Descartes' Error* and John Searle's *Mind, Language and Society* appeared in many Polish bookstores, and were often displayed in the same window (Damasio 1999, Searle 1999). Most readers (like the booksellers who composed the window displays) can see at a glance that these two books are at many essential points devoted to the same topic, that is, the relationship between the brain and the mind, and yet there would seem to be no point of contact between them. Not only do the two authors not cite each other, in fact they do not seem to have read any of the same books—with the interesting exception of Descartes, the favorite whipping boy of twentieth-century thought. In fact, scarcely a single book or author appears in the bibliographies of both books. Damasio and Searle are discussing the same phenomena, but within two realms of discourse, each of which seems oblivious to the other's existence. More importantly, both these discourses are badly, not to say fatally flawed by the absence of precisely that awareness. Searle's effort to find a *via tertia* between dualism and materialism would benefit greatly from contemporary insights into how the brain works, but in fact much of this information is still available only to a limited number of specialists who read the right journals and speak the lingo. As for Damasio, his assumption that developments in the neurosciences have simply rendered obsolete the concept of a mind as something other than a brain is to say the least philosophically naive (McGinn 2003).

Neuropsychology as a general rule has always tended to be about brains, not minds. The latter term is sometimes used, to be sure, in such stereotyped expressions as "changing one's mind," rather uncritically, or as a convenient way of talking about mentation, typically understood as an otherwise unspecified brain function, that which is left over when the other cognitive functions (memory, attention, perception, and so forth) are removed.

More often, though, the mind (or the soul, or the psyche, or whatever term is used to designate the putative non-material dimension of human existence and cognition) is ignored or explicitly rejected as a concept irrelevant to an empirical science, such as neuropsychology is or aspires to be. A brain is a concrete object that can be measured, photographed (after a fashion), even removed from the skull and studied in the finest detail, while a mind is something whose existence we can infer, but cannot demonstrate. Not surprisingly, then, essentially mechanical idioms and metaphors representing the brain as a kind of biological computer dominate our thinking about thinking in the neurosciences, so that neuropsychology can begin to look like a certain kind of bioengineering. As perhaps inevitably happens (Lakoff 1987, Johnson 1987), the metaphor used to illustrate the concept begins to drive the concept, controlling what can and cannot be conceived. The brain is no longer *like* a computer, it *is* a computer, built of hydrocarbons instead of silicon, with nerves instead of wires and ganglia instead of circuit boards. Human language comes to be seen as an imperfect, quaint precursor of computational language, enabling the smooth flow of input and output. The mind is the software, and the brain is the hardware.

There are, of course, many reasons why the human brain cannot really be conceived as a computer. Even if we were to decide that what a computer does can be called "thinking," certain stubborn biological facts remain. Computers do not grow, and when damaged, they do not repair themselves, but brains do both of these things (Cappa 1998, Papathanasiou 2003). Computers do not think (again, presuming that the operations a computer performs constitute "thinking") in and for themselves, but rather react to the commands they receive from a user; brains, by contrast, execute commands they generate themselves—unless, that is, we conceive of the brain as a kind of instrument used by a distinct entity known as "the mind." The mind, in this view, sits at the keyboard of the nervous system and looks at the screen of perception, using the brain exactly as the author of these words is using the computer. This seems a neat solution, but neither neuropsychologists nor philosophers are likely to find it particularly attractive, and in fact it begs the main questions posed by dualism and materialism. For the present purposes, however, the point is that a materialist account of the brain as a computer is confronted by the nearly insoluble problem of the "user," without whom the computer has no input, and the output has no meaning.

Cognitivist theories of mind, on the other hand, can construct plausible, intellectually satisfying models of mental process (primarily cognition) precisely by setting aside the annoying details of brain and neuronal architecture. One postulates mental modules, each of which receives information from other modules, processes that information in a particular way, and then conveys the new information to the next module for further processing. Thoughts, behaviors, speech acts are broken down into elements in order to determine what transformations are needed to produce the observed articulations, which in turn indicates what "processors" or "modules" are needed in the model of the mind in order to account for these transformations (Jackendoff 2000). The difficulties in finding actual neural correlates for these processors, or the presumed connections between them, are taken as purely empirical problems, waiting for an answer until enough data have been amassed. The stubborn refusal of observable neural structures in the human brain to fall into a pattern of modules connected by transmission lines does not seem to have had much impact on the way thinking is modeled in cognitivist theory. Emotions, then, constitute the smoke, dust, and noise produced in the inner workings of the brain-machine, an approach that very much echoes the attitude towards emotion found in the works of many philosophers since at least the sixth century BCE. We are left with the unchallenged assumption that emotions and cognition belong to two entirely separate systems, as so eloquently stated by Pascal: "Le cœur a ses raisons, que la raison ne connait pas" ("The heart has its reasons, which reason does not know"—*Meditations* 4.277).

One of the implications that emerges clearly from these arguments and counterarguments, models constructed and deconstructed, is that clinical material based on the behavior of persons with brain damage continues to be a largely untapped source of verification or refutation for most, if not all of the proposed models of both brain work and mind work. If we assume that the brain works in thus-and-such a way, then it should be possible to predict what the consequences for thinking would be if particular parts of the brain were to be "switched off," that is, destroyed or otherwise taken "off line." If that which we are calling "the mind" is affected by something that happens to the brain, and if the effects of brain pathology seem to display certain patterns of regularity and predictability, then this fact seems to have important implications for the brain-mind relationship. Indeed, upon further reflection it seems clear enough that no theory of thinking that fails to account in some way for the clinical effects of brain damage can possibly be valid, especially since thinking, in both broader and narrower senses, is almost always affected by such damage. Thus the potential for neuropsychology to enrich and perhaps constrain philosophical discourse about the mind remains a goal worth pursuing, despite the obvious difficulties in initiating and maintaining dialogue.

Both the creative potential and the daunting barriers entailed by dialogue between the neurosciences and philosophy are clearly revealed by a consideration of the history of microgenetic theory in neuropsychology. This history has a beginning in the holistic thinking of such pioneer neurologists as J. Hughlings Jackson and Kurt Goldstein, the evolutionary thought of Paul Maclean and others, and the important work of Karl Pribram, Alexander

Luria, and other prominent figures in neuropsychology, consistently voicing reasoned doubts about the usefulness of the essentially connectionist theories that have dominated neuropsychology since the days of Carl Wernicke. For neuropsychology, however, the history of microgenetic theory consists primarily in the scholarly biography of Jason W. Brown, the American neurologist who first began the systematic application of process thought to behavioral neurology and neuropsychology in the 1970s (Brown 1988, Hanlon 1991). The result is a fascinating corpus of work that has had considerable difficulty finding readers able to follow the arguments, which begin in the arcana of neuroanatomy and aphasiology, and end in process philosophy, influenced at certain crucial points by Buddhist thought and German Idealism. Almost every reader will inevitably get lost at least once along the way. Thus both the theory and its founder are treated with great respect among neuropsychologists, but alas, with little actual understanding (Pachalska 2002). This is all the more regrettable because microgenetic theory has the potential to become a veritable Copernican revolution in the neurosciences, and at the same time to renew the lapsed dialogue between them and philosophy.

A Brief Introduction to Microgenetic Theory

The essence of microgenetic theory in neuropsychology is an account of the phases in brain process through which successive mind/brain states arise and perish over the duration of the psychological present, measured in milliseconds. According to the theory, mental states are rhythmically generated out of a "core" (Brown 2000) in the anatomically deepest and phylogenetically oldest parts of the central nervous system, over phases to the outermost and youngest regions of the brain, the gray matter that constitutes the neocortex. The progression in each mental state, then, runs through layers deposited by millions of years of evolution, and by the growth processes of ontogenesis, which in a general way replicate the course of evolution.

It is essential in this context to bear in mind the nature of evolutionary change, since in microgenetic theory the principles that apply to phylogenesis over eons of evolution and ontogenesis over years of growth are equally applicable to the formation of a behavior over the milliseconds required for a neural impulse to travel up through the successive layers of the central nervous system. Evolutionary change occurs as new layers are constantly deposited on the surface, covering but not supplanting the older layers beneath, as the lava from successive eruptions builds up the classic volcanic cone. When higher species, then, begin to evolve from lower ones, the latter do not simply disappear. The appearance of the human species did not render chimpanzees obsolete; rather, about 4–6 million years ago there took place a bifurcation in the evolution of the ape, so that one branch became chimpanzees, and the other human beings. Evolution is generally a matter of bifurcation and branching, characterized by splits and discontinuities, rather than the kind of gradual transformation commonly (but mistakenly) associated with the word "evolve." The evolution of a species does not take place within a generation or a lifetime, but in the succession between generations and individuals, and in the discontinuities that prevent this succession from being an incessant repetition of the same patterns. That is why the branching process of evolution, the precise moment at which a split takes place, is seldom perceptible when it happens.

The layers deposited in the human brain by evolutionary and growth processes can be represented in several different ways, but the "triune brain" model of Paul MacLean (Figure 11.1) is a good starting point (MacLean 1991).

The brainstem and midbrain of the human being differ rather little from that of reptiles, fish, and amphibians. In other words, any vertebrate has a structure at the upper end of the spinal cord that looks very much like a human brainstem, relative of course to the size of the animal (only the structure

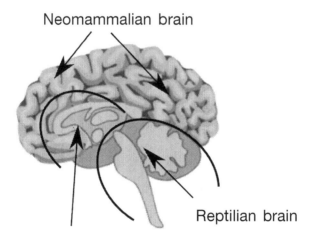

Fig. 11.1. Schematic representation of the three primary planes of evolutionary development in the human brain (adapted from MacLean 1967).

called the "pons" is slightly fatter, proportionally, in the human brain). The difference is that in the lower orders these structures constitute the entire brain, while in the higher orders there are additional layers. Thus the evolution of the earliest mammalian species was accompanied by the appearance of new neural structures that branched out from the midbrain, and organized themselves into the structures known as the limbic system (largely responsible for the basic emotions) and the cerebellum (whose Latin name, a diminutive from *cerebrum* 'brain," reflects its nature as a more or less self-contained center for movement and sensation). These structures constitute the middle layer on Figure 11.1, the paleo-mammalian brain. The important point, again, is that the paleomammalian brain does not replace or even strictly speaking subsume the reptilian brain that precedes it, but rather has been deposited on top of it. In the same way, then, the final layer of the human brain, the cortex (especially the forebrain), overlies the reptilian and paleomammalian brains. The layering here is a matter of visible, anatomical structure, which can be revealed by dissection, and at the same time is reflected in function. Brain function is layered because the respective layers are not modules on a production line, but rather brains-in-the-making. This means that each of them can do what a brain does, that is, produce behavior.

As Brown points out (2000), it is essential here to distinguish sensori-motor reflex, which is linear and circular, like the inhale-exhale cycle, from an action-perception construct, which is simultaneous and parallel. As neural processing expands beyond the reflex level (i.e., above the lower brainstem), both sensation and movement are physical events that take shape outside cognition. On the level of the reptilian brain, then, the sensation-reaction cycle closes very quickly, differing little from a reflex arc. The brainstem is involved in many involuntary brain functions fundamental for life (pulse, respiration, the sleep-wake cycle), which is why damage to the brainstem almost always leads to either death or coma. Thus behaviors mediated primarily by the brainstem seem automatic, innate, and by the same token primitive. The frog, for example, has a rather fixed repertoire of reactions to stimuli and is capable of only a limited degree of adaptation. There is no perception in any meaningful sense of the word, but only a kind of gross sensation limited to detection of whole objects and motion, qualitatively undifferentiated for the most part; action is whole-body, immediate, algorithmic and inflexible. The focus is on survival, or perhaps more broadly, biological success: finding food and drink, avoiding threats, reproducing the species. Behavior is primarily approach-avoidance, modulated by drives and instinctive reactions. Upon hearing a sudden loud noise, the whole body tenses (producing the leap of the frog, the startle reaction in a higher animal) and the autonomic nervous system immediately raises the pulse rate, blood pressure, and respiration rate, long before the rest of the brain has taken in the stimulus, analyzed and identified it, and decided upon the appropriate reaction. Time here is the pulse and rhythm of heart and lungs, actions and reactions in a Newtonian system of balanced mechanics.

The limbic system, as previously mentioned, is the primary source of emotion, understood for the present purposes as a biochemical reaction to a stimulus. The brainstem works primarily with bioelectrical impulses, while the limbic system modulates the working of the nervous system through hormones, neurotransmitters, and the like. The world takes on color, in both a literal and figurative sense, and the approach-avoidance scheme of behavior is replaced by like-dislike, which in turn signals much more clearly the presence of a will and a self, entering into relations with objects that are liked and disliked. There is an element of decision in the limbic system, as action here is less automatic and algorithmic. While the "reptilian" brainstem is oriented toward avoiding pain, that is, avoiding danger and satisfying drives (the organism eats to assuage hunger, copulates to assuage tension, etc.), the "paleomammalian" limbic system is largely obedient to the pleasure principle. Perception on this level emerges from anxiety and desire, as objects are endowed with a highly subjective, emotional loading that takes precedence over their objective features, which in fact have not yet evolved into a perception. There is a different, more developed intentionality on this level, an "I-thou" that does not (yet) have a concept of the third person (Pachalska and MacQueen 2002). Limbic perception is thus the perception of memory, dream, and hallucination, much more connected to the inner life of the perceiver than to any outer reality. Action is no longer restricted to whole-body movements, but begins to be goal directed, controlled by the cerebellum. The stiff and awkward movement of a patient with cerebellar damage is also the gait of a sleepwalker: arms stretched out, ankles stiff, eyes fixed forward.

Limbic time, as Brown points out (1996), is the floating, recurrent time of dream consciousness. Events have a before-and-after sequence, McTaggart's "A Series" (1934/68), but are not placed in a progressive time frame consisting of past, present and future (the "B Series"). Things happen, but they have already happened, and will happen again, perhaps differently, perhaps the same. The inability of this subcortical brain to discriminate objects on the basis of their articulated features means that there is no psychological basis for saying that one event is different from another. Everything is blended into everything else, identities shift and flow, images fade in and out. The present is not only constantly compared to the past, it *is* the past, recurring yet again. More importantly, however, the action/perception cycle takes on a rather different character, so much so, in fact, that the whole distinction of action and perception, which seems so obvious, makes little sense at the limbic level. Feeling, a subliminal and perceptually informed affective engagement with images, is the fundamental action of the limbic system, not something prior to and motivating action, as we usually think of stimulus-response cycles. Both action and perception are guided by a pleasure orientation and unfold together, simultaneously.

The level of conscious reasoning, of that which we usually call "thought," is the cortex, the layer of gray matter (about a centimeter deep) that overlies and surrounds the entire brain (hence the name, "cortex," which in Latin means "bark"). Although the cellular architecture of the cortex is in fact quite complex (several areas, phylogenetically and ontogenetically older than the rest, make up the "limbic cortex," as opposed to the "neocortex"), the gross structure of the cortex, unlike that of the limbic system, does not consist of distinguishable clusters of tissue that form organ-like structures, but is rather a complex, ramified surface, whose anatomical divisions into lobes and regions are to some extent arbitrary. This fact, apparent to the naked eye, is not without significance. The modular approach to cognition seems to imply that the cortex should be made up precisely of modules (the boxes in a cognitivist "flow-chart") connected by "wires," and yet nothing in the physical appearance of the cortex suggests that it is built in this way. To be sure, the evidence from more than a century of systematic study of the symptoms produced by damage to specific regions of the brain seems to indicate very clearly that the cortex is not a completely homogenous mass, not the *sensorium commune* of pre-nineteenth-century medicine. Yet attempts to "map" the brain have produced results of rather dubious value, and more recent studies using new neuroimaging techniques have complicated rather than simplified the task of the map-makers (Andrewes 2001).

It is in the cortex that perception and action reach the level of conscious decision. The brain forms articulated pictures or representations of what is out there in the world, and of what has been out there in the world, and the play of these images constitutes conscious perception. What is more—and this has only recently begun to be a subject of interest for neuropsychology (MacQueen 2002)—the cortex is capable of forming images of what might be or could be out there, or could have been, or should have been, and was not. It is not that hard to form a coherent theory of how the brain forms an image of something the eyes are seeing or have seen, but it is quite another thing to explain how the "mind's eye" works in terms of brain structure and function.

For the present purposes, however, the most important fact about the cerebral cortex is that both perception and action at this stage are character-ized by detail, discrimination, and analysis. The reptilian brain sees a large moving object, to be avoided, or seized, or ignored; the paleomammalian brain sees a human figure, producing an affect, positive or negative; the cortex sees features, details, a face, and can put a name to it, or not. The complexity of perception results from the fact that these three images come into existence independently and sequentially, though there is only one perceiver and one object, and the entire process takes milliseconds to complete. The conscious mind, then, typically experiences its perception as a single, simple act of seeing. According to microgenetic theory, however, this single act is a multilayered actualization, the tip of an iceberg that floats to the surface and then subsides, containing within itself the traces of all that has gone before, in phylogeny, ontogeny, and microgeny (Pachalska 2002).

As objects take on their objective character in a sculpting process constrained by sensory data, time becomes a dimension of the subject-object system, along with space, which expands beyond the arms reach and the immediate visual field. The mind can conceive of places other than "here," and time other than "now." There is past, present, and future, which come into existence as concepts when the fluid before-and-after sequences of limbic time are projected out into the world and fixed to something that at least seems to be objective. This is not to say, of course, that the time of our consciousness is the same as clock time, or even that our ordinary assumptions about the three domains of time (past, present, future) are as natural or self-evident as they may seem. As Brown continually reminds us (1996, 2000, 2004), time is a central issue for microgenetic theory, where the crucial point is the duration or "thickness" of the "now." Given that time-space is actually a continuum, the "forward" movement of time is more a psychological than a physical fact (Germine 2004). The past is a construct that is created and re-created at each moment of the now; the future is an extrapolation resulting from the experience of a certain "forward" momentum in the resurgence of the "now" over the rapidly receding past.

Thus from the physical (and metaphysical) point of view, the present is a dimensionless boundary between the fully actualized past, which having exhausted its potential no longer exists, and the potential future, which does not yet exist. When an arrow is shot from a bow at a target, its flight seems a single event, but this is a psychological fact, and not a physical one. Whether or not the arrow strikes the target at which it was aimed depends, of course, upon a number of variables: the skill of the archer, the distance, the wind, the movement of the target, etc. At the moment the archer releases the arrow, the range of possible outcomes is still very wide. With the proper video equipment, however, we can break this event down into a series of states, frozen on film, and at each of these "nows" the number of possible trajectories is significantly reduced, as is the number of possible interfering factors. With each successive frame, then, it becomes easier to predict whether or not the arrow will strike the target, and at some point it becomes reasonably easy to predict exactly where it will strike the target. At 100 milliseconds before impact there is no real doubt what is about to happen.

The point of this example is that every mental act is in fact played out in the same way as the flight of this hypothetical arrow, and this is what forms the essence of time as the cortex learns to manipulate it. In fact, though the time in which cortex operates may seem more objective, closer to the fourth dimension of physical objects than the free-floating sequences of limbic time, the operations involved in creating past, present, and future are ultimately subjective in nature. Patients with various kinds of brain disorders typically exhibit specific dysfunctions in the area of their experience of time, though for lack of theoretical groundwork there has been relatively little research done on this issue. Moreover, much of what has been done on the pathology of "orientation in time" is based on philosophically naive assumptions and has so far produced little of interest. The exception that proves the rule is Pöppel's work (1988), which is much admired but seldom imitated. In most of the work on temporal orientation, the conventional past-present-future framework is taken as a self-evident reality against which the disturbances typical of, for example, Alzheimer's dementia are measured. Few if any have taken up the challenge of exploring how the brain *creates* time.

The Archaeology of the Brain

Sigmund Freud, as is generally known, was fond of remarking that psycho-analysis is "the archaeology of the soul" (Jones 1960/1962). The metaphor is often cited, but its meaning has seldom been explored. The image of the psychoanalyst digging in the rubbish of the past seems obvious, even stereo-typical, but the notion of the present as a surface overlying successive deposits, and then itself subsiding to form yet another layer of substrate—this is a much richer metaphor. Memory is not a structure of interactive data bases in which information is shuttled through various connections and interfaces, but a layered, stratified structure made up of the "shells" of all the "nows" that have gone before. The deeper the layer, the more it is subject to a certain flattening, although the essential contours somehow persist.

The familiar Freudian models of the psyche (of which the "archaeo-logical" model is only one, and perhaps the least developed in Freud's own work) have been replaced over the last century by more fashionable models, which sometimes proceed by mapping mental functions to neuroanatomical models, sometimes by mapping neuroanatomy to models of mental functions, but most often by mapping either neuroanatomy or mental functions with only a passing nod in the other direction. The problem of the architecture of the psyche and its relation or lack of relation to the architecture of the brain and its billions of neurons has been largely marginalized, which may well be one of the primary reasons why microgenetic theory still struggles for a hearing, even though it presents an elegant solution to a problem that should be central to the neurosciences.

The problem, of course, is much older than either microgenetic theory or psychoanalysis. Indeed, there are ancient precedents in philosophy for MacLean's "triune brain" structure, of which one of the most interesting is surely Plato's "tripartite soul," particularly in the version developed in the *Republic*, which in turn influenced St. Augustine and those medieval philosophers whose thought was shaped by him. As the population of the ideal city is divided into three classes—workers, warriors, and rulers—so the soul, Socrates argues, is divided into three elements:

1. The desiring part (*to epithymetikon*), the seat of bodily appetites, corresponding to the workers, whose *raison d'être* is the consumption and production of goods.

2. The spirited part (*to thymoeides*), consisting of the "social" emotions characteristic of warriors, who must be prepared to sacrifice their lives for the common good.

3. The rational or calculating part (*to logistikon*), the ruling element, shaped by philosophy to strive for self-control and ever greater understanding.

Though of course Plato can have had no idea of the evolutionary development of the brain (indeed, in the fifth century BCE it was not at all clear that the brain, the contents of the skull, had any essential role in thinking), it is not hard to see that the elements of cognition, perception, and action have been arranged in much the same way as the sequence from reptilian (brainstem) to paleomammalian (limbic system) to neomammalian (cortex) proposed by MacLean and developed by Brown in microgenetic theory.

In the *Republic*, Socrates argues that in a well-ordered city (or soul), good order and harmony depend on the ability of the *nous* to keep the lower impulses of *epithymia* and the "spiritedness" of the *thymos* under control. Yet the *epithymetikon* and the *thymoeides* are essential parts of the soul (*psyche*): for all the purity of its thought, the Platonic *nous* does not exist separately. Thus the goal of philosophy for Socrates is not to dispose of emotions and passions, but rather to somehow harness them, or more precisely, to bring sensation, feeling, and cognition into a "well-ordered state." Later, the Stoics consigned emotions to the category of *pathemata*: that is, an emotion is an event, something that happens *to* the soul, and not something the soul *does*, which would belong to *praxis*. When an adverse event occurs, as for example when one's house burns down, the event itself is a *pathema*, and so is one's emotional reaction to the event, that which we would today call "affect."

Thus the Sage must be on his guard not to allow *pathemata* to steer *praxis,* a perversion of the natural order as the Stoics conceived it. This leads by a series of steps to the formation of that tradition in Western philosophy enthroning reason as the Good King and consigning the "passions" (*passio* is Latin for *pathema*) to the role of Evil Pretender. Pascal demurred, Nietzsche and Schopenhauer rebelled, the twentieth century went to the barricades, but even in' the works of Freud, who is generally credited with disenthroning Reason and giving power to the lawless Id, the relative valuation of conscious reason and surging passion is constantly in the background. Freud's volcanic Id and the "dark horse of the soul" in Plato's *Phaedrus* are clearly drawn from the same source.

This same problem, though couched in different terms, arises in microgenetic theory. The perception and action of the later phases of a mental act would appear at first glance to be superfluous, since the stimulus-response arc is closed very quickly in the brainstem. In order to allow for behavior shaped by higher levels of processing, it is necessary that the brain possess a mechanism to prolong, retard, suspend, or even interrupt the flow of the process, to allow successively higher (and slower) levels to operate. In evolutionary theory, one speaks of "neoteny," the prolongation of a phase in development, which is often necessary in order to allow for elaboration of function; the prolonged helplessness of the human infant, for example, is both cause and effect of the fact that a much greater percentage of our behavior is learned, rather than innate. In microgenetic terms, neoteny in behavior suspends the immediate closure of the stimulus-response arc, an essential precondition for the heuristics of thoughtful behavior. This explains why the psychological time frames are increasingly broader as the mental act moves upward through the evolutionary planes. The "now" of the reptilian brain is the handful of milliseconds that elapses from the moment the frog sees a fly until it thrusts out its tongue to catch it; the limbic "now" is an envelope of cyclical dream time, in which hours seem like minutes and minutes seem like hours; the "now" of the cortex is the sum of everything that lies within the envelope of consciousness, created, as Brown suggests (1996), by the interval of time that exists between the arising of a psychological moment and its extinction, prolonged by the fact that the self and its objects do not disappear from one moment to the next, but rather linger, more or less successfully resisting decay. This overlapping of "nows" is illustrated by Figure 11.2.

Each of the three "triangles" in this figure represents a behavioral cycle completed within one phase of the "triune brain" described above. The first cycle, A, is closed so quickly that in essence it differs little from a reflex arc. The reaction at time T_1 results directly and immediately from the nature of the stimulus (at T_0), consistent with a limited repertoire of instinctive or learned automatic behaviors. The second cycle, B, which begins at the same

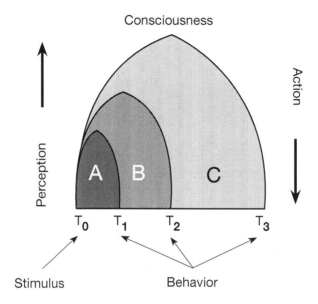

Fig. 11.2. A microgenetic model of behavior.

moment (T_0) in the "paleomammalian" brain, takes somewhat longer to be realized, at T_2, which also means that cycle A as a whole is part of the environment to which the brain in cycle B (the limbic brain) is responding. In the same way, cycle C (the neocortex) takes in the two previous cycles, since it requires yet more time before a behavior emerges at T_3. To some extent, the inhibition (or at least temporary suspension) of behaviors issuing from cycles A and B at T_1 and T_2 is a precondition for any behavior to be realized by cycle C at T_3, since otherwise cycle C is perfectly superfluous. This suppression function, as is well known, is especially associated with the frontal lobes, which have many projections back to the limbic system and the basal ganglia. At the same time, however, cycle C never appears completely independently of cycles A and B, which always form a part of the substructure for cycle C.

An important qualification is necessary at this point. We do not have three brains inside one skull, but rather one, vertically layered brain, in which at least three phases, corresponding to stages in phylogenesis, can be identified. The human brainstem may grossly resemble the brain of a frog, but unlike a frog, a human being cannot survive, even in a coma, if the cortex and subcortical structures are stripped away. If we actually had a self-sufficient frog brain inside our skulls, we would leap from lily pad to lily pad and catch flies with our tongues, and the higher levels of the nervous system would be no more than superfluous spectators to behaviors that have already been realized. In an evolutionary system, newer forms appear *on the base of* older forms, which may or may not persist. Thus in the ecosystem of which the newer form is now an element, the older form can exist in two ways:

1. As a continuation of itself, though as part of a changed system, as lemurs and macaques persist in the presence of more advanced ape species;

2. As an archaic layer in the substance of the newer form, as in the 95% of the human genome that does not differ from that of the chimpanzee.

The same applies, then, to mental process: the functions of the lower, deeper, older layers of the nervous system persist as behaviors that in certain circumstances emerge directly, and as the archaic substrate of everything that is done at higher levels. The force fields that allow the respective layers of the brain to interact with each other, inside or outside the field of consciousness, are as yet only beginning to be understood, which explains why reductionist models of behavior (such as that of behaviorism) come and go so quickly.

Action and perception in the cortex take distinct neural pathways, unfolding from memory (hippocampus and association cortex) outward to the anterior and posterior parts of the brain. It is not the case—the point must be stressed—that action in the anterior brain is bound to or emerges from perception in the posterior brain in a cause-effect relationship, or even that (as the "S-R" cycle of behaviorist psychology would have us believe) in a fixed temporal sequence. Action unfolds from memory, through the frontal lobes to the precentral gyrus and then out to the peripheral nerves and muscles, while perception, as Brown points out (2004), moves from parietal association cortex (again, memory) to primary visual and acoustic cortex in the occipital and temporal lobes, respectively. This is no longer anything like the reflex arc; it results, rather, from the specialization of areas of the cortex to control the formation of percepts or acts. This parcellation of tasks on the motor level is what enables the fingers, under the control of the motor cortex, to move independently; on the cognitive level, parcellation means that the whole brain does not do everything that the brain does. Just as animals and plants in an ecosystem find a niche for themselves, or perish, so neurons in the cortex find a niche, a particular task that they can do better than other neurons can do them, or they perish.

The part of the cortex that is involved in movement can be mapped with considerable precision to the various parts of the body, but it is important to recall that the motor regions of the cortex are not "circuit boards." It is not the case that every muscle in the body is directly wired to (and thus controlled by) the motor cortex, which by the same token is not the point of origin for gross motor behavior. Rather, the "body map" in the motor cortex is mostly devoted to those parts of the musculo-skeletal system that perform delicate, articulated movements. Not surprisingly, then, the face and the hands (from forearm to fingers) are disproportionately represented in the motor cortex. When a person plays the violin, the cortex sculpts the grasp reflex into the fingering of the strings. The difficulty most people have in moving the little finger without moving the adjacent fingers or the whole hand is a result of incomplete sculpting in the motor cortex, not a mechanical problem in the hand itself.

Fully developed, rational behavior is thus formed by the elimination of excess, the trimming or parsing of the irrelevant, the inappropriate, the undesirable. The suspension of brainstem and limbic impulses enables the cortex to make its analysis of wholes to parts, or of potential to actual, in a process of creation that is more like the sculpting of a block into a figure than the modeling of a figure from a shapeless mass of elements. The essential notion here is of constraints, the factors that allow a thing to become what it is by not allowing it to become something else. Constraint, as Hume argued in his essay *On liberty and necessity* (1909–1914), is not the same thing as necessity, or causation. The banks of a river constrain, but do not cause its flow. The river flows because of the force of gravity and the pressure of the water, but it flows here or there because of the constraints of the landscape. Analogously, then, the cortex (especially the frontal lobes) does not so much cause behavior as constrain it, shape it, sculpt it to fit more precisely the situation into which the behavior evolves.

Anatomically, this is reflected in the extensive connections (visible in Figure 11.3) between the frontal lobes and the limbic system (Pachalska 2003). The frontal lobes impose a kind of neoteny in behavior, a suspension or even interruption of algorithmic stimulus-response mechanisms, to allow parcellated perception and action to develop. This mechanism surely accounts, at least in part, for the intuitive conviction that "good" behavior is characterized by restraint (read: self-imposed constraints), and for psychological theories from Socrates to Freud, according to whom there is a constant struggle within the psyche between impulse and inhibition. The same thing goes on within each cell of the organism, as changes in the chemical and physical environment cause various genes in the DNA strands to be activated or deactivated, and specific receptors in the cell walls are opened by agonists or closed by antagonists. Nature displays a great conservatism of principle, constantly repeating the same themes at different levels of organization, from atoms and molecules through cells and tissues up to human societies and the cosmos.

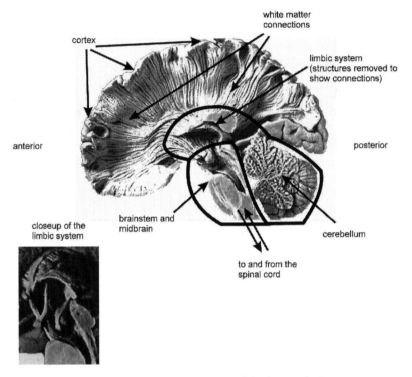

Fig. 11.3. Medial cross-section of the human brain.

In microgenetic theory, the flow of mental process is from the archaic to the recent in forebrain evolution, from the continually reactivated past to the present moment, which is born and immediately dies and decays. Momentary cognitions are extrapolated from memory to perception, and from the intrapsychic to the extrapersonal in spatial and temporal representation. Mental process is unidirectional, obligatory, and recurrent, like the flow of a fountain, whose water continually circulates in such a way that the stream, though in reality it is constantly changing, seems to be constantly the same. What is fixed in a given state of mind is the cumulative series of phases traversed in a given actualization as it rises and falls in this "fountain" structure. Continuity, the ability to sustain a thought, an argument, a train of associations, even a mood, results from the constant repetition of these actualizations, which to the last moment traverse the same routes, and from the fact that a new actualization always appears before the last has faded. This overlapping of past and present gives the thickness of the psychological present, which for William James (1890) was one of the central questions of psychology (cf. Brown 1996, 2000, 2004).

Each present moment, then, is derived out of the memory and past experience of the antecedent state. It appears, perishes, and is replaced, like the overlapping pulses or drops of experience described by James, or the succession of *ksana* ("point-instants") in Buddhist metaphysics. External and internal constraints on this process, such as sensation and habit, determine the degree of novelty in the mental contents. Concepts and categories may control the process in an algorithmic manner, virtually a reflex, and be deduced all the way down to objects perceived in the world without pausing to consider alternatives, or the cognitive process may undergo neoteny at an earlier, imaginal or conceptual phase, to serve as a springboard for the propagation of novel content. This is, once again, the evolutionary principle of branching: novelty does not appear from a relentless forward movement, but from a branching that occurs at some point before the main process reaches its natural endpoint. The content of the neotenous image may be reproductive, as in the case of a memory image, or productive, as in imagination (or hallucination). There is, to be sure, some novelty in every act of cognition (no two moments are ever exactly alike), but what is productive should be interpreted as a deviation from a more general trend to repetition. Without the stability of this repetition the mind/brain would jump from one world to the next in each blink of the eye, which is exactly what seems to be occurring in some kinds of psychosis.

Most of us are aware that when we look at a film sequence, we are actually looking at a series of still photos, projected in such rapid succession that the images seem to flow together, creating the illusion of motion. The illusion is dependent, however, on there being relatively little change between one frame and the next; otherwise, the images jump and flash, spoiling the illusion of reality. According to microgenetic theory, all our perception in fact occurs in an analogous manner. Memory is a film to which new frames are continually being added, but each frame (that is, each perception) is itself the result of a series of transformations up through the evolutionary layers of the nervous systems. Thus there seems to be movement in two planes, horizontal and vertical, time and space, though in reality there is one movement, up-and-out. The brainstem's Gestalt becomes the limbic system's image, and finally the articulated object of the cortex, which does not mean that we see three different objects in three different worlds. Rather, the object being perceived flows through these phases in a process of continuous change, more or less what one would expect from a nervous system that seems to consist entirely of connections (i.e., neurons) without any fixed point of destination for the information that is being conveyed along the "wires." The principle is one of movement and change, where stability is provided by reiteration.

One essential point that emerges from this discussion is that the conventional distinction made in neuropsychology (and elsewhere) between structure and function is not as sharp as it may seem in naive intuition. The infant brain, which is still only to a limited extent capable of exercising voluntary control over the rest of the body, exhibits a pattern of exuberant neuron growth, creating a veritable jungle of synaptic connections. As maturity approaches, the development of new synapses slows markedly, and the superfluous ones begin to be trimmed away. Once again, the principle is one of sculpting, removing from a shapeless mass whatever is unnecessary, so that the desired form, whether of structure or of function, can emerge untrammeled. Maturity, in fact, is marked by a kind of shift from process that deposits structure to process that deposits function, though there is no real discontinuity between these moments in time, and the same process of discarding what is superfluous is still the guiding principle (Brown and Pachalska 2003). This sculpting process—or rather, to use the more precise term, parcellation—continues to the end of life, unless the atrophic, involutionary processes associated with dementia (as in persons with Alzheimer's Disease) erode the neural architecture of the brain to such an extent that the elaborate dance of impulse and constraint breaks down. From the microgenetic point of view, then, dementia is precisely the result of involution, or perhaps more strictly, demented behavior is the result of "microphthisis," as normal behavior results from microgenesis.

Symptoms

The claim was made earlier that any theory of thinking has to be able to account for the disturbances of thinking that occur when the brain is damaged. In the light of the foregoing, all-too-brief sketch of how the brain works, from the standpoint of microgenetic theory, it is possible to account for a great deal of what one actually observes in clinical practice with persons who have suffered brain damage, whether localized to one particular place (in what is called a "focal lesion") or spread out over much or all of the brain.

Each of the three levels of brain structure exhibits a similar relation of symptom type to lesion and anatomical phase. For example, evolutionarily recent, or surface, formations are associated with the analysis of form in expanded realms of space and time, while older, deeper, formations are associated with concepts and meanings in personal space, that is, within the immediate field of vision or the arm's reach. Typically, in the deeper structures it is bilateral lesions that produce the characteristic symptoms, with increasing laterality and specificity closer to the surface. The higher the point at which the lesion occurs, the more specific the symptoms, where by "higher" we mean, at one at the same time, "more advanced" and "farther removed from the base," that is, the brainstem. Both structure and function in the brain "branch out" from the brainstem (*truncus cerebri* in Latin), and the degree of elaboration and specification is to a large extent a function of the distance from that "trunk."

These general principles are illustrated by the pathological phases in the realization of an action. In the condition known as akinetic mutism, a common early phase in recovery from prolonged coma after head injury, the patient lies motionless and does not vocalize, but there is no paralysis. The interpretation is that the envelope or kernel of the action is disrupted at the phase of its initiation. This in turn results from the fact that coma is usually caused by an insult to the brainstem, which is responsible for, among other things, the sleep-wake cycle. In akinetic mutism, then, the limited, stereotyped reactions that the "reptilian" brainstem originates are suspended, even though the cortex remains theoretically capable of moving the limbs. What the cortex cannot do unassisted, it would seem, is to set the body in motion. Many patients later report that during this phase of their recovery, they seem to remember conversing with people and even walking around the room, and then being puzzled that no one seems to react; in reality, they have been all this time in "akinetic mutism," and their memory has recorded *what they meant to do or say* as being *what they actually did or said.*

The converse situation arises when there is damage to the motor areas of the cortex (a band of gray matter about 2 centimeters wide just in front of the central fissure that divides the frontal lobes from the parietal and temporal lobes). The ultimate effect may seem at first glance to be the same, in that the patient is unable to move the affected limb, but the differences between paralysis and akinetic mutism are extremely significant. To begin with, in akinetic mutism there is no initiation of movement in any limb, while the patient with a paralyzed limb can usually move the other limbs. Even more importantly, the patient with paralysis resulting from damage to the cerebral cortex can actually perform gross movements of the limb (e.g., the arm moves at the shoulder), but is unable to make the finer movements needed for any kind of manipulation (e.g., is completely unable to move the fingers).

Indeed, the sequence of purely motor symptoms caused by nerve damage reveals very clearly how actions (in this case, movements) are created microgenetically, as one moves the point of damage higher and higher in the central nervous system, from the spinal cord through the base of the skull into the brain. To begin with, if there is serious damage to the spinal cord in the lumbar or thoracic segments, the result is paraplegia, when the patient cannot walk; if higher, the arms are also affected, a condition which is called "tetraplegia" (or "quadriplegia"). In either case, the patient cannot move or feel either of the affected limbs below the level corresponding to the point where the cord is damaged. The mental image of what motion and sensation actually feel like is unaffected, but the programmed activation of the effectors in the musculo-skeletal system to produce movement (a process not directly accessible to consciousness) is interrupted. Tetraplegics and paraplegics know all too well what they would do with their limbs, if only they could. The action (wiggling the fingers, moving the arm, walking) remains a potential object of cognition, even though the physical movement has become impossible.

If the damage is very high in the spinal cord, in the top two vertebrae or near the area where the cord passes into the brain at the base of the skull and becomes the lower end of the brainstem, the result is the "locked-in" syndrome, where the patient is fully conscious but unable to initiate any movement. Sometimes the eyelids are spared, sometimes the facial muscles, sometimes the vocal apparatus as well, all depending on how high the point of damage is and how completely the cord is severed. There is still full consciousness of what motion is, despite the complete inability to perform it, which makes the locked-in syndrome a "fate worse than death" for most patients and a major ethical dilemma for physicians and families.

If the brainstem itself is damaged (serious damage here is invariably fatal, since the brainstem controls pulse and respiration), there is akinetic mutism, in which, as described above, the patient lies motionless, and may even be "conscious" of movement that is not actually occurring in the limbs. Consciousness at this stage is fitful, as the patient drifts in and out, and the danger of dying or falling into a persistent vegetative state is very great.

If there is damage to the cerebellum, movement is possible, but it is discoordinated, awkward, jerky, often out of sequence (a condition referred to by neurologists as "cerebellar ataxia"). The patient can often learn to walk again, though slowly and with difficulty. Many patients report a persistent fear of falling, or even a sensation of falling when walking, which causes them to lunge forward or backward to regain balance, when in fact they have not lost their balance at all. Interestingly, we have observed in our own clinical practice that patients at this stage are unable to walk and talk at the same time: if one speaks to them while they are learning to walk, they will either ignore the interlocutor, or stop the effort to walk in order to enter into conversation. Clearly, at this level, movement and language are using many of the same (compromised) brain resources, so that the two activities must compete for access.

When the basal ganglia are compromised, the patient's motor behavior is slowed, becoming stiff and stereotyped. The face assumes a mask-like, impassive expression that gives little outward clue to what the patient is actually feeling or thinking. Trembling of the hands is common; as some readers will doubtless have noticed, this is the classic picture of Parkinson's Disease, which tends to attack the basal ganglia first. If the limbic system is attacked, as in Tourette's Syndrome, facial mimicry is exaggerated, motor behavior is disorganized by sporadic jerks and violent tics, and the patient often exhibits a symptom known as "coprolalia": the involuntary utterance of foul words. Interestingly enough, coprolalia in one form or another is also encountered in stroke patients with subcortical damage, and in many persons at an early stage in regaining consciousness after general anesthesia.

If there is damage only to the motor area of the cortex, the result is hemiplegia, that is, paralysis affecting one side of the body, left or right. The paralysis can be spastic or flaccid, depending on the exact nature of the damage and several other factors, but this is a peripheral issue for the present purposes. The main point is that the cortex is primarily engaged in complex, articulated actions, and damage to this area disrupts primarily (though not exclusively) the ability to operate with the muscles of the face and hands. In some cases, cortical damage produces a symptom called "apraxia," in which the patient loses the ability to execute voluntary, learned movements, especially of the hands and fingers (sometimes the facial muscles as well), despite intact neurological function.

From this brief description of motor symptoms resulting from nerve damage at various levels, it becomes possible to infer how a normal action unfolds, since the symptoms here described constitute derailments of normal process at specific points, with consequences as predicted by microgenetic theory. The picture of action that emerges here begins with an incipient action that is first prefigured in body space, then initiated, and then projected out into extrapersonal space. The act unfolds from gross movements along body axes to fine distal articulations, from egocentric body space to extrapersonal space, finally to motor implementation, as actions in the mind become movements in the world. The act develops over tiers of spatial representation, from the space of the body through the action perimeter, the space of the arm's reach (Bradford 1992), to an effectuation on objects in extrapersonal space.

The speech act, though obviously far more complex than limb motion, unfolds in an analogous manner, and the range of speech disturbances associated with damage occurring at specific points along the older-to-newer, inner-to-outer, self-to-world lines of microgeny can be explained in much the same way. As Brown points out (1988), the word selection errors seen in patients with aphasia do not represent a pattern of random mistakes:

> Some patients regularly commit errors in word choice that show wide semantic distance from targets, e.g. "wheelbase" for *chair*. This is called "semantic jargon" or "jargon aphasia," a form of Wernicke's aphasia, in which patients use words that bear little

or no actual relation to the intended word, and not infrequently are not words at all.

With "anomic" or "amnestic" aphasia, the errors tend to be in the same object category as the target word, for example, "table" for chair, or the word may be semantically constrained but not evoked, the so-called "tip-of-the-tongue" state, often leaving the patient very frustrated.

In "conduction aphasia," the lexical item is available but does not achieve an adequate phonemic encoding. For example, these patients say "chore" for *chair*, "predisent" for *president*, and so on, and cannot repeat a sentence immediately after hearing it; they seem unaware of their errors and seldom correct themselves.

In "apraxia of speech," the phonemic realization of the words is likewise distorted, but there are frequent efforts to correct; the patient seems "tongue-tied," as though every sentence were a tongue-twister, and struggles to be understood. The patient is frustrated by the fact that what is coming out of his mouth is not the speech act formed in his mind.

In "dysarthria," the patient is unable to make the speech apparatus obey the intention to speak. There is a fully formed and completely normal speech act in the mind, but its physical execution is faulty because one or more of the components of the peripheral speech apparatus (mouth, lips, tongue, palate, voice box, diaphragm) does not "fire" properly or at the proper time.

When these errors are correlated with the location of the lesions, it becomes clear that the progression from word meaning to word form is again occurring over growth planes in forebrain evolution. Respectively, then:

- In jargon aphasia, the lesion most often occurs in limbic-temporal cortex, the oldest part of the cortex, richly connected to and arising from the limbic structures (see Figure 11.3);

- In anomic and amnestic aphasia, the lesion is likely to be in association or integration neocortex in the left hemisphere (phylogenetically and ontogenetically younger than limbic cortex but older than focal cortex);

- In conduction aphasia, apraxia of speech, and dysarthria, very specific areas of focal cortex in the language-dominant hemisphere (usually the left hemisphere in right-handed persons) are affected, so that specific functions involving the transition from lexical selection to phonetic realization are knocked out or disorganized by the lesion.

What emerges from the symptoms is progressive specification within the lexicon, a zeroing-in on the target item, using first semantic criteria, and then phonological. In other words, this is parcellation on the microgenetic scale. The major forms of what is usually called "receptive" aphasia (primarily affecting the understanding of speech acts, including one's own) can be interpreted as disruptions at successive phases in the perceptual actualization of an utterance. The same holds true for the various forms of "expressive" aphasia (primarily affecting the ability to produce speech acts), where again (though the demonstration is lengthy, cf. Brown 1988) the various syndromes we see in the clinic reflect varying points in normal processing where the interference occurs. There is normal processing up to a certain point, then a derailment or gap, and then a resumption of normal process with some elements missing or out of place (Brown and Pachalska 2003).

In language, as in action, microgeny actualizes through a sequence of context-item transformations. The symptom reveals correlation with evolutionary growth, and is also the key to understanding the process. What then is a symptom? Instead of the unreflective assumption that a lesion destroys or disables a center, an operation or a representation, brain process should be conceived in terms of wave-fronts or recurring fields, and a lesion as a disruption in the flow, comparable to a rock in a stream. The rock produces an eddy or whirlpool that retards flow but does not stop it (which is to say, neoteny occurs, a heterochrony of flow in the water above, below, and beside the lesion). The extent to which the process is restored to normal flow depends, then, on how large the rock is, and where it occurs in relation to the point where the stream is measured. What emerges as a symptom is not a deficit, not an empty place where a behavior used to be, but a fragment of a normal process, prematurely brought to the surface by the "rock in the stream." This is one of the fundamental problems of neuropsychology, which remains to be solved: so long as we use tests only to measure what the patient cannot do, we do not really understand what the symptom is, or what it means. Microgenetic theory (Brown and Pachalska 2003) suggests how symptoms reveal the inner structure of behavior.

To summarize: the mental state develops out of reflex systems in the brainstem, where the purely sequential nature of sensorimotor reflex arcs undergoes a shift to a simultaneous act-object. This cognitive core is surrounded by a multi-tiered layering of physical input and output. The pattern of a continuous sheet of thinking that flows from self out to world, characterized by a wave of whole-to-part transformations sculpted by sensory constraints, activating a series of motor keyboards, becomes the model for successive levels of derivation. The progression is from unity to multiplicity, with reiteration of the sequence within the state and across states in overlapping waves. The model requires that events within the same phase are simultaneous from one domain to another (for example, movement and speech), and that all events pass through each phase in the series.

The Neuropsychology of Consciousness

Although consciousness has always been an important topic for philosophy and psychology, neuropsychology until recently has not ventured into this territory (Brown 1996, 2000). There are several reasons for this, one of which is surely the problem that consciousness is so variously defined. A scientist or clinician who is trying to solve a particular concrete problem can perhaps be forgiven for attempting to sidestep this difficult issue. In neurology, consciousness is normally defined as the nervous system's readiness to receive sensory stimuli and react to them on an ongoing basis. In psychology, on the other hand, there are as many definitions of consciousness as there are schools of psychological thought, but at the risk of some simplification it can be said that consciousness from a psychological perspective is most often defined in a somewhat circular fashion, as the individual's awareness of being aware: if I know that I know something, then I am conscious of knowing something, and thus I am conscious. Even Freud's discovery of the unconscious is at some level based on just such a definition, since the fundamental doctrines of psychoanalysis emerge from the premise that we can know something and not know that we know it, which is precisely what the unconscious is.

Although Freud was a neurologist by training and generally very interested in the brain (Brown 2000, Wallesch 2004), his views on the nature of the psyche and the inner life put him at odds with the pioneers of neuropsychology, such as Carl Wernicke. He never tried to place the unconscious (or the Id) in the brain, and despite his lifelong fascination with Darwinian evolution he made only sporadic and not very systematic efforts to apply evolutionary thinking to his psychological doctrine until his last great work, *Moses and Monotheism*. Nowadays, the idea of applying neuropsychological methods to such fundamental problems of psychoanalysis as consciousness, or conversely, of applying psychoanalysis to neuropsychological research, will strike many specialists on both sides of this divide as a very dubious undertaking. The result of this mutual suspicion, however, is that an extremely important area of inquiry has remained largely a no-man's land (or perhaps, to update the metaphor, a "free-fire zone"). There is, to be sure, an admirable journal called *Neuropsychoanalysis*, but it has been dogged by marketing problems from the beginning, which perhaps serves to prove the point. This is much to be regretted. Neuropsychology, by focusing largely on specific cognitive processes (leaving emotion and even mentation for separate treatment) without having a coherent theory of consciousness, identity, or personality, may well be making bricks without straw. On the other hand, theorizing about consciousness without taking the brain into account would seem to be an undertaking at least equally dubious.

The primary reason why neuropsychology has not produced a theory of consciousness (and has thus remained largely a marginal contributor to the philosophy of mind) is that the dominant views of brain function in the neurosciences make such a theory all but impossible to conceive. A modular mind/brain made up of discrete processors shuttling bits of data back and forth does not need to be conscious in order to do its job. If computers were to become conscious they would by the same token cease to be useful as computers, and if we conceive of our brains as organic computers, as is fashionable nowadays, then the same applies to them. For Damasio, for example (2003), all mental states (emotions, cognitions, and consciousness) are perceptions of the body, so that the very notion of consciousness becomes superfluous, an anachronistic and misleading name for the fact that a mental state exists in a given person at a given time. As McGinn points out, however (2003), Damasio has neglected the intentionality of mental states and reduced subjects to objects (as one might expect from the author of *Descartes' Error*), avoiding the "homunculus" trap but falling straight into another, yet more insidious. Even if I say, "My consciousness is a perception of my body," what is the meaning of the first person singular "my"? One should say, "*This* consciousness is a perception of *this* body," as a computer would say, since the very word "my" brings the homunculus right back out of the waste basket. But if first-person-ness is not simply a verbal artifact left over in the language from a long rejected paradigm, like "sunrises" and "sunsets," if the brain-damaged patient who says "he" in reference to himself is in fact displaying a loss of some essential element of consciousness, and not just language competence, then the simple reduction of consciousness to perception and perception to bodily sensation propounded by Damasio gives us no basis whatever for understanding the basic problem. If neuropsychology is to make a contribution to philosophical discourse about consciousness, then we need to find another way to do it.

To the present authors, it seems clear that microgenetic theory, based on process thinking on the one hand, and acute observation of clinical phenomena on the other, is precisely the path that we should be taking. Consciousness is not simply a particular state of the mind/brain, something predicated of the brain as one of many possible attributes. It is, rather, the mental process by which the self creates itself. As perception and action percolate upwards through the nervous system, through the evolutionary planes of brain growth, consciousness emerges in three primary stages:

1. In the midbrain core, perception and action are indivisible and fully complementary parts of a single event, and the self functions automatically, purely ecologically, as a part of the

environment. There is no distinction between inner and outer worlds, self and other, so that even the notion of "self" at this stage is an interpretation from the perspective of the observer. There is the natural selfishness of the organism striving to survive at all costs, reacting instinctively to threats and drives, but this is not the same thing as self-consciousness.

2. In the next stage, the limbic self turns inward from the outer environment and creates a dream world of pure feeling. The world consists of the self and the objects that lie within its cocoon. This is an animist world, in which the objects perceived by the self are all "thou," seen as sentient beings endowed with intentionality.

3. In the cortical self, perception and action are constrained by an awareness of the existence of self as subject and a world populated by objects. There is a theory of mind, which enables the self to distinguish between objects that are sentient and those that are not.

Consciousness is usually seen by neurologists as a phenomenon of the cortex. When we sleep, it is precisely the electrical activity of the cortex that is most affected. In dream, the limbic system is in active dialogue with the sensory cortex, but the pons (a brainstem structure), having set the dream process in motion, shuts down the flow of sensation (in dream, after all, we "see" with our eyes shut). This does not mean, however, that this "cortical" consciousness is something entirely separate from or antagonistic to the lower layers of the self. Extensive bilateral damage to the cortex also produces coma, even when the brainstem is untouched. A patient in the final stages of a neurodegenerative disease, such as Alzheimer's disease or the MELAS syndrome (Pachalska and MacQueen 2001), which gradually destroys the cortex, is mostly conscious in the strictly neurological sense, since the central nervous system is in a state of readiness to receive sensory stimuli and react to them, but in any other sense of the word consciousness has been lost. What this means is that the cortex, with its characteristic functions of analysis, discrimination, and articulation, is no longer able to control either perception or action. There are other neurodegenerative diseases in which the pathological process begins at a lower level, such as Parkinson's Disease, and the cortex is largely spared until the disease progresses. Functions deteriorate and there is steady decline, but until the brainstem ceases to function the cortex does its work. Although dementia does sometimes occur with Parkinson's Disease, its symptoms and course are quite different from those of Alzheimer's Disease, since the derailment occurs at a deeper level and does not have much direct effect on consciousness until the disease is far advanced.

Consciousness is not purely a cortical phenomenon, from the microgenetic point of view, but emerges precisely from the process of evolution, passing from an undifferentiated core, through an animist dream world, to a world of self and objects. It is the whole process, not just its endpoint, that constitutes and creates consciousness. This is illustrated by Figure 11.4.

The self arises at a phase in the forming of the object prior to the resolution of clear mental images in sensory cortex, but it is not reducible to an image, even a reflective one. The duration of brain process creates an envelope of time and space; the self gazes at this envelope and feels itself present in the moment, which is the essence of consciousness. The overlapping of these moments and the continuing presence of the conscious self over the flow of time creates identity, which in this way can be approached as a neuropsychological problem. Consciousness, in the microgenetic concept, is not a sort of homunculus sitting upon the rumbling volcano of the id and praying that it will not erupt, as in the Freudian psyche, but rather the product of the self pushing its way up through the evolutionary planes and perceiving itself in action.

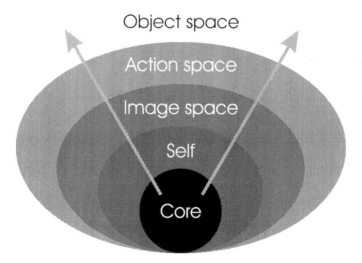

Fig. 11.4. Levels in the mental state. Self, image, and objects are stages in the unfolding between an intrapersonal core and the representation of extrapersonal space.

Conclusion

The preceding reflections could easily constitute the first chapter in an entire book, which would be devoted in full to illustrating how microgenetic theory, rooted in process thought, is supported by the observable symptoms of brain damage. What often happens in clinical practice is that the bewildering array of symptoms conceals the regularities and patterns that underlie them (Pachalska 1999). Most clinicians will immediately recognize the symptoms we have already discussed here, in terms of motor dysfunction and language disturbances, and could easily add a host of additional categories and sub-categories. Our purpose here, however, was to present an overview of this difficult and complex subject matter for readers who presumably know quite a lot about the philosophy of mind and perhaps rather little about neuro-anatomy and the various pathomechanisms of organic brain damage. It is easy to hide behind professional jargon and expertise, so as not to be forced into the uncomfortable position of revealing the limits of what one actually knows. Our purpose here was to venture into this dangerous territory, fully aware of the perils, and also of the enormous potential.

Of course the clinical applications are only one aspect of the creative potential of microgenetic theory. Indeed, the elegance of the theory consists in the way in which it can be extended into a number of different fields of endeavor, providing a kind of "unified field theory" for the explanation of often rather diverse phenomena (MacQueen 2003). High time, then, for neuropsychology and neurolinguistics to resume the interdisciplinary discourse they were founded to conduct.

Acknowledgments

The authors would like to thank Dr. Jason W. Brown for his invaluable comments and suggestions on the successive drafts of this paper, which he was kind enough to review. A particular debt of gratitude is owed to Dr. David Bradford, whose careful and incisive reading of an early version of this chapter helped the authors clarify a number of difficult points and avoid some serious errors.

References

Andrewes, D. 2001. *Neuropsychology: From Theory to Practice*. Hove and New York: Psychology Press.
Bradford, D.T. 1992. *Interpretive Reasoning and the Halstead-Reitan Tests*. North Tonawanda, NY: Multi-Health Systems.
Brown, J. 1988. *Life of the Mind*. Hillsdale, NJ: Lawrence Erlbaum.

Brown, J. 1991. *Self and Process.* New York: Springer-Verlag.

Brown, J. 1996. *Time, Will and Mental Process.* New York: Plenum.

Brown, J. 2000. *Mind and Nature. Essays on Time and Subjectivity.* London: Whurr Publishers.

Brown, J. 2004. "A Microgenetic Approach to Time and Memory in Neuropsychology." *Acta Neuropsychologica* 2 (1): 1–12.

Brown, J., and M. Pachalska. 2003. "The Nature of the Symptom and Its Relevance for Neuropsychology." *Acta Neuropsychologica* 1 (1): 1–11.

Cappa, S.F. 1998. "Spontaneous Recovery in Aphasia." In *Handbook of Neurolinguistics*, B. Stemmer and H.A. Whitaker, eds., 536–544. San Diego: Academic Press.

Damasio, A. 1999. *Blad Kartezjusza. Emocje, rozum i ludzki mozg.* Trans. M. Karpinski. Poznan, Poland: Rebis (trans. of *Descartes' Error. Emotion, Reason, and the Human Brain.* New York: Putnam, 1994).

Damasio, A. 2003. *Looking for Spinoza: Joy, Sorrow, and the Feeling Brain.* New York: Harcourt.

Germine, M. 2004. "Why Time Moves Forward." In *Mind and Time: The Dynamics of Thought, Reality and Consciousness*, A. Combs, M. Germine, and B. Goertzel, eds., 227–233. Creskill, NJ: Hampton Press.

Hanlon, R.E., ed. 1991. *Cognitive Microgenesis. A Neuropsychological Perspective.* New York: Springer-Verlag.

Hume, D. 1909–1914. *An Enquiry Concerning Human Understanding.* Part VII: On Liberty and Necessity. Harvard Classics. Cambridge, MA: Harvard University Press.

Jackendoff, R. 2000. "Fodorian Modularity and Representational Modularity." In *Language and the Brain: Representation and Processing*, Y. Grodzinsky, L. Shapiro, and D. Swinney, eds. San Diego: Academic Press.

James, William. 1890. *Principles of Psychology.* New York: Holt.

Johnson, M. 1987. *The Body in the Mind: The Bodily Basis of Meaning, Imagination and Reason.* Chicago: University of Chicago Press.

Jones, Ernst. 1960–1962. *Das Leben und Werk von Sigmund Freud.* In 3 vols. Bern: H. Huber.

Lakoff, G. 1987. *Women, Fire and Dangerous Things.* Chicago: University of Chicago Press.

MacLean, Paul D. 1967. "The Brain in Relation to Empathy and Medical Education." *Journal of Nervous and Mental Disease* 144:374–382.

MacLean, Paul D. 1991. "Neofrontocerebellar Evolution in Regard to Computation and Prediction: Some Fractal Aspects of Microgenesis." In *Cognitive Microgenesis: A Neuropsychological Perspective*, Robert E. Hanlon, ed., 3–31. New York: Springer-Verlag.

MacQueen, B.D. 2002. "Imagining the Brain." *Medical Science Monitor* 7 (4): 564–566.

MacQueen, B.D. 2003. "How a Sentence Unfolds." *Acta Neuropsychologica* 1 (4): 382–406.

McGinn, C. 2003. "Fear Factor." New York Times Book Review, 23 February 2003, 11.

McTaggart, J. 1934/1968. *Philosophical Studies.* New York: Books for Libraries.

Pachalska, M. 1999. *Afazjologia*. Cracow and Warsaw: PWN [in Polish with English summary].

Pachalska, M. 2002. "The Microgenetic Revolution. Reflections on a Recent Essay by Jason Brown." *Neuropsychoanalysis* 4 (1–2): 108–116.

Pachalska, M. 2003. "Neuropsychological Rehabilitation for Post-traumatic Frontal Syndrome in Patients Recovering from Prolonged Coma: A preliminary Report." *Acta Neuropsychologica* 1 (2): 164–227.

Pachalska, M., and MacQueen, B.D. 2001. "Episodic Aphasia with Residual Effects in a Patient with Progressive Dementia Resulting from a Mitochondrial Cytopathy (MELAS)." *Aphasiology* 15 (6): 599–615.

Pachalska, M., and MacQueen, B.D. 2002. "The Collapse of the US-THEM Structure in Aphasia: A Neuropsychological and Neurolinguistic Perspective." In *Us and Others*. A. Duszak. ed., 481–503. Amsterdam: John Benjamins.

Papathanasiou, I. 2003. "Nervous System Mechanism of Recovery and Plasticity Following Injury." *Acta Neuropsychologica* 1 (3): 345–354.

Pöppel, E. 1988. "Time Perception." In *Encyclopedia of Neuroscience*, vol. 2. Boston: Birkhauser.

Searle, J. 1999. *Umysl jezyk spoleczenstwo. Filozofia i rzeczywistosc*. Trans. Dominika Ciesla. Warsaw: CiS & W.A.B (trans. of *Mind, Language, and Society: Philosophy in the Real World*. New York: Basic Books, 1998).

Wallesch, C.-W. 2004. "The History of Aphasia: Freud as an Aphasiologist." *Aphasiology* 18 (4): 389–399.

12

From Coma to Consciousness

Recovery and the Process of Differentiation

Avraham Schweiger, Michael Frost, and Ofer Keren

This chapter will focus on an overarching homomorphism among four different processes in nature, spanning very different time scales. Of the four, three are quite familiar, their shared dynamics having already been pointed out in the past (see Brown 2002). They are phylogeny, ontogeny, and microgeny. These processes represent the basic dynamic of life: differentiation at all levels, from the unified to the diversified, but also from the diffuse to the individuated. It is the process whereby simple organisms develop specialized organs; neuronal networks evolve into emergent consciousness; simple motor reflexes transform into rational thought; and moment-to-moment nerve firings dissolve into embodied awareness.

The fourth process, which occupies a midway position along the temporal scale between microgeny and ontogeny, is the process of recovery from coma. Our working hypothesis is that recovery from coma, which unlike the others is a pathological process, is also a process of successive differentiation and specification, from a state of total unresponsiveness, through diffuse, uncoordinated interactions with the surroundings, to a fully conscious state. At the latter point the organism responds to individuated objects (both animate and inanimate) and exhibits goal-directed behavior.

Homomorphism in such a progression from smaller to larger scales is in the spirit of Whitehead's analysis of the two species of process: the microscopic and the macroscopic, the former nested within the latter (PR, pt. 2, ch. 10). Furthermore, Whitehead stated that what he termed "organic process," the formation of an actuality, ". . . repeats in microcosm what the universe is in macrocosm" (PR 215). Our approach here is motivated by this view as it provides a framework for understanding all levels of processual analyses of living matter. In fact, all four processes can be seen as homomorphic in fractal perspective: at different levels of analysis the process is the same, each constituted by the previous level and incorporated at the subsequent one.

The microgenetic approach of Brown (e.g., 2002) will serve here as a dynamic model to anchor the discussion of the four processes, as it emphasizes the continuous renewal, at the level of moment-to-moment realization, of the conscious object/subject, rather than specific stages. Brown's approach, developed in part to explicate clinical phenomena in brain damaged patients, is also very well suited to articulate clinical description of recovery from pathological states.

In the spirit of Brown's microgenesis, we will assume that treating consciousness as a process entails that our phenomenal experience, our subjective ontogeny of awareness and intentionality, and especially our interactions with the aspectual world, are continuously unfolding phenomena. It is the moment-to-moment end product of successive phases of realization leading toward a specific conscious event (the figure) out of amorphous interactions with the surroundings (the background). Thus consciousness is not a static phenomenon but a condition in a constant state of becoming. Every conscious moment is an "event," and conscious flow is the flow of such events.

Viewing consciousness as an emergent property of a process of differentiating unified experience into individuated objects/events is in contrast to much of the current zeitgeist in cognitive science, according to which phenomenological appearances of objects/events represent properties of "reality." The latter view leads to a variety of well-known, persistent, and intractable problems in theories of brain functioning, such as the homunculus and the "binding problem." In contrast, the contents of conscious states in our view are assumed to unfold through developmental stages. It is this process of unfolding as a whole, over several temporal epochs that is of present interest. As this unfolding is not accessible directly to our phenomenological experience, examining its homomorphic manifestations in different time scales may facilitate appreciation for the shared biological basis of the process.

Initially, three perspectives of developing consciousness and their contextual time frames will be considered:

1. The phylogenic perspective, considering consciousness in its evolutionary antecedents. Here we examine the evolutionary course of consciousness development. Within this perspective unfolding/development from unicellular organisms to consciousness are on a very large time frame measured in millions (even billions) of years.

2. The ontogenetic perspective, here considering developmental stages of human cognitive abilities and consciousness from infancy to adulthood. This is a view of temporal development within a time frame on the order of years.

3. The microgenetic perspective, viewing brain functioning, perceptual and conscious processes on a brief time scale (measured in milliseconds).

These perspectives are obviously not mutually exclusive, but rather nested within each other. Thus the phylogenic process includes the ontogenetic processes of the individual organism, and the latter, of course, exhibits microgenetic processes. The time frame is different, but the processes are homomorphic in their dynamics. Attempt is made to unify some empirical findings emerging from these strategies, and we suggest that each perspective reveals consciousness development to be a process of differentiation from the global and diffuse to the individuated object/event. This developmental differentiation can be analyzed into at least three general stages (although it is fundamentally a continuum):

1. Undifferentiated, diffused, and global state.

2. More elaborated object formation through interactions with the environment.

3. Externalized and individuated objects, seemingly "independent" of mind but serving as its content, in concrete surroundings.

The first part of this chapter will focus on this differentiation process as revealed in phylogenic, ontogenetic, and neurological research. Next we consider another phenomenon that should shed light on conscious development: the process of recovery from coma following severe brain damage. This phenomenon is appropriate as it gives us a different time frame from the ones manifested in phylogenic, ontogenetic, or microgenetic processes: not as slow as the ontogenetic, but slower than the very rapid microgenetic processes. In it we see a "natural" manifestation of the successive formation of conscious "becoming," unfolding from an initially nonresponding organism.

For reasons of clarity and consistency, each process will be presented using a specific theoretical model. These expositions are brief, and they are only intended to give a global picture of these approaches and their findings regarding consciousness development. The phylogenic/evolutionary perspective will be represented through the work of Maturana and Varela (1998). The ontogenetic perspective will be presented using Jean Piaget's ontogenetic theory (Piaget and Inhelder 2000), and the microgenetic perspective will be presented through Jason Brown's writings (2002). All three can be thought of as theorizing within the process approach, in the sense that a process is "an actual or possible occurrence that consists of an integrated series of connected development unfolding in programmatic coordination" (Rescher 2000).

The Phylogenic Perspective

Maturana and Varela (1998) suggested that the defining essence of a living being is autopoiesis (self-making and self-defining through interactions with the environment). The organic system interacts with the environment at any specific moment according to its ontogenetic and evolutionary history of "structural coupling" (i.e., the history of the recurrent interactions of the organism with its environment, leading to a structural "congruence" between the autopoietic system and its environment). In that sense, every living being "behaves" and has "knowledge," even before the development of a nervous system. Every autopoietic unit "specifies a realm of perturbations and maintains its organization owing to the changes of state that these perturbations trigger in it" (Maturana and Varela 1998, 142). Perhaps the most significant feature of phylogenic history is the development of a nervous system, as it plays a crucial part in this dance of structural coupling. Briefly, it enlarges the realm of possible behaviors and cognitive abilities, by expanding the repertoire of the environment/organism coupling. But what does "expand" mean and what does that expansion have to do with consciousness development?

When Maturana and Varela examine the behavior of the simplest autopoietic system, such as chemotaxis of a single cell (the movement towards zones of greater concentration of significant substances), they explain this process from the cell's standpoint: chemotaxis is an autopoietic process involving maintenance of a certain internal cellular correlation between a structure capable of admitting certain perturbations (sensory surface) and a structure capable of generating movement (motor surface). Thus both the sensory and motor surfaces are the cell (i.e., their coupling is immediate). The behavior of these cells is relatively limited because there is a rather limited number of perturbations that can affect these cells and to which the organism reacts globally. On the next phylogenic level, they examine multi-cellular autopoietic systems (consisting of aggregates of cells). These systems develop further structural differentiation between the sensory surface and the motor surface. At some point in this phylogenic development, a system of intermediary cells appears that coordinates the coupling of sensory and motor cells: the neurons. The hydra's behavior (feeding, flight, reproduction), for example, is the result of the different ways in which these two surfaces (sensory and motor) are dynamically related via the interneuronal network (i.e., its primitive nervous system). The hydra's behavior is more differentiated and complex than the single cell behavior due to this further differentiation and connectivity between different aggregates of cells. "This is the key mechanism whereby the nervous system expands the realm of interactions of an organism: it couples the sensory and motor surface through a network of neurons whose pattern can be quite varied" (Maturana and Varela 1998, 159). The basic architecture of the nervous system is universal, but the form in which this network is embodied and its connections can vary from one animal species to another.

In Maturana and Varela's view, the nervous system does not operate as a relay system between sensory and motor surfaces; its functioning is such that external perturbations only modulate the constant coming and going of internal balances of sensorimotor correlations. An example might be an image projected on the retina (perturbation), and its effect is "relayed" through neurons to the lateral geniculate nucleus (LGN) and then to the visual cortex. But, for every neuron on the retina projecting to the LGN there are thousands other neurons from other zones of the nervous system projecting to the LGN (including the visual cortex to which the cells of the LGN eventually project), which influence what comes out of the LGN toward the visual cortex. Thus, the nervous system does not enrich the field of behavior by relaying more efficiently the "outside world." Rather, it enriches the field of possible sensorimotor correlations (i.e., the autonomous autopoietic existence). It expands the cognitive abilities in two complementary ways: expending the realm of possible sensorimotor states (behavior) and opening new dimensions of structural coupling by allowing the organism to associate many different internal states with different interactions within its environment. This ongoing structural/functional differentiation implies a system in a continuous structural change (plasticity), but in a different sense in this context than changes due to plasticity as a compensatory reorganization during recovery.

As a next important step after the level of a multicellular organism with a nervous system, consider the continual structural couplings of an organism with other members of its kind (this is a rather large jump, which took millions of evolutionary years to appear). Maturana and Varela (1998) define this as "third order coupling," and this may be regarded as "social behavior." From an evolutionary perspective, this structural coupling is highly important for the continuity of organic lineage, enhancing survival through reproduction and social cooperation. Although a general phenomenon, this structural coupling occurs in different animal groups under a variety of forms, depending upon the structure, size and internal complexity of their nervous system and the unique history of their structural couplings. Reciprocal and constant coordination between members of a social unit is communication, and this communication has both apparently "instinctive" and "learned" components. At the social level, humans exhibit a unique and distinctive behavioral feature: the ability to communicate about their communication and reflexively to make linguistic distinctions *about* their linguistic distinctions. According to Maturana and Varela, humans are able to differentiate and objectify communicative actions and behaviors (i.e., the "World" they bring about with other members of their social groups), and to contemplate these communicative and behavioral distinctions as abstract objects, in the sense that they are distinct from themselves. Humans are able to externalize differentiated objects as entities "independent" from mind and thus show the unique cognitive ability of reflexivity. We might note that biologically, this ability seems related to the highly developed human frontal lobes.

Maturana and Varela thus create a compelling theory about the evolutionary phylogeny of cognition/consciousness: (1) cognition is always self-embodied (later, Varela et al. 1991 would define this as "enacted"). It does not represent the "World" that exists outside, but rather brings forth a "World," depending upon the specific autopoietic structure by virtue of the history of social and environmental structural coupling of the species. Human cognition is likewise dependent on this development and shows the unique feature of reflexivity; (2) cognitive abilities, which are further differentiated, are always an expansion of primitive sensorimotor actions from the basic phylogenic core; (3) the evolution of humanity corresponds to the developmental process suggested earlier regarding developing autopoietic systems, from a single cell to multicellular organisms: consciousness is essentially the development of more specification and differentiation of cognitive abilities out of the primitive sensorimotor couplings. That is, it arises from undifferentiated organic structures and sensorimotor systems, developing toward more differentiated, specialized and semi-independent constellations. Such developed constellations correspond to more specific, varied levels of behavioral abilities and finally to cognitive abilities. In a simple cell with a very global and undifferentiated existence, no separation between sensory and motor surface exists: behavior is global and limited in range (due to the limited set of perturbations that can affect it). Sensory and motor systems differentiate increasingly into seemingly more independently functioning subunits. Thus an intricate environmental sphere is developed, and the organism's world begins to differentiate into more discrete and specific objects. At the most complex phylogenic level, at which consciousness appears, we find humans who possess the ability to fully individuate objects and talk "about" them as separate and discrete entities in the external world, including relating to themselves as "objects."

The Ontogenetic Perspective

The constructivist process seen at the phylogenic level is also evident on the ontogenetic level as described by Jean Piaget. Piaget considers the human organism (following von Bertalanfy) as an open system, which retains its form only through continued flow and exchange with the environment. The particular risk to an open system is that its immediate environment will not supply the necessary elements for its survival, and thus its "openness" is a source of constant threat. According to Piaget (1976), the development of human cognitive abilities is grounded upon this systematic ontogenetic threat. The open system of an organism is in constant struggle with its environment to ensure survival and to close itself (a goal continuously pursued but never achieved), which is done by expanding the realm of interactions with the environment (Inhelder and Chipman 1976).

There is substantial homomorphism between Maturana and Varela's view and Piaget's: both view cognitive abilities as developmental processes that enrich the ways of interacting with the environment. They also agree upon the basic structural autonomy of the human organism, and upon the notion of hierarchical development of cognitive abilities, the higher ones grounded upon sensorimotor functions (the first stage of children's cognitive development according to Piaget). They also concur that cognition is neither preformed nor merely a mechanism for creating a copy of reality in the mind. Rather, it develops within an interactional process, characterized by Piaget as a process of adaptation through assimilation and accommodation (resembling closely the structural coupling of Maturana and Varela). Although ontogenetic development of human cognitive abilities does not necessarily copy its phylogenic development, Piaget's developmental theory (Piaget and Inhelder 2000) entails that both share the process of increased differentiation, specifically with regard to cognitive abilities, to which we now turn.

During Piaget's "sensorimotor" stage (roughly the first two years of life), the human infant exhibits (developmental) progression from reflexive schemata to repetitive actions, to intentional coordination and finally to goal directed behavior. Self-centered behavioral habits develop toward externalized behaviors. The child begins to form habits within its concrete environment. Thus, the child's behavior appears less and less global as it becomes more specific and goal directed, differentiating specific realms of behavior and repeating them as specified units of action. This is quite different from the previous global and undifferentiated reactions. At the end of this stage, the child's behavior or interactions with its environment become more efficient and specific because it can individuate a target, differentiate it from its surrounding, and form the means for its attainment.

Piaget specified various (interconnected) areas of cognitive development at the sensorimotor stage, but here only his studies of causality will be utilized for illustration. Initially, the child's notion of causality is concentrated upon its own behavior regardless of the spatial connection between cause and effect. Later the child begins to develop a sense of causality, which is evident, for example, in searching for the hanging rope holding an object placed above it. Later, the child can recognize the causes over which it has control, and those belonging to different objects; it can "recognize" the fact (constructed out of its experience) that a casual connection between two objects, or their activities, obligates physical and spatial proximity between them. The child begins to exhibit intention toward specific results, without being bound to specific means, and eventually it finds new means through contemplation (insight). This development exhibits the same phases suggested above: at first, the child's behavior and cognitive world are undifferentiated and global. Later, the child begins to form an actual world of objects. But this world is still highly dependent upon the immediate surroundings, including the child's own point of view and actions. Eventually, the child externalizes objects into its world (using "representations"), and treats them as individuated objects, independent of mind (an ability that only develops later in childhood).

Regarding the self, Piaget described the child as showing an egocentric stance toward the universe during the sensorimotor stage (Piaget and Inhelder 2000). There is no difference between internal world and external reality, and there is no sense of self-awareness, as the self has not individuated yet. At the end of this stage the child learns it is one among "others," beginning to differentiate self from objects and to recognize the self as an agent of actions and intentionality. These are the early signs of consciousness, albeit not yet in the adult sense of a fully developed consciousness. The achievement of object permanence, for instance, is one of the signs that the child differentiates its own existence from that of other objects. At the "pre-operational" stage (the second stage of children's cognitive development according to Piaget), Piaget noted the appearance of "representations" through which the child begins to perceive more intricate relationships between its self and objects. The development of language skills brings forth a world that is populated with objects and subjects (with their own view of reality), which the child has to incorporate into its schemes. At the last stage of "formal operation," the child begins to use its representational abilities to form theories and hypotheses about self and world. Here the individuated objects (one of which is the self) and actions achieve such fine level of differentiation that they can be manipulated and projected into the future: they can be separated from their concrete spatial/temporal context, and be combined and recombined *ad infinitum*. This progression from the diffuse to the specific, evident at both the phylogenic and ontogenetic levels, is also expressed at the microgenetic level as described by Brown (e.g., 2002).

The Microgenetic Perspective

Historically, the microgenetic approach to consciousness has its roots in various fields of research, such as the Würzburg research group around the turn of the twentieth century (mainly through introspective methods), Gestalt theory, and the work of some neurologists (such as Arnold Pick and, currently, Jason Brown) and different psychologists/psychiatrists (such as Heinz Werner and Paul Schilder). Very loosely, the term *microgenesis* refers to processes at the micro-temporal level that underlie formations of objects in perception and of thoughts, beginning in diffuse meaning and culminating in discrete objects. This research was aimed at identifying the progression of this unfolding, sketching its stages and the brain mechanisms involved. There is common agreement among microgenetic theorists that conscious content development is unidirectional and that it begins as a diffuse and global state, moving through progressive differentiation until it becomes a distinct configuration in consciousness. It is also agreed that some aspects of "subconscious" operations (such as symbolic operations, imagery) are pre-liminary stages of the formation of conscious content, and that the meaning and affective states associated with conscious contents are formed in this "subconscious" realm before the object becomes conscious (Brown 2002). Also worth noting is that the microgenetic approach (especially Werner's) treats the momentary unfolding of cognition as a retracing of levels, or stages, in evolution and ontogeny.

Microgenesis has been kept "alive" as a central concept in the general theorizing of brain functioning in Brown's writing (cf. Brown 1988, 2002, 2003). In brief, Brown regards symptoms of brain pathology as the exposed stages in the microgenetic progression from diffuse meaning to individuated entities. For instance, a brain-damaged patient may read the word "DOG" but say aloud "CAT." For Brown, this "symptom" does not represent distorted behavior, but rather the derailment of the process prior to its phonological completion. That is, after constructing the seen word's meaning, the symp-tom exposes the process of specification of that meaning into the correctly differentiated item but before its completion due to damage. The result is a response that reveals the formation of meaning (a four-legged domestic animal) without its final differentiation (individuation) into the correct item ("dog"). Many examples exist in the clinical literature describing this kind of derailment, typically outside the patient's awareness. For instance, patients with the so-called "letter-by-letter" dyslexia can demonstrate behaviorally appreciation for the meaning of words exposed briefly for them on a screen (say, by pointing to the right objects corresponding to the flashed words), all the while vehemently denying they have "read" these words.

Thus, Brown described a mental process, such as perceiving an object, as a fountain, always moving from diffuse content towards further specification, with its climax in conscious experience of object concretization. Mental processes do not occur at the conscious level, but the outcome of this unfolding is conscious experience of a "representation," a word, an object or idea. Every conscious moment "relives" the phylogenic and ontogenetic development in a fraction of a second (approximately a 10th of a second) and then decays and overlaps with the next occurrence. This movement gives us the sense of continuity and a sense of time. Brown distinguishes in this development at least four phases (Brown 2002):

1. Pure wakefulness—a state of arousal without focus or intent, a global undifferentiated pre-object awareness without any sense of self, image, and object. It is a state that relates to functioning of the upper brain steam. Note the parallel here to Maturana and Varela's description of organisms prior to appearance of the nervous system.

2. Dream consciousness—the forming object undergoes selection through a system of personal memory and "dream work mentation" to constitute an image space. Dreams and hallucinations are the objects at this mental level; this space is a plastic and changing one that lacks depth. Prior sensory information at the upper brain stem constrains the development of the object but the content of the image tends to represent the personal meaning of the object. The self in this state is passive, charged with affect and shares affect with objects around it (i.e., incomplete detachment of self and objects). This stage is related to functioning of the limbic system and temporal lobe. Note here the parallel to early sensorimotor stages of Piaget.

3. Object awareness—the developing object is refined by distant memory of categories of things and events encountered before; not only meaning but the broader context of life experience enters the process. The sensations derived from the direct contact with the evolving object further sculpt the affective meaning into specific shape, size, texture, and so on. The image becomes more like an object. Space becomes more like object space, and it elaborates the immediate space that is directly encountered; an immediate action space is formed. As images resolve into objects, a sense of self-awareness also begins to form. This stage is related to functioning of the frontal neocortex.

4. Analytic perception and the separation of self and the world—the transition here is from a proximate space of objects in the reach of the senses into a fully developed space of fully externalized and public objects, with detailed features and a seemingly independent life of their own. At this stage the "mind" brings forth a sense of agency that is not embedded in the world: the independent self. This is our everyday conscious experience.

In summary, the microgenetic model is homomorphic both to Piaget's and to Maturana and Varela's models: in the nested stages of its microgenesis, the embodied and constructed nature of mind parallels the priority of sensorimotor action to higher forms of cognitive abilities, as reflected in Piaget's developmental hierarchy, and is tightly bound to the nested hierarchy of nervous system centers, whose evolutionary sequence, as Maturana and Varela stress, sustain a development toward more differentiated cognitive abilities and consciousness. Microgenetic theory of conscious content describes the same developmental dimension of progression from the global and diffuse, to the concrete and to the fully individuated and externalized objects/events. All three perspectives share this formal similarity in progressing from the global and diffuse to the specific and "objectified." They all share a view of consciousness as becoming. Differences between the three perspectives do exist; for example, consciousness appears fairly early in ontogenetic development relative to the latest stages of formal operation in Piaget's theory, but in a different sense than it appears later, fully populated with a social world of ideas.

The Recovery from Coma

Now we turn briefly to recovery from coma, starting with a brief description of the process, and then discussing its characteristics in the context of emerging consciousness.

Coma State can be caused by cardiac arrest, drug overdose, and head trauma (to name the major causes; De Giorgio et al. 1991). People in coma exhibit no awareness; they do not respond in any way to pain, do not have sleep/wake cycles or purposeful movement, may have depressed respiratory functions, and the absence of spontaneous eye opening is considered unique to coma (Wilson et al. 2001). Due to improved medical technology, a patient might progress to a *Vegetative State* (no awareness, no pain response, no purposeful movement, but patients do show sleep/wake cycles and normal respiratory functions), and further to *Minimally Conscious State* (limited self-awareness, some pain response, patients may also show sleep/wake cycles and severely limited movement), which may lead to further recovery or deteriorate to death (Wilson et al. 2001).

In addition to etiology, assessment tools evaluating level of coma (its depth and duration) and levels of cognitive functioning were found to be important in predicting recovery outcome. These scales typically describe a sequence of behaviors and responses appearing through the emergence from coma, and thus provide a recounting of the process. These scales can be viewed as indicators of the hierarchical process underlying consciousness development during recovery, while bearing in mind the limitations: first, since consciousness has the inherent property of "ontogenetic subjectivity" (it is always experienced by an agent and never by an outside observer; Searle

1999), conscious states can only be inferred from behaviors and verbal communications. Thus, inferring conscious states (especially in the initial phases of coma recovery) from these scales based on patients' observed behavior, or from later self-reports, are inherently limited and ambiguous. Second, these assessment tools are not very sensitive to individual variations. They are general, and so the borderline between levels seems fuzzy and even arbitrary at times. Two such assessment scales, frequently utilized by clinicians to evaluate coma state and its recovery, will be considered.

The first scale of interest is the Glasgow Coma Scale (GCS, Teasadale and Jennet 1974). The GCS is a numeric scale ranging from 3 (deepest coma) to 15 (awake and oriented), and is the most common tool used to assess level of coma severity. Three dimensions are assessed, with scores on each dimension added for the global score. To provide a flavor of the unfolding behaviors during emergence from coma, the scoring of stages is as follows (these stages describe the severity of the coma but not the stages of emergence out of it):

> Eye opening—the patient: (1) does not open eyes to pain, (2) does open eyes to pain, (3) does open eyes when asked to in a loud voice, (4) does open eyes on his or her own.
>
> Verbal behavior—the patient: (1) makes no noise, (2) makes sounds that examiner can't understand, (3) talks so examiner can understand him, but makes no sense, (4) seems confused or disoriented, (5) carries on a conversation correctly and tells examiner where he or she is and the year and the month.
>
> Best motor response—the patient: (1) has no motor response to pain, (2) exhibits decerebrate posture, (3) exhibits flexion in response to pain (decorticate posturing), (4) pulls a part of his or her body away on painful stimuli, (5) exhibits purposeful movement in response to painful stimulus, (6) obeys commands for movement.

A lower combined score reflects a more grievous condition. It may be observed that this scale defines a hierarchy of behaviors to evaluate conscious state, the guiding observations being that the more goal oriented a behavior is (within a given domain), the higher the level of consciousness: from the lowest level of no response, through some global response, to only partial response, to a self-initiated specific response to pain and finally to purposeful actions.

The GCS is limited because it does not provide a detailed cognitive picture of recovery. For these reasons, other instruments were developed, such as the Rancho Los Amigos Scale that is frequently used to track improvement and evaluate the patient's cognitive abilities until complete recovery. The scale is divided into eight stages, each with its specific behavioral markers:

The Eight Levels of Cognitive Functioning of the "Rancho Scale"

This list is adapted from Lezak (1995).

1. *No Response*: The patient is in deep coma and completely unresponsive.

2. *Generalized Response*: The patient reacts inconsistently and nonpurposefully to stimuli.

3. *Localized Response*: The patient reacts specifically but inconsistently to stimuli, orienting, withdrawing, or even following simple commands.

4. *Confused–Agitated*: The patient is in a heightened state of activity with severely decreased ability to process information.

5. *Confused–Inappropriate, Nonagitated*: The patient appears alert and is able to respond to simple commands fairly consistently; however, with increased complexity of commands or lack of any external structure, responses are nonpurposeful, random, or at best fragmented in relation to any desired goal.

6. *Confused–Appropriate*: The patient shows goal directed behavior, but is dependent on external input for direction

7. *Automatic–Appropriate*: The patient appears oriented and responds appropriately within hospital and home settings, goes through daily routines automatically, but frequently robot-like, with minimal to no confusion, and has shallow recall of what he or she has been doing.

8. *Purposeful and Appropriate*: The patient is alert and oriented, is able to recall and integrate past and recent events, and is aware of, and responsive to his or her environment.

Like the GCS scale, this scale is based on progressively differentiated abilities, and on a similar progression from diffuse and global behaviors to specific, self-directed ones. It is noteworthy that this scale's recovery stages correspond to the phases of conscious development we suggested and to Brown's microgenetic developmental stages.

From Diffuse to Specific Responses in Recovery

At first, at level two of the Rancho Scale (the first signs of responsiveness), the patient's behavior is totally nonspecific and undifferentiated. The patient exhibits no concrete awareness, and the patient's mental existence is probably one of complete "void" (much like Brown's "Pure Wakefulness," the first microgenetic stage). It is characterized, for example, by the reappearance of primitive reflexes, such as righting movements and rooting reflexes. Then (level three), the patient slowly begins to react specifically to her or his surroundings, suggesting that within her or his own world, he or she begins to differentiate specific features of the environment into meaningful entities. But the responses are still generalized. This meaningful contact then becomes more specific, but still inconsistent, confused and agitated (levels four and five), suggesting that it is not relevant features of the environment that guide behavior but the patient's own inner states in their momentary and immediate contact with this environment. This whole picture is that of the diffused and global state we suggested at the core of conscious development.

Regarding this state of awareness, it seems clear that patients in this state have some form of "consciousness," but that it is diffused, dependent upon their own inner states and emotions, lacking clear aspectual characteristics. The very few postrecovery accounts (i.e., of people having been themselves through the process of recovery) suggest that this interpretation is fairly accurate: they recall knowing and seeing things that were happening around them but they cannot comprehend these events around them. This stage seems as one big nightmarish, blurred existence with words sounding like noise and people around them lacking in depth and specific character. Patients also report feelings of terror and confusion in this state, which is reasonable, considering the chaotic world characterizing their existence: they emerge from comatose state, into a world devoid of context or means of organizing experience, probably enhanced by the helplessness and the constant medical treatment, the latter usually including invasive procedures and pain. There are even some postrecovery complaints from patients claiming that the staff did not treat them well during this state. Some patients report later they would have preferred to receive explanation of what is being done to them and be spoken to even if the staff thought they did not "understand" (Wilson et al. 2001). This conscious state is not entirely meaningless, and consequently they may require help in forming more concrete "meaning" in this traumatic situation. This stage corresponds to the second stage of Brown's microgenetic conscious development, the "Dream Consciousness" stage, in which the patient's own set of personal meanings and emotional state define much of the patient's interactions with the surroundings.

At the next stage (level six), the patient begins to form some goal directed behavior and is able to understand and communicate to a certain degree of complexity. But these behaviors are still bound within the actual surroundings, needing constant external input to structure them. This stage corresponds to that of creating a concrete action world containing objects that have their own existence regardless of the patient's perceptions. Here the patient is more capable of differentiating certain features of his or her world. But the main point is that this world is very much the patient's own immediate "action sphere," and it requires constant structured and concrete physical contact with the environment in order to function properly. This corresponds to the second stage suggested in consciousness development (Piaget's pre-operational stage of more elaborated object formation heavily dependent upon the concrete surrounding); it also corresponds to Brown's third stage of "object awareness" (see Table 1 below).

At last, the patient is able to expand this immediate sphere of action and thought. The progress witnessed is the increased ability to "represent" the world symbolically (at first very literally, during which the patient might seem like a robot following rules—this being level seven), and later (level eight) the patient is able to manipulate this world mentally without the same rigidity. This can be thought of as exemplifying Brown's fourth stage. The final developmental stage of object and world externalization is complete.

Specific clinical predictions follow from this view of recovery. For example, restoration will exhibit certain sequential patterns and not others, in accordance with their phylogenic and ontogenetic order of acquisition. Or the unfolding of recovery may indicate interventional approaches that capitalize on the diffuse character of preconscious stage. Such predictions and others remain to be investigated. Conceptually, the recovery process as presented here, together with the other three perspectives, suggest that consciousness as a property of brain functioning emerges at a point where neuronal tissue achieves sufficient inner complexity (both in structure and function) as to allow construction of unlimited distinctions, categories, relations and actions, including a reflexive self. The homomorphism of the four processes discussed above points to an underlying unitary dynamics driving development in all organic systems: from simple wholes, towards progressively greater individuation into complex, coordinated parts.

Summary

The comparison of all four temporal scales of development indicates that coma recovery follows the general outline of conscious development: progressing from initial "void," through gradually differentiated responses to more and more detailed features of the environment, culminating in a sense of self independent of others and capable of forming goals and carrying them out. Table 1 summarizes the overall homomorphism.

In all three "normal" processes, consciousness arises at some point where sufficient individuation of objects and actions (including individuation of the self) is achieved, and these are projected into an external world "out there." It appears when organisms exhibit sufficiently complex nervous systems with trillions of inter-connections/correlations, thus allowing "checks and balances" (phylogeny), and supporting reflexive abstraction of referents independent of the environment (ontogeny). These large scale processes occur also on a moment-to-moment basis, as waves of brain activities retrace remote and immediate past activities, constrained by sensorimotor interactions with the environment, and emerge from diffuse meaning into individuated world and consciousness (Brown's microgeny). Thus, not only ontogeny recapitulates phylogeny, and microgeny repeats both, but following severe brain damage,

Table 12.1. The Homomorphism of the Four Processual Spheres*

Microgeny	Ontogeny	Phylogeny	Recovery from Coma
Pure Wakefulness	Early Sensorimotor Stage: Primitive Reflexes	Mono-cellular Organisms	Rancho Scale 2: Generalized Responses
Dream Consciousness	Later Sensorimotor Stage: Causality Appears, Purposeful Movements	Animals with Specialized Sense Organs and Nervous Systems Appear	Rancho Scale 3–5: Localized, but Confused Responses
Object Awareness	Pre-operational Stage: Concrete-bound Operations, Reasoning	Primates: Primitive Cognition, Tool Use, Social Behavior	Rancho Scale 6–7: Dependence on Structure, Some Mechanical Purposeful Behavior
Analytic Perception and the Separation of Self and World	Formal Operations, Logico-mathematical Thinking	Embodied Consciousness, Self-reflection, Language and Culture	Rancho Scale 8: Fully Conscious Behavior, Appropriate and Purposeful

*Consciousness appears gradually across the stages, not necessarily at the same rate in each processual sphere.

recovery can also be seen to recapitulate in its form, albeit on a different time scale, all three. And as this process flows onward at all levels, one is reminded of Whitehead's apt description: "an organism . . . is an incompletion in process of production."

References

Brown, J.W. 1988. *Life of the Mind: Selected Papers.* Hillsdale, NJ: Lawrence Erlbaum.

Brown, J.W. 2002. *The Self-Embodying Mind.* Barrytown: Station Hill Press.

Brown, J.W. 2003. "What Is An Object?" *Acta Neuropsychologica* (3): 239–259.

De Giorgio, Christopher M., and Mark F. Lew. 1991. "Consciousness, Coma, and the Vegetative State: Physical Basis and Definitional Character." *Issues in Law and Medicine* 6 (4).

Inhelder, B., and H.H. Chipman, eds. 1976. *Piaget and His School: A Reader in Developmental Psychology.* New York: Springer-Verlag.

Lezak, M.D. 1995. *Neuropsychological Assessment.* 3rd ed. New York/Oxford: Oxford University Press.

Maturana, M., and F. Varella. 1998. *The Tree of Knowledge.* Boston: Shambhala Publications.

Piaget, J. 1976. "Biology and Cognition." In Inhelder and Chipman 1976.

Piaget, J., and B. Inhelder. 2000. *The Psychology of the Child.* New York: Basic Books.

Pinker, S. 1999. *Words and Rules.* New York: Basic Books.

Rescher, N. 2000. *Process Philosophy.* Pittsburgh: University of Pittsburgh Press.

Searle J. 1999. *Mind, Language and Society.* London: Weidefeld and Nicolson.

Teasadale G., and B. Jennet. 1974. "Assessment of Coma and Impaired Consciousness: A Practical Scale." *Lancet* 2:81–84.

Varela, F.J., E. Thompson, and E. Rosch. 1991. *The Embodied Mind.* Cambridge, MA: MIT Press.

Whitehead, A.N. 1978. *Process and Reality.* Corrected edition by D.R. Griffin and D.W. Sherburne. New York: The Free Press.

Wilson, B.A., F. Gracey, and K. Bainbridge. 2001. "Case Study—Cognitive Recovery from Persistent Vegetative State: Psychological and Personal Perspectives." *Brain Injury* 15 (12): 1803–1092.

13

Consciousness and Rationality
from a Process Perspective

Michel Weber

The nature of consciousness is highly debated these days; and, interestingly enough, a definition of this very complex and diffuse phenomenon is rarely attempted. In most cases, psychological studies focus on a particular contextual aspect, and a vague description is followed by a speedy operational definition—the mindset being: let us deal with measurements only. For its part, the nature of rationality itself is intrinsically tricky, all the more so since it is to reason that the question is posed.

It is not difficult to identify the few broad, remnant presuppositions haunting consciousness studies: since consciousness is necessarily coextensive with rationality, it pertains to human beings only ("species solipsism"[1]); more precisely, it cannot be predicated of new born babies and the like. Not too long ago, some would have even claimed that it is primarily a man's characteristic. In other, more inclusive, words, there is only one such "function" called consciousness: it is a *human rational* phenomenon. Although a certain conceptual carefulness is noticeable since James' publication of "Does 'Consciousness' Exist?" in 1904, philosophers have obviously never gone far from Aristotle's definition of human beings as "rational animals" [*zōion logon echon*], unless it is to embrace his alternative definition in terms of "political animals" [*zōion politikon*]. (See mainly Aristotle's *Politics* and *Nicomachean Ethics*.) This is so much the case that the forthcoming analysis can be said to evince the intricate interplay between the rational pole of consciousness, traditionally self-centered, and the political pole, traditionally others-centered.

We speak of "intricacies of interplay" because "consciousness" stands for a function; it is a peculiar "scene effect"[2] allowing the following working hypothesis: consciousness is an activity of unification directed toward various ends,[3] the main one being still, for most of us who are locked in the *vita activa*, survival in a more threatening than peaceful environment. It is a dynamic coordination, a capacity of multiplying oneself in space and time without dividing oneself.[4] Far from being a substantial metamental loop, consciousness primarily means eventful con-sciousness, manifold entanglement, togetherness of elements that can be heuristically pooled in two sets: private and public. Consciousness is so to speak Janus-like, facing two directions: first-personness and third-personness, unity and plurality, privacy and publicity.

This paper intends to give a philosophical analysis of the concepts of consciousness and rationality, and particularly to display the correlation existing between what is usually called the "normal state of consciousness" and what should be called the "normal state of rationality." Eventually, it draws consequences for the correlation between "altered/aberrant states of consciousness" and "altered/aberrant rationality."[5] Although it argues from a broad phenomenological perspective, its grounding technicalities belong to the field of *process thought*, as fleshed out by the later Alfred North Whitehead (1861–1947). Furthermore, the path we have chosen to exploit is intermediate between the carving out of the (more or less) elastic definitions advocated by many[6] and the giving of the (more or less) articulated descriptions lauded by others—"descriptionism," taken here as a subcategory of phenomenological nominalism. (See, of course Husserl or, more recently, Strawson 1959.) Since we start from a set of undemonstrated (and maybe indemonstrable), allegedly self-evident, propositions, we will speak of axioms, in the loose sense of the term. The key criterion will be axiomatic coherence, as Whitehead himself would have claimed.[7]

The cornerstone of the paper is the following: in order to do justice to the numerous semantic layers embedded in the notion of normal consciousness (or *consciousness-zero*, as we have called it elsewhere), one needs to define an Archimedean point (a point of leverage outside of normal consciousness) whose access is, by definition, forbidden by substantialism. The substantialistic account of consciousness can indeed be boiled down to a triad (see below): (1) consciousness is a well-defined entity (principle of identity); (2) one cannot be at the same time conscious and unconscious (non-contradiction); and (3) one has to be either conscious or unconscious (excluded middle). With the help of a multilayered processual—genetic—perspective, it becomes feasible to show how normal consciousness is a construct in the double sense that (1) it is processed by developmental structures in ontogeny, evolution, and socialization, and (2) it is a concept carved out, precisely, by the rationality at work in the normal state. In other words, the reader should keep in mind the idea of a spectrum of consciousness unfolding within normal consciousness (actualizing it) *and* without normal consciousness (from the perspective of the continuum in which it is inscribed). The spectrum is compatible with clinical tools like the *Glasgow Coma Scale*, but the question of its quantification is not analyzed here.

It occurred very early to the author of this chapter that the study of consciousness must begin with the careful use of introspection, that is, with the linguistically articulated consciousness of the adult socialized human being (who in this case happens to be a white male living in continental Europe). Symmetrical patterns have been used to help build the argument in the following way: first, all the main characteristics of normal consciousness have been identified; second, their overlappings have been named; and, third, one possible set of nested characteristics has been selected from the perspective of a sharp articulation of the public/private axis. By doing so, we basically followed a heuristic hunch that played out well. This paper bypasses the organic causes of consciousness-alteration or dementia insofar as they are likely to be independent of the will of the patient and of the actors constituting his or her social sphere (Parkinson's disease, Alzheimer's disease, Down's syndrome, etc.).

The paper proceeds in three main stages. First, it sketches the various semantic layers embedded in the concept of everyday (or "normal") consciousness and contextualizes their interanimation, thereby activating a "nuclear pivotal model of normal consciousness." Second, focusing on the strict correlation between "normal" consciousness and "normal" rationality, it proposes an analysis of "normal" and "abnormal" rationalities. Third, it investigates the necessity of using an "abnormal rationality" for the clinical treatment of "altered/aberrant states of consciousness." A brief conclusion suggests some ways of opening our argument toward further researches.[8]

The Nuclear Pivotal Model of Normal Consciousness

For the sake of clarity, unless specified otherwise, the term of "consciousness" itself is used in these lines only in the sense of "normal consciousness," in other words, of the everyday alchemy between the respective layers of private and public awareness: it is a particular existential rhythm made of shared interactive levels between "always already" social individuals. Operating at the intersection of the individual matrix and the social one, consciousness is the key feature of our being in the world, of our public privacy. The paper's basic instrumental abstraction is thus the differentiation of private and public spheres; and it is part of its endeavor to point to the vices and virtues of such a polarization. Evolving within that working hypothesis, we will first singularize one individual and: (1) hierarchize private and public abstractions; (2) state the interactive overlappings between these abstractions; (3) draw conclusions opening the argument to a society of individuals. (The analytical skeleton of the pivotal model is to be found in Figure 13.1.)

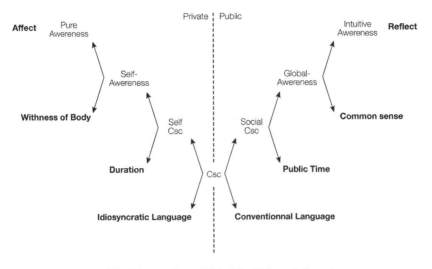

Fig. 13.1. The Nuclear Pivotal Model of Normal Consciousness.

Pivotal Model

Axioms

PRIVATE

Private realms are traditionally the domain of philosophy, especially since Descartes chose to lock himself in his stove ("*poële*," i.e., heated study) to look for a reliable foundation of his world. This allusion to the French philosopher is not gratuitous, since we will proceed from clear and distinct characteristics to vague and indistinct ones. From the private standpoint, consciousness is essentially a "self-consciousness" lived through a "linguistic stream." The notion of "self-consciousness" will be fleshed out in a moment; for the time being, let us agree that it covers the idea of a prelinguistic embodied identity, with its urges, needs, and spatio-temporal contingencies.

Idiosyncratic Language. We live, without a doubt, under the law of language. Even a superficial introspection teaches us that consciousness is conceptual in character: we experience consciousness as a linguistic flux, that is, as an endless chat evolving from a free association of ideas (truly stochastic or not) to the tight weaving of an argument (conceptual linearization respectful of rules debated in the next section). At one end of the linguistic spectrum we have poetic texts and mantic utterings, at the other, the univocity of syllogistic constructs.

The question of idiosyncratic language (or speech in Saussure) can receive some clarification from a study of the notion of "style." Each individual has her own way of appropriating the constraints of her mother tongue: choice of the words used (possibly the framing of neologisms), grammatical preferences, play with the Russellian-Batesonian "logical types" . . . In other words, a personal style depicts holistically the way an individual makes use of language to express herself. The necessities of a constant hermeneutical struggle with authors like James and Whitehead have led us in the direction of an analysis of style with the help of two subordinated notions: the global semantic level that is style overlaps the conceptual and propositional levels; at the conceptual level, the key is polysemiality, at the propositional, it is interanimation.[9]

Having said this, to define the essence of normal consciousness as verbal does not mean that it is possible to encapsulate all forms of consciousness verbally: it is perfectly possible to have somebody being self-conscious (and thus conceptualizing) without being able to use language (i.e., verbalizing). Self-consciousness of pain is furthermore possible without the concept of "pain." In the "boxed-in (or locked-in) syndrome," experienced in rare cases during surgery, a state of full awareness deprived of the ability to do anything or to communicate anything is endured (!) by the patient. Moreover, everybody experiences, now and then, states of arousal—or even thoughts—that cannot be clearly expressed. In some cases, this is just a transient state, like a delay in the access to the linguistic register; in other cases, it is a definitive incapacity: some experiences are simply not susceptible to being verbalized. They are at the edge of normal consciousness. It is definitely not by accident that Husserl developed a shorthand to be able to put on paper thoughts at the same speed with which they occurred to him. Whitehead is very clear in that regard:

> Language is not the essence of thought. But this conclusion must be carefully limited. Apart from language, the retention of thought, the easy recall of thought, the interweaving of thought into higher complexity, the communication of thought, are all gravely limited. Human civilization is an outgrowth of language, and language is the product of advancing civilization. Freedom of thought is made possible by language: we are thereby released from complete bondage to the immediacies of mood and circumstance. It is no accident that the Athenians from whom we derive our Western notions of freedom enjoyed the use of a language supreme for its delicate variety.[10]

And indeed, as our figure intends to show, consciousness' private core, self-consciousness, is preconceptual.[11]

Duration. Now, if we dig further and analyze what is meant by "self-consciousness," we have to carve out further abstractions, leading us, quite paradoxically, to sink into vagueness. We have indeed argued for prelinguistic thoughts, and, although this claim has no dogmatic pretensions, its consequences are paradoxical in the sense that abstractions, usually associated with very sharp notions, are here associated with plastic phenomena. Bergson himself expressly asked for a reformed, authentic, dynamic rationalism, a *rationalism of the fluid concept* that will encounter the richness and the qualitativeness of the stream of experience.[12]

Self-consciousness is made of "self-awareness" and durational awareness. The embodied mood that is "self-awareness" will need one further abstractive step; but first let us contemplate the temporal dimension that has just been extracted. Evolving in a Plotinian-Augustinian tradition (see the *Confessions' "distentio animi"*), Bergson's investigation of the "immediate data of consciousness" leads to his insistence on their heterogeneous continuity, in one word, to his concept of duration. The famous meditation on the concept of number gives the second chapter of the *Essai* (Bergson 1889; English translation 1910) the opportunity to contrast the two fundamental types of multiplicity disclosed by experience: the multiplicity of the purely affective states of mind ("*états purement affectifs de l'âme*"), and the multiplicity of the material objects localized in space. The former is solidarity, fusion, mutual penetration of heterogeneous moments; the latter is a bare *partes extra partes* juxtaposition of homogeneous moments. In duration, there is an organic continuity modulated by qualitative fluctuations. The subject experiences herself as shot through and through by a double internal tension: on the one hand, there is retention (or memory) anchoring subjectivity in past events; on the other, there is protention (or intention) luring each durational slab toward its successors. In conclusion, everyday consciousness does not house a pure present: the conscious subject lives in a past stretched toward a probable/willed future. Whitehead's analysis of conscious perception in terms of *symbolic reference* and later his genetic analysis of the process of concrescence arrive at the exact same conclusions:

> No actual entity can be conscious of its own satisfaction; for such knowledge would be a component in the process, and would thereby alter the satisfaction. In respect to the entity in question the satisfaction can only be considered as a creative determination, by which the objectifications of the entity beyond itself are settled. (PR 85)

Withness of the Body. Retention and protention—that, according to Whitehead, correspond to the old efficient and final causes—install a very basic dialectic animating all sentient beings. But even more basic is their lived embodiment. Before reaching the core of private consciousness—affect—the "withness of the body" has to be spelled out; and that crucial Whiteheadian concept can be approximated through a perusal of the classical concept of coenaesthesia. How is it that the body can say "I" alone?[13] Sherrington (who invented the concept of "proprioception") identifies three complementary sets of sensory receptors (Sherrington 1906 and Sherrington 1940).

Exteroception is constituted by the five senses open to the external world: sight, hearing, smell, taste, and touch (including the various modes of cutaneous sensitivity). They constitute what is commonly called "sense perception" and deliver a rather clear-cut picture of our surroundings. Now, thinkers like Bergson and Whitehead insist on the contingency of that perspective, that it is as precise as it is superficial: from a broad evolution-ist viewpoint, it is but the triumph of one possible type of specialization, and of dualistic thought. Interoception denominates the internal sensitivity complementing the exteroceptive one. Most of the time, its messages, coming from receptors housed by all organs and tissues, do not "reach" consciousness: they are, through reflex action, the source of a harmonious bodily life. One can distinguish internal pains (cephalalgia, colic . . .), internal taste (chemical sensitivity ruling various reflex activities), and internal touch (sensitivity to variations of pressure, like distension of the bladder or the rectum, stomach contractions, antiperistaltic contractions of the esophagus, determining the nausea feeling). So, for instance, the entire intestinal motility is nervously coordinated by the unconscious messages of receptors sensitive to distension.[14] Proprioception denominates the messages of position and movement allowing, with the help of the internal ear's semi-circular canals, a spatialization—and thereby a full (ap)propriation—of the body. Proprioceptive perception issues from sensorial receptors[15] delivering data about the position and the rela-tive movements of the different parts of our body. Through reflex action, it regulates the muscular tone and helps us to localize ourselves in space and to create a sense of depth (stereognosy). Proprioception also includes the muscular sensitivity that complements exteroceptive touch in offering estimates of the weight and volume of the prehended or moved object. The structuration of our proprioceptive field provides for the fundamental organic anchorage of our identity. Thanks to that capacity of experiencing "my body" as being "me," I am plunged into the world. A proprioceptive loss blinds the "eyes of the body" (Sacks 1985, 47), thereby depriving the patient of his physical identity and jeopardizing his being-in-the-world.
Now, since that organic anchorage is actually the product of the *synergy* of these different perceptive modes, the concept of coenaesthesia (or synesthe-sia) is the most appropriate to suggest the essence of the withness of the body, which Bradley called the "felt surplus in our undistinguished core."[16]

All feelings go hand in hand—which does not mean that their respective data blend together: we are not concerned here with the involuntary experience of a cross-modal association (see Cytowic 1989). For Whitehead and Merleau-Ponty, there is a mutual immanence of the body and the world, a co-belonging or chiasmus between the flesh of the body and the flesh of the world. The body is the locus of an exploratory strategy; it is the field of localization of experience (Merleau-Ponty 1968, 113–115). More precisely, the withness of the body is a bipolar reality: on the one hand, it denominates the fact that the body is the starting point for our knowledge of the circumambient world, that it is "through" it that we prehend everything;[17] on the other hand, the most primitive perception we have is the one of our bodily functionings: if all our sensory windows were occluded, we would only be a pure embodiment. Here again the Greek language is revelatory: *synaisthēsis* means common feeling, sympathy, and consciousness.

Affect. We have spoken of an embodied *mood* to qualify "self-awareness"; if one last bracketing is made (the speculative bracketing of the body—that could actually be equated with its complete cosmic correlation), we are left with the very experiential core of self-consciousness: "pure" awareness, which is affectivity.[18] In so doing, we follow Whitehead and, to some extent, Michel Henry, but also—and this is remarkable—what psychotherapists have learned from the use of clinical hypnosis. According to the former, enjoyment is at the very heart of actuality; it is its quintessential mystery. For his part, Henry speaks of *"pâtir"* and *"passion,"* terms broader than sufferance, but linked with it. On the other hand, Chertok spoke of hypnosis as a *purely affective relation* whose discovery occasioned a fourth narcissistic wound in the European mind.

The cognitive role of emotion—however crucial[19]—matters less here than its bare pristine character. "The basis of experience is emotional" (AI 176): in the immediate experience a proximity indicates itself. It is a proximity that is first and foremost affectivity, the reaching of a pure emotional intensity: "The organic philosophy interprets experience as meaning the self enjoyment of being one among many, and of being one arising out of the composition of many" (PR 145.) One will rediscover later the opening of that intrinsically private concept to the public sphere. For the time being, let us underline that by no means are we arguing here that emotions are independent of embodiment.

PUBLIC

Let us now attempt a symmetrical journey into the public realm. From the public standpoint, consciousness is first and foremost a "social consciousness" shot through and through by a conventional—rationalized—language. The introductory statement to our "private" section alluded to Cartesian modes of thought; it is furthermore remarkable that his foundational project eventually relied totally upon the benevolent existence of an *Other*. In the same way the notion of "self-consciousness" covers the idea of a prelinguistic embodied identity, the notion of "social consciousness" covers the idea of a prelinguistic social identity. The feeling of belonging to a certain social body (among other things, the unconscious knowledge—or symbolic violence[20]—of the "pecking order"), is sustained by a certain language, whose appropriate manipulation is crucial.

Conventional Language. "Language is a social art" (Quine 1960, ix); it is nothing other than the *key* to common life (remember the Agora). The idiosyncratic language evoked earlier is a personalization of the common language, that is, of the language that enables one individual to communicate efficiently with another (set of) individual(s).

The public use of language is traditionally the domain of Rhetoric; notwithstanding, the present speculation needs a broader generalization of our discussion of idiosyncratic language. With Hagège, one could define language in the following way: a language is an organic system of signs investing the phonic substance with the intention to signify—and especially to communicate these significations—by drawing the outlines of sets through the opacity of events.[21] A word belonging to a natural language, or a philosophical concept stratified in a categoreal scheme, does not reproduce the concrete eventful-ness, but classifies it by naming some of its recognizable features. It is thus more cautious to speak of "filtering through classification" rather than mere "cutting out." Language reinvents the world; it does not picture it. Since it is particularly at this point of our diagram that the structural influence of rationality is made obvious, and since this question will be the object of our next section, we postpone its further development.

Public Time. If we dig further again and analyze what is meant by "social consciousness," we have to differentiate "global awareness" and temporal awareness. Global awareness is an *atmospheric mood* that will be later defined by "intuitive awareness" and "common sense."

The concept of public time that is used here is a "soft" one: it does not correspond to the "hard" concept of physical time, operationalized in the sciences, or even to the concept of natural time, metaphysical in its essence. It refers (1) to the *commonly lived time*, which Hall's studies of the pecu-liarities of socially acceptable temporality have so much clarified (see, e.g., Hall 1959, 1966, 1984); (2) to historicity, which embodies the way a given society profiles itself in its own historical adventure; (3) to the *eschatological horizon*, which manifests a properly religious anchorage by speculating on the possibility of an individual and/or collective postmortem career or even a prenatal one (see Pomian 1984).

Common Sense. The global awareness—or atmospheric mood—that constitutes, with public time, social consciousness, is susceptible to a bipolar analysis distinguishing "common sense" and "reflect" (reflect denominates here the public experiential core corresponding to affect).

Testis unus, testis nullus. "Atmospheric" refers to the *feeling of feelings* in a shared world and culture, that is, to the senses in common in the social cosmos. For the sake of our specular analysis, which postulates that the structure of public consciousness mirrors that of private consciousness, it is to the old concept of *sensus communis* that we have to appeal. Of its threefold meaning—concerted functioning of the five senses (more precisely, coenaesthesia), sharing with others of the world *qua* context, sharing with other living creatures of the world as environment[22]—, the second one is particularly relevant here (the third will resonate with our genetic discussion of consciousness). It is through a constant interchange of data about the appearances that an individual can be confident in her own perception. They are "real" because they reach the common world. Only the fitting of the objects in an identity-giving context creates the feeling of reality. The coenaesthesia approximating the withness of the body is not enough for existing meaningfully in the world: without confirmation and reinforcement of percepts, chaos still reigns. The withness of the social body is required; departing from it can lead straight to insanity. (There is one painful additional question that should be examined here: how far could the delusion of one individual validate the delusion of another?)

A later section will raise the question of the genesis of that contextual evidence. For the time being, we have to point to two essential phenomenological concepts: Husserl's *Lebenswelt* (Husserl 1954)—that will be approached below by the concept of *Urdoxa*—and Heidegger's *Umwelt* (Heidegger 1927, §§ 15–18). We belong to the world and necessarily live in the firm belief of that vital binding: "To be born is both to be born of the world and to be born into the world."[23] What makes sense is the intentional unity contextualizing human beings' percepts, concepts and affects. Now, it is remarkable that there is a cultural valuation of senses. Let us take two examples. On the one hand, the association of sight with Greek culture and of hearing with Hebrews is now well known, since the conflict of these two ground metaphors are at the basis of European (Christian) civilization. The metaphor of vision is central to Greek culture and consequently exercised a heavy influence on the emergent philosophical science. Jonas has shown very straightforwardly the inevitable bias of their concepts, mainly in terms of the neutralization of time and causation. To say it in another way: the metaphor of vision imposes the idea of the *spectator-subject*, that is, of a totally passive onlooker factually unaffected by the scenery (Jonas 1966). It is that ideal of a pure objective knowledge that has opened the doors to a technoscience that manipulates things and renounces living in them.[24] The Hebrews, for their part, emphasized hearing and interiority. The blurred, cryptic, dialogue that occurs between human beings and god weaves bonds of proximity that transform the story of certain communities into holy history (see Boman 1954). To the Greek static and dualistic propensity (taken over by Plotinus and Augustine, and culminating in Descartes) answers the dynamic and globalized anthropo-theology of the Hebrews. A human being is a fleshed breath, a breathed flesh, an undivided and fluctuating globality.[25]

On the other hand, communication in the social body happens at various complementary levels, not the least of which is the gestural or "kinesic" one. Among the conventions defining the public sphere, there are of course all the explicit and implicit signs of recognition and gratefulness conveyed by the various social rules, including the rules of politeness. Less obvious are the different forms of territorialism and the sort of tactile (palpable) sense of space and time required by social life. Even less obvious are the kinesics that rule meta-communication. Bateson has asked, "Why do Frenchmen wave their arms about?" (Bateson 1972, 9–13) and the answer is not that simple to spell out. Although the old Greek dichotomy claiming that only language expresses thought while body expresses merely emotions dies hard, the "Palo Alto school" has accumulated evidence showing the intimate (and possibly necessary) relationship between certain structured body motions and spoken language forms (Birdwhistell 1970, 128; see, e.g., Scheflen 1972). Moreover, kinesics provide essential metasignals about the relationship: the codes discriminating the different logical types are mainly nonverbal (posture, gesture, facial expression, intonation), the verbal media (vocabulary) being particularly poor in that regard.[26] Multiple typing, that is, the capacity of identifying and hierarchizing the different types of messages, is indispensable to communication (even in animals): not being able to assign the correct communicational mode, for example, not being able to properly label metaphors, dangerously impairs the adequate handling of signals. This is so much the case that, according to the famous double-bind theory, such dysfunctions open the door to schizophrenia: a breakdown in the ability to discriminate types prevents the decoding of paradoxical instructions propagated at the lexical and kinesic levels.

Reflect.   According to our chart, the public experiential core is an intuitive awareness fairly remote from the categories of everyday language. Instantaneous, gut-like, deep, it installs a vivid sympathy between its subject and its object. That reflective mood concerns both our fellow human beings and the cosmos as a totality. Actually, it blurs the difference between subject and object, sheer individuality and the overwhelming experience of in-finitude. Bergson has described that blissful awareness under the label of "intuition";

more precisely, it is one meaning of the concept that conveys the experience we are looking for. Let us quickly unfold this. Sometimes, Bergson uses the concept of intuition to speak of the fugitive focal center around which a speculative system orbits. In sealing his system, the philosopher does not arrive at unity, but has started from it.[27] What stands out here is the dialectic intuition/intelligence that weaves the systematic attempts. More relevant for our purpose is a complementary threefold meaning of the concept, that is, a meshing between three different submeanings of the concept of intuition: subjective, objective, and sympathetic.

The restricted—subjective—sense of the concept of intuition belongs to the (metaphysical) binomial "intuition/intelligence," originating in the (psychological) binomial "duration/time." The concept of intuition spreads out from the concept of duration in so far as intuitive thought is durational thought, and this duration is first a subjective, inner growth operating in the secret of our immediacy.[28] Physical time, homogeneous, measurable, and reversible is not internal temporality, which is heterogeneous, nonmeasurable and irreversible.[29] In this intuitive "pure perception,"[30] the world is seen *sub specie durationis*, that is, in a heterogeneous duration in which all moments penetrate each other. It is less a vision than an immediate contact bypass-ing—not obliterating—rationality: actually, intuition, and intelligence work hand in hand;[31] its main task is to rediscover the rhythm of creative evolution by localizing oneself at its heart (Bergson 1959, 1327).

When Bergson expands the field of applicability of the subjective concept of intuition to the "objective" world, when he installs duration and freedom at the heart of things,[32] he realizes a speculative feat comparable to Whitehead's reformed subjectivism (see below). The subject/object difference, still sensitive in the *Essai* (1889), shades off in *Matière et mémoire* (1896). The "*Introduction à la métaphysique*" (1903) claims that our private consciousness, in its perpetual flux, introduces us inside a reality that has to be the model for any reality whatsoever.[33] The intuition of our duration puts us in contact with a continuity of durations that we can try to track either upstream or downstream (Bergson 1959, 1419). It is an effort of conscious dilation to seize nature round the waist, to grasp it in its deepest being—which is also, to a different degree, our own.

Now that the brotherhood between subjective and objective mundane features is established, the mysterious connivance that we can entertain with "things" becomes a precious clue. The coincidence, in a simple act, with what is unique (and as a result inexpressible),[34] should allow us to avoid the forgetfulness of the cosmic dynamism (i.e., its obliteration by sense-percep-tion) and thereby to ground a method overcoming the problematic stabilizing (rigidifying) effect of every conceptualization (Bergson 1959, 1276). Bergson is looking for a rationalism of the fluid concept. In his own words:

Intuition, then, signifies first of all consciousness, but immediate consciousness, a vision which is scarcely distinguishable from the object seen, a knowledge which is contact and even coincidence. —Next, it is consciousness extended, pressing upon the edge of an unconscious which gives way and which resists [. . .].[35]

AXIOMATIC OVERLAPPINGS

"When we conceptualize, we cut out and fix, and exclude everything but what we have fixed. A concept means a *that-and-no-other*," insists James (1977, 113). However, the cruel contingency of our linguistic tool is problematic only if the abstractions framed are uncritically considered. Once this dogmatic trend is recognized for itself, temperate carving and weaving of meaningful abstractions become possible again.[36] Nothing would be worse than a tessellated view of our framework, and now that the axioms have been introduced, we have to highlight their possible overlappings and suggest what existential picture their interanimation generates. Out of the various overlappings due to the limitedness (and the heuristic nature) of the categories used, let us gather the following four chiasmi. By displaying how one concept is inseparable from its specular brother, we will take the first step in the direction of proving the coherence of the entire categorial set.

The "stylistic" grid used to analyze the peculiarities of personal language aims at displaying how an individual appropriates the polysemiality of his or her mother tongue and how the interanimation of sentences is achieved. Conventional language remains the basic semantic framework defining normal consciousness through normal rationality: on the one hand, the idiosyncrasies of a private language are always found adhering to public language; on the other, private language creates neologisms and grammatical inflections that can have an impact on public language itself. Let us give a quick philosophical example. Whitehead's relation to language is quite complex; for the sake of the present inquiry, it can be linearized in the following way: he first identifies the fallacies of everyday, scientific and philosophical languages, denouncing the faulty categories. It is mainly substantialism and its heir, materialism, that are incriminated. Second, he scrutinizes his own "subjective" experience in order to reveal what impregnates every actuality[37] and contemplates the necessity of redesigning language in order to be able to systematize these ultimate generalities. He consequently advocates a careful analogical expansion of the current semantic horizon of the words. Everyday language is designed only for everyday purposes; the ultimate asks for a reformed language, even if it means that common sense (nontechnical use of the term) is overthrown. In order to manifest his own intuitions, the philosopher implements choices, reappropriations, and conceptual creation.

He thus first uses everyday terms whose meaning have been purified and extended: *feeling, experience, enjoyment, value* or *God* gain a valence foreign to ordinary language, while still keeping a grasp on normal experience. However, even when ordinary language has reached its maximum stretch, its tribulations remain very far from full-fledged concreteness. The, so to speak, deviant ontology and habits of thought induced by its concepts are still active. Then the creation of concepts takes place with "neologisms" like *creative advance, unison of becoming, hybrid prehensions*, or *ingression*. But still, there is a stretching, not a total breaking with the linguistico-cultural landscape: the price paid to allow a possible communication is to leave the grammatical structure more or less untouched. The key to the differentiation between a very personal use of language and a pathological one is perhaps the state in which the grammatical structure is left, allowing, or not allowing, some access to communication.

In regard to duration and time, suffice it to say that duration can be projected, bent, constricted in physical time (think of Bergson having to wait for the dissolution of his lump of sugar). Ontologically speaking, it is furthermore possible to argue along with Whitehead for a durational genesis of time.

With regard to the proximity of the "withness of the body" and "common sense": whereas the former anchors the individual in her body and, thereby, in the world, the latter anchors the individual in her social tissue. Neither can work without the other.

Eventually, the toppling effects between the two specular core concepts, affect and reflect, have to be underlined. The marrow of the private (subjective) side of consciousness has been described with the concepts of enjoyment and affectivity; the marrow of the public (objective) side has been spelled with the concept of intuition. We have taken some time to spell the valences of Bergson's concept of intuition precisely because that concept allows the categorial bypassing of subjectivity and objectivity. Pure awareness (affectivity) necessarily opens itself to the Whole, and intuitive awareness is in its essence affectivity. Very suggestive complementary concepts are James' "pure experience" and its Nishidan appropriation, but their examination would lead us too far.[38] The "self-centric" mode of existence is a particularity of the "normal" state of consciousness; the "cosmocentric" (Nishitani 1984; see also Deikman 1996) mode in which we escape from historical thought belongs to "altered" states. A more pragmatic exemplification is offered by the hypnotic state of consciousness that is introduced below.

It is solely with the total reappropriation of the structure of our modes of relationality that the cosmic structure itself will be understood. This is remarkably epitomized in Whitehead's "reformed subjectivist principle" that can be expressed very simply: what we learn through our personal—embodied—experience can be generalized to any experience whatsoever. In fact, not only can it be, but it *must* be if we claim that no bifurcation can disinherit humanity from its natural filiation. Now, what this experience teaches us above all else is its pure experiential factuality: "to be" is to be experiencing; nothing "is" that is not experiencing or experienceable.[39] And every experience has necessarily some intrinsic value conferred by its inalienable "enjoyment." Consequently, it is absolutely appropriate to speak of *panexperientialism*. To belong to a world is to be both the product and the actor of an ontological weaving. Technically speaking, it is to be an actual entity, a pulse in existence, a windowed monad.

As Hegel beautifully uttered, *das Wahre ist das Ganze* (Hegel 1937, 21). The axioms here proposed make sense fully only when they are interanimated, that is, when their coherence allows the projection of the reader in their own semantic space. It is impossible to freeze a meaning: only a total processualization makes sense. To picture the conscious state analytically evoked, one has to realize an incessant back and forth, introspective movement between each of the arborescences and their experiential focus.

Nuclear Pivotal Model

According to our speculative wager, the subtle synergy between the various private and public levels of awareness defines normal human consciousness. The model so far introduced is pivotal: the structural skeleton we have skimmed through defines normal consciousness as the eventful pivot energizing the togetherness of private and public modes of awareness of a given human individual. But there are two qualifications we must consider. One is that the various dimensions of experience we have mapped represent a quality space that is not equally saturated with consciousness throughout. Normal consciousness is only a focal selection of this space, the rest of which functions as a dim and nebulous horizon. It is therefore expedient to introduce the idea of the nuclear pivot. The second qualification is that the individual pivot is, by its very nature, a collective pivot as well. To determine the conditions of possibility of the pivotal tuning, we have to contemplate the social individual. As we will see in our next section, if the pivot is not shared, the individual consciousnesses are not attuned, and the question of the sanity of (some of) the implicated individuals immediately arises.

Emphasis has traditionally fallen on language and sense perception, whose meshing was said to rule consciousness: they are but (crucial) ingredients of a more holistic picture. The nucleus of conscious experience is constituted by a chiasmus between languaged "self-consciousness" and languaged "social consciousness": everyday interactions usually bracket the other private and public characters, which are thus unconscious. As a matter of fact, the appeal to personal experience shows straightaway that most of the categories involved are often factually shaded, if not obliterated in social interaction. What is conscious and what is not is not only a matter of degree; it is a matter of fluctuating degree: within the "normal consciousness pattern," all the items presented can receive special attention, either because the subject chooses to do so, or because some "unwilled" event imposes itself.[40] The subject can, for instance, decide to explore the existential ramifications of intuitive awareness; or he can be the victim of a toothache leading him to feel the heaviness of embodiment more cruelly than usual. . . . To go into retreat in one's solitary stove puts into brackets, even before the launching of the hyperbolical doubt, social consciousness, maybe even conventional language itself. To choose, like most of our contemporaries, to live only "socially" (i.e., scattered), leads to the forgetfulness of the other ineffective modes of awareness.[41]

James' concept of a "fringe of experience" is helpful to polish the concept of *nuclear* pivot: the *Principles of Psychology* distinguishes between the experiential nucleus (which is definite) and its fringe, halo, or penumbra (constituted by the more or less vague contextualization, that is, the web of meaning-giving relations).[42] The clear and distinct phenomena receive their significance and value from this "penumbra that surrounds and escorts it" (James 1950, 254–255). That Jamesean couplet finds a worthy heir in Whitehead's *early* distinction between sense perception and sense-awareness, which actually announces his *late* distinction between presentational immediacy and causal efficacy.[43] "Nature as perceived always has a ragged edge" (CN 50). In the very same way James re-establishes the pedigree of the idea of "vagueness," Whitehead considers vagueness as primordial as value: the fundamental is not, and does not have to be, settled, clear and distinct.

To rephrase our conclusion: pivotal consciousness is the characteristic of the individual experiential flux weaving the existence of societies of human beings and rooting these societies in their cosmic environment; nuclear pivotal consciousness denominates the chiaroscuro highlighting *some* features of that complex socio-environmental rooting. The latter is not simply an abstraction of the former in the conceptual sense of the term: there is a filtration of experience that transforms an indistinct eventful wealth of prehensions into an ordered universe. Consciousness is selectiveness of enjoyment: "We experience more than we can analyze. For we experience the universe, and we analyze in our consciousness a minute selection of its details" (MT 89). According to process philosophy, enticity is a matter of degree *and* convention (see Galin 1999). A being appears isolated only from a narrow perspective, and thanks to the instability of the innumerable links it entertains with the cosmos.[44]

The concept of fringe directs our attention (no pun intended, but appropriate) toward the filtrating business of consciousness in a rather simpler way than Whitehead's difficult categorialization he calls "the genetic analysis of concrescence." Out of the interconnected manifold, only a few stabilized relationships reach consciousness: the selectiveness of enjoyment in the higher animals that "arises from expression coordinating the activities of physiological functionings" is the *triumph of specialization* (MT 29 and 121). Three steps are observed: first the filtration—or negation—of some data; second, the comparison—or contrast—of the selected data; third, their structuration into a world "of my own." More precisely, consciousness arises with a counterfactual contrast, that is, when a fact is contrasted with a possibility (which it is not, or is, but need not have been): the conscious subject does not only perceive, say, "this stone as grey," but also perceives "this stone as *grey*" (the stone *is* something it need not be) or "this stone as *not* white" (the stone is not something it could have been). Consciousness is the feeling of negation; it involves the rise into importance of the contrast (PR 161 referring himself to "Part III, for the full account"). "Consciousness is an ever-shifting process of abstracting shifting quality from a massive process of essential existence. It emphasizes. And yet, if we forget the background, the result is triviality" (MT 108).

Normal and Abnormal Rationalities

So far, we have proposed a new cartography of normal consciousness; to do so, we have had to focus on one single individual. It is now time to use the nuclear model to approach rationality in a society of individuals. From a process perspective, negation, contrast, and structuration can operate in various ways in an ever-fluctuating universe; there are, in other words, numerous ways to "cut" into the concrete; and to claim that some ways are more straightforward than others requires the use of a more or less conventional criterion.[45] As a result, the Parmenidian understanding of the conditions of possibility of science as the discourse on the immutable, on the unchanging—a point of view appropriated by Plato, and that has framed the modern way of talking of knowledge—is definitely not applicable anymore. What is at stake here is the strict correlation between normal consciousness and normal—normative—rationality.

It is too obvious that what is rational from the perspective of a given system of thought might not be so from the perspective of another one—and hence that objectivity varies for different cultures and even for different sub-cultures: not only does a Melanesian not have the same "world" as a Bantu or an Asian-American, but among the latter, there are various *Weltanschauungen*. A golfer does not "exist" with the same mental picture as a nuclear scientist; a public school kid does not sympathize with the world in the same way as a gardener or an agricultural engineer. What becomes apparent here is precisely the scattered worldview in the "civilized" West: on the one hand the world of life, on the other, the world(s) of science. There is no mystery as to why meaning was *given* in "traditional" societies, and is *pulled apart* in "modern" ones. To be as straightforward as possible: the way an individual *cuts out* reality depends on her way of positioning herself in front of the Totality. It depends on a metaphysical decision that can be ultimately reduced, from the viewpoint of the history of (Western) philosophy, to "substance or flux."[46] Needless to say that substance ontology has so far installed itself as the paradigmatic worldview, setting into movement Modernity and its trail of pitiful bankruptcies. Hence the baffling claim that can be found in some "Nietzschean" (Buddhist, if you like) thinkers—and particularly in Whitehead and Nishida: the substance-attribute/subject-predicate ontology is at the root of all evils, in the strong sense of the term. Now, within a given culture, there are so to speak micro-fluctuations that have led to the various figures of the concept of madness, something that will especially occupy us in the third part of the paper.

Rationality, Irrationality, and Arationality

A straightforward distinction between rational, irrational, and arational realms enables us to name the cultural relativity mentioned above while preserving a healthy realism. A rational proposition is congruent with a set of given rules of relevance; an irrational proposition is not congruent, but could become so, once some fixing-up is provided; the *arational* is definitely incommensurable with reason.[47] The simplest way of discussing this is to take a quick look at Aristotelian logic, understood since the seventeenth century as defined by three principles. The principle of identity states that we come to know all things in so far as they have some unity and identity. It has naturally to be linked with the substance-attribute ontology granting permanence amid flux. The principle of contradiction is somewhat the negative side of the principle of identity: it claims that the same attribute cannot, at the same time and in the same respect, belong and not belong to the same subject. According to the principle of *excluded middle*, there cannot be an intermediate between contradictories: of one subject we must either affirm or deny any one predicate.[48] Consequently, any proposition that does belong to the territory marked out by these three principles is, from an Aristotelian perspective, rational; if it does not, it is irrational (further specifications are of course needed to take account of limit-cases like the predication regarding future contingents). A contradiction is not irrational, since it possesses a clear status in the system: it is a statement that is always false and *everybody agrees* that it is so because some mistake must have occurred in the chain of reasoning. A paradox, however, is irrational: as its etymology shows, it is a contradiction that has the appearance of truth, with the result that there are numerous *opinions* regarding the way of understanding them; no consensus prevails. The arational is for him *matter* [*hylē*] (the complement of *form* [*morphē*] in his hylomorphism).

Reasonableness

Up to this point, we have relativized rationality with the help of the concepts of irrationality and arationality. Even if there are numerous possible rationalities, the definition of the "normal" rationality is nonetheless still pending. Since discrimination needs a *meta*-criterion, a supplemental distinction has to be introduced between rational and reasonable, that is, between to convince and to persuade: one can be convinced by an argument, that is, recognize its complete rationality, and nevertheless not be persuaded at all of its immediate implications for oneself. In such a case, the universal validity of the argument is acknowledged, but it is rejected on the basis of its irrelevance.

The Greeks understood very quickly that discursivity requires founding principles coming from another faculty; hence Plato's distinction (*Republic* VI) of *noēsis* and *dianoia*, the former providing the anhypothetical principles of the latter, purely hypothetico-deductive, faculty. Later on, Aquinas differentiated "*intellectus*" (the intuitive faculty) and "*ratio*" (the argumentative faculty), and Kant stratified "*Verstand*" and "*Vernunft*." Closer to us, it is remarkable that Jung also used "*psychologische Typen*" to discriminate arguments (Jung 1921). Two questions are directly relevant to our argument: On the one hand, what are the necessary characteristics of the reasonable? On the other, what can be said of its contingent characteristics? To circumscribe them, one can appeal, first, to the now famous Husserlian *doxa* (or *Urglaube*) and its Merleau-Pontian appraisal,[49] and second, to a genetic discussion. Our question becomes: what is the origin of the "rules of relevance" evoked earlier to define rationality; why is a given set of rules socially preferred to another; why is one rationality defined as more reasonable than another? For instance, what licenses the Aristotelian principle of contradiction that seems to be a primordial requirement of any rational system?

The Urdoxastic Ontological Security

We are born with instinctive expectations to find regularities and useful stabilities; we are fully equipped to discover them—read: to construct them—and failing to do so inevitably immerses us in the abyss of "ontological insecurity."[50] In the elusive flux of events (an apparent redundancy that barely expresses the paradoxicality of the continuous emergence of totally new cosmic features), there has to be a rock upon which we could build our lives. One recognizes here of course the Cartesian question, which is merely a modern reformulation of the old existential puzzling that has lead, through the quest for the *principle* [*archē*], to the concept of *substance* [*ousia*]. Furthermore, as Russell constantly warns us, the very dynamic of the subject-predicate languages is to transform verbs and adjectives into nouns, that is, to "transubstantiate" processes into things.

The Urdoxastic theme is present throughout Husserl's thinking, from the published work to the *Nachlaß*: in § 104 of the first volume of the *Ideen* (1913), in his "pre-Copernican" essay (1988), and in the Introduction of *Erfahrung und Urteil* (1954); it is crucial to the foundation of the "phenomenological science." The "Urdoxa" is the "perceptive faith" (Merleau-Ponty 1964, 17–30 and *passim*) that characterizes our belonging to the world: not only are we sure that what we perceive is real, but a momentary suspension of perception does not nullify that certainty. Intersubjectivity is there to warrant the durability of the concrete, the intrinsic coherence of the unfoldment of its profiles. Solipsistic thought is blatantly in contradiction with the most elementary data of our conscious experience. Each and every perception occurs with the world as background: to perceive something is also to perceive its (always already given) horizon of meaning. The Earth does not move: she is the unmoving familiar ground allowing the existence of rest and movement; she is the root, the stock, the original ark in which our spatiality is rooted. Common sense is undoubtedly pre-Euclidean in the sense that our personal universe is finite and spherical, it has a center: ourselves (Cornford 1936).

Aristotle is entirely relevant to our argument because his system can be said to *adhere* to common sense, that is, to the evidences that ground everyday life. This well-known strength became its main weakness when philosophy and science opened new paths of thought by essentially obliterating substantialism. Anyway, we are in good company here since Whitehead and Piaget make basically the same claim (see MT 74 and Piaget 1949, 70–79). Whitehead argues that, whereas the Presocratic speculations, and especially the Platonic mathematicism, attempted to overcome common sense, Aristotle's biocentrism systematized it. According to him, spontaneous thought is phenomenist, that is, prelogical, in a similar way in children and in primitive societies: both make extensive use of animistic teleology and prenumerical symbolism; there is no clear distinction between appearance and reality, subjectivity and objectivity. The world has a center[51]. The difference between children and societies is the egocentrism of the former, basically confident in his way toward socialization, and the sociocentrism of the latter, basically distressed vis-à-vis a threatening environment. Before going forward with our argument, two things need to be said in the light of the discussion of "irrational" statements: first, although Lévy-Bruhl's "pre-logical" statements have to be manipulated with great care, all the more so since he eventually renounced his own concept, there is nothing intrinsically wrong with "mystical participation" (Lévy-Bruhl 1910, Lévy-Bruhl 1922). Second, Piaget seems to adulate normal rationality: in the Western imagination, "primitive" modes of thought have always been down-valued, and cultures making use of participatory or even paradoxical concepts speculatively slaughtered. He basically asks: who could *seriously* think of making any use of Indian philosophies that take their start from the paradox of simultaneous antagonisms?[52]

Let us finally pinpoint a recent similar attempt in Whiteheadian studies. Griffin speaks of hardcore commonsense notions (Griffin and Smith 1989, esp. 90–91) to qualify the universal and primordial beliefs that human beings do not question *in practice*: their fundamental freedom, the causal efficacy of their actions, the existence of values and of a temporal drift. All this in a realistic atmosphere. In conclusion: what is fundamentally (necessarily) reasonable is what does not endanger the Urdoxastic vital—carnal—link we maintain with the perceived world. Further thoughts are nevertheless needed to specify the debated meta-criterion.

The Genetic Approach: Pivotal Tuning

How was the flesh made consciousness? Asking how consciousness actually did arise is a question lying beyond the present inquiries (and perhaps beyond any inquiries whatsoever); we will raise more modestly the question that can be approximated by our working hypothesis: how are the individual consciousnesses in tune; how do the different pivots synchronize? This is the question of the unity in multiplicity of consciousness. The first thing to state explicitly is that there is "nothing" prior to the tuning: it is only the rationalization of an all-embracing process that gives the impression of such a consecution (sequence): "But in point of fact nature doesn't make eggs by making first half an egg, then a quarter, then an eighth, etc., and adding them together. She either makes a whole egg at once of none at all, and so of all other units" (James 1977, 103).

So far, even when the public pole was examined, the focus was on the individual. We have now to offer paths to understand the double-faced tuning that defines normal consciousness. The first (synchronic) tuning is manifested by the pivotal skeleton: there are structural adjustments to allow the state of consciousness of one individual to be leveled with the state of consciousness of other individuals. This is a collective state (or level) of consciousness that is nothing less than the product of the successive adjustments that evolution has imposed on the individuals of the different species and that education has inculcated (and sophisticated) in the case of human beings (second twofold tuning, which is the diachronic one).

Furthermore, as mental illness testifies, two geneses are possible: harmonization (attunement, evolution) of the different rational consciousnesses present, and disharmonization (involution) of these structures. With regard to evolution, three broad keys are useful: the biological, the topological, and the ethological factors: the first denominates the organic support of the embodied interacting structures; the second denominates the discrete but omnipresent environment; the third denominates the innate or learned behavioral habits. They will be used in triplets articulating the twofold stabilization—the (etho-topo)-biological "interactive diachronization" and of the (bio-topo)-ethological "integrative synchronization"—and its specular double, destabilization. With regard to involution, it is mainly the concept of schismogenesis that will hold our attention. Let us thus examine the bipolar origin of the contingent features of the reasonable—evolution in the biosphere and education in the ethosphere—in order to assess normal rationality in the context of the nuclear pivotal model of normal consciousness.

ATTUNEMENT

Normal consciousness manifests the unison of experiences occurring in the historical biosphere, defined by natural selection (term used in a broad, non-technical, way) and sealed by a particular culture. Normality is conventional (ethological integrative synchronization), but first there is a fundamental bio-topological foundation. Hence our two steps: evolution in the biosphere and education in the ethosphere.

What is called the "genetic" or "biological" theory of knowledge, or even "evolutionary epistemology," is commonly used to understand the interactive diachronic tuning. But in the same way that in evolutionary theory itself the majority of contributors agree on the principles without being able to create a consensus supported by the facts, no applicable genetic model has yet reached maturity. Its intuition is the following: the cognitive functions of the human mind are not static operators; they are the transient phylogenetic result of a long adaptive process. Under the pressure of environmental adjustment (better knowledge allows a better chance for survival), intellect has become a master in the logic of solid bodies (linear causality, Euclidean geometry, etc.). This is, however, just an evolutionary adjustment to a limited—perceived—segment of a throbbing and coalescing world. This narrow scope is defined by the possibility of action in the context of natural selection. Knowledge is purely practical, utilitarian: what is reasonable is the rationality that works in everyday life, in other words, that is applicable within our practical scope. Nowadays, cognitivists argue for an overtaking of the old "evolutionary epistemology" by a constructivist evolutionary epistemology where theoretical terms are defined as invariants of operations represented by physical measurement devices and observational terms are the phylogenetically evolved features of human perception and interpretation, defined operationally as invariants of certain actions and transformations.[53]

According to the diachronic tuning hypothesis, the categories that are *a priori* for the individual are *a posteriori* for the species. The evolutionary success of the "*Homo approximatus*" (see Galin 2003) lies in the fortunate oversimplifications the species has achieved, mainly through cultural endeavors. Let us now see how the synchronic tuning defines the normal—common—level of consciousness of contemporary individuals. To denominate the process of integrative synchronic tuning and contrast it with the schismogenesis[54]—or progressive differentiation—that will be tackled later, we use the concept of koinogenesis (from *koinos*, meaning "common," "public"). Koinogenesis is the process of convergence of individual consciousness through learning. *Learning* does not here mean simply the institutionalized educational processes from child-rearing to postgraduate studies but, more comprehensively, all the forms of communication that exploit reinforcement loops to "tune-in" individuals, all the skills of navigation in society and in the world that are "broadcasted." Tuning does not mean unification—pluralism is preserved—but the conventional locking of a set of categories and of behavioral constraints, in short: the adjustment to common values. These values, for being "consensually" validated, are basically decreed by the dominant group(s) of the society. It is not the place to analyze this, but one cannot avoid being reminded of the brilliant arguments given by Foucault, especially now that we have a better knowledge of what happened in the former USSR (Foucault 1972, Fulford 1993). In the same way medicalization of mental disorders is driven by social norms; what is called "scientific objectivity" is actually just another guise of consensual (and hence contextual) judgment (see, e.g., Stengers 1992). A quick exemplification can be given with the problem of the demonstration of the principle of noncontradiction. Although noncontradiction has appeared for a long time as an obvious basic requirement of reason, Aristotle's so-called demonstration has always been considered as flawed. This tricky issue has received a truly insightful solution with Lukasiewicz's arresting remark that the principle is actually ethico-practical. He has been followed by Apel who develops that thesis: the logical principle of noncontradiction is grounded on an ethical principle securing the possibility of *individual action* within a community (Lukasiewicz 1910, Apel 1973).

DISCORDANCY

How could the concert of consciousness go out of tune? Again, two steps are expedient: involution in the biosphere and corruption in the ethosphere.

A global involution in the biosphere would be a mystery (although perhaps no more than evolution itself) unless one dares to appeal to theological concepts. . . . *Local* involutions—degenerative dementias, consciousness impairment in brain-damaged individuals, epilepsy, the enigmatic dementia praecox, and the like, are, however, frequent (see, e.g., Stevens 1984). The fields involved in these puzzling out-tunings—evil and diseases—are too remote from our main thread to be treated in these lines.

Corruption in the ethosphere is directly relevant to our argument, and the key concept is, as announced, schismogenesis. Bateson defines it as *a process of differentiation in the norms of individual behavior resulting from cumulative interaction between individuals* (Bateson 1958, 175; see especially the "Epilogue 1958," 280–303). He further distinguishes symmetrical schismogenesis that occurs when there is mutual emulation, competition, rivalry (positive feedback) and complementary schismogenesis that occurs when there is mutual fitness, dominance-submission, dependence-nurturance patterns, etc. (negative feedback). Cumulation is essential—each party reacts to the reactions of the other—because it allows auto-organization and opens the doors to a synchronic understanding of pathologies, as opposed to the Freudian emphasis upon the diachronic. The concept of schismogenesis finds its origin in the anthropological research related in *Naven*, but Bateson expects to recognize it "in the progressive maladjustment of neurotic and prepsychotic individuals" (Bateson 1958, 179). For reasons that will be approached in the following discussion of Watzlawick, the schizophrenic is engaged in "security operations" (Laing 1961, 36, citing H.S. Sullivan) to restore her ontological security (see the discussion of the *Urdoxa*). These operations consist of a sustained misconstrual of experience that, instead of curing the ontological insecurity, give root to mental illnesses, that is, lock in the loss of tuning. The growing discrepancy between the patient's construal and other members of the society's construal, instead of spurring insight, leads to further delusional constructions (positive feedback). In conclusion, what is *contingently* unreasonable is what leads to schismogenesis.

Abnormal Rationality

He is not in his right mind: in everyday language, to be insane is not to be reasonable anymore. It is to have lost the discriminative criterion that allows the tuning-in with other consciousnesses, which involves the recognition and the use of normative rationality. As a result, the patient adopts one or more alternative rationalities, even if normative rationality can still be used sporadically, according to the mood, in the strong sense of the term. The rational loss induced by the criterial destruction thus means that reason gets scattered, that it "goes irrational." It is thus correct, but not enough, to equate insanity and serious impairment of the capacity for rational thought (Fulford 1986, 126–127), or to say that the criterion for mental health is the degree of agreement between two people, one being, by common accord, sane (Laing

1960, 44). Some light needs to be thrown, even fleetingly, on the complex entanglement between modes of consciousness and modes of rationality. Two main cases have been observed: with regard to the necessary feature of reasonableness, we have seen that the "Urdoxastic loss" leads to a total cosmic estrangement;[55] with regard to the contingent features of reasonableness, we have seen that if there can be an *objective* discrepancy between the modes of interaction of an individual and the socially recognized modes—that objective alienation is rooted in a collective *subjective* decision.

Aberrant Consciousness and Abnormal Rationality

A pragmatic way of approaching the problem of the status of the abnormal rationality that, so to speak, structures aberrant consciousness is to study the ins and outs of successful psychotherapies. We will look at two kinds of nonintellectual therapies, the Palo-Alto or Watzlawickian therapy and hypnosis.

Ferenczi and Rank were perhaps the first to have questioned the usefulness of intellect in the process of therapeutic change.[56] Against the theoretical knowledge of the analyst, they put forward real-life as it is lived (*"erleben"*). The "process thought" of Paul Watzlawick (1921–), which attempts to give a rational framework to Don D. Jackson's (1920–1968) and Milton H. Erickson's (1901–1980) rather intuitive therapeutic strategies offers a good exemplification of that much needed debate. Let us resume the discussion that started in *Searching for New Contrasts*.

Watzlawick is enormously indebted to Bateson's speculations for two complementary keystones of his systematic attempts. On the one hand, his double-bind theory shows how the entrapment in a closed network of paradoxical relations favors—if not generates—schizophrenia. On the other, his generalization of the concept of feedback causation, and especially of negative feedback, provides the tool to understand the internal equilibrium some pathological systems reach through repeated auto-corrections. Double bind and feedback rely on the idea that relationships are always the product of multiple descriptions, they cannot be internal to one single individual:

> Only if you hold on tight to the primacy and priority of relationship can you avoid dormitive explanation. The opium does not contain a dormitive principle, and the man does not contain an aggressive instinct. [. . .] If you want to talk about, say, "pride," you must talk about two persons or two groups and what happens between them. [. . .] As binocular vision gives the possibility of a new order of information (about depth), so the understanding (conscious and unconscious) of behavior through relationship gives

a new logical type of learning. (In *Steps to an Ecology of Mind*, I
have called this Learning II, or deutero-learning.)[57]

The Ariadne's clew is the well-known Palo-Alto claim (made as far back
as the 1960s): the vast majority of psychopathologies are due to trouble
with communication (see, e.g., Ruesch and Bateson 1951). It is worth
reminding ourselves that this claim can actually be traced back to Milton
Erickson's reading of Ernest-Charles Lasègue (1816–1883) and Jules Falret's
(1824–1902) seminal paper "La folie à deux" (1877), where the ego-logical
and organic etiology was really undermined for the first time (see Rausky
1998). What is furthermore of the highest interest in that paper is the use
of hypnosis to understand the (linear) induction of the pathology. In other
words, the biology and the rationality of psychopathologies were relegated
to a position of secondary importance while the affective dimension was
gaining decisive impetus.

Three steps would be expedient to address the nucleus of Watzlawick's
system of human communication and, hence, of therapeutic process; we
provide here only a brief synopsis of the synthesis available in our "Art of
Epochal Change."[58] First step: to explore the axiomatic of communication of
his *Pragmatics of Human Communication*. Of the five interdependent axioms
it carves out, let us remind ourselves of the first one: it is impossible *not* to
communicate.[59] Second step: to question how this theoretical frame results
in the structuration of *Change, Principles of Problem Formation and Problem
Solution* around the following pragmatic binomial: first-order change is a
change occurring *within* a given system—which remains itself unchanged;
second-order change is constituted by the *alteration* of the structure of a
given system—which is thus intrinsically modified, restructured. Third step:
to specify the status of paradoxes with the help of *The Language of Change*,
and thereby to show how Watzlawickian brief therapy argues for the usefulness (if not the necessity) of using a so-to-speak abnormal rationality to
deal with aberrant states of consciousness. The keystone is the direct access
paradoxical utterances give to the affective core of any state of consciousness
(see above). Unsurprisingly, we meet again with hypnosis (or, come to think
of it, with the mysterious Freudian transference): when a rationality different
from the normal rationality is being used, the state of consciousness—the
way a given individual relates to herself, to others, and to the world—gets
modified. The use of paradoxes induces, *volens nolens*, a consciousness that
is not fully attuned with normal consciousness. Specularly, it is well known
that the depiction of the non-normal states requires different categories and
structures of thought than the account of everyday experiences.

Hypnosis ranks, with hysteria and dreams, among the main clues that
put psychologists on the path of the extra-marginal. Let us introduce its

characteristics with the help of François Roustang's powerful speculations, inspired in part by Léon Chertok and Milton H. Erickson.[60] Chertok proposes a few provisional definitions of the hypnotic state stemming from the old—but still relevant—concept of animal magnetism[61] and insisting on the affective core of the hypnotic trance; it is a natural potentiality that manifests itself already in the relation of attachment to the mother; it is the matrix, the crucible in which all subsequent relations will come within its scope; its essence is very archaic, prelinguistic, presexual.[62] Keeping this in mind, let us first sketch the induction of the hypnotic state. For the sake of the present argument, we can bypass the distinction between self-hypnosis and hypnosis suggested on a willing and cooperative subject by a clinician. The basic conditions for entering hypnosis are fairly simple: it is just a matter of fixation of ones own attention. As one concentrates on a single stimulus by gradually bracketing most of the other afferent stimuli, attention becomes more and more invasive and the waking state gets dramatically transformed: sense perception is now nuclear, while action becomes cataleptic and reason drifts from its judgmental concern to get closer to affects. Discussing the related topic of attention, a major mystic of the twentieth century—Simone Weil—puts it this way: "attention consists in the suspension of one's thought, in making oneself available, empty and penetrable by the object; it consists in keeping in oneself the proximity of thought and of the various acquired knowledge that one is usually forced to use, but at a lower level and without contact with it."[63]

What about the characteristics of this gradual relaxation or sleepiness? Hypnotic wakefulness features indeed, as its etymology suggests, many affinities with ordinary sleep: muscular relaxation and redistributed brain activity (patterns that remind us of paradoxical sleep as disclosed in EEG and EMG), anesthesia and/or hyperesthesia (although not genuinely sensorial), amnesia (while hypermnesia is possible), perceptive distortions (including hallucinations), increased suggestibility (besides post-hypnotic—that is, deferred—suggestions) and the possibility of role-enactment and of alteration of the personality.

But it features as well remarkable differences (that James would claim are only of degree) with ordinary sleep; to outline them coherently, it is essential to go through the four (non-necessary) steps to full hypnotic actualization. First, the induction of the hypnotic state occurs through perceptive fixedness; fascination starts where ordinary perception stops. Second, the hypnotic state installs indetermination: all customary differences can be abolished, paving the way for confusion, blindness, loss of reference point, and possible feeling of helplessness. Third, the positive side of the dispersed attitude of attention is the opening of the possible: resting on this indeterminate waiting, spring dissociations, withdrawal and hallucinations; and with them the possibility of transforming one's appraisal of life. Everything can be reframed: percepts can be put in a wider context by reverie, absence, or imagination. Fourth, the hypnotic trance displays itself as enhanced vigilance, mobilized power, energy ready to implement action, that is, to shape the world. All the acquired knowledge is gathered, actively taken in, and one has them at one's disposal. This explains why the hypnotherapist suggests only what is possible for the patient; he reveals the power the patient has over his own becoming.

Roustang concludes: "to understand something of paradoxical wakefulness, we have to do violence to ourselves and—at a great expense—invent in our culture a new cosmology and a new anthropology."[64] All the consequences of the contiguum of the states of consciousness and of the levels of beings, that is, of bodies, have to be thought. This is exactly what panexperientialism provides: one single onto-psychical field that allows, so to speak, only unwillingly, the bifurcation of subject and object. Since there is one organizing and differentiating power endowed by many centers of forces, the mesocosmic perception of an object by a subject ceases to be mysterious: in pure experience, subject and object, subject and subject, grow together and reciprocally (com-)prehend one another.[65] Each experience has both a physical and a mental dimension that can be pulled apart only in abstraction. The concreteness of experience, in other words, goes beyond the limited perspectives of physicality and mentality. After many others, Deleuze has suggested the metaphor of the fold to intuit how such a bimodal ontology is possible; James provides us with a concept, Whitehead with a categoreal scheme.

Conclusions

This chapter has tried to clear the way for a more holistic, less eliminative topology of consciousness. Its goal—a philosophical analysis of the intricacies of the concepts of consciousness and rationality—was undoubtedly very bold and its author will be happy even if only a partial success is acknowledged. A few last clarifying remarks are now advisable.

First, the nuclear pivotal model has been designed to meet normal (instrumental) consciousness as it is lived. To the nuclear restriction, one has to add the varying emphasis that, in each individual, inevitably falls on this or that feature of the scheme. Moreover, this precaution is especially relevant when understanding the slow access of children to fully constituted, normal consciousness matters: that long process could be described as a journey from the private and public edges of the diagram, through self-consciousness and social consciousness, to its core, together with the synchronic tuning evoked.

Second, the proper theorization of altered states of consciousness is likely to require a start from a different pivotal model; only experience could decide here on its characteristics: don't we speak of mystical experience as transcending language, time, (social) embodiment and even sometimes affect and reflect? Is it feasible to argue for one single core concept anyway?

Third, the quest for a criterion defining normal consciousness and normal rationality finally results in elevating the praxeological constraints. The conditions of the possibility of acting—within and upon the socionatural environment in a competitive context—asks for filtration, comparison, and structuration of data according to rules that have converged through a long phylogenetic and koinogenetic process. A certain rationality allowing the exploitation of clear and distinctly localized images delivered by sense-perception, their strict objectification, the correlative distinction of a "*subjectum*"—or substantial self—separate from others by sharp boundaries has been selected. That self-centered awareness is often contrasted with the cosmocentric awareness of mystics, where acting is replaced by renunciation, the boundaries are blurred or merged, self is undifferentiated, nonlocalized, not distinct from (but resonant with) environment, and the stretch of protention-retention is replaced by a focus on the experiential "now." However, there are *various types* of "receptive consciousness" and that simplistic bipartition (see Deikman 1996) does not do justice to their express characteristics (a distinction should be made, at the very least, between ecstasy and trance). Besides that, being capable of acting in a competitive context makes the fundamental difference between the ill and the sane. Actually, adaptability, opening to the opening that is the world, makes the difference as well between the ill and the mystic. To be a patient is no longer to be fully an agent (Fulford 1994): the psychotic cannot, or is not willing to, share his world (i.e., world-sharing is an activity, not a totally passive synthesis). In the complex landscape established by the synergy of hallucination, delusion, and lack of insight, the patient apparently rules as the absolute sovereign on a purely chimerical world—and suffers precisely from this watertight closing (it only seems agentive, it is really totally passive). Smothering by the chimerical world is the price to pay for absolute domination in dementia (the price of the illusion of absolute unrestricted agency is absolute unrestricted passivity). But the world is real precisely because it is always different from what the subject thought, because it has, so to speak, a life of its own, a nonrationality in James' terms. Made frozen, strictly predictable, mechanistic in dementia, its full-fledged reality vanishes, its causality is denied, and the sheet anchor of the body becomes an eerie trap. To put it in another way: when in dementia agency has become only devoted to chimerical world-building, it is, from the perspective of the individuals dwelling in the common world, a purely passive activity.

Fourth, a subsidiary question gets mentioned: the status of animal consciousness. Here again, the nuclear pivotal model can serve only as an analogy. However, if we accept the necessity of following the path Whitehead named the "reformed subjectivist principle"—to start from our experience and to carefully determine what can be generalized from it—it becomes a necessary analogy. According to the philosopher, there is no doubt that all (higher) animals enjoy nonverbal thinking, aesthetic experience, and even moral experience; as their behavior displays, they no doubt have a self- and global-awareness. Griffin's criterion (see his contribution to this volume) is basically adaptiveness, behavioral versatility: consciousness confers a significant adaptive advantage that is noticeable in terms of problem solving (Griffin 1981, Griffin 1984). Since there is a qualitative evolutionary continuity of mental experiences among multicellular animals, that is, no dichotomy between human language and animal communication, he raises the White-headian "panpsychic" hypothesis. By definition, indeed, all beings are plugged into reality and endure some reactivity: from simple responsiveness (reaction triggered by stimulus—or let's even think of Newton's third law of motion: "action/reaction") to creativity.

Forthcoming issues of the WPN Studies will feature an examination of the conditions of possibility of the definition of a spectrum of consciousness and of its correlate, an ontological scale that bypasses the difficulties of materialistic dualism, vitalism and panpsychism. It will be the occasion as well to dive into *Process and Reality*'s genetic analysis of consciousness.

Notes

1. See Griffin 1984, 88. (Notice the difference between the late Harvard zoologist/ethologist Donald Redfield Griffin and the Claremont theologian David Ray Griffin.)

2. "La prise de conscience est un certain effet de scène" (Derrida 1972, 329).

3. "La conscience est une mise en faisceau, une organisation de connaissances (*cum scrire*) donc une opération unifiante accomplie avec intention et suivant un dessein. [...] Elle ramasse un être dispersé" (Pradines 1943, 6).

4. "Un être capable de se multiplier sans se diviser, d'étendre au loin son regard dans l'espace sans perdre la référence des points aperçus au lieu où il se trouve, de rappeler semblablement son passé sous la perspective du présent qui s'en distingue tout en l'utilisant, est par là con-scient" (Pradines 1943, 7).

5. We use aberrant in order to avoid the usual direct correlation between "altered states of consciousness" and "drug-induced states."

6. "Definitions are like belts; the shorter they are, the more elastic they need to be" (Toulmin 1961, 18).

7. Part I of his magnum opus, *Process and Reality*, actually employs five criteria to define speculative philosophy (consistency, coherence, applicability, adequation, and necessity). A fair interpretation of that set of constraints is a demanding task, far

beyond our present goal. One twofold point is, however, relevant: the requirement of an *applicable* categoreal *democracy*. Applicability is basic insofar as full-fledged concreteness is to be in the scheme's sight; democracy names the double subconstraint: independence (or contributivity, i.e., concepts are not reciprocally deducible) and interdependence (co-presuppositionality). The limited nature of this paper necessitates only a tangential approach to these core criteria, for a more exhaustive treatment see Weber 2006.

8. An earlier version of this paper was presented at the Fourth International Conference on Philosophy and Psychiatry, Madness, Science and Society, in Florence, August 26–29, 2000. Its argument does not presuppose the speculations of our "The Art of Epochal Change" (to be found in the first Whitehead Psychology Nexus Studies: Riffert and Weber 2003, 252–281), but its reading would help setting the stage of numerous discussions.

9. A polysemial concept—or "polyseme"—is simply a concept that carries various meanings. Instead of having a one-to-one relationship between the signifier and the signified, there is a one-to-many correspondence. One can speak of the leg of a human being, of a horse, of a table, or of a cooked lamb lying on one's plate, without generating much confusion. Polysemiality is indeed a very common—and harmless—feature of natural language as it is currently used (i.e., in everyday life): the contextualization of the actual utterances usually prevents any difficulties. Reading a speculative philosopher confronts us nevertheless with a particular form of the hermeneutical problem: how to make sense out of texts that champion polysemiality? A polyseme acts as a semantic cluster focused on one privileged experience synthesizing "in the flesh" all the partial meanings constituting the cluster. There is a movement of overtaking, from the hierarchy of the various meanings to a "primordial" experience that is the author's, as purified (universalized, i.e., rationalized) from its personal contingencies as possible. That raw *experience* is, quite obviously, richer than the partial converging meanings: it embodies the ontological excess, or surplus, that lies at the center of the cluster, constituting its nucleus. Solely the beatings of this experiential heart can nourish the hierarchized network's dynamism. Polysemiality occurs at the conceptual or lexical level. Of course, communication does not happen with the occasional uttering of single words, whose intrinsic richness would be sufficient to trigger the manifestation of an entire worldview. (This being perhaps the case in most animal forms of communication.) A similar semantic overtaking mechanism takes place at the propositional or syntactical level. It is embodied by what Quine calls the "interanimation of sentences." The discursive concatenation of sentences introduces a semantic vitality that opens the text to the concrete (or at least to a "meta" level). There is, in other words, a prismatic virtue of propositional chains that explains how intentionality imposes itself, so to speak, *interstitially* (see Merleau-Ponty 1992, 46–47 and 61–62; Quine 1960; Richards 1965).

10. MT 35. In his last philosophical paper (Whitehead 1936), he claims: "If the experience be unusual, verbalization may be, for us, impossible. We are then deprived of our chief instrument of recall, comparison, and communication."

11. Besides Hegel, James, Bergson, Whitehead, Merleau-Ponty and the like, see, for example, Hurley 1997 or Lucas 1972. Armstrong-Buck (1989) defines self-consciousness in the following way: "subjective form characterized by a vivid feeling

of 'mineness' as it unifies high-grade multiple contrasts." Interestingly enough, her argument offers some similarities with ours (that was developed independently), as when she articulates "agent self-consciousness," "public self-consciousness," "private self-consciousness" and "pure self-consciousness."

12. See below our comment on Bergson's "fluid images" in his "Introduction to Metaphysics," reprinted in *The Creative Mind: An Introduction to Metaphysics* (Bergson 1975).

13. "Le corps sait dire je tout seul" (Serres 1985, 16).

14. Bergson alludes to these messages when he speaks of "sensations de 'toucher intérieur' émanant de tous les points de l'organisme, et plus particulièrement des viscères" (in Bergson 1959, 883).

15. Articular capsule, periosteum, tendons, joints, muscles house sensitive corpuscles and nerve endings similar to the skin's (see Sherrington 1906, 132–133 and 1940, 309).

16. "At any moment of our waking life, one part of our experience is a mass of obscure sensation connected with breathing and digestion, the pressure of clothes, vague hungers and fatigues, our bodily fitness or unfitness. We seldom think of these feelings, but they are there undoubtedly [. . .]" (Blanshard 1939, vol. 1, 67, citing Bradley's *Appearance and Reality*, 2nd ed., 293).

17. PR 81 (and see 64, 119–122, 176–180, 311–318). In Merleau-Pontian terms, "la conscience est l'être à la chose par l'intermédiaire du corps," "la chose [. . .] se constitue dans la prise de mon corps sur elle" (1945, 161 and 369).

18. "Ce qui sent sans que ce soit par l'intermédiaire d'un sens est dans son essence affectivité. [. . .] L'affectivité est l'essence de l'ipséité" (Henry 1963, 577 and 581).

19. See the following conceptual bounds: James 1884; Sousa 1987; Cytowic 1989; Brown 1988; Lazarus 1991; Damasio 1994.

20. For Pierre Bourdieu's cardinal concept, see, for example, Bourdieu 1994.

21. Definition adapted from Hagège 1986, 131, 143, 202.

22. "A three-fold commonness" (Arendt 1978, 50). This has to be read with the Greek idea of truth as common logos in mind.

23. "Naître du monde et naître au monde"; Merleau-Ponty continues: "The world is already constituted; in the first case we are acted upon, in the second case we are open to an infinite number of possibilities. [. . .] It is impossible to determine precisely the 'share contributed by the situation' and the 'share contributed by freedom'" (Merleau-Ponty 1945, 517).

24. "La science manipule les choses et renonce à les habiter" (Merleau-Ponty 1964, 9 et 12–13).

25. "Les deux racines hébraïques majeures qui servent de pivot au réseau sémantique qui véhicule la pensée biblique du corps sont ruah et bâsâr: le souffle et la chair. Un être humain est une chair insufflée, un souffle charnel, une globalité dynamique et indivise" (Malherbe 1987, 56–57).

26. Bateson, Jackson, Haley and Weakland 1956. See, for example, Bateson 1979, 127–128 on Pavlov's paradigm of experimental neurosis.

27. "Le philosophe n'est pas venu à l'unité, il en est parti" (Bergson 1959, 1362). "À mesure que nous cherchons d'avantage à nous installer dans la pensée du philosophe au lieu d'en faire le tour, nous voyons sa doctrine se transfigurer. [. . .]

Tout se ramasse en un point unique [. . .] en ce point est quelque chose de simple, de si extraordinairement simple que le philosophe n'a jamais réussi à le dire. Et c'est pourquoi il a parlé toute sa vie [. . .] il n'a fait autre chose [. . .] que rendre avec une approximation croissante la simplicité de son intuition originelle. Toute la complexité de sa doctrine, qui irait à l'infini, n'est donc que l'incommensurabilité entre son intuition simple et les moyens dont il disposait pour l'exprimer" (Bergson 1959, 810).

28. "L'intuition dont nous parlons porte donc avant tout sur la durée intérieure. Elle saisit une succession qui n'est pas juxtaposition, une croissance par le dedans, le prolongement ininterrompu du passé dans un présent qui empiète sur l'avenir" (Bergson 1959, 1272–1273).

29. "Concentrons-nous donc sur ce que nous avons, tout à la fois, de plus détaché de l'extérieur et de moins pénétré d'intellectualité. Cherchons, au plus profond de nous-mêmes, le point où nous nous sentons le plus intérieur à notre propre vie. C'est dans la pure durée que nous replongeons alors, une durée où le passé, toujours en marche, se grossit sans cesse d'un présent absolument nouveau. Mais, en même temps, nous sentons se tendre, jusqu'à sa limite extrême, le ressort de notre volonté. Il faut que, par une contraction violente de notre personnalité sur elle-même, nous ramassions notre passé qui se dérobe, pour le pousser, compact et indivisé, dans un présent qu'il créera en s'y introduisant. Bien rares sont les moments où nous nous ressaisissons nous-mêmes à ce point: ils ne font qu'un avec nos actions vraiment libres" (Bergson 1959, 664–665).

30. "nous sommes véritablement placés hors de nous dans la perception pure, [. . .] nous touchons alors la réalité de l'objet dans une intuition immédiate" (Bergson 1959, 222).

31. "Cette intuition, on ne nous la communiquera jamais toute faite, car le langage qu'on nous parle, si spéciaux et si appropriés qu'on en suppose les signes, ne peut exprimer que des ressemblances, et c'est d'une différence qu'il s'agit" (Bergson 1903, viii–ix).

32. "La durée et le libre choix" (Bergson 1959, 729).

33. "La conscience que nous avons de notre propre personne, dans son continuel écoulement, nous introduit à l'intérieur d'une réalité sur le modèle de laquelle nous devons nous représenter les autres" (Bergson 1959, 1420).

34. "Nous appelons ici intuition la *sympathie* par laquelle on se transporte à l'intérieur d'un objet pour coïncider avec ce qu'il a d'unique et par conséquent d'inexprimable" (Bergson 1959, 1395).

35. "Intuition signifie donc d'abord conscience, mais conscience immédiate, vision qui se distingue à peine de l'objet vu, connaissance qui est contact et même coïncidence.—C'est ensuite de la conscience élargie, presant sur le bord d'un inconscient qui cède et qui résiste, qui se rend et qui se reprend [. . .]" (Bergson 1959, 1273; trans.: Bergson 1946, 35–36).
See "L'intuition philosophique," in Bergson 1959, 1365.

36. See what has been said earlier of Whitehead's criterion of axiomatic coherence.

37. See his "reformed subjectivist principle" (PR 160) evoked below.

38. Nishida 1990. See also Heidegger 1927, § 29 on the concept of *Befindlichkeit*.

39. In this, Whitehead follows the path cleared by Bergson, but also by James: "The principle of pure experience is also a methodological postulate. Nothing shall be admitted as fact, it says, except what can be experienced at some definite time by some experient; and for every feature of fact ever so experienced, a definite place must be found somewhere in the final system of reality. In other words: Everything real must be experienceable somewhere, and every kind of thing experienced must be somewhere real" (James 1976, 160).

40. "The animal consciousness does not easily discriminate its dependence on detailed bodily functioning. Such discrimination is usually a sign of illness. When we observe the functionings of our viscera, something has gone wrong. We take the infinite complexity of our bodies for granted" (MT 29).

41. See the Heideggerian binomial *Sorge/besorgen*.

42. The *Principles of Psychology* indicates that there are various categories of fringe experiences. Rather than attempting an exhaustive list or a systematic analysis of their relations to each other, it offers a few examples: feelings of familiarity (James 1950, 252), feelings of knowing (251), feelings of relation (245), feelings of action tendency (253), attitudes of expectancy (250), feelings of "rightness" or being "on-the-right-track" (259–261). For all this, see Galin 1994.

43. His last book presents his views in a non-technical manner: see MT 110.

44. "À partir de la *connaissance*, l'existence d'une personne n'est isolée de celle de l'ensemble que d'un point de vue étroit et négligeable. Seule l'instabilité des liaisons (ce fait banal: quelque intime que soit un lien, la séparation est aisée, se multiplie et peut se prolonger) permet l'illusion de l'être isolé, replié sur lui-même et possédant le pouvoir d'exister sans échange" (Bataille 1973, 100).

45. See, for example, Edward Sapir, Benjamin Lee Whorf, Edward E. Evans-Pritchard, Paul K. Feyerabend.

46. More fundamentally, the way the individual *trusts* the World should be pictured with the help of the Husserlian concept of *Urdoxa* and its Merleaupontian cartography.

47. See *A Pluralistic Universe*'s concept of "non-rational."

48. See, respectively, *Metaphysics* Beta, 4 and Iota, 1; *Metaphysics* Gamma, 3 and *Posterior Analytics* I, 77a10–22; *Metaphysics* Gamma, 7 and *Posterior Analytics* I, 77a22–25.

49. Merleau-Ponty 1965, 266. See Merleau-Ponty 1945, 85, 395, 491; Merleau-Ponty 1964, 17, 41, 222, 234, 270, 272, 286, 292, 308, 312. Unfortunately, we cannot discuss here Santayana's "animal faith."

50. Laing's term (1960) was inspired by Tillich's *The Courage to Be* (1952).

51. See Eliade powerful (however controversial) inquiries.

52. See, for example, Heinrich Robert Zimmer and Sarvepalli Radhakrishnan.

53. Diettrich 1998. For the main inflections of this fairly simple grounding principle, see M. Weber's Introduction in Weber 2004.

54. We borrow of course Bateson's term: see, for example, Bateson 1935, 178–183.

55. The link that Laing exploits between existentialists philosophies and psychopathologies could be fruitfully put in perspective with the help of the cross-examination of Heideggerian concepts and Gnostic dogmas: see Jonas 1934.

56. According to Léon Chertok (1989, 226), who cites Ferenczi 1924.

57. Bateson 1979, 143. See as well Huxley's *Point Counter Point* and Durrell's *Alexandria Quartet*.

58. See (1) Watzlawick 1967, (2) Watzlawick 1974, and (3) Watzlawick 1978.

59. "Behavior has no opposite [. . .] there is no such thing as nonbehavior or, to put it even more simply: one cannot *not* behave" (Watzlawick 1967, 48).

60. See especially Roustang's *Qu'est-ce que l'hypnose?* (1994).

61. The concept has been recently reboosted by Boris Cyrulnik (see, e.g.,Cyrulnik 1997).

62. "On peut seulement affirmer que c'est au niveau de l'affect, c'est-à-dire de la réalité la plus évidente, puisqu'elle est de l'ordre du vécu, et la plus difficile à comprendre. [. . .] C'est un quatrième état de l'organisme, actuellement non objectivable (à l'inverse des trois autres : veille, sommeil, rêve : une sorte de potentialité naturelle, de dispositif inné prenant ses racines jusque dans l'hypnose animale, caractérisé par des traits qui renvoient apparemment aux relations pré-langagières d'attachement de l'enfant et se produisant dans des situations où l'individu est perturbé dans ses rapports avec l'environnement. L'hypnose garde sa spécificité par rapport à la sugges-tion, bien que celle-ci, sous quelque forme qu'elle se manifeste, soit nécessaire à la production de celle-là. La suggestion nous apparaît ainsi comme la relation primaire, fondamentale entre deux êtres, la matrice, le creuset dans lequel viendront s'inscrire toutes les relations ultérieures. Nous dirons encore qu'elle est une entité psycho-socio-biologique indissociable, agissant à un niveau inconscient très archaïque, pré-langagier, pré-sexuel, et médiatisant l'influence affective que tout individu exerce sur un autre" (Chertok 1989, 260–261).

63. "L'attention consiste à suspendre sa pensée, à la laisser disponible, vide et pénétrable à l'objet, à maintenir en soi-même la proximité de la pensée, mais à un niveau inférieur et sans contact avec elle, les diverses connaissances acquises qu'on est forcé d'utiliser" (Weil 1957, 76–77).

64. "Pour comprendre quelque chose de la veille paradoxale, il faut nous faire violence et inventer dans notre culture, à grands frais, une nouvelle cosmologie et une nouvelle anthropologie" (1994, 98–99).

65. "Grâce à cette puissance qui organise et différencie, représentée par l'anticipation, toute une série de faux problèmes tombent d'eux-mêmes. Il n'y a plus à se demander comment un sujet peut percevoir un objet, puisque l'un et l'autre grandissent ensemble et s'appréhendent dans une action réciproque, ni comment un humain peut en comprendre un autre, puisqu'ils n'existent dès l'origine que par cette compréhension, ni comment peuvent se tisser entre eux des interrelations: l'identification et le lien affectif n'ont dû être inventés que par la supposition erronée que les individus d'abord confondus, ont été ensuite séparés" (1994, 87).

References

Apel, Karl Otto. 1973. *Transformation der Philosophie. II. Das Apriori der Kommuni-kationsgemeinschaft.* Frankfurt am Main: Suhrkamp.

Arendt, Hannah. 1978. *The Life of the Mind.* 1-vol. ed. San Diego, New York, London: Harcourt Brace Jovanovich.

Armstrong-Buck, Susan. 1989. "Nonhuman Experience: A Whiteheadian Analysis." *Process Studies* 18 (1): 1–18.

Bataille, Georges. 1973. *L'expérience intérieure.* Paris: Gallimard.

Bateson, Gregory. 1935. "Culture Contact and Schismogenesis." *Man* 35:178–183. Reprinted in *Steps to an Ecology of Mind*, 61–72.

Bateson, Gregory. 1958/1936. *Naven: A Survey of the Problems Suggested by a Composite Picture of the Culture of a New Guinea Tribe Drawn from Three Points of View.* 2nd ed. Stanford: Stanford University Press.

Bateson, Gregory. 1972. *Steps to an Ecology of Mind: Collected Essays in Anthropology, Psychiatry, Evolution, and Epistemology.* San Francisco: Chandler.

Bateson, Gregory. 1979. *Mind and Nature: A Necessary Unity.* London: Wildwood House.

Bateson, Gregory, D.D. Jackson, Jay Haley, and John J. Weakland. 1956. "Toward a Theory of Schizophrenia." *Behavioral Scientist* 1:251–264.

Bergson, Henri. 1889. *Essai sur les données immédiates de la conscience.* Paris: Librairie Félix Alcan (*Time and Free Will: An Essay on the Immediate Data of Consciousness.* Trans. by F.L. Pogson. New York: Macmillan, 1910).

Bergson, Henri. 1903. "Préface." In Émile Lubac, *Esquisse d'un système de psychologie rationnelle. Leçons de psychologie.* Paris: Félix Alcan, viii–ix.

Bergson, Henri. 1911. "L'intuition philosophique." In Bergson 1959, 1345–1365.

Bergson, Henri. 1946. *The Creative Mind.* Trans. by Mabelle L. Andison. New York: Greenwood Press.

Bergson, Henri. 1959. *Œuvres.* Textes annotés par André Robinet. Introduction par Henri Gouhier. Paris: Presses Universitaires de France.

Birdwhistell, Ray L. 1970. *Kinesics and Context: Body Motion Communication.* Philadelphia: University of Pennsylvania Press.

Blanshard, Brand. 1939. *The Nature of Thought.* London: George Allen & Unwin Ltd.

Boman, Thorlief. 1954. *Das hebraïsche Denken im Vergleich mit dem Griechischen.* Göttingen: Vandenhoeck & Ruprecht.

Bourdieu, Pierre. 1994. *Raisons pratiques: Sur la théorie de l'action.* Paris: Éditions du Seuil.

Brown, Jason W. 1988. *The Life of the Mind: Selected Papers.* Hillsdale: Lawrence Erlbaum.

Chertok, Léon. 1989/1959. *L'Hypnose: Théorie, pratique et technique.* Édition remaniée et augmentée. Paris: Éditions Payot.

Cornford, Francis MacDonald. 1936. "The Invention of Space." In *Essays in Honor of Gilbert Murray*, 215–235. London: Allen & Unwin. Reprinted in *The Concepts of Space and Time: Their Structure and their Development*, Milic Capek, ed., 3–16. Dordrecht and Boston: D. Reidel, 1976.

Cyrulnik, Boris. 1997. *L'ensorcellement du monde.* Paris: Éditions Odile Jacob.

Cytowic, Richard E. 1989. *Synesthesia: A Union of the Senses.* New York: Springer-Verlag.

Damasio, Antonio R. 1994. *Descartes' Error: Emotion, Reason, and the Human Brain.* New York: Putnam.

Deikman, Arthur J. 1996. "Intention, Self and Spiritual Experience: A Functional Model of Consciousness." In *Toward a Science of Consciousness. The First Tucson Discussions and Debates*, Stuart R. Hameroff, Alfred W. Kaszniak, A.C. Scott, eds., 695–706. Cambridge, MA/London: A Bradford Book. MIT Press.

Derrida, Jacques. 1972. *La Dissémination*. Paris: Éditions du Seuil.

Diettrich, Olaf. 1998. "On Some Relations between Cognitive and Organic Evolution." In *Evolutionary Systems*, Gertrudis van de Vijver, Stanley N. Salthe, M. Delpos, eds., 319–340. Dordrecht: Kluwer.

Ferenczi, Sándor, und Otto Rank. 1924. *Entwicklungsziele der Psychoanalyse*. Leipzig/Wien/Zürich: Internationaler Psychoanalyticher Verlag.

Foucault, Michel. 1972. *Histoire de la folie à l'âge classique*. Paris: NRF Éditions Gallimard.

Fulford, K.W.M. 1986. "Insanity." In *Dictionary of Philosophy and Psychology*, Rom Harré and Roger Lamb, eds., 126–127. Oxford: Blackwell.

Fulford, K.W.M., Alex Smirnoff, and Elena Snow. 1993. "Concepts of Disease and the Abuse of Psychiatry in the USSR." *British Journal of Psychiatry* 162:801–810.

Fulford, K.W.M. 1994. "Value, Illness, and Failure of Action: Framework for a Philosophical Psychopathology of Delusions." In *Philosophical Psychopathology*, George Graham and G. Lynn Stephens, eds., 205–233. Cambridge, MA: MIT Press.

Galin, David. 1994. "The Structure of Awareness. Contemporary Application of William James's Forgotten Concept of 'the Fringe.'" *Journal of Mind and Behavior* 15 (4): 375–400.

Galin, David. 1999. "Separating First-Personness from the Other Problems of Consciousness or 'You Had to Have Been There !'" *Journal of Consciousness Studies* Special Issue (Feb.–Mar.): 341–348.

Galin, David. 2003. "Untangling 'Self,' 'Person,' and 'I,'" in Riffert and Weber 2003, 313–331.

Griffin, David Ray, and Huston Smith, 1989. *Primordial Truth and Postmodern Theology*. Albany: State University of New York Press.

Griffin, Donald Redfield. 1981. *The Question of Animal Awareness: Evolutionary Continuity of Mental Experience*. Revised ed. New York: Rockefeller University Press.

Griffin, Donald Redfield. 1984. *Animal Thinking*. Cambridge, MA: Harvard University Press.

Hagège, Claude. 1986. *L'homme de paroles: Contribution linguistique aux sciences humaines*. Paris: Gallimard.

Hall, Edward T. 1959. *The Silent Language*. New York: Doubleday.

Hall, Edward T. 1966. *The Hidden Dimension*. New York: Doubleday.

Hall, Edward T. 1984. *The Dance of Life. The Other Dimension of Time*. Garden City: Anchor Press.

Hegel, Georg Wilhelm Friedrich. 1937. *Phänomenologie des Geistes*. Leipzig: Felix Meiner.

Heidegger, Martin. 1927. *Sein und Zeit*. Tübingen: Niemeyer.

Henry, Michel. 1963. *L'essence de la manifestation*. 2 vols. Paris: Presses Universitaires de France.

Hurley, S.L. 1997. "Nonconceptual Self-Consciousness and Agency: Perspective and Access." *Communication and Cognition* 30 (3/4): 207–248.

Husserl, Edmund. 1913. *Ideen zu einer reinen Phaemenologie und phaemenologische Philosophie.* Jahrbuch für Philosophie und phämenologische Forschung. Pt. 1. Halle: Max Niemeyer.

Husserl, Edmund. 1954. *Die Krisis der Europäischen Wissenschaften und die Transzendentale Phänomenologie.* The Hague: Martinus Nijhoff Publishers.

Husserl, Edmund. 1954/1939. *Erfahrung und Urteil: Untersuchungen zur Genealogie der Logik. Redigiert und herausgegeben von Ludwig Landgrebe.* Zweite unveränderte Auflage. Hamburg: Claassen & Goverts.

Husserl, Edmund. 1988/1934. "Die Urarche Erde bewegt sich nicht." In *Philosophical Essays in Memory of E. Husserl,* 307–325. New York: Greenwood Press.

James, William. 1884. "What is Emotion?" *Mind* 9:188–205.

James, William. 1950/1890. *The Principles of Psychology.* New York: Dover Publications.

James, William. 1976. *Essays in Radical Empiricism* (posthumously published by Ralph Barton Perry, 1912). Ed. by Fredson Bowers et al. Cambridge, MA: Harvard University Press.

James, William. 1977/1909. *A Pluralistic Universe.* Hibbert Lectures at Manchester College on the Present Situation in Philosophy. Ed. by Fredson Bowers and Ignas K. Skrupskelis. Cambridge, MA: Harvard University Press.

Jonas, Hans. 1934. *Gnosis und späntantiker Geist.* Teil 1: *Die mythologische Gnosis, mit Einer Einleitung zur Geschichte und Methodologie der Forschung.* Göttingen: Vandenhoeck & Ruprecht.

Jonas, Hans. 1966. *The Phenomenon of Life: Toward a Philosophical Biology.* Chicago and London: University of Chicago Press.

Jung, Carl Gustav. 1921. *Psychologische Typen.* Zürich: Rascher.

Laing, Ronald David. 1960. *The Divided Self: An Existential Study in Sanity and Madness.* London: Tavistock.

Laing, Ronald David. 1961. *The Self and Others: Further Studies in Sanity and Madness.* London: Tavistock.

Lazarus, Richard. 1991. *Passion and Reason.* Oxford: Oxford University Press.

Lévy-Bruhl, Lucien. 1910. *Les fonctions mentales dans les sociétés inférieures.* Paris, Félix Alcan, Éditeur.

Lévy-Bruhl, Lucien, 1922. *La mentalité primitive.* Paris: Librairie Félix Alcan.

Lucas, John. 1972. "Consciousness Without Language." In *The Nature of Mind,* A.J.P. Kenny, H.C. Longuet-Higgins, John Randolph Lucas, and C.H. Waddington, 108–122. Gifford lectures 1971/1972. Edinburgh: Edinburgh University Press.

Lukasiewicz, Jan. 1910. "Über den Satz von Widerspruch bei Aristoteles." *Bulletin international de l'Académie des Sciences de Cracovie.* Classe d'histoire et de philosophie, 15–38. English trans. by Vernon Wedin: "On the Principle of Contradiction in Aristotle." *Review of Metaphysics* 24 (March 1971): 485–509.

Malherbe, Jean-François, 1987. *Pour une éthique de la médecine.* Paris: Larousse.

Merleau-Ponty, Maurice. 1945. *Phénoménologie de la perception.* Paris: NRF Éditions Gallimard.

Merleau-Ponty, Maurice. 1964. *Le Visible et l'Invisible. Suivi de Notes de travail.* Texte établi par Claude Lefort. Paris: Éditions Gallimard.

Merleau-Ponty, Maurice. 1964. *L'œil et l'esprit.* Préface de Claude Lefort. Paris: Éditions Gallimard.

Merleau-Ponty, Maurice. 1965. "Husserl et la notion de Nature. Notes prises au cours de Merleau-Ponty." *Revue de Métaphysique et de Morale* 3:257–269.

Merleau-Ponty, Maurice. 1968. *Résumés de Cours. Collège de France 1952-1960.* Édités par Claude Lefort. Paris: NRF Éditions Gallimard.

Merleau-Ponty, Maurice. 1992. *La prose du monde.* Texte établi et présenté par Claude Lefort. Paris: Éditions Gallimard.

Nishida, Kitarô. 1990. *An Inquiry into the Good.* Trans. by Masao Abe and Christopher Ives (Zen no Kenkyû, 1911). New Haven and London: Yale University Press.

Nishitani, Keiji. 1984 "The Standpoint of Zen." Trans. by John C. Maraldo. *The Eastern Buddhist* 17 (1): 1–26.

Piaget, Jean. 1949. *Introduction à l'épistémologie génétique. Vol. 2, La pensée physique.* Paris: Presses Universitaires de France.

Pomian, Krzysztof. 1984. *L'ordre du temps.* Paris: NRF Éditions Gallimard.

Pradines, Maurice. 1943. *Traité de psychologie générale.* Vol. 1. Paris: Presses Universitaires de France.

Quine, Willard Van Orman. 1960. *Word and Object.* Cambridge, MA: MIT Press.

Rausky, Franklin. 1998. "Communication hypnotique et délire familial." In *Hypnose, Langage et Communication*, Didier Michaux (sous la dir. de). Paris: Éditions Imago.

Richards, Ivor Armstrong. 1965. *The Philosophy of Rhetoric.* The Mary Flexner Lectures on the Humanities 3, delivered at Bryn Mawr College, February and March 1936. New York: Oxford University Press.

Riffert, Franz G., and Michel Weber, eds. 2003. *Searching for New Contrasts. Whiteheadian Contributions to Contemporary Challenges in Neurophysiology, Psychology, Psychotherapy and the Philosophy of Mind.* Frankfurt am Main: Peter Lang.

Roustang, François. 1994. *Qu'est-ce que l'hypnose?* Paris: Éditions de Minuit.

Ruesch, Jurgen, and Gregory Bateson. 1951. *Communication: The Social Matrix of Psychiatry.* New York: Norton.

Sacks, Oliver. 1985. *The Man Who Mistook his Wife for a Hat and Other Clinical Tales.* London: Gerald Duckworth.

Scheflen, Albert E. (with the contribution of Alice Sheflen). 1972. *Body Language and Social Order: Communication as Behavioral Control.* Englewood Cliffs: Prentice-Hall.

Serres, Michel. 1985. *Les Cinq Sens. Philosophie des corps mêlés.* Paris: Éditions Bernard Grasset.

Sherrington, Sir Charles Scott. 1906. *The Integrative Action of the Nervous System.* Cambridge, MA: Harvard University Press.

Sherrington, Sir Charles Scott. 1940. *Man on his Nature.* Cambridge: At the University Press.

Sousa, Ronald de. 1987. *The Rationality of Emotion.* Cambridge, MA: MIT Press.

Stengers, Isabelle. 1992. *La volonté de faire science: À propos de la psychanalyse.* Paris: Édition des Laboratoires Delagrange.

Stevens, Robin (ed.). 1984. *Aspects of Consciousness. Vol. 4: Clinical Issues.* London: Academic Press.

Strawson, Peter Frederick. 1959. *Individuals: An Essay in Descriptive Metaphysics.* London: Methuen.

Tillich, Paul. 1952. *The Courage to Be.* New Haven: Yale University Press.

Toulmin, Stephen E. 1961. *Foresight and Understanding: An Inquiry into the Aims of Science.* London/Bloomington: Hutchinson's University Library and Indiana University Press.

Watzlawick, Beavin, Helmick, and Jackson, 1967. *Pragmatics of Human Communication: A Study on Interactional Patterns, Pathologies and Paradoxes.* New York: Norton.

Watzlawick, Paul, 1978. *The Language of Change: Elements of Therapeutic Communication.* New York: Basic Books.

Watzlawick, Paul, John Weakland, and Richard Fisch. 1974. *Change: Principles of Problem Formation and Problem Solution.* New York: Norton.

Weber, Michel. 2003. "The Art of Epochal Change." In Riffert and Weber 2003, 252–281.

Weber, Michel. 2004. "Introduction." In *After Whitehead: Rescher on Process Metaphysics.* Frankfurt: Ontos Verlag.

Weber, Michel. 2006. *Whitehead's Pancreativism: The Basics.* Foreword by Nicholas Rescher. Frankfurt/Paris: Ontos Verlag.

Weil, Simone. 1957. *Attente de Dieu.* Paris: La Colombe, Éditions du vieux colombier.

Whitehead, Alfred North. 1936. "Remarks to the Eastern Division of the American Philosophical Association." *Proceedings and Addresses of the American Philosophical Association* 10:178–186.

Part V

History (and Future?) of Philosophy

14

Consciousness, Memory, and Recollection According to Whitehead

Xavier Verley

Since Descartes, mental life has found its source in consciousness. In his *Meditations*, he begins by purifying the soul of everything that came from the senses, from tradition, and from memory. Thus reduced to a point related only to the thinking subject, the mind is disclosed as a consciousness that judges, senses, wills, and desires. Reduced to a pure act of the mind, consciousness is a relation of itself to itself. One might then suppose that what is at issue here is a return to a deeper foundation within oneself [*en soi*], and solipsism would thus appear as a return to the primordial form of the subject.

The Cartesian approach illustrates the procedure of reversal that implies the passage from exteriority to interiority, from the world to the "me" [*le moi*] and the self [*le soi*]. But the beginning of the *Meditations* reveals that for Descartes hyperbolic doubt poses the question not only of the relation to the senses, but also of the relation to good sense. By doubting too much what the senses teach us, one ends by losing one's sense and becoming literally senseless (insane):

> But even though the senses deceive us sometimes concerning things scarcely perceptible or very distant, perhaps many others are met with about which one cannot reasonably doubt, although we know them by means of the senses: for example, that I am here, seated near the fire, dressed in a dressing gown, having this paper between my hands, and other things of this nature. And how is it that I could deny that these hands and this body right here are mine? Unless perhaps I compare myself to those who are insane, of whom the brain is so far disturbed and clouded

by the black vapors of bile that they assure themselves constantly that they are kings when they are very poor, that they have robes of gold and crimson when they are naked, or imagine themselves to be ceramic or to have a head of glass. (Descartes 1953, 268/1964–1976, 7:18–19/1984, 2:12–13)

Since the subject and consciousness rise up from doubt, doubt ends by reducing the "me" [*le moi*] to a point, to knowing the "I" [*le "je"*], which is different from the "me" [*le moi*] and the self [*le soi*]. Identifying itself with the consciousness it has of itself, the subject reduces itself to the "I" grasped in the instant, and it ends by losing any relation to its memory, which links it to its past and to its habits. It exists only in the present reflection of the "me," isolated from the world, from others. In such a case, its solipsistic and narcissistic existence becomes incapable of integrating memory and self-consciousness, and it is able to advance in the creation of itself only by dint of the freedom that the understanding must concede to the will insofar as the infinite scope of willing exceeds the limited scope of the understanding.[1] Without this relation to itself, to others, and to God, consciousness risks disappearing in an alienated existence.

Whitehead inverts this perspective completely. For he admits that it is futile to look for the clear and distinct in connection with the self-consciousness of the one who is engaged in scrutinizing experience. If consciousness is a light, it is shrouded in darkness. How to escape the impasse of solipsism that threatens us with madness? How to regain in perception and in memory a relation to oneself [*à soi*] that would not be a simple consciousness of oneself in the other. We would like to show that consciousness can regain its relation to itself only by way of memory and can achieve self-consciousness only by recollection.

Consciousness and the Power of Judgment

Whitehead mentions Descartes often, sometimes to underscore the difference that separates them in their understanding of matter or the nature of the mind, sometimes to make him a sort of precursor to the philosophy of organism. In *Science and the Modern World* he reminds us how modern philosophy and theology are imbued with subjectivism. While the Catholic Church taught what believers were required to think about the nature of God and the mysteries (the Trinity, the Incarnation, and Redemption), the Reformation turned to the existence of the individual in order to elucidate its relation to justification and faith, thus restoring a meaning to the individual experience of believers:

> At the Reformation, the Church was torn asunder by dissension as
> to the individual experiences of believers in respect to justification.
> The individual subject of experience had been substituted for the
> total drama of all reality. Luther asked, "How am I justified?";
> modern philosophers have asked, "How do I have knowledge?"
> The emphasis lies upon the subject of experience. (SMW 140)

But before highlighting the "subject of experience," the return to the individual had paved the way for the advent and supremacy of consciousness in
the life of the mind.

Whitehead thinks that Descartes played a primary role in the new
orientation assumed by modern philosophy. The author of the *Discourse on
Method* identifies the subject of experience with the subject that speaks of
its intellectual life in the first person. Subjectivity comes to light in the "I,"
the concentrated locus of past and present life. But Whitehead interprets
the Cartesian *cogito* not as an act tied to pure consciousness, but as an act
of experience: "For each time he pronounces 'I am, I exist,' the actual occasion, which is the ego, is different; and the 'he' which is common to the two
egos is an eternal object or, alternatively, the nexus of successive occasions"
(PR 75). Thus, Whitehead conceives the subject that says "I" ["*je*"] not as
the subject of a thinking substance, but as an index that changes with time.
The possibility of an "I" that transcends what changes in experience depends
on an eternal object—not on the universal subject, but on the "it," a subject
that is anonymous and as impersonal as the green perceived when I look at
the leaves of a tree.

The identification of the subject with the "I" that speaks of its spiritual
search reveals that the "I" is no longer the simple individuality or personality of Descartes, but the most intimate source where the union of thought
and being is realized, and because of this transcendence in relation to his
individuality, the "I" that speaks is united to that self-consciousness that
every human being can retrieve from within.

The soul that Descartes discovers is no longer the one that is gripped
in the drama of the universe, but the one which, anxious about its immortality and its justification, finds itself gripped in the interior drama of its
responsibility in the face of falsehood and error.

Accompanying the discovery of the identity of the "I" and the universality of consciousness is that omnipotence attested by the will, that is, by
the freedom dwelling in the very heart of all the soul's activities. Thus, the
consciousness of wanting or feeling imply not only the capacity of judgment,
but also the intervention of the will, which always has the power of approv-
ing or disapproving what consciousness envisions. It is in this relationship
that spiritual freedom is constituted.

From this involution of interiority there results the opposition between the soul and the body, mind and matter, but also the separation of metaphysics and science. If philosophers such as Spinoza and Leibniz did not follow Descartes on this subjectivist path, others, such as Hume, Locke, and Kant continued to be imbued with the belief that the reality of the mind comes from its self-consciousness at the moment of thought. The power of judgment proper to the mind implies that the ego that thinks is the subject and that the consciousness that accompanies thought depends on a predicate inwardly attached to the subject so that one can say that to think is to judge.

Whitehead disputes that perception and sensible impressions of which the mind can be conscious depend on the power of judgment alone. At issue is a prejudice based on the dualism of the universal (the subject that thinks) and the particular (the sensible impressions as attributes of the soul). Thus, the universality of the subject that says "I" rests on a logico-metaphysical prejudice according to which every judgment assumes a subject and a predicate.

Subjectivism, understood as a theory of mind identified with subjective consciousness, implies the substantial character of the subject and of its consciousness.[2] Even if, like Kant, one rejects the substantiality of the "I think" in order to retain only the form, prefixed to every judgment, the consciousness of oneself at the moment of judgment is indispensable for comprehending how certitude accompanies consciousness and how there can be truth. Thinking consciousness remains the universal form inherent in all consciousness.

Subject and Primary Substance

Descartes' idea of thinking substance and extended substance proceeds from prejudices that are unacknowledged but which, according to Whitehead, have continued to influence subsequent ideas. Convinced that the act of thought can be only an act of experience, Whitehead believes that the analysis of this experience yields premises that explain why consciousness can be interpreted as a substance or a form.

Not only does Descartes adopt the dyad substance-quality as the foundation of his ontology, but he also takes up the Aristotelian theory according to which primary substance is always a subject and never a predicate. Descartes is thus able to make of the subject of experience a primary substance. Whitehead recognizes the importance of subjectivity in the synthesis of experience, but he shows that from Descartes to Kant the "subjectivist principle" is based entirely on what he calls the "sensationist principle." According to the first principle, the act of experience implies the relation of a particular, the Ego of Descartes, to a universal, the idea that he has of a thing. Perception of things and others happens by a sort of inspection (*inspectio*) that is not yet an intuition (*intuitio*). The power of judgment, which connects the universal to the particular—just as much as the consciousness that accompanies it—is indispensable for compensating for the gaps and the passivity of the eyes' vision. The second principle, the sensationist principle, interprets the act of perception as a simple receptivity to the given, thereby effectively excluding the subjective forms of apprehension, such as emotion, attraction, aversion, resulting in the illusion of a pure sensation.

In a general way the principle of subjectivity appeals to an ontology of substance that implies, first, the substance-quality dyad in the analysis of experience, then the theory of primary substance, which is always subject and never attribute, and, finally, the theory according to which the subject that experiences is always a primary substance. Whitehead never ceases to remind us that the analysis of experience that begins with the dyads "universal-particular" and "substance-quality" results from a prejudice because experience (in the sense that he gives to this term) implies, to paraphrase Aristotle, an act common to what is sensing and what is sensed.

Whitehead's critique of the logical analysis of experience proceeds from this principle: the community of the sensing and the sensed in the act of experience. If one takes this principle seriously, then it is necessary to renounce the identification of substance and subject and to conclude, quite contrary to the doctrine of Aristotle, that even though a substance is not present in a subject, nevertheless, an actual entity is truly present in the heart of other actual entities. It is appropriate then for Whitehead to substitute for the metaphysical principle that starts by opposing substance to accident and then shows the necessity of including the multiplicity of accidents in the unity of a substance a principle of relativity that shows how an entity can be present in another entity.

Whitehead criticizes Descartes, Locke, and Hume, but accords them a place in the philosophy of organism. Of Locke, he says:

> The philosophy of organism in its appeal to the facts can thus support itself by an appeal to the insight of John Locke, who in British philosophy is the analogue to Plato, in the epoch of his life, in personal endowments, in width of experience, and in dispassionate statement of conflicting intuitions. (PR 60)

If the author of the *Essay Concerning Human Understanding* had been able to free himself from the subject-predicate thought scheme, which entails the adoption of certain metaphysical categories, he would not have retained the opposition perception-understanding.

Whitehead recognizes in Locke the merit of having carried out an analysis pertinent to the type of experience had by an actual entity: the complete experience of such an entity shows that there isn't anything more in understanding than in perception, which obviates the necessity of an intervention by the will in order to apprehend from the side of understanding what is missing from the grasp of perception.

Consequently, each entity "possesses its own measure of absolute self-realization," and Whitehead proposes the term "prehension" to signify both the process of each thing's self-realization in experience and at the same time the synthetic activity by which other things intervene in the concresence of that experience. In order to account for the fact that the relation of things in experience is not static, but dynamic, Whitehead speaks of transaction:

> The "prehension" of one actual entity by another actual entity is the complete transaction, analysable into the objectification of the former entity as one of the data for the latter, and into the fully clothed feeling whereby the datum is absorbed into the subjective satisfaction—"clothed" with the various elements of its "subjective form." (PR 52)

If experience implies a synthesis, this synthesis can only come from the act of a subject that unifies the multiplicity of impressions that would be the predicates: the synthesis is more than a union, it is a transaction.

Hume inherits the logico-metaphysical prejudice founded on the dualism of the subject-predicate opposition, which entails the soul-body dualism. In maintaining that mind is a subject and that its contents are its predicates, he has accentuated the subjectivist conception of the mind by dividing the totality of the mind's perceptions into impressions and ideas:

> The perceptions, for Hume, are what the mind knows about itself; and tacitly the knowable facts are always treated as qualities of a subject—the subject being the mind. His final criticism of the notion of the "mind" does not alter the plain fact that the whole of the previous discussion has included this presupposition. Hume's final criticism only exposes the metaphysical superficiality of his preceding exposition. (PR138)

The impressions of sensations are the predicates of the soul. In other words, the mind is only a substance passively receiving the impressions that will become "phenomena" in Kant.

Such a doctrine implies that, similar to substance, only the subject can integrate its accidents. And as the subject is a substance only if it is present to itself, subjectivity ends by identifying itself with the fact of being itself [*soi-même*] at the present instant. Whitehead often evokes the formula of Santayana on the "solipsism of the present moment," which makes the impressions of memory an attribute of subjectivity: "Even memory goes: for a memory-impression is not an impression of memory. It is only another immediate private impression" (S 33).

In order to comprehend the relation of the universal to the particular, Kant gives to the subject and to the consciousness present in every judgment a function of synthesis that is brought about with representation as its starting point.

Repetition and Memory According to Hume

From the notion of substance as from that of modality, Hume retains the idea of collections of simple ideas, united by the imagination, and to which one attributes a specific name. Hume maintains that the simple ideas are copies of simple impressions, but he has to admit that one can perceive the nuances of color that are missing on a graduated scale. This applies also to the sensations of sound, to odors, and to all the registers of sensations. Can these nuances be derived from the simple power of imagining? Hume believes in the freedom of the imagination, but Whitehead remarks that "[i]magination is never very free" (PR 132).

When the issue is to understand how simple ideas get united in a complex idea, Hume appeals to customary conjunction. Ideas can copy impressions only if the latter are repeated. But in the relation of cause to effect repetition does not allow us to understand how one passes from the multiplicity of the impressions to the idea of necessary connection among them. Experience reduced to sensible impressions and to images of memory allows nothing but a multitude to come before consciousness. The repetition of impressions and ideas does not suffice to produce the unity of a new idea. In other words, Hume seems to confuse memory and imagination just as if he conceived a progression going from impressions to memories and to ideas.

Whitehead denies the Humean analysis in the name of facts:

> This doctrine is very unplausible; and, to speak bluntly, is in contradiction to plain fact. But, even worse, it omits the vital character of memory, namely, that it is *memory*. In fact the whole notion of *repetition* is lost in the "force and vivacity" doctrine. What Hume does explain is that with a number of different perceptions immediately concurrent, he sorts them out into three different classes according to force and vivacity. But the repeti-

tion character, which he ascribes to simple ideas, and which is the whole point of memory, finds no place in his explanation. Nor can it do so, without an entire recasting of his fundamental philosophic notions. (PR135)

Thus, Hume, who has divided the life of the mind into impressions and ideas, brings in the notion of repetition, which does not correspond to any impression. If repetition comes from memory, it can only be considered as bound to a particular impression. Whitehead faults the Humean analysis for being too narrow a conception of experience, reducing it to a mass of impressions and in the end making memory useless and inactive. In other words, repetition is possible only because it is fundamentally associated with memory. Had Hume set out from the experience of feeling, he would not have been able to effect this division and he would not have been able to isolate the impressions as one isolates the grains in a pile of sand. The experience of feeling reveals the primordial character of memory as repetition:

> The first point to notice is that Hume's philosophy is pervaded by the notion of "repetition," and that memory is a particular example of this character of experience, that in some sense there is entwined in its fundamental nature the fact that it is repeating something. Tear "repetition" out of "experience," and there is nothing left. On the other hand, "immediacy," or "first-handedness," is another element in experience. Feeling overwhelms repetition; and there remains the immediate, first-handed fact, which is the actual world in an immediate complex unity of feeling. (PR 135)

Whitehead speaks of persistence in change rather than of repetition. This Humean doctrine, which pulverizes becoming into instants and the experience of the mind into a scattering of impressions and ideas proceeds from the Cartesian precept that enjoins us to begin with the simple in order to obtain subsequently what is complex. But this precept also assumes that what is given in experience presents itself to us as individual, independent entities, which removes any possibility of becoming and repetition: "These various aspects can be summed up in the statement that *experience* involves a *becoming*, that *becoming* means that *something becomes*, and that *what becomes* involves *repetition* transformed into *novel immediacy*" (PR 136–137). In order to understand how something novel appears, it is important to understand that repetition is closely connected with becoming and that it exists in the very act of becoming. Thus, Whitehead can say that repetition is fundamental in the philosophy of organism.

The Humean doctrine, which divides the givens of the mind into impressions and ideas, is only an extension of the idea of a matter divisible into points that one can localize, and this theory is only another expression for what Whitehead calls "the fallacy of simple location." This prejudice concerning material things extends also to the experience we have of them. Humean impressions, elements of the subject analogous to the points and instants of extension, fragment and deform perceptual experience and the knowledge we can have of it. Against Hume, Kant, and Descartes, Whitehead holds that we have a direct intuition of inheritance and memory—but these philosophers do not succeed at integrating these data in their description of experience.

The Reformed Subjectivitst Principle and Its Impact on the Concept of Consciousness

Whitehead says occasionally that a philosophy concerned with preserving the relations between the concrete and the abstract in experience cannot bypass subjectivity. If he criticizes the principle of subjectivity, it is because it is associated with an erroneous logic founded on the substance-attribute dyad and with a metaphysics that identifies logical subject and primary substance. But the universal-particular dyad is of scarcely greater value for describing experience. If the universal serves to qualify particulars, particulars cannot serve to describe other particulars. Like primary substances, particulars do not enter into the composition of other particulars:

> An actual entity cannot be described, even inadequately, by univer-
> sals; because other actual entities do enter into the description of
> any one actual entity. Thus every so-called "universal" is particular
> in the sense of being just what it is, diverse from everything else;
> and every so-called "particular" is universal in the sense of entering
> into the constitution of other actual entities. (PR 48)

From this critique of the universal-particular dyad there results for the philosophy of organism the necessity of reforming the principle of subjectivity, which rigidifies the description of experience and prohibits the perceiving subject from being in harmony with the rest of the universe. If one adopts the principle according to which it belongs to the nature of a being to be a potential for every becoming, one rejects the doctrine of primary substance, which makes an entity into a being in itself and for itself. One ought thus to admit that an actual entity can be present in the heart of other actual entities.

Such a principle, called the principle of relativity, combined with the ontological principle—which says that everything is positively situated some-where *in actu*, and everywhere in potency—permits the reinterpretation of the principle of subjectivity. At the heart of the subject, delivered from the guardianship of substance, what is revealed is not the identity of thought and being, but the identity of being and becoming, which erupts from the deepest stratum of experience:

> The way in which one actual entity is qualified by other actual entities is the "experience" of the actual world enjoyed by that actual entity, as subject. The subjectivist principle is that the whole universe consists of elements disclosed in the analysis of the experiences of subjects. Process is the becoming of experience. It follows that the philosophy of organism entirely accepts the subjectivist bias of modern philosophy. (PR 166)

Whitehead proposes a recasting of the principle of subjectivity in order to render it more in conformity with the description of what is given in experience: "Finally, the reformed subjectivist principle must be repeated: that apart from the experiences of subjects there is nothing, nothing, nothing, bare nothingness" (PR 167). The reform of the principle of subjectivity entails in turn a reevaluation of the role of consciousness in experience. For Descartes and Kant, the subjectivity inherent in experience would be incomplete without consciousness. Whether it be *inspectio* or *intuitio*, perception implies consciousness and the power of judgment; also, the foundation of all synthesis, that of pure intuition as well as that of the understanding which judges, is the "I think" that accompanies not just judgment, but all representations. Instead of making consciousness a center of experience, Whitehead sees in it only a particular element in the midst of experience:

> The principle that I am adopting is that consciousness presupposes experience, and not experience consciousness. It is a special element in the subjective forms of some feelings. Thus an actual entity may, or may not, be conscious of some part of its experience. Its experience is its complete formal constitution, including its consciousness, if any. (PR 53)

For Whitehead, William James represents a decisive step in the evolution of the critique of consciousness in that he considers consciousness as a function of knowledge and not as a substance. In this reassessment of consciousness, the role of sciences such as medicine and physiology were decisive. James maintains a monistic doctrine intended to resolve dualisms—those of subject and object, but equally those of the image and the thing. He praises Berkeley for having reminded us that our sensations are not some interior doubles of the things, but the things themselves. The concern is to show that the reality of the thing is in its image. In a text written in French, "La notion de conscience," James says:

> I conclude then that—although there is a practical dualism, since images are distinguished from objects, take their place, and lead us to them—there is no need to attribute to them a difference in essential nature. Thought and actuality are made of one and the same stuff, which is the stuff of experience in general. (James 1912, 216)

Whitehead, too, shares this conception of experience, which no longer permits opposing the knowing subject to the object known, the interiority of consciousness to the exteriority of the object. But now is the appropriate time to evaluate the function of consciousness in experience.

Consciousness as the Power of Contrast

If for Descartes the *cogito* is dedicated to consciousness as the source that illuminates experience and makes it possible, the act of consciousness is an act of synthesis that springs from pure thought. Whitehead envisions consciousness only as a stage in a process of integration or again as an attribute of certain perceptions:

> Descartes' "Cogito, ergo sum" is wrongly translated, "I *think*, therefore I am." It is never bare thought or bare existence that we are aware of. I find myself as essentially a unity of emotions, enjoyments, hopes, fears, regrets, valuations of alternatives, decisions—all of them subjective reactions to the environment as active in my nature. My unity—which is Descartes' "I am"—is my process of shaping this welter of material into a consistent pattern of feelings. (MT 166)

Thus, the unity of what one calls the "me," does indeed spring from a synthesis, but one that is less a synthesis of consciousness than a synthesis of becoming or of a causal activity that comes from the experience of the body and produces the "me." Perception no longer depends on judgment, but on an activity that arises in the experience of things without my knowing whether it is the things that act on me [*moi*] or I [*moi*] who acts or reacts upon things.

If one set out from the proposition "This stone is gray," the analysis of this proposition in the context of the principle of subjectivity shows that

perception consists of grasping a universal quality at the moment when the
quality is in the process of determining a particular substance:

> Now if we scan "my perception of this stone as grey" in order
> to find a universal, the only available candidate is "greyness."
> Accordingly for Hume, "greyness," functioning as a sensation
> qualifying the mind, is a fundamental type of fact for metaphysi-
> cal generalization. (PR 159)

According to Whitehead, Hume limits himself to deducing consciousness
from the perception of the gray stone whereas in fact the consciousness
appears negligible. To say that it is negligible is not to deny it, but to reduce
it to the role of a resultant:

> Consciousness flickers; and even at its brightest, there is a small
> focal region of clear illumination, and a large penumbral region
> of experience which tells of intense experience in dim apprehen-
> sion. The simplicity of clear consciousness is no measure of the
> complexity of complete experience. Also this character of our
> experience suggests that consciousness is the crown of experience,
> only occasionally attained, not its necessary base. (PR 267)

Elsewhere Whitehead says that consciousness appears only after syntheses
and integrations are formed. In other words, consciousness cannot intervene
in the physical composition of experience:

> Blind physical purposes reign. It is now obvious that blind
> prehensions, physical and mental, are the ultimate bricks of the
> physical universe. They are bound together within each actuality
> by the subjective unity of aim which governs their allied genesis
> and their final concresence. (PR 308)

Conscious perception is characterized by negation. In perceiving this
stone as gray, the gray, an eternal object, makes an incursion into my experience and compels me to decide between gray and nongray. The eternal
objects constitute potentialities for the actual entities given in experience.
Potentiality makes up part of what is given; and being that is given insofar
as it is potential implies being limited, possibly denied, in order to be capable
of being sensed in experience: "'Potentiality' is the correlative of 'givenness.'
The meaning of 'givenness' is that what *is* 'given' might not have been
'given;' and that what *is not* 'given' *might have been* 'given'" (PR 44). In the
proposition affirming the gray character of the stone, the gray is detached

as something novel in experience, at the same time that it is in conformity
with what is given; thus its character is accentuated. An alternative discloses
itself in experience and it makes the given appear as being capable of not
being given in such a way; consequently the given appears as something novel
that cannot be explained simply as the product of the past. Consciousness
belongs to the subject whenever it perceives a "contrast between the eternal
objects designated by the words 'any' and 'just that.' Conscious perception is,
therefore, the most primitive form of judgment" (PR 161–162). It remains to
be considered why certain eternal objects are prehended positively and other
negatively, or again why certain ones are felt and other not.

> Consciousness is the feeling of negation: in the perception of "the
> stone as grey," such feeling is in barest germ; in the perception of
> "the stone as not grey," such feeling is in full development. Thus
> the negative perception is the triumph of consciousness. It finally
> rises to the peak of free imagination, in which the conceptual
> novelties search through a universe in which they are not datively
> exemplified. (PR 161)

Thus, consciousness illuminates or highlights only the higher phases in the
genesis of experience and leaves in the shadows what is more primitive and
accessible only to memory. If consciousness is light, illumination, it is necessary to add that it illuminates only what is recent and near to the present,
but it cannot reach what is long past or future.

Memory, Causal Efficacy of the Body

Whitehead accords the greatest importance to the problem of causality, but
he thinks that it was posed altogether badly by Hume and by Kant. If one
concedes to credit perceptual experience with our power of learning something
in the external world, then it appears that in regard to the external world
we have at our disposal two sources of information of different origin. The
perception of external things is given under two modalities, presentational
immediacy and causal efficacy. In perception by presentational immediacy
we apprehend things given in space-time with their qualities, colors, flavors,
sounds, etc. From perception by presentational immediacy we discover that
the sensuous data depend upon the perceiving organism and its relations to
other organisms. This form of perception, which allows us to localize things in
space, makes its appearance only in a small number of higher organisms.

In perception by causal efficacy, the accent is placed on the action of
the body that makes possible the representation of the data of experience.

If, in the eyes of Whitehead, Hume and Kant had good reason to bring the role of causality into the foreground, they did not see its true place in experience. They situated causal action at the level of the relations of things that are given in space-time. Hume sees in it only a habit of thinking and Kant a category of the understanding. Both have rightly seen the link of causal efficacy to time, but they have proceeded from a false conception of time—time reduced to pure succession. In other words, these two philosophers reduce causality to the projection of an intuition, a habit, or a judgment, onto the data of experience, and they do this because, under the pretext of apprehending what is immediate in experience, they grasp only what consciousness would see there. If time is given to us from experience, it is not the consciousness of the succession of acts and events relative to them that is capable of giving us that which is primordial in time. Whether it concerns impressions or phenomena, nothing given in experience is simple or pure. This pure succession, the object of a specific intuition according to Kant, results from an abstraction:

> Time is known to us as the succession of our acts of experience, and thence derivatively as the succession of events objectively perceived in those acts. But this succession is not pure succession: it is the derivation of state from state, with the later state exhibiting conformity to the antecedent. Time in the concrete is the conformation of state to state, the later to the earlier; and the pure succession is an abstraction from the irreversible relationship of settled past to derivative present. The notion of pure succession is analogous to the notion of colour. There is no mere colour, but always some particular colour such as red or blue: analogously there is no pure succession, but always some particular relational ground in respect to which the terms succeed each other. The integers succeed each other in one way, and events succeed each other in another way; and, when we abstract from these ways of succession, we find that pure succession is an abstraction of the second order, a generic abstraction omitting the temporal character of time and the numerical relation of integers. (S 35)

Hume and Kant thus did not grasp the true nature of time because they were prisoners to the principle of subjectivity, which binds the subject to consciousness.

If one adopts along with Whitehead the reformed subjectivist principle, then the truth issuing from experience can no longer come from a subject that receives impressions or that, setting out from its experience, represents objects as phenomena.

The principle of relativity, which governs all subjective experience, implies that all truth bearing on a thing is relative to all the other things that are produced in the universe. Experience can present the subject with something given only because the actuality of the act of experience does not simply imply the habits of experience or the conditions of its possibility, but fundamentally refers the source of every condition back to the universe.

In adopting the reformed subjectivist principle, it appears that efficient causality, independent of logical thinking, is given from an experience of time that is the experience of the conformity of the immediate present to the immediate past. From there one will be able to recognize as well the conformity of a fact connected with present action to the fact which immediately precedes that action. Contrary to perception by presentational immediacy, this perception does not turn the subject toward space, but to its body, and so perception by causal efficacy acts in every organism, however elementary it may be:

> My point is that this conformation of present fact to immediate past is more prominent both in apparent behaviour and in consciousness, when the organism is low grade. A flower turns to the light with much greater certainty than does a human being, and a stone conforms to the conditions set by its external environment with much greater certainty than does a flower. A dog anticipates the conformation of the immediate future to his present activity with the same certainty as a human being. When it comes to calculations and remote inferences, the dog fails. But the dog never acts as though the immediate future were irrelevant to the present. Irresolution in action arises from consciousness of a somewhat distant relevant future, combined with inability to evaluate its precise type. (S 41–42)

If this givenness of the experience of time escaped Descartes and his posterity, this is because the consciousness that conditions every act of perception and judgment implies attention and is therefore possible only from the starting point of the moment in which time is immobilized in a present lifted out from the pure intuition of time.

The reformed subjectivist principle thus comprises not only a principle of relativity but also a principle of conformity, which stipulates that what has been determines what is actual and what shall come. This conformity presents itself at once as a primitive experience of time referring to the continuity of corporeal life and ultimately to the continuity of the universe, but it is also given as an experience of the agreement between the presentational immediacy of things, according to which they appear as *"partes extra partes,"* and the experience of causal efficacy. Whitehead gives the name symbolic reference to the agreement between the two aspects of perception, which show at the same time the completion and the incompletion of the process: indeed, in presentational immediacy things follow one another in succession and perish, while in the experience of causal efficacy we get the experience of a continuity. Hence the diversity of subjective forms in feeling, which is always bipolar, namely, mental and physical.

This double aspect of perception eludes us in everyday perception, which is given most often as presentational immediacy, but sometimes it wells up from artistic and poetic experience. Art has the ability to rouse this double aspect of life, which is made of permanence (space) and becoming (time):

> "Pereunt et imputantur" is the inscription on old sundials in "religious" houses: "The hours perish and are laid to account." Here "Pereunt" refers to the world disclosed in immediate presentation, gay with a thousand tints, passing, and intrinsically meaningless. "Imputantur" refers to the world disclosed in its causal efficacy, where each event infects the ages to come, for good or for evil, with its own individuality. Almost all pathos includes a reference to lapse of time. (S 47)

Consciousness and Recollection

Thus, the continuity of experience does not come, as with Descartes, from a God who welds acts and instants together, or, as with Kant, from a pure intuition of succession as the form that orders empirical diversity. The body and time are not objects—or even subjects—of experience, but they enable us to understand how the life of the body actualizes what is given to us in experience. One can no longer say with Descartes that there is a body, and an environment that acts on it, and consciousness, which, at a distance, objectifies and neutralizes all these factors. Descartes, Hume, Locke, and Kant do not seem to have understood the true nature of time. Reduced to the repetition of sensations, the subject—caught in the contradiction between finite understanding, which sees, and infinite will, which affirms or negates—cannot act, or create, for it is outside of time. Only the divine will can reassemble the instants and the points of extension because the existence of the subject (just as that of extension) remains suspended in the continual creation accomplished by the divine will. But the continual creation secures only the continuity of the creation willed by God in the beginning. It does not extend to the "I," which is at once both substance (being in itself) and freedom (being for itself). To the extent that consciousness identifies itself with the "I," it appears as a relation between freedom, by which it can provisionally suspend the evidence coming from the understanding, and necessity, which comes from that same understanding when the truth guaranteed by God is imposed upon it. This relationship between freedom and necessity makes possible a creation of the subject that comes from the subject itself without having to realize an essence that God would have conceived at the moment of creating the world. Consciousness then appears as a relation between the will and the understanding that isolates the subject in a sort of solipsism and ends by making it a stranger to itself, namely, to its past and its body. Consciousness thus springs from a progressive purification that reduces time to the present instant and knowledge of time to the certitude of being in the present.

The Transmission of Feeling and Corporeal Inheritance

If Whitehead eschews this solipsistic conception of mind, it is because the conservation of the past does not isolate it from the present and the future as a truncated experience of time might make us believe. Whitehead's thesis begins from a physical experience of time. Indeed, if he were to adhere to this thesis strictly, his naturalism would become indistinguishable from a materialism that supposed memory derives its foundation from the fact that causal efficacy applies not only to phenomena, but also to the body and to the brain, without which there would not be any presentational immediacy.

The experience of the perceiving subject is no doubt an experience of feeling, but for higher beings it is both physical and mental at the same time. The perception of the gray stone is more than a simple visual display: "The 'stone' has a reference to its past, when it could be used as missile if small enough, or as a seat if large enough. A 'stone' has certainly a history, and probably a future" (PR 121). Thus, the physical feeling, when it is not reduced to the visual display of the qualities of things, reveals that nature—both physical and physiological—is not reducible to pure receptivity, but that it is transmission as well.

This is what gives perception is vectorial character:

> Pure receptivity and transmission give place to the trigger-action of life whereby there is release of energy in novel forms. Thus the transmitted datum acquires sensa enhanced in relevance or even changed in character by the passage from the low-grade external world into the intimacy of the human body. The datum transmitted from the stone becomes the touch-feeling in the hand, but it preserves the vector character of its origin from the stone. The touch-feeling in the hand with this vector origin from the stone is transmitted to the percipient in the brain. Thus the

final perception is the perception of the stone through the touch in the hand. In this perception the stone is vague and faintly relevant in comparison with the hand. But, however dim, it is there. (PR 119–120)

From the fact of this receptivity and this transmission, rendered possible by the causal efficacy that acts as much in nature as it does in the body, one can say that direct perception is inheritance.[3] If perception is not simply presentation but prolongation of the past, it is because things are given to us with their history. Whitehead even speaks of a physical memory. Causality and subsistence in time concern physical nature as well as organic nature:

> Again fatigue is the expression of cumulation; it is physical memory. Further, causation and physical memory spring from the same root: both of them are physical perception. Cosmology must do equal justice to atomism, to continuity, to causation, to memory, to perception, to qualitative and quantitative forms of energy, and to extension. But so far there has been no reference to the ultimate vibratory characters of organisms and to the "potential" element in nature. (PR 239)

What is true of physical feeling, which experiences causal efficacy with the body, is also true of mental feeling, which apprehends the contemporaneity of things in space. When mental feeling becomes a conceptual feeling, the subject experiences a perception of objects that would not be possible without an internal relation to eternal objects.

In this case perception preserves the character of receptivity and transmission originally manifested in physical feeling in the function of corporeal inheritance. Perception of the object through presentational immediacy calls for a decision that makes it possible to define what is given and delineate it from what is not given. In order to define the object starting from the representation, it is necessary to bring in positive prehensions when the object approximates to the datum, and negative ones when it deviates from it. Consciousness comes about when a decision obtains on whether or not the potentiality of the eternal object is actualized in the experience of the object represented in space-time.

Conclusion

According to Whitehead, the alienation of consciousness isolated like a point springs foremost from a bifurcation of nature into what is in itself and what is for us. This bifurcation is repeated by a split in the mind between what the mind is in itself and what it is for itself. The reconciliation of mind with itself requires a dialectical movement in the course of which the mind finally recovers its lost unity while preserving the history of its odyssey. In the case of bifurcation, the subject that is a relation of consciousness to self-consciousness needs an infinite time in order to realize itself. It is the end that pilots the process.

For Whitehead, self-realization concerns nature as well as spirit, for they are inseparable. In maintaining the thesis that every actualization is bipolar, at once both physical and mental, Whitehead exorcises the madness that menaces the mind when it doubts and reflects the doubt by a doubting of that doubt. Reflection and critique do not convey the true nature of the mind, which is a relation between becoming and permanence, a connection of the self [*le soi*] of memory and the me of consciousness [*le moi de la conscience*].

If consciousness is only a modality of the life of the subject and not a center, one can perhaps better understand how the return to oneself is accomplished by memory and how memory acts in every actualization in the occasion of experience.

Translation by Anderson Weekes[4]

Notes

1. Descartes understands freedom as the result of an asymmetrical relationship between will and understanding: "So what then is the source of my mistakes? It must be simply this: the scope of the will is wider than that of the intellect; but instead of restricting it within the same limits, I extend its use to matters which I do not understand" (Descartes 1953, 306/1964–1976, 7:58/1984, 2:40).

2. "The simple notion of an enduring substance sustaining persistent qualities, either essentially or accidentally, expresses a useful abstract for many purposes of life. But whenever we try to use it as a fundamental statement of the nature of things, it proves itself mistaken. It arose from a mistake and has never succeeded in any of its applications. But it has had one success: it has entrenched itself in language, in Aristotelian logic, and in metaphysics" (PR 79).

3. "The crude aboriginal character of direct perception is inheritance. What is inherited is feeling-tone with evidence of its origin: in other words, vector feeling-tone. In the higher grades of perception vague feeling-tone differentiates itself into various types of sensa—those of touch, sight, smell, etc.—each transmuted into a definite prehension of tonal contemporary nexūs by the final percipient" (PR 119).

4. The translator would like to thank Michel Weber for invaluable assistance with the translation and Xavier Verley for graciously answering so many questions about argument, interpretation, and phrasing.

References

Descartes, René. 1953. *Œuvres et Lettres*. Textes présentés par André Bridoux. Paris: Gallimard, Bibliothèque de la Pléiade.

Descartes, René. 1964–1976. *Œuvres de Descartes*. Ed. by Ch. Adam and P. Tannery. Revised ed. Paris: Vrin/C.N.R.S.

Descartes, René. 1984. *The Philosophical Writings of Descartes*. 3 vols. Trans. by John Cottingham, Robert Stoothoff, Dugald Murdoch. Cambridge: Cambridge University Press.

James, William. 1912. *Essays in Radical Empiricism*. New York/London/Toronto: Longmans, Green, and Co.

15

Consciousness and Causation in Whitehead's Phenomenology of Becoming

Anderson Weekes

Consciousness and causation are topics that intersect in two obvious ways. We can ask what the cause of consciousness is and we can ask how we become conscious of causation. Both questions take us back to seminal figures in the history of modern philosophy and both questions continue to be the subject of intense debate.

Early in the twentieth century, Alfred North Whitehead proposed a radical solution to both questions by treating them as the *same* question. It is lamentable that Whitehead's elegant solutions are so little discussed in the intellectual mainstream. Like the philosophy of Aristotle, Ockham, or Kant, Whitehead's is no doubt in the final analysis all wrong. Nevertheless, like theirs, Whitehead's system of thought possesses a degree of rigor and analytic nuance, as well as a comprehensiveness of scope that makes it an ideal tool for exploring the structure of philosophical problems, which—just because they are philosophical—reveal their contours only through our failed attempts to solve them.

This investigation seeks to make Whitehead's consolidated answer to these two important philosophical questions more accessible to the intellectual mainstream by carefully relating his theorems to well-established issues and ideas in Continental and Anglo-American philosophy and the history of philosophy as they understand it. I limit my discussion to the concepts of consciousness and causation as we have inherited them from the early modern tradition: consciousness as a form of seemingly private self-presence attending all our encounters with objects, real and imaginary; causation as a logically necessary or somehow physically impelled diachronic sequence of empirical phenomena, that is, efficient causation.

This focus on Whitehead's account of efficient causation (and our consciousness of it) also serves a secondary purpose. There is a not uncommon tendency among Whitehead enthusiasts to be lopsidedly concerned with human freedom, which they seek to preserve through an interpretation of his cosmology that amounts to eliminating physical necessity and efficient causation from the world. But Whitehead was as concerned to solve the problems of induction and the necessary connection between cause and effect as he was to vindicate freedom and personal responsibility. He did not seek to vindicate one side at the expense of the other. On the contrary, he expressly sought an integrated solution, the general structure of which he thought could be gleaned from a phenomenon such as consciousness, which he thought was a coherent nexus of both action and passion. By focusing primarily on Whitehead's defense of necessary causal connection rather than on freedom, this investigation hopes to rebalance the wider scholarly discussion.[1]

Background: History of the Two Problems and their Involution

Causation of Consciousness

Descartes is famous for being the first philosopher to circumscribe consciousness as an autonomous domain of reflection. For him consciousness had no cause other than God. Under the rubric of *res cogitans* it was a substance all its own, and in its reflection it was effectively *causa sui*. Others such as Hobbes and Gassendi believed the body was the cause of consciousness. In the eighteenth and nineteenth centuries, consciousness as self-cause became the leading theme of the idealistic philosophy developing in Germany, while consciousness as an effect or epiphenomenon of material organization was an idea pursued by the French materialists. What kind of causal relations—if any—obtain between consciousness and matter was a question that permitted a compact spectrum of answers and under the name of the mind-body problem continues to be recognized as one of the great philosophical questions.

Most recently, the apparent successes of cognitive psychology in explaining perception and cognition in terms of information processing routines and of neurobiology in finding the physiological mechanisms by which these processing routines are carried out have had paradoxical results. While seeming to make clear headway towards solving the mystery of how the mind depends on and arises from the brain, they have in fact forced the mind-body problem into its most aggravated form. The traditional assumption was that consciousness is necessary for the execution of sophisticated forms of cognition. However, there is no obvious reason why the sort of processing routines that have been successful in modeling cognition need to be accompanied by consciousness, and very often they are not. Advances in cognitive psychology and neuroscience have therefore made the biological explanation of consciousness a more rather than less daunting prospect. Why should the organism's processing of information from the environment—at least in certain distinctive cases—have a quality that is subjectively felt in an inner world of self-presence? Following David Chalmers (1995), this has come to be known as the "hard problem" of cognitive psychology and has generated a huge literature.

The hard problem results from the enigma of a relationship it plausibly assumes must exist. It makes the naturalistic assumption that matter in some form of organization gives rise to or must be attended by consciousness. What I am calling *causation of consciousness* is this assumed relationship, defined in its greatest possible generality. It is the determination according to which an inner world comes into being in dependency on features of the outer world (such as the neural organization of the brain). Excluded thereby is only the idea that matter is altogether something to which mind gives rise (idealism) or that there is no necessary link between them (occasionalism, preestablished harmony). No particular way of construing this determinative relationship (e.g., genesis, function, supervenience, emergence) is ruled out *a priori*.

Consciousness of Causation

How we become conscious of causation was a question raised by Locke in seeking the empirical origin of our various ideas—in this case the idea of "power." But it was Hume, disappointed by Locke's account, who subjected to rigorous critique the idea that one thing can bring about another. Like Locke, Hume asked what empirical basis there was for this idea. Famously, he found none and offered instead a psychological explanation of our propensity to believe in causation. Subsequently, no science seeking its foundations has been able to remain indifferent to Hume's question about the nature of causation and our knowledge of it.

Hume's analysis of causation is distinguished in historical effect. Philosophically conceived problems—even the ones felt to be the most revolutionary in their day—become quaint when the context of discussion shifts. Hume's argument did not. It not only brought on one of the great upheavals in intellectual history, but it also retained its cogency and long outlived the intellectual climate that fostered it. It remains a fundamental point of reference for contemporary discussion, where it is the centerpiece of what is known as the problem of induction or the problem of verification.

The problem of induction comes down to this: Unless the correlations we can document empirically result from the necessity of some kind of real causal connectedness, it's unclear what justification we could have for generalizing them. For all we know, they may be coincidences. Verifying a conjunction *de facto* would thus offer no grounds for induction, which entails generalizing the conjunction to unobserved (or even unobservable) instances. Induction seems to presuppose, if not that we understand how causation operates, at least that we know that it exists and that its operation is the reason for a given conjunction. Only then can we generalize.

We can distinguish a conceptual as well as an empirical aspect to the causality/induction problem. Philosophers, as we shall see in due course, often raise questions about the logical coherence of the very idea of causation (conceptual problem). But what engages the sciences is a legitimately empirical concern about the applicability of such a concept to experience. Of course, philosophical objections based on the alleged logical incoherence of the concept of causation are *a fortiori* objections to its empirical applicability. In this way the philosophers' arguments bear on empirical concerns. But even if the idea is not incoherent, empirical concerns remain. For even granting the coherence of the idea of causation, we still do not know if it applies to anything we actually experience. Furthermore, even if we know in general that it applies, how do we know in individual cases whether we are dealing with causation or coincidence? It is worth emphasizing that scientific induction is not the only relevant case of causal thinking applied to experience. The commonsense assumption that beliefs influence behavior is an everyday example of causal thinking, just as the idea of "character" is an everyday example of induction, without which behavior could never be predicted or anticipated.

There are two approaches to solving these problems that need to be distinguished before we can proceed to catalog the objections to them. It is possible to secure and define the applicability of causation to experience transcendentally or descriptively. The transcendental approach is the one first employed by Kant, arguing that causal structure is the very condition of the possibility of experience, and hence that any experience is causally structured. The attractiveness of this approach lies mainly in avoiding the notorious difficulties of the other way. In and of itself, Kant's transcendental apparatus of *a priori* conditions finds little favor. Because it is nothing empirical, it seems "metaphysical" and theoretically unwieldy. But the transcendental approach, stripped of its unwieldiness and cast in a form that still deserves serious consideration, has been kept alive in our time by pragmatism, which replaces the mysteriously *a priori* conditions of the possibility of experience with the pragmatic conditions of the possibility of successful engagement.[2] The other way tries to justify the empirical applicability of the idea of causation more simply: by showing that it is in fact empirically derived. This is what Locke tried to do and what Hume argued could not be done.

We need to be clear about what is required by this second approach. It requires not simply that we understand causation conceptually and be able to infer that it exist, which would be the transcendental approach, but rather that its very operation fall within the purview of consciousness. What I am calling *consciousness of causation* is therefore a condition of any empirical or phenomenological justification for the application of causal thinking to experience. (Henceforth in place of "empirical or phenomenological" I shall say descriptive.) The descriptive approach presupposes a conscious experience by means of which we become directly acquainted with causal action; that is to say, it presupposes "knowledge by acquaintance" in Bertrand Russell's sense. On the other hand, a "knowledge by description" in the specific sense defined by Russell (which is not a descriptive report on the content of first-hand acquaintance, but the conceptual specification of identity conditions), would seem to suffice for the transcendental approach.[3] However, I will argue in the following paragraphs that consciousness of causation is also—albeit less directly—a condition of the transcendental justification. Let's look first at the objections to the descriptive approach, which refine the causation problem into a set of specific counterarguments against the attempted descriptive solutions.

Arguments against the second approach to justifying causal thinking—the approach based on the description of causation as a phenomenon falling within the purview of consciousness—take several forms, which span the full spectrum from purely empirical to purely conceptual arguments. In practice the distinctions tend to blur, but in theory we can distinguish four. I list them in ascending order of logical strength: in each case, the weaker objection holds *a fortiori* if the stronger one does, the last and strongest argument being the philosophers' argument from logical incoherence. (1) A conscious experience of causation has not been found (*de facto*); (2) a conscious experience of causation cannot be found because such an experience is impossible on psychological or phenomenological grounds; (3) a conscious experience of causation cannot be found because causation is impossible on physical or metaphysical grounds; (4) a conscious experience of causation cannot be found because causation is impossible on logical or conceptual grounds.[4]

We now need to notice that objections (3) and (4), because they concern the very possibility of causation, and objection (2), because it concerns its thinkability, pose as much of a threat to the transcendental approach as they do to the descriptive approach. It may be that objections (2), (3), and (4) can be neutralized only by a descriptive finding of decisive importance (the "proof is in the pudding" rebuttal). Indeed, if the concept of causation is as paradoxical as Hume and its other critics allege, then the transcendental approach could never be assured of the concept's empirical applicability based on discursive considerations alone. The situation is not unlike wave-particle complementarity in physics: it's so paradoxical that no one would believe it if it weren't empirically documented, regardless of the strength of theoretical arguments. Similarly, the transcendental approach must either relieve the concept of causation from its burden of paradox or be ready to make the pudding. It must be able to render the phenomenon of causation transparent *in actu exercito*, which requires exhibiting its reality or at least being able to imagine its real possibility *in concreto*. The inevitable conclusion is that actual consciousness of causation is not just a condition of the success of the descriptive approach, but also of the transcendental approach to the justification of causal thinking.

Two Problems or One?

It is noteworthy that the causation/induction problem and the mind-body problem are seen as two distinct problem clusters and are rarely discussed together. But it was surely only a matter of time until the one problem would be applied to the other: how can we hope to understand how consciousness is brought about if we have no consciousness of how one thing brings about another? The fact that this involution has explicitly taken place in the journal literature is the instigation for this paper. The arguments are refereed below and set the stage for my discussion of Whitehead's theory of consciousness. For Whitehead believes that the mind-body problem and the induction problem are the same problem, and that the problem arises as the result of a skewed and incomplete phenomenology of consciousness, one that arbitrarily ignores the genetic dimension of experience. When this dimension is ignored, says Whitehead, the reality of causation and the relationship of consciousness to the reality that causes it are both eclipsed.

My point of departure is a provocative article on the psychology of explanation by Eleanor Rosch (1994) in the first issue of the *Journal of Consciousness Studies*, "Is Causation Circular?" As an extreme radicalization of Hume's skepticism, Rosch suggests that, apart from the explanatorily useless limiting case of tautology, a necessary (or even intelligible) connection between cause and effect is not just empirically unattested, but altogether impossible. This lends our stubborn propensity to believe in causation a pathological aspect that her sympathies with Buddhism do not deflect. In fact, her analysis employs the analytic framework of the Mādhyamika, the skeptical dialecticians of early and medieval Buddhism, but it could equally well have drawn on Western precedents. On the grounds—not unfamiliar to the Western reader—that identity or tautology is the only logical necessity, she endorses Hume's argument that separate (i.e., nonidentical) phenomena cannot be necessarily related. But for Rosch, Hume's argument is just a special case of the Mādhyamika's dialectical argument. According to the Mādhyamika, we can in effect classify all relations into relations of identity and relations of difference. It's not hard to see that being different, in and of itself, is not enough to establish a necessary connection between any two things. If the only other kind of relation is the relation of identity (construed perhaps as the pseudo-relation of single-itemhood), then identity will be the only kind of necessity possible (although not all identities need be necessary).

Rosch's account of the psychology of explanation found its inevitable application to the problem of explaining consciousness in a subsequent issue of the same journal. In an article entitled "Should We Expect to Feel as if We Understand Consciousness?" M.C. Price (1996) uses Rosch's analysis to argue that the famous "hard problem" of explaining consciousness is nothing more than a particularly conspicuous instance of the impossibility of cogently explaining anything. We could, according to Price, never have the intellectual satisfaction of feeling like we have explained something unless, Hume to the contrary, causation were something that could be rendered intelligible. And we have just clarified what that would mean. The operation of causation must be brought within the purview of consciousness and rendered perspicuous. The supposed necessary connection of separate phenomena ("ideas") is something that otherwise remains unintelligible. But Price is confident that it is inherently unintelligible. Following Rosch (following the Mādhyamika), Price proposes that "separate, but dependent/interdependent" is just plain contradictory. Consequently, the idea of causal operation will never be perspicuous, and the most we will ever know about the relationship of mind and animal body—the most that there is to know—is that up until now they have always been constantly conjoined.

This result is intriguing. It means that we could never explain consciousness without first (or at least at the same time) documenting that we do have some legitimate consciousness of causation to model our explanation on. Otherwise the best we get is a self-contradictory concept and a set of inscrutable correlations. In short, explaining consciousness requires solving the intractable problem of causal connection, which Rosch's analysis has inflated into an archetypal problem of metaphysics, the insolubility of which seems to her to call for a religious rather than a scientific response.

Archetypal Status of the Causation Problem

There is something to be said for the archetypal status of this problem. It erupts with a certain amount of intellectual violence in every major philosophical tradition. A rejection of causation based on the impossibility of a necessary connection between distinct individuals makes what is probably its earliest philosophical appearance in ancient Greece. It played an important role in the skepticism of the New Academy (ca. third century BCE) and is documented for us in the compendia of skeptical arguments preserved for us by Sextus Empiricus (third century CE).[5]

In Indian philosophy, critical discussion of causation dates from the earliest times (Kalupahana 1975, chs. 1–2), but the dialectical critique of causation has its beginning with Nāgārjuna and the Mādhyamika in the first century CE (Inada 1993, Kalupahana 1986, McCagney 1997). The specific argument predicated on the impossibility of necessary connection between distinct individuals played an understandably prominent role in Buddhism due to the doctrine of momentariness of all being (the question being "how can phenomena isolated in independent moments of time be connected?"). While the Mādhyamika in particular rejected this doctrine and operated with more abstract categories (e.g., same and other), the schools accepting it (Sautrāntika, Yogācāra) advanced a critique of causation that is virtually indistinguishable from its western counterparts. It can be found, for example, in Dharmakīrti (seventh century CE) or in Śāntarakṣita's *Tattvasangraha* and its commentary by Kamalaśīla (both eighth century CE).[6]

The argument then makes a dramatic appearance in the context of Islamic theology (Kalām). First a polemical weapon of the reactionary al-Ash'arī[7] (tenth century), who saw the rationalizing tendencies of early Kalām (i.e., the Mu'tazila) as anathema to religion, it was famously taken over by al-Ghazālī (eleventh century) in his similarly motivated attack on science and philosophy, *The Incoherence of the Philosophers*.[8] Like the *Tattvasangraha*, *The Incoherence of the Philosophers* is a kind of elenchtic encyclopedia—not a systematic compendium of knowledge, but a systematic compendium of knowledge claims and their unrelenting refutation. In both cases the objective was religious. In this regard, both works bear a strong and arguably not coincidental resemblance to the compendia of skeptical arguments composed by Sextus Empiricus. The *Outlines of Pyrrhonism* and the sequence of works *Against the Professors* constitute an exhaustive elenchtic encyclopedia, the purport of which is not theoretical but expressly spiritual: inducing peace of mind (*ataraxia*) by exposing the vanity of all claims to knowledge.

In its last major eruption before the modern period, the argument is a natural consequence of the kind of nominalism popular in the Latin West of the fourteenth century. It makes a first appearance in a very limited context in the writings of William of Ockham, but quickly breaks out of all bounds, making an explicit stand in the famous condemned letters of Nicholas of Autrecourt (Maier 1963, Weinberg 1969 and 1977).

In sum, there are rich and formidable traditions behind Rosch's argumentation. Furthermore, Price's application of it seems unavoidable: if causation is something impossible or the possibility of which is at any rate off-limits to consciousness, then consciousness itself is one of the things we can't explain.

Prospect

Many will want to challenge different steps in the arguments of Rosch and Price or make distinctions that seem neglected here. I doubt these stratagems will help in the long run. What I want to explore is something different. As the philosophy of A.N. Whitehead demonstrates, it is possible to concede almost every point to Rosch and Price—even to the Mādhyamika—and still hold out for a different result. In fact, the trajectory I have described, since it implies that the mind-body problem cannot be solved apart from the induction problem, can be seen as partial corroboration of Whitehead's belief that they are the same problem. What Whitehead adds of course is that the induction problem cannot be solved apart from the mind-body problem either.

We will see that Whitehead offers a unique solution to the causation problem and in so doing makes a positive contribution to the phenomenology of consciousness. This phenomenology yields at one stroke his solution to the problem of induction and to the mind-body problem. Whitehead believes that consciousness is at bottom an experience of its own causal emergence out of the physical world it is conscious of. Consequently, we do not have to go far to find an authentic experience of causation. All consciousness involves an experience of causation, and in being conscious we already possess a paradigm of what causation is. What this means, of course, is that consciousness must have all of the same problematic features that have made causation so controversial. For Whitehead, therefore, the challenge of explaining consciousness is even greater, but the trade-off is that if he can explain how consciousness is possible, he will have explained at the same time how causation is possible.

Whitehead's psychology is unconventional. For one thing, he does not believe that all experience is conscious. On the contrary, he thinks consciousness is a uniquely convoluted form of experience that is comparatively rare. As one might expect, his explanation of consciousness is correspondingly convoluted. Furthermore, his theory of nonconscious experience becomes the staging area for his famously bold experiment in metaphysical cosmology. This, too, makes his psychology a challenge to conventional wisdom and easy interpretation. These complications dictate the course of our investigation. Before harvesting Whitehead's theory of consciousness for his solution to the causation problem, we will have to outline the unorthodox psychology at the heart of his theory of experience and his metaphysics insofar as it bears on this psychology. And before that, we will have to deal with the obvious question: if the experience of causation is so readily available, why has the existence of such an experience been so widely and successfully disputed throughout the history of philosophy? The Whiteheadian answer I will elaborate is: consciousness is always an experience of causation (both final and efficient), but it is never more than barely consciousness of causation. In short, it is true that no one will find causation among the well-identified objects of consciousness, but there are other places to look that have traditionally been ignored (cf. Weekes 2006). What Whitehead thinks we find by looking back at experience that was nonobjectified as it was occurring is a universal model for understanding causal operation. We discover process as a quasi-organic event whose germinal reality is unavoidably characterized by a logical and ontological fuzziness. This process is not vulnerable to the demands that power the dialectical arguments against causation, namely, the demands for a stark disjunction between identity and difference, same and other, separate and interdependent, or distinct and internally related.

Using nonobjectified experience as his model, Whitehead's metaphysics proposes a radically original ontology of events. All things are made of events, and all events have the structure of experience, even if its intensity is in most cases so attenuated as to be negligible. Whitehead's proposal to use psychology as a model for a new metaphysics strikes many as outlandish. Yet it is an idea whose time seems to have come as a growing body of literature explores the possibility that the features of consciousness that are hardest to explain are a macro-manifestation of essential properties of physical micro-structure. But it is not just physics that Whitehead transforms with a psychological reading. He also transforms psychology with a physical or physiological reading that counteracts its inherent tendency toward some form of subjective idealism. The result is a psychology that avoids many of the snares of modern philosophy that still trapped the Phenomenology of Husserl and continue to lurk in many proposals of cognitive psychology. My final objective, however, is not to defend or critique this theory, although I attempt to present it in a sympathetic light, but to make it available to ongoing discussion. It fills an unsuspected gap in the spectrum of possible answers to the much-debated question of the nature of consciousness.

Rosch: Circularity and Incoherence in Causal Thinking

In her article, Eleanor Rosch offers a psychological analysis of the perception and ascription of causality. Examining a wide cross-section of samples—from science to superstition—as well the results of controlled experiments, she finds that the explanatory patterns of both scientific and everyday thinking illustrate the same dubious logic. Despite themselves, common sense and scientific practice corroborate the most extreme views of the philosophers. She takes as undisputed that no one—scientist or layman—accepts as valid an explanation that analysis and reflection reveal to be a mere tautology. But her data suggest that no one—scientist or layman—finds an explanation coherent until it has in fact been reduced to a tautology. Since explicit tautology is not accepted, the sense that explanation has done its job successfully comes from the degree to which we have managed to deceive ourselves about the fallacy we have committed.

In effect, Rosch provides an empirical confirmation of the extreme critique of causality. If the philosophers are right, then what passes for successful explanation must involve an element of deception. Empirical psychology seems to confirm this. Since Whitehead's view is the opposite—that common practice attests veridically to causality—Rosch's analysis merits our detailed attention.

Rosch's Argument

First, Rosch analyzes causation into three elements: "Any coherent event or event sequence can be conceived in terms of three parts: a *ground* out of which the event can be seen to arise, something that *happens*, and an *outcome*. The happening is the connecting link between the ground and the outcome" (51). Then she applies the Mādhyamika's typology, which is meant to encompass all logically possible relations between ground and outcome. Since the Mādhyamika's dialectic is unconventional in the extreme, a short introduction may be in order.

According to the Mādhyamika there are four ways to understand the arising of events. Either an event arises out of a cause that is the same as, different from, both the same as and different from, or neither the same as nor different from itself (this is the logical format of the Mādhyamika's so-called "tetralemma"). Taking the extreme cases under each heading, the first alternative is said to be self-causation, a thing arising from itself (identity being the limit of sameness), and the second is said to be causation by something wholly other. Anything intermediate between these two extremes (causation by something similar, for example) is seen as somehow composed of or mediated by these two extremes and so falls under alternative three, which in its own extreme formulation divides into two alternatives: "causation by something *both* wholly identical *and* wholly other" or "causation by something in part identical and in part other." Finally, the last alternative is identified with having no cause at all, things arising by pure chance.

It should not be difficult to see how the Mādhyamika's typology lends itself to destructive dialectic. I will review the lemmas in reverse order, reserving critique for the next section. The idea that everything arises completely by chance squares poorly with the evident order and regularity in a world of heterogeneous events. Instead, we should expect wild irregularities and/or by the law of large numbers a chaos converging on complete uniformity. I have already set the third alternative up in a way to foreground its putative inadequacy. "Both wholly identical and wholly other" is rejected as a bald contradiction, and "in part identical and in part other" obviously resolves itself into "one part wholly identical" and "one part wholly other," in other words into a straightforward conjunction of the first two alternatives. Accordingly, this construal of the third alternative will stand or fall with each of them. The second alternative, by reducing the connection of cause and effect to sheer difference, fails to explain why any two arbitrarily taken events cannot stand in the relation of cause and effect as long as they are different. The first alternative runs up against a number of fascinating logical puzzles that cannot be explored here. The most important is the obvious one: if cause and effect are truly identical, then there is no dyadic relation of two terms, no progression from one to the other, in short, no causality. Alternatively, if there is such a self-reproduction, it should reiterate indefinitely. The overall conclusion, then, is that causation cannot be understood in any of the four ways that are logically conceivable. In short, causation is impossible.

Dialectical arguments of this type, so common in antiquity both East and West, may not be as easily dispatched as modern thinkers would like to believe, and we shall see that Rosch has done a remarkable job of showing this in the case at hand.

Rosch suggests that we always justify the ascription of causal connectedness by an appeal to some kind of identity across difference. She associates this tactic with the Mādhyamika's first construal of causation. She catalogues four basic types of putative "self-causation." (1) Seeing the ground and outcome as the same entity, only transformed in some way. Examples: object constancy amid variations in visual perception. An object looks different not despite its being the same object, but under the circumstances because it is the same object. (2) Seeing the transfer of a property from ground to outcome. Examples: apparent motion transfer in apparent collisions; sympathetic magic; affective association. A feature of the ground is directly conveyed to the outcome. (3) Seeing an object as causing our perception of it or our intention as causing our action. Examples: "the tacit assumption that objects have the properties we see in them;" explanation by motives, by unconscious intentions, by unconscious information processing, by instinct. (4) Seeing something as the manifestation of its essence. Examples: explanation by attribution of character traits, dispositions, the "nature" of the thing, genetics, faculties.

But this appeal to identity has the result that explanations we initially find acceptable turn out to be scientifically useless tautologies. Her thesis:

> [T]o be perceived as coherent, events must normally be seen to
> arise from themselves. [. . .] any event—temporal or deductive—

will be seen to be coherent (or causally bound) to the extent that the outcome is seen to be already in the ground. The connecting link must also be the appropriate sort to transform the outcome as it is contained in the ground into the actual outcome; however, the more identical the outcome in the ground is to the actual outcome, the more minimal need be an account of the happening which connects them. Although this is the natural mode of explanation, when we reflect upon such accounts we find them tautological and demand of scientific explanations that events be shown to arise from what is other than themselves. It is from this demand that the other three types of explanation arise. (52)

But attempts at scientific explanation are doomed to failure because identity is the only standard of coherence we know:

> A real account of causes, a noncircular explanation, a scientific account, must show how something arises from what is not already itself. [...] But however long the chain, explanations which derive outcomes from what is entirely other than themselves face an interesting difficulty. As long as an event comes from a ground which is strictly and thoroughly other than the outcome, the relationship between ground and outcome remains incoherent. [...] all explanations deriving events from something completely other than themselves become explanations because somewhere along the way they introduce the outcome itself and thus turn the account into one in which the outcome is already contained in the ground. (57–58)

The identity requirement aligns with the Mādhyamika's first alternative, the difference requirement with the second. Rosch does not believe the two requirements are compatible any more than the Mādhyamika did, but an adequate explanation would have to be one that satisfied both requirements simultaneously: establishing identity without abrogating difference. The argument is deceptively simple. What impresses is the way empirical data about human behavior appear to support its conclusions. Rosch's most striking examples are drawn from psychology: cognitive science and behaviorism.

Rosch's Documentation

Rosch stresses the explanatory satisfaction cognitive science finds in isomorphisms: in "a computational account of form perception [...] [r]etinal stimulation goes through a series of stages at each of which the representation looks more and more like the percept. In fact, 'looks like' is taken somewhat literally by the computationalists." Rosch takes this to be a clear case of explaining something through itself. Furthermore, where first-order isomorphism between neurophysiology and experience cannot be found, as in the case of color perception ("there are obviously no first-order-isomorphisms between neural representations, which are not coloured, and the percept which is"), second-order isomorphisms are sought: "In regard to colour, the structure of neural representations at the cortical level can be said to *map* the structure of the colour solid. The more similar the better" (59).

It might seem that the idea of second-order isomorphism is just what is needed, since it satisfies the identity requirement without abrogating the difference requirement. So don't we have it: identity without tautology? Rosch does not address this consideration expressly, and frankly I think she has not exploited the full power of her own example. Since it will become relevant when we turn to the problem of explaining consciousness below, let the following be noted as a rejoinder of the Mādhyamika's type: while "second-order isomorphism" may appear to be a coherent, nontautological way of explaining qualitative aspects of perception such as color, it resolves itself—just as the Mādhyamika's dialectic predicts—into two parts, a part that is tautological because it asserts that a structure remains the same as itself, and a part that is incoherent because it spans a gap of unmediated and unbridgeable difference. This is the "hard problem": how the qualities of subjective experience can arise from a purely physical substrate like the brain. What the fairly broad contemporary consensus about the hard problem comes down to is this: at least in the case of explaining consciousness, the Mādhyamika's analysis is right on target.

Rosch does not believe that the logical problem of explanation is unique to the hard problem of consciousness or the methodological program of cognitive psychology. She gives examples from the history of behaviorism that that are equally remarkable for the way second-order isomorphism is superimposed on unexplained difference.[9]

Rosch also finds tautology concealed in types of explanation that do not employ the concept of isomorphism, such as multi-factorial and statistical explanations. Here she finds that the bias for circularity disguises itself as a demand for "causal relevance." Rosch documents a general tendency for people to disbelieve that things can have more than one cause, as well as a (presumably related) tendency in avowedly multi-factorial explanation to downplay factors that are merely correlations and to emphasize one (and usually just one) that seems to have intrinsic relevance because it really conceals a tautology. Multi-factorial explanation—not as it is envisioned, but as it is practiced—is thus a case of the Mādhyamika's third alternative. It tends to reduce to a factor that is considered "relevant" because circular and others whose relevance is considered opaque and unsatisfactory because they are not circular, but simply other.

Statistical explanations and explanations that eschew the notion of causation or causal relevance in the name of mere correlations or their frequencies Rosch compares to the Mādhyamika's fourth alternative. Here she rightly notes that no laymen or practicing scientist really operates on a regularity interpretation of causality. Only regularities that are relevant within the context of an inclusive theory of how things work are considered causal: "we do not think for a minute that our belief that rice plants will grow from rice seeds is only an expectation generated from the constant conjunction of these events in the past; we understand this regularity within our theory of genetics, which itself is part of our general theory of biological systems. [...] [C]onstant conjunction [...] will not be taken as causality itself unless it is embedded in an appropriate theory" (61). But what the embedding theory provides, as we saw above from Rosch's discussion of behaviorism and cognitive psychology, is a surreptitious way to think of certain regularities as circularities.

Finally, Rosch notes the frequency with which statistical explanations commit the fallacy of computing probability based on assumptions of representativeness rather than on base-rates:

> Thus, the probability of a given person being a librarian is computed, not on the basis of the (low) rate of occurrence of librarians in the population sampled, but by how closely the individual in question matches the stereotype of a librarian, a category essence relationship. This may not be simply a technical error in computing probability, as it is often treated, but a downright refusal on the part of subjects to take the situation as probabilistic. Subjects are quite capable of using base rates when those are presented as causally relevant. (62)

Upshot of her Analysis

Rosch's defense of the Mādhyamika's thesis is no doubt off-putting, but the identification of necessity or logical coherence with analyticity or formal tautology in twentieth-century logic lends support to their view. Indeed, the impossibility of reducing causation to formal logical necessity (to identity or tautology) is the core of Hume's critique of science that empiricism still accepts. In its usual form the critique makes the following assumptions: (a) that logical necessity (or something as strong as logical necessity) is what is required in scientific explanations, (b) that only logical necessity satisfies condition (a) because nothing else is as strong as logical necessity, (c) that identity and tautology are the only logical necessities, and (d) the relationship between putative cause and effect cannot be reduced to identity or tautology. It is not only possible to find each of these assumptions in Hume's *Treatise*, but it is also possible to show that they are not simply prejudices of empiricism. For it is precisely because the rationalists Leibniz and Wolff accepted (a), (b), and (c), that they saw a need to rescue the law of causation by attempting to disprove (d).[10] Leibniz at least was quick to realize that (d) could not be disproved and sought instead ingenious ways to qualify it.[11]

The argument of the Mādhyamika and their Western counterparts is logical: coherence that is not simply identity is an incoherent notion. Rosch wants to show that this seemingly daring thesis is something everyone, including the scientist, implicitly already believes. Rosch's thesis poses an unusual evidentiary burden on its opponents. For it is an empirical claim that could be refuted only by a logical argument: to show that belief in successful explanation is not always deceptive, we would have to adduce an instance of truly successful (logically unexceptionable) explanation. Those who invoke intellectual seriousness as a reason to put aside the Scholasticism of purely verbal arguments, enjoining us to focus on propositions of empirical importance, will find themselves uncomfortably cornered. Whether or not Rosch has exposed deception at the heart of explanation, she has exposed the shallowness of positivistic posturing.

Outline of Whitehead's Solution

We seem to be left with the classic dilemma: tautologies are not acceptable explanations, but explanations whose necessity falls short of the logical necessity of tautologies are not accepted either. We see why the law of causality came to be associated with what Kant described as synthetic knowledge *a priori*. If explanation is to be both compelling and noncircular, a necessity that is not a formal-logical tautology must be possible. And short of this vexed Kantian solution, it's not clear that Rosch's argument won't carry the day—a triumph few will welcome.

If this situation piques interest in alternatives, few are in the offing. Most philosophers either give up on nontautological necessity or attempt variations on Kant's aprioristic solution using transcendental arguments about the conditions of the possibility of cognitive engagement with the world. Whitehead, on the other hand, offers a genuine alternative. He proposes process as the basis for necessary synthesis.

Whitehead sets out to find the conditions of the possibility of existence in time. We take it for granted that the world at any moment is overwhelmingly like but distinct from the world of the immediately preceding moment and that it will turn out to have been overwhelmingly like but distinct from the immediately following moment. This continuity is the most rudimentary basis for induction. But, just as for Hume, induction will have no scientific justification—only a psychological explanation—unless this process of similar continuation is somehow necessary. The assimilation of the past to the present and the accommodation of the present to the past must be metaphysically obligatory. Otherwise our expectation of a greater or lesser degree of continuity at every moment will remain a leap of faith.

Whitehead believes the continuity of things existing in time is the external appearance or result of what are really discrete acts of continuation. This is the lesson he chose to take from the earliest discoveries in quantum theory. Taking his next cue from Bergson, he thinks we can have some idea what this time-creating process looks like from the inside by looking at the most primitive aspects of our own experience of time, which is characterized by the organic wholeness of experience within the brief duration of the specious present. This unlikely fusion of Bergson's theory of duration with quantum theory yields the following (possibly incredible) thesis: manifest physical time is an accretion of lifeless deposits left behind by countless minute durations of lived time, which succeed one another in a dense volley of surges, each having the briefest possible duration. Whitehead proposes that inside the durational process there is a dyadic relation that is the basis for such distinctions as present and past, subject and object, effect and cause, all of which collapse into one distinction. In outline: the present corresponds to mind (lived duration) and the past to matter (lifeless deposit left by previously expired durations). Matter is analogous to the animal body, which is both the material substrate upon which the functioning of mind depends (or that from which it emerges) and the primary object that mind experiences. The past is both substrate and object of the present. Before going any further into Whitehead's ideas, we need to finish our examination of the sort of position to which he offers an alternative.

Whitehead Agrees with Price: The "Hard Problem" of Explaining Consciousness Is Hume's Problem of Causation

Price's Argument

Drawing on Rosch's analysis, M.C. Price (1997) suggests a novel solution to the hard problem of physically explaining experienced qualia. Price concedes that there is an "explanatory gap" between our objective accounts of brains and our first-person subjective viewpoints, but for him this is not the problem: "I would like to suggest (1) that explanatory gaps are in fact ubiquitous in our causal explanations of the world, (2) that we are just very good at covering up these gaps, and (3) that what is special about consciousness is not the presence of a gap, but the fact that the gap just happens to be particularly obvious and difficult to obscure" (83). Accepting Rosch's analysis of the psychology of the feeling of causal closure and Hume's regularity account of causation, Price concludes that the hard problem is an illusion. Causation is simply regular correlation. Never is it the case that there is transparent connection between cause and effect. Sounding like the Mādhyamika, he argues: "The idea of a causal nexus is in principle non-sensical because ground A and outcome B cannot at the same time be different from one another *and* account for each other. We seek to link two different states of affairs, but, by virtue of the very fact that they are different, an explanatory gap must remain between them. Causation 'as it really is' consists just of regularities in the relationships between states of affairs in the world (Hume's 'constant union and conjunction of like objects')" (85).

According to Price we *feel* as if an explanation is adequate when it meets one of the four conditions of concealed tautology described by Rosch (or similar conditions—Price notes that Rosch's catalog might be incomplete). Price then considers each of the possibilities (in a somewhat different order than Rosch) in regard to the causation of consciousness: (1) where consciousness is the outcome, could we see qualitative subjectivity as a property transferred from the brain as ground? Obviously not—that's the whole hard problem in a nutshell; (2) but neither, he claims, can we see consciousness as the result of perceiving an object or intending an action: "[T]he hard question of consciousness is not about how particular objects of perception or particular actions map onto particular *contents* of consciousness—it is about how our internal representations are conscious at all" (88). (3) Can we see consciousness as the same thing as the brain, only transformed in some way? This is the view, he notes, implied by the mind-brain identity thesis and the dual aspect theory, but neither theory meets the psychological requirement: "it is all very well to think of consciousness and its ground as the same thing viewed from differing perspectives, but this merely begs the question of how such radically differing perspectives can come about" (89); (4) finally, Price proposes panpsychism as a paradigm example of the fourth type of explanation, which he formulates somewhat differently from Rosch: seeing the outcome as a property of a category to which the ground belongs. But seeing consciousness as a property of matter to begin with, he claims, just pushes the explanatory gap back; it doesn't bridge it. Price concludes: the hard problem is a psychological problem, not a scientific one. There is no reason to expect we will feel satisfied with even a perfectly adequate explanation of consciousness because, unlike folk explanations that involve concealed tautologies, truly scientific explanations are just correlations and never "bridge" the explanatory gap.

Reservations and Critical Responses

Taking stock of the arguments of Rosch and Price, we must ask how serious a triumph this is for the Mādhyamika. Some important reservations need to be granted. For a sophisticated solution we can turn to chaos theory and nonlinear dynamics, which have taught us that random events need not average out into a state of zero complexity. Self-organization is compatible with the second law of thermodynamics, which presumably has implications for information theory. This would circumvent the rejection of alternative four, and Rosch acknowledges the importance of this prospect (64). But the discomfort of common sense lies elsewhere.

The first two alternatives, given their extreme formulation ("self-same" or "simply other"), are logically hopeless construals of causation. But what about less extreme formulations? Common sense can go along with the idea that anything less extreme will fall "between" these two extremes and should be treated under the heading of alternative three ("same *and* not the same"), but common sense probably can't help suspecting that alternative three has not gotten a fair shake. Recall that "both the same and not the same" was construed to mean either "in part the same and in part not the same" or "both *wholly* the same and *wholly* not the same." The former was rejected as a straightforward conjunction of alternatives ones and two and hence no better than either, while the latter was rejected as an intolerable contradiction. In both cases the assumption is that alternative three simply resolves itself back into the mere conjunction of the first two alternatives—generating a contradiction if the conjuncts are not differently distributed and offering nothing over and above one and two if they are. Two response strategies are pertinent here: (1) on the one hand, why should we go along with the damaging claim that alternative three simply resolves itself back into the mere conjunction of the first two alternatives? (2) On the other hand, even if it does, why can't the conjunction of one and two solve the problem each suffers in isolation?

The former option—the one I pursue in this paper—leads to a highly unconventional solution that happens to lie at the heart of Whitehead's theory of causation and consciousness. The latter option leads to the most conventional attempt at a solution. Both are motivated by the *prima facie* plausibility that between identity and otherness there must be some intermediate that would allow cause and effect to be distinct, yet related in a nonarbitrary way. Similarity is an obvious candidate here and one that was traditionally chosen for this job ("effects must be like their causes"), and there are many other familiar constraints (spatio-temporal contiguity, conserved or expended quantities, patterns of invariance, regular deformation) that would infuse relevance into the relation of things numerically distinct. One of the virtues of Rosch's analysis lies in showing how easily this demand for relevance falls prey to the Mādhyamika's dialectic. A theory of causation that was successful by traditional standards would be one that, pursuing strategy (2), successfully factored causation into identity and difference without simply becoming the conjunction of a tautology and an incoherence. Showing that this requirement is difficult to meet—which is what Rosch has done—is not the same as showing that it is impossible—which is what Hume and the Mādhyamika believe themselves to have done. On the other hand, the only way to show that this requirement can be met is to meet it ("the only proof is in the pudding"), which arguably has never been done. But the problem may not be with causation. It may be that the challenge itself is misconceived, unjustifiably demanding the impossible. The long-standing stalemate over this issue makes alternative approaches that might otherwise seem far-fetched worth exploring.

Pursuing strategy (1) leads to the unconventional results that interest me. If we could find a relevance relation that was immune to the stark same-or-different, identity-or-otherness disjunction, then alternative three would simply not resolve back into alternatives one and two combined. I suggest that similarity, if rightly construed, is a candidate here. Wittgenstein is famous for having opposed the classical notion (so ably defended by Husserl in his *Logical Investigations* and, before him, by Herbart) that similarity is self-contradictory if it cannot be factored into a part or aspect that is wholly identical and a different part or aspect that is wholly other. Using the now-famous metaphor of "family resemblance" he proposed instead similarity as an irreducible primitive. On this telling, similar things would not be identical in one respect and different in another. Rather, they would be both the same and different and in the same respect: in respect of being similar. In the context of the Mādhyamika's dialectic we can see that Wittgenstein's obstinacy is well motivated. It suggests a different way to approach the analysis of relations such as causation, one that offers a unique possibility for solving the causation dilemma. Tautology and incoherence—or the unmitigated superposition of tautology and incoherence—cease to be the only viable alternatives. Causes can be both the same as and different from their effects in the same respect without this being self-contradictory if the respect in which they are both is their similarity as a vague or fuzzy but irreducibly primitive relation. Another way to put this will become important in section seven below: the relation between cause and effect will be both internal and external at the same time. The end-result of such an approach may not be so different from what the Mādhyamika themselves had in mind—experience freed from the presumed strict demarcation of concepts.

How Whitehead Turns the Tables

This is the context in which Whitehead becomes relevant. Whitehead claims that we do have an experience of causation and could therefore possess a concept of it that is both coherent and nontautological. And this experience is nothing other than the experience of being conscious itself. Consciousness is always the experience of its own arising out of an antecedent and ambient physical world. It should be obvious that this viewpoint corresponds roughly to one of Rosch's four types of felt causation: seeing our perception as being caused by its object. In fact, in the conclusion of this chapter, I will claim that it corresponds to each of Rosch's four types, without being tautological. Instead, it is a relation of vague but primitive similarity.

The connection that Whitehead sees between the induction problem and the mind-body problem can now be stated in briefest outline. The induction problem takes us back to the causation problem, which is the problem of necessary synthesis. To solve these problems, Whitehead proposes a unique concept of process—the process by which the present accommodates the past. If we demand to know what empirical justification there is for this clever notion, he tells us that consciousness experiences itself as just such a process. The induction problem is thus solved by exhibiting the experience of being conscious as the paradigm of a process that makes causation intelligible. But since the particular process that consciousness exemplifies is, according to Whitehead, none other than the emergence of the mind out of the body (and its worldly environment), it turns out that the induction problem is solved only by solving the mind-body problem—and vice versa. Just as for Price the mind-body problem is simply the causation problem applied to consciousness, so for Whitehead the *solution* to the mind-body problem is simply his solution to the causation problem applied to consciousness. But Whitehead goes much further than this. Shifting the focus from consciousness to experience, he proposes that experience isn't just a paradigm case of process, but the key to its essential structure. All process involves the emergence of something ever so briefly mind-like out of the physical, creating some modicum of both novelty and continuity through an assimilation and accommodation between what already is and what is, more or less creatively, just now becoming.

Consciousness: Classical Phenomenology vs. Whitehead's Phenomenology

To see how Whitehead documents the veridical experience of causation, we must first familiarize ourselves with some of his operative concepts and

critical distinctions. Then we can confront what he thinks he's finding with
the methodologies that can't find it.

Whitehead's Basic Concepts and Distinctions

According to Whitehead a careful and unbiased description of experience
finds the bodily subject enjoying two fundamentally different kinds of perception, which Whitehead distinguishes as presentational immediacy and
causal efficacy (PR 117, 121–124, 168, 174–178). A third, derivative kind
of perception, which arises from their relation, he calls symbolic reference
(PR 168–183). Experience in the "natural attitude" is almost always a case
of symbolic reference, meaning that it is a hybrid arising from the correlation of the two "pure" modes of perception. Information from one mode
thus becomes relevant to information from the other mode. According to
Whitehead, this is the most fundamental semiotic relation. The *perceptum*
of one mode functions as the meaning that the *perceptum* of the other mode
comes naturally and automatically to signify. Normally, the two pure modes
are therefore unconsciously commingled. Only by distinguishing them carefully
can we assess their respective contributions to everyday experience.

Presentational immediacy is Whitehead's name for what is usually just
called perception. But he finds this usual concept unduly narrow and so gives
it a special name. For one thing, he notes that "perception" is typically but
tacitly narrowed to cover perception only at peak acuity and optimal function. He believes that there is good phenomenological justification for this
narrow concept—it names a natural kind, if you will—but no justification for
thinking it is the only kind of perception there is. It is assumed, for example,
that disturbed organic functioning results in perception that is simply a deficient mode of presentational immediacy. Whitehead believes that this is an
inaccurate description of our most intimate experience. It is, in other words,
phenomenologically false. In illnesses, when the organism is not functioning
properly, we typically become more or less directly aware of the animal body
producing the sense of being that we are experiencing. Organic disturbance
thus involves a different kind of perception than presentational immediacy.
It is direct perception of causal efficacy. Outside of such exceptional cases as
organic disease, does phenomenological description supports Whitehead's dual
typology of perception? This is the crucial question we are working toward
answering. First let's see how Whitehead characterizes the types.

In presentational immediacy the world is a contemporaneous manifold
present to consciousness in the vivid actuality of the moment. It appears spread
out in space, geometrically structured, and saturated with sensuous qualities
more or less sharply delineated. In short, presentational immediacy is clear
and distinct and always marks the knife-edge of the present. These are its

paramount phenomenological features. Causal efficacy, on the other hand, is the bodily feeling we have of being affected by and dependent upon an ambient physical milieu, as well as the feeling we have of the organic body itself as the most proximate milieu of this sort. Our experience feels its own emergence from the animal body. It also expresses itself in the animal body and feels that expression washing back as more experience emerging from the body. For example, I think of something that makes me angry and then I feel my body tense, my pulse quicken.

In contrast to presentational immediacy, consciousness of perception in the mode of causal efficacy is vague, unspecific, and diffuse. It is mostly visceral in locus and affective in content. It is characteristically vector-like in conveying vague but imperative information about how what's proximate and just past is impinging on the present actuality of experience, or how what's present and actual is going to impinge on its immediate sequel.

Presentational immediacy is something private—the sensuous representation of the world endowed with qualities, such as colors, sounds, and tastes that depend for their felt qualities on the anatomy and physiology of the percipient organism and accordingly are enjoyed in supreme indifference to the real state of the external world—as mirrors, hallucinogens, and electrical stimulation of the brain amply demonstrate (PR 64, 122; AI 247). Confined to the present, presentational immediacy is necessarily static, like a tableau. Relegated to privacy, it lacks real import, like an illusion. It is only in the feeling of causal efficacy that the percipient has direct access to the public domain of things-in-themselves—and this is its paramount feature. However vague and diffuse, it is nonetheless a veridical feeling of the transcendent world. For this reason alone can its vague message be so imperative. Presentational immediacy tends to affective neutrality because, despite its vivid variegation, its information is inert. Only causal efficacy can relieve or terrify. The organism experiences its own contingency in the perceptual mode of causal efficacy because it is in that mode that it experiences the reality of a world upon which its existence decisively depends. Through symbolic reference, the finely discriminated items localized in presentational immediacy take on the relevance of what is disclosed in the feeling of causal efficacy (PR 178). They are perceived as being causally efficacious entities in the public world around us. In this way they acquire the meaning of reality, which only causal efficacy could bestow.

Phenomenology

Whether there is normally such a thing as a feeling of causal efficacy and whether such a feeling can be veridical are of course the matters in dispute, and like all phenomenological findings one either finds them or not. But it is important—and must be stressed—that the dispute is not a dispute about the relevance of phenomenology to epistemology, but about what phenomenology finds. What Whitehead says of Hume, for example, tells us how he stands on the importance of methodologically rigorous description:

> Hume's demand that causation be describable as an element in experience is [...] entirely justifiable. The point of the criticisms of Hume's procedure is that we have direct intuition of inheritance and memory: thus the only problem is, so to describe the general character of experience that these intuitions may be included. (PR 166–167)

If we are right in finding phenomenological motives in Whitehead, the question naturally arises as to the difference between his phenomenology and that of the practitioners who were responsible for making this methodology famous.[12] As it turns out, clarifying this brings the question we are discussing to the forefront: whether phenomenology can lay hold of causality and if so, why it has so famously eluded pursuit.

Whitehead took no notice of Phenomenology, but it is not difficult to establish points of fundamental agreement and disagreement. Whitehead would agree with the classical Phenomenology of Husserl or Merleau-Ponty that philosophy must ground itself in the description of pure experience in its immediate actuality and cannot accept as *given* anything that is not given *to experience*. Another important point of agreement, to be discussed more fully in the next section, has to do with the subject-object relation. Whitehead and Phenomenology both see the subject-object relation as fundamental to experience. Phenomenology terms this relation intentionality, and Whitehead calls it prehension. But this is a point of agreement around which many important disagreements cluster. Besides the differences to be stressed in the next section, we can note the following. For Husserl, the intentional object is an "ideality" that is immanent in the act that relates to it, and it exists simultaneously with that act. For Whitehead, the object is a reality that transcends and temporally precedes the act that relates to it. Furthermore, intentionality is understood exclusively as a kind of final causation. Husserl speaks of motivation as defining intentionality and opposes it to causation, by which he means efficient causation (Husserl 1952, §§ 55 and 56). This has the important result that intentionality is possible only in the abeyance of efficient causation. For Phenomenology, efficient causation and meaning conferment are mutually exclusive: what is caused is *ipso facto* not motivated and *vice versa*. But prehension is supposed to be causation and meaning conferment at one and the same time, just viewed from different perspectives. This is supposed to be possible because it integrates final and efficient causation, both freedom and necessity, in a single, albeit complex act. The analysis of this act and its contrast with intentionality will concern us below. Now we turn to a broad characterization of the most fundamental and principled differences between Phenomenology and process philosophy. Whitehead stands in sharpest disagreement with Phenomenology as Husserl or Merleau-Ponty practiced it on two cardinal issues: the descriptive status of causation and the general relevance of consciousness to description.

Phenomenology and Causation

First, Phenomenology considers the causal dependency of perception on its object (Rosch's third type of causation) to be a prejudice of the "natural attitude" rather than a primitive datum. In fact, the idea that experience arises by some kind of actuation by transcendent things is singularly important to Phenomenology because it is precisely by suspending this natural assumption that Phenomenology is supposed to become possible, where Phenomenology is construed as description rigorously limited to what is *actually given*. Of course, there is a circularity here: if description is considered "pure" only if it does not admit causal affection, then obviously pure description will never discover causal affection. Bracketed at the outset, it will not subsequently be found. But the important test for Phenomenology will not be the evasion of logical circles in getting started, but whether it can carry its project through to the end, describing the constitution of the whole wealth of the world we live in without leaving anything of importance out or making an illicit appeal to the causal efficacy of transcendent things. Whitehead thought modern philosophy was already engaged in this very project and consistently failed. Two very striking passages merit quotation at length:

> The discussion of the problem constituted by the connection between causation and perception has been conducted by the various schools of thought derived from Hume and Kant under the misapprehension generated by an inversion of the true constitution of experience. The inversion was explicit in the writings of Hume and Kant: for both of them presentational immediacy was the primary fact of perception, and any apprehension of causation was, somehow or other, to be elicited from this primary fact. This view of the relation between causation and perception, as items in experience, was not original to these great philosophers. It is to be found presupposed in Locke and Descartes; and they derived it from medieval predecessors. (PR 173)

Owing to its long dominance, it has been usual to assume as
an obvious fact the primacy of presentational immediacy. We
open our eyes and our other sense-organs; we then survey the
contemporary world decorated with sights, and sounds, and
tastes; and then, by the sole aid of this information about the
contemporary world, thus decorated, we draw what conclusions
we can as to the actual world. No philosopher really holds that
this is the sole source of information: Hume and his followers
appeal vaguely to "memory" and to "practice," in order to supplement their direct information; and Kant wrote other Critiques in
order to supplement his Critique of Pure Reason. But the general
procedure of modern philosophical "criticism" is to tie down opponents strictly to the front door of presentational immediacy
as the sole source of information, while one's own philosophy
makes its escape by a back door veiled under the ordinary usages
of language. (PR 174)

It is striking how close the concept of "pure appearance" in Phenomenology is to Whitehead's concept of presentational immediacy. In this connection
we can reassess the significance of Husserl's claim that Phenomenology is the
"secrete longing" of modern philosophy. Whitehead would have agreed. Only
he would have identified this longing as the source of its downfall rather than
its prescient greatness. The contrast could not be greater. Husserl believes
that he successfully consummated the very project Whitehead pronounced
impossible—reconstituting the whole world out of elements drawn exclusively
from presentational immediacy. Either Whitehead was wrong and the project
is feasible—or his critique must apply *mutatis mutandis* to Phenomenology.
Whether Phenomenology is indeed equally guilty of sneaking out the back
way to rendezvous unnoticed with the causation it had barred from front-
door entry is an important question that must be left for another occasion.
For now our question must be limited to why Phenomenology does not in
the first place allow causation to come in through the front, which brings
us to the second crucial disagreement Whitehead would have with classical
Phenomenology. It concerns the role of consciousness itself in philosophy
and experience.

Phenomenology and Consciousness

Phenomenology identifies experience with conscious experience, and more
specifically the kind of experience that can be identified in reflective self-
consciousness for "just what it is" (even if it normally is not so objectified, it
is all-important that it can be). It is this consciously nailed-down ("objecti-

fied") experience that Phenomenology describes (Husserl 1950, §§ 63–79). Here again what Whitehead diagnoses as a pervasive tendency in modern philosophy, Phenomenology propounds as an explicit principle. Whitehead thinks the first of these principles (the denial of causation as a datum) follows from the second (the aggrandizement of consciousness), and he rejects them both. What Whitehead believes a careful description finds is that experience is a process. It is a process that always originates in the resonations of the organic body with its environment and their manifold disruptions by more or less discrete thrusts of transcendent things impinging on and affecting it. These irruptions are at once dim and overwhelming, heavy with the meaning of emotion. Sometimes experience does not progress beyond this, as appears to be evident from states of borderline and transitional consciousness such as result from intoxication and morbid conditions, physical or emotional trauma, or the gradual recovery from unconsciousness (coma, narcosis, even deep sleep). When, by contrast, experience discloses to us the geometrically structured manifold of vivid, but affectively neutral sense-qualities spread out in presentational immediacy, we are never without a residual sense of causal efficacy and its vague, but insistent affective relevance, always tending to invest the items of presentational immediacy with existential meaning. In fact, we always experience the content of presentational immediacy as more or less dependent upon the antecedent functioning of the organic body: Whitehead claims that we do not infer, but feel that we see with our eyes and touch with our hands. Presentational immediacy therefore represents a secondary phase of experience in which bodily feeling that was "vague, ill defined, and hardly relevant [...] becomes distinct, well defined, and importantly relevant [...]" (172). Finally, we can recall many experiences where we were presentationally aware, but consciousness did not achieve its peak intensity of explicit, focal-thematic awareness. Consciousness thus appears to be a particularly sophisticated fruition of experience that is not necessary for the other phases. What consciousness does is consummate the process of experience with the retrospective illumination of that process (PR 161, 242). Since what consciousness illuminates is its own process of coming to be, what finds illumination in consciousness is clear and distinct in proportion to its genetic proximity to this final phase, which has the important consequence that for consciousness the dative phase of causal efficacy *will always have a fugitive character* (PR 173). The denial that causal efficacy is a datum is therefore already implicit in Phenomenology's insistence on the methodological primacy of acute consciousness.

According to Whitehead, therefore, when there is consciousness there will always be some measure of consciousness pertaining to each of the three kinds of perception: symbolic reference, presentational immediacy, causal efficacy. But insisting that the findings of philosophical reflection all be rendered with the certainty and clarity of consciousness at its most focused and intense guarantees that the most primitive data will be misconstrued as deficient modes of consciousness, rather than as the genetic residue of something more primitive than consciousness. Their cognitive value will be misconstrued accordingly.

Whitehead believes that if we look at experience without prejudging questions about the experiential primacy of consciousness or the cognitive value of lucid, reflective consciousness, the idea that perception is caused by its object ceases to be far-fetched, no matter how scientifically sophisticated we are. On the contrary, it becomes a patent truism of everyone's experience. The same pervasive phenomena that modern philosophy and Phenomenology alike have so much trouble accommodating (and accordingly like to ignore) can now be accepted as so many examples of things or events in the experience-transcending world (the "external" world) causing a subjective experience. A catalog of such phenomena drawn from Whitehead's scattered observations includes: memory, reflex, habituation, fatigue, embodiment, continuity over time, and time itself.[13]

What these phenomena have in common is that their intelligibility depends on real causal dependency of the present on the past. They cannot be understood as the result of an act of meaning conferment executed in the present. They cannot, in other words, be explained without conceding transcendent causal action—that is, without abandoning the constraints of Phenomenology.

For Phenomenology, anything beyond the limits of "pure" or "absolute" consciousness arises from a meaning conferred *by* pure or absolute consciousness on something within itself. Being actual only, pure or absolute consciousness is essentially always present. Anything external to actual consciousness such as the material world or anything past, including past states of consciousness, can exist only as products of consciousness-immanent acts of meaning conferment, executed by actual consciousness in the present. Thus, the Phenomenological account of experience perfectly illustrates what Whitehead, borrowing a phrase from Santayana, derides as the "solipsism of the present moment." Hume's regularity interpretation of causation, we should note, anticipates Phenomenology because it turns causation into a *meaning conferred in the present* rather than an effect of something actually past. The refutation of Hume should thus apply *mutatis mutandis* to Phenomenology. Let's take the example of reflex. The very first time a child touches a candle flame she reflexively pulls away and feels quite certain that she pulled away because the flame burned her finger. There's no constant conjunction here and no prior expectations on the part of the child. Hume's account may hold a shred of plausibility in regard to the psychologist who expects children to behave in certain ways around candles, but it doesn't make any sense for the child or for the psychologist when he gets burned himself. This distinction is critical. The psychologist objectifies the reactions of the child as observed phenomena and asks what relationship they bear to another observed phenomenon, the candle. The child may adopt an objectifying attitude to her own reactions at a later time, but when they are happening they are lived through in a way that is not objectifying. These attitudes are as different as listening to a piece of music and performing it. For convenience, I will call the nonobjectifying attitude *performative*. Whitehead's thesis is that causation is always a performative phenomenon. It is the performative aspect of experience itself.

Similar arguments can be derived from the phenomena of fatigue and habituation. They result from experiencing the same stimulus or exertion over time. There can be no Phenomenological explanation for this. What all the noted biological phenomena have in common is the conditioning of present activity by past activity—not by the appearance or (re)presentation of past activity in the present or the present interpretation of something *as* past, but by past activity itself. They presuppose that events over time have a cumulative effect and hence that the world does not in effect begin anew at each moment in time. The idea that the world begins anew in each moment is a position that Descartes expressly advocates with his idea of continual recreation by God (Descartes 1964–1976, 8:48–49, 109, 8A:13; 1984, 2:33, 78–79, 1:200), and with few exceptions it lies in one form or another at the heart of all modern philosophy. Its recurrence is easy to spot in Locke's account of memory in the second edition of the *Essay* (memory is the present having of an idea to which is annexed a further present idea of "being had before") (Locke 1959, 1:111–113 and 194) or in Hume's temporal atomism (Hume 1978, 73–82 and 233).[14] In fact, it frames the whole development of modern thought, with its roots in the skepticism of al-Ghazālī and the Nominalism of the fourteenth century and its final fruition in Phenomenology.

Whitehead, by contrast, believes that as the present becomes past it accretes to the new present in a way that determines or constrains it. Only by accommodating the past can the present build on it. Contrariwise, if the present did not accommodate the past, there would be no reason for the world at present to be like or even to depend upon the past at all. For example, at each new moment in which consciousness repeats, as Descartes says, "I am, I exist" (Descartes 1964–1976, 8:25; 1984, 2:17), it would establish its present reality as an absolute that has no necessary connection with any previous act of self-establishment or anything that had happened before. This implies that the world essentially does (or might as well as or could just as well as) begin anew at every moment of transcendent time and that the experienced richness of phenomenological time with its past and future is an internal *distentio animi* confined to an instant of transcendent time—like the vertical axis of Husserl's famous time diagram, which represents lived time and intersects the horizontal axis ("real" time) *at a point*. This point is none other than Descartes' Archimedean point, possessing itself totally at the expense of real connection to anything else.

We should also say a few words about the importance of embodiment. Whitehead lays great stress on the fact that we are always conscious of perceiving the various sense-qualities *with* the respective sense organ. He calls this the "withness of the body," which is also a performative rather than an objectifying experience. We know from idealists such as Berkeley that it is (perhaps) not impossible to ignore this experience and to think of the organic body as an ideational construct, but we know how strange and cumbersome this project becomes. Probably the greatest difficulty faced by the Way of Ideas lies here with embodiment. For having eliminated the animal body as a real condition of experience, it can no longer explain the passivity of the subject. If the body is only another ideational construct, a mosaic of ideas like any other, then there is no easy way to explain the difference between *having an idea* and *suffering its impingement*. Thus, with the animal body, the possibility of distinguishing between imagination and perception also disappears. Ultimately we lose sight of any reason for the subject to suffer anything at all, that is, to be finite or mortal. Husserl's puzzling (bizarre?) claim that the transcendental ego is immortal[15] is directly related to Locke's difficulty distinguishing perception from imagination[16] and Berkeley's similar difficulty distinguishing the suffering of pain from merely knowing what it is (since both according the *via idearum* would amount to the very same thing: having the idea).[17]

It should be clear by now that the key to Whitehead's rehabilitation of causality is time. Whitehead understands causation as a diachronic process in which causes precede their effects. In fact, he endorses a causal theory of time according to which time is sustained by causation (PR 237). The power of his arguments against the denial of causal efficacy can now be stated succinctly. If the events contained in successive moments in time are not causally related, there is no reason for them to be continuous or cumulative in any way. If we admit that they are continuous and cumulative, this needs explaining. If we abstain from what Phenomenology would call an "unphenomenological" explanation, we are forced back to the idea that experienced continuity and apparent cumulative effect, along with all the phenomena we have just noted (reflex, habituation, fatigue, memory, embodiment, time), are things somehow created out of and inhabiting only the present moment: not the result of transcendent causes operating from the past, but of immanent motivation and meaning-conferment operating in the present on present experience. This consequence is unavoidable: since the past (the real as opposed to the intended past) is transcendent, it should not, according to Phenomenology, make any difference to the descriptive content of present experience whether the past really existed or not. In other words, for all consciousness is concerned, the world might as well begin anew with every moment. If this is absurd, Whitehead thinks we should concede that causal efficacy is after all the respectable phenomenon it appears to be, manifesting itself continuously in the very continuity of existence in time.

Two Central Concepts in Whitehead's Psychology: Nonobjectifying Experience and Centripetal Objectivation

Classical Phenomenology speaks for the mainline tradition of modern philosophy when it declares the subject-object relation to be the foundation of experience. Whitehead agrees. The subject-object relation is a kind of phenomenological first principle that defines the structure of experience. But agreement stops there, and caveats begin. Two crucial differences concern us. First, Whitehead protests that modern philosophy narrowly identifies the subject-object relation with the relation of knower to known. Whitehead is surely right about this. For although there are exceptions, such as Herder or Main de Biran, they are figures whose ideas never entered the mainstream. Secondly, Whitehead wants to reverse the tropism usually ascribed to the relation.

Objectification

Identifying *subject-object* with *knower-known* assumes that all experience is essentially cognition and that the subject of every experience is consciousness. This is the fundamental commitment of the mainstream of modern philosophy from the Way of Ideas to Transcendental Phenomenology. The concept of "objectification," which owes its current philosophical acceptation to the Phenomenology of Husserl (in its last phase), has its relevance here. Although Whitehead does not make use of this concept and in fact uses the term objectification to mean something else,[18] the Husserlian acceptation aptly designates one of the principal fallacies Whitehead characterizes.

In cognition the object is thematized *as object*. Cognition is therefore said to be an "objectifying" attitude. The object is not just experienced—as being hot or cold or threatening, for example. It is experienced as *being an object* with such and such qualities, of such and such a description. It is of course true of every object that it is an object, but objectification makes this fact about the object become a phenomenological property of it—a descriptive feature in the "narrow content" of the experience. The modern equation of object with *cognitum* implies that every object is objectified in this way, in short, that all experience is objectifying. We could write the equation: "*object = object* qua *object.*" Even Husserl came to reject this position, to say nothing of later phenomenologists. Not only is experience much wider than knowledge, but also the attempt to know the phenomena that fall in the margins of cognition often denatures them. Emotions offer easy examples: it is impossible to objectify one's anger and still be angry. But that means anger *in actu exercito* has in fact not been objectified at all. It has slipped away, and what we are objectifying is past anger by way of our memory of it. The difference between *anger being experienced* and *anger remembered* is nontrivial, for it is unlike, say, the difference between an experienced and a remembered fact. A remembered fact may still be a fact, but remembered anger is not anger any more than melted snow is snow. Being drunk or sleepy are equally good examples of things that cannot be objectified without ceasing to be what they were. In these cases the object never equals the object *qua* object.

Whitehead rightly insists that the greatest part of our experience falls into this category of nonobjectifiable actuality: experience whose objectification is incompatible with its present actuality. Obviously the experience of causal efficacy belongs here, too. In fact, everything performative falls into this category. Once objectified, it is no longer performance (unless it be someone else's). The concept of objectification thus brings to light the epistemologically crucial difference between perception in the mode of presentational immediacy and perception in the mode of causal efficacy. Whitehead's failure to circumscribe the operation of objectification by attaching a unique name to it left the essential disparity between the two pure modes of perception inadequately characterized. He stressed their difference descriptively in terms of "clear and distinct" *vs.* "vague and visceral," which is accurate and important, but fails to reveal that the difference is not one of degree, even extreme degree, but of altogether heterogeneous function and structural valence. The content of presentational immediacy is not something performative. Therefore, the content of presentational immediacy *can* be objectified without undergoing significant alteration in content. Causal efficacy cannot. A great part of the modern prejudice in favor of presentational immediacy has its roots here. The factors singled out by Whitehead for mention—a preference for the clear and distinct over the vague and obscure or for vision over the bowels—have a deeper root. Assuming that objectified being is being "as it really is," modern philosophy had little respect for anything skittish under the lens of objectification. Truth, it assumed, was precisely what could be objectified.

We should perhaps pause here to note that the identification of experience with objectifying experience is what motivates the otherwise preposterous question whether animals "have experience." Descartes, who more than anyone was responsible for this identification, is not coincidentally the one who fathered the unfortunate notion that animals are not subjects of experience. Almost certainly they are not subjects of objectifying experience. But once we jettison the constricting notion that objectifying experience is all the experience there is, we can begin to see the world with very different eyes: there is a spectacular amount of experience teeming throughout the world, and objectifying experience is a small part, almost vanishingly small.

Whitehead was particularly clearheaded about the tight logical connection between the concept of experience as objectification (as a kind of "knowing" in his language) and the primacy ascribed to consciousness in modern philosophy. Cognition is a function of consciousness. If all experience is objectifying, then subjectivity is simply consciousness. Letting go of the restrictive concept of experience thus allows us to embrace a broader and richer concept of subjectivity. Nonconscious subjectivity is really the centerpiece of Whitehead's metaphysical cosmology. Once subjectivity is no longer identified narrowly with a single type of subjectivity, one that happens to be the rarest of all because it represents the extreme top on the scale of sophistication, then we are free to wonder philosophically how far downscale subjectivity reaches and accordingly how widespread its least sophisticated types may be. For present purposes we can make do with the descriptive finding that our own conscious life is buoyed up by a rush of more primitive experience that is not intrinsically conscious and is never really objectified.

One of the main constructive proposals of this paper lies here. It is that "non-conscious subjectivity" need not be an empty cipher for us: the experience that is unconscious in other kinds of subjects need not be entirely inaccessible to consciousness in human beings. It overlaps at least in part with the nonobjectifiable experience that haunts the margins of objectifying consciousness. I suggest that what Whitehead (PR 58) calls consciousness of "presentational objectification" (which would be presentational objectivation in the language of this paper) is objectifying consciousness; what he calls consciousness of "causal objectification" (which would be causal objectivation in the language of this paper) is nonobjectifying consciousness that is only obliquely available to us in vague, fleeting, or marginal ways. On the interpretation proposed here the content of nonobjectifying consciousness would significantly overlap with the content of the "unconscious" experience assumed to exist in Whitehead's metaphysical psychology.

Objectivation

The second critical difference in the way Whitehead wants us to understand the subject-object relation concerns what I have called its tropism. If we agree that experience is a process, then the question naturally arises how the subject-object relation maps on to this process. The two most obvious possibilities are the ones that will concern us. Experience can be a process directed from the subject to the object or from the object to the subject. Subject-to-object is the tropism exclusively preferred by the mainstream of modern philosophy, while Whitehead proposes seeing it the other way around (PR 156). He makes room for the subject-to-object tropism with his concept of presentational immediacy, which does seems to project the physiologically conditioned qualities of bodily experience out into space. But this, he insists, is secondary and in some respects illusory. The real structure of experience is the object-to-subject tropism of causal efficacy. Regardless of direction, it will be convenient to have a generic designation available. For reasons soon to be clear, I call the directional character of the experiential process "objectivation" (although Whitehead calls it objectification). The difference and connection between objectification and objectivation (as I employ them) will emerge presently. Let's look at the two simplest interpretations of objectivation, which happen to be the most influential historically.

It is characteristic of modern philosophy to construe objectivation as a centrifugal process. This can be attributed to its exclusive focus on presentational immediacy. Accordingly, the experienced world is understood as a sort of projection radiating out from the subject as the center of experience. This is just as evident in the Rationalism and Empiricism of the seventeenth century or in twentieth century movements such as Phenomenology and Positivism as it is in the Idealism of Kant and Fichte. Immanence comes first, methodologically and even ontologically.[19] Consciousness is a domain of immediate self-presence. It finds within this domain (within itself) various contents (ideas, sense-data, immediate givens, nonintentional experiences). Under specific conditions and constraints some of these contents are objectivated, which here means that they are transcendently apperceived—they are judged or interpreted or constructively appropriated to be external things, or the appearance of external things. In this way, modern philosophy typically concerns itself with the construction or constitution of the external world out of elements that are really (or at least originally) internal to consciousness.

An important question is how we supposedly become aware of this original state of affairs. How does consciousness become aware of its content as such, independent of objectivation? Are these contents really knowable? The standard answer is that they are known to consciousness by way of the self-objectifying attitude of reflection. It is all-important to notice here that self-objectification is not an objectivation. It is a form of immanence or self-coincidence, not a centrifugal process. Objectivation, on the other hand, always concerns the relation of subject as self and object as other (regardless of tropism direction). While modern philosophy thus holds that objectification is not necessarily an objectivation (because self-objectification is not objectivating), it denies the converse, characteristically assuming that objectivation is always and necessarily objectifying. It is simply the objectification of the contents of consciousness as the appearance of another rather than as the being of the self—as perception rather than as reflection. There is simply no room in this scheme for a nonobjectifying relation to things.

Whitehead by contrast aligns himself with a premodern heritage that leaves important traces in early modern philosophy, but is more characteristic of the conservative strains in Scholasticism. Objectivation in this context is a *centripetal* process, from the ambient world into the mind as the focus of experience.[20] The important concept here is *res objectiva* as distinguished from *res formalis*. Things—conceived in terms of the Aristotelian criteria of substantiality, autonomy, independence—are said to have *formal reality* as they exist in the world independent of being thought about. This is also called their subjective reality—subjective in the Aristotelian sense of being an independently existing substrate supporting accidents. But insofar as they are experienced in any way—known or perceived or desired—they are said to be objects and to have *objective reality* in the mind. Descartes uses the term *realitas objectiva*; Spinoza uses *essentia objectiva*. In medieval philosophy the terms are objective being (*esse objectivum*) or intentional being (*esse intentionale*) or simply object (*objectum*).

Apparently without appreciating its rich Scholastic heritage, Whitehead finds this concept of objective reality still present in early modern thought—it figures famously in Descartes' proof for the existence of God, for example, and its interpretation becomes a point of controversy between Descartes and the respondents to his *Meditations*. But Whitehead astutely notices how unhappily this concept coexists with the new orientation of the Way of Ideas. It is easiest to contrast the two orientations if we look at the causal structure of ideation. On the Scholastic understanding, thinking and perceiving are passions wrought upon the mind by the agency of the worldly thing. The conditions under which such agency could take place were an important topic in Scholastic psychology that need not detain us. What's important here is that the thing possesses a measure of activity or actuality by virtue of its subjective or formal reality, which allows it to have an effect upon the mind under appropriate circumstances. This effect is its objective being in the mind, its being thought about. We find the causal structure of ideation reversed in the modern period, where knowledge is an act of the knowing subject rather than of the thing known. In this scheme, formal or "subjective" being is assigned not to the known thing, but to the mind—a famous shift that occurs conceptually with Descartes, but terminologically with Hobbes and Berkeley, who first speak of *the subject* as the subject of experience, and Kant, who first speaks of subjectivity in the modern sense—so that the mind becomes the agent, rather than the patient in ideation. Objectivity is now something that results from appropriate activities of the mind, not something it undergoes. Objectivity results when our originally subjective impressions or presumptions have been validated or recast in a form that is valid vis-à-vis a mind-transcending reality.

Whitehead bills his organic philosophy as a return to pre-Kantian modes of thinking (PR xi). But he establishes beyond any doubt that within the early modern tradition there are already disparate tendencies, the one which clearly triumphs in the eighteenth century in Hume and Kant, and the one he champions, which, unbeknownst to him, was a vestige of Aristotelianism. In this respect, it might be better to go the whole way and say his organic philosophy is a return to pre-Cartesian modes of thought. In any case, it is to Whitehead's credit as a self-taught philosopher and historian of philosophy that he discovered and convincingly documented these conflicting tendencies in early modern thought. Standing on his shoulders we can now see that this conflict resulted in part from the short-lived overlap of an old tradition on its way out and forward-looking movement that was just beginning. But Whitehead also identifies the substantive reasons why the new tradition could not remain true to itself and would always be forced to equivocate on fundamental principles: its bias for objectification obscures or misrepresents everything performative, which it nevertheless cannot do without (PR 49–60, 73–76, 113, 122–123, 130–156, 158). Thus, Whitehead thinks that Hume's problem with causation is a direct consequence of the new Way of Ideas that he has set out on, while the older tradition either does not generate this problem or at least harbors prospects for solving it.

In brief: by trying to objectify causation, modern philosophy makes it disappear and cannot recover it without stealth. Causation will never reveal itself to the objectifying attitude. Thus, although the raw, pre-objectified experience that consciousness normally objectifies is itself causally structured in its relation to the subject, this causal structure does not survive its objectification. What survives objectification is always static and thing-like, never dynamic and process-like. Similarly, it must be conceded or even stressed that consciousness itself is a causal experience. The subject after all is necessarily active in performing the objectification that constitutes consciousness. But this experience of the subject is never the object it is conscious of. Performance itself is never objectified as long as it is being performed, although it is always experienced. It does not even become a candidate for objectification until it is no longer a performance (in memory). If correct, this finding has extraordinary implications. It means that the principle methodological assumption of modern philosophy, including Transcendental Phenomenology, is wrong. The nature of consciousness is *never* disclosed in reflection (see also Weekes 2006).

This explains why objectification inflicts the greatest damage on consciousness itself. As soon as consciousness assumes that its own being is revealed by being objectified, it reduces itself to the content of its own reflection, which means that it has isolated itself from time and confined itself to the moment of self-objectification.[21] Despite the efforts of Descartes, or Kant, or Husserl, there is no way back to the world from here. Descartes' Archimedean point is really a point of no return.

The historical uniqueness of Whitehead's program is his insistence on embracing the modern concept of subjectivity while retaining the medieval concept of objectivation. The key to its success lies in broadening the concept of subjectivity to include more than objectifying consciousness and thereby allowing objectivation to operate free and clear of objectification. The feeling of causal efficacy is the objectivation of the world in the subject. Experience is the "enjoyment" of this process. Here we begin to broach the technicalities of Whitehead's thought, which need some elucidation before we can appreciate their application to the problem of causation.

Whitehead's Metaphysical Scheme and its Descriptive Implications for Psychology

Experience

First of all, why is there experience? This is a question that has received a lot of attention in the wake of David Chalmers' book, *The Conscious Mind* (1996). Assuming there is such a thing as causal action of one thing upon another, why should the effect of such causal action ever be associated with experience? Here is where Whitehead's most speculative ideas become relevant. He proposes that experience is not something superadded to certain peculiar effects (such as stimulation of the nervous system). It is simply the obverse side of causation—what it looks like from the perspective of the effect or the patient undergoing the effect. If A affects B, then B "experiences" A, where experience can be understood as minimally as a physical or chemical reaction.[22] The reaction has the intentional structure of experience to the extent that the effect is (can be construed as) a sign of the cause. It seems to lack the intentional structure of experience insofar as it is not for itself such a sign of its cause. In the always-useful language of Peirce, a reaction seems to display Secondness, but not Thirdness. Whitehead's proposal, which doesn't seem too far from Peirce, is that this lack of reflexivity is an illusion. Pure Secondness is possible only as a kind of limiting case of Thirdness, where the difference between what a thing is for itself and what it is through and for others becomes vanishingly small.

Now recall the question raised above: if a subjectivity more primitive than consciousness is possible, how far downscale does subjectivity go? Whitehead's answer is all the way down. How widespread? Across the board. In the same way, for example, that dynamics needs to think of rest as an infinitely slow motion in order to avoid antinomies, Whitehead thinks we can avoid the great antinomies of modern philosophy if we think of inanimate physical interactions as a kind of experience, one that is infinitely impoverished. The specific application of this concept of experience to the problem of causation this paper began with requires us to have before us at least the outline of Whitehead's famously speculative proposal for a twentieth-century metaphysics that takes stock of special relativity and the discovery of the discrete quanta of energy.

Whitehead's Metaphysical Scheme

Whitehead begins[23] with the intuition that nothing can be for an instant only or at a point only. There is a minimum time it takes for anything to be at all and a minimum space it takes up. This least unit of being is the actual occasion. The minimum time of the actual occasion is its duration, which is privately lived before it leaves a sort of fossil of itself as an increment of measurable physical time. The minimum space of the actual occasion becomes its scalar localization in the universe. Everything exceeding this minimum space and time must be some kind of aggregate society composed of actual occasions as its constituent atoms. The extensive continuum, which in our cosmic epoch manifests as a four-dimensional space-time continuum, is suffused throughout with actual occasions, creating what Whitehead at one point refers to as an "ether of events" (CN 78). It is the nature of occasions not just to happen at a discrete location, but also to exercise an unbounded causal influence. This manifests as a physical effect that propagates with finite velocity throughout our four-dimensional space-time. For each occasion this propagation will corresponds to the forward light-cone in Minkowski space, representing that occasion's being-for-others (that is, for other occasions of experience). The backward light-cone will represent its own "experience" (the being of other things for it).

   Now since occasions have the briefest possible duration, the question naturally arises where the new ones keep coming from. This question offers a vantage from which we can survey Whitehead's metaphysics in a clear if foreshortened form.

   Whitehead's philosophy consciously operates in the grand tradition of metaphysics. His fundamental postulate is *Creativity*, which he compares to Aristotle's matter, Spinoza's one substance, and Bradley's Absolute (PR 7, 21, 31, 200). It recalls—deliberately—Bergson's *élan vital* and—not so deliberately—Nietzsche's will to power. In important ways it is more like

Aristotle's actuality than his matter, and for similar reasons looks a lot like the Thomistic or Avicennan *esse*.

Whitehead sees creativity as a metaphysical urge toward unity and coherence that pervades the extensive continuum.[24] Because the effects of past occasions propagate indefinitely, there is at every locus in the extensive continuum a convergence of indefinitely many effects. Subjectivity is the (inevitable) manifestation of the creative urge at any given locus of convergence. It wants to unify the many converging effects. The urge is satisfied when the manifold data have been integrated in a way that is harmonious and results in a fully determinate individual or concretum (PR 84). When this satisfaction is achieved, subjectivity is extinguished and instead of being a subject of active ("living") experience it becomes the inactive ("dead") "superject" that remains as the end result after that particular fruition of experience has been achieved. Now the occasion begins its career as the propagating after-shock of its having happened, that is to say, as an object for future subjects. At any locus, subjectivity emerges out of the chaotic fund of objects, which are simply the objectification of subjects extinguished in the past. We see here how causality suffered and causality initiated are interdependent and both required by the scheme. Objectification is causality suffered, and unification is causality initiated. It is impossible to have one without the other. Without objectification there would be nothing to unify. Without unification there would be no experience to receive the converging objectifications. It is important to note that unification is never simply reducible to the conjoined effects of converging objectifications. Whitehead thinks the conjoined effects of objectification are at any given locus always more or less incompatible. Consequently, there must always be some element of creative initiative, however attenuated it may be, effecting reconciliation of data as the condition of unification.[25] This is the spontaneity and novelty intrinsic to all subjectivity. Because the universe is fundamentally many, it can never achieve a new unity without effecting a creative synthesis. At the same time, as Whitehead stresses, each such achievement simply adds one more datum to a universe always seeking novel unity, impelling the cycle to commence anew.

We come now to an important point. Although the satisfaction of the occasion consists in its achievement of complete determinacy, its purpose is actually intensity in the enjoyment of experience. Experience is understood as the process of achieving the satisfaction. Whitehead calls the process *concrescence* because the result is something that has become concrete. The occasion aims at satisfaction (being concrete), but its purpose is in the process (becoming concrete). The coherence of this particular theorem of Whitehead's metaphysics might be challenged, but it makes sense. In order to enjoy the game you have to play to win. But you don't play the game in order to win; you play in order to enjoy the playing.

Consciousness and Subjective Form

In addition to the objective content of experience, Whitehead believes there is also a wholly subjective component, which is how the content is felt and appropriated. Whitehead calls this the *subjective form* of the experience. Subjective form accounts for the qualitative feel of experience, and there is always a strict correlation between the subjective form of the experience and what kind of object is being experienced, for example, green is felt greenly, anger irately, sharpness sharply. Subjective form is what characterizes the enjoyment of experience, and it is what vanishes when subjectivity has exhausted itself in the achievement of concrete determinacy.

Whitehead claims that *consciousness* is a subjective form (PR 162 and 241). It is the subjective form of an especially complex experience, one whose object is a proposition involving the negation of a contrast between actuality and potentiality (or factuality and possibility). We are conscious of an individual when we "feel" the absence of a difference between that individual (indicated indexically in actual perception) and the concept (or "description") of that individual (PR 161, 266–273, esp. 267 and 269).

Even if we let Whitehead's explanation of consciousness go as another arabesque in his metaphysical constructions, it has aspects that will interest the phenomenologist and the cognitive psychologist. The idea that consciousness is a subjective form has descriptive relevance. It means that consciousness is not a faculty, or even a thing (much less an "absolute being"), but rather the adverbial *how* of a process. It also means that consciousness is not the only way that objects can be felt, but also that objects felt consciously are not identical to objects that are (or can be) felt unconsciously. Consciousness, then, is not like a searchlight, indifferent to the kind of objects it can illuminate. Rather, it arises in strict conformity to a specific kind of object and excludes others in principle (PR 241). Therefore, the world as an object of consciousness cannot, strictly speaking, be the same world that is enjoyed in other ways, although the specifics of Whitehead's theory of consciousness mitigate the implications of this statement somewhat: in consciousness one experiences that something is not different from a description it satisfies.

Most important for our purposes is the idea that consciousness is not, as it was for Descartes (and arguably for Husserl, too), a thing. Consequently, if the description of consciousness proceeds on the assumption that what it is describing is some sort of thing, the resulting description will be systematically skewed. Things are what survive (or emerge from) objectification. Whatever cannot be objectified (without being transformed) is not a thing. The thing assumption goes hand in hand with the idea that the being of consciousness is to be found in its self-objectification in reflection, which is thought of as a sort of absolute self-possession. Whitehead is rightly skeptical of this odd notion. He thinks it distorts our experience and creates problems like the mind-body problem and the induction problem. We don't need to endorse Whitehead's metaphysics to find his clinical diagnosis compelling: these problems are symptoms peculiar to the way modern philosophy has distorted experience. A more faithful description should therefore be able to avoid them. The challenge is how to go about describing consciousness without reifying it. How are we to understand and capture the being of a non-thing? Whitehead may not have the right answer to this, but he merits our attention because he is one of few who understand the problem and at least have *an* answer, which we can use to assess the unusual demands of the problem.

Whitehead's Model Solution to the Archetypal Problems of Metaphysics and Epistemology

Metaphysical Uniqueness of Subjectivity

We can explicate the difficult idea that consciousness is not a thing by looking at several surprising and mostly neglected implications of Whitehead's metaphysics. We will see that they offer us impressive tools to tackle our original problem regarding the experience of causation. Notice first of all that the subjective form of experience, whether it is conscious or not, must be entirely a private affair. An occasion can never be prehended by another before its own subjective enjoyment has perished, making the act (but not the object) of experience wholly private. Furthermore, the process of experience itself does not happen in the public time of the extensive continuum (PR 283), whose elements are what get experienced. This may be easier to demonstrate than to understand. Consider the following: if an occasion must occupy a least amount of time in order to exist at all, it cannot come into being gradually. It must come in to being as a whole. But obviously an incomplete being cannot come into being as a whole. So it cannot come into being before its process of individuation has reached completion in the satisfaction. But this means that the time in which enjoyment takes place is not the time in which the satisfaction manifests itself as a minimum duration. "Objective time" is a summation of these minute intervals in which satisfied individuals come into being in microscopic spurts. But this aggregation of satisfaction times nowhere contains enjoyment or the time in which it seems to happen.

Finally, this account imputes a still more remarkable characteristic to experience, as well as to subjectivity, which experience defines: it is not fully individuated (PR 152, 255). The only individuality it enjoys is the solipsistic individuality of being wholly alone with itself in a world that it privately possesses (PR 69, 80–81, 200). This private world, strictly speaking, contains no other subjects. The subject's world is what falls in the backward light cone of Minkowski space and contains only objects. Objects, on the other hand, enjoy the individuality of complete determination in respect to one another and in respect to every possible predicate. They either include or exclude every "eternal object"—*tertium non datur; contradictio non est.* Subjectivity, on the other hand, necessarily lacks this sort of individuality. It is unique in its world, but not because it differs in definite ways from all other entities of the same type. It is unique because it is alone. It does not share its world with any entities of comparable type. There is, consequently, no metaphysical reason why the subject in its own being as an experiencing actuality must comply with the law of excluded middle or even with the law of noncontradiction. In fact, it necessarily cannot since it is the very process by which that compliance is first achieved.

Causation Revisited

These unusual features of subjectivity are key to Whitehead's theory of causation. To understand causation, we need to see how the past can—indeed, must—project itself into its own future so as to create the base line of the present. This is precisely the process that the traditional dialectic seizes upon to destructive effect. Something is either past and not present or present and not past, but not somehow both. ("Still present" may seem, but is not relevant here, since it is not the past that is still present!) In the same way we can trigger the classic problem of epistemology, even if we want to allow subject and object to enjoy an asymmetrical relationship that is internal for the subject and external for the object. For if the experience is internally related to the object, then the object must be immanent in the experience. But if the object of present experience is immanent, then the object, too, must be present and not past (because *immanent in the present experience* can only mean *present in its content*). If, on the other hand, the object is past, then it must be transcendent with respect to the present experience and its content, and so the relation becomes symmetrically external. It follows that the present and the past cannot be internally related, whether symmetrically or asymmetrically.

Whitehead, I submit, does not doubt for a minute that these are irrefutable arguments—but only as long as we look at time with objectifying eyes. Even nonobjectifying experience fails to find internal relations between objects. Whether thematized as objects or not, objects are related to one another only externally. This is a necessary consequence of their complete determinacy: an internal relation to something else would mean that they were incomplete taken by themselves (MT 164).

Here we hit upon a treasure buried in Whitehead's metaphysics. Whitehead identifies the logical deep structure common to all the historical manifestations of what I have called the "archetypal" problem of metaphysics. Hume's argument against causation has the same structure as (and is indirectly derived from) similar and equally celebrated arguments against causation from Nominalism in the fourteenth century (Ockham and Nicholas of Autrecourt) and from Kalām in the tenth and eleventh centuries (al-Ashʿarī and al-Ghazālī). Furthermore, these arguments are similar to (and possibly influenced by) those advanced in medieval Indian philosophy (Dharmakīrti, Śāntarakṣita, Kamalaśīla) in its assault on causation. In each case the argument is that each real thing in the world is a fully determinate individual and as such possesses an "absolute" being. Absolute in this acceptation means self-sustaining and independent of other things (just like Husserl's Absolute Consciousness). The argument is: if fully individual, then lacking nothing, complete without anything else, *ergo*, absolute. This logic is expressed in Scholasticism by saying that there exists a real distinction between any two individuals, which means that it is at least possible for God to create the one without the other. Otherwise they would not each be completely realized individuals, but somehow abstract, partial, or incomplete as long as they were (thought of as) separated from the other. In that case, indeed, they would not be "absolute" beings, but relative, dependent ones. This logic shows up in Hume's *Treatise* in the form of the all-important (but phenomenologically unjustified) assumption that any two ideas that are distinct must also be separable. It shows up in Descartes' philosophy in the often-enunciated principle that two ideas are necessarily related if and only if it is impossible to conceive one or both of them distinctly in separation from the other. In each case the same conclusion follows. A necessary connection between distinct things is impossible.

Whitehead in effect agrees with these great philosophical traditions, albeit it with a decisive qualification. It's true that we cannot avoid the conclusion that necessary connections between distinct phenomena are impossible. *But this holds only as long as we are quantifying over fully determinate individuals.* This is the paramount insight to which Whitehead's metaphysics inspired him. He proposes that we concede the arguments of the tradition and affirm categorically: among fully determinate individuals there can be only external relations. But this is not the same thing as affirming that among *distinguishable* individuals there can be only external relations. Thus, Whitehead—always an adventurer in the world of thought—asks us to consider the contrapositive: if related internally, then not fully determinate. If there are distinguishable, but inseparable things (i.e., distinct, but internally or necessarily related things, whose stated interconnection would thus represent a "synthetic judgment *a priori*"), then at least one of them cannot be a completely determinate individual. It would have to be some kind of "indeterminate individual" or an incompletely individuated thing or perhaps not even a thing in any important sense—without, however, forfeiting its distinguishable individuality. Why should something of that sort be impossible? Whitehead believes that there is something of that sort.

As discussed at the beginning of this section, experience has some very remarkable characteristics. On Whitehead's account, experience—and that includes conscious experience—necessarily belongs to the preterminal stage of concrescence. When we are conscious, we are conscious of the satisfaction of other things, things whose experience is terminated, but our own experience is to a greater or lesser degree indeterminate and still seeking its satisfaction. Thus, Whitehead can say that "[n]o actual entity can be conscious of its own satisfaction; for such knowledge would be a component in the process, and would thereby alter the satisfaction" (PR 85). Thus, while consciousness belongs to a very late stage of concrescence, it can never belong to the end-point of full concretion, which means that consciousness itself will never be altogether concrete. A residual abstractness or indeterminacy always characterizes it.

Due to the inchoative character of experience, the relationship of subject to object is necessarily to some extent vague and fuzzy. The asymmetry of the logical relationship between them is secondary to the asymmetry of their ontological status. The object is a definite individual; the subject is inchoate. This allows the subject's experience to maintain an internal relation to something from which it is in the very process of distinguishing itself. Because it is still in the process of separating itself from the object or the event that just happened, that is, because it has not yet fully consummated its differentiation from the past, it remains internally related to it. At the same time, it is distinct from it by virtue of the subject-object polarity defining experience. The subject enjoys the object immediately (internal relation between subject and object), but the subject alone possesses immediacy of enjoyment (subject and object are distinct). It is, in other words, the subject's lonesome pseudo-individuality that keeps it distinct from the same object to which it is necessarily related.

It should be clear from this short treatment how the process of differentiation of subject from object mandates some modicum of spontaneity and provides the latitude for creativity and freedom so important to Whiteheadians. At the same time, no differentiation can take place that is not differentiation *from the immediately past object*, which means that the present can enact itself only on the basis of the immediate past. This is the constraint we have been calling efficient causation and necessary synthesis. It manifests as the impossibility that any new and present actuality be an abrupt total departure from everything that went before. To the extent that the present is different from the past, it must create that difference on a foundation or baseline of sameness. Regardless of the degree of difference, therefore, the present will always be to some extent like the past from which it is distinguishing itself because it is only a modified continuation of it. Accordingly, Whitehead holds that the primary function of efficient causation is the repetition of the immediate past in the present, which appears from the standpoint of the present as its obligatory accommodation of and conformation to the immediate past.

Now let's try to work the Mādhyamika's dialectic. Whitehead's analysis of causation seems to yield quickly to its first approach. In the present moment there is a part that is different from the immediately past moment (the contribution of spontaneous creativity) and a part that is the same (the replication of the past). But when in the next step the dialectic tries for decisive victory, it fails. Are the past and its present replication the same or different? Obviously they are neither one hundred percent. So if, alternatively, they are similar, what is the element of sameness and what is the element of difference that combined together make them similar? Are they perhaps "qualitatively" the same but "numerically" different? The dialectic wants to proceed: If they really are numerically distinct (that is, two things rather than one), then they must be separable, so how can they be internally related? And if they are not numerically distinct, then we don't really have two things at all. We just have the past and something that is still not different from it. Hence, no question of relations arises.

However, it is simply not possible to factor Whitehead's repetition into identity and difference. The process of concrescence happens privately, outside of measurable, physical time, and within this process we find a logical twilight. The subject is both the same as and different from the object, or neither, if you like. Together they are both one and not one, two and not two. The subject is above all not "partly" different from the object and "partly" the same. It is wholly both and neither, as a process unfolds that presupposes (in the sense that it "aims" at) its own completion. The completion realizes the mutual externality of cause and effect, and its presupposition is testimony to the synthetic aspect of the relation. But insofar as the process is still going on, externality between cause and effect is still incompletely realized, keeping them internally related, which is essential to the necessary aspect of the relation.

It follows on this analysis that the object is both immanent in and transcendent to the experience of the subject as long as the experience is still actively going on. For the same reasons, it is both present and past, both ideal and real, both mental and physical. Since mind is always on its way to concretizing as an experientially precipitated physical fact,[26] the experiential process is the brief and vanishing bridge between successive concreta. Because mind is a state of incomplete differentiation from matter, it is both the same as and different from matter.

Whitehead proposes process, thus understood, as the metaphysical basis for the synthetic necessity Kant was looking for. Cause and effect are internally and necessarily related insofar as they are one and the same. Cause and effect are distinct and synthetically related insofar as they are not the same. When the causal/experiential process is consummated, what's left are things that are now related only externally. That's why causation will never be found among facts. It resides and operates only in the subjective process through which new events come to pass by differentiating themselves from the facts left by still prior processes. The only direct and nonanalogical access we have to this process is in our own perception, but this becomes a basis for understanding the causal process in everything that happens.

A nice theory, but does it work empirically? Whitehead believes that if we adopt what amounts to a phenomenological attitude to the performative dimension of our own experiencing, we will notice something that we otherwise take for granted. Our experience always has a greater or lesser degree of continuity over time. This continuity manifests a compulsion that each state of our being has not to change totally and abruptly, but to continue with some degree of ontological *vis inertiae*. This compulsion is entirely performative and nonobjectifiable. We feel it constantly from two paramount sources: from our immediate experiential past, with which we are in direct contact, and from our bodies, with which we are also in direct contact. We experience the tangency of these two kinds of ontological otherness with an immediacy that no amount of theorizing can circumvent. It defies the Cartesian will to doubt. Through our bodies there is also a vague but imperious feeling of the world beyond, whose extreme vagueness does not compromise its value as metaphysical knowledge. The impingement of these forms of transcendent otherness on our vital subjectivity cannot be coherently or consistently denied. Whitehead thinks they convey at every moment of our life descriptive proof that our subjectivity undergoes action inflicted upon it by something other than subjectivity.

At the heart of Whitehead's metaphysical constructions we find phenomenology—and an implicit phenomenological challenge to Phenomenology. But we also find metaphysical generalization. Whitehead proposes that our experience at its least sophisticated may be the most valuable philosophically. Since what the phenomenology of rudimentary existence in time discloses is not necessarily unique to human experience, Whitehead wonders if it might be the secrete of time itself. He proposes to understand all events in the universe on this model, which means that objective time comes to be as an accretion of deposits left by countless small performative events—the brief coruscations of experiential time, every one of which effects a necessary causal synthesis sustaining the possibility of spontaneity.

On traditional metaphysical models, we face such intractable questions as: How can consciousness be conscious of anything besides its own content? And how can it contain anything that transcends consciousness? For example, how can consciousness be conscious of (i.e., "contain") matter? How can consciousness, if its being is simply being conscious, have any relationship (besides otherness) to matter, the being of which is thought to be (to consist in) not being conscious? Or, how can consciousness be conscious of the past, that is, how can the present (present consciousness) contain the past? How can any two distinct moments in time be internally related? How can there be a necessary connection between cause and effect if they occupy distinct moments of time?

However, on Whitehead's model, we have no need to deny that consciousness contains what is transcendent or that the present contains the past or that mind contains matter. In concrescence, the world is both immanent (a content) and transcendent (a reality). In the logical twilight of genesis, either-or gives way to both-and/neither-nor. The past is not what is no longer present, but what the present is immediately transcending. Thus, it both contains and transcends the past. It contains the past by still incompletely transcending it, that is, by still being in the process of transcending it. When this process of transcending is complete, the past will indeed be something wholly transcendent to the present, which by the same token forfeits is claim to immediate presence. But until that point its transcendence depends on something more subtle than mutual ontic externality. The still living present transcends the past (and is transcended by it) through living possession of the immediacy of enjoyment that the past has extinguished. The actual (still living) present is therefore distinct from the past without being wholly other than the past and hence without being logically separable from it. The key notion here is "inchoative transcendence," which makes sense only if we understand the link between the terms as process. Matter is not what is other than consciousness, but that to which consciousness is giving vivid immediacy as it emerges from it. Consciousness contains the body because it is still emerging from it. Consciousness transcends the body (and is transcended by it) by containing it as experienced rather than experiencing. This differs from idealism because consciousness itself depends upon the prior (and hence transcendent) reality of this experienced "content." The process of "immediately transcending" enjoys a connection with what is being immediately transcended that is necessary, yet synthetic. Transcending and being-transcended are one without being identical; they are two without being separable. As Aristotle would have said, they are one in number but two in essence or being.[27] Consciousness, like experience in general, is a process of immediately transcending things, and by dint of this enjoys a relationship with things that is both necessary and synthetic. Such a process is possible because consciousness is not itself a thing, but on its way to thinghood—not yet an *ens creatum*, but an *ens creatandum*.

Conclusion: Whiteheadian Response to Price's Objections to Explaining Consciousness

In conclusion, I offer a schematic of Whiteheadian answer to Price. Price looked at each of Rosch's four types of felt causation and denied that consciousness could be understood as caused in any of these four ways. Given the model elaborated in this paper, it is possible to rebut each of Price's objections. Whitehead gives us the means to understand how each of Rosch's four types identifies a way that consciousness is caused as well as a way that consciousness enjoys a veridical experience (but not an objectified consciousness) of the causal process. In each case the process results in an assimilation of the past to the present and an accommodation of the present to past. In one mechanism this process explains how mind is related to matter and how events unfold with enough continuity to sustain induction. Mind in its most rudimentary form is simply the inner dynamic of time—a dynamic whose function is always a more or less creative revival of the immediate past.

Identity

What could be the thing that remains identical across the causation of consciousness, only transformed in some way? Whitehead: the world. The world as superject becomes the world of the subject. This happens in the logical and ontological twilight in which past and present overlap in the ambivalent process of becoming. We experience this psychologically as "making sense of our surroundings."

Property Transfer

What property could the object be bestowing upon the subject? Whitehead: concreteness. The concreteness of the objects is conferred upon the subject and becomes a constituent in its own concreteness (hence the idea that it is a unique "concrescence" of them). We experience this psychologically as the impossibility of dating internal events in the history of our own states of mind except in reference to the dating of events in the history of our environment.

Animate Causality

How can consciousness be caused by its objects? Whitehead: by the conformal feeling that is the felt origin of all events. Price's problem: how can the object be the cause of consciousness rather than of its content? Because consciousness is the subjective form corresponding to certain kinds of contents. It's true that for Whitehead this content would not come about without the intervention of concepts, and his theory of concepts (eternal objects) is unappealingly metaphysical, but it is enough to rebut Price if the object plays any felt role in the causation of consciousness. We should also note that Price's distinction—where does the consciousness come from, not the content—is more troublesome for Price than for Whitehead. Price assumes that qualia are peculiarly bound up with consciousness, not features of the content. So his question, how can the object cause consciousness, is really: how can it cause qualia? But for Whitehead qualia do not depend on consciousness. They are universals (eternal objects) and their instantiation depends not on consciousness, but on subjectivity. Any effect is some kind of subjectively felt quality. The initial locus of this quality-token is in the content, and the corresponding subjective form arises in response. So if Price's question is how the object causes qualities to be felt subjectively, then Whitehead's answer is: this is the one and only thing that objects do, and it is our most primitive and pervasive experience. We experience this psychologically as continuity with our own immediate past.

Essence

How is consciousness the manifested essence of the object? Whitehead: in a sense, all things are intrinsically subjects because subjectivity alone gives rise to concreteness and individuality. Many things are of course just aggregates, but they are concrete only because they are aggregates of real individuals. Being experienced is the way the extinguished subjectivity of objects is rekindled. We feel this because we feel ourselves constituting our own individuality out of the individuality of the objects we encounter, our own subjectivity out of theirs. Whitehead's agreement with this fourth construal of causation (as the manifestation of a thing's "essence") can be inferred with confidence. He says on the one hand that what a feeling feels is the feelings of antecedent subjects. But he says on the other hand that no occasion can be felt (prehended) before its own process of concrescence is terminated and its living subjectivity is extinguished. Feeling is therefore tantamount to reviving the feelings that resulted in an antecedent thing's concreteness. We experience this psychologically as the so-called pathetic fallacy.

The reader must decide for herself whether to assess these proposals as contributions to a heavyweight metaphysics of the future or as a source of inspiration for something less freighted. I present them partly "for the record"—as a contribution to Whitehead scholarship—and partly for the impetus they may provide to innovative work in phenomenology, psychology, and the philosophical frontiers of semantics.

Notes

1. In the points made in this paragraph I am in full agreement with Elizabeth Kraus (1985), although her analysis of Whitehead's concept of efficient causation has an entirely different focus from mine. She focuses on the way Whitehead's occasions are supposed to anticipate the effects they will have in the future. It does not seem to me that her analysis, which explains how the future can be immanent in the present, really succeeds at explaining the converse: how causes can be immanent in their effects. However, I would characterize her analysis as incomplete rather than incorrect. It does not seem to be incompatible with the arguments advanced later in this chapter.

2. Think of the work of Nicholas Rescher, Karl-Otto Apel, and others inspired by Peirce.

3. The reader should not confuse Russell's "knowledge by description" with what I am calling the "descriptive approach," by which I mean the kind of knowledge captured in the empirical or phenomenological *description* of an object of direct acquaintance. What I am calling description therefore corresponds to Russell's knowledge by acquaintance, and Russell's knowledge by description corresponds to what I am calling the transcendental approach.

4. Hume makes arguments (1), (2), and arguably (4). Argument (3) was made by Greek skepticism, medieval Buddhism (Dharmakīrti, Śāntarakṣita, Kamalaśīla), and medieval Islam (al-Ash'arī and the Asharite Kalām, al-Ghazālī). Argument (4) was made by Greek skepticism and by Nāgārjuna (and the other Mādhyamika).

5. *Pyrrhoneae Hypotyposes* 2, chs. X–xi, §§ 97–135; *Adversus Mathematicos* 8, ch. 3, §§ 145–299.

6. For Dharmakīrti, see V.N. Jha's translation (1990) of the *Sambandha-parīkṣā* (*Theory of Relations*); for the *Tattvasangraha* (with Kamalaśīla's indispensable commentary), see G. Jha's translation (1937). The *Tattvasangraha* examines causality in the chapters on "permanence" (8), on "the relation between actions and their results" (9), and on the Vaishēsika categories of "quality" (11) and "action" (12). The successful defense of causation announced in Kamalaśīla's commentary to § 532 is belied by the refuge taken in a strict regularity theory of causation in § 438, which has the expected nominalist consequences for dynamics. A quality such as momentum, which is a force of diachronic determination, is impossible (§§684–687). The

Buddhist doctrine of momentariness thus leads to the same problem with projectile motion that plagued Aristotle.

7. The *locus classicus* for the doctrines of Asharite Kalām is the summary provided by the unsympathetic Maimonides in Book I, chapter 73 of his *Guide of the Perplexed* (Pines 1963, I 194–214).

8. "Discussion 17" ["On Causality and Miracles"] of Ghazālī's *Tahāfut al-falāsifa* (Marmura 1997, 170–181).

9. "Hull's initial theoretical machinery operated to get the rat into the maze, but before the rat got to the reinforcement at the end, Hull was forced to introduce a mediating variable called 'fractional antedating goal responses.' These are just what they sound like, miniature versions of the outcome. Skinner's dictum of the organism as a black box allowed for no intervening variables at all. Coherence in his explanations came from second-order isomorphisms; certain characteristics of stimuli are correlated with equivalent aspects of response. Amount of bar pressing to get food is a simple function of number of hours of food deprivation. The temporal characteristics of responses on a fixed interval schedule mirror the intervals of the schedule. Where such elegant relationships cannot be found, a Skinnerian analysis breaks down." (59)

10. Zocher 1952, "Anhang;" Wolff 1736, § 70 ("Principium rationis sufficientis probantur").

11. Leibniz argued that even if contingent propositions are not true analytically, there is nevertheless always a reason why they are true, and that having a reason always means being analytic at some level of analysis. What distinguishes contingent from necessary propositions is simply that their analyticity would be evident only in the total context of all events, which means their analyticity would be evident only to God. Causal necessity for Leibniz is therefore a special case of logical necessity: a logical necessity whose demonstration requires an infinite number of middle terms. See, for example, Leibniz 1989, 96, 98–101.

12. I confine myself to the most rudimentary comparison of Whitehead with classical Phenomenology, which I take to be represented best by Husserl. To avoid confusion, I adopt the upper-case orthography to designate the core doctrines and methods of the classical phase of the movement that expressly styled itself "phenomenological," and I employ the lower-case orthography to designate the practice of intimate psychological description to which no school can lay proprietary claim. It is found abundantly, for example, in Hodgson, Bergson, Mach, Bradley, James, and of course in Whitehead.

13. PR 120, 122 (memory); 174 (reflex); 175 (habituation); 239 (fatigue); 81, 176 (embodiment); 137, 237–8 (time, causation, continuity).

14. "Hume's impressions are self-contained, and he can find no temporal relationship other than mere serial order" (PR 137).

15. Readers of *Ideas I* or the *Phenomenology of Internal Time-Consciousness* did not seem to realize Husserl was being both serious and literal when he argued that the stream of transcendental consciousness must be infinite. No doubt can be left about this from *Analysen zur passiven Synthesis*, Beilage 8, § 10, on the "immortality of the transcendental ego" and "the impossibility that the transcendental ego should be born." See Husserl 1950, § 82; 1966b, § 13; 1966a, 377–381.

16. Perception differs from imagination according to Locke because in perception we know noninferentially that the idea we are having is at that moment an idea of something really existing. But Locke also claims that all knowledge is of the agreement or disagreement of ideas, all of which are universals or clusters of universals. Locke is therefore being consistent when he says in Book 4, chapter 1 of the *Essay* (1959, 2:171–172) that knowing something exists is merely perceiving the agreement between the idea of it and the idea of existence, which is a simple idea of perception and reflection (1959, 1:161). It is impossible on this analysis to see how perception differs from imagining something to exist. Locke was challenged on this and expressly defends his position in the correspondence with Stillingfleet (1963, 360–361). As Whitehead shows (PR 51–60, 113, 122–123, 138, 146–147, 149, 152, 157), the untenability of this position forced Locke to betray the *via idearum* when it became too inconvenient: he often invokes, without acknowledging the inconsistency, peripheral stimulation as the defining factor in perception, as in Book 4, chapter 11.

17. Berkeley 1954, "Third Dialogue" (esp. 87–89). Berkeley's genius is evident in his remarkable success in finding a consistent way to construe suffering an idea (as opposed to merely having one) as itself being a relation of ideas, which Locke failed to do. When having one idea is contingent on first having another idea (specifically an idea of the felt body), then the former idea is suffered. Without this condition, it is had (thought, imagined, etc.), but not suffered. In the Third Analogy of Experience Kant harvested Berkeley's genius for a general solution to the problem causation poses for the Way of Ideas: how a causal sequence can be anything more than a temporal sequence. Let a and b be two ideas, and let A and B be the classes of ideas the same in content as a and b respectively. Two consecutive ideas, a and b, constitute a causal sequence if ideas from the class A and ideas from the class B can only be had in the temporal sequence AB, never in the temporal sequence BA. If on the other hand A and B are reversible in their time sequence, they represent things that are simultaneous and so not causally ordered. On closer inspection, however, we see that Kant's effort fails in just the way Whitehead leads us to expect. What Kant overlooks is the modality implicit in his concepts of reversible and irreversible, and the conditions of the possibility of realizing such modality in the subject. It is not enough for idea sequences to be unreversed. Some must prove to be irreversible: causal sequences are not just unreversed sequences; they are irreversible sequences. But by the same token, some must prove reversible. If we were unable to reverse any idea sequences, then irreversible (as opposed to unreversed) would have no meaning. But arbitrary reversibility is possible only because we inhabit an organic body, and the order of our perceptions is dependent on its motility. Reversible idea sequences are those registering the motion of our own bodies, which we can reverse at will, looking up instead of down or down instead of up. Irreversible idea sequences are those that are not controlled by the movement of our own bodies. It follows that the entire "objective" ordering of perceptions depends on the intervention of the organic body in the process of perception. Kant's "transcendental" constitution of space as the order of objective simultaneity and of causality as the order of objective succession is therefore predicated on the unacknowledged presupposition of something that does not and cannot have any transcendental status. It is predicated on the reality of what

for Kant can only be an idea of reason: the organism. This is the result Whitehead would lead us to expect: the attempted constitution of the world out of presentational immediacy succeeds only to the extent that it tacitly appeals to the living body and its experience of causal efficacy.

18. Whitehead uses objectify/objectification to indicate the process I am calling *objectivation* (v., objectivate), the meaning of which I explain below.

19. It comes first ontologically, for example, insofar as the being of things comes to be identified with their being-for-consciousness or simply insofar as subjective being comes to be identified as the truly paradigmatic kind of being.

20. See PR Index for *"realitas objectiva."*

21. I am indebted to Xavier Verley for the clarity of this insight. See his contribution to this volume.

22. To emphasize the experiential aspect of the relationship, Whitehead uses the term "feeling." Later occasions *feel* the former ones. But in order to avoid misleading associations with *conscious* experience, he also employs the term "prehension" in deliberate imitation of Leibniz: as Leibniz's *perception* is to his *apperception*, so Whitehead's *prehension* is to *apprehension*. Prehension, he says, is an "uncognitive apprehension" (SMW 69–70).

23. The reader may wish to compare the following précis with Whitehead's own outline of his system (PR 20–30).

24. Does creativity presuppose the extensive continuum or *vice versa*? This difficult and important question is beyond our present scope.

25. "[P]rocess is the way by which the universe escapes from the exclusions of inconsistency" (MT 54).

26. The word "fact," coming from Latin, *factum*, meaning *(something) made* seems ideally suited to express the fully concrete, but lifeless deposit left behind by consummated experience.

27. Aristotle's paradigm example is sound and hearing: in number they are two, in actuality they are one and the same. See chapter 3, note 77.

References

Berkeley, George. 1954/1713. *Three Dialogues between Hylas and Philonous.* Ed. by Colin M. Turbayne. Indianapolis: Bobbs-Merril Company.

Chalmers, David. 1996. *The Conscious Mind: in Search of a Fundamental Theory.* New York: Oxford University Press.

Chalmers, David. 1995. "Facing up to the Problem of Consciousness." *Journal of Consciousness Studies* 3:200–219. Reprinted in Shear 1998, 9–30.

Descartes, René. 1964–1976. *Œuvres de Descartes.* Ed. by Ch. Adam and P. Tannery. Revised ed. Paris: Vrin/C.N.R.S.

Descartes, René. 1984. *The Philosophical Writings of Descartes.* 3 vols. Trans. by John Cottingham, Robert Stoothoff, Dugald Murdoch. Cambridge: Cambridge University Press.

Hochstetter, E., ed. 1952. *Leibniz. Zu Seinem 300. Geburtstag. 1646–1946.* Berlin: Walter de Gruyter and Co.

Hume, David. 1978. *A Treatise of Human Nature.* Analytical Index by L.A. Selby-Bigge. 2nd ed. with text revised and notes by P.H. Nidditch. Oxford: Clarendon Press.

Husserl, Edmund. 1950/1913. *Ideen zu einer reinen Phänomenologie und phänomenologischen Philosophie I: Allgemeine Einführung in die reine Phänomenologie.* Husserliana 3. Haag: Martinus Nijhoff.

Husserl, Edmund. 1952. *Ideen zu einer reinen Phänomenologie und phänomenologischen Philosophie II: Phänomenologische Untersuchungen zur Konstitution.* Husserliana 4. Haag: Martinus Nijhoff.

Husserl, Edmund. 1966a. *Analysen zur passiven Synthesis.* Aus Vorlesungs- und Forschungsmanuskripten 1918–1926. Husserliana 11. Haag: Martinus Nijhoff.

Husserl, Edmund. 1966b. *Zur Phänomenologie des inneren Zeitbewusstseins (1893–1917).* Husserliana 10. Haag: Martinus Nijhoff.

Inada, Kenneth K., trans. 1993. *Nāgārjuna, a Translation of His Mūlamadhyamakakārikā.* Delhi: Sri Satguru Publications.

Jha, Ganganatha, trans. 1937. *The Tattvasangraha of Śāntarakṣita with the Commentary of Kamalaśīla.* 2 vols. Baroda: Oriental Institute.

Jha, V.N., trans. 1990. *The Philosophy of Relations.* Containing the Sanskrit text and English translation of Dharma Kīrti's *Sambandha-parīksā* with Prabhācandra's Commentary. Delhi: Sri Satguru Publications.

Kalupahana, David J., trans. 1986. *Mūlamadhyamakakārikā: the Philosophy of the Middle Way* (Nāgārjuna). Albany: State University of New York Press.

Kalupahana, David J. 1975. *Causality—the Central Philosophy of Buddhism.* Honolulu: University Press of Hawaii.

Kraus, Elizabeth M. 1985. "Existence as Transaction: A Whiteheadian Study of Causality." *International Philosophical Quarterly* 25(4): 349–366.

Leibniz, G.W. 1989. *Philosophical Essays.* Ed. and trans. by Roger Ariew and Daniel Garber. Indianapolis and Cambridge: Hackett.

Locke, John. 1959/1690. *An Essay Concerning Human Understanding.* Complete and unabridged. Collated and annotated by Alexander Campbell Fraser. 2 vols. New York: Dover Publications.

Locke, John. 1963/1823. *The Works of John Locke.* A new edition, corrected. 10 vols. Vol. 4. Aalen: Scientia Verlag.

Maier, Anneliese. 1963. "Das Problem der Evidenz in der Philosophie des 14. Jahrhunderts." *Scholastik* 38:183–225. Reprinted in Maier 1964–1967, vol. 2, 366–418.

Maier, Anneliese. 1964–1967. *Ausgehendes Mittelalter: gesammelte Aufsätze zur Geistesgeschichte des 14. Jahrhunderts.* 2 vols. Roma: Edizioni di storia e letteratura.

Marmura, Michael E., trans. 1997. *The Incoherence of the Philosophers* (al-Ghazālī). Provo: Brigham Young University Press.

McCagney, Nancy. 1997. *Nāgārjuna and the Philosophy of Openness.* Lanham: Rowman and Littlefield.

Mookerjee, Satkari. 1975/1935. *The Buddhist Philosophy of Universal Flux: An Exposition of the Philosophy of Critical Realism as Expounded by the School of Dignāga.* Delhi: Motilal Banarsidass.

Pines, Shlomo, trans. 1963. *The Guide of the Perplexed* (Moses Maimonides). 2 vols. Chicago: University of Chicago Press.

Price, Mark C. 1997/1996. "Should We Expect to Feel As If We Understand Consciousness?" In Shear 1997, 83–93. Originally published in *Journal of Consciousness Studies* 3 (4): 303–312.

Rosch, Eleanor. 1994. "Is Causality Circular? Event Structure in Folk Psychology, Cognitive Science and Buddhist Logic." *Journal of Consciousness Studies* 1 (1): 50–65.

Shear, Jonathan, ed. 1997. *Explaining Consciousness—The Hard Problem*. Cambridge, MA/London: MIT Press.

Weekes, Anderson. 2006. "The Many Streams in Ralph Pred's *Onflow*." In *Chromatikon II: Annuaire de la philosophie en process*, Michel Weber and Pierfrancesco Basile, eds., 227–244. Louvain: Presses universitaires de Louvain.

Weinberg, Julius R. 1969/1948. *Nicolaus of Autrecourt: A Study in 14th Century Thought*. With a preface to the Greenwood reprint by the author. New York: Greenwood Press.

Weinberg, Julius R. 1977. *Ockham, Descartes, and Hume: Self-knowledge, Substance, and Causality*. Madison: University of Wisconsin Press.

Wolff, Christian, Freiherr von. 1736. *Philosophia prima, sive ontologia, methodo scientifica pertractata, qua omnis cognitionis humanæ principia continentur*. Francofurti and Lipsiæ, prostat in Officina libraria Rengeriana.

Zocher, Rudolf. 1952. "Leibniz' Erkenntnislehre." *Lieferung* 7 of Hochstetter 1952.

Contributors

Michael Frost completed his BA in psychology at the Academic College of Tel Aviv, in addition to two years of study in philosophy at the University of Tel Aviv and New York University. At the same time, he was active as a professional musician, working live with singers as well as in television productions. Today he is a full-time musician, playing bass and guitar and producing music.

David Griffin is Professor Emeritus of Philosophy of Religion at Claremont School of Theology and Claremont Graduate University and a Director of the Center for Process Studies. His books include *Archetypal Process: Self and Divine in Whitehead, Jung, and Hillman* (ed., 1989), *Parapsychology, Philosophy, and Spirituality* (1997), *Unsnarling the World-Knot: Consciousness, Freedom, and the Mind-Body Problem* (1998), *Religion and Scientific Naturalism* (2000), and *Reenchantment without Supernaturalism: A Process Philosophy of Religion* (2001).

The late *Donald Redfield Griffin* (1915–2003) was Professor Emeritus at Rockefeller University and Research Associate at the Museum of Comparative Zoology, Harvard University. His principal books are *Listening in the Dark, The Acoustic Orientation of Bats and Men* (1958), *The Question of Animal Awareness, Evolutionary Continuity of Mental Experience* (1976), and *Animal Minds, Beyond Cognition to Consciousness* (2001).

Michael Katzko received his PhD in theoretical psychology at the University of Alberta, Edmonton. He is currently Research Associate at Netherlands Psychoanalytic Institute. He has taught and carried out research in Europe, Indonesia, and Peru. In addition to a general interest in the methodological and metaphysical foundations of psychology, his current research interests include the relation between self and social contexts, and the rhetorical structure of academic research.

Ofer Keren obtained his medical degree at Ben-Gurion University of the Negev. Specializing in clinical neurology, he has practiced rehabilitative medicine as

Attending Physician at the Greenery Rehabilitation Center (Boston) and as Staff Attending Physician in the Department of Traumatic Brain Injury at the Loewenstein Rehabilitation Center (Raanana), where he subsequently also served as Director of the Clinical Neurophysiology Unit. He is currently the Director of the Department of Rehabilitation, Alyn Hospital, Pediatric and Adolescent Rehabilitation Center, Jerusalem.

Bruce Duncan MacQueen is Professor of Comparative Literature at the University of Silesia and Visiting Professor of Psychology at the University of Gdańsk. He is the author of two monographs in classical and comparative literature, including *Myth, Rhetoric and Fiction* (listed as one of the Outstanding Academic Books for 1991 by the American Association of College and Research Libraries), several book chapters in literary studies and in neurolinguistics, published both in Polish and in English, and numerous articles in both fields.

Maria Pachalska is Professor at the Institute of Psychology, Gdansk University, consultant in the Center for Cognition and Communication in New York, founder and President of the Polish Neuropsychological Association, founder and President of the Foundation for Persons with Brain Dysfunctions, Editor-in-Chief of the quarterly *Acta Neuropsychologica* and the quarterly *Disability and Health*, and a member of numerous editorial boards, including *Aphasiology* and *Medical Science Monitor*, both listed in Current Contents. She has more than 100 publications in neuropsychology, including authorial methods of neuropsychological diagnosis and therapy and is the author of nine books, including *Clinical Neuropsychology: Traumatic Brain Injury* (2007), *Neuropsychological Rehabilitation* (2008), and *Aphasiology* (1999), and co-author of two books, including *Identity and Microgenetic Theory*, written (in Polish) with B. Grochmal-Bach (2004). She is also the author of more than 30 book chapters, including: "The collapse of the US-THEM Structure in Aphasia: A Neuropsychological and Neurolinguistic Perspective" (in *Us and Others*, A. Duszak, ed., 2003) and "Process Neuropsychology, Microgenetic Theory and Brain Science," in *Handbook of Whiteheadean Process Thought* (M. Weber and W. Desmond, eds., 2008). She is editor or co-editor of six books, including *Identity in an Interdisciplinary Perspective* (2005), co-edited with B.D. MacQueen and B. Grochmal-Bach, and a member of numerous national and international scientific associations.

Gregg Rosenberg received his PhD in Philosophy and Cognitive Science from Indiana University in 1997. He currently works in the private sector as a Senior Director and Practice Manager at the Corporate Executive Board, in Washington DC. His book on consciousness, *A Place for Consciousness*, was published by Oxford University Press as part of their Philosophy of Mind Series in 2004.

Avraham Schweiger (PhD in psychology, UCLA, major in cognitive psychology) is Associate Professor and head of the graduate program in Neuropsychology at Academic College of Tel Aviv & Loewenstein Rehabilitation Center, Israel, and Research Associate at Souraski Medical Center, Tel Aviv, Division of Advanced Brain Imaging. His current research interests focus on functional imaging of recovery following brain damage using fMRI and PET scans and the application of the process approach in the context of such brain imaging studies.

George W. Shields received his PhD from the University of Chicago and did further study at Oxford University. He is the 2000–01 University Distinguished Professor, Professor of Philosophy, and Chair of the Division of Literature, Languages, and Philosophy at Kentucky State University, Frankfort, KY. Among other works, he is editor and co-author of *Process and Analysis: Whitehead, Hartshorne, and the Analytic Tradition* (also published by State University of New York Press). He serves as a member of the International Advisory Board of *Process Studies*, and has authored some 100 articles, reviews, introductions, and critical studies in a wide variety of scholarly books, conference proceedings, and peer-reviewed journals.

Max Velmans is currently Emeritus Professor of Psychology at Goldsmiths, University of London and Visiting Professor of Consciousness Studies at the University of Plymouth. He has more than 90 publications on consciousness including *Understanding Consciousness* (2000), *How Could Conscious Experiences Affect Brains?* (2003), *Investigating Phenomenal Consciousness: New Methodologies and Maps* (2000), *The Science of Consciousness: Psychological, Neuropsychological and Clinical Reviews* (1996), and the jointly edited *Blackwell Companion to Consciousness* (2007). He co-founded and from 2003 to 2006 chaired the Consciousness and Experiential Psychology Section of the British Psychological Society.

Xavier Verley is Professeur agrégé and senior lecturer at the Université de Toulouse le Mirail. His research interests are in symbolic logic, epistemology, philosophy of sciences and psychology. He has published on Mach, Carnap, Frege, Husserl, and Whitehead.

Michel Weber obtained his PhD in Philosophy from the Université catholique de Louvain (Belgium). He is the director of the Centre for philosophical practice "Chromatiques whiteheadiennes." In 2008–2009, he is visiting Professor at the New Bulgarian University (Sofia), Department of Cognitive

Science and Psychology and Department of Philosophy and Sociology. He has edited numerous books on Whitehead and published *La dialectique de l'intuition chez A. N. Whitehead* (2005), *Whitehead's Pancreativism* (2006), and *L'épreuve de la philosophie* (2008).

Anderson Weekes works as an educational consultant in the private sector. He holds a doctorate in philosophy from the State University of New York at Stony Brook. Trained in Ancient Philosophy, German Idealism, and Phenomenology, his research compares the treatment of similar ("perennial") problems across different philosophical traditions. His publications have examined Whitehead's metaphysics in the larger context of the history of western philosophy. He is Secretary of the "Whitehead Psychology Nexus."

Index

Made in the USA
Lexington, KY
20 December 2015